FOOD & WINE ANNUAL COOKBOOK 2004
EDITOR Kate Heddings
ART DIRECTOR Liz Quan
SENIOR EDITOR Pamela Mitchell
COPY EDITOR Lisa Leventer
PRODUCTION ASSOCIATES Ethan Cornell, Griffin Plonchak
PHOTO ASSISTANT Lisa S. Kim
EDITORIAL BUSINESS ASSOCIATE Jessica Magnusen-DiFusco
EDITORIAL ASSISTANT Beth Collins

SENIOR VICE PRESIDENT, CHIEF MARKETING OFFICER Mark V. Stanich
VICE PRESIDENT, BOOKS AND PRODUCTS Marshall Corey
DIRECTOR, BRANDED SERVICES AND RETAIL Tom Mastrocola
CORPORATE PRODUCTION MANAGER Stuart Handelman
MARKETING MANAGER Bruce Spanier
SENIOR OPERATIONS MANAGER Phil Black
BUSINESS MANAGER Doreen Camardi

FRONT COVER
Chicken with Riesling, p. 113
PHOTOGRAPH BY Jim Franco
FOOD STYLING BY Rori Trovato

BACK COVER
PHOTOGRAPHS BY (left to right) Lucy Schaeffer, Quentin Bacon, John Kernick, Quentin Bacon

FLAP PHOTOGRAPHS
DANA COWIN PORTRAIT BY Andrew French
KATE HEDDINGS PORTRAIT BY Emily Wilson

AMERICAN EXPRESS PUBLISHING CORPORATION

Copyright 2004 American Express Publishing Corporation

ISBN 0-916103-93-5
ISSN 1097-1564

Published by American Express Publishing Corporation
1120 Avenue of the Americas, New York, New York 10036

Manufactured in the United States of America

FOOD & WINE MAGAZINE
EDITOR IN CHIEF Dana Cowin
CREATIVE DIRECTOR Stephen Scoble
MANAGING EDITOR Mary Ellen Ward
EXECUTIVE EDITOR Pamela Kaufman
EXECUTIVE FOOD EDITOR Tina Ujlaki
WINE EDITOR Lettie Teague

FEATURES
FEATURES EDITOR Michelle Shih
TRAVEL EDITOR Salma Abdelnour
SENIOR EDITOR Kate Krader
ASSOCIATE STYLE EDITOR Charlotte Druckman
ASSISTANT STYLE EDITOR Lauren Fister
EDITORIAL ASSISTANTS Ruby Cutolo, Ratha Tep

FOOD
SENIOR EDITORS Lily Barberio, Kate Heddings, Jane Sigal
TEST KITCHEN SUPERVISOR Marcia Kiesel
SENIOR TEST KITCHEN ASSOCIATE Grace Parisi
KITCHEN ASSISTANT Jim Standard

ART
ART DIRECTOR Patricia Sanchez
PHOTO EDITOR Fredrika Stjärne
DESIGNER Andrew Haug
ASSOCIATE PHOTO EDITOR Lucy Schaeffer
PRODUCTION ASSOCIATE Griffin Plonchak
PHOTO ASSISTANT Lisa S. Kim

COPY & RESEARCH
ASSISTANT MANAGING EDITOR William Loob
SENIOR EDITOR Martha Crow
COPY EDITOR Maggie Robbins
ASSISTANT RESEARCH EDITOR Carla Ranicki
EDITORIAL BUSINESS ASSOCIATE Jessica Magnusen-DiFusco

annual cookbook

AN ENTIRE YEAR OF RECIPES 2004

FOOD&WINE annual cookbook 2004

American Express Publishing Corporation, New York

FOOD&WINE
BOOKS

contents

foreword

One of the most interesting things about putting together FOOD & WINE's annual cookbook is reflecting on how culinary trends change from year to year. Here are a few that were big this year.

Global comfort food In addition to all-American dishes like macaroni and cheese, F&W published an unprecedented number of delicious homey recipes from such countries as India (Chicken Tikka Masala), Morocco (Lamb Tagine with Toasted Almonds and Prunes) and Mexico (Turkey Breast Escabeche with Onions and Poblanos).

Protein, protein and more protein F&W published more than a hundred poultry, beef and lamb recipes this year. Some of our favorites were Roast Chicken with Grapes, Chestnuts and Tarragon Butter, Beef Sirloin with Piquillo Peppers and Lamb Steaks with Shallot-Anchovy Relish.

Power brunches Perhaps because brunch is one of the simplest and tastiest meals to serve guests, F&W emphasized easy and elegant recipes such as Banana Waffles with Pecans, Leek and Gruyère Tart and Canadian Bacon and Cheddar Cheese Flan.

Classic desserts revamped From Strawberry Shortcake with Star Anise Sauce to Pumpkin Cheesecake Tart with Cranberry Gelée, F&W noted the trend for old-fashioned desserts with a modern twist.

Beyond the recipes, you'll see other changes in this 2004 annual as well. We've paired each main course (and all the hors d'oeuvres and appetizers) with an easy-to-find wine; look for our revised wine glossary on page 352. We've also added great new test kitchen tips to every chapter and fun Q&A's on topics that range from avoiding soggy French toast to mixing the perfect vinaigrette.

Finally, we're proud to say that there are over 35 more recipes in this annual than in last year's, which is the equivalent of almost an entire extra issue of the magazine. With so many great recipes, we hope this book inspires you to start cooking immediately.

Dana Cowin
Editor in Chief
FOOD & WINE Magazine

Kate Heddings
Editor
FOOD & WINE Cookbooks

SPICY CHICKPEA CHAT, P. 22

starters

HERB-ROASTED OLIVES

GARLICKY ROASTED BELL PEPPERS

Herb-Roasted Olives

ACTIVE: 10 MIN; TOTAL: 25 MIN

MAKES 2 CUPS ● ● ●

- 2 cups mixed green and black olives (¾ pound)
- 2 tablespoons extra-virgin olive oil
- 2 garlic cloves, minced
- ¼ teaspoon dried oregano, crumbled
- ¼ teaspoon fennel seeds
- ¼ teaspoon crushed red pepper
- ½ teaspoon kosher salt
- ½ teaspoon freshly ground black pepper
- 1 teaspoon finely grated orange zest
- 1 tablespoon chopped flat-leaf parsley
- ½ teaspoon coarsely chopped rosemary

Preheat the oven to 450°. On a small baking sheet, toss the olives, oil, garlic, oregano, fennel seeds, crushed red pepper, salt and black pepper. Roast until sizzling, about 15 minutes. Transfer the olives to a bowl and toss with the orange zest, parsley and rosemary. Serve warm or at room temperature. —*Sally Sampson*

MAKE AHEAD The olives can be refrigerated for up to three days.

WINE Aromatic, zesty Albariño.

Garlicky Roasted Bell Peppers

TOTAL: 35 MIN

6 TO 8 SERVINGS ● ● ●

- 3 large green bell peppers
- 3 large red bell peppers
- ⅓ cup extra-virgin olive oil
- 1 tablespoon finely chopped garlic

Salt and freshly ground pepper

Warm crusty bread, for serving

ı. Preheat the broiler. Put the bell peppers on a large rimmed baking sheet. Broil as close to the heat as possible, turning frequently, until blackened and blistered on all sides, about 15 minutes.

2. Transfer the peppers to a medium bowl, cover with plastic wrap and let them steam for 10 minutes.

3. Set a coarse strainer or a colander over a bowl. Working over the strainer, peel the peppers and discard the stems and seeds. Reserve the pepper juices.

4. Cut the peppers lengthwise into ½-inch-wide strips; transfer the strips to a clean bowl. Pour the strained pepper juices over the peppers and add the olive oil and garlic. Season the peppers generously with salt and pepper and serve with crusty bread. —*Gloria Pépin*

MAKE AHEAD The peppers can be refrigerated in a container for up to 3 days. Serve chilled or at room temperature.

WINE Light, dry Soave or similar white.

Roasted Pepper, Mozzarella and Anchovy Involtini

ACTIVE: 30 MIN; TOTAL: 1 HR

MAKES 2 DOZEN ROLLS ●

Involtini are Italian stuffed rolls. Here, roasted red bell peppers are rolled around a spicy, tangy cheese filling. These hors d'oeuvres make a great addition to a plate of antipasti.

- 4 large red bell peppers
- Vegetable oil, for rubbing
- 2 tablespoons minced parsley
- 1 tablespoon minced drained capers
- 1 tablespoon extra-virgin olive oil
- 1 small garlic clove, minced
- Salt and freshly ground pepper
- ½ pound buffalo mozzarella, cut into 2-by-⅓-inch matchsticks
- One 2-ounce can flat anchovies, rinsed and halved lengthwise

1. Preheat the oven to 500°. On a large baking sheet, lightly rub the red bell peppers with vegetable oil. Roast for about 20 minutes, turning the bell peppers halfway through, until blackened in spots. Transfer the peppers to a bowl, cover with plastic and let cool. Peel the peppers and cut them lengthwise into thirds; discard the stems, cores and seeds.

2. In a small bowl, combine the parsley with the capers, olive oil and garlic, season lightly with salt and pepper and mix well. Spread the roasted peppers on a work surface. Lay the mozzarella sticks on the short ends of the peppers and top with the anchovy fillets. Spoon the parsley mixture on top and roll into tight cylinders. Trim the ends of the peppers and cut the rolls in half. Pierce with toothpicks, arrange on a platter and serve. —*Grace Parisi*

MAKE AHEAD The rolls can be kept at room temperature for up to 4 hours or covered and refrigerated for up to 8 hours. Bring to room temperature before serving.

WINE Light, dry Soave or similar white.

Herb-Stuffed Zucchini

ACTIVE: 1 HR; TOTAL: 2 HR 20 MIN

4 SERVINGS ● ●

- 4 round zucchini (10 ounces each)
- 2 tablespoons plus ½ teaspoon olive oil, plus more for brushing
- 1 small zucchini (6 ounces), cut into ½-inch dice
- Salt and freshly ground pepper
- 2 tablespoons minced onion
- 1 garlic clove, minced
- 1 medium tomato, finely chopped
- ½ cup diced ham (2 ounces)
- ½ cup cooked basmati rice
- 1 tablespoon chopped parsley
- 1 teaspoon chopped thyme
- ¼ cup packed fresh bread crumbs

1. Preheat the oven to 375°. Cut a thin slice off the tops of the round zucchini and discard them. Using a small spoon, scrape out the flesh, leaving a ¼-inch-thick wall. Coarsely chop the flesh and squeeze dry.

2. Heat 1 tablespoon of the olive oil in a large skillet. Add the diced zucchini, season with salt and pepper and cook over moderately high heat, stirring, until barely tender, about 3 minutes. Transfer to a bowl.

3. Heat 1 tablespoon of the olive oil in the skillet. Add the onion, garlic, tomato and scraped out zucchini flesh and cook over high heat, stirring occasionally, until tender, about 4 minutes. Add to the bowl and refrigerate for 20 minutes. Stir in the ham, rice, parsley and thyme and season with salt and pepper.

4. Season the zucchini cups with salt and pepper and brush the outsides generously with olive oil. In a small bowl, using your fingers, rub the bread crumbs with the remaining ½ teaspoon of olive oil. Mound the stuffing in the zucchini cups and top with the crumbs. Set the zucchini on a baking sheet and bake for about 40 minutes, or until tender and heated through. Serve hot or at room temperature. —*Eric Ripert*

MAKE AHEAD The zucchini can be kept at room temperature for up to 6 hours.

WINE Round, rich Sauvignon Blanc.

Pan-Fried Cheese with Salsa Verde

TOTAL: 20 MIN

4 SERVINGS ●

This recipe calls for scamorza, an Italian cow's-milk cheese that resembles a dry mozzarella. It holds its shape when cooked, oozing just the right amount in the center.

- 2 cups basil leaves
- 2 tablespoons packed flat-leaf parsley leaves
- 1 tablespoon packed mint leaves
- 4 anchovy fillets, rinsed
- 2 tablespoons freshly grated Pecorino Romano cheese
- 1 tablespoon drained capers
- ½ cup plus 1 tablespoon extra-virgin olive oil
- Salt and freshly ground pepper
- ¼ cup all-purpose flour
- Four ⅓-inch-thick slices of scamorza (1½ to 2 ounces each)
- 4 thick slices of peasant bread, toasted

1. In a food processor, combine the basil, parsley and mint with the anchovies, Pecorino and capers and pulse until finely chopped. With the machine on, add ½ cup of the olive oil in a steady stream and process until smooth. Season with salt and pepper.

2. Spread the flour in a pie plate. Add the cheese slices and dredge lightly, gently tapping off the excess flour. In a medium nonstick skillet, heat the remaining 1 tablespoon of olive oil. Add the cheese and fry over moderate heat, turning once, until golden all over, about 3 minutes. Transfer the fried cheese to 4 plates, drizzle with the salsa verde and serve with the toasted bread. —*Michael White*

WINE Simple, fruity Chianti.

starters

Crispy Asiago Frico

TOTAL: 20 MIN

6 SERVINGS ● ●

- 1 pound aged Asiago cheese, coarsely shredded

Optional seasonings: sesame seeds or finely chopped macadamia nuts

Sprinkle 6 tablespoon-size mounds of the cheese in a large nonstick skillet. Top each mound with a pinch of the seasonings. Cook the frico over moderately high heat until lacy and slightly set. Using a thin, flexible metal spatula, loosen and flip each frico and cook for 1 minute longer, or until crisp and golden. Transfer to paper towels to drain. Wipe out the skillet and repeat. —*Grace Parisi*

WINE Dry, crisp sparkling wine.

Spicy Cocktail Shortbreads

ACTIVE: 10 MIN; TOTAL: 2 HR

MAKES ABOUT 2 DOZEN
SHORTBREADS ●

- 1½ sticks (6 ounces) unsalted butter, at room temperature
- ¼ cup sugar
- 1½ cups all-purpose flour
- 1⅛ teaspoons mild curry powder
- 1 teaspoon fine sea salt
- ¾ teaspoon sweet paprika
- ¾ teaspoon ground turmeric
- ¼ teaspoon chili powder
- ⅛ teaspoon freshly ground black pepper
- ⅛ teaspoon cayenne pepper

1. Using a handheld electric mixer, beat the butter and sugar at medium speed until fluffy, about 2 minutes.
2. Sift the flour, curry powder, salt, paprika, turmeric, chili powder and black and cayenne peppers. Add the dry ingredients to the butter; beat until blended.
3. Scrape out the dough onto plastic wrap or parchment paper and pat it into a log 1¼ inches in diameter. Pat the log into a rectangle and wrap it up. Refrigerate until firm, about 1 hour.

4. Preheat the oven to 350°. Cut the dough into ¼-inch-thick slices and arrange on 2 parchment-lined baking sheets. Prick the tops of the shortbreads all over with a fork and bake them for 20 minutes, or until golden. Slide the parchment onto a wire rack and let the shortbreads cool. —*Gail Monaghan*
MAKE AHEAD The cooled shortbreads can be stored in an airtight container at room temperature for up to 1 week or frozen for up to 1 month.

WINE Dry, light, crisp Champagne.

Porcini Mushroom Tartlets

ACTIVE: 15 MIN; TOTAL: 1 HR 15 MIN

MAKES 4 TARTLETS ●

- 1 cup walnuts
- 10 ounces frozen all-butter puff pastry, thawed and chilled
- 3 tablespoons unsalted butter
- 2 large onions, cut into very thin slices

Salt and freshly ground pepper

- ¾ pound medium porcini or cremini mushrooms, trimmed

Extra-virgin olive oil, for brushing
Snipped chives

1. Preheat the oven to 350°. In a pie plate, bake the walnuts for about 8 minutes, or until lightly browned, then let cool and coarsely chop. Line a medium baking sheet with parchment paper.
2. Unfold the puff pastry and cut out four 4-inch rounds about ⅛ inch thick. Transfer the rounds to the prepared baking sheet and prick all over with a fork. Cover with another sheet of parchment paper and set a baking sheet on top. Bake the pastry for about 25 minutes, or until it is cooked and browned; remove the pastry from the oven. Increase the oven temperature to 400°.
3. Meanwhile, melt the butter in a large skillet. Add the onions and cook, stirring, over moderately high heat for 4 minutes; then cook over low heat, stirring, until soft and golden, about

50 minutes; let cool. In a food processor, coarsely puree the onions and walnuts. Season with salt and pepper.
4. In a saucepan of boiling water, blanch the mushrooms until tender, 2 minutes. Drain and cut into ¼-inch-thick slices.
5. Spread the pastry rounds with the puree and arrange the mushrooms, overlapping, on top. Brush with olive oil and bake for 10 minutes, or until hot. Garnish with chives and serve.
—*Jean-Georges Vongerichten*
MAKE AHEAD The recipe can be prepared through Step 3 up to 1 day ahead. Wrap the pastry rounds in plastic and refrigerate the onion-walnut puree.
SERVE WITH Frisée and herb salad.
WINE Tart, low-tannin Barbera.

Chunky Guacamole with Cumin

TOTAL: 20 MIN

6 SERVINGS ● ● ●

- ½ teaspoon cumin seeds
- 5 large Hass avocados, halved and pitted
- 3 tablespoons fresh lemon juice
- 2 tablespoons chopped cilantro
- 1 small onion, minced
- 1 large garlic clove, minced
- 1 jalapeño, with some seeds, minced

Salt

1. In a skillet, toast the cumin seeds over moderately high heat, shaking the skillet constantly, until fragrant, about 30 seconds. Transfer the cumin seeds to a mortar to cool completely, then finely grind with a pestle.
2. Scoop half of the avocados into a large bowl and coarsely mash them with a fork. Stir in the lemon juice, cilantro, onion, garlic, jalapeño and ground cumin. Scoop chunks of the remaining avocados into the bowl; stir lightly with a spoon. Season the guacamole with salt and serve at room temperature or lightly chilled. —*Marcia Kiesel*
WINE Tangy, crisp Vernaccia.

PORCINI MUSHROOM TARTLETS

MELTED TALEGGIO FLAT BREADS WITH TOPPINGS

OVEN-ROASTED TOMATO TART

Melted Taleggio Flat Breads with Three Toppings

TOTAL: 30 MIN

12 SERVINGS ●

Twelve 7-inch flat breads or
    pocketless pita breads

Extra-virgin olive oil, for brushing

  3 large jalapeños

1¾ pounds Taleggio cheese, at room
    temperature, rind removed and
    cheese cut into 12 pieces
    (see Note)

Two 6½-ounce jars marinated
    artichoke hearts—drained, patted
    dry and thinly sliced

 ½ cup Spanish green olives,
    pitted and chopped

 ½ cup chopped salted
    roasted almonds

1. Preheat the oven to 350°. Lightly brush the flat breads on both sides with olive oil. Toast them directly on the oven rack for 6 minutes, or until golden.

2. Brush the jalapeños lightly with olive oil. Roast them over a gas flame or under the broiler until softened and blackened in spots, about 4 minutes. Transfer the jalapeños to a bowl, cover with plastic and let cool. Peel, seed and cut the jalapeños into thin strips.

3. Spread the Taleggio on the breads, leaving a 1-inch border all around. Top 4 of the breads with the jalapeño strips, 4 with the artichoke hearts and 4 with a mix of the olives and almonds.

4. Just before serving, bake the flat breads directly on the oven racks for 5 minutes, or until the bottoms are crisp and the cheese is melted. Cut into wedges and serve. —*Grace Parisi*

NOTE Taleggio is a rich, semisoft cow's-milk cheese from Italy. You can also make these toasts with mozzarella, Monterey Jack or Muenster.

MAKE AHEAD The flat breads can be prepared through Step 3 earlier in the day and refrigerated.

WINE Light, spicy Pinot Grigio.

Oven-Roasted Tomato Tart

ACTIVE: 30 MIN; TOTAL: 2 HR

8 SERVINGS ●

- 3 pounds ripe plum tomatoes, halved lengthwise and seeded
- ¼ cup extra-virgin olive oil
- 1 tablespoon thyme leaves

Kosher salt and freshly ground pepper

- 2 garlic cloves, thinly sliced

About 1 cup all-purpose flour

- 6½ tablespoons cold unsalted butter, cut into ½-inch pieces
- ¼ cup ice water
- 2 tablespoons crème fraîche
- 1 tablespoon whole-grain mustard
- ½ cup shredded Gruyère cheese

I. Preheat the oven to 350°. Toss the tomatoes with the olive oil and thyme; season with salt and pepper. Spread the tomatoes halves, cut side down, on a rimmed baking sheet. Roast in the oven for 35 minutes. Pull off the skins. Turn the tomatoes cut side up, top with the garlic and roast for 35 minutes longer, or until slightly dried and the garlic is golden. Let cool, then blot dry with paper towels. Leave the oven on.

2. Meanwhile, in a food processor, combine 1 cup of flour with a pinch of salt. Add the butter and pulse until it is the size of small peas. Sprinkle on the ice water and pulse just until a dough forms. Wrap the dough in plastic and refrigerate until chilled, about 30 minutes.

3. On a lightly floured surface, roll out the dough to an 11½-inch round about ⅛ inch thick; fit it into a 9½-inch tart pan with a removable bottom. Fold in the overhang to reinforce the sides. Trim off any excess dough. Chill the tart shell.

4. Line the tart shell with foil and fill with pie weights. Bake the tart shell for 35 minutes, or until just set. Carefully remove the foil and weights and bake for 5 minutes longer, or until golden.

5. Mix the crème fraîche and mustard and spread over the prebaked tart shell. Sprinkle the cheese all over.

Arrange the tomatoes in the shell in 2 layers, cut side up, seasoning between the layers. Bake the tart for 25 minutes, or until the tomatoes are just beginning to brown. Serve hot or at room temperature. —*Grace Parisi*

MAKE AHEAD The tart can be kept at room temperature for up to 6 hours.

WINE Tart, low-tannin Barbera.

Gruyère Toasts with Caramelized Onions and Sherry

ACTIVE: 25 MIN; TOTAL: 1 HR 20 MIN

MAKES 4 DOZEN TOASTS ●

- ¼ cup extra-virgin olive oil
- 4 large onions, thinly sliced
- ¼ cup fino sherry
- 1½ teaspoons caraway seeds, lightly toasted

Kosher salt and freshly ground pepper

- 12 slices of rye bread from a square loaf of rye or European pumpernickel bread
- ½ cup whole-grain mustard
- 10 ounces Gruyère cheese, shredded

I. Heat 2 tablespoons of olive oil in each of 2 large skillets. Add half of the onions to each skillet and cook over moderately low heat for 1 hour, or until nicely browned, stirring occasionally. Scrape all of the onions into 1 skillet. Stir in the sherry and caraway seeds and cook until the sherry is completely absorbed, about 1 minute. Season with salt and pepper.

2. Preheat the oven to 400°. Lightly spread 1 side of each slice of bread with the mustard and arrange on a large baking sheet. Top with the onions and cheese. Season with pepper.

3. Bake the open-faced sandwiches for 6 minutes, or until the cheese is melted and the edges of the bread are toasted. Transfer the toasts to a cutting board and cut each into 4 triangles.

—*Tom Colicchio and Sisha Ortuzar*

MAKE AHEAD The recipe can be prepared through Step 2 up to 4 hours ahead.

WINE Medium-bodied, round Pinot Blanc.

Fried Green Tomatoes with Anchovy and Lemon

TOTAL: 30 MIN

8 SERVINGS ●

- ½ cup all-purpose flour
- ½ teaspoon kosher salt
- ¼ teaspoon cayenne pepper
- 2 large eggs
- 2 tablespoons water
- 2 cups fine fresh bread crumbs (from six 1-ounce slices of bread, crusts removed)
- 4 green tomatoes (¾ pound each), cut crosswise into ¼-inch-thick slices (see Note)
- ½ cup extra-virgin olive oil
- 8 large anchovy fillets, halved lengthwise

Lemon wedges, for serving

I. In a shallow bowl, mix the flour with the salt and cayenne. In another shallow bowl, beat the eggs with the water. Spread the bread crumbs in a third shallow bowl.

2. Dredge 4 of the tomato slices in the flour and shake off the excess. Dip them in the egg, then coat with the bread crumbs, shaking off the excess. Repeat with the remaining tomato slices.

3. Heat the olive oil in a large nonstick skillet until shimmering. Add half of the breaded green tomato slices and fry them over moderately high heat until crisp and golden brown, about 2 minutes per side. Drain the tomato slices on paper towels and transfer them to a large platter. Repeat with the remaining tomato slices. Top each fried tomato slice with an anchovy strip and a lemon wedge and serve immediately.

—*Michael Tusk*

NOTE The medium-size green tomato is a distinct variety. Its zesty flavor makes it excellent for frying, broiling and adding to relishes. Green tomatoes are available at specialty food stores and well-stocked produce markets.

WINE Lively, assertive Sauvignon Blanc.

starters

Chickpea Fries with Sage and Parmesan

ACTIVE: 30 MIN; TOTAL: 2 HR 30 MIN

12 SERVINGS ● ●

2 ¾ cups milk

1 ½ teaspoons unsalted butter

1 small garlic clove, minced

1 cup chickpea flour, sifted if lumpy (see Note)

Coarse salt and freshly ground pepper

Canola oil, for frying

2 tablespoons finely chopped sage

½ cup grated Parmesan cheese

1. In a medium saucepan, combine the milk, butter and garlic and bring to a boil over high heat. Reduce the heat to moderately low and gradually whisk in the chickpea flour until smooth. Stir constantly with a rubber spatula until the mixture thickens, about 2 minutes. Season with salt and pepper.

2. Scrape the mixture into a nonstick 9-by-13-inch rimmed baking sheet or baking dish that has been lightly sprayed with vegetable oil spray; spread into a ¼-inch layer. Cover with parchment paper and refrigerate until firm, 2 to 3 hours.

3. Pour 1 inch of canola oil into a wide skillet and heat it to 350°, or until a piece of bread bubbles rapidly when added to the hot oil. Meanwhile, cut the chickpea mixture into 2-inch squares. Fry the squares in batches until golden brown, about 1 minute per side. Transfer the squares to a rack lined with paper towels to drain, then keep them warm in a low oven while you fry the rest.

4. In a bowl, mix the sage and Parmesan cheese. Toss the fries in the cheese and sage mixture until coated; serve warm.
—*Tom Valenti*

NOTE Chickpea flour is available at Indian markets and health food stores.

MAKE AHEAD The recipe can be prepared through Step 3; refrigerate overnight. Re-crisp the fries in a 350° oven. Toss with the sage and Parmesan before serving.

WINE Dry, rich Champagne.

Walnut Pesto and Goat Cheese Dip

TOTAL: 30 MIN

MAKES ABOUT 4 CUPS ● ●

Pesto is the Italian word for "pounded," and here it refers to ingredients that are crushed together in a food processor. Walnuts, goat cheese and watercress form the basis for this delectable dip.

14 ounces walnuts (2 ¼ cups)

½ cup extra-virgin olive oil, plus more for drizzling

Kosher salt and freshly ground pepper

10 ounces fresh goat cheese, at room temperature

4 small shallots, minced

½ cup finely chopped watercress leaves

¼ cup fresh lemon juice

3 Hass avocados, cut into ½-inch dice

Small radishes and assorted vegetable sticks, such as celery, fennel and carrots, for serving

1. Preheat the oven to 350°. Spread the walnuts on a rimmed baking sheet and toast for 7 minutes, or until golden. Transfer to a plate and let cool. In a food processor, working in 2 batches, pulse the walnuts until coarsely chopped. Return all of the walnuts to the food processor and pulse in the ½ cup of olive oil. Do not overprocess; the pesto should be slightly chunky. Season with 2 teaspoons of salt and ½ teaspoon of pepper and stir to mix.

2. Transfer the pesto to a medium bowl. Mix in the goat cheese, shallots, watercress and lemon juice. Season with salt and pepper. Fold in the avocados. Drizzle the dip with olive oil and serve with radishes and assorted crisp vegetables.
—*Tom Colicchio and Sisha Ortuzar*

MAKE AHEAD The dip can be refrigerated overnight without the avocados. Bring to room temperature and fold in the diced avocados before serving.

WINE Round, rich Sauvignon Blanc.

White Bean Dip with Herbs

TOTAL: 10 MIN

MAKES ABOUT 3 CUPS ● ● ●

¼ cup plus 2 tablespoons extra-virgin olive oil

3 garlic cloves, very finely chopped

1 teaspoon finely chopped sage

½ teaspoon finely chopped rosemary

Two 19-ounce cans cannellini beans, drained

2 tablespoons water

Salt

Cayenne pepper

Pita chips, for serving

1. In a medium skillet, heat ¼ cup of the olive oil until shimmering. Add the garlic, sage and rosemary and cook over moderately high heat, stirring, until fragrant and the garlic is just beginning to brown, about 1 minute. Add the beans and toss to coat.

2. Transfer the bean mixture to a food processor. Add the water, season with salt and cayenne and process to a fairly smooth puree.

3. Transfer the dip to a small serving bowl, drizzle the remaining 2 tablespoons of olive oil on top and serve with pita chips. —*Grace Parisi*

WINE Tangy, crisp Vernaccia.

Bruschetta of Spring Vegetables

ACTIVE: 1 HR; TOTAL: 1 HR 20 MIN

8 SERVINGS ●

The challenge of preparing spring vegetables is preserving their fragile color, texture and sweetness. Chef Paul Bertolli's approach is to stew them gently with shallots, garlic and olive oil; the vegetables cook gradually in the water they render. Since the cooking time for each one varies, simply add the next vegetable when the previous one has lost some of its crunch but is not softened to the core. The flavors will remain distinct yet also blend harmoniously. Spring vegetables are most flavorful when served lukewarm.

BRUSCHETTA OF SPRING VEGETABLES

WHITE BEAN DIP WITH HERBS

6 baby artichokes (about 1 pound)
½ lemon
1 cup shelled fresh fava beans
    (from 1 pound in the pod)
6 tablespoons extra-virgin olive oil,
    plus more for brushing
8 small spring garlic cloves or 4
    medium garlic cloves, thinly sliced
1 small shallot, minced
8 medium asparagus, peeled
    and cut on the diagonal into
    ½-inch lengths
12 scallions, cut into 1-inch lengths
1 cup shelled fresh peas (from
    1½ pounds in the pod)
Salt
1 tablespoon chopped parsley
½ tablespoon finely chopped chives
½ teaspoon finely chopped tarragon
Eight ½-inch-thick slices of sourdough
    bread, crusts removed

1. Preheat the oven to 375°. Pull the outer leaves off the artichokes until you reach the yellow inner leaves. With a small, sharp knife, trim the stems and any dark green spots from the artichoke bottoms. Rub with the lemon. Cut the artichokes lengthwise into ⅛-inch-thick slices and place in a bowl; squeeze the lemon half over them and toss to coat with juice.

2. Blanch the fava beans in a medium saucepan of boiling water for about 15 seconds to loosen their skins. Drain and let cool, then peel the fava beans.

3. In a large, deep skillet, warm the 6 tablespoons of olive oil. Add the garlic and shallot and cook over moderate heat until fragrant, about 3 minutes. Stir in the artichokes until coated with oil and spread in an even layer. Cover with a round of parchment paper an inch larger than the skillet, pressing it directly over the artichokes. Cover the skillet with a lid and cook over moderately low heat until the artichokes are barely tender, about 3 minutes. Add the asparagus, cover with the parchment and lid and cook for about 3 minutes.

4. Repeat the procedure with the scallions, peas and fava beans, adding them at approximate 3-minute intervals and adjusting the heat so that all the vegetables sweat but do not brown. Season with salt, stir in the herbs and remove the skillet from the heat.

5. Put the bread slices on a baking sheet, lightly brush both sides with olive oil and bake until golden brown, about 4 minutes per side. Set the toasts on plates, spoon the vegetables on top and serve. —*Paul Bertolli*

WINE Medium-bodied, round Pinot Blanc.

EGG SALAD CROSTINI WITH WHITE ANCHOVIES

MUSHROOM AND FONTINA CROSTINI

Egg Salad Crostini with White Anchovies

ACTIVE: 30 MIN; TOTAL: 1 HR 20 MIN
MAKES ABOUT 4 DOZEN
CROSTINI ● ●

- 2 tablespoons extra-virgin olive oil, plus more for brushing
- 1 large onion, thinly sliced
- Kosher salt and freshly ground pepper
- 1 thin baguette, cut into ¼-inch-thick slices
- 1 large garlic clove, halved
- 6 large eggs, at room temperature
- 1 tablespoon finely chopped chives
- 1 teaspoon white wine vinegar
- 24 white anchovy fillets or pickled herring pieces—drained, patted dry and halved crosswise

1. Heat 1 tablespoon of oil in a skillet. Add the onion; cook over moderately low heat, stirring occasionally, until browned, 1 hour. Season with salt and pepper.

2. Preheat the oven to 300°. Lightly brush both sides of the bread slices with olive oil and arrange on a large baking sheet. Bake the crostini for 5 minutes, or until crisp but not golden. Immediately rub 1 side of each crostini with the garlic. Let cool on the baking sheet.

3. Meanwhile, prepare an ice-water bath. Bring a small pot of water to a boil. Add the eggs and return to a boil, then boil for 7 minutes. Immerse the eggs in the ice-water bath until completely cool, then peel and transfer to a medium bowl. Lightly mash the eggs with a large fork. Gently stir in the chives, vinegar and the remaining 1 tablespoon of olive oil. Season with salt and pepper.

4. Top each crostini with onion, followed by egg salad and a piece of anchovy.
—*Tom Colicchio and Sisha Ortuzar*

MAKE AHEAD The soft-boiled eggs can be refrigerated overnight. The crostini toasts can be stored in an airtight container overnight. Assemble the crostini up to 30 minutes before serving.

WINE Dry, fruity sparkling wine.

Mushroom and Fontina Crostini

TOTAL: 35 MIN

4 SERVINGS ● ●

In this dish, Italian Fontina cheese melts beautifully, but young Gouda would be equally delicious.

Four ½-inch-thick slices of peasant
    bread, halved diagonally
5 tablespoons extra-virgin olive oil
1½ pounds white mushrooms
2 tablespoons unsalted butter
2 medium shallots, finely chopped
1 large garlic clove, minced
1 teaspoon chopped thyme
3 tablespoons water
Salt and freshly ground pepper
¼ pound Fontina cheese, coarsely
    shredded (about 1 cup)
1 tablespoon chopped parsley

1. Preheat the oven to 400°. Arrange the bread on a baking sheet and drizzle with 3 tablespoons of the olive oil. Toast for 12 minutes, until slightly golden around the edges. Turn the broiler on.

2. Meanwhile, thinly slice the mushrooms. In a large skillet, cook the butter over high heat until lightly browned, 2 minutes. Add the remaining 2 tablespoons of olive oil and the mushrooms and cook undisturbed until the mushrooms are browned on the bottoms, 2 minutes. Continue to cook, stirring occasionally, until browned all over, 10 minutes. Add the shallots, garlic and thyme, lower the heat to moderate and cook until the shallots are tender, 5 minutes. Add the water and scrape up any browned bits from the bottom of the pan, then cook for 3 minutes longer. Season the mushrooms with salt and pepper and remove from the heat.

3. Spoon the mushroom mixture on the toasts and sprinkle the cheese on top. Broil for 2 minutes, or until the cheese is melted. Transfer the crostini to a platter, sprinkle with the parsley and serve.
—*Maria Helm Sinskey*

WINE Light, zesty, fruity Dolcetto.

Lima Bean Puree with Olives and Shaved Pecorino

TOTAL: 35 MIN

10 SERVINGS ● ● ●

4 cups fresh lima beans (from
    about 5 pounds in the pod) or
    two 10-ounce packages frozen
    baby limas, thawed
¾ cup plus 1 tablespoon
    extra-virgin olive oil
1 rosemary sprig
2 garlic cloves, minced
2½ tablespoons fresh lemon juice
Kosher salt and freshly ground pepper
¾ cup oil-cured black olives (about
    4 ounces), pitted and halved
¼ cup coarsely chopped
    flat-leaf parsley
One 2-ounce piece of Pecorino
    Romano cheese, shaved with
    a vegetable peeler (¾ cup)
Thin baguette slices, toasted

1. If using fresh limas, blanch them in a large saucepan of boiling salted water until just tender, about 5 minutes; drain.

2. In a large saucepan, heat ¾ cup of the olive oil with the rosemary. Add the lima beans and garlic and cook over moderate heat until the limas are soft, about 10 minutes. Drain the beans in a fine sieve set over a heatproof bowl. Discard the rosemary sprig and reserve the oil.

3. Transfer the lima beans to a food processor and pulse until pureed. With the machine on, gradually add the reserved oil and process until smooth. Add 2 tablespoons of the lemon juice and season with salt and pepper.

4. In a bowl, combine the olives, parsley and the remaining 1 tablespoon of oil and ½ tablespoon of lemon juice. Add half of the cheese and toss gently.

5. Spoon the lima puree onto a serving platter or into a serving bowl. Scatter the olive mixture and the remaining cheese on top and serve right away, passing the baguette toasts alongside.
—*Suzanne Goin*

MAKE AHEAD The lima bean puree can be refrigerated overnight. Serve at room temperature.

WINE High-acid, savory Vermentino.

Two-Cheese Panini with Tomato-Olive Pesto

TOTAL: 45 MIN

MAKES ABOUT 40 SMALL PANINI ●

⅔ cup drained oil-packed sun-dried
    tomatoes, coarsely chopped
⅓ cup oil-cured black olives,
    pitted and coarsely chopped
1 teaspoon dried oregano
Freshly ground pepper
1 pullman loaf (20 slices)
    of white bread
Extra-virgin olive oil, for brushing
10 thin slices of provolone cheese
1 pound fresh mozzarella, cut into
    ¼-inch slices

1. In a food processor, process the sun-dried tomatoes, olives and oregano to a coarse paste. Season with pepper.

2. Brush 1 side of each slice of bread with olive oil and set on a baking sheet, oiled side down. Top half of the bread with the provolone, spread each of these with 1 tablespoon of the tomato-olive pesto and top with the mozzarella. Close with the remaining bread, oiled side up.

3. Heat a griddle or a very large skillet. Arrange 3 or 4 sandwiches on the griddle and top with a cast-iron skillet; do not press the pan down. Cook the sandwiches over moderately high heat until golden on the bottoms, 2 minutes. Flip the sandwiches and cook until browned and the cheese is melted, 2 minutes longer. Transfer to a wire rack to cool. Repeat with the remaining sandwiches.

4. Cut the crusts off the sandwiches, then cut into 4 triangles and serve.
—*Tom Colicchio and Sisha Ortuzar*

MAKE AHEAD The panini can be prepared through Step 3 up to 6 hours ahead (leave on the rack). Crisp in a 350° oven.

WINE Light, spicy Pinot Grigio.

starters

Classic Hummus

TOTAL: 5 MIN

MAKES ABOUT 1¼ CUPS ● ● ●

- 1   cup cooked chickpeas, drained
- 2   large garlic cloves, chopped
- 2   tablespoons tahini

Juice of 1 lemon

- ½   cup extra-virgin olive oil

Salt and freshly ground pepper

In a food processor, puree the chickpeas, garlic, tahini and lemon juice. Gradually add the olive oil until incorporated. Season the hummus with salt and pepper and scrape it into a bowl. Refrigerate until ready to serve or use.

—Jehangir Mehta

WINE Dry, crisp sparkling wine.

Crostini of Squid Stewed in Red Wine

ACTIVE: 30 MIN; TOTAL: 1 HR 35 MIN

MAKES 16 CROSTINI ● ●

- 3   tablespoons extra-virgin olive oil, plus more for brushing
- 2   garlic cloves, 1 halved, 1 pounded in a mortar or minced
- 2   pounds cleaned small squid, bodies cut into ¼-inch-thick slices, large tentacles halved

Salt

- 2   medium leeks, white parts only, thinly sliced
- ¼   teaspoon crushed red pepper
- 2   teaspoons all-purpose flour
- 1   medium tomato—peeled, seeded and finely chopped
- 1   cup fruity, young red wine

Freshly ground black pepper

Sixteen ½-inch-thick slices of French bread

- ½   cup mayonnaise

Fresh lemon juice

- 1   cup shredded arugula

I. Preheat the oven to 375°. In a large skillet, heat 1 tablespoon of the olive oil until shimmering. Add half of a garlic clove and cook over high heat, stirring frequently, until golden brown.

Using a slotted spoon, discard the garlic. Spread half of the squid evenly in the skillet and season with salt. Cook without stirring for 1 minute, then transfer the squid to a large bowl. Repeat with 1 tablespoon of the olive oil and the remaining garlic clove half and squid.

2. Add the remaining 1 tablespoon of olive oil, the leeks and crushed red pepper to the skillet. Cook over low heat, stirring occasionally, until the leeks are softened, about 8 minutes. Stir in the flour and cook for 1 minute. Add the tomato and wine and bring to a simmer, stirring well to scrape up any browned bits on the bottom of the skillet. Return the squid and its juices to the skillet and simmer, stirring occasionally, until the stew has thickened and the squid is very tender, about 50 minutes. Season with salt and black pepper.

3. Meanwhile, arrange the bread slices on a large rimmed baking sheet. Brush the slices with olive oil and bake for 8 minutes, or until golden brown. In a small bowl, mix the mayonnaise with the pounded garlic and season with lemon juice and salt.

4. Mound the squid on the crostini. Top with aioli and the arugula and serve.

—Michael Tusk

WINE Bright, fruity rosé.

Eggplant and Goat Cheese Crostini

ACTIVE: 25 MIN; TOTAL: 45 MIN

MAKES 32 CROSTINI ●

The eggplant spread for this recipe keeps beautifully and is tasty with grilled fish, chicken or steak.

- 1   tablespoon extra-virgin olive oil
- 1   pound eggplant, peeled and cut into ½-inch dice
- 1   medium tomato, cut into ½-inch dice
- 1   yellow bell pepper, cut into ½-inch dice
- ¼   cup sherry vinegar

- 1   garlic clove, minced
- 1   teaspoon ground cumin
- 1   tablespoon finely chopped parsley
- ½   teaspoon coarsely chopped thyme

Pinch of cayenne pepper

Salt and freshly ground pepper

- 1   baguette, cut into ½-inch-thick slices and toasted
- 1½ cups soft goat cheese (¾ pound)

I. Heat the olive oil in a large skillet. Add the eggplant, tomato, bell pepper, vinegar, garlic and cumin and bring to a boil. Cover and cook over moderately low heat, stirring occasionally, until thickened, about 20 minutes. Uncover and cook, stirring, until the liquid has evaporated, about 2 minutes. Stir in the parsley, thyme and cayenne and season with salt and pepper. Let cool.

2. Spread each slice of toasted baguette with 2 teaspoons of the goat cheese, and then dollop 1 tablespoon of the eggplant spread on top. Arrange the crostini on a platter and serve.

—Joshua Wesson

MAKE AHEAD The eggplant spread can be refrigerated for up to 1 week.

WINE Lively, assertive Sauvignon Blanc.

Green Olive and Walnut Crostini

TOTAL: 25 MIN

MAKES 16 CROSTINI ● ●

This chunky, nutty green-olive topping was inspired by tapenade, the Provençal black-olive spread.

- ½   cup walnut pieces (2 ounces)
- ¼   pound Picholine or other green olives, pitted and finely chopped
- 3   tablespoons extra-virgin olive oil
- 2   anchovy fillets, finely chopped
- 1   garlic clove, minced
- ½   baguette, cut into ½-inch-thick slices and toasted
- ¾   cup soft goat cheese (6 ounces)

I. Preheat the oven to 350°. Spread the walnuts in a pie plate and bake for about 10 minutes, or until lightly browned. Let cool, then finely chop.

2. In a medium bowl, mix the olives, walnuts, olive oil, anchovies and garlic.

3. Spread each slice of the toasted baguette with 2 teaspoons of the goat cheese and top with 1 tablespoon of the olive mixture. Arrange the crostini on a platter and serve. —*Marcia Kiesel*
WINE Round, rich Sauvignon Blanc.

Artichoke and Goat Cheese Bruschetta

TOTAL: 30 MIN

MAKES 16 BRUSCHETTA ●

- 2 tablespoons extra-virgin olive oil, plus more for brushing
- 2 garlic cloves, cut into paper-thin slices
- 1 bay leaf
- 5 thyme sprigs
- One 10-ounce package frozen artichoke hearts, thawed and squeezed dry
- ½ teaspoon finely grated lemon zest
- ¼ pound mild fresh goat cheese, softened (½ cup)
- 2 teaspoons fresh lemon juice

Salt and freshly ground pepper

- 16 thin baguette slices

1. Preheat the broiler. In a medium skillet, heat 2 tablespoons of olive oil until shimmering. Add the garlic, bay leaf and thyme sprigs and cook over moderate heat until fragrant, 2 minutes. Add the artichokes and lemon zest and cook, stirring, until lightly browned, 5 minutes. Scrape the thyme leaves into the skillet; discard the sprigs and bay leaf.

2. Transfer the artichoke mixture to a food processor. Add the goat cheese and lemon juice; pulse until pureed. Season with salt and pepper. Transfer to a serving dish, cover and keep warm.

3. Brush the bread slices with olive oil and broil for 1 minute, turning once, until golden and crisp. Serve the artichoke spread with the baguette slices.
—*Laura Chenel*
WINE Round, rich Sauvignon Blanc.

Bean Sprout Chat

TOTAL: 30 MIN

4 TO 6 SERVINGS ● ●

Chat is a crunchy Indian noodle snack. About the ingredients: Tamarind chutney is a sweet, tangy condiment made from the fruit of the tropical tamarind tree. The sticky pulp is strained to remove the seeds and stringy fibers, then sweetened and enhanced with ginger, chiles and other spices. *Chat masala* is a spicy seasoning blend that flavors a host of Indian snack foods and salads. It usually includes black salt, which provides smokiness, and *amchoor* (powdered dried green mango), for tang. *Sev* are mild, fragrant or fiery snacks made from broken fried chickpea-flour noodles. All these ingredients are available by mail order from Kalustyan's in New York City (123 Lexington Ave.; 212-685-3451 or www.kalustyans.com).

- 1 baking potato (½ pound), peeled and cut into ½-inch dice
- 3 cups sprouted mung beans
- ¼ cup prepared tamarind chutney
- ¼ cup fresh lime juice
- 3 tablespoons plain yogurt
- 3 tablespoons extra-virgin olive oil
- 1 tablespoon chopped chives
- 1 tablespoon ground cumin
- 1 teaspoon *chat masala*

Pinch of sugar

- 1 Granny Smith apple—peeled, cored and cut into ½-inch dice
- 2 tablespoons finely chopped red onion
- 2 tablespoons green mango, cut into ¼-inch dice (optional)
- 1½ cups *sev,* plus more for garnish

Salt and freshly ground pepper

1. In a small saucepan of boiling water, cook the potato until just tender, about 4 minutes; drain. In a small saucepan of boiling salted water, blanch the mung beans for 3 minutes; drain and cool.

2. In a medium bowl, mix together the chutney, lime juice, yogurt and olive oil. Stir in the chives, cumin, *chat masala* and sugar. Fold in the mung beans, apple, onion, green mango, potato and 1½ cups of the *sev.* Season with salt and pepper. Sprinkle more *sev* on top of the chat and serve right away.
—*Floyd Cardoz*
WINE Light, soft Chenin Blanc.

TASTE TEST | supermarket cheddar cheese

In a taste test, the F&W staff sampled a dozen Cheddar cheeses sold at supermarkets nationwide and rated these four best.

PRODUCT	F&W COMMENT	INTERESTING BITE
Cabot Sharp	"Nice nutty flavor."	In 2000, Cabot made the world's largest grilled cheese—320 lbs.
Cracker Barrel Sharp	"Great tang, kind of addictive."	Cracker Barrel will celebrate its 50th birthday in 2004.
Sargento Sharp White	"Good creaminess, perfect for grilling."	See their Web site for cheese—wine pairings (www.sargento.com).
Heluva Good Sharp	"Creamy and sharp—but not too sharp."	Unlike many large producers, Heluva Good ages its cheese naturally.

---

starters

Spicy Chickpea Chat

ACTIVE: 20 MIN; TOTAL: 1 HR 20 MIN

MAKES 4 CUPS ● ●

We like to serve this snack in the crisp lentil-flour wafers called pappadams sold at every Indian market.

½ cup plain yogurt
2 medium tomatoes, seeded and cut into ½-inch dice
⅔ cup chopped cilantro
1 small sweet onion, finely diced
2 jalapeños, seeded and minced
¼ teaspoon turmeric
One 19-ounce can chickpeas— drained, rinsed and patted dry
Salt and freshly ground pepper

In a large bowl, mix the yogurt with the tomatoes, cilantro, onion, jalapeños and turmeric. Stir in the chickpeas, season with salt and pepper and refrigerate for at least 1 hour. Serve chilled or at room temperature. —*Jehangir Mehta*

WINE Dry, fruity sparkling wine.

Red Potato and Green Pea Samosas

ACTIVE: 1 HR; TOTAL: 1 HR 40 MIN

MAKES 40 SAMOSAS ●

Samosas are a popular Indian snack food served at teatime and with drinks. This lighter version is baked instead of fried.

¾ pound red potatoes, peeled and cut into ¼-inch dice
1 cup frozen peas
1 teaspoon chili powder
½ teaspoon caraway seeds
½ teaspoon garam masala
Kosher salt and freshly ground pepper
14 sheets of phyllo dough
5 tablespoons unsalted butter, melted
Sweet-and-Sour Tamarind Chutney (recipe follows), for serving

I. Preheat the oven to 350°. In a medium saucepan of boiling salted water, cook the potatoes and peas until tender when pierced, about 6 minutes.

Drain well and transfer to a bowl. Stir in the chili powder, caraway seeds and garam marsala until combined. Season with salt and pepper.

2. Spread 1 sheet of phyllo on a work surface with a long side facing you. Brush the sheet with melted butter and set another sheet on top of it. Cut the sheets crosswise into 2-inch strips. Set 1 teaspoon of the filling at the bottom end of a strip; fold the corner over the filling to form a triangle. Continue folding the phyllo up and over, onto itself like a folded flag, sealing the last fold with melted butter. Transfer to a baking sheet and brush with melted butter. Repeat to form the remaining samosas.

3. Bake the samosas in the oven for about 25 minutes, or until they are golden brown. Serve hot or at room temperature with the tamarind chutney alongside. —*Jehangir Mehta*

MAKE AHEAD The samosas can be refrigerated, covered, overnight before baking. Brush with butter just before baking.

WINE Ripe, creamy-textured Chardonnay.

Sweet-and-Sour Tamarind Chutney

ACTIVE: 10 MIN; TOTAL: 30 MIN

MAKES ABOUT ½ CUP ● ● ●

2 cups water
½ cup tamarind paste (4 ounces; see Note)
2 tablespoons sugar

In a medium saucepan, combine the water, tamarind paste and sugar and bring to a boil over moderate heat. Reduce the heat to moderately low and simmer until the liquid has reduced by half, about 20 minutes. Strain the tamarind through a coarse sieve, pushing on it with a rubber spatula to release all of the paste from the seeds. —*J.M.*

NOTE Tamarind paste is available at Indian markets.

MAKE AHEAD The chutney can be refrigerated for up to 4 days.

Tomato-Cilantro Raita

ACTIVE: 15 MIN; TOTAL: 1 HR 15 MIN

MAKES 2 CUPS ● ●

1 cup plain yogurt
2 medium tomatoes, seeded and cut into ½-inch dice
½ cup coarsely chopped cilantro
⅛ teaspoon cayenne pepper
Salt and freshly ground pepper
20 large black-pepper pappadams

I. Whisk the yogurt, tomatoes, cilantro and cayenne; season with salt and pepper. Refrigerate for 1 hour or overnight.

2. Preheat the broiler. Broil 1 pappadam on a baking sheet as close to the heat as possible with the oven door open until the pappadam begins to puff, about 5 seconds. Turn the pappadam 180 degrees and broil until the pappadam is dimpled and puffed, about 3 seconds longer. Transfer the pappadam to a wire rack and repeat with the remaining pappadams. Serve with the raita. —*Jehangir Mehta*

WINE Lively, assertive Sauvignon Blanc.

Spicy Clams with Tomatoes

TOTAL: 25 MIN

4 SERVINGS ● ●

¼ cup extra-virgin olive oil
2 tablespoons finely chopped garlic
½ teaspoon crushed red pepper
2 medium plum tomatoes—peeled, seeded and coarsely chopped
¼ cup dry white wine
2 pounds cockles, rinsed
¼ cup finely chopped parsley

Heat the olive oil in a deep skillet. Add the garlic and red pepper and cook over low heat until fragrant, 1 minute. Add the tomatoes and cook over moderately high heat for 2 minutes. Add the wine, bring to a boil and reduce by half. Add the cockles and cook over high heat, stirring, until they open, 5 minutes. Sprinkle the parsley on top and serve. —*Gianfranco Becchina*

WINE High-acid, savory Vermentino.

RED POTATO AND GREEN PEA SAMOSAS, WITH SWEET-AND-SOUR TAMARIND CHUTNEY

starters

Shrimp Fritters

TOTAL: 50 MIN

MAKES 20 FRITTERS ●

- 1 pound medium shrimp—shelled, deveined and coarsely chopped
- 3 slices of firm white sandwich bread, crusts removed, bread cut into ¼-inch dice
- 1 medium onion, minced
- ⅓ cup coarsely chopped cilantro
- 4 jalapeños, seeded and minced
- 6 garlic cloves, finely chopped
- 1 large egg, beaten
- 1 teaspoon turmeric
- ½ teaspoon cumin seeds
- ½ teaspoon fresh lemon juice
- 1 teaspoon salt
- 1 cup fine dry bread crumbs
- 2 cups vegetable oil, for frying

I. In a large bowl, combine the chopped shrimp with the bread, onion, cilantro, jalapeños, garlic, egg, turmeric, cumin, lemon juice and salt. Shape the shrimp mixture into 20 balls, using 2 table- spoons of the mixture for each. Transfer to a baking sheet and refrigerate until firm, about 30 minutes.

2. Preheat the oven to 350°. Spread the bread crumbs in a shallow bowl. Roll the shrimp balls in the crumbs, patting to adhere. Shake off any excess. In a skillet, heat the oil until shimmering. Fry the shrimp fritters, without crowding,

over moderately high heat until browned, 2 minutes per side. Drain the fritters on a wire rack. Repeat with the remaining fritters. When all of the fritters have been fried, arrange on a baking sheet well apart and bake until cooked through, about 5 minutes. —*Jehangir Mehta*

MAKE AHEAD The shrimp fritters can be made through Step 1 and refrigerated overnight, or fried up to 1 day ahead and then finished in the oven just before serving. Bring the shrimp fritters to room temperature before baking them.

WINE Medium-bodied, round Pinot Blanc.

Shrimp and Green Papaya Summer Rolls

TOTAL: 30 MIN

MAKES 6 SUMMER ROLLS ● ● ●

Green papayas (oval, pale green and cucumber-like) are available at Asian markets and some supermarkets. You can also substitute shredded cabbage.

- 3½ tablespoons Asian fish sauce
- 3½ tablespoons fresh lime juice
- 3 tablespoons sugar
- 1 small green papaya (about 1½ pounds)—peeled, seeded and coarsely shredded
- 2 carrots, coarsely shredded
- 3 tablespoons chopped cilantro
- 3 tablespoons chopped mint

Six 9-inch round rice paper wrappers, plus more in case they tear
- ½ cup unsweetened coconut milk
- ¼ cup unsalted dry-roasted peanuts
- 2 tablespoons water
- 1½ tablespoons hoisin sauce
- 1 small garlic clove, smashed

Kosher salt
- 18 shelled, cooked large shrimp (about ½ pound), halved lengthwise

I. In a large bowl, mix 3 tablespoons each of the fish sauce and lime juice with the sugar; stir until the sugar is dissolved. Add the papaya, carrots, cilantro and mint and toss to combine.

2. Fill a large bowl halfway with cold water. One at a time, submerge the rice paper wrappers in the water and let soak together for 5 minutes, or until pliable.

3. Meanwhile, in a blender, puree the coconut milk with the peanuts, water, hoisin sauce, garlic and the remaining ½ tablespoon each of fish sauce and lime juice. Transfer the dipping sauce to a bowl and season lightly with salt.

4. Set a strainer over a bowl and drain the papaya salad well. Divide the salad into 6 portions. Drain the rice paper wrappers and pat dry. Arrange 3 wrap- pers on a dry work surface, keeping the rest covered with a damp towel. Arrange 3 shrimp halves in a neat row, facing the same direction, just below the cen- ter of each wrapper; top with the papaya salad and 3 more shrimp halves. Fold the bottom edge of the wrappers over the filling and roll them into tight cylin- ders, tucking in the sides as you roll. Transfer the finished rolls to a plate and cover. Repeat to form the remaining 3 rolls. Serve the summer rolls with the dipping sauce on the side. —*Melissa Clark*

MAKE AHEAD The summer rolls can be covered and refrigerated for up to 4 hours.

WINE Bright, citrusy Riesling.

Sardine and Celery Salad

TOTAL: 20 MIN

4 SERVINGS ● ● ●

- ¼ cup coarsely chopped cilantro
- 3 tablespoons extra-virgin olive oil
- 2 tablespoons grainy mustard
- 2 tablespoons Dijon mustard
- 1 small red onion, cut into very thin slices
- 2 tablespoons fresh lemon juice
- 1 teaspoon finely grated lemon zest

Four 4⅜-ounce cans sardines in oil, drained and coarsely chopped
- 4 large celery ribs, peeled and cut into 1-inch matchsticks

Salt and freshly ground pepper

TUNA AND WHITE BEAN ANTIPASTO SALAD

SARDINE AND CELERY SALAD

In a large bowl, mix the chopped cilantro with the olive oil, grainy and Dijon mustards, red onion and the lemon juice and zest. Gently fold in the sardines and celery and season with salt and pepper. Refrigerate the salad and serve chilled.
—*Marcia Kiesel*

SERVE WITH Rye crackers.

WINE Dry, medium-bodied Pinot Gris.

Lemony Tuna and White Bean Antipasto Salad

TOTAL: 35 MIN

8 SERVINGS ● ● ●

This quick and easy salad offers all the variety and freshness of a great antipasto. The quality of this dish ultimately depends on the quality of the tuna: Using an imported Italian or Spanish variety packed in olive oil makes the salad extraordinary.

¼ cup plus 2 tablespoons fresh lemon juice

¼ cup plus 2 tablespoons fruity extra-virgin olive oil, plus more for drizzling

Two 6-ounce cans olive oil–packed tuna, drained and broken into large chunks

One 19-ounce can cannellini beans, drained and rinsed (about 1½ cups)

24 pitted Calamata olives, coarsely chopped

2 cups thickly sliced celery hearts and leaves

2 tablespoons capers, drained, or if packed in salt, rinsed

2 heaping tablespoons finely chopped flat-leaf parsley

2 teaspoons grated lemon zest

1 teaspoon minced garlic

Freshly ground pepper

2 roasted red peppers from a jar or 4 piquillo peppers from a jar

Kosher salt

4 lemon slices, for garnish

1. Pour the lemon juice into a large bowl and slowly whisk in ¼ cup plus 2 tablespoons of the olive oil. Add the tuna, cannellini beans, olives, sliced celery, capers, parsley, lemon zest and garlic and toss gently. Season with pepper, cover and set aside.

2. Halve the roasted red peppers lengthwise and arrange on plates, drizzle with olive oil and season with salt. Spoon the tuna salad over the peppers and drizzle with more olive oil. Garnish with the lemon slices and serve.
—*David Rosengarten*

SERVE WITH Crusty French bread.

WINE Tangy, crisp Vernaccia.

starters

Steamed Squid and Shrimp Salad with Arugula

TOTAL: 30 MIN

4 SERVINGS ● ○

If you don't have a steamer, improvise by setting a colander or strainer in a large pot over boiling water. Close the lid tightly to prevent steam from escaping. You can use foil if you don't have a lid.

- ½ pound medium shrimp, shelled and deveined
- ½ pound small squid, cleaned, bodies cut into ¼-inch-thick rings, tentacles left whole (see Note)
- 3 cups packed arugula (2 ounces)
- 2 tablespoons extra-virgin olive oil, plus more for serving

Sea salt and freshly ground black pepper

Lemon wedges, for serving

1. Oil a large steamer basket and set it in a large saucepan over ½ inch of simmering water. Spread the shrimp in an even layer in the basket, then cover and steam over moderately high heat for 1 minute. Scatter the squid over the shrimp, cover and steam until the squid and shrimp are just done, about 2 minutes longer. Remove the steamer basket from the pan.

2. Meanwhile, in a large bowl, toss the arugula with 2 tablespoons of the olive oil and season with sea salt and pepper. Mound the arugula on plates and top with the shrimp and squid. Serve the salad with lemon wedges, olive oil and sea salt. —*Gianfranco Becchina*

NOTE For the best results, buy the smallest squid you can find.

WINE Aromatic, zesty Albariño.

Mini Herb Frittatas with Smoked Salmon

TOTAL: 1 HR

MAKES ABOUT 50 FRITTATAS ●

- 20 large eggs, lightly beaten
- ½ cup crème fraîche, plus more for topping
- ⅓ cup finely chopped tarragon
- ⅓ cup finely chopped dill, plus small sprigs for garnish
- ⅓ cup finely chopped chives
- 4 scallions, white and tender green parts only, thinly sliced

Salt and freshly ground pepper

- 2 tablespoons extra-virgin olive oil
- ½ pound thinly sliced smoked salmon, cut into 1-inch strips

1. Preheat the oven to 325°. In a bowl, whisk the eggs with the ½ cup of crème fraîche, the tarragon, chopped dill, chives and scallions. Season with 1½ teaspoons of salt and ½ teaspoon of pepper.

2. In a 10-inch ovenproof nonstick skillet, heat 1 tablespoon of the olive oil. Add half of the eggs and cook over moderately low heat, stirring gently, for 5 minutes; keep the heat low enough so the eggs do not begin to scramble. Cook the eggs, undisturbed, for 5 minutes longer. Transfer the skillet to the oven and bake for 10 minutes, or until the eggs are set around the edge and just firm in the center.

3. Loosen the side of the frittata with a spatula and gently turn it out onto a wire rack to cool completely. Repeat with the remaining oil and eggs.

4. Cut the frittatas into 1-inch squares and place on a serving platter. Garnish with the crème fraîche, salmon and dill sprigs and serve at room temperature. —*Tom Colicchio and Sisha Ortuzar*

MAKE AHEAD The frittatas can be baked up to 3 hours ahead. Cover tightly and keep at room temperature.

WINE Dry, light, crisp Champagne.

Smoked Salmon and Herbed Egg Salad Involtini

ACTIVE: 40 MIN; TOTAL: 1 HR

MAKES 2 DOZEN ROLLS ●

- 6 hard-cooked large eggs, chopped
- ¼ cup crème fraîche
- 2 tablespoons snipped chives
- 1 tablespoon finely chopped tarragon
- 1 teaspoon Dijon mustard

Salt and cayenne pepper

- 1 pound thinly sliced smoked salmon, cut into twelve 6-by-3-inch rectangles
- 2 medium radishes, cut into fine julienne strips

1. In a medium bowl, mix the eggs with the crème fraîche, chives, tarragon and mustard; season with salt and cayenne.

2. Spread the salmon slices on a work surface. Mound 1½ tablespoons of the egg salad on the short ends. Top with a few radish sticks and roll into tight cylinders. Cover and refrigerate until chilled, at least 20 minutes. Trim the ends and cut the rolls in half. Garnish with the remaining radishes and serve. —*Grace Parisi*

MAKE AHEAD The rolls can be refrigerated overnight.

WINE Dry, rich Champagne.

WINE PAIRING TIP

wine and cheese

- **Drink high-acid wines with younger, more acidic cheeses** sauvignon blanc with goat cheese

- **Choose light wines for young cheeses** orvieto with young pecorino

- **Try lower–acid wines with older cheeses** chardonnay with gruyère

- **Pour a sweet dessert wine with a salty cheese** sauternes with roquefort

- **Pair big red wines with creamy cheeses** cabernet with brie de meaux

- **Have strong wines with strong cheeses** syrah with aged cheddar

- **Match earthy wines with herbed cheeses** corsican red with brin d'amour

Q+A
cheese

fondue

Q: I'm a fondue failure. Whenever I try to make it, I end up with a stringy, gloppy mess.

A: Maybe you add the cheese too quickly; maybe you use too much cornstarch; maybe there isn't enough acid in the wine you cook with. Or perhaps you don't have a good recipe! Chef Terrance Brennan, of Artisanal in New York City, has a great fondue recipe. You can make the recipe below with cheeses other than the ones suggested, but don't use blues (they'll overpower the others), goats (they don't melt nicely) or dry, aged, Parmesan-like cheeses (they remain grainy). And remember, the best way to swirl your bread in the fondue is in a figure 8!

Artisanal's Cheese Fondue
TOTAL: 20 MIN
6 SERVINGS ●
- 1 garlic clove, halved
- 1 cup Sauvignon Blanc
- 2 teaspoons fresh lemon juice
- ¾ pound rindless cheese, such as Emmentaler, Gruyère, Comté and Appenzeller, coarsely shredded
- 1 tablespoon cornstarch

Salt and freshly ground pepper

Vigorously rub the garlic clove all over the inside of a fondue pot or medium saucepan; discard the garlic. Add the wine and lemon juice to the fondue pot and bring to a boil. In a bowl, toss the shredded cheese with the cornstarch. When the wine boils, gradually add the cheese by the handful, whisking constantly until it is fully melted before adding more. Once all of the cheese has been incorporated, simmer the fondue over moderate heat for 1 minute, stirring constantly. Remove from the heat and season with salt and pepper. Serve hot, with cubes of crusty peasant bread, boiled fingerling potatoes, cornichons or sautéed beef tips.

soufflé

Q: Wow! That fondue was amazing. On to my next cheese obsession—soufflés. Mine never rise, and they're always bland. What can I do?

A: You could always add another beaten egg white, but it really doesn't matter if your soufflé doesn't reach the sky. In fact, some people prefer a flatter soufflé, which has more crust. Blandness is easy to fix—just taste the soufflé base before adding the eggs and be sure it's highly seasoned, with tasty cheese, a bit of mustard or simply salt and pepper. You can also use all the odds and ends in your cheese bin—but avoid mozzarella, which gets stringy. Serve this soufflé straight from the baking dish, with a salad or steak.

Fallen Cheese Soufflé
ACTIVE: 10 MIN; TOTAL: 30 MIN
6 SIDE-DISH SERVINGS ●
- 4 tablespoons unsalted butter
- ¼ cup all-purpose flour
- 1½ cups milk
- 1 to 1½ cups coarsely chopped, crumbled or shredded cheese

Dijon mustard (optional)

Salt and freshly ground pepper
- 6 large eggs, separated

Freshly grated Parmesan cheese

1. Preheat the oven to 400°. Butter an 8-by-12-inch glass or ceramic baking dish. In a medium saucepan, melt the butter over moderate heat. Add the flour and whisk until blended and bubbling. Gradually whisk in the milk and bring to a boil, whisking constantly; simmer for 3 minutes. Gradually whisk in the cheese until melted. Add mustard if desired and season generously with salt and pepper. Whisk in the egg yolks.

2. In a bowl, beat the egg whites until firm. Whisk half of the whites into the soufflé base, then fold the base into the remaining whites. Pour the mixture into the baking dish and sprinkle with Parmesan. Bake for 20 minutes, or until puffed. Serve hot. —*Tina Ujlaki*

starters

Roast Beef and Watercress Involtini

TOTAL: 30 MIN

MAKES 2 DOZEN ROLLS ● ● ●

1½ tablespoons extra-virgin olive oil
1½ tablespoons fresh lemon juice
1½ packed cups small
     watercress sprigs
 ¾ cup finely shredded red cabbage
 ¼ cup very thinly sliced red onion
Salt and freshly ground pepper
16 slices of rare roast beef
     (about 1 pound)
Pesto, for garnish

1. In a medium bowl, whisk the olive oil with the lemon juice. Add the watercress, cabbage and onion, season with salt and pepper and toss.

2. Spread the roast beef slices on a work surface in pairs, overlapping them slightly along the sides, so you have eight 7-by-8-inch rectangles. Season the roast beef with salt and pepper. Mound the watercress salad on the meat and roll into tight cylinders. Trim the ends and cut the rolls into thirds. Sprinkle with salt, dot with pesto and serve. —*Grace Parisi*

MAKE AHEAD The rolls can be refrigerated for up to 1 hour.

WINE Simple, fruity Chianti.

Prosciutto and Marinated Artichoke Involtini

TOTAL: 40 MIN

MAKES 2 DOZEN ROLLS ●

 1 teaspoon extra-virgin olive oil
 ½ cup slivered blanched almonds
     (2 ounces)
One 6.5-ounce jar marinated artichoke
     hearts, drained and patted dry
 ¼ cup cream cheese, softened
 2 tablespoons freshly grated
     Parmesan cheese
 ½ teaspoon finely grated lemon zest
Salt and freshly ground pepper
18 thin slices of prosciutto
     (about 7 ounces)

1. Heat the olive oil in a small skillet. Add the slivered almonds and cook over moderate heat, stirring frequently, until golden, about 5 minutes. Transfer to a plate and let cool.

2. In a mini food processor, pulse the artichoke hearts with the almonds until finely chopped. Add the cream cheese, Parmesan and lemon zest and process to a paste. Season with salt and pepper.

3. Lay 3 prosciutto slices on a work surface, overlapping them slightly along the sides. Spoon 2 tablespoons of the artichoke filling onto the short end and roll into a tight cylinder. Repeat with the remaining prosciutto and filling. Trim the ends, cut into quarters and serve. —*Grace Parisi*

MAKE AHEAD The rolls can be refrigerated for up to 2 days.

WINE Fruity, low-oak Chardonnay.

Prosciutto-Wrapped Shrimp with Orange Marmalade

TOTAL: 30 MIN

4 SERVINGS ● ●

 ¼ cup orange marmalade
 4 teaspoons soy sauce
 4 teaspoons fresh lemon juice
 1 teaspoon minced fresh ginger
 1 large garlic clove, minced
 2 scallions, finely chopped
12 jumbo shrimp—shelled,
     deveined and butterflied
12 thin slices of prosciutto
     (about 4 ounces)
 2 tablespoons vegetable oil

1. In a bowl, mix the marmalade, soy sauce, lemon juice, ginger, garlic and scallions. Add the shrimp and toss to coat. Lay a slice of prosciutto on a work surface and fold it in half lengthwise. Wrap the prosciutto around the middle third of 1 of the shrimp. Repeat with the remaining shrimp and prosciutto.

2. In a large skillet, heat the oil until shimmering. Add the shrimp and cook over moderate heat, turning once or twice, until golden and cooked through, about 8 minutes. Transfer to a plate and serve warm or at room temperature. —*Megan Moore*

MAKE AHEAD The shrimp can be kept at room temperature for up to 2 hours.

WINE Light, spicy Pinot Grigio.

Prosciutto and Foie Gras Roulades with Fig Compote

ACTIVE: 45 MIN; TOTAL: 2 HR 45 MIN

MAKES ABOUT 3 DOZEN CANAPÉS ●

 ½ pound dried figs, stems discarded
 ¾ cup dry red wine
 1 tablespoon port
1¼ teaspoons balsamic vinegar
 1 teaspoon honey
 ¼ pound thinly sliced prosciutto
 ¼ pound foie gras mousse, at room
     temperature (see Note)
36 thin baguette slices,
     lightly toasted

ENTERTAINING TIP

dinner party menu planning

HERE ARE SOME TIPS THAT WE THINK WOULD HELP before planning your next dinner party.

1. Take an equipment inventory. Don't decide to roast a turkey if your pan can only hold a quail.

2. Mix textures and colors. You don't want everything on the plate to be round or brown. Look to vegetables for added color.

3. Play to your audience. Avoid messy foods if your guests are bringing kids.

4. Think like a food stylist. For a buffet, serve dishes that will still look good after guests dig in.

5. Give yourself time to hang out. Avoid having more than one dish that needs last-minute attention.

1. In a saucepan, combine the figs, wine, port, balsamic vinegar and honey and bring to a boil. Reduce the heat to moderate and simmer until the liquid is absorbed and the figs are tender, 15 minutes. Let cool, then puree in a food processor. Transfer ½ cup to a pastry bag fitted with a ½-inch round tip. Reserve the remaining compote to serve with cheese or cured meat.

2. Line a baking sheet with plastic wrap. Overlap the prosciutto slices on top to form a 9-by-12-inch rectangle. Using an offset spatula, spread the foie gras mousse over the prosciutto in a very thin layer. Pipe the fig compote along one 9-inch edge of the rectangle. Beginning there, roll up the prosciutto tightly, using the plastic wrap to guide you. Wrap the prosciutto roll in plastic and refrigerate until firm, at least 2 hours.

3. To assemble the roulades, slice the prosciutto roll on the diagonal ⅛ inch thick and set the slices on the baguette toasts. Transfer to a platter and serve. —David Waltuck

NOTE Foie gras mousse is available at specialty shops or by mail order from D'Artagnan (800-327-8246 or www.dartagnan.com).

MAKE AHEAD The unsliced prosciutto roll can be refrigerated overnight.

WINE Round-textured Sémillon.

Bacon Rings with Avocado

ACTIVE: 25 MIN; TOTAL: 1 HR 10 MIN

MAKES 16 RINGS

- 16 thin slices of lean bacon (about ¾ pound)
- 4 large carrots (1½ inches in diameter)
- 2 tablespoons mayonnaise
- 2 teaspoons hot sauce
- Salt
- 1 small avocado, cut lengthwise into ¼-inch-thick slices, the slices halved crosswise
- 1 cup alfalfa sprouts

1. Preheat the oven to 425°. Lay 4 slices of the bacon side by side on a work surface. Place a carrot at 1 end and roll up the carrot in the bacon slices. Transfer the carrot to a rimmed baking sheet. Repeat with the remaining bacon and carrots. Bake for about 45 minutes, or until the bacon is crisp. Let cool slightly, then carefully loosen each bacon ring and slide it off the carrot, keeping the ring intact. Stand the rings upright and let them cool.

2. In a small bowl, mix the mayonnaise with the hot sauce and season with salt. When a carrot is cool enough to handle, cut it into 3-inch-long matchsticks. Save the other carrots for another use.

3. To assemble a bacon ring, gently press 3 of the carrot sticks together with 2 of the avocado slices. Spread a thin layer of the mayonnaise mixture all around them and then roll the bundles in alfalfa sprouts. Gently press this vegetable filling into a bacon ring, pushing it in only halfway or just far enough to hold together. Repeat to form the remaining bacon rings. Transfer to a platter and serve at room temperature. —Marcia Kiesel

MAKE AHEAD The unfilled bacon rings can be refrigerated overnight. Reheat them in a 350° oven for 2 minutes, or until sizzling.

WINE Bright, fruity rosé.

Pu-Pu Platter Pineapple with Bacon

ACTIVE: 25 MIN; TOTAL: 45 MIN

MAKES ABOUT 2 DOZEN PIECES ●

The inspiration for this whimsical snack is rumaki, the classic chicken liver and bacon hors d'oeuvre. The quality of the pineapple is very important: Look for one that's slightly soft to the touch and golden in color (too much green means it's underripe, dark spots mean it's overripe), with nice green leaves (no brown or yellow tips) and a wonderful fragrance.

- ½ pound thinly sliced bacon (about 11 slices), halved crosswise
- 1 teaspoon curry powder
- One ¾-pound pineapple—peeled, cored and cut into 1-inch cubes (about 22 to 24 cubes)

1. Preheat the oven to 450°. Lay the bacon slices on a work surface and sprinkle with the curry powder. Roll up a pineapple cube in each bacon slice and transfer the bundles to a rimmed baking sheet.

2. Bake the bacon-pineapple bundles in the upper third of the oven for about 20 minutes, or until the bacon is crisp and brown. Serve hot or at room temperature. —Marcia Kiesel

MAKE AHEAD The bacon-wrapped pineapple can be refrigerated overnight. Bring the hors d'oeuvre back to room temperature before baking.

WINE Spicy New World Gewürztraminer.

Pancetta-Wrapped Mushrooms

ACTIVE: 25 MIN; TOTAL: 40 MIN

MAKES 2 DOZEN HORS D'OEUVRES ●

Serve these mushrooms as an hors d'oeuvre or as an accompaniment to a beef or veal roast.

- 24 medium porcini or cremini mushrooms
- 3 medium garlic cloves, thinly sliced
- 3 ounces thinly sliced pancetta, torn into thin strips
- 1 tablespoon extra-virgin olive oil

Preheat the oven to 450°. Make a cut in the center of each mushroom stem down to the cap. Insert a garlic slice in each stem, wrap a pancetta strip around it and secure with a toothpick. Spread the mushrooms on 2 large baking sheets, brush with the olive oil and bake for about 14 minutes, or until browned and crisp. Remove the toothpicks, transfer to a platter and serve. —Jean-Georges Vongerichten

WINE Light, dry Soave or similar white.

FRISÉE SALAD WITH BAKED GOAT CHEESE AND BACON

Frisée Salad with Baked Goat Cheese and Bacon

TOTAL: 40 MIN

4 SERVINGS

A hot disk of tangy goat cheese set on a tangle of frisée is one of the glories of the French bistro kitchen. So is a salad of vinegary greens tossed with rich cubes of bacon. This dish is a combination of the two.

- 3 ounces thickly sliced bacon, cut crosswise into ¼-inch strips
- 3 tablespoons red wine vinegar
- 3 tablespoons grapeseed oil
- 2 tablespoons walnut oil
- 2 teaspoons Dijon mustard

Salt and freshly ground pepper

- 4 slices of country bread
- 1 tablespoon plus 1 teaspoon unsalted butter, softened

Two 3½-ounce round goat cheeses, such as Crottin de Chavignol, halved horizontally

- ½ pound frisée lettuce (8 cups)
- ¼ cup minced chives

I. Preheat the oven to 350°. In a skillet, fry the bacon over moderate heat until crisp, 6 minutes. Pour off the fat. Add 1 tablespoon of vinegar to the bacon and cook until evaporated.

2. In a small bowl, whisk the grapeseed oil with the remaining 2 tablespoons of red wine vinegar, the walnut oil and mustard until thoroughly emulsified. Season with salt and pepper.

3. On a baking sheet, spread the bread with the butter. Bake for 6 minutes, or until golden. Top each toast with a cheese half. Bake the toasts for about 8 minutes, or until the cheese is warmed and soft throughout.

4. Meanwhile, in a large bowl, toss the frisée, bacon, chives and vinaigrette. Mound the salad on plates and set a goat cheese toast alongside. Grind some pepper over the cheese and serve. —*Christophe Gerard*

WINE Lively, assertive Sauvignon Blanc.

Smothered Meatballs in Red Chile Sauce

TOTAL: 40 MIN

4 TO 6 SERVINGS ●

- 4 small ancho chiles (1½-ounce package)—stemmed, seeded and torn into 2-inch pieces
- 1 cup water

One 28-ounce can Italian peeled tomatoes, drained

- 4 medium garlic cloves, very finely chopped
- 4 medium scallions, coarsely chopped
- 1 tablespoon ground cumin
- 1 teaspoon coriander
- 1 cup chicken stock or canned low-sodium broth

Kosher salt and freshly ground pepper

- 1 pound lean ground pork
- 1 pound ground sirloin
- 2 large eggs, beaten
- ½ cup freshly grated Parmesan cheese
- ¼ cup plain dry bread crumbs
- ½ teaspoon dried thyme
- 2 tablespoons vegetable oil
- 3 red or yellow bell peppers, cut into ½-inch strips

I. In a microwavable bowl, cover the ancho chiles with the water, then cover the bowl and microwave the chiles on high for 2 minutes. Transfer the chiles and ½ cup of their soaking liquid to a blender. Add the tomatoes, 2 of the garlic cloves, 2 of the scallions, 1 teaspoon of the cumin, the coriander and the chicken stock. Season the chile sauce with salt and pepper and puree until smooth.

2. In a large bowl, mix the pork and beef with the eggs, Parmesan, bread crumbs, thyme, 1 tablespoon of kosher salt, ¼ teaspoon of pepper and the remaining 2 garlic cloves, 2 scallions and 2 teaspoons of cumin. Form the meat into 18 meatballs.

3. In a 10-inch cast-iron skillet, heat the oil until shimmering. Add the meatballs and cook over moderately high heat until browned all over, about 6 minutes. Add the peppers and cook, stirring occasionally, until softened, 2 to 3 minutes. Add the chile sauce and bring to a boil. Simmer over moderate heat until the sauce is thickened and the meatballs are cooked through, about 10 minutes. Serve at once. —*Grace Parisi*

MAKE AHEAD The meatballs can be refrigerated for up to 2 days.

SERVE WITH Sliced bread and crumbled farmer cheese.

WINE Bright, fruity rosé.

Spicy Korean Pork Buns

TOTAL: 20 MIN

MAKES 10 BUNS ●

- ¼ pound breakfast sausage, casings removed (½ cup)
- ¼ cup chopped drained kimchi (see Note)
- 1 scallion, finely chopped

Pinch of sugar

- 1 package (7½ ounces) refrigerated buttermilk biscuit dough

Soy sauce, for serving

I. In a bowl, combine the sausage, kimchi, scallion and sugar. On a work surface, flatten each biscuit to a 3-inch round. Place 1 tablespoon of the filling in the center of each biscuit and pull up the edges around the filling. Moisten the edges and pinch the seam to seal.

2. Line a bamboo or metal steamer with a sheet of lightly oiled wax paper. Place the buns on the wax paper, seam side up. Cover and steam for 10 minutes. Serve the steamed buns at once, passing soy sauce on the side. —*Younhee Choi*

NOTE Kimchi is a spicy Korean condiment made of fermented vegetables, such as cabbage. It is sold in the refrigerated section of Asian markets and some supermarkets.

WINE Dry, fruity sparkling wine.

WATERCRESS AND MANGO SALAD WITH GINGER DRESSING, P. 44

salads

WILTED AUTUMN GREENS WITH SYRAH VINAIGRETTE

MOROCCAN ARUGULA SALAD

Spinach-Watercress Salad with Candied Walnuts

TOTAL: 45 MIN

4 SERVINGS

- ½ cup walnut halves
- ½ cup sugar
- 1 cup water

Salt

- 1 tablespoon unseasoned rice vinegar
- 1 tablespoon orange juice
- 2 tablespoons grapeseed oil or other mild vegetable oil
- 1 tablespoon extra-virgin olive oil
- ¼ teaspoon Asian sesame oil

Freshly ground pepper

- 5 ounces baby spinach (8 loosely packed cups)
- 1 medium bunch watercress, tough stems discarded
- 2 plums, cut into ½-inch wedges
- 1 crisp, tart apple—peeled, halved, cored and cut into ½-inch wedges
- ¾ cup shredded Gruyère cheese (about 2 ounces)

I. Preheat the oven to 350°. In a small saucepan, combine the walnuts, sugar and water; bring to a boil, stirring, until the sugar dissolves. Cook over moderate heat, stirring, for 5 minutes. Using a slotted spoon, transfer the walnuts to a pie plate and sprinkle lightly with salt. Bake for 7 minutes, or until the nuts are fragrant and lightly caramelized. Let cool.
2. In a small bowl, whisk the vinegar, orange juice, grapeseed oil, olive oil and sesame oil; season with salt and pepper.
3. In a bowl, toss the spinach with the watercress, plums, apple and Gruyère. Add the dressing, season with salt and pepper and toss. Scatter the walnuts on top and serve. —*Chip Angell*

Wilted Autumn Greens with Syrah Vinaigrette

TOTAL: 40 MIN

4 SERVINGS ●

- ½ cup Syrah
- 2 small shallots, minced
- 2 small garlic cloves, minced
- 1 small beet (2 ounces), peeled and cut into ¼-inch dice

Pinch of freshly grated nutmeg

Salt and freshly ground pepper

- 3 ounces baguette, cut into ½-inch dice (2 cups)
- ¼ cup extra-virgin olive oil
- 2 ounces watercress, stemmed
- 2 ounces arugula
- 2 ounces spinach, stemmed
- 2 ounces small kale leaves, stemmed
- 1 large Belgian endive (6 ounces), cored and cut crosswise into 1-inch-thick slices

1. Preheat the oven to 400°. In a small saucepan, boil the wine over high heat until reduced to ⅓ cup, about 2 minutes. Add the shallots, 1 garlic clove, the beet and nutmeg and season with salt and pepper.

2. On a rimmed baking sheet, toss the bread with 1 tablespoon of the olive oil. Bake for about 8 minutes, or until crisp and golden.

3. In a large skillet, heat the remaining 3 tablespoons of olive oil until shimmering. Add the remaining 1 clove of garlic, then add the watercress, arugula, spinach, kale and endive. Toss over moderate heat until just wilted, about 40 seconds. Add the wine mixture, toss to coat and season with salt and pepper. Mound the salad in bowls, top with the croutons and serve. —Colin Alevras

MAKE AHEAD The recipe can be prepared 1 day ahead through Step 2. Refrigerate the wine mixture. Keep the croutons in an airtight container at room temperature.

Moroccan Arugula Salad with Beets and Ricotta Salata

ACTIVE: 20 MIN; TOTAL: 1 HR

6 SERVINGS ●

- 1 pound small red or golden beets, tops trimmed
- 3 tablespoons extra-virgin olive oil
- 1½ tablespoons fresh orange juice
- 1 tablespoon white wine vinegar
- ¼ teaspoon ground cumin
- ¼ teaspoon ground coriander

Salt

Cayenne pepper

- ½ pound young arugula, trimmed
- ¼ cup crumbled ricotta salata

1. Preheat the oven to 400°. Spread the beets in a small baking dish and add ¼ inch of water. Cover and roast for 35 minutes, or until tender. Let cool slightly. Peel and cut into ¼-inch wedges.

2. In a medium bowl, whisk the olive oil with the orange juice, vinegar, cumin and coriander. Season with salt and cayenne.

Add the beets and the arugula and toss. Mound the beet salad on plates, sprinkle with the cheese and serve at once. —Annie Somerville

Midsummer Market Salad

ACTIVE: 30 MIN; TOTAL: 1 HR

6 SERVINGS ● ●

- 10 small turnips (¾ pound), peeled
- ½ pound baby carrots, peeled

Six 2-inch baby onions, peeled

- ¼ cup plus 2 tablespoons extra-virgin olive oil
- 2 tablespoons red wine vinegar
- 1 tablespoon French walnut oil or extra-virgin olive oil
- 1 teaspoon Dijon mustard

Salt and freshly ground pepper

Two 6-ounce heads Bibb lettuce (8 cups)

- 3 ounces baby spinach (4 cups)
- 4 baby bok choy (6 ounces), thickly sliced crosswise
- 3 small kirby cucumbers (½ pound), cut crosswise into ¼-inch-thick slices
- 1 cup packed small basil leaves
- ½ cup lightly packed small chervil or parsley sprigs

1. Bring a large saucepan of salted water to a boil. Add the turnips and boil until just tender, about 5 minutes. Using a slotted spoon, transfer the turnips to a platter. Repeat with the carrots, cooking them for 3 minutes, and then repeat with the onions, cooking them for 2 minutes. Refrigerate the vegetables until chilled. Halve the turnips and thickly slice the onions.

2. In a small bowl, whisk the olive oil with the vinegar, walnut oil and mustard and season with salt and pepper.

3. In a salad bowl, toss the Bibb lettuce, spinach, bok choy, cucumbers, basil, chervil and the cooked vegetables with the vinaigrette and serve. —Tony Maws

MAKE AHEAD The cooked vegetables can be refrigerated overnight.

Summer Fruit Salad with Arugula and Almonds

ACTIVE: 20 MIN; TOTAL: 35 MIN

10 SERVINGS ● ●

You can make this savory and sweet salad with whatever fruit looks best at the market. Ripe green or black figs are wonderful, and a few crushed ones can be used in the vinaigrette in place of the nectarines.

- 1 cup whole blanched almonds (5½ ounces)
- 1 tablespoon plus ½ teaspoon almond oil or additional olive oil

Kosher salt

- 4 large nectarines (2 pounds), 3 cut into ¼-inch-thick slices, 1 coarsely chopped
- 1 small shallot, minced
- 3 tablespoons sherry vinegar
- ¼ cup plus 2 tablespoons extra-virgin olive oil

Freshly ground pepper

- 1 pint blackberries or Persian mulberries
- 4 bunches arugula (1¼ pounds), large stems discarded

1. Preheat the oven to 375°. Spread the almonds in a small pie plate and toast them in the oven for 8 minutes, until fragrant. Toss with ½ teaspoon of the almond oil and kosher salt.

2. In a mini food processor, puree the chopped nectarine. Transfer to a small bowl and add the shallot, vinegar and ½ teaspoon of kosher salt. Let stand for 5 minutes, then whisk in the extra-virgin olive oil and the remaining 1 tablespoon of almond oil. Season with kosher salt and pepper.

3. In a bowl, mix the sliced nectarines and blackberries with one-third of the vinaigrette; season with salt and pepper. In a shallow bowl, season the arugula with salt and pepper and toss with the remaining vinaigrette. Gently toss in the fruit. Add the almonds and serve. —Suzanne Goin

salads

Arugula Salad with Potatoes and Green Beans

ACTIVE: 30 MIN; TOTAL: 1 HR

6 SERVINGS ●

Use fingerling, Yellow Finn or Yukon Gold potatoes in this salad and toss them gently with the vinaigrette so they keep their shape.

2 pounds small potatoes

2 teaspoons minced garlic

6 tablespoons plus 1 teaspoon extra-virgin olive oil

Salt and freshly ground pepper

½ pound green beans, halved crosswise

3 tablespoons red wine vinegar

1 tablespoon grainy mustard

½ small red onion, finely diced

Boiling water

1½ tablespoons capers, rinsed

½ pound young arugula, trimmed

1. Preheat the oven to 400°. In a shallow baking dish, toss the potatoes with the garlic and 1 teaspoon of the olive oil. Season with salt and pepper, cover and roast for 35 to 40 minutes, or until tender. Let cool slightly.

growing arugula

EVEN IF YOUR TOMATOES get black spot and your zucchini plants never fruit, you can still grow arugula. This resilient green, which thrives in window boxes or gardens, needs only three hours of direct sunlight each day. Arugula can produce greens continuously from April through October. Pinch off the outer leaves and ignore the center ones. Once a plant flowers, leaf production drops, but the flowers can be used in salads or as a garnish. Contact Shepherd's Garden Seeds (www.shepherdseeds.com) for more information.

2. Meanwhile, bring a large saucepan of water to a boil. Add the green beans and boil until just tender, 2 to 3 minutes. Drain and rinse under cold water, then drain again.

3. In a large bowl, whisk the remaining 6 tablespoons of olive oil with 2½ tablespoons of the vinegar and mustard. Season with salt and pepper.

4. In a glass measuring cup, cover the red onion with boiling water and let stand for 30 seconds. Drain and stir in the remaining ½ tablespoon of vinegar.

5. Halve or quarter the potatoes. Add them to the vinaigrette with the onion, capers and any garlic from the baking dish and toss gently. Add the arugula and green beans, toss again and serve. —*Annie Somerville*

MAKE AHEAD The potato salad can be made up to 4 hours ahead. Add the arugula and green beans before serving.

Shaved Asparagus Salad with Oranges and Pecorino

TOTAL: 20 MIN

6 SERVINGS ● ●

1 large bunch thick asparagus (2 pounds), trimmed

One 1½-ounce piece of Pecorino Romano cheese

3 tablespoons fresh orange juice

1½ tablespoons snipped chives

1½ teaspoons Champagne vinegar or white wine vinegar

¼ teaspoon finely grated orange zest

¼ cup hazelnut oil

1½ tablespoons grapeseed oil

Kosher salt and freshly ground pepper

1 navel orange

2 tablespoons toasted hazelnuts, coarsely chopped (optional)

1. Using a mandoline (or a sturdy vegetable peeler) set over a bowl, shave the asparagus lengthwise. Shave the Pecorino Romano cheese into the bowl.

2. In a blender, puree the orange juice, snipped chives, vinegar and orange zest.

With the machine on, add the hazelnut and grapeseed oils in a thin stream and process until emulsified; season with salt and pepper. Pour over the asparagus and let stand for 5 minutes, until the asparagus is slightly wilted.

3. Peel the orange, removing all of the bitter white pith. Working over a bowl, cut in between the membranes to release the sections. Add the orange sections to the asparagus. Mound the salad on a platter, garnish with the hazelnuts and serve. —*Melissa Clark*

Spicy Orange and Jicama Salad

ACTIVE: 30 MIN; TOTAL: 2 HR 30 MIN

6 SERVINGS ● ●

6 small navel oranges

1 small red onion, thinly sliced

1 cup jicama sticks (3 by ½ inches)

½ cup coarsely chopped cilantro

Salt

Cayenne pepper

Working over a bowl, using a small knife, cut in between the membranes to release the orange sections; pour off and reserve the juice for another use. Toss the orange slices with the onion slices, jicama sticks and cilantro; season with salt and cayenne. Cover the salad and refrigerate until chilled, about 2 hours. Serve cold. —*Patricia Quintana*

MAKE AHEAD The salad can be refrigerated overnight.

Beet and Raspberry Salad

ACTIVE: 25 MIN; TOTAL: 1 HR 25 MIN

4 SERVINGS ●

5 small beets (2 ounces each)

¼ cup extra-virgin olive oil

2 tablespoons white wine vinegar

Salt and freshly ground pepper

3 ounces mesclun (6 cups)

½ cup small cilantro sprigs

½ cup small dill sprigs

1 cup raspberries

1 Hass avocado, cut lengthwise into ¼-inch-thick slices

1. Preheat the oven to 350°. Wrap the beets in foil and bake for 1 hour, or until tender. Let cool slightly, then peel and halve or quarter.

2. Combine the olive oil and vinegar and season with salt and pepper. Toss 2 tablespoons of the dressing with the beets. Toss the mesclun, cilantro and dill with 2 tablespoons of the dressing. Mound on plates and top with the raspberries, avocado and beets. Drizzle with the remaining dressing and serve.
—*Janie Hibler*

Green Salad with Garlic Crunch

ACTIVE: 10 MIN; TOTAL: 35 MIN

4 SERVINGS ●

- 3 large garlic cloves, thinly sliced
- 1 cup old-fashioned rolled oats
- 1 tablespoon melted unsalted butter
- 2 tablespoons honey

Salt

- 5 ounces soft goat cheese
- 2 tablespoons flat-leaf parsley leaves
- 2 teaspoons thyme leaves
- 2 teaspoons red wine vinegar
- 1 scallion, chopped
- ½ cup skim milk
- ¼ cup extra-virgin olive oil

Freshly ground pepper

- 8 cups packed Boston lettuce leaves (from 1 large head)
- 16 cherry tomatoes, halved

1. Preheat the oven to 300°. In a baking pan, toss the garlic with the oats, butter and honey and season lightly with salt. Spread the oats in an even layer and bake for about 25 minutes, stirring occasionally, until lightly browned. Spread the garlic crunch on a plate and let cool completely, until crisp.

2. Meanwhile, in a blender, combine the goat cheese, parsley, thyme, vinegar, scallion, skim milk and olive oil and blend until smooth. Scrape the dressing into a bowl and season with salt and pepper.

ASPARAGUS SALAD WITH ORANGES AND PECORINO

ARUGULA SALAD WITH POTATOES AND GREEN BEANS

GARLICKY CAESAR SALAD

TOMATO SALAD WITH CRISPY SHALLOTS

3. In a large bowl, toss the lettuce and tomatoes with ½ cup of the dressing. Sprinkle some of the crunch over the salad and serve. Reserve the remaining dressing and crunch for another use.
—*Marcia Kiesel*

VARIATIONS You can also sprinkle the toasted garlic crunch on top of mashed potatoes or rice.

Garlicky Caesar Salad
TOTAL: 30 MIN

6 SERVINGS ●

This Caesar salad gets a flavor wallop from substantial doses of chopped fresh garlic and oil-packed anchovies. The creamy dressing is made with raw egg yolks; if you prefer a cooked-egg alternative, coddle the eggs by placing them in their shells in boiling water for just 3 minutes.

One 2-ounce can anchovies packed in olive oil—drained, rinsed and finely chopped—plus 8 anchovy fillets for garnish
1 tablespoon very finely chopped garlic
¼ cup fresh lemon juice (from about 1 large lemon)
4 large egg yolks
½ cup freshly grated Parmesan cheese, plus ½ cup Parmesan shavings
1 cup extra-virgin olive oil
About 5 romaine lettuce hearts, cut into 1½-inch pieces (24 cups)
2 cups large croutons made from a loaf of country bread (see Note)
2 teaspoons freshly cracked black pepper

1. In a large wooden or ceramic bowl, mash the chopped anchovies and garlic to a paste with a large wooden spoon. Whisk in the lemon juice. Whisk in the egg yolks and stir in the grated Parmesan cheese. In a slow, steady stream, whisk in the extra-virgin olive oil until blended.

2. Add the romaine hearts, croutons and pepper to the dressing and toss to coat. Add the Parmesan shavings and toss lightly. Transfer the Caesar salad to individual bowls or plates, garnish with the anchovy fillets and serve immediately.
—*Terrance Brennan*

NOTE To make basic croutons, toss stale bread cubes with melted unsalted butter in a large bowl. Pour onto a baking sheet and spread out in a single layer. Toast the bread cubes in a 350° oven for about 10 minutes.

Baby Romaine with Green Goddess Dressing

TOTAL: 35 MIN

6 SERVINGS ● ● ●

The dressing here makes more than enough for this salad, so serve the extra with cold poached fish. Or use it in lobster rolls instead of mayonnaise.

- 1 small shallot, minced
- 1 garlic clove, minced
- 1 tablespoon white wine vinegar
- 1 tablespoon fresh lemon juice
- 2 teaspoons fresh lime juice
- 1 large egg yolk, at room temperature (optional)
- ½ cup extra-virgin olive oil
- ½ ripe avocado, mashed
- 3 tablespoons chopped parsley
- 1 tablespoon chopped tarragon
- 1 tablespoon chopped basil
- 1 tablespoon chopped cilantro
- 1 tablespoon chopped chives

Salt and freshly ground pepper

- 1½ pounds baby romaine lettuce heads, halved or quartered

1. In a small bowl, combine the shallot with the garlic, vinegar and lemon and lime juices. Let stand for 5 minutes.
2. In a medium bowl, beat the yolk with a whisk. Gradually add half of the olive oil in a thin drizzle, whisking constantly. Add 1 tablespoon of liquid from the shallot mixture, then whisk in the remaining olive oil. Add the avocado and mash it in with a fork. Whisk in the remaining shallot mixture and the herbs and season with salt and pepper.
3. Add the lettuce to bowls, top with some of the Green Goddess Dressing and serve. —*Fanny Singer*

Escarole Salad with Creamy Garlic Dressing

TOTAL: 15 MIN

6 SERVINGS ● ●

- 2 garlic cloves, minced
- 1 tablespoon red wine vinegar
- 1 tablespoon Dijon mustard
- ¼ cup extra-virgin olive oil

Salt and freshly ground pepper

- One 1-pound head escarole or chicory, torn into bite-size pieces (8 packed cups)

In a large bowl, mix the garlic with the vinegar, mustard and olive oil until blended. Season with salt and pepper. Add the escarole and toss until coated. Transfer to plates and serve at once. —*Jacques Pépin*

MAKE AHEAD The dressing can be refrigerated for up to 4 days.

Escarole and Roquefort Salad with Crispy Croutons

TOTAL: 30 MIN

12 SERVINGS ●

- ½ loaf whole wheat bread (about 1 pound), crusts trimmed, bread cut into ½-inch dice
- ¾ cup plus 1½ tablespoons pure olive oil

Salt and freshly ground pepper

- ⅓ cup red wine vinegar
- ¾ teaspoon dried thyme
- ¾ teaspoon dried oregano
- 1 garlic clove, minced
- 1 small shallot, minced

Pinch of sugar

- ¼ cup freshly grated Parmesan cheese
- 5 heads escarole (about 4 pounds), dark green leaves discarded, the rest torn into bite-size pieces
- 6 ounces Roquefort cheese, crumbled, at room temperature

1. Heat the oven to 400°. On a large baking sheet, toss the diced bread with 1½ tablespoons of olive oil and season with salt and pepper. Toast for 10 minutes, stirring once, until golden brown.
2. In a small bowl, whisk the remaining ¾ cup of olive oil with the wine vinegar, thyme, oregano, garlic, shallot, sugar, Parmesan cheese and 1 teaspoon each of salt and pepper.

3. In a large bowl, toss the escarole hearts with the dressing. Garnish with the croutons and Roquefort and serve. —*Tom Valenti*

MAKE AHEAD The escarole can be cleaned ahead of time and refrigerated overnight. The croutons can be toasted and stored overnight in an airtight container at room temperature.

Tomato Salad with Crispy Shallots

TOTAL: 30 MIN

6 SERVINGS ● ●

- 3 large shallots (½ pound), cut crosswise into ¼-inch-thick slices and separated into rings, plus 1 small shallot, minced
- 1 tablespoon red wine vinegar
- 2 tablespoons extra-virgin olive oil

Salt and freshly ground pepper

- 1 cup canola oil
- 3½ pounds assorted ripe tomatoes, sliced, or halved if cherry

Small basil leaves, for garnish

1. In a small bowl, combine the minced shallot with the vinegar and let stand for at least 5 minutes. Whisk in the olive oil and season with salt and pepper.
2. Meanwhile, in a medium saucepan, heat the canola oil until shimmering. Add half of the sliced shallots and cook over moderately high heat, stirring occasionally, until browned, about 5 minutes. Using a slotted spoon, transfer the shallots to paper towels to drain and season with salt. Repeat with the remaining sliced shallots.
3. Spread the tomatoes on a large platter, season with salt and pepper and drizzle with the vinaigrette. Scatter the fried shallots and basil leaves over the tomatoes and serve. —*Fanny Singer*

MAKE AHEAD The fried shallots can be kept at room temperature for 2 hours. Salt them just before using.

salads

Mom's Marinated Tomato Salad

ACTIVE: 25 MIN; TOTAL: 2 HR 35 MIN

10 SERVINGS ●

David Lentz names this salad in honor of his mother, who makes it with big red beefsteak tomatoes.

¼ cup minced shallots

2 garlic cloves, minced

¼ cup red wine vinegar

Kosher salt

¼ cup fresh lemon juice

Freshly ground pepper

2 basil sprigs, plus ¼ cup chopped leaves

1 cup extra-virgin olive oil

3 pounds ripe tomatoes, cut into ½-inch-thick slices

6 ounces sharp provolone cheese

I. In a medium bowl, combine the shallots, garlic, vinegar and 1 teaspoon of salt; let stand for 5 minutes. Add the lemon juice and season with pepper. Break up the basil sprigs in your hands to release their flavor and add them to the bowl. Whisk in the oil and let stand for 10 minutes; discard the basil sprigs.

2. Spoon one-quarter of the vinaigrette onto a large, shallow platter. Arrange half of the tomato slices in overlapping circles on the platter and season with salt and pepper. Using a sturdy vegetable peeler, shave half of the provolone over the tomatoes. Spoon half of the remaining vinaigrette on top and sprinkle with half of the chopped basil. Repeat with the remaining tomatoes, cheese, vinaigrette and basil, seasoning with salt and pepper between layers. Cover with plastic wrap and refrigerate for 2 hours before serving. —*Jean Lentz*

Green Tomato, Scallion and Corn Bread Panzanella

TOTAL: 15 MIN

6 SERVINGS ● ●

For this riff on an Italian bread salad, try using day-old corn bread, which soaks up the dressing really well.

¼ cup extra-virgin olive oil

2 tablespoons cider vinegar

Kosher salt and freshly ground pepper

Hot sauce

2 large green tomatoes (6 to 8 ounces each), cut into ½-inch pieces

1 medium green bell pepper, finely diced

½ cup coarsely shredded basil leaves

4 scallions, thinly sliced

One 5-inch square of store-bought corn bread, cut into ¾-inch cubes (4 cups)

In a salad bowl, combine the olive oil and vinegar; season with salt, pepper and hot sauce. Add the green tomatoes, green pepper, basil and scallions and toss. Just before serving, add the corn bread and toss gently. —*Melissa Clark*

Bread Salad with Roasted Tomatoes and Capers

TOTAL: 30 MIN

4 SERVINGS ● ● ●

If you omit the caperberries, double the amount of capers in the salad.

1 pint grape tomatoes

5 tablespoons extra-virgin olive oil

1 garlic clove, minced

1 teaspoon chopped thyme

Kosher salt and freshly ground pepper

4 cups diced baguette (½-inch dice)

2½ tablespoons fresh lemon juice

½ European seedless cucumber, peeled and thinly sliced

⅓ cup pitted Calamata olives

2 teaspoons drained capers

6 caperberries, halved lengthwise (optional)

2 tablespoons chopped basil leaves

I. Preheat the oven to 400°. In a medium glass baking dish, toss the tomatoes with 1 tablespoon of the olive oil, the garlic and thyme and season with salt and pepper. On a rimmed baking sheet, toss the bread with 1 tablespoon

of the olive oil. Bake the tomatoes and bread for about 10 minutes, or until the tomato skins are just beginning to split and the bread is golden.

2. Meanwhile, in a bowl, mix the lemon juice with the remaining 3 tablespoons of olive oil; season with salt and pepper. Add the cucumber, olives, capers, caperberries, basil, tomatoes and bread, toss and serve. —*Megan Moore*

MAKE AHEAD The salad can be kept at room temperature for up to 3 hours.

Warm Green Bell Pepper and Tomato Salad

TOTAL: 1 HR

8 SERVINGS ● ●

¼ cup vegetable oil

1 pound small green bell peppers, stems trimmed

1 tablespoon extra-virgin olive oil

1 large garlic clove, minced

1 teaspoon ground cumin

2 pounds tomatoes—peeled, seeded and cut into 1-inch pieces

1 teaspoon distilled white vinegar

Salt

¼ cup flat-leaf parsley leaves

I. Heat the vegetable oil in a large skillet. Poke a hole or make a small slit in the side of each pepper and add them to the skillet. Cook over moderate heat, turning frequently, until browned and softened all over, about 20 minutes. Drain on paper towels and let cool. Peel, core and seed the peppers, then cut them into ½-inch-wide strips.

2. In another large skillet, heat the olive oil. Add the garlic and cumin and cook over low heat, stirring, until fragrant, about 1 minute. Add the tomatoes, bell pepper strips and vinegar, season with salt and cook, tossing frequently, just until heated through. Transfer to a bowl and stir in the parsley. —*Hajja Halima*

MAKE AHEAD The salad can be made up to 4 hours ahead. Stir in the parsley just before serving.

Q+A
salad savior

lively mesclun

Q: I get so tired of wilted heads of lettuce and mesclun mix, and my salads always seem a little limp. Is there anything I can do to keep my salad greens crisp?

A: This sounds obvious, but try to start out with really fresh greens. If the leaves have gone a little limp on the way home from the market, revive them with a brief soak in a bowl of very cold water—they'll perk up perfectly. Then lift them out and dry them thoroughly in a salad spinner. (The Zyliss and OXO versions are terrific.) If you don't plan to use them right away, wrap them in a cotton kitchen towel or lightly dampened paper towels and seal them in a plastic bag—they'll be fine for at least a day. You can also store the washed and dried greens right in the salad spinner overnight in the refrigerator.

If you'd like to make your mesclun mix a little more exciting, add a bitter bite with sliced Belgian endive, radicchio, chicory, escarole or frisée, or go for a peppery tang with arugula, watercress or mizuna. Don't forget about sprouts—sunflower and radish especially—and fresh herbs like parsley, dill or cilantro sprigs and mint and tarragon leaves.

flawless vinaigrette

Q: I'm in a vinaigrette rut! I always make my mother's recipe, with honey, mustard, oil and vinegar, but I never get the proportions right—and frankly, I'm a little sick of it.

A: Here's a recipe from F&W friend Charles Pierce, a salad whiz. It's perfect for dressing green salads, tomatoes, avocados, mushrooms, beets and just about any other vegetable. You could also dress it up with chopped herbs, olives, diced fresh or sun-dried tomatoes or minced anchovies and serve it with grilled or poached fish or shellfish, poultry or meat.

Classic Vinaigrette
MAKES ENOUGH FOR 10 TO 12 CUPS OF SALAD GREENS ●
1 rounded teaspoon Dijon mustard
2 tablespoons red wine vinegar
Scant 1 teaspoon fresh lemon juice
Scant ¼ teaspoon salt
5 twists of a pepper mill
Scant ¼ cup olive oil
2 tablespoons vegetable oil
In a small bowl, combine the mustard with the red wine vinegar, lemon juice, salt and pepper; whisk to dissolve the salt. Gradually whisk in the olive oil and then the vegetable oil in a very thin stream until combined.

quick dressings

Q: Sometimes I want a lighter dressing than vinaigrette, with a different flavor. Do you have any ideas?

A: To make a dressing with Asian flavors, begin with vegetable oil and rice vinegar and add a splash of soy sauce, freshly grated ginger, a bit of minced garlic and a little sesame oil; for heat, add chili sauce, chili-garlic sauce or chili oil; for sweetness, add a touch of honey; for a creamy dressing, stir in light miso or peanut butter.

When time is really tight—don't tell the salad police—you can always just dress the salad right in the bowl. Sprinkle on a good everyday balsamic vinegar (such as Cavalli or Fini), the finest olive oil you have in the house, a bit of crunchy salt (kosher, sea or fleur de sel) and a couple of twists of fresh black pepper, then toss everything together. If you don't get the balance right the first time, add a little more of whatever's missing to even it out. You might replace the balsamic with any other vinegar (red or white wine, sherry, Champagne, rice) or a fresh citrus juice (anything from mild, sweet orange, grapefruit or clementine to tangy lime or lemon).

salads

Spicy Asian Tofu with Cucumber Salad

TOTAL: 20 MIN

6 SERVINGS ● ● ●

Kimchi is a traditional spicy-hot Korean condiment made with fermented cabbage (and, sometimes, other vegctables). It's available in the refrigerated section of some supermarkets and at most Asian markets.

One 14-ounce package extra-firm tofu, drained and patted dry

1 cup kimchi, finely chopped (7 ounces)

¼ cup low-sodium soy sauce

2½ tablespoons rice vinegar

1 teaspoon Asian sesame oil

2 large European seedless cucumbers (2 pounds total)— peeled, halved lengthwise and thinly sliced crosswise

2 tablespoons mirin

Kosher salt

2 scallions, white and light green parts only, finely chopped

1. Place the tofu between 2 plates. Weight the top plate with a heavy can and refrigerate for 15 minutes.

2. Meanwhile, in a medium bowl, combine the chopped kimchi with the soy sauce, 1 tablespoon of the rice vinegar and ½ teaspoon of the sesame oil. Drain the tofu and pat dry. Cut the tofu into ¼-inch-thick slices and then cut each slice into 2 triangles. Arrange the tofu triangles on a platter and spoon the kimchi dressing on top. Refrigerate the dressed tofu for 5 minutes.

3. Meanwhile, in a medium bowl, toss the cucumbers with the remaining 1½ tablespoons of vinegar, ½ teaspoon of sesame oil and the mirin. Season with salt. Scatter the scallions over the tofu and serve right away, passing the cucumber salad on the side.

—*Melissa Clark*

MAKE AHEAD The recipe can be prepared through Step 2 and refrigerated for up to 6 hours.

Edamame with Tofu, Bean Sprouts and Seaweed

ACTIVE: 15 MIN; TOTAL: 35 MIN

4 SERVINGS ● ●

¼ cup lightly crumbled wakame seaweed (about ¼ ounce)

1 cup boiling water

1½ teaspoons sesame seeds

1 tablespoon unseasoned rice vinegar

1½ teaspoons low-sodium soy sauce

1 teaspoon finely grated fresh ginger

1½ tablespoons peanut oil

½ teaspoon Asian sesame oil

Salt

Cayenne pepper

½ pound extra-firm tofu, cut into ½-inch dice

1 pound frozen shelled edamame (2¾ cups)—thawed, rinsed and patted dry

¼ pound mung bean sprouts (1½ cups), both ends trimmed

1. In a heatproof bowl, cover the wakame with the boiling water and let stand until softened, about 15 minutes. Drain the wakame and press to remove any excess water.

2. Toast the sesame seeds in a small skillet over moderate heat, stirring, for 3 minutes. In a medium bowl, whisk the rice vinegar with the soy sauce and ginger. Whisk in the peanut and sesame oils. Season with salt and cayenne.

3. Add the tofu to the dressing and let stand for 5 minutes. Transfer the tofu to a small plate. Add the edamame, bean sprouts and wakame to the dressing and toss to coat. Fold in the tofu. Transfer to a scrving bowl, sprinkle with the sesame seeds and serve.

—*Grace Parisi*

MAKE AHEAD The wakame, sesame seeds and dressing can be prepared through Step 2 up to 4 hours ahead.

Edamame and Pea Salad with Sweet Onions and Goat Cheese

TOTAL: 40 MIN

4 SERVINGS ●

¼ cup extra-virgin olive oil

¼ pound thickly sliced bacon, cut into ¼-inch dice

1 Vidalia onion (¾ pound), cut into ½-inch wedges through the root end

1 large garlic clove, thinly sliced

1 cup frozen shelled edamame (6 ounces), thawed

1½ cups frozen peas (6 ounces), thawed

2 cups sugar snap peas (6 ounces)

3 tablespoons fresh lemon juice

1 teaspoon Dijon mustard

2 teaspoons coarsely chopped mint

Kosher salt and freshly ground pepper

2 ounces aged goat cheese, crumbled (½ cup)

1. In a large skillet, heat 1 teaspoon of the olive oil. Add the bacon and cook over moderate heat, stirring occasionally, until crisp, about 5 minutes. Transfer the bacon to a plate. Add the onion wedges to the skillet and cook, turning occasionally, until golden and softened, about 8 minutes. Add the garlic and cook until golden, 2 minutes. Transfer the onions and garlic to a plate.

edamame

INGREDIENT TIP

FRESH GREEN SOYBEANS, a.k.a. edamame, are a rich source of isoflavones, compounds that may help reduce cholesterol, fight cancer and strengthen bones. They're also a great source of protein, fiber and B vitamins. Look for the plump, dark green pods in produce markets. They are also available year-round in the supermarket freezer section.

EDAMAME WITH TOFU, BEAN SPROUTS AND SEAWEED

2. Meanwhile, bring a large saucepan of salted water to a boil. Add the edamame, peas and sugar snap peas and cook until the sugar snaps are crisp-tender, about 4 minutes. Drain and cool under running water. Pat dry.

3. In a large bowl, mix the lemon juice with the mustard and the remaining 3 tablespoons plus 2 teaspoons of olive oil. Add the edamame, peas, sugar snaps, bacon, onion wedges, garlic and mint. Season the salad with salt and pepper and toss until combined. Sprinkle the goat cheese over the salad and serve at room temperature.

—*Megan Moore*

MAKE AHEAD The salad can be kept at room temperature for up to 3 hours.

Glazed Tofu-Mushroom Salad

TOTAL: 25 MIN

4 SERVINGS ● ●

Ketchup, a Western ingredient that has been adopted by the Japanese, helps form a sweet glaze on both the mushrooms and tofu.

- ¼ cup ketchup
- 2 tablespoons soy sauce
- 2 teaspoons dry sherry
- ½ teaspoon Asian sesame oil
- 1 tablespoon fresh lemon juice
- 1 pound shiitake mushrooms, stems discarded
- 2 tablespoons vegetable oil

Salt and freshly ground pepper

- ½ pound firm tofu, cut into ½-inch-thick slices
- 1 scallion, thinly sliced
- 1 large tomato, coarsely chopped
- 1 cup mung bean sprouts

I. Preheat the broiler. In a small bowl, combine the ketchup, soy sauce, sherry and sesame oil. In another small bowl, blend 1 tablespoon of the ketchup sauce with the lemon juice and reserve.

2. Arrange the mushroom caps on a cookie sheet, stemmed side down; brush with the vegetable oil and season with salt and pepper. Broil 6 inches from the heat for 4 minutes, rotating the pan if necessary, until browned. Turn the caps and broil for 3 minutes, or until lightly browned. Brush the caps with some ketchup sauce and broil for 30 seconds, or until crisp and deeply browned. Turn, brush again with sauce and broil for 30 seconds longer. Stack the caps and slice into ¼-inch strips.

3. On the cookie sheet, brush the tofu on both sides with some of the ketchup sauce. Broil for 1 minute, or until deeply browned and crisp. While still on the sheet, gently cut into 1-inch cubes.

4. In a bowl, toss the mushrooms, scallion, tomato and sprouts with the lemon dressing; season with salt and pepper. Using a spatula, transfer the tofu to the salad, toss lightly and serve.

—*Marcia Kiesel*

Green and Yellow Bean Salad with Ricotta Salata

TOTAL: 25 MIN

4 SERVINGS ● ●

Kosher salt

- ½ pound thin green beans
- ½ pound yellow wax beans
- ¼ cup plus 1 tablespoon extra-virgin olive oil
- 2 tablespoons sherry vinegar
- 1½ tablespoons minced shallots
- ½ pint cherry tomatoes, halved
- 3 tablespoons Niçoise olives, pitted and halved
- ¼ pound ricotta salata, thinly sliced (1 cup)

Freshly ground pepper

I. Bring a large saucepan of salted water to a boil and fill a large bowl with ice water. Add the green beans to the saucepan and boil until just tender, about 5 minutes. Using a slotted spoon, transfer the beans to the ice water. Return the water to a boil. Add the yellow wax beans and cook until just tender, 5 to 6 minutes. Transfer to the ice water and let cool. Drain all the beans and pat dry with paper towels.

2. In a large bowl, whisk the olive oil with the vinegar and shallots. Add the beans, tomatoes, olives and half of the ricotta salata and toss; season with salt and pepper. Transfer the salad to plates, sprinkle the remaining cheese on top and serve. —*Daniel Boulud*

Watercress with Pears and Macadamia Nuts

TOTAL: 20 MIN

6 SERVINGS ●

You can substitute ¼ cup vegetable oil mixed with 2 tablespoons of walnut or hazelnut oil for the macadamia-nut oil.

- 1 tablespoon minced shallot
- 1 teaspoon Dijon mustard
- 3 tablespoons pear or white wine vinegar
- ¼ cup plus 2 tablespoons macadamia-nut oil

Salt and freshly ground pepper

- 3 large bunches of watercress, thick stems discarded (16 loose cups)
- 2 ripe Anjou pears—peeled, cored and thinly sliced
- 3 ounces Parmesan cheese, thinly shaved (1½ cups)
- ½ cup coarsely chopped salted macadamia nuts

In a bowl, whisk the shallot, mustard and vinegar. Slowly whisk in the nut oil and season with salt and pepper. Add the watercress, season with salt and pepper and toss. Add the sliced pears, Parmesan and macadamia nuts, toss gently and serve. —*Grace Parisi*

Watercress and Mango Salad with Ginger Dressing

TOTAL: 30 MIN

8 SERVINGS ● ●

- 2 tablespoons canola oil
- 2 tablespoons minced peeled fresh ginger

2 tablespoons fresh lime juice

1 tablespoon unseasoned
rice vinegar

½ teaspoon chili paste or
Tabasco to taste

½ teaspoon minced garlic

Pinch of sugar

½ teaspoon Asian sesame oil

¼ cup extra-virgin olive oil

Salt and freshly ground pepper

2 tablespoons finely chopped
cilantro

1 scallion, thinly sliced

Three 6-ounce bunches watercress,
tough stems discarded

1 small red onion, thinly sliced

1 mango, cut into ½-inch dice

1 Hass avocado, cut
into ½-inch dice

1. Heat the canola oil in a small skillet. Add the ginger and cook over moderate heat until just golden and fragrant, about 2 minutes. Transfer the ginger to a small bowl and let cool. Stir in the lime juice, rice vinegar, chili paste, garlic, sugar and sesame oil. Slowly whisk in the olive oil and season with salt and pepper. Stir in the cilantro and scallion.

2. In a bowl, toss the watercress, onion and dressing; season with salt and pepper. Add the mango and avocado, toss gently and serve. —*Gail Monaghan*

MAKE AHEAD The dressing can be refrigerated for up to 2 days. Stir in the cilantro and scallion just before serving.

Endive and Bacon Salad with Avocado Dressing

TOTAL: 30 MIN

4 SERVINGS ●

DRESSING

½ Hass avocado, coarsely chopped

¼ cup plus 2 tablespoons buttermilk

1 tablespoon white wine vinegar

1 small shallot, coarsely chopped

1½ teaspoons minced flat-leaf parsley

1 small garlic clove, smashed

¼ cup vegetable oil

Kosher salt and freshly ground
white pepper

SALAD

¾ pound applewood-smoked bacon

4 thin slices of sourdough bread

1 tablespoon extra-virgin olive oil

4 medium Belgian endives
(1 pound), cut crosswise into
1-inch pieces

¼ cup plus 1 tablespoon
snipped chives

Kosher salt and freshly ground pepper

1 Hass avocado, cut into
thin wedges

1. MAKE THE DRESSING: In a blender, combine the avocado with the buttermilk, vinegar, shallot, parsley and garlic and process until smooth. With the machine on, add the vegetable oil in a thin stream and process the avocado dressing until smooth. Season the dressing with salt and white pepper.

2. MAKE THE SALAD: Preheat the broiler and position a rack 8 inches from the heat source. In 2 large skillets, cook the bacon over moderate heat, turning once, until crisp, about 6 minutes. Drain the bacon on paper towels, then break it into 1-inch pieces. Brush the bread on both sides with the olive oil and broil until toasted, about 45 seconds per side. Cut each slice in half diagonally.

3. In a bowl, toss the endives, ¼ cup of the chives and the bacon. Add ½ cup of the dressing and toss to coat; refrigerate the remaining dressing to use within 3 days. Season the salad with salt and pepper. Arrange the toast on 4 large plates. Mound the salad on top and tuck in the avocado wedges. Sprinkle with the remaining 1 tablespoon of chives and serve. —*Scott Tycer*

MAKE AHEAD The avocado dressing can be refrigerated for up to 3 days.

TASTE TEST supermarket olive oil

You don't have to shop at a specialty-food store to find a decent olive oil. We tasted 12 brands sold at local supermarkets and turned up four that offer a pleasing depth of flavor for a fraction of the cost.

PRODUCT	F&W COMMENT	INTERESTING BITE
Patsy's Extra Virgin Olive Oil ($8.59 for 17 oz.)	"Spicy, with a lingering finish and a good balance of acidity and richness."	Produced by Patsy's Restaurant in New York City, this is made with only Italian olives.
Monini Extra Virgin Olive Oil ($10 for 17 oz.)	"Great fruity flavor with a fiery bite."	Two well-known Italian foodies, Sophia Loren and Luciano Pavarotti, use Monini in their kitchens.
Bertolli Classico ($4.19 for 8.5 oz.)	"Pleasantly light body and nice aftertaste."	Bertolli was one of the first manufacturers to package oil in glass bottles instead of cans.
Lucini Extra Virgin Olive Oil ($8 for 17 oz.)	"Zippy flavor; grassy and refreshing."	The striking octagonal bottle was inspired by the Duomo in Florence.

ROASTED PINEAPPLE AND AVOCADO SALAD

MARINATED CARROT SALAD

Fennel, Apple and Celery Salad with Watercress

TOTAL: 25 MIN

12 SERVINGS ● ●

- ¾ cup extra-virgin olive oil
- 3 tablespoons fresh lemon juice, plus ½ lemon
- 3 tablespoons balsamic vinegar

Salt and freshly ground pepper

- 6 medium celery ribs, peeled and thinly sliced crosswise on a mandoline
- 4 medium fennel bulbs—halved, cored and thinly sliced on a mandoline
- 2 Granny Smith apples—halved, cored and thinly sliced on a mandoline

Three 6-ounce bunches watercress, large stems discarded

- 1 cup seedless red grapes, halved
- ¾ cup chopped flat-leaf parsley

1. In a small bowl, mix the olive oil, lemon juice and vinegar. Season with salt and pepper. In a large bowl, squeeze the ½ lemon over the celery, fennel and apples and toss well.

2. In another large bowl, toss the watercress with ¼ cup of the vinaigrette. Add the grapes, parsley and the remaining vinaigrette to the celery, fennel and apples and toss. Arrange over the watercress and serve. —*Elisabeth Prueitt*

Fennel and Apple Salad with Blue Cheese and Pecans

TOTAL: 30 MIN

6 SERVINGS ●

- 1½ tablespoons fresh lemon juice
- 1½ teaspoons white wine vinegar
- 1 teaspoon Dijon mustard
- ¼ cup extra-virgin olive oil

Kosher salt and freshly ground pepper

- 1 large fennel bulb—halved lengthwise, cored and sliced crosswise paper-thin
- 1 tablespoon finely chopped fennel fronds

1 Granny Smith apple, peeled and cut into matchsticks

1 cup crumbled blue cheese (about 4 ounces)

¾ cup pecan halves, toasted

In a large bowl, whisk the lemon juice, vinegar and mustard. Gradually whisk in the oil and season with salt and pepper. Add the fennel, fennel fronds and apple, season with salt and pepper and toss. Garnish with the blue cheese and pecans and serve. —*Maile Carpenter*

Fennel Salad with Parmesan

TOTAL: 20 MIN

12 SERVINGS ● ●

½ cup plus 2 tablespoons extra-virgin olive oil

½ cup fresh lemon juice

Salt and freshly ground pepper

6 fennel bulbs—halved, cored and very thinly sliced on a mandoline

1½ cups Parmesan shavings made with a vegetable peeler (3 ounces)

In a large bowl, whisk the olive oil with the lemon juice and season with salt and pepper. Add the fennel and toss to coat. Transfer to a platter, top with the Parmesan and serve. —*David Waltuck*

Roasted Pineapple and Avocado Salad

ACTIVE: 15 MIN; TOTAL: 25 MIN

4 SERVINGS ● ●

1 pound peeled and cored fresh pineapple, cut into ¾-inch chunks (2 cups)

½ teaspoon light brown sugar

Kosher salt

1½ tablespoons extra-virgin olive oil

1½ tablespoons balsamic vinegar

2 Hass avocados, cut into ¾-inch chunks

4 ounces cleaned baby spinach (4 cups)

12 mint leaves

Freshly ground pepper

Lime wedges, for serving

1. Preheat the oven to 400°. In a medium bowl, toss the pineapple with the brown sugar and ½ teaspoon of salt. Spread the pineapple on a baking sheet and roast in the upper third of the oven for about 10 minutes, or until softened and just beginning to brown.

2. In a medium bowl, whisk the olive oil with the vinegar. Add the avocados, spinach and mint, season with salt and pepper and toss. Transfer the salad to plates, top with the pineapple and serve with lime wedges. —*Sally Sampson*

Marinated Carrot Salad

ACTIVE: 35 MIN; TOTAL: 4 HR 40 MIN

4 SERVINGS ● ●

This garlicky salad travels well. Pack it in a container for a potluck supper or serve it as a side dish with anything from pork and steak to chicken and fish.

Salt

1 pound carrots, thinly sliced on the diagonal or julienned

¼ cup extra-virgin olive oil

2 tablespoons sherry vinegar or red wine vinegar

2 garlic cloves, minced

1 tablespoon fresh lemon juice

1 tablespoon minced shallot

1 tablespoon chopped parsley

1 teaspoon Dijon mustard

1 teaspoon sugar

Freshly ground pepper

1. Bring a medium saucepan of water to a boil. Salt the water, then add the carrots and cook until they are barely tender, about 3 minutes; drain them.

2. In a large bowl, whisk the olive oil with the vinegar, garlic, lemon juice, shallot, parsley, mustard and sugar and season with salt and pepper. Add the carrots and toss to coat. Refrigerate for at least 4 hours or overnight. Serve the carrot salad chilled or at room temperature. —*Andrew J. Powning*

MAKE AHEAD The marinated carrots can be refrigerated for up to 2 days.

Red Pepper and Endive Slaw with Soppressata

TOTAL: 20 MIN

6 SERVINGS ●

2 tablespoons sherry vinegar

1 tablespoon minced shallot

1 tablespoon Dijon mustard

⅓ cup extra-virgin olive oil

Kosher salt and freshly ground pepper

2 large red bell peppers, very thinly sliced lengthwise

2 large Belgian endives (about 1 pound total), cored and thinly sliced crosswise

3 ounces thick-sliced soppressata, cut into matchsticks

¼ cup shredded basil

In a large bowl, mix the vinegar with the shallot and let stand for 5 minutes. Whisk in the mustard, then slowly whisk in the olive oil; season with salt and pepper. Add the red peppers, endives, soppressata and basil and toss to combine. Season the salad with salt and pepper, transfer to a bowl and serve. —*Melissa Clark*

Smoky Eggplant Salad with Cucumber Raita

ACTIVE: 1 HR; TOTAL: 1 HR 45 MIN

8 SERVINGS ● ●

Broiling the baked eggplants until their skins are black and blistered is the key to their smoky flavor here.

Six 1-pound narrow eggplants

2 garlic cloves, minced

¼ cup extra-virgin olive oil

¼ cup chopped mint

¼ preserved lemon, peel only, minced (optional; see Note)

1½ tablespoons fresh lemon juice

¼ teaspoon finely grated lemon zest

Salt and freshly ground pepper

1 medium cucumber—peeled, halved lengthwise, seeded and finely diced

1 cup plain whole milk yogurt

2 tablespoons grated onion

salads

1. Preheat the oven to 500°. Prick the eggplants in a few places with a sharp knife. Bake them on 2 rimmed baking sheets until very soft, about 50 minutes.

2. Preheat the broiler. Broil the eggplants 3 inches from the heat until blackened on top, about 3 minutes. Let cool slightly. Slit the eggplant skins and scrape out the flesh, discarding as many seeds as possible. Finely chop the eggplants, transfer to a bowl and pour off any accumulated eggplant liquid.

3. Stir the garlic, olive oil, mint, minced preserved lemon peel, lemon juice and grated lemon zest into the chopped eggplant. Season with salt and pepper.

4. Put the cucumber in a colander set over a bowl and sprinkle with a large pinch of salt. Let stand for 10 minutes. Rinse the cucumber and pat thoroughly dry. Transfer to a bowl and stir in the yogurt and grated onion. Season with salt and pepper. Serve the cucumber raita and eggplant salad together, at room temperature. —*Gail Monaghan*

NOTE Jarred preserved lemons are available at specialty shops and Middle Eastern markets.

COOKING TIP

main-dish salads

TO CREATE A MAIN-DISH SALAD follow these guidelines:

• Match assertive greens (such as arugula, dandelion, chicory, endive, frisée and radicchio) with strong-flavored dressings and hearty ingredients like beef or sausage.

• Coat milder greens (romaine, Boston, Bibb and red-leaf lettuces) with subtle dressings that won't overpower them.

• Serve starch-based salads (pasta, potatoes, bread or grains) at room temperature, not chilled.

MAKE AHEAD The eggplant salad and cucumber raita can be refrigerated overnight. Bring them to room temperature before serving.

Cobb Salad with Pancetta Chips

TOTAL: 1 HR

4 SERVINGS

- 4 thin slices of pancetta
- 5 large eggs, at room temperature
- 2 tablespoons sherry vinegar
- 1½ teaspoons water
- ½ teaspoon Dijon mustard
- 6 tablespoons grapeseed oil
- 6 tablespoons extra-virgin olive oil

Salt and freshly ground pepper

- 6 slices of thick-cut bacon, cut into ¼-inch matchsticks
- 1 pound hearts of romaine lettuce, cut crosswise into ½-inch ribbons
- 2 Hass avocados, cut into ½-inch wedges
- 2 tomatoes, halved and cut into ¼-inch-thick slices
- 4 grilled or roasted skinless, boneless chicken breast halves, thickly sliced
- 3½ ounces dry-aged blue cheese, shaved or crumbled

1. Preheat the oven to 350°. Lay the pancetta on a baking sheet, cover with parchment paper and place another baking sheet on top. Bake for 15 minutes, or until browned. Blot dry.

2. Meanwhile, add the eggs to a saucepan of boiling water; cook for exactly 6 minutes. Transfer to an ice-water bath for 10 minutes, then peel. Scoop the soft-cooked yolk out of 1 egg and transfer to a blender. Add the vinegar, water and mustard and puree. With the machine on, slowly add the 2 oils and blend. Season with salt and pepper.

3. In a small skillet, cook the bacon over moderate heat, stirring occasionally, until just crisp. Drain on paper towels.

4. In a bowl, toss the romaine with ½ cup of the dressing, season with salt

and pepper and mound on 4 plates. Arrange the avocados, tomatoes and chicken on the plates; drizzle with ¼ cup of the dressing. Scatter the bacon and blue cheese on top. Carefully slice off 1 end of each of the remaining eggs to expose the yolks; set an egg in the center of each salad. Top with the pancetta and serve with the remaining dressing. —*Josiah Citrin*

Mexican Chopped Salad

ACTIVE: 1 HR; TOTAL: 2 HR 15 MIN

6 SERVINGS ●

Los Angeles is known for its salads and also for its large Latin population. This salad pays homage to both.

- 1¼ cups plus 2 tablespoons canola oil
- 7 tablespoons fresh lime juice
- 1½ tablespoons minced garlic
- 1 small jalapeño—stemmed, seeded and minced

Kosher salt

- 6 skinless, boneless chicken breast halves
- 2 red bell peppers
- 1 green bell pepper
- 6 corn tortillas, cut into 2-by-¼-inch strips
- 1 cup tightly packed coarsely chopped cilantro
- 1 tablespoon sugar
- 1 tablespoon cider vinegar

Freshly ground pepper

- 2 tomatoes, seeded and diced
- 2 ripe Hass avocados, cut into ½-inch dice
- 1 medium red onion, finely diced
- 1 small jicama (1 pound), peeled and cut into ½-inch dice
- 5 large tomatillos, husked and cut into thin wedges

1. In a large nonreactive baking dish, mix ¼ cup plus 2 tablespoons of the canola oil with 3 tablespoons of the lime juice, the garlic, jalapeño and 1 teaspoon of salt. Add the chicken breasts, turn to coat thoroughly and let stand at

room temperature for 1 hour or refrigerate for up to 4 hours.

2. Roast the red and green peppers under the broiler or directly over a gas flame, turning occasionally, until charred all over, about 10 minutes. Transfer to a bowl, cover with plastic wrap and let steam for 10 minutes. Peel the peppers, discard the stems and seeds, then dice.

3. Meanwhile, in a medium skillet, heat ¼ cup of the oil until shimmering. Add the tortilla strips and fry over high heat, turning frequently, until golden, about 2 minutes. Drain on paper towels and sprinkle with salt.

4. In a blender, combine the remaining ¾ cup of oil with the cilantro, sugar, vinegar and the remaining ¼ cup of lime juice and puree until smooth. Season the vinaigrette with salt and pepper.

5. Heat a large cast-iron grill pan and lightly rub the inside with oil. Remove the chicken from the marinade and scrape off any garlic and jalapeño. Grill the chicken over moderate heat, turning occasionally, until browned and cooked through, 10 to 12 minutes. Transfer to a work surface and let stand for 10 minutes, then cut into ¾-inch dice.

6. In a large bowl, combine the roasted peppers with the tomatoes, avocados, onion, jicama, tomatillos and chicken. Add the vinaigrette and toss gently to coat; season with salt and pepper. Transfer the salad to a large platter, scatter the fried tortilla strips on top and serve.
—*Alexandra Angle*

Sweet Pepper Salad with Manchego and Almonds

TOTAL: 20 MIN

4 SERVINGS ● ●

- 2 teaspoons vegetable oil
- ½ cup whole blanched almonds
- 2 cups roasted bell peppers, cut into 2-inch strips
- ¼ cup extra-virgin olive oil
- 2 tablespoons sherry vinegar

- 1 large garlic clove, minced
- 1½ teaspoons chopped drained capers
- ½ teaspoon finely chopped thyme
- ½ teaspoon minced marjoram
- Salt and freshly ground pepper
- 20 small pitted green olives
- ¼ pound Manchego cheese, cut into ¼-inch-thick slices
- 1 tablespoon minced flat-leaf parsley
- Crusty bread, for serving

1. In a medium skillet, heat the vegetable oil. Add the blanched almonds and cook over moderate heat, stirring constantly, until golden, about 5 minutes; transfer to paper towels and let cool, then coarsely chop.

2. Arrange the roasted peppers on serving plates. In a small bowl, combine the olive oil, vinegar, garlic, capers, thyme and marjoram; season with salt and pepper. Drizzle the dressing over the peppers. Top with the olives, chopped almonds and cheese. Sprinkle with the parsley and serve with crusty bread.
—*Laura Chenel*

Quick Thai Beef Salad

TOTAL: 15 MIN

4 SERVINGS ● ●

This pungent, tangy salad is astonishingly fast to make. Other versions of this recipe require you to marinate and cook the meat, which can take hours; this variation calls for store-bought roast beef instead.

- ¼ cup plus 2 tablespoons fresh lime juice
- ¼ cup plus 1 tablespoon Asian fish sauce
- 2 Thai chiles, minced
- 1 teaspoon sugar
- ½ pound thinly sliced rare roast beef
- 5 small scallions, cut into 1-inch lengths
- 3 medium shallots, thinly sliced
- 1 medium tomato, halved lengthwise and thickly sliced

- 1 cup thinly sliced peeled cucumber
- ½ cup chopped celery leaves

In a large bowl, mix the lime juice, fish sauce, chiles and sugar; stir to dissolve the sugar. Add the beef slices, scallions, shallots, tomato, cucumber and celery leaves; toss gently and serve.
—*Sompon and Elizabeth Nabnian*

Sliced Beef with Lemony Arugula and Mushroom Salad

TOTAL: 25 MIN

4 SERVINGS ●

To save time, have the butcher at the supermarket pound the beef thin.

- ¼ cup plus 2 tablespoons olive oil
- 1 tablespoon chopped garlic
- 2 teaspoons chopped rosemary
- Four ¾-inch slices of beef tenderloin, pounded ½ inch thick
- 2 teaspoons mayonnaise
- 2 teaspoons fresh lemon juice
- 1 teaspoon finely grated lemon zest
- Kosher salt and freshly ground pepper
- 5 ounces arugula leaves (2 cups)
- 1 cup very thinly sliced mushrooms
- ¼ pound Parmesan cheese, shaved with a vegetable peeler

1. In a shallow dish, mix ¼ cup of the olive oil with the garlic and rosemary. Add the meat and turn to coat.

2. In a small bowl, whisk the mayonnaise, lemon juice, lemon zest and the remaining 2 tablespoons of olive oil. Season with salt and pepper.

3. Set a large grill pan or cast-iron skillet over high heat. When the pan is very hot, remove the meat from the marinade and season generously with salt and pepper; discard the marinade. Add the beef to the grill pan and cook until nicely browned, 30 seconds per side. Transfer to plates and top with the arugula, mushrooms and Parmesan shavings. Drizzle the dressing over the salads and serve. —*Bruce Aidells*

PORCINI-ONION SOUP WITH GRUYÈRE TOASTS, P. 64

soups

MINI CHILLED BEET SOUPS

GREEN PAPAYA SOUP WITH PICKLED PAPAYA

Mini Chilled Beet Soups

ACTIVE: 15 MIN; TOTAL: 4 HR

12 SERVINGS ● ●

- 3 large beets (1½ pounds), quartered
- 2 quarts chicken stock
- 1 medium onion, coarsely chopped
- 2 garlic cloves, coarsely chopped
- 1 tablespoon red wine vinegar
- 1 tablespoon balsamic vinegar

Salt and freshly ground pepper

Crème fraîche and small dill sprigs, for garnish

1. In a large saucepan, combine the beets, stock, onion, garlic, wine vinegar and balsamic vinegar; bring to a boil. Reduce the heat to moderate; simmer until the beets are tender, 45 minutes.

2. Strain the soup in a colander set over a large heatproof bowl. Let the vegetables cool slightly, then peel the beets and cut them into chunks. Transfer the beets, onion and garlic to a blender. Add 2 cups of the cooking liquid and puree until silky. Stir the puree into the remaining cooking liquid; season with salt and pepper. Chill for at least 3 hours. Serve in small cups, garnished with crème fraîche and dill sprigs. —*David Waltuck*

MAKE AHEAD The soup can be refrigerated for up to 2 days.

Green Papaya Soup with Pickled Papaya

ACTIVE: 1 HR 10 MIN; TOTAL: 3 HR 10 MIN

4 SERVINGS ●

PAPAYAS

- ½ cup unseasoned rice vinegar
- 2 cups sugar
- 4 cups water
- 1 teaspoon mustard seeds
- 1 teaspoon whole black peppercorns
- 1 star anise pod
- 1 whole clove

Sea salt

- 1 small ripe papaya—peeled, seeded and cut into ½-inch dice
- 4 mint sprigs
- ½ large unripe green papaya— peeled, seeded and cut into 1-inch pieces

COCONUT BROTH

- 1½ teaspoons coriander seeds
- 1½ teaspoons fennel seeds
- 1 teaspoon whole cloves
- 1 teaspoon allspice berries
- 1 star anise pod
- 2 tablespoons vegetable oil
- 1 carrot, finely chopped
- 1 medium celery rib, very finely chopped
- 1 medium onion, very finely chopped

½ cup thinly sliced peeled
    fresh ginger

1 stalk of lemongrass, chopped

1 cup dry white wine

One 13½-ounce can unsweetened
    coconut milk

Six 1-inch strips of lime zest
    (from 1 lime), plus extra
    zest for garnish

4 basil sprigs

4 cilantro sprigs

½ cup plus 1 tablespoon
    fresh lime juice

½ cup very cold water

Sea salt

Hot sauce

1 cooked lobster tail (about
    3 ounces), cut crosswise
    into ⅓-inch-thick slices

I. PREPARE THE PAPAYAS: In a small saucepan, combine the unseasoned rice vinegar with ½ cup of sugar, 1 cup of water, the mustard seeds, peppercorns, star anise, clove and 2 tablespoons of sea salt. Bring the pickling liquid to a boil. Put the ripe papaya in a heatproof bowl and pour the hot pickling liquid over it. Let stand for 1 hour, until cool.

2. Meanwhile, in a large saucepan, combine the remaining 1½ cups of sugar with the remaining 3 cups of water and the mint sprigs and bring to a boil, stirring until the sugar dissolves. Add the green papaya and cook over moderate heat until tender, about 45 minutes. Strain the papaya and let cool slightly; discard the mint. Transfer the cooked papaya to a blender and puree until smooth. Transfer to a bowl and refrigerate until cold.

3. MAKE THE COCONUT BROTH: In a small skillet, toast the coriander seeds, fennel seeds, whole cloves, allspice berries and star anise pod over moderate heat, shaking the pan, until fragrant, about 2 minutes. Transfer the toasted spices to a plate to cool.

4. Heat the vegetable oil in a medium saucepan. Add the carrot, celery, onion, ginger and lemongrass and cook over moderate heat, stirring, until the vegetables are softened, about 7 minutes. Add the toasted spices and the wine to the saucepan and cook over moderately high heat, stirring, until the wine has evaporated, about 5 minutes. Add the coconut milk, 6 lime zest strips, basil and cilantro and bring to a boil. Cover and let stand off the heat for 30 minutes. Strain the coconut broth through a fine sieve set over a medium bowl, pressing hard on the solids with the back of a spoon to extract as much liquid as possible. Refrigerate the coconut broth until well chilled.

5. Drain the pickled papaya and pick out the peppercorns, star anise and clove; pat the papaya dry. Add the green papaya puree, lime juice and cold water to the coconut broth; season with salt and hot sauce. Ladle the papaya soup into shallow bowls, mound the lobster in the center of each bowl and arrange the pickled papaya on top. Garnish the papaya soup with lime zest and serve at once. *—David Myers*

MAKE AHEAD The green papaya puree and the coconut broth can be refrigerated separately overnight. The drained pickled papaya can be refrigerated overnight.

Creamy Artichoke and Sunchoke Soup

ACTIVE: 40 MIN; TOTAL: 1 HR 10 MIN
4 TO 6 SERVINGS

Artichokes are part of the thistle family, while sunchokes (Jerusalem artichokes) are related to sunflowers. Their complementary nutty flavors add a lovely complexity to this soup.

1 lemon, halved

4 large artichokes, stemmed

1 pound sunchokes

¼ cup olive oil

¼ pound chopped pancetta

½ cup finely chopped onion

¼ cup finely chopped carrot

¼ cup finely chopped celery

3 medium garlic cloves, very
    finely chopped

2 marjoram sprigs

2 thyme sprigs

½ cup dry white wine

About 4½ cups chicken stock or
    canned low-sodium broth

¼ cup heavy cream

Salt and freshly ground white pepper
Crusty bread, for serving

I. Squeeze the lemon juice into a bowl of cold water and add the lemon halves. Using a sharp knife, halve the artichokes crosswise. Discard the tops. Working with 1 artichoke at a time, pull off all the outer green leaves until you reach the tender yellow leaves. Trim off the dark green skin. Scrape out the hairy choke with a teaspoon, then quarter the heart and drop it into the lemon water.

2. Peel and coarsely chop the sunchokes. Add them to the artichokes in the lemon water.

3. In a large enameled cast-iron casserole, heat the olive oil. Add the pancetta, onion, carrot, celery and garlic and cook over high heat, stirring occasionally, until softened, 5 to 6 minutes. Drain the artichokes and sunchokes and add them to the casserole along with the marjoram and thyme and cook, stirring, for 3 minutes. Add the white wine and boil until almost evaporated.

4. Add 4 cups of chicken stock to the casserole and simmer until the vegetables are tender, about 30 minutes. Discard the herb sprigs. Add the heavy cream and bring to a simmer.

5. In a blender, puree the soup until smooth. If the soup is too thick, add the remaining ½ cup of stock and rewarm. Season with salt and white pepper and serve hot, with crusty bread.
—Michael White

soups

Avocado and Grapefruit Soup

TOTAL: 30 MIN

4 SERVINGS ● ● ●

- 1 large Ruby Red grapefruit
- 1 bunch watercress (6 ounces), stems discarded
- 3 medium Hass avocados, peeled and pitted
- 1½ teaspoons finely grated fresh ginger

Juice of 1 lime

- 1 cup vegetable broth, chilled
- ¾ cup ice water

Kosher salt

- ⅓ cup finely diced peeled and seeded cucumber
- 1 tablespoon snipped chives

1. Using a sharp knife, peel the grapefruit, removing all of the bitter white pith. Working over a strainer set over a medium bowl, cut in between the grapefruit membranes to release the sections into the strainer. Squeeze the grapefruit juice from the membranes through the strainer. Reserve the juice and grapefruit sections separately.

2. Bring a small saucepan of water to a boil; fill a medium bowl with ice water. Blanch the watercress in the boiling water just until limp, about 30 seconds. Drain the watercress and plunge it in the ice water to stop the cooking. Drain the watercress again thoroughly, squeezing out any excess liquid. Finely chop the watercress.

3. In a blender or food processor, puree the avocados with the blanched watercress, ginger, lime juice and the reserved grapefruit juice. With the machine on, add the chilled vegetable broth and the ¾ cup of ice water and puree the avocado soup until combined. Season the soup with salt and ladle it into bowls. Just before serving, garnish with the cucumber, chives and grapefruit sections. —*Megan Moore*

MAKE AHEAD The Avocado and Grape-Fruit Soup can be kept chilled for up to 3 hours.

Cordovan Gazpacho

ACTIVE: 30 MIN; TOTAL: 9 HR

4 SERVINGS ● ●

The soup must be refrigerated overnight, so plan accordingly.

- 2 pounds tomatoes
- 3 cups cubed stale crustless peasant bread (½-inch cubes)
- 1 large garlic clove

Coarse salt

- ⅓ cup coarsely chopped green or red bell pepper
- ⅓ cup extra-virgin olive oil
- ¼ cup water
- 2 teaspoons aged sherry vinegar

Pinch of sugar

Freshly ground pepper

- ⅓ cup slivered Serrano ham (1 ounce)
- 2 hard-cooked egg whites, finely diced

1. Roast the tomatoes over an open flame or in a hot cast-iron skillet, turning, until the skins slip off. Let cool, then peel and halve crosswise. Set a coarse strainer over a large bowl and squeeze the tomato seeds into the strainer. With a spoon, press the seeds to release the juices into the bowl. Chop the tomatoes and add them to the bowl. Add the bread, toss well and let stand until softened, at least 20 minutes.

2. On a work surface, crush the garlic and sprinkle it with 1 teaspoon of coarse salt; mince and mash the garlic with the salt. Add the garlic to the tomato and bread mixture along with the bell pepper, olive oil, water, sherry vinegar and sugar. Working in batches, puree the tomato and bread mixture in a blender until smooth. Cover and refrigerate overnight.

3. Thin the gazpacho with cold water if it is too thick. Season the soup with salt and pepper and ladle it into small bowls. Garnish with the Serrano ham slivers and finely diced egg whites and serve cold. —*Richard Stephens*

MAKE AHEAD The gazpacho can be refrigerated for up to 2 days.

Strawberry, Tomato and Fennel Gazpacho

ACTIVE: 40 MIN; TOTAL: 1 HR 10 MIN

8 SERVINGS ● ●

One 7-inch piece of baguette, crust removed

- 2 pounds tomatoes, 2 tablespoons finely diced, the rest chopped
- 2 pounds strawberries, hulled, 2 tablespoons finely diced, the rest chopped
- 1 large green bell pepper, 2 tablespoons finely diced, the rest chopped
- ¼ medium fennel bulb, 2 tablespoons finely diced, the rest thinly sliced
- 1½ cups sparkling mineral water
- 2 garlic cloves, minced

Salt

Extra-virgin olive oil, for drizzling

1. Preheat the oven to 350°. Cut the bread into 1-inch cubes. (You will need about 1 cup.) Scatter the bread cubes on a baking sheet and bake for 7 minutes, or until crisp. Let cool.

2. In a large bowl, combine the chopped tomatoes, chopped strawberries and chopped bell pepper with the sliced fennel, mineral water, minced garlic and toasted bread cubes. Toss well. Working in 2 batches, puree the mixture in a food processor. Strain the gazpacho through a fine sieve set over another large bowl. Season the soup with salt and refrigerate for about 25 minutes, or until chilled.

3. Meanwhile, in another large bowl, combine the diced tomatoes, strawberries, pepper and fennel. Refrigerate until chilled.

4. Spoon the diced mixture into shallow soup bowls and ladle the gazpacho on top. Drizzle each bowl of soup with olive oil and serve. —*Adolfo Muñoz*

MAKE AHEAD The gazpacho and the diced-vegetable garnish can be refrigerated separately for up to 6 hours.

Chilled Green Tomato Soup with Tomato Confit

ACTIVE: 1 HR 10 MIN; TOTAL: 2 HR 20 MIN

4 SERVINGS

- 12 large plum tomatoes (2 pounds)— peeled, seeded and quartered lengthwise
- ¾ cup extra-virgin olive oil
- 1 tablespoon fresh thyme
- 1 large garlic clove, minced
- 1 tablespoon plus 1 teaspoon sugar

Kosher salt and freshly ground white pepper

- 1 small artichoke (about 5 ounces)
- 1½ pounds unripe green tomatoes (preferably heirlooms), halved crosswise
- 1 small white onion, finely chopped
- 1 medium shallot, finely chopped
- ½ green bell pepper, coarsely chopped
- ½ cup heavy cream
- ½ cup ice water
- ¼ cup finely chopped basil
- 1½ cups mixed yellow and red pear tomatoes, quartered lengthwise

1. Preheat the oven to 225°. In a medium bowl, toss the plum tomatoes with ½ cup of the olive oil, the thyme, garlic, sugar and 2 teaspoons of kosher salt; season with white pepper. Spread the tomatoes out on a rimmed baking sheet and bake for 1 hour and 20 minutes, turning them over halfway through cooking. Let cool. Transfer to a bowl and refrigerate until chilled.

2. Meanwhile, snap off the tough outer leaves of the artichoke until you reach the pale green leaves. Using a sharp knife, cut off the top two-thirds of the leaves, then peel the base and stem. Using a spoon or melon baller, scoop out the hairy choke. Cut the artichoke into ½-inch pieces.

3. Squeeze the green tomato halves to soften, then scoop out the seeds and discard. Quarter each half. In a saucepan, heat the remaining ¼ cup of oil.

AVOCADO AND GRAPEFRUIT SOUP

CORDOVAN GAZPACHO

soups

Add the onion, shallot, green pepper and artichoke, season with salt and cook over moderate heat until softened, 10 minutes. Add the green tomatoes, cover and cook over moderately low heat, stirring, until softened and most of the liquid has evaporated, about 1 hour.

4. Transfer the vegetables to a blender and puree until smooth. Strain the puree through a fine sieve set over a medium bowl and refrigerate until chilled. Stir in the cream and water, season with salt and white pepper and refrigerate.

5. Drain the plum tomatoes and pat dry with paper towels. Finely chop the tomatoes and transfer to a bowl. Add 2 tablespoons of the basil and season lightly with salt and white pepper. In another bowl, season the pear tomatoes with salt and white pepper.

6. Place a 3-inch round ring mold or biscuit cutter in the bottom of each of 4 shallow bowls. Press the plum tomato mixture into the molds, then carefully remove the molds. Mound the pear tomatoes on top. Pour the soup all around, garnish with the remaining 2 tablespoons of basil and serve. —*Gabriel Kreuther*

MAKE AHEAD The baked plum tomatoes can be refrigerated for up to 2 days. The green tomato puree can be refrigerated overnight. Stir in the cream and water before serving.

INGREDIENT TIP

fresh chestnuts

IF YOU CAN'T FIND BOTTLED chestnuts for the Silky Chestnut Soup (right), you can prepare fresh ones. Score an "X" on the top of each nut. Boil the nuts for 5 to 8 minutes, until tender; remove and peel them one by one. Then, either roast them at 350° or sauté them with butter until tender, about 15 minutes.

Grape and Almond Gazpacho

ACTIVE: 20 MIN; TOTAL: 2 HR

6 SERVINGS ● ●

- 2 pounds seedless green grapes
- 1 medium cucumber—peeled, seeded and coarsely chopped
- ¼ cup roasted unsalted almonds
- 2 scallions, white and light green parts only, coarsely chopped
- ¼ cup unseasoned rice vinegar
- ½ cup plain yogurt
- 3 ounces cream cheese
- ¼ cup buttermilk
- 2 tablespoons extra-virgin olive oil
- 2 large dill sprigs, minced

Pinch of cayenne pepper

Salt and freshly ground white pepper

Thinly sliced cucumber and minced chives, for garnish

1. In a blender, combine the grapes, cucumber, almonds, scallions, rice vinegar, yogurt, cream cheese, buttermilk and olive oil. Blend until almost smooth. Stir in the dill and cayenne, season with salt and white pepper and chill.

2. Serve the gazpacho in well-chilled shallow bowls, garnished with the cucumber slices and chives. —*Cindy Pawlcyn*

MAKE AHEAD The soup can be refrigerated overnight

Silky Chestnut Soup

ACTIVE: 25 MIN; TOTAL: 1 HR

6 SERVINGS ●

- 4 tablespoons unsalted butter
- 1 medium carrot, finely chopped
- 1 celery rib, finely chopped
- ½ medium onion, finely chopped
- 2 cups cooked chestnuts (from one 14.8-ounce vacuum-packed jar)
- 1 cup ruby port
- 1 thyme sprig
- 3 cups chicken stock or broth
- ½ cup heavy cream

Salt and freshly ground pepper

1. Melt the butter in a medium saucepan over moderately low heat. Stir in the chopped carrot, celery and onion.

Cook, stirring, until softened, about 10 minutes. Add the chestnuts and cook for 4 minutes. Add the port and thyme and cook over moderately high heat until the port is reduced by half, about 4 minutes. Add the stock and bring to a boil. Cover partially and simmer over low heat for 30 minutes. Discard the thyme sprig.

2. Add the cream to the soup. Working in batches, puree the soup in a blender. Return the soup to the saucepan and bring to a simmer. Season with salt and pepper and serve. —*Wolfgang Puck*

Thirty-Minute Minestrone

TOTAL: 30 MIN

6 SERVINGS ● ● ●

- 2 tablespoons extra-virgin olive oil
- 6 shiitake mushrooms, stemmed, caps cut into ½-inch pieces
- 3 large garlic cloves, minced
- 1 leek, white and tender green parts only, halved lengthwise and sliced
- 6 cups vegetable stock
- 1 cup drained canned Italian tomatoes, coarsely chopped

Salt and freshly ground pepper

- 1 cup tubetti pasta (¼ pound)
- ½ pound wax beans, cut into 1-inch pieces
- ½ pound baby zucchini, cut into ½-inch rounds
- 1 cup drained canned white beans
- ½ cup frozen baby peas, thawed
- 2 tablespoons chopped basil

Heat 1 tablespoon of the olive oil in a large casserole. Add the mushrooms, garlic and leek and cook over moderate heat, stirring, until barely softened. Add the stock and tomatoes, season with salt and pepper and bring to a boil. Add the pasta and cook until barely softened, about 4 minutes. Add the wax beans, zucchini and white beans, cover the pan partially and cook until tender. Stir in the peas and basil. Drizzle with the remaining 1 tablespoon of olive oil and serve. —*Grace Parisi*

Smoked Tomato Soup

TOTAL: 1 HR

4 SERVINGS ● ●

- ¼ cup apple, pecan or hickory wood chips (preferably ½ inch or smaller)
- 10 large plum tomatoes (about 2½ pounds), halved and seeded, 8 coarsely chopped
- ¼ cup extra-virgin olive oil
- 1 large onion, finely chopped
- 1 large leek, halved lengthwise and thinly sliced crosswise
- 1½ teaspoons coriander seeds
- 2 garlic cloves, smashed
- 2 bay leaves
- 1 teaspoon finely grated fresh or drained bottled horseradish
- 1 cup chicken stock or canned low-sodium broth

Pinch of sugar

- 4 tablespoons unsalted butter, softened

Salt and freshly ground pepper

Small basil leaves, for garnish

1. Scatter the wood chips in a medium cast-iron skillet and cover the skillet tightly. Heat the chips over moderately high heat until smoking. Place the tomato halves on a rack and set the rack in the skillet. Cover and smoke the tomatoes for 2 to 3 minutes, or until barely softened. Transfer the tomatoes to a plate and let cool slightly, then peel.

2. In a large saucepan, heat the olive oil until shimmering. Add the onion and leek and cook over moderate heat, stirring frequently, until softened but not browned, about 10 minutes. Add the coriander seeds, garlic, bay leaves and horseradish and cook until fragrant, about 2 minutes. Add the chopped tomatoes, chicken stock and sugar, cover and cook over moderate heat until the tomatoes are nicely softened, 10 minutes. Discard the bay leaves.

3. Working in batches, puree the soup with the butter and smoked tomatoes until smooth. Strain the soup into a clean saucepan; season with salt and pepper. Serve the soup in bowls, garnished with basil. —*Dan Barber*

MAKE AHEAD The soup can be refrigerated overnight.

Lettuce Soup with Watercress-Herb Puree

ACTIVE: 1 HR; TOTAL: 1 HR 30 MIN

8 SERVINGS ● ●

To demonstrate how much Italians love a hit of bitterness, chef Sergio Sigala tops his mild lettuce soup with a peppery watercress-herb puree.

LETTUCE SOUP

- 2 tablespoons extra-virgin olive oil
- 3 medium leeks, white and light green parts only, coarsely chopped
- 3 medium celery ribs, coarsely chopped
- 1 large baking potato (10 ounces), peeled and cut into 1-inch dice
- 2 pounds Boston lettuce (about 6 heads), coarsely chopped
- 1 quart vegetable stock, preferably homemade

Salt and freshly ground pepper

WATERCRESS-HERB PUREE

One 6-ounce bunch watercress, thick stems discarded

- 2 cups packed basil leaves
- ¼ cup water
- ¼ cup chopped chives
- 3 tablespoons extra-virgin olive oil
- 1 teaspoon marjoram leaves

Salt and freshly ground pepper

Peppery extra-virgin olive oil, preferably Tuscan, for drizzling

1. MAKE THE LETTUCE SOUP: Heat the olive oil in a very large saucepan. Add the leeks, celery and potato and cook over moderately low heat, stirring often, until the vegetables are slightly softened, about 10 minutes. Add the chopped lettuce by large handfuls, stirring each batch until wilted before adding the next. Add 2 cups of the vegetable stock and season with salt and pepper. Reduce the heat to moderately low. Cover and simmer the soup, stirring often, until the vegetables are very soft, about 20 minutes. Add the remaining 2 cups of stock, cover and cook for 20 minutes longer.

2. Working in batches, carefully puree the hot soup in a blender. Pour the soup into a clean saucepan and season with salt and pepper.

3. PREPARE THE WATERCRESS-HERB PUREE: In a medium bowl, prepare an ice-water bath. Set aside 8 small watercress sprigs. In a medium saucepan of boiling salted water, blanch the remaining watercress and the basil leaves for 5 seconds. Drain and plunge into the ice-water bath to cool. Drain again and squeeze out any excess water, then coarsely chop. Transfer the chopped watercress and basil to a blender. Add the water, chives, extra-virgin olive oil and marjoram and blend until emulsified. Transfer the puree to a bowl and season with salt and pepper.

4. Gently reheat the soup and ladle into warmed shallow bowls. Drizzle some Tuscan olive oil and a rounded tablespoon of the watercress puree over the soup. Garnish with the reserved watercress sprigs and serve.

—*Sergio Sigala*

MAKE AHEAD The lettuce soup and the watercress-herb puree can be refrigerated separately overnight in airtight containers.

Soft-Cooked Eggs and Artichokes in Broth

TOTAL: 35 MIN

4 SERVINGS ● ●

- 1 lemon, halved lengthwise
- 2 large artichokes
- 1 tablespoon extra-virgin olive oil
- 1 garlic clove, thinly sliced
- 4 cups chicken stock, preferably homemade

Salt and freshly ground pepper

soups

8 cremini mushrooms, thinly sliced

4 large eggs

2 scallions, thinly sliced

Freshly grated Parmesan cheese and
    crusty bread, for serving

1. Fill a bowl with water and squeeze a lemon half into it. Working with 1 artichoke at a time, snap off the tough outer leaves and trim the stem to 1 inch. Using a sharp knife, cut off the top two-thirds of the artichoke. With a teaspoon, scoop out the furry choke. Peel the artichoke base, removing the dark green skin, and add to the lemon water. Very thinly slice the artichoke bottoms and return to the water. Cut the remaining lemon half into 4 wedges.

2. In a large, deep skillet, heat the oil. Add the garlic and cook over moderately high heat until softened, 30 seconds. Add the stock, season with salt and pepper; bring to a boil. Drain the artichokes, add to the skillet and simmer until crisp-tender, 3 minutes. Add the mushrooms; simmer for 2 minutes.

3. Crack the eggs into the soup, leaving space between them. Cook gently over moderately low heat until the whites are set but the yolks are still runny, about 2 minutes. Carefully spoon each egg into a bowl, then ladle the soup on top. Sprinkle the soup with the scallions and serve with the lemon wedges, Parmesan cheese and bread. —*Anne Quatrano*

COOKING TIP

making stock

HOMEMADE STOCK MAKES the best soup. For chicken stock, cover 4 pounds of chicken parts with cold water. Add a chopped onion, carrot and celery rib (and herbs as desired). Simmer for 3 hours, skimming and adding more water as needed. Strain and let cool. Discard the fat, then use or freeze for up to 2 months.

Creamy Asparagus Soup with Lemon Dumplings

ACTIVE: 55 MIN; TOTAL: 2 HR 30 MIN

6 SERVINGS ● ○

4 tablespoons unsalted butter

1 tablespoon extra-virgin olive oil

2 large shallots, thinly sliced (1½ cups)

2 pounds medium asparagus, 1½-inch tips reserved, spears coarsely chopped

Salt and freshly ground pepper

1 quart chicken stock or low-sodium broth

1 cup heavy cream

24 Lemon Dumplings (recipe follows)

1. In a large saucepan, melt 2 tablespoons of the butter in the olive oil. Add the shallots and cook over low heat until softened, about 5 minutes. Add the chopped asparagus, season with salt and pepper and cook, stirring, until softened, about 5 minutes. Add the chicken stock and cream and bring to a boil over moderately high heat. Reduce the heat to moderately low and simmer until the asparagus is very tender, about 15 minutes.

2. Meanwhile, bring a medium saucepan of water to a boil. Add salt and the asparagus tips and cook until just tender, about 3 minutes. Using a slotted spoon, remove the tips and reserve them; keep the water boiling.

3. Puree the soup in batches in a food processor and strain it through a coarse sieve, pressing on the solids. Return the soup to the large saucepan, season with salt and pepper and add the asparagus tips. Keep hot.

4. Add the Lemon Dumplings to the boiling water and cook until just tender, about 1½ minutes; drain. Melt the remaining 2 tablespoons of butter in the same saucepan over moderately high heat. Add the Lemon Dumplings and carefully swirl them in the butter to coat. Add 4 dumplings to each soup plate,

ladle the asparagus soup over them and serve at once.
—*Jean-Georges Vongerichten*

MAKE AHEAD The soup and cooked asparagus tips can be refrigerated for up to 2 days. Reheat gently.

Lemon Dumplings

ACTIVE: 30 MIN; TOTAL: 2 HR 30 MIN

MAKES 24 DUMPLINGS ● ●

These dumplings are filled with a lemon jelly that liquefies when cooked. They would be equally delicious in a good chicken broth, chicken and rice soup or egg drop soup.

2 large lemons

1 envelope unflavored powdered gelatin

½ tablespoon extra-virgin olive oil

1 teaspoon sugar

Salt

Cayenne pepper

24 square wonton wrappers

1. Finely grate the zest of ½ lemon. Peel all of the lemons, removing the skin and white pith. Working over a large non-reactive saucepan to catch the juice, cut in between the membranes to release the sections. Squeeze the juice from the membranes into the pan. There should be 2 tablespoons of juice. Finely chop the lemon sections and add to the pan. Sprinkle the gelatin over the lemon mixture and let stand until jellied, about 3 minutes.

2. Set the saucepan over low heat and swirl the pan a few times until the mixture is barely hot and the gelatin has melted, 40 to 50 seconds. Pour the mixture into a shallow glass baking dish, stir in the olive oil and sugar and season with salt and a pinch of cayenne. Refrigerate until very firm, about 2 hours.

3. Scrape the gelatin onto a cutting board and finely chop. Lay 4 wonton wrappers on a work surface and moisten the edges with water. Mound 1 teaspoon of the lemon gelatin just

ASPARAGUS SOUP WITH LEMON DUMPLINGS

BITTER GREENS WITH CHEESE DUMPLINGS

below the center of each wrapper. Bring 2 opposite corners together over the filling to form a triangle. Press all around the filling to release any air pockets and seal the dumplings. Moisten the opposite tips, bring them together and press to seal. Repeat with the remaining wrappers and gelatin. —*J.-G. V.*

MAKE AHEAD The lemon gelatin can be refrigerated for up to 2 days. The lemon dumplings can be frozen for up to a month (do not defrost—cook the dumplings frozen).

Soup of Bitter Greens with Cheese Dumplings

ACTIVE: 25 MIN; TOTAL: 1 HR

4 SERVINGS

- 1 cup slightly packed freshly grated Parmesan cheese (about 4 ounces)
- 1 cup slightly packed freshly grated Pecorino Romano cheese (4 ounces), plus more for serving
- ¾ cup fine dry bread crumbs (3 ounces)
- 1 tablespoon finely chopped flat-leaf parsley
- 4 large eggs, lightly beaten
- 2 garlic cloves, minced
- 2 tablespoons extra-virgin olive oil
- ½ pound bitter greens, such as escarole or chicory, coarsely chopped
- 2 quarts chicken stock or canned low-sodium broth

Salt and freshly ground pepper

I. In a bowl, combine the Parmesan cheese with the 1 cup of Pecorino, the bread crumbs, parsley, eggs and half of the garlic and stir gently until a soft dough forms. Using moistened hands, roll the dumpling mixture into ¾-inch balls and arrange in a single layer on a baking sheet lined with plastic wrap. Refrigerate until chilled and firm, about 30 minutes.

2. Meanwhile, in a medium saucepan, heat the olive oil until shimmering. Add the remaining garlic and cook over moderately high heat until softened, about 30 seconds. Add the greens and cook, stirring, until wilted and just beginning to brown, 3 to 4 minutes longer. Add the stock and bring to a simmer. Drop the dumplings into the simmering stock and cook until they rise to the surface, about 5 minutes. Season the soup with salt and pepper and serve in bowls, passing extra Pecorino at the table. —*Michael White*

MAKE AHEAD The uncooked dumplings can be refrigerated overnight.

BUTTERNUT SQUASH SOUP WITH CRISP PANCETTA

Butternut Squash Soup with Crisp Pancetta

ACTIVE: 45 MIN; TOTAL: 1 HR 45 MIN

12 SERVINGS ●

- 4 medium butternut squash (6 pounds)
- 6 tablespoons unsalted butter, cut into 8 pieces

Kosher salt and freshly ground pepper

- 12 very thin slices of pancetta (3 ounces)
- 2 tablespoons extra-virgin olive oil, plus more for drizzling
- 1 large Spanish onion, chopped
- 6 thyme sprigs
- 1 bay leaf
- 2 quarts chicken stock or low-sodium broth
- 2 tablespoons heavy cream

Sugar (optional)

1. Preheat the oven to 400°. Halve the squash lengthwise and scoop out the seeds. Set the squash on a rimmed baking sheet, cut sides up. Put a piece of butter in each cavity and season generously with salt and pepper. Drape the squash halves with the pancetta slices. Roast the squash for 45 to 50 minutes, or until tender.

2. Transfer the pancetta to paper towels to drain. Crumble and set aside. Scoop the squash out of the skins into a bowl.

3. In a large, heavy stockpot, heat the 2 tablespoons of olive oil until shimmering. Add the onion, season with salt and pepper and cook over moderately high heat, stirring, until softened but not browned, about 6 minutes. Add 3 of the thyme sprigs and the bay leaf. Stir in the squash and the stock and bring to a boil over high heat, stirring frequently. Reduce the heat and simmer the soup for 15 minutes, stirring occasionally.

4. Pick out and discard from the soup the thyme and bay leaf. Working in batches, transfer the soup to a blender or food processor and puree until thick and creamy, about 1 minute per batch.

Transfer the soup to a clean saucepan. Stir in the heavy cream and season with salt and pepper (and sugar if desired).

5. Reheat the soup if necessary. Ladle into 12 bowls. Garnish the soup with the pancetta, the leaves from the remaining 3 thyme sprigs and a drizzle of olive oil.
—*Tom Valenti*

MAKE AHEAD The soup and roasted pancetta can be refrigerated for up to 2 days. Reheat the soup and recrisp the pancetta before serving; the soup may need to be thinned with stock or water.

Butternut Squash and Leek Soup

ACTIVE: 35 MIN; TOTAL: 1 HR

6 SERVINGS ●

- 2 tablespoons unsalted butter
- 4 leeks, white and tender green parts only, coarsely chopped
- 1 celery rib, chopped
- 1 garlic clove, smashed
- 1 quart chicken stock, preferably homemade
- 1 large butternut squash, peeled and cut into ½-inch dice (3 cups)
- 1 tablespoon tomato paste
- 1 large bay leaf

Sea salt and freshly ground pepper

- ¼ cup flat-leaf parsley leaves
- ½ cup heavy cream

1. Melt the butter in a large, heavy saucepan. Add the leeks, celery and garlic and cook over moderate heat, stirring occasionally, until softened, 7 to 8 minutes. Add the stock, squash, tomato paste and bay leaf. Season with salt and pepper and simmer over moderately low heat until all the vegetables are tender, about 25 minutes. Discard the bay leaf and add the parsley.

2. Puree the soup in a blender, then return it to the saucepan. Stir in the cream and cook just until heated through. Season with salt and pepper and serve. – *Barbara Damrosch*

MAKE AHEAD The soup can be refrigerated overnight.

Curried Winter Squash Soup with Cheddar Crisps

ACTIVE: 1 HR 15 MIN; TOTAL: 4 HR

12 SERVINGS ●

- 4 tablespoons unsalted butter
- ¼ cup vegetable oil
- 1 medium sweet onion, coarsely chopped (2 cups)
- 2 large garlic cloves, thinly sliced
- 2 tablespoons medium-hot Madras curry powder
- 7 pounds winter squash, such as butternut, buttercup or kabocha—peeled, seeded and cut into 1-inch chunks (about 16 cups)

About 8 cups Rich Turkey Stock (recipe, p. 125)

- ¾ pound sharp white Cheddar cheese, cut into twenty-four 1½-inch squares ¼ inch thick
- 1 teaspoon cumin seeds
- 2 tablespoons sliced blanched almonds

Salt and freshly ground pepper

1. In a large stockpot, melt the butter in the vegetable oil. Add the onion and garlic and cook over high heat, stirring, until softened but not browned, about 4 minutes. Add the curry and cook, stirring, for 1 minute. Add the squash and cook, stirring, for 4 minutes. Add 6 cups of the stock and bring to a boil. Cover and simmer over moderately low heat until the squash is tender, 30 minutes.

2. Arrange 4 of the Cheddar squares in a large nonstick skillet and cook over moderate heat until bubbling, 1½ minutes. Sprinkle each with a pinch of the cumin seeds and 3 or 4 almond slices; cook until the edges are golden, about 1½ minutes longer. Using a spatula, flip the crisps and cook until the almonds are browned, about 20 seconds longer. Transfer to a baking sheet lined with paper towels; let cool until crisp. Wipe out the skillet. Repeat with the remaining Cheddar, cumin seeds and almonds.

soups

3. Working in batches, puree the soup in a blender. Return the soup to the pot and gradually stir in about 2 cups of stock, until the soup has a silky, bisque-like consistency. Season with salt and pepper and keep warm over low heat.
4. Ladle the soup into shallow bowls and pass the Cheddar crisps alongside for dipping or crumbling. —*Grace Parisi*
MAKE AHEAD The soup can be refrigerated for up to 3 days. The Cheddar crisps can be stored overnight in an airtight container. Recrisp on a baking sheet in a 350° oven and let cool.

Spicy Carrot Soup
ACTIVE: 30 MIN; TOTAL: 45 MIN
8 SERVINGS ● ●
- 5 cups chicken stock or broth
- 1 pound carrots, coarsely chopped
- 2 medium celery ribs, coarsely chopped
- 1 large onion, coarsely chopped
- 1 leek, white and tender green parts only, coarsely chopped
- 1 small baking potato (6 ounces), peeled and coarsely chopped
- 1½ teaspoons ground cumin
- 1 teaspoon sweet paprika
- ¼ teaspoon cayenne pepper
- 1 cup low-fat buttermilk or yogurt
- Salt and freshly ground pepper
- 2 tablespoons chopped parsley

1. In a large pot, combine the stock with the carrots, celery, onion, leek, potato, cumin, paprika and cayenne and bring to a boil. Cover and simmer over low heat until the vegetables are tender, about 15 minutes.
2. Working in batches, puree the soup in a blender or food processor, then return to the pot. Stir in the buttermilk and season with salt and pepper. Reheat gently. Ladle into bowls, sprinkle with the parsley and serve.
—*Andrew J. Powning*
MAKE AHEAD The soup can be refrigerated overnight.

Tunisian Chickpea Soup with Harissa
TOTAL: 1 HR
8 SERVINGS ● ●
- 2 tablespoons extra-virgin olive oil, plus more for serving
- 2 garlic cloves, minced
- 5 cups veal or chicken stock or low-sodium broth
- Two 15-ounce cans chickpeas, drained and rinsed
- 1 red bell pepper
- 8 large eggs, at room temperature
- 3 cups diced stale bread (½-inch dice)
- Salt and freshly ground pepper
- Harissa (recipe follows)
- Ground cumin
- 2 tablespoons drained capers
- ¼ cup green olives, such as Picholine, pitted and chopped
- Lemon wedges, for serving

1. In a large saucepan, heat the 2 tablespoons of olive oil. Add the garlic and cook over low heat until fragrant, about 2 minutes. Add the stock and chickpeas and bring to a boil. Cover and simmer over low heat for 15 minutes.
2. Roast the bell pepper over an open flame or under a broiler until charred all over. Transfer the pepper to a plate to cool for 5 minutes. Remove the skin, seeds and stem. Dice the pepper.
3. Fill a large saucepan with water and bring to a simmer over moderate heat. Add the eggs and simmer for 7 minutes. Drain the eggs and gently crack the shells all over, then cover the eggs with cold water and let cool for 2 minutes.
4. Divide all the bread cubes among 8 shallow soup bowls. Season the piping-hot chickpea soup generously with salt and pepper and ladle it into the bowls. Drizzle about 1 tablespoon of the *harissa* into each bowl and sprinkle with a small pinch of cumin.
5. Drain the eggs, then peel. Break the eggs in half crosswise, setting each into

a bowl. Scatter the capers, olives and diced red bell pepper over the chickpeas. Garnish the soup with lemon wedges and serve, passing additional olive oil at the table. —*Paula Wolfert*
MAKE AHEAD The recipe can be prepared through Step 2 up to 2 days in advance. Refrigerate the soup and diced red bell pepper separately.

Harissa
TOTAL: 25 MIN
MAKES ABOUT ¾ CUP ● ● ●
This somewhat mild, creamy version of the Tunisian chile sauce is a very versatile condiment. You can use it as a dip or spread for bread, slather it on skewered shrimp before grilling or spread it on grilled chicken or lamb.
- 2 dried New Mexico chiles or 1 ancho and 1 guajillo chile— stemmed, seeded and torn into 2-inch pieces
- 1 large sun-dried tomato
- 1 garlic clove
- ½ teaspoon ground coriander
- ⅛ teaspoon ground caraway seeds (optional)
- 2 tablespoons extra-virgin olive oil
- ½ cup water
- Fresh lemon juice
- Salt

1. In a medium bowl, soak the dried chiles and the sun-dried tomato in warm water until softened, about 20 minutes. Drain the chiles and the tomato and squeeze dry.
2. In a blender, combine the dried chiles and the sun-dried tomato with the garlic, ground coriander and caraway seeds and pulse until a paste forms. Add the olive oil and water and blend until the paste is smooth. Stir in about ½ teaspoon of lemon juice, or more to taste, and season the *harissa* generously with salt. —*P.W.*
MAKE AHEAD The *harissa* can be refrigerated for up to 1 week.

Turkish Red Lentil Soup

ACTIVE. 25 MIN; TOTAL: 1 HR

4 SERVINGS ●

- 4 tablespoons unsalted butter
- ½ cup grated onion
- 1 garlic clove, minced
- 6 cups water
- 2 cups chicken or beef stock
- 1 cup red lentils (6½ ounces)
- 2 tablespoons short-grain rice
- 1½ tablespoons tomato paste
- Salt and freshly ground pepper
- 4 slices of peasant bread, cut into ½-inch cubes
- 2 tablespoons all-purpose flour
- 2 teaspoons crushed red pepper
- 1 teaspoon dried spearmint

1. Melt 1 tablespoon of the butter in a medium saucepan. Add the onion and garlic and cook over moderate heat, stirring, until softened, about 5 minutes. Add the water, stock, red lentils, rice and tomato paste, cover and bring to a boil. Skim the soup, then cover and cook over moderately low heat, stirring occasionally, until the lentils have dissolved, about 45 minutes. Pass the soup through the fine disk of a food mill; season with salt and pepper. Return the soup to the saucepan and bring to a simmer over low heat.

2. Meanwhile, preheat the oven to 375°. Spread the bread on a baking sheet and toast until golden and crisp, 8 minutes.

3. In a small skillet, melt 2 tablespoons of the butter. Stir in the flour and cook over moderate heat, whisking, until a smooth brown roux forms. Gradually whisk the roux into the soup and simmer for 5 minutes. Wipe out the skillet.

4. Working over the small skillet, rub the crushed red pepper and mint through a fine sieve. Add the remaining 1 tablespoon of butter to the skillet and heat until sizzling. Ladle the soup into bowls. Drizzle with the sizzling butter and sprinkle with the croutons; serve. —*Arif Dcveli*

MAKE AHEAD Refrigerate the soup overnight. Swirl in the butter before serving.

TUNISIAN CHICKPEA SOUP WITH HARISSA

TURKISH RED LENTIL SOUP

soups

Porcini-Onion Soup with Gruyère Toasts

ACTIVE: 40 MIN; TOTAL: 1 HR 15 MIN

4 SERVINGS

- 4 cups low-sodium chicken broth
- 1 ounce dried porcini mushrooms (see Note)
- 1 cup water
- 1 tablespoon plus 1 teaspoon unsalted butter
- 2 pounds medium onions, cut into very thin slices

Salt

- ½ teaspoon sugar
- ½ cup dry white wine
- 1 teaspoon thyme leaves

Freshly ground pepper

- 1 small baguette, cut into 8 slices on an extreme diagonal
- ¼ pound Gruyère cheese, shredded
- 1 tablespoon freshly grated Parmesan cheese

COOKING TIP

five steps to soup

1. SIMMER A LIQUID Healthy options include stock, water, low-fat milk and buttermilk.

2. ADD VEGETABLES Toss in one or more aromatic vegetables— onion, leek, garlic, celery, carrot.

3. ENRICH THE POT with meats, poultry or seafood. Long-simmered soups make great use of tough beef cuts or mature chickens. Quick soups use chicken breast, beef tenderloin, shrimp and fish.

4. STIR IN A THICKENER Rice, potatoes, pasta, dried peas, bread, flour (mixed into the vegetables as they sauté) and cornstarch (whisked into the finished, simmering soup) all lend body.

5. GARNISH Choices include toast, dumplings, choux pastry.

1. In a medium saucepan, combine the chicken broth, dried porcini and water and bring to a boil over high heat. Reduce the heat to low and simmer for 20 minutes. Strain the broth through a fine sieve set over a bowl or very large measuring cup, pressing down on the mushrooms to extract as much liquid as possible and stopping when you reach the grit at the bottom of the pan. You should have 1 quart of broth; if necessary, add water. Rinse the porcini to remove any grit, then pat dry and coarsely chop.

2. In a large, deep skillet, melt the butter. Stir in the onions and 1 teaspoon of salt. Cover and cook over moderately low heat, stirring occasionally, until the onions have released some of their liquid, about 10 minutes. Raise the heat to moderate and cook, uncovered, stirring occasionally, until the liquid has evaporated, about 10 minutes. Add the sugar and continue cooking, stirring frequently, until the onions are golden brown, about 15 minutes longer. Raise the heat to high. Add the wine, thyme and chopped mushrooms. Cook, stirring, until the wine is completely evaporated and the onions have begun to brown again, about 7 minutes. Add the porcini broth, reduce the heat to low and simmer for 5 more minutes. Season with salt and pepper.

3. Meanwhile, preheat the broiler and arrange the bread on a baking sheet and toast under the broiler 3 inches from the heat until golden. Turn the bread, sprinkle the Gruyère and Parmesan on top; broil until bubbling and golden.

4. Ladle the soup into shallow bowls and serve with the toasts. —*Sally Schneider*

NOTE Imported dried porcini, also called cèpes or king boletes, are available at specialty food stores.

MAKE AHEAD The porcini broth can be refrigerated for up to 2 days; refrigerate the chopped porcini separately.

Barley Soup with Porcini Mushrooms

ACTIVE: 30 MIN; TOTAL: 10 HR

6 SERVINGS ● ●

- 2 ounces dried porcini mushrooms (2 cups)
- 2 cups warm milk
- 2 tablespoons extra-virgin olive oil, plus more for serving
- 1 medium onion, finely chopped
- 1 medium celery rib, finely chopped
- 1 small carrot, finely chopped
- 1½ quarts chicken stock or canned low-sodium broth
- 1 bay leaf
- ½ pound pearl barley (1¼ cups), soaked overnight and drained
- ¾ pound Yukon Gold potatoes, peeled and cut into ½-inch dice

Salt and freshly ground pepper

Freshly grated Parmesan cheese, for serving

1. In a bowl, cover the porcini with the warm milk and let stand until softened, about 20 minutes. Rub the porcini in the milk to rinse off any grit, then coarsely chop them. Reserve the milk.

2. In a large saucepan, heat the 2 tablespoons of olive oil. Add the onion, celery and carrot and cook over moderate heat until browned, about 15 minutes. Add the porcini and cook for 1 minute, stirring. Add the stock, bay leaf and barley and bring to a boil. Cover and simmer over low heat for 30 minutes, stirring occasionally. Add the potatoes, cover and simmer until the barley and potatoes are tender, about 30 minutes. Stir in the reserved milk, stopping when you reach the grit at the bottom. Simmer for 5 minutes. Discard the bay leaf and season with salt and pepper. Ladle the soup into bowls and serve, passing olive oil and Parmesan cheese at the table. —*Marika Seguso*

MAKE AHEAD The soup can be refrigerated for up to 2 days. Add more stock when reheating if the soup is too thick.

Mushroom Dumplings in Brodo
TOTAL: 1 HR 10 MIN
6 SERVINGS ●

As an alternative to serving the boiled dumplings in broth, sauté them in butter and sprinkle with Parmesan cheese.

1 tablespoon extra-virgin olive oil
½ pound white or other mushrooms, such as shiitake, cut into ¼-inch-thick slices
1 medium shallot, thinly sliced
1 large egg yolk
1 teaspoon finely chopped flat-leaf parsley
3 tablespoons freshly grated Parmesan cheese, plus more for serving
Salt and freshly ground pepper
36 square wonton wrappers
6 cups homemade chicken stock, or best-quality low-sodium broth, piping hot

1. Heat the olive oil in a large skillet. Add the mushrooms and cook over low heat until the liquid they release has evaporated, about 5 minutes. Add the shallot and cook, stirring, until the shallot is softened and the mushrooms are lightly browned, about 5 minutes. Transfer the mushrooms and shallot to a cutting board and let cool, then finely chop.
2. In a medium bowl, mix the mushrooms with the egg yolk, parsley and 3 tablespoons of Parmesan. Season with salt and pepper.
3. Lay 4 wonton wrappers on a work surface and moisten the edges with water. Mound 1½ teaspoons of the mushroom filling just below the center of each wonton wrapper. Bring 2 opposite corners together over the filling to form a triangle. Press all around the filling to release any air pockets and seal the dumplings. Moisten the opposite tips, bring them together and press to seal. Repeat the procedure with the remaining wonton wrappers and mushroom filling.

4. Warm the chicken stock over moderate heat. Bring a large saucepan of water to a boil. Season with salt and add the dumplings. Cook the dumplings until they are just tender, about 1½ minutes. Drain them and transfer to shallow bowls. Pour the hot stock over the dumplings and serve. Pass the remaining grated Parmesan at the table.
—*Jean-Georges Vongerichten*

MAKE AHEAD The mushroom filling can be covered and kept refrigerated for up to 2 days. The dumplings can be frozen for up to 1 month (do not defrost—cook the dumplings frozen).

Potato, Leek and Radish Green Vichyssoise
ACTIVE: 30 MIN; TOTAL: 1 HR 45 MIN
6 SERVINGS ●

2 tablespoons unsalted butter
2 medium leeks, white and tender green parts, coarsely chopped
1¼ pounds Yukon Gold potatoes, peeled and cut into ½-inch dice
Salt and freshly ground pepper
1 quart chicken stock or low-sodium broth
1 quart water
8 cups packed radish greens (from 2 pounds radishes)
1 cup crème fraîche
3 tablespoons finely chopped chives

1. Melt the butter in a large saucepan. Add the leeks and potatoes, season with salt and pepper and cook over moderately low heat, stirring occasionally, until the leeks are softened, about 8 minutes. Add the chicken stock and water and bring to a boil over high heat. Reduce the heat to moderately low and simmer until the potatoes are tender, about 15 minutes.
2. Add the radish greens and crème fraîche to the soup. Simmer the greens over low heat until softened, about 2 minutes.

3. Working in batches, puree the soup in a blender on low speed until smooth and flecked with bits of green. Transfer to a large bowl, season with salt and pepper and refrigerate, stirring occasionally, until chilled, about 1 hour.
4. Ladle the chilled soup into bowls, top with the chives and serve at once.
—*Tony Maws*

MAKE AHEAD The soup can be refrigerated for up to 2 days.

Scallop and Mushroom Soup with Ginger and Leeks
TOTAL: 30 MIN
4 SERVINGS ● ●

¾ pound sea scallops
1 tablespoon unsalted butter
Salt and freshly ground pepper
¾ pound oyster mushrooms, cut into ¼-inch-thick slices
1 large leek, white and tender green parts only, finely julienned
2 tablespoons finely julienned peeled fresh ginger
1 quart chicken stock or low-sodium broth
1 tablespoon coarsely chopped cilantro

1. Preheat the oven to 400°. Thinly slice the scallops crosswise. Spread them in 4 ovenproof soup plates. Melt the butter in a medium saucepan. Brush the scallops with some of the butter and season with salt and pepper.
2. Add the mushrooms to the remaining butter in the saucepan. Season with salt and pepper and cook over moderately high heat until lightly browned, about 5 minutes. Add the leek and ginger and cook, stirring, until wilted, about 3 minutes. Add the stock and bring to a boil. Season with salt. Keep hot.
3. Bake the scallops in the oven for about 30 seconds, or until the bowls are hot. Pour the hot soup over the scallops, garnish with the cilantro and serve.
—*Jean-Georges Vongerichten*

soups

Bok Choy and Rice Noodle Soup with Turkey Meatballs

TOTAL: 50 MIN

4 SERVINGS ● ●

½ pound thin rice noodles
6 ounces low-fat firm tofu
½ pound ground turkey
3 tablespoons finely chopped water chestnuts
2 scallions, finely chopped
1 tablespoon very finely chopped fresh ginger
⅓ cup plus ½ cup coarsely chopped cilantro leaves
2 tablespoons low-sodium soy sauce
   Salt and freshly ground white pepper
2 tablespoons canola oil
2 medium shallots, cut into very thin slices
7 cups chicken stock or low-sodium broth
1 small red chile, very finely chopped
2 teaspoons fresh lime juice
1 teaspoon sugar
1 pound baby bok choy, sliced crosswise into ¼-inch strips
1 tomato, cut into ½-inch dice

1. In a large bowl, soak the rice noodles in hot water for 10 minutes, then drain. Cut the noodles into 4-inch lengths.

2. In a medium bowl, mash the tofu until it resembles cottage cheese. Mix in the turkey, water chestnuts, scallions, ginger, ⅓ cup of the cilantro, 1 tablespoon of the soy sauce, ½ teaspoon of salt and ¼ teaspoon of white pepper. Form into 1-inch balls and transfer to a plate. Cover with plastic and refrigerate.

3. Heat the oil in a small skillet. Add the shallots and cook over moderate heat, stirring constantly, until golden, 7 to 8 minutes. Drain on paper towels.

4. In a large saucepan, combine the stock with the chile, lime juice, sugar and the remaining 1 tablespoon of soy sauce. Season with salt and pepper and bring to a boil. Reduce the heat to moderately low, add the meatballs and cook for 3 minutes. Stir in the bok choy and tomato and cook for 1 minute. Add the rice noodles and cook over moderate heat until slightly softened, about 2 minutes. Ladle the soup into bowls, garnish with the fried shallots and the remaining ½ cup of cilantro and serve.

—*Jeannie Chen*

Hot-and-Sour Shrimp Soup

TOTAL: 50 MIN

4 SERVINGS

Growing up, chef Ming Tsai loved the flavors of traditional Chinese hot-and-sour soup, but he didn't like the heavy texture. This is his riff on that soup, with a much lighter and tangier broth.

2 tablespoons vegetable oil
¾ pound shiitake mushrooms, stemmed, caps cut into ¼-inch-thick slices
   Salt and freshly ground pepper
4 Thai chiles, minced
3 stalks of fresh lemongrass, inner bulbs only, thinly sliced
1 pound medium shrimp, shelled and deveined, shells reserved
1 large onion, chopped
½ cup thinly sliced fresh ginger
¼ cup Asian fish sauce
2 quarts chicken stock or canned low-sodium broth
¼ cup fresh lime juice
½ cup small basil leaves

1. In a large, deep skillet, heat 1 tablespoon of the oil. Add the shiitake and season with salt and pepper. Cover and cook over moderate heat, stirring a few times, until tender, 5 minutes. Uncover and cook, stirring, until the shiitake are golden, 3 minutes. Transfer to a plate.

2. Add the remaining 1 tablespoon of oil to the skillet. Add the chiles, lemongrass, shrimp shells, onion and ginger and cook over moderate heat, stirring occasionally, until the onion is softened and golden, about 7 minutes. Add the fish sauce and stock and bring to a boil. Simmer over moderate heat for 10 minutes. Strain the shrimp broth into a large bowl.

3. Return the broth to the skillet; bring to a simmer over moderate heat. Add the shrimp and shiitake and cook until the shrimp are pink and curled, 1 minute. Add the lime juice and season with salt and pepper. Ladle the soup into bowls, garnish with the basil leaves and serve.

—*Ming Tsai*

Shrimp Soup with Black Beans and Hominy

ACTIVE: 30 MIN; TOTAL: 2 HR 30 MIN

6 SERVINGS ●

1 meaty ham hock (1½ pounds)
2 large carrots, halved
4 large garlic cloves, halved
1 small onion, halved
1 celery rib, halved
1 bay leaf
3 quarts water
One 15-ounce can white hominy, drained and rinsed
One 15-ounce can black beans, drained and rinsed
1 red bell pepper, diced

BOK CHOY AND RICE NOODLE SOUP WITH TURKEY MEATBALLS

soups

1 ancho chile—stemmed, seeded and cut into very thin strips

Salt and freshly ground pepper

1 pound shrimp, shelled and deveined

3 tablespoons fresh lime juice

1 Hass avocado, half diced, half sliced, for garnish

⅓ cup cilantro sprigs, for garnish

1. In a large pot, bring the ham hock, carrots, garlic, onion, celery, bay leaf and water to a boil. Cover partially and simmer over low heat for 2 hours. Strain, return to the pot and boil until reduced to 10 cups, 10 minutes; skim.

2. Add the hominy, black beans, red bell pepper and ancho; season with salt and pepper. Simmer until the bell pepper is tender, about 6 minutes. Add the shrimp and cook until pink. Add the lime juice. Ladle into bowls, garnish with the avocado and cilantro and serve. —*Grace Parisi*

RECIPE TIP

global soups

EVERY COUNTRY in the world makes healthy and delicious soups. Here are four standouts.

BORSCHT/RUSSIA Of peasant origins, a soup of beets, green cabbage and potatoes often enriched with beef shank.

MINESTRONE/ITALY A chunky vegetable soup with shell beans and pasta laced with tomatoes, basil and garlic.

PHO/VIETNAM A rice-noodle soup with thick or thin noodles and a choice of the cut of meat and garnishes: bean sprouts, herbs and chiles.

RASAM/INDIA Sometimes called pepper water, a spicy broth made with small yellow lentils and tomatoes.

Tortilla-Crab Soup with Tomatillo Crème Fraîche

TOTAL: 1 HR

12 SERVINGS ● ●

½ pound tomatillos—husked, rinsed and quartered

1 cup cilantro leaves

¼ cup plus 2 tablespoons crème fraîche or sour cream

2 tablespoons fresh lime juice

Salt and freshly ground pepper

Vegetable oil, for frying

Eight 6-inch yellow or white corn tortillas, cut into ½-inch strips

4 tablespoons unsalted butter

6 ounces thick-cut bacon

1 medium sweet onion, cut into ½-inch pieces (about 2 cups)

3 large garlic cloves, thinly sliced

1 large jalapeño, seeded and chopped

4 large scallions, white parts finely chopped, light green parts thinly sliced and reserved separately

¼ cup all-purpose flour

½ teaspoon ground cumin

½ teaspoon ground coriander

8 cups fish stock or 4 cups bottled clam juice mixed with 4 cups water

1½ cups frozen baby peas, thawed

1 pound jumbo lump crabmeat, picked over

Lime wedges and green hot sauce, for serving

1. In a blender or food processor, puree the tomatillos with ½ cup of the cilantro, the crème fraîche and the lime juice. Season with salt and pepper.

2. In a medium skillet, heat ½ inch of vegetable oil until shimmering. Add the tortilla strips in several batches and fry over moderately high heat, stirring occasionally, until lightly golden, about 2 minutes per batch. Using a slotted spoon, transfer the tortilla strips to a plate lined with paper towels. Sprinkle with salt.

3. Melt the butter in a stockpot. When the foam subsides, add the bacon and cook over moderate heat until crisp, about 8 minutes. Using tongs, transfer the bacon to a plate lined with paper towels and reserve for another use.

4. Add the onion, garlic, jalapeño and scallion whites to the pot and cook over moderate heat until softened but not browned, 7 to 8 minutes. Whisk in the flour, cumin and coriander and cook for 1 minute, whisking constantly. Whisk in the fish stock and bring to a boil. Reduce the heat to moderately low and simmer the soup for 15 minutes, stirring occasionally. Add the peas, scallion greens and the remaining ½ cup of cilantro and bring the soup to a simmer over moderate heat.

5. To serve, mound the crabmeat in the center of 12 deep soup bowls and ladle the soup over the crab. Garnish with the tomatillo crème fraîche and tortilla strips. Pass the lime wedges and hot sauce alongside. —*Grace Parisi*

MAKE AHEAD The tomatillo crème fraîche can be refrigerated overnight. The tortilla strips can be stored in an airtight container overnight. The soup can be prepared through Step 4; refrigerate overnight, but add the peas, cilantro and scallion greens just before reheating.

Chicken Soup with Whole Wheat Dumplings

ACTIVE: 25 MIN; TOTAL: 45 MIN

6 SERVINGS ● ● ●

8 cups chicken stock

¾ pound skinless, boneless chicken breast halves

¼ cup all-purpose flour

¼ cup whole wheat flour

2 tablespoons freshly grated Parmesan cheese

2 tablespoons skim milk

1 large egg

Salt and freshly ground pepper

1 carrot, cut into ½-inch pieces

1 large parsnip, cut into ½-inch pieces

½ small butternut squash—peeled, seeded and cut into ½-inch pieces

1 large turnip, peeled and cut into ½-inch pieces

1 leek, white and tender green parts only, halved lengthwise and cut into 1-inch pieces

I. In a pot, bring the stock to a simmer. Add the chicken breasts and simmer over moderate heat until just cooked through, about 20 minutes. Transfer the chicken to a plate to cool, then shred.

2. Meanwhile, in a medium bowl, mix the flours with the Parmesan, milk and egg. Season with ¼ teaspoon of salt and ¼ teaspoon of pepper. Transfer to a pastry bag fitted with a ¼-inch round tip.

3. Add the carrot, parsnip, squash and turnip to the stock and season with salt and pepper. Cover partially and cook over moderate heat until the vegetables are just tender, about 10 minutes. Add the leek and cook until tender, about 3 minutes. Holding the pastry bag in one hand and a table knife in the other, cut 1-inch lengths of the dumpling dough into the simmering soup. When all of the dough has been added, stir gently and cook until tender, about 2 minutes. Add the chicken, cook until heated through and serve. —*Grace Parisi*

Yucatán Lime and Chicken Soup

ACTIVE: 1 HR; TOTAL: 2 HR 15 MIN

6 SERVINGS ●

4 medium tomatoes

1 large white onion, unpeeled, plus ½ cup minced onion for garnish

21 garlic cloves, peeled (2 heads)

3 whole bone-in chicken breasts (about 1¼ pounds each)

3 quarts chicken stock or broth

2 limes, zest finely grated and limes halved, plus wedges for serving

20 allspice berries

1 tablespoon dried oregano, plus more for sprinkling

Salt and freshly ground pepper

1 cup plus 2 tablespoons vegetable oil

6 large scallions, minced

Twelve 6-inch corn tortillas, cut into thin strips

2 banana chiles or jalapeños, seeded and minced, for serving

I. Preheat the oven to 500°. Arrange the tomatoes on a small rimmed baking sheet. Set the unpeeled onion in a pie plate with 6 of the garlic cloves. Roast the vegetables on the top rack of the oven until blackened on top and tender, about 10 minutes for the garlic, 20 for the tomatoes and 30 for the onion. Let cool slightly, then cut the onion in half. Press the tomatoes through a coarse strainer.

2. In a large saucepan, cover the chicken breasts with the stock. Add the lime zest and lime halves, allspice, oregano, the remaining 15 garlic cloves and a pinch each of salt and pepper and bring to a boil over moderately high heat. Add the roasted onion, reduce the heat to low and simmer until the chicken is cooked through, about 30 minutes.

3. Transfer the chicken to a platter and let cool. Gently simmer the broth for 10 minutes, then strain. Wipe out the saucepan. Remove the chicken from the bones and tear it into thick shreds.

4. Heat 2 tablespoons of the oil in the saucepan. Add the scallions and roasted garlic; mash the cloves to a paste with a fork. Cook over moderately high heat until the scallions are browned, 4 minutes. Add the strained tomatoes and simmer until the fat separates from the sauce, about 5 minutes. Add the strained broth and bring to a boil; reduce the heat to low and simmer for 10 minutes. Season with salt and pepper.

5. Meanwhile, in a large skillet, heat the remaining 1 cup of oil until shimmering. Add one-fourth of the tortilla strips and fry over moderately high heat, stirring

occasionally with a slotted spoon, until golden brown, about 2 minutes. Transfer to a paper towel–lined baking sheet and season with salt. Repeat with the remaining tortilla strips, lowering the heat if the oil gets too hot.

6. Add the chicken to the broth and cook until heated through. Ladle the soup into bowls, top with the tortilla strips and sprinkle with oregano. Serve, passing lime wedges, minced onion and banana chiles at the table.
—*Patricia Quintana*

MAKE AHEAD The chicken soup can be prepared through Step 5 up to 1 day ahead. Refrigerate the shredded chicken and broth separately. Keep the fried tortilla strips in an airtight container.

Chunky Bean Soup with Ham and Kale

ACTIVE: 20 MIN; TOTAL: 2 HR 30 MIN, PLUS SOAKING BEANS OVERNIGHT

6 SERVINGS

The Jacob's cattle beans called for here are striking in appearance: white with dark red speckles. Their meaty, creamy texture makes them great in soup. Pinto beans are a fine substitute.

½ pound Jacob's cattle beans (1¼ cups), soaked overnight and drained

1 meaty ham hock (1½ pounds)

5 large carrots, 4 sliced into ½-inch rounds

3 large garlic cloves, smashed

1 celery rib, halved

2 small onions, 1 coarsely chopped

Bouquet garni: 1 teaspoon dried thyme, 1 teaspoon black peppercorns, ½ teaspoon herbes de Provence and 1 bay leaf, tied in cheesecloth

2½ quarts water

6 cups chicken stock or broth

Salt and freshly ground pepper

6 kale leaves, stems and ribs discarded, leaves chopped

VEGETABLE TURKEY SOUP WITH CORNMEAL NOODLES

CORN CHOWDER WITH BACON AND SEA SCALLOPS

1. Put the beans in a large soup pot. Add the ham hock, whole carrot, garlic, celery, whole onion, bouquet garni and water and bring to a boil. Cover partially and cook over moderate heat until the beans are just barely tender, about 1½ hours.

2. Using a slotted spoon, discard the carrot, celery and onion. Add the sliced carrots, chopped onion and stock; season with salt and pepper. Cover partially and simmer until the beans are tender, about 45 minutes. Remove the hock and let cool slightly, then shred the meat and return to the soup. Add the kale and cook until tender, 10 minutes. Discard the bouquet garni, season with salt and pepper and serve. —*Grace Parisi*

Vegetable Turkey Soup with Cornmeal Noodles

ACTIVE: 1 HR; TOTAL: 5 HR

6 SERVINGS ●

- 2 large eggs, at room temperature
- ½ cup milk
- 1 tablespoon snipped chives
- 1 tablespoon minced parsley
- 1 cup all-purpose flour
- ¼ cup cornmeal

Pinch of cayenne

Pinch of dried sage

Kosher salt

- 2 tablespoons extra-virgin olive oil
- 2 medium leeks, white and tender green parts only, very thinly sliced
- 2 large carrots, thinly sliced
- 2 quarts Rich Turkey Stock (recipe, p. 125)
- ½ pound white button mushrooms, quartered
- 1 cup frozen baby peas, thawed

Freshly ground pepper

- 1¼ pounds roast turkey, preferably dark meat, shredded (4 cups)

1. In a medium bowl, whisk the eggs with the milk, chives and parsley. Add the flour, cornmeal, cayenne, sage and 1 teaspoon of salt; stir until evenly moistened.

2. Heat 1 tablespoon of the oil in a large stockpot. Add the leeks and carrots and cook over moderate heat, stirring occasionally, until crisp-tender, about 8 minutes. Add the stock and bring to a simmer. Cook over moderate heat until the carrots are tender, about 5 minutes.

3. Meanwhile, heat the remaining 1 table-spoon of oil in a medium skillet. Add the mushrooms and cook over high heat until browned, about 5 minutes. Add the mushrooms and the peas to the soup. Season with salt and pepper. Let the soup simmer over moderate heat.

4. Spread ½ cup of the noodle batter onto the center of an inverted cake pan. Using a large offset spatula, scrape ¼-inch strips into the soup, creating long, thin noodles. Repeat with the remaining batter. Gently stir the soup to separate the noodles and cook until tender, about 2 minutes. Add the turkey and cook just until hot, then serve.
—*Grace Parisi*

Corn Chowder with Bacon and Sea Scallops

ACTIVE: 25 MIN; TOTAL: 1 HR 5 MIN

4 SERVINGS

Look for sugar-cured bacon, which is smoky and sweet but mild enough not to overpower the other flavors here.

- 6 ounces thickly sliced bacon, coarsely chopped
- 1 large red onion, very finely chopped
- ¼ cup finely chopped celery
- 15 ounces frozen corn, thawed (3 cups)
- 3 cups whole milk
- 1 pound red potatoes, scrubbed and cut into ½-inch dice
- ½ cup heavy cream
- 2 tablespoons minced chives, plus more for garnish

Salt and freshly ground pepper

Tabasco

- ½ pound medium sea scallops

1. In a large saucepan, cook the bacon over moderately low heat until nice and crisp, about 10 minutes. Transfer the bacon to paper towels to drain. Pour off 2 tablespoons of the bacon fat and reserve. Add the onion and celery to the pan. Cook over low heat until soft-ened, about 12 minutes.

2. Meanwhile, in a food processor, puree 1 cup of the corn with 1 cup of the milk. Add the corn puree to the saucepan along with the remaining 2 cups each of corn and milk. Stir in the potatoes and simmer over low heat until they are tender, about 20 minutes. Stir in the cream, chives and bacon until thoroughly incorporated. Season the chowder with salt, pepper and Tabasco sauce and keep warm.

3. In a large skillet, heat the reserved 2 tablespoons of bacon fat until shim-mering. Add the scallops, season with salt and pepper and cook over moder-ately high heat, turning once, just until browned, about 1½ minutes per side. Ladle the soup into serving bowls; top with the scallops and chives and serve.
—*Grateful Palate*

MAKE AHEAD The recipe can be prepared through Step 2; refrigerate overnight (reserve the bacon fat separately).

Rustic Meatball Soup

ACTIVE: 40 MIN; TOTAL: 1 HR 15 MIN

6 SERVINGS ●

- 1 pound ground beef
- 6 large garlic cloves, minced
- 1 large onion, finely chopped (about 3 cups)
- 2 medium green bell peppers, finely chopped
- 2 teaspoons dried oregano
- ¾ teaspoon ground cumin

Kosher salt

- 1 large egg, lightly beaten
- ½ cup stone-ground yellow cornmeal
- 2 tablespoons peanut oil

- 1 pound plum tomatoes, seeded and cut into ¼-inch dice
- 1 large carrot, cut into ¼-inch dice
- 2 quarts plus 2 cups water
- 6 cilantro sprigs, plus 1 tablespoon finely chopped cilantro leaves for garnish
- ½ cup long-grain rice

Freshly ground pepper

Lime wedges, for serving

1. In a large bowl, gently mix the ground beef with half of the minced garlic, 1 cup of the chopped onion, 1 cup of the chopped bell peppers, the oregano, cumin, 1 teaspoon of salt and the egg. Add the cornmeal in 2 batches, mixing gently until combined. Shape the meat mixture into 1½-inch meatballs. Trans-fer to a plate and refrigerate.

2. In a medium stockpot, heat the oil until shimmering. Add the remaining minced garlic and cook over moderate heat until golden, about 30 seconds. Add the remaining chopped onion and cook, stirring frequently, until softened, about 4 minutes. Add the remaining chopped bell peppers and cook, stirring often, for 3 minutes longer. Add the tomatoes and cook until soft-ened, about 5 minutes. Add the carrot and cook, stirring, for 1 minute. Add the water, cilantro sprigs and 2 teaspoons of salt and bring the soup to a boil. Reduce the heat to moderately low and simmer the soup for 10 minutes.

3. Stir the rice into the soup and simmer for 10 minutes longer.

4. Add the meatballs to the soup and simmer over moderately high heat until they are cooked through and the rice is tender, about 15 minutes. Skim the fat from the surface of the soup and season with salt and pepper. Ladle the meat-ball soup into bowls and garnish with the chopped cilantro. Serve the soup with lime wedges. —*Maricel Presilla*

MAKE AHEAD The soup can be refriger-ated overnight.

soups

French Farmer Soup

ACTIVE: 45 MIN; TOTAL: 2 HR 45 MIN

4 SERVINGS ●

Traditional versions of this soup are very rich, containing goose or duck confit, a variety of sausages and cuts of pork. But this lighter, simpler example, made with smoked pork shoulder, is as deeply flavored and satisfying.

- 3 quarts water
- 1½ pounds trimmed smoked pork shoulder or smoky ham or 2 pounds very lean slab bacon, trimmed of all fat
- ½ pound dried cannellini, navy or white kidney beans, rinsed and picked over
- 4 cups coarsely chopped green cabbage
- 3 medium carrots, cut into ½-inch pieces
- 2 medium potatoes, peeled and cut into ½-inch pieces
- 1 large parsnip, cut into ½-inch pieces
- 1 large leek, white and tender green parts only, halved lengthwise and cut into ½-inch pieces
- 1 large celery rib, cut into ½-inch pieces

Salt and freshly ground pepper

Four ¼-inch-thick slices of country bread, lightly toasted

- 1 cup shredded Gruyère cheese (3 ounces)

I. In a large pot, combine the water, smoked pork shoulder and dried beans and bring to a boil. Skim the surface with a metal spoon, then cover the pot and reduce the heat to low. Simmer the soup for 1 hour. Add the green cabbage, carrots, potatoes, parsnip, leek, celery rib and a large pinch each of salt and pepper. Stir well, cover the pot and simmer until the pork shoulder, beans and vegetables are very tender, about 1 hour longer.

2. Using tongs, remove the pork shoulder from the soup and let cool slightly, then cut the meat into 1-inch pieces. Discard any fat. Return the pork shoulder to the soup and season with salt and pepper.

3. Preheat the broiler. Arrange the slices of toasted bread on a baking sheet and top each slice with ¼ cup of the Gruyère. Broil the toast 6 inches from the heat for about 2 minutes, or until the cheese is bubbling. Ladle the soup into bowls, top with the cheese toasts and serve at once. —*Jacques Pépin*

MAKE AHEAD The soup can be refrigerated for up to 5 days. Reheat gently and season the soup again if necessary.

Classic Beef Consommé

ACTIVE: 1 HR; TOTAL: 15 HR

MAKES 2 QUARTS ● ●

Perfect consommé is a crystal-clear soup that has all the flavor of the meat it is made from but none of the fat. The key to a consommé's success is the raft, or solid layer that forms on top of the stock as it simmers. When making the stock, be sure to use bones that have no fat on them; a little lean meat is fine. Serve the consommé on its own or garnished with a very fine julienne of blanched carrots and leeks.

STOCK

- 1 large unpeeled onion, halved, and 1 medium onion, peeled and studded with 3 whole cloves
- 4½ quarts cold water
- 4 pounds beef shin bones
- 1 teaspoon peppercorns
- 1 bay leaf

Kosher salt

RAFT

- 6 large egg whites
- 2 medium leek greens, thinly sliced crosswise
- 1 pound very lean ground beef
- 1 large carrot, thinly sliced
- 1 medium tomato, finely diced
- 1 cup cold water
- ½ cup coarsely chopped celery leaves
- ½ cup coarsely chopped parsley
- 2 bay leaves, crumbled
- 2 teaspoons chopped tarragon
- ½ teaspoon thyme leaves
- ½ teaspoon peppercorns

I. MAKE THE STOCK: In a medium cast-iron skillet, cook the onion halves, cut side down, over low heat until charred, about 15 minutes.

2. In a large stockpot, combine the water, beef bones, charred onion, clove-studded onion, peppercorns, bay leaf and 2 teaspoons of salt. Bring to a boil, reduce the heat to low and simmer for 5 hours, skimming occasionally. Strain into a heatproof bowl. Let cool to room temperature, then refrigerate overnight.

3. Using a spoon, scrape the fat from the surface of the cold stock and discard. Pour the stock into a stockpot and bring to a bare simmer over moderate heat. Remove from the heat.

4. MAKE THE RAFT: In a large bowl, mix all of the raft ingredients. Add to the stock and bring to a boil, stirring constantly. Stop stirring, reduce the heat to low and let the consommé simmer gently until a solid raft forms on top, about 10 minutes. Using a chopstick, gently poke 2 holes in the center of the raft to allow steam to escape. Simmer for 1 hour. Remove from the heat and let stand for 15 minutes.

5. Place a fine sieve lined with 4 layers of dampened cheesecloth over a large pot. Ladle the consommé into the sieve, leaving as much of the raft behind in the stockpot as possible. Season the consommé with salt and reheat very gently, without boiling, before serving. —*Jacques Pépin*

MAKE AHEAD The stock can be refrigerated for up to 3 days or frozen for up to 2 months. The consommé can be refrigerated for up to 2 days.

FRENCH FARMER SOUP

MACARONI AND CHEESE WITH BUTTERY CRUMBS, P. 82

pasta

PENNE WITH RED PEPPER SAUCE

SPAGHETTINI WITH TOMATOES AND EGGPLANT

Penne with Red Pepper Sauce

TOTAL: 30 MIN

4 SERVINGS ● ●

- ¾ pound penne rigate
- ¼ cup extra-virgin olive oil
- 1 large Spanish onion, thinly sliced lengthwise
- Salt and freshly ground black pepper
- 2 large red bell peppers—cored, seeded and sliced lengthwise
- 1 tablespoon drained capers
- ½ teaspoon crushed red pepper
- ¼ cup red wine vinegar
- 1 cup tomato sauce, preferably homemade
- 2 tablespoons shredded basil
- ¼ cup freshly grated pecorino cheese

1. In a large pot of boiling salted water, cook the penne until al dente. Drain, reserving ¾ cup of the cooking water.

2. Meanwhile, in a large, deep skillet, heat the olive oil until shimmering. Add the onion, season with salt and pepper and cook over moderately high heat until softened and just beginning to brown, about 5 minutes. Add the bell peppers, capers and crushed red pepper and cook, stirring occasionally, until the peppers are softened and lightly browned in spots, about 10 minutes. Stir in the vinegar and cook until nearly evaporated, about 2 minutes. Add the tomato sauce and cook for 5 minutes.

3. Add the penne and the reserved cooking water to the sauce, season with salt and pepper and simmer, stirring, until thickened, about 2 minutes. Stir in the basil. Transfer the pasta to bowls, sprinkle with the pecorino and serve.
—Scott Conant

WINE Medium-bodied, round Pinot Blanc.

Linguine with Fresh Tomatoes, Basil and Garlic

TOTAL: 20 MIN

4 SERVINGS ● ●

The easy sauce for this dish can be made while the pasta water comes to a boil. Or for more flavor, make the sauce ahead, letting the garlic and basil steep in the olive oil for an hour before adding the tomatoes and cheese.

- 2 tablespoons sliced garlic
- ½ teaspoon sea salt
- ½ cup extra-virgin olive oil
- ½ cup slivered basil leaves
- 2 tablespoons fresh lemon juice
- 1 pound tomatoes—peeled, seeded and thinly sliced lengthwise
- ¼ cup freshly grated Pecorino Toscano or mild Pecorino Romano cheese, plus more for serving
- 1 pound linguine

1. In a mortar, pound the garlic to a paste with the salt. Stir in the olive oil, then add the basil and lemon juice and pound gently until the basil is bruised. Scrape the sauce into a large pasta bowl and add the tomatoes and ¼ cup of Pecorino Toscano cheese.

2. In a large pot of boiling salted water, cook the linguine until al dente. Drain lightly. Transfer the pasta to the bowl and toss until coated with the sauce. Serve at once, passing more Pecorino at the table. —*Gianfranco Becchina*

WINE Light, spicy Pinot Grigio.

Spaghettini with Pesto Tomatoes and Grilled Eggplant

TOTAL: 1 HR

6 SERVINGS

    2 medium garlic cloves, smashed
    2 cups basil leaves, chopped
    ¾ cup plus 2 tablespoons
       extra-virgin olive oil
Salt and freshly ground pepper
    1 pint each red and yellow cherry
       tomatoes, halved or quartered
One 1¼-pound eggplant, cut into
       ½-inch-thick slices lengthwise
       or crosswise
    6 ounces ricotta salata, cut into
       ¼- to ⅓-inch-thick slices
    ¾ pound spaghettini

1. In a mortar, pound the garlic to a very coarse paste with a pestle. Add the chopped basil in 2 batches and pound to a coarse paste. Stir in ¾ cup of the olive oil. Season the pesto with salt and pepper, then transfer all but 3 tablespoons to a large bowl. Add the yellow and red cherry tomatoes to the bowl. Season with salt and pepper and let stand for 15 minutes.

2. Meanwhile, light a grill. Brush the eggplant with the remaining 2 tablespoons of olive oil and season lightly with salt. Grill the eggplant over a medium-hot fire, turning occasionally, until tender and browned, 8 to 10 min-

utes. Brush the eggplant with 2 tablespoons of the reserved pesto and grill for 30 seconds longer per side. Transfer to a plate and cover loosely with foil.

3. Brush the ricotta salata with the remaining tablespoon of reserved pesto and grill until the cheese is lightly charred, about 30 seconds per side. Add to the plate with the eggplant.

4. In a large pot of boiling salted water, cook the spaghettini until al dente. Reserve 2 tablespoons of the cooking water; drain the pasta and transfer to a bowl. Add the marinated tomatoes and the reserved cooking water and toss well. Season with salt and pepper. Arrange the eggplant on plates and top with the spaghettini. Garnish with the ricotta salata and serve. —*Grace Parisi*

WINE Complex, savory Chianti Classico.

Eggplant, Tomato and Fresh Ricotta Farfalle

TOTAL: 30 MIN

4 SERVINGS ● ●

    1 medium eggplant (1¼ pounds),
       peeled and cut into ¾-inch dice
Salt
    ¾ pound farfalle
    ¼ cup vegetable oil
    ¼ cup extra-virgin olive oil
    1 large garlic clove, thinly sliced
    1 pint red grape tomatoes, halved
    1 teaspoon finely chopped oregano
    ¼ to ½ teaspoon crushed red pepper
Freshly ground black pepper
    2 tablespoons freshly grated
       Parmesan cheese, plus more
       for serving
    ¼ cup fresh ricotta cheese
    2 tablespoons shredded basil

1. In a colander, toss the eggplant with 1 teaspoon of salt and let stand for 10 minutes. Pat dry with paper towels.

2. Meanwhile, in a large pot of boiling salted water, cook the farfalle until just al dente. Drain, reserving ½ cup of the cooking water.

3. In a large, deep skillet, heat the vegetable oil until shimmering. Add the eggplant and cook over high heat, stirring occasionally, until tender and golden, about 5 minutes; transfer to a paper towel–lined plate. Wipe out the skillet.

4. Heat the olive oil in the skillet over moderately high heat. Add the garlic and cook for 1 minute. Add the tomatoes, oregano, crushed red pepper and a pinch of black pepper. Cook, crushing the tomatoes, about 3 minutes. Add the farfalle, the reserved cooking water and the eggplant and cook over moderate heat, stirring, until the pasta is heated through, 3 minutes; season with salt. Transfer to bowls and sprinkle with the Parmesan. Top with the ricotta and basil and pass extra Parmesan at the table. —*Scott Conant*

WINE Simple, fruity Chianti.

Vegetarian Red Curry Noodles

ACTIVE: 30 MIN; TOTAL: 45 MIN

4 SERVINGS

This dish is a showcase for the flavors of Southeast Asia: It's spicy, tart, creamy and slightly sweet. Use the extra sauce as a marinade for chicken or pork.

    ¼ cup vegetable oil
    4 large garlic cloves, minced
    3 large shallots, thinly sliced
    3 Thai chiles, minced
    3 stalks of fresh lemongrass, inner
       bulbs only, thinly sliced
    ¼ cup minced fresh ginger
    2 tablespoons light brown sugar
    2 tablespoons ground coriander
    1½ cups unsweetened coconut milk
    ¼ cup fresh lime juice
    ¼ cup Asian fish sauce
Salt and freshly ground pepper
    1 cup snow peas
    1 pound thin dried Chinese
       egg noodles or spaghettini
    1 small red bell pepper, thinly sliced
    1 cup chopped napa cabbage
    ½ cup shredded carrot

● FAST   ● HEALTHY   ● MAKE AHEAD   ● STAFF FAVORITE

pasta

I. In a large, deep skillet, heat the oil. Add the garlic, shallots, chiles, lemongrass and ginger and cook over moderate heat, stirring, until the aromatics are softened and golden, about 5 minutes. Add the brown sugar and coriander and cook until the sugar is melted, about 20 seconds. Add the coconut milk and simmer, stirring, for 2 minutes. Transfer to a food processor and blend until pureed. Blend in the lime juice and fish sauce. Scrape the sauce into a glass measuring cup and season with salt and pepper. Leave the skillet on the stove.
2. Bring a large pot of salted water to a boil. Add the snow peas and blanch until bright green, about 40 seconds. Using a slotted spoon, transfer them to a plate to cool. Add the noodles to the pot and cook, stirring, until al dente. Drain, reserving ¼ cup of the cooking water.
3. Add 1 cup of the curry sauce to the skillet and bring to a simmer over moderate heat. Add the noodles, snow peas, red pepper, cabbage and carrot and toss well to coat the noodles. Add some of the reserved cooking water if the noodles seem dry. Season with salt and pepper and serve the pasta right away. —*Ming Tsai*

MAKE AHEAD The sauce can be refrigerated for up to 2 weeks.

WINE Bright, citrusy Riesling.

Fregola with Grilled Red Onions and Pine Nuts

ACTIVE: 45 MIN; TOTAL: 1 HR 30 MIN
10 SERVINGS ● ●
Also known as Italian couscous, fregola is made from semolina flour; grains of the medium variety are about the size of small capers. You can find it at specialty food shops and Italian markets.

- 7½ tablespoons extra-virgin olive oil
- 3 tablespoons sherry vinegar
- Kosher salt and freshly ground pepper
- 2 large red onions, cut into ½-inch-thick slices
- 1¼ pounds medium fregola (about 3 cups)
- 1 cup pine nuts (5 ounces)
- 4 medium carrots, cut into ¼-inch dice
- 3 medium celery ribs, cut into ¼-inch dice
- ⅓ cup very finely chopped cilantro leaves
- ⅓ cup very finely chopped flat-leaf parsley leaves

I. On a shallow platter or large plate, combine 2 tablespoons of the olive oil with 2 tablespoons of the vinegar and season generously with salt and pepper. Add the onion slices and turn to coat, keeping them intact; let stand at room temperature for 30 minutes.
2. Light a grill or preheat the broiler. Grill the onions over a medium-hot fire or broil for about 8 minutes, until softened and charred in spots. Return to the platter and let cool. Coarsely chop the onions and transfer them to a large bowl.
3. In a pot of boiling salted water, cook the fregola until al dente. Drain well, shaking off any excess water. Return the fregola to the pot, add ¼ cup of the oil and toss to coat. Spread the fregola out on a rimmed baking sheet to cool.
4. In a skillet, heat ½ tablespoon of the oil. Add the pine nuts and cook over moderate heat, stirring constantly, until golden, about 4 minutes. Drain on paper towels and let cool. Add the remaining 1 tablespoon of oil to the skillet with the carrots and celery and cook over moderate heat until softened, 4 minutes. Transfer to a plate and let cool.
5. Add the fregola to the bowl with the grilled onions. Add the carrots and celery, pine nuts, cilantro, parsley and the remaining 1 tablespoon of vinegar. Season with salt and pepper and serve. —*Suzanne Goin*

MAKE AHEAD The salad can be refrigerated overnight.

WINE Ripe, creamy-textured Chardonnay.

Fettuccine with Wilted Escarole and Mushrooms

TOTAL: 25 MIN
4 SERVINGS ● ●
- ¾ pound fettuccine
- ¼ cup extra-virgin olive oil
- 4 garlic cloves, cut into very thin slices
- ½ teaspoon crushed red pepper
- 1½ cups thinly sliced white mushrooms (5 ounces)
- Salt and freshly ground black pepper
- 1 small head escarole (about ½ pound), cored and cut into 1-inch ribbons (see Note)
- 6 tablespoons freshly grated Parmesan cheese, plus more for serving

I. In a large pot of boiling salted water, cook the fettuccine until just al dente. Drain the fettuccine, reserving 1 cup of the cooking water.
2. In a large, deep skillet, heat the olive oil until shimmering. Add the garlic and crushed red pepper and cook over moderately high heat until fragrant but not browned, about 30 seconds. Add the mushrooms, season with salt and pepper and cook until softened and just beginning to brown, about 5 minutes.
3. Add the escarole to the skillet and cook, stirring, until wilted. Add the fettuccine and the reserved cooking water and cook, tossing gently, until the sauce is slightly thickened, about 2 minutes. Season the fettuccine with salt and pepper. Add the 6 tablespoons of Parmesan cheese and toss to coat well. Transfer the pasta to plates or bowls and pass extra Parmesan at the table. —*Scott Conant*

NOTE Escarole, a variety of endive and a member of the same botanical family as chicory, has broad, curved leaves and a milder flavor than either Belgian endive or curly endive. It's available year-round.

WINE Round-textured Sémillon.

Pasta with Parmesan and Fried Eggs

ACTIVE: 20 MIN; TOTAL: 30 MIN

4 SERVINGS ● ○

Soft-cooked egg yolks and Parmesan enrich the luscious sauce for this quick carbonara-inspired dish. Also try adding roasted peppers and onions to the pasta before topping it with the eggs.

- ¾ pound spaghetti or linguine
- 4 large eggs
- 2 teaspoons extra-virgin olive oil
- 1 garlic clove, thinly sliced
- 1 large rosemary sprig, halved

Salt and freshly ground pepper

- ½ cup plus 2 tablespoons freshly grated Parmesan cheese
- ¼ cup coarsely chopped parsley

1. In a large pot of boiling, generously salted water, cook the pasta until almost al dente. Drain the pasta, reserving ½ cup of the pasta cooking water.

2. Meanwhile, crack the eggs into 4 ramekins without breaking the yolks. Heat the oil in a large nonstick skillet. Add the garlic and rosemary. Cook over moderate heat for 1 to 2 minutes, or until the oil is fragrant. Discard the garlic and rosemary. Carefully add the eggs to the skillet and season with salt and pepper. Reduce the heat to low, cover and cook until the egg whites are set and the yolks are still runny, about 3 minutes. Separate the cooked eggs with a spatula.

3. Return the pasta to the pot. Add ⅓ cup of the reserved pasta cooking water and 6 tablespoons of the Parmesan and toss until the pasta is coated with a creamy sauce; add some of the remaining pasta water if the pasta appears dry. Season generously with salt and pepper.

4. Transfer the pasta to plates and sprinkle with some of the remaining Parmesan. Top the pasta with the eggs and sprinkle with the remaining cheese and the parsley. Serve at once.
—*Sally Schneider*

WINE Light, zesty, fruity Dolcetto.

FETTUCCINE WITH WILTED ESCAROLE AND MUSHROOMS

PASTA WITH PARMESAN AND FRIED EGG

pasta

Spaghetti with Garlicky Marsala Mushrooms

TOTAL: 30 MIN

4 SERVINGS ●

 5 tablespoons extra-virgin olive oil
 1 pound white mushrooms, caps quartered
 1 pound shiitake mushrooms, stems discarded, caps quartered
 Salt and freshly ground pepper
 4 large garlic cloves, 2 thinly sliced, 2 minced
 1 medium shallot, thinly sliced
 1½ teaspoons minced rosemary
 ½ cup dry Marsala wine
 3 tablespoons balsamic vinegar
 6 Calamata olives, pitted and coarsely chopped
 ¾ pound spaghetti
 2 tablespoons unsalted butter
 ⅓ cup freshly grated Parmesan cheese, plus more for serving
 2 tablespoons minced chives

1. In a very large skillet, heat 2 tablespoons of the olive oil. Add the white and shiitake mushrooms, season with salt and pepper, cover and cook over moderately high heat for 5 minutes, stirring once. Uncover and cook over high heat, stirring once, until the mushrooms are browned all over, about 3 minutes. Add the sliced garlic, the shallot and rosemary and cook, stirring, until fragrant, about 2 minutes. Add the Marsala and cook until evaporated, about 30 seconds. Add the vinegar and cook, stirring, for 30 seconds. Stir in the minced garlic, olives and the remaining 3 tablespoons of oil and season with salt and pepper. Cover and keep warm.

2. In a pot of boiling salted water, cook the spaghetti until al dente; drain. Return the spaghetti to the pot. Stir in the butter and mushrooms and season with salt and pepper. Stir in ⅓ cup of the Parmesan. Transfer the pasta to bowls, sprinkle with the chives and serve, passing more Parmesan at the table. —*Marcia Kiesel*

VARIATIONS The mushrooms can be folded into an omelet or served with chicken breasts or cheese grits.
WINE Soft, earthy Rioja.

Egg Noodle Gratin with Gruyère

ACTIVE: 25 MIN; TOTAL: 1 HR 10 MIN

4 TO 6 SERVINGS ●

 1 pound wide egg noodles
 7 tablespoons unsalted butter
 1 cup plain dry bread crumbs
 ¼ cup all-purpose flour
 6 cups whole milk
 1 bay leaf
 1 small onion, coarsely chopped
 Salt and freshly ground pepper
 ¾ pound Gruyère cheese, coarsely shredded (about 3 cups)

1. Preheat the oven to 350°. Butter a 9-by-13-inch glass or ceramic baking dish. In a large pot of boiling salted water, cook the noodles until al dente; drain and rinse well under cool water to stop the cooking. Drain again. Spread the noodles in the baking dish.

2. Meanwhile, in a medium skillet, melt 3 tablespoons of the butter. Stir in the crumbs just until evenly moistened. Remove from the heat.

3. In a large saucepan, melt the remaining 4 tablespoons of butter over moderate heat. Whisk in the flour and cook, whisking constantly, for 2 minutes. Remove from the heat. Whisk in the milk. Return the pan to moderate heat and bring the white sauce to a simmer, whisking constantly. Add the bay leaf and onion and cook over low heat, stirring, until thickened, about 10 minutes. Season with salt and pepper.

4. Strain the sauce over the noodles. Stir in the Gruyère until combined. Sprinkle the bread crumbs over the noodles. Bake for 35 minutes, or until bubbling and golden, then serve. —*Maria Helm Sinskey*
MAKE AHEAD The baked gratin can be refrigerated for up to 2 days.
WINE Medium-bodied, round Pinot Blanc.

Rigatoni with Roasted Butternut Squash and Pancetta

TOTAL: 35 MIN

4 SERVINGS ●

 One 1¾-pound butternut squash, peeled and cut into ½-inch dice (2 cups)
 ¼ cup extra-virgin olive oil
 Salt
 ¾ pound rigatoni
 3 ounces thickly sliced pancetta, cut into ¼-inch dice
 2 shallots, thinly sliced
 12 sage leaves, torn
 ¼ teaspoon crushed red pepper
 Freshly ground black pepper
 ½ cup freshly grated pecorino cheese, plus more for serving

1. Preheat the oven to 425°. On a medium rimmed baking sheet, toss the squash with 1 tablespoon of the olive oil. Roast for 15 minutes, tossing once, until browned and tender; season with salt.

2. Meanwhile, in a large pot of boiling salted water, cook the rigatoni until just al dente. Drain, reserving 1 cup of the cooking water.

3. Heat the remaining 3 tablespoons of olive oil in a large skillet. Add the pancetta and cook over moderate heat until lightly browned, about 5 minutes. Add the shallots, sage, crushed red pepper and a generous pinch of black pepper and cook until the shallots are soft, about 4 minutes. Add the squash, rigatoni and the reserved cooking water and cook over moderate heat, tossing gently, until the sauce is thickened and the pasta is al dente, 2 to 3 minutes; season with salt. Stir in the ½ cup of pecorino. Serve the pasta in deep bowls, passing extra pecorino at the table.
—*Scott Conant*

MAKE AHEAD The roasted butternut squash can be refrigerated for up to 2 days. Bring to room temperature before proceeding with the recipe.
WINE Tangy, crisp Vernaccia.

RIGATONI WITH ROASTED BUTTERNUT SQUASH AND PANCETTA

pasta

Baked Pasta with Four Cheeses

TOTAL: 35 MIN

4 SERVINGS ●

- ½ pound small pasta, such as ditalini
- 2 tablespoons unsalted butter
- 1 large garlic clove, minced
- 1 teaspoon finely chopped oregano
- 6 ounces Fontina cheese, coarsely shredded (1½ cups)
- 4 ounces mozzarella cheese, coarsely shredded (1 cup)
- 3 ounces freshly grated Pecorino Romano cheese (¾ cup)
- 2 ounces freshly grated Parmesan cheese (½ cup)
- 2 tablespoons minced parsley

Salt and freshly ground pepper

1. Preheat the oven to 350°. Position a rack in the upper third. Lightly butter a shallow 2-quart baking dish.

2. In a large pot of boiling salted water, cook the pasta until al dente. Drain, reserving ¼ cup of the cooking water.

3. In a skillet, melt the butter over moderate heat. Add the garlic and cook for 1 minute. Add the oregano and cook for 30 seconds. Remove from the heat.

4. Return the pasta to the pot and add the Fontina, mozzarella, Pecorino and half of the Parmesan. Stir in the garlic butter, parsley and the reserved pasta water and season with salt and pepper.

5. Spread the pasta in the baking dish and sprinkle the remaining Parmesan on top. Bake for about 10 minutes, or until the cheese is melted. Turn on the broiler and broil the pasta for 1 minute, or until the top is golden brown. Serve.

—*Laura Chenel*

WINE Rich, smoky-plummy Shiraz.

Three-Cheese Baked Pasta with Porcini and Radicchio

ACTIVE: 50 MIN; TOTAL: 1 HR 15 MIN

8 SERVINGS ● ●

- 1 ounce dried porcini (1 cup)

Boiling water

- 5 tablespoons unsalted butter
- 2 tablespoons extra-virgin olive oil
- 2 ounces sliced pancetta, cut into ½-inch pieces
- 4 large garlic cloves, minced
- 2 heads radicchio (1¼ pounds total), each cut into 8 wedges through the core

Salt and freshly ground pepper

- 2 teaspoons chopped fresh sage
- 1 pound lumache pasta or medium shells
- ¼ cup all-purpose flour
- 2 cups milk
- 1½ cups heavy cream

Pinch of freshly grated nutmeg

- ¼ pound Asiago cheese, grated (about 1⅓ cups)
- 6 ounces Fontina cheese, grated (about 1½ cups)
- ¼ cup freshly grated Parmesan cheese

1. Preheat the oven to 350°. Butter a 3-quart baking dish. In a heatproof bowl, soak the porcini in boiling water until softened, 15 minutes. Rinse the porcini well, then drain and chop them. Discard the soaking liquid.

2. In a large, deep skillet, melt 2 tablespoons of the butter in the olive oil. Add the porcini, pancetta and one-third of the garlic and cook over moderately high heat, stirring, until the garlic is golden and fragrant, about 3 minutes. Using a slotted spoon, transfer to a plate.

3. Add the radicchio wedges to the skillet in a slightly overlapping layer and cook over moderately high heat until wilted and beginning to brown, about 4 minutes. Add the remaining garlic, season with salt and pepper and cook, stirring, until the radicchio is slightly caramelized, 5 minutes longer. Stir in the porcini mixture and the sage. Transfer the mixture to a large bowl.

4. Cook the pasta in a large pot of boiling salted water until al dente. Drain very well. Meanwhile, in a medium saucepan, melt the remaining 3 tablespoons of butter. Add the flour and cook over moderately high heat, stirring, until foamy, about 2 minutes. Gradually whisk in the milk and bring to a boil; cook, whisking, until thickened, about 4 minutes. Add the cream and nutmeg and season with salt and pepper. Transfer the sauce to the bowl with the radicchio.

5. Add the pasta to the bowl along with the Asiago and Fontina; toss well. Transfer the pasta to the prepared baking dish. Sprinkle with the Parmesan cheese. Bake for 20 minutes, or until heated through.

6. Preheat the broiler. Broil the pasta for 2 minutes, until the top is golden and bubbling. Let stand for 10 minutes; serve.

—*Grace Parisi*

WINE Light, zesty, fruity Dolcetto.

Macaroni and Cheese with Buttery Crumbs

ACTIVE: 45 MIN; TOTAL: 1 HR 30 MIN

6 SERVINGS ● ●

Small chunks of Cheddar and Colby cheeses throughout give this classic American dish a perfect hit of flavor and a fabulous gooey texture.

5 tablespoons unsalted butter

3 tablespoons all-purpose flour

2½ cups half-and-half or whole milk

1 pound sharp Cheddar cheese, cut into ½-inch pieces

½ pound Colby cheese, cut into ½-inch pieces

1 tablespoon Dijon mustard

Pinch of freshly grated nutmeg

Pinch of cayenne pepper

Salt and freshly ground pepper

1 pound elbow macaroni

¾ cup plain dry bread crumbs

1. Preheat the oven to 350°. Generously butter a shallow 2-quart baking dish. Melt 3 tablespoons of the butter in a large saucepan. Add the flour and cook over moderate heat for 2 minutes, stirring constantly. Add the half-and-half and cook over moderate heat, whisking constantly, until thickened, about 3 minutes. Add one-half of the Cheddar and Colby cheeses and cook over low heat, stirring, until melted. Stir in the mustard, nutmeg and cayenne; season with salt and pepper.

2. Meanwhile, in a large pot of boiling salted water, cook the elbow macaroni until al dente. Drain very well. Return the macaroni to the pot. Add the cheese sauce and the remaining cheese and stir until combined. Spread the macaroni in the prepared baking dish.

3. Place the remaining 2 tablespoons of butter in a small glass bowl and melt in a microwave oven. Add the bread crumbs, season generously with salt and pepper and stir until evenly moistened. Sprinkle the buttered crumbs over the macaroni and bake for 45 minutes, or until bubbling and golden on top. Let stand for 15 minutes before serving. —*Grace Parisi*

MAKE AHEAD The assembled dish can be refrigerated overnight. Bring the macaroni to room temperature and then bake it as directed.

WINE Round, supple, fruity Syrah.

Spaetzle with Gruyère and Caramelized Onions

ACTIVE: 25 MIN; TOTAL: 1 HR 25 MIN

6 SERVINGS ●

1¾ cups milk

4 large egg yolks

1 large egg

3 cups all-purpose flour

¼ teaspoon freshly grated nutmeg

Salt and freshly ground pepper

2 tablespoons peanut oil

1 tablespoon unsalted butter, cut into small pieces

1½ cups shredded Gruyère cheese (5 ounces)

1 medium white onion, thinly sliced

1. In a small bowl, whisk the milk with the egg yolks and egg. In a large bowl, whisk the flour with the nutmeg, 1 teaspoon of salt and ¼ teaspoon of pepper. Using a wooden spoon, stir the egg mixture into the flour, leaving a few lumps. Cover and refrigerate the batter for at least 1 hour or overnight.

2. Bring a pot of salted water to a boil. Prepare a large bowl of ice water. Carefully hold a colander with large holes over the boiling water. Add about ½ cup of the batter to the colander and press it into the simmering water with a spatula or the back of a spoon. Repeat until all of the batter has been used. Cook the spaetzle for 2 minutes longer, then drain. Immediately transfer the spaetzle to the ice water, swirling the dumplings until the ice melts. Drain and transfer to a bowl. Stir in 1 tablespoon of the oil, season with salt and pepper and toss to coat.

3. Preheat the oven to 400°. Oil a 9-by-13-inch baking dish. Spread the spaetzle in the dish and dot with the butter. Sprinkle with the cheese and bake for about 20 minutes, or until the spaetzle is hot and the cheese is just melted.

4. Meanwhile, in a medium skillet, heat the remaining 1 tablespoon of oil. Add the onion and cook over high heat until softened, about 1 minute. Reduce the heat to moderately low and cook, stirring occasionally, until lightly browned, about 15 minutes. Scatter the onion over the spaetzle and serve. —*Wolfgang Puck*

MAKE AHEAD The spaetzle can be prepared through Step 2 and refrigerated for up to 1 day.

WINE Ripe, creamy-textured Chardonnay.

Creamy Goat Cheese and Asparagus Orecchiette

TOTAL: 25 MIN

4 SERVINGS ● ●

¾ pound orecchiette

¼ cup extra-virgin olive oil

½ medium red onion, finely diced

¾ pound medium asparagus spears, cut into ½-inch lengths

½ teaspoon crushed red pepper

2 tablespoons fresh lemon juice

1 teaspoon finely grated lemon zest

Salt and freshly ground black pepper

2 tablespoons fresh goat cheese

1 tablespoon snipped chives

Freshly grated Parmesan cheese, for serving

1. In a large pot of boiling salted water, cook the orecchiette until just al dente. Drain the orecchiette, reserving ⅔ cup of the cooking water.

2. Meanwhile, in a large, deep skillet, heat the olive oil until shimmering. Add the onion and cook over moderately low heat until softened, about 5 minutes. Add the asparagus and crushed red pepper and cook over moderate heat until crisp-tender, about 5 minutes.

3. Add the orecchiette and the reserved cooking water to the skillet along with the lemon juice and zest; season with salt and pepper. Cook, stirring, until the orecchiette is al dente and the asparagus is just tender, about 2 minutes. Add the goat cheese and chives and stir until melted. Transfer the pasta to bowls and serve with Parmesan cheese. —*Scott Conant*

WINE Round, rich Sauvignon Blanc.

pasta

Linguine with Mussels and Kale

TOTAL: 25 MIN

4 SERVINGS ● ●

- ¾ pound linguine
- ¼ cup plus 2 tablespoons extra-virgin olive oil
- 1 medium onion, quartered lengthwise and thinly sliced crosswise
- 2 garlic cloves, thinly sliced
- ½ teaspoon crushed red pepper
- 2 pounds mussels, scrubbed and debearded
- 6 large kale leaves, stems and inner ribs discarded, leaves coarsely chopped

Salt

1. In a large pot of boiling salted water, cook the linguine until just barely al dente. Drain, reserving ½ cup of the pasta cooking water.

2. Meanwhile, in a large, deep skillet, heat ¼ cup of the olive oil until shimmering. Add the onion, garlic and crushed red pepper and cook over high heat until softened, about 2 minutes. Add the mussels and cook, tossing, until half of them open, 2 to 3 minutes. Add the kale leaves and cook, tossing, until wilted, 3 to 4 minutes. Add the linguine and the reserved cooking water and cook, tossing, until the linguine is al dente, the mussels are open and the sauce is thickened, about 2 minutes longer. Discard any unopened mussels. Season the linguine generously with salt. Transfer the linguine to shallow bowls, drizzle each with ½ tablespoon olive oil and serve at once. —*Scott Conant*

WINE High-acid, savory Vermentino.

Farfalle with Lobster, Favas and Peas

ACTIVE: 1 HR 10 MIN; TOTAL: 2 HR 20 MIN

8 SERVINGS ●

Salt

Three 1¼-pound lobsters

- ¼ cup plus 2 tablespoons extra-virgin olive oil
- 2 fennel stalks, thinly sliced
- 1 medium leek, white and light green parts only, thinly sliced
- 1 garlic clove, thinly sliced
- 1 large shallot, thinly sliced
- 1 teaspoon tomato paste
- 1 cup dry white wine
- 1 quart water
- 6 parsley sprigs
- 3 mint sprigs, plus ¼ cup small mint leaves
- 2 cups shelled and peeled fava beans (2 pounds in the shell)
- 1 pound farfalle
- 1 cup shelled peas (4 ounces)
- 3 tablespoons unsalted butter
- 1 cup nasturtium flowers

1. Bring a large pot of water to a boil. Add salt, then add the lobsters head-first and cook them until red all over, about 5 minutes. Transfer the lobsters to a large bowl and let cool to room temperature. Twist off the tails and claws. Using scissors, cut down the backs of the tails and remove the tail meat, then remove the intestinal veins. Crack the claws and knuckles and remove the meat. Slice the lobster tails crosswise ¼ inch thick and coarsely chop the claw and knuckle meat; cover and refrigerate. Tear the heads into large pieces and reserve with the other shells.

2. Heat ¼ cup of the olive oil in a large saucepan. Add all of the reserved lobster shells and cook over moderately high heat, stirring occasionally, until they start to brown, about 8 minutes. Add the fennel stalks, leek, garlic, shallot and ½ teaspoon of salt. Cook, stirring, for 2 minutes. Add the tomato paste and cook, stirring, for 2 minutes. Add the wine and stir to scrape up the browned bits on the bottom.

3. Add the water and parsley and mint sprigs to the saucepan and bring to a boil. Skim the foam off the surface and simmer over moderately low heat for 40 minutes. Strain the stock, leaving the red layer of oil on top. Wipe out the saucepan and return the stock to the pan. Boil over high heat until reduced to 1 cup, about 12 minutes.

4. Bring a large pot of salted water to a boil. Put the fava beans into a small colander or strainer that fits into the pot. Lower the favas into the boiling water and cook until just tender, about 3 minutes; remove. Add the farfalle to the pot and cook until al dente; drain.

5. In the same pot, heat the remaining 2 tablespoons of olive oil. Add the peas and favas and warm for 2 minutes. Add the lobster meat and reduced stock and bring to a simmer. Stir in the farfalle, then the butter to thicken the sauce. Season with salt and spoon into bowls. Top with the mint leaves and nasturtiums and serve. —*Michael Tusk*

MAKE AHEAD The lobster meat, reduced lobster stock and cooked fava beans can be refrigerated separately overnight.

WINE Dry, full-flavored Alsace Riesling.

HEALTH TIP

nutritious tomatoes

WHICH IS MORE NUTRITIOUS, a summer tomato just off the vine or ketchup? The answer, which might surprise you, is ketchup. That's because foods made with cooked tomatoes (tomato paste, tomato soup, canned tomatoes, tomato sauce) and sun-dried tomatoes are more concentrated sources of lycopene, a cancer-fighting antioxidant. Although tomatoes are fairly modest in vitamins and minerals, because we eat so many of them (both raw and cooked) they rank high as an overall source of vitamins A and C in the American diet.

Q+A
tomato sauce

roasted

Q: I know everything Marcella Hazan does is perfect. So I'm sure I did something wrong when I made her roasted tomato sauce and it was watery. What was my mistake?

A: Making sauce with oven-roasted tomatoes is a brilliant idea—you don't have to fuss with peeling and seeding the tomatoes or contend with spatters as they simmer on the stove. Plus, roasting concentrates the tomato flavor while keeping it fresh and vibrant. Maybe the holes in the disk of your food mill were too small or the disk was attached too loosely to the machine, so the pulp that would have thickened the sauce didn't get pushed through. Or maybe your tomatoes were too juicy, with too little pulp to counter-balance all the liquid. Plum tomatoes would certainly yield a thicker sauce, but they're probably not the ones Marcella intended. Give the recipe another whirl using ripe local tomatoes, and be sure to drain them very well before transferring them to the food mill.

P.S. Pour the olive oil and tomato roasting juices that get left behind in the baking dish (when you add the tomatoes to the food mill) over grilled tuna and arugula: delicious.

Pasta with Spicy Oven-Roasted Tomato Sauce

ACTIVE: 15 MIN; TOTAL: 2 HR

4 TO 6 SERVINGS ● ●

This recipe is adapted from *Marcella's Italian Kitchen* by Marcella Hazan (1986).

2 ¼ **pounds ripe tomatoes**
 3 **tablespoons chopped parsley**
 2 **tablespoons chopped garlic**
Salt and freshly ground pepper
 ½ **cup extra-virgin olive oil**
 1 **pound fusilli or spaghetti**
Crushed red pepper

1. Preheat the oven to 400°. Halve the tomatoes crosswise and arrange them, cut side up, in a glass or ceramic baking dish. Sprinkle the parsley and garlic over the tomatoes and season with salt and pepper. Pour ¼ cup of the olive oil over the tomatoes and bake for about 1 hour and 15 minutes, or until they are very tender, shrunken slightly and browned at the edges; let cool slightly.

2. Lift the tomatoes with a fork, letting them drain well, and transfer them to a food mill fitted with a medium disk. Puree the tomatoes into a bowl.

3. Bring a large pot of salted water to a boil. Add the fusilli and cook, stirring, until al dente; drain. Add the pasta to the tomato sauce and toss. Add the remaining ¼ cup of olive oil and some crushed red pepper, season with salt and pepper, toss again and serve.

uncooked

Q: Thanks! I could live on pasta and tomatoes. But my uncooked sauces always end up tasting like chunky salad dressing. Any suggestions?

A: There's nothing like a raw tomato sauce in the summer—on pasta, fish, arugula, beans, chicken breasts, fresh mozzarella or grilled meats. The recipe here is based on one from Michael Romano at Union Square Cafe in Manhattan that we featured in F&W years ago.

Cut 1 pound of tomatoes (use heirlooms if you can), into ½- to ¾-inch pieces. In a bowl, toss them with ½ teaspoon of coarse salt and let stand for 10 minutes. Add 12 torn basil leaves, 2 lightly crushed garlic cloves (remember to pick them out before serving) and ⅓ cup of extra-virgin olive oil. Set aside for at least 1 hour and up to 8.

It's as simple as that. Depending on what you're having the sauce on, you could add lemon or orange zest, fresh mint, oregano, parsley, onion, jalapeños, capers, anchovies, sun-dried tomatoes, olives, salami or prosciutto. Of course, this recipe demands incredible tomatoes. When shopping at a farmers' market, buy a tomato and taste it —if it's great, buy more. If not, move on.

pasta

Venetian Spaghetti with Sardines

TOTAL: 40 MIN

6 SERVINGS ● ●

- 2 tablespoons unsalted butter
- 2 tablespoons extra-virgin olive oil
- 2 medium onions, finely chopped
- One 4-ounce can olive oil–packed sardines (120 grams)—drained, boned and finely chopped
- 2 tablespoons water
- 1 cup whole milk
- Salt and freshly ground pepper
- 1 pound spaghetti

I. In a large, deep skillet, melt the butter in the olive oil over low heat. Add the onions and cook, stirring occasionally, until softened and golden, about 20 minutes. Add the sardines and water and cook, stirring, until hot, about 2 minutes. Add the milk and simmer until the sardines dissolve into a thick sauce, about 6 minutes. Season with salt and pepper.

2. Meanwhile, in a large pot of boiling salted water, cook the spaghetti until al dente. Drain and add the spaghetti to the skillet. Toss the spaghetti with the sauce and season with salt. Transfer to bowls and serve at once with freshly ground pepper. —*Marika Seguso*
WINE Flinty, high-acid Chablis.

Spicy Garlic Shrimp and Tomato Spaghetti

TOTAL: 25 MIN

4 SERVINGS ● ●

- 2 tablespoons dry bread crumbs
- ¼ cup plus 1 tablespoon extra-virgin olive oil
- ¾ pound spaghetti
- ½ pound shelled and deveined medium shrimp, cut into ½-inch pieces
- ½ pint small yellow pear or red grape tomatoes
- 2 garlic cloves, minced
- 1 teaspoon minced rosemary
- 1 teaspoon crushed red pepper
- Salt and freshly ground black pepper

I. In a small skillet, cook the bread crumbs in 1 tablespoon of the olive oil over moderate heat, stirring occasionally, until golden and crisp, 2 to 3 minutes. Scrape the bread crumbs onto a plate.

2. In a large pot of boiling salted water, cook the spaghetti until just barely al dente. Drain the spaghetti, reserving ½ cup of the cooking water.

3. Meanwhile, in a large, deep skillet, combine the remaining ¼ cup of olive oil with the shrimp, tomatoes, garlic, rosemary and crushed red pepper. Add the spaghetti and the reserved cooking water to the skillet and season with salt and pepper. Cook over moderately high heat, tossing the pasta and lightly crushing the tomatoes, until the sauce is slightly thickened and the shrimp are cooked through, about 4 minutes. Transfer the spaghetti to bowls, sprinkle the bread crumbs on top and serve.
—*Scott Conant*
WINE Ripe, creamy-textured Chardonnay.

Toasted Orzo and Chicken Pilaf with Green Olives and Peas

TOTAL: 35 MIN

4 TO 6 SERVINGS ● ●

- 2 tablespoons extra-virgin olive oil
- 1½ pounds skinless, boneless chicken thighs, cut into 2-inch pieces
- Salt and freshly ground pepper
- 1½ cups orzo (10 ounces)
- 2 scallions, thinly sliced
- 1 large garlic clove, minced
- Pinch of crushed red pepper
- One 14-ounce can diced Italian tomatoes, drained
- 3 cups chicken stock or canned low-sodium broth
- ¾ cup pitted green olives (3 ounces), coarsely chopped
- ¾ cup frozen baby peas
- 1 tablespoon finely chopped flat-leaf parsley

I. In a large nonstick skillet, heat the olive oil until shimmering. Season the chicken with salt and pepper, add it to the skillet and cook over high heat, stirring, until browned, about 8 minutes. Transfer the chicken to a plate.

2. Add the orzo to the skillet and cook, stirring, for 3 minutes. Add the scallions, garlic and red pepper and cook, stirring, for 30 seconds. Stir in the tomatoes, chicken stock, olives and peas, scraping up any browned bits from the pan. Stir in the chicken along with any accumulated juices. Cover and simmer until the broth is nearly absorbed and the orzo is al dente, about 15 minutes. Stir in the parsley and fluff with a fork. Spoon into bowls and serve at once. —*Grace Parisi*
WINE Light, spicy Pinot Grigio.

Fusilli Salad with Grilled Chicken and Zucchini

TOTAL: 30 MIN

4 SERVINGS ● ● ●

- ½ pound whole wheat fusilli
- 4 small zucchini (about 1½ pounds)
- 3 tablespoons fresh lemon juice
- Salt and freshly ground pepper
- 1 pound skinless, boneless chicken breast halves
- 2 tablespoons plus 2 teaspoons extra-virgin olive oil
- 3 anchovy fillets, finely chopped
- 2 garlic cloves, minced
- 1 red bell pepper, thinly sliced
- ½ cup chopped basil

I. Preheat a grill or grill pan. In a pot of boiling salted water, cook the fusilli until al dente; drain. Transfer to a large bowl.

2. Halve the zucchini lengthwise and brush the cut sides with 1 tablespoon lemon juice; season with salt and pepper. Grill, cut side down, over a medium-hot fire until lightly charred, about 3 minutes. Turn the zucchini and move to the sides of the grill. Brush the chicken breasts with 2 teaspoons olive oil; season with salt and pepper. Grill the chicken breasts

FUSILLI SALAD WITH GRILLED CHICKEN

ASIAN CHICKEN AND RICE-NOODLE SALAD

until cooked through, turning once, about 10 minutes. Transfer the chicken and zucchini to a platter; let stand for 5 minutes.
3. Combine the anchovies, garlic and remaining 2 tablespoons lemon juice and olive oil; season with salt and pepper.
4. Cut the chicken and zucchini into bite-size pieces and add them to the fusilli. Add the red pepper and the anchovy dressing and toss well. Sprinkle the basil on top, season with salt and pepper, toss again and serve. —*Marcia Kiesel*
WINE Dry, medium-bodied Pinot Gris.

Asian Chicken and Rice-Noodle Salad with Peanuts
TOTAL: 30 MIN

4 SERVINGS ● ● ●

  8 ounces rice noodles
     (pad thai noodles)
1½ tablespoons chopped fresh ginger

  2 small Thai chiles—stemmed, seeded and chopped—or 1 jalapeño with seeds, stemmed and coarsely chopped
  1 scallion, cut into 2-inch pieces
  1 garlic clove, smashed
  3 tablespoons Asian fish sauce
  2 tablespoons fresh lime juice
1½ tablespoons sugar
  1 roasted whole chicken breast, skin and bones discarded, meat shredded (2 cups)
  2 carrots, coarsely shredded
  1 kirby cucumber—peeled, seeded and thinly sliced
  2 large radishes, thinly sliced
  ⅓ cup torn cilantro leaves
  ⅓ cup torn mint leaves
  ¼ cup roasted unsalted peanuts (1 ounce), coarsely chopped
Lime wedges, for serving

1. In a large saucepan of boiling salted water, cook the rice noodles until they are al dente, 6 to 7 minutes. Drain and rinse them under running water until cold. Shake out the excess water and pat the noodles thoroughly dry with paper towels.
2. In a blender or food processor, combine the coarsely chopped ginger with the Thai chiles, scallion pieces and smashed garlic and pulse until chopped. Add the fish sauce, lime juice and sugar and process until smooth.
3. Transfer the rice noodles to a large serving bowl. Add the chicken, carrots, cucumber, radishes, cilantro and mint and toss. Add the dressing and toss until evenly coated. Sprinkle the rice noodles with peanuts and serve with lime wedges. —*Grace Parisi*
WINE Light, soft Chenin Blanc.

SPAGHETTI WITH BOLOGNESE SAUCE

Three-Cheese Linguine with Chicken and Spinach

TOTAL: 35 MIN

4 SERVINGS ●

- 12 ounces linguine
- ¼ cup extra-virgin olive oil
- 1 large garlic clove, minced
- 1 teaspoon finely chopped thyme
- ½ teaspoon finely chopped marjoram
- 1 pound skinless, boneless chicken breast, cut into 3-by-½-inch strips

Kosher salt and freshly ground pepper

Two 5-ounce bags prewashed baby spinach

- 3 ounces Asiago cheese, coarsely shredded (1 cup)
- 3 ounces Fontina cheese, coarsely shredded (¾ cup)
- 3 ounces finely grated Parmesan cheese (¾ cup)

1. In a large pot of boiling salted water, cook the linguine until al dente. Drain, reserving 1 cup of the cooking water.

2. In a bowl, combine 3 tablespoons of olive oil with the garlic, thyme and marjoram. Add the chicken; season with salt and pepper and toss.

3. Heat a large skillet. Add the spinach and cook over moderate heat, stirring, until wilted. Transfer to a colander and drain well. Wipe out the skillet.

4. Heat the remaining 1 tablespoon of olive oil until shimmering. Add the chicken and marinade. Cook over moderately high heat until just cooked through, about 3 minutes. Toss in the spinach.

5. Return the pasta to the pot. Add the chicken, spinach, Asiago, Fontina and half of the Parmesan. Add ¾ cup of the reserved water. Cook over low heat, tossing, until creamy, 1 minute; add more water if needed. Season with salt and pepper. Transfer to a bowl, sprinkle with the remaining Parmesan and serve. —*Laura Chenel*

WINE Rich, earthy Pinot Noir.

Soba with Lemon, Cream and Prosciutto

TOTAL: 25 MIN

4 SERVINGS ●

The buckwheat noodles called soba, a staple of Japanese cooking, get a Mediterranean treatment here; cream and lemon brighten and enhance their earthy flavor. Be sure to buy soba made with some wheat flour; 100 percent buckwheat-flour pasta breaks and overcooks easily.

- 1 tablespoon unsalted butter
- 2 tablespoons shredded sage leaves
- 4 ounces prosciutto, sliced ⅛ inch thick and cut into matchsticks
- ½ cup heavy cream

Finely grated zest of 1 small lemon

Salt and freshly ground pepper

- ¾ pound buckwheat noodles (soba)
- ¼ cup freshly grated Parmesan cheese, plus more for serving

1. Melt the butter in a large skillet. Add the sage leaves and cook over moderately high heat until very fragrant and golden, 1 to 2 minutes. Add the prosciutto and cook, stirring occasionally, until sizzling, about 2 minutes. Stir in the cream and lemon zest and season with salt and pepper. Remove from the heat, cover and keep warm.

2. In a large pot of boiling salted water, cook the buckwheat noodles until just barely al dente, about 4 minutes. Drain in a colander, reserving 1 cup of the pasta cooking water.

3. Add the cooked soba noodles, the reserved cooking water and ¼ cup of the Parmesan cheese to the skillet and cook briefly over moderate heat, gently tossing and stirring, until the sauce is slightly thickened and thoroughly coats the pasta. Transfer the pasta to a large serving platter and serve at once, passing additional Parmesan at the table. —*Sally Schneider*

WINE Dry, full-flavored Alsace Riesling.

Spaghetti with Bolognese Sauce

ACTIVE: 45 MIN; TOTAL: 2 HR 15 MIN

6 SERVINGS ● ●

- 1 tablespoon unsalted butter
- 1 tablespoon extra-virgin olive oil
- 4 garlic cloves, minced
- 3 ounces sliced pancetta, chopped
- 1 medium carrot, finely diced
- 1 medium onion, finely diced
- 1 celery rib, finely diced
- 1 pound coarsely ground beef chuck
- 1 pound coarsely ground pork
- ¼ pound mortadella, cut into ¼-inch dice (optional)
- 1 tablespoon tomato paste
- 1 cup dry white wine

One 28-ounce can Italian tomatoes, chopped, juices reserved

- 1½ cups chicken or beef stock
- ¼ teaspoon freshly grated nutmeg
- 3 tablespoons chopped parsley
- 2 tablespoons chopped basil

Salt and freshly ground pepper

- 1 pound spaghetti
- ¼ cup heavy cream

Freshly grated Parmesan cheese

1. In an enameled cast-iron casserole, melt the butter in the oil. Add the garlic, pancetta, carrot, onion and celery and cook over moderately low heat until the onion is golden, about 5 minutes. Add the ground beef and pork and cook over moderate heat, breaking up the meat with a spoon, until no pink remains, about 8 minutes. Stir in the mortadella and tomato paste and cook for 2 minutes. Add the wine and cook, stirring, until reduced by half, about 3 minutes. Add the tomatoes with their juices, the stock, nutmeg and 1 tablespoon each of the parsley and basil and bring to a boil. Season with salt and pepper and simmer over low heat, stirring occasionally, until very thick, about 1½ hours. Keep warm.

2. In a large pot of boiling salted water, cook the spaghetti until al dente. Drain and return it to the pot.

pasta

3. Stir the cream and the remaining 2 tablespoons of parsley and 1 tablespoon of basil into the meat sauce. Season the sauce with salt and pepper, then add 2 cups to the spaghetti and toss. Transfer the spaghetti to a large bowl, top with the remaining sauce and serve. Pass the Parmesan cheese at the table. —*Marcia Kiesel*

MAKE AHEAD The Bolognese sauce can be refrigerated for up to 5 days.

WINE Deep, pungent, tannic Barolo.

Creamy Spaghetti Carbonara

TOTAL: 20 MIN
4 SERVINGS ●

- 1 pound spaghetti
- 2 large egg yolks
- ½ cup heavy cream
- 1 tablespoon extra-virgin olive oil
- 6 ounces thickly sliced pancetta, cut into ⅛-inch dice
- 2 garlic cloves, thinly sliced
- 1 cup freshly grated Parmesan cheese (3 ounces)

Pinch of freshly grated nutmeg

Freshly ground pepper

1. In a large pot of boiling salted water, cook the spaghetti until just al dente. Drain, reserving ½ cup of the pasta cooking water.

2. Meanwhile, in a small bowl, whisk the egg yolks and cream. In a large, deep skillet, heat the oil. Add the pancetta and cook over moderately high heat, stirring, until crisp, 4 minutes. Add the garlic and cook until golden, 1 minute.

3. Add the spaghetti to the skillet. Cook over low heat, tossing, until coated. Slowly add the reserved pasta cooking water and beaten egg yolks. Toss until coated with a creamy sauce, about 1 minute. Add the 1 cup of Parmesan and the nutmeg; season with pepper. Transfer to bowls and serve, passing extra Parmesan. —*Anne Quatrano*

WINE Round-textured Sémillon.

Spinach Cannelloni with Bacon and Walnuts

ACTIVE: 1 HR 45 MIN; TOTAL: 2 HR 20 MIN
6 SERVINGS

- 2 tablespoons extra-virgin olive oil
- 1½ cups minced onions (2 medium)
- 1 teaspoon dried oregano
- 1 teaspoon sugar

Kosher salt and freshly ground black pepper

- ¼ cup dry red wine
- 1 cup canned tomato sauce
- ½ cup water
- 4 tablespoons unsalted butter
- ¼ cup plus 2 tablespoons all-purpose flour
- 1 quart milk
- 1 cup freshly grated Parmesan cheese
- ¾ teaspoon freshly grated nutmeg

Pinch of white pepper

- 2 pounds fresh spinach, large stems discarded
- ¼ pound bacon, cut into ¼-inch strips
- 4 large garlic cloves, minced
- ¼ cup finely chopped walnuts

Basic Crêpes (recipe follows)

1. In a skillet, heat 1 tablespoon of the olive oil. Add 1 cup of onions and cook over moderately high heat, stirring, until golden. Add the oregano and sugar; season with salt and black pepper. Cook for 1 minute. Add the wine and simmer, stirring, for 1 minute. Add the tomato sauce and water and simmer until slightly thickened, 10 minutes. Remove from the heat.

2. Melt the butter in a medium saucepan. Add ¼ cup of the onions and cook over moderate heat, stirring, until softened, about 4 minutes. Whisk in the flour until combined. Add the milk in 2 batches, whisking constantly until smooth before adding more. Bring to a boil, then simmer over moderate heat until thickened, about 2 minutes. Whisk in ¼ cup of the Parmesan cheese, the nutmeg, white pepper and ¾ teaspoon of salt. Remove from the heat and press a piece of plastic wrap directly on the surface of the white sauce.

3. In a large skillet over high heat, add the spinach by handfuls and toss until wilted. Squeeze the spinach dry, then finely chop. Wipe out the skillet.

4. In the same skillet, heat the remaining 1 tablespoon of olive oil. Add the bacon and cook over moderately high heat until golden, about 3 minutes. Add the garlic and cook, stirring, until fragrant, about 30 seconds. Add the remaining ¼ cup of chopped onion and cook until translucent, about 3 minutes. Add the spinach and cook, stirring, for 2 minutes. Add 1 cup of the white sauce and 1 teaspoon each of salt and black pepper. Remove from the heat and stir in ½ cup of the Parmesan cheese and the walnuts.

5. Preheat the oven to 400°. Lay out 16 crêpes on a work surface and spread 3 tablespoons of the spinach filling in a strip down the center of each one. Tightly roll the crêpe around the filling, tucking in the edges as you roll it up to form a neat cylinder. Repeat with the remaining filling and crêpes.

6. Spread ¼ cup of tomato sauce on the bottom of a 9-by-13-inch baking dish. Arrange the cannelloni over the tomato sauce. Spread the remaining white sauce over the cannelloni. Drizzle the remaining tomato sauce on top and sprinkle with the remaining ¼ cup of Parmesan. Bake for 25 minutes, or until the cheese is golden and the cannelloni are heated through. Let stand for 10 minutes before serving. —*Maricel Presilla*

MAKE AHEAD All the components can be made up to 2 days ahead and assembled just before baking.

WINE Simple, fruity Chianti.

Basic Crêpes

ACTIVE: 25 MIN; TOTAL: 1 HR 30 MIN

MAKES 16 TO 18 CRÊPES ●

- 4 large eggs
- 1½ cups milk
- 1½ teaspoons sugar

Pinch of salt

- 1 cup all-purpose flour
- 1 tablespoon melted unsalted butter, plus more for cooking

1. In a medium bowl, whisk the eggs, ½ cup of the milk and the sugar and salt until combined. Whisk in the flour until the batter is smooth. Whisk the remaining 1 cup of milk and the 1 tablespoon of melted butter into the batter. Let stand at room temperature for 1 hour.

2. Heat a 7-inch crêpe pan over moderate heat and brush with melted butter. Pour 3 tablespoons of the crêpe batter into the pan and immediately rotate the pan to coat the bottom evenly. Cook the crêpe until lightly browned on the bottom, about 30 seconds. Flip the crêpe and cook until brown dots appear on the second side, about 10 seconds longer. Transfer the crêpes to a large plate as they are cooked. Continue making crêpes with the batter, adding melted butter as needed, to make 16 to 18 crêpes. —*M.P.*

MAKE AHEAD The crêpes can be refrigerated overnight.

Penne with Cauliflower, Bacon and Creamy Tomato Sauce

ACTIVE: 45 MIN; TOTAL: 1 HR 30 MIN

12 SERVINGS ●

One 2½-pound head cauliflower, cut into 1-inch florets

- 2 tablespoons extra-virgin olive oil

Salt and freshly ground pepper

- 1 pound thick-sliced bacon
- 2 pounds penne

One 28-ounce can crushed tomatoes

- 2½ cups heavy cream
- 2 garlic cloves, minced
- 2 teaspoons chopped thyme
- 1 teaspoon crushed red pepper
- 2½ cups shredded Italian Fontina cheese (14 ounces)
- ¾ cup plus 2 tablespoons freshly grated Parmesan cheese
- ¼ cup finely chopped flat-leaf parsley

1. Preheat the oven to 450°. On a large rimmed baking sheet, toss the cauliflower with the olive oil and season with salt and pepper. Roast for 40 minutes, or until tender and browned; let cool.

2. Meanwhile, in a large skillet, working in 2 batches, cook the bacon over moderate heat until crisp, about 4 minutes per side. Drain on paper towels, then coarsely chop the bacon.

3. Butter 2 large shallow baking dishes. In a large pot of boiling salted water, cook the penne just until al dente; drain. Return the penne to the pot.

4. Stir the roasted cauliflower, tomatoes, cream, garlic, thyme, crushed red pepper, 2 cups of the Fontina cheese and ¾ cup of the Parmesan into the penne. Season with salt and pepper. Transfer the pasta to the prepared baking dishes and sprinkle with the remaining ½ cup of Fontina cheese and 2 tablespoons of Parmesan. Bake for 15 minutes, or until bubbling and lightly browned. Sprinkle the pasta with the parsley and chopped bacon and serve. —*Ken Oringer*

MAKE AHEAD The pasta can be assembled and refrigerated overnight. Bring to room temperature before baking.

WINE Complex, savory Chianti Classico.

TASTE TEST canned tomatoes

F&W editors taste-tested 13 brands of canned tomatoes. Our favorites use San Marzanos from Italy, recognizable by a government seal and the term D.O.P. *(Denominazione di Origine Protetta)* on the label.

PRODUCT	F&W COMMENT	INTERESTING BITE
Famoso San Marzano (www.famosofoods.com)	"No tinny taste like some brands."	A tasting team travels to Italy to select the crop for this American brand.
Pastene San Marzano (www.pastene.com)	"Real tomato flavor. They're a little soft but great for sauce."	Pastene began as a pushcart operation in Boston's North End in 1848.
Vantia San Marzano (718-326-9696)	"Tastes just like fresh tomatoes. Very nice."	Dozens of small family farms grow these special tomatoes for Vantia.

pasta

Ricotta Cavatelli with Bacon and Zucchini

ACTIVE: 25 MIN; TOTAL: 35 MIN

8 SERVINGS ●

Chef Sergio Sigala turns out homemade cavatelli with a professional-style pasta machine. Since making it by hand is time-consuming, we substituted fresh or frozen store-bought pasta.

- 1 tablespoon extra-virgin olive oil
- ½ pound speck or lean slab bacon, sliced ¼ inch thick and cut into 1-inch strips
- 2 medium zucchini, cut into 1½-by-¼-inch matchsticks

Salt and freshly ground pepper

- 2 pounds fresh or frozen ricotta cavatelli or gnocchi
- 1 large tomato, cut into ½-inch dice
- ½ cup shredded basil
- ⅓ cup freshly grated Parmesan cheese, plus more for serving

1. In a large, deep skillet, heat the olive oil. Add the speck and cook over moderate heat until crisp, about 8 minutes. Transfer to paper towels to drain.

2. Pour off all but 1 tablespoon of the speck fat. Add the zucchini; season with salt and pepper. Cook over moderately high heat, stirring, until barely softened, about 2 minutes. Return the speck to the skillet and remove from the heat.

3. In a large pot of boiling salted water, cook the cavatelli until al dente. Drain, reserving ¼ cup of the pasta cooking water. Add the cavatelli, reserved cooking water and tomato to the skillet. Season with salt and pepper. Toss gently over moderate heat until warm.

4. Transfer the pasta and sauce to a large, shallow bowl and toss with the shredded basil and ⅓ cup of the Parmesan cheese. Serve the pasta immediately, passing additional Parmesan at the table. —*Sergio Sigala*

WINE Fruity, low-oak Chardonnay.

Farfalle with Bacon and Endives

ACTIVE: 20 MIN; TOTAL: 50 MIN

4 TO 6 SERVINGS

Coarsely chopped curly green chicory is a great alternative to the endives; both offer a marvelous bitter edge and refreshing crunch.

- 1 quart chicken stock or low-sodium broth
- 1 pound farfalle
- 1 tablespoon extra-virgin olive oil
- ½ pound thickly sliced bacon, cut crosswise into 1-inch pieces
- 4 medium Belgian endives, cored and cut crosswise into 1-inch-thick slices
- 3 large garlic cloves, thinly sliced
- ¼ cup coarsely chopped flat-leaf parsley
- 1 teaspoon finely grated lemon zest
- ¼ cup freshly grated Parmesan cheese

Salt and freshly ground pepper

1. In a saucepan, boil the stock until reduced to 1 cup, about 20 minutes.

2. Meanwhile, in a large pot of boiling salted water, cook the farfalle until it is al dente.

3. In a large, deep skillet, heat the olive oil. Add the bacon and cook over moderately low heat until slightly crisp, about 7 minutes. Transfer the bacon to paper towels to drain. Pour off all but 2 tablespoons of the fat. Add the endives and garlic to the skillet and cook over moderately high heat, tossing, until the endives are just wilted but still crisp, about 4 minutes.

4. Drain the farfalle and add it to the skillet. Add the reduced chicken stock, parsley, lemon zest and bacon and toss well. Remove from the heat. Stir in the Parmesan and season the pasta with salt and pepper. Transfer to a large bowl and serve at once. —*Marcia Kiesel*

MAKE AHEAD The reduced stock can be refrigerated overnight.

WINE Full-bodied, fragrant Viognier.

Gemelli with Sweet Sausage and Spinach

TOTAL: 30 MIN

4 SERVINGS ●

- ¾ pound gemelli or penne
- 2 tablespoons extra-virgin olive oil
- 1 large onion, quartered lengthwise and thinly sliced crosswise
- 1 pound sweet Italian sausages, casings removed
- ½ teaspoon crushed red pepper
- 2 cups coarsely chopped baby spinach (4 ounces)
- ½ pint red grape tomatoes

Salt

- ½ cup grated Parmesan cheese

1. In a large pot of boiling salted water, cook the gemelli until just al dente. Drain, reserving 1 cup of the water.

2. In a large, deep skillet, heat the olive oil until shimmering. Add the onion and cook over moderately high heat, stirring, until softened, 4 to 5 minutes. Add the sausage and crushed red pepper and cook, breaking up the meat, for 5 minutes. Add the spinach and tomatoes and cook until softened, about 3 minutes.

3. Add the gemelli and reserved water and cook, lightly crushing the tomatoes, until heated, about 2 minutes; season with salt. Transfer to bowls, sprinkle with the Parmesan and serve. —*Scott Conant*

WINE Tannic, full-bodied Barbaresco.

Antipasti Pasta

TOTAL: 25 MIN

4 SERVINGS ●

- ¾ pound penne
- ¼ cup extra-virgin olive oil
- 1 cup jarred roasted red peppers, drained and cut into strips
- 2 large garlic cloves, thinly sliced
- ¼ teaspoon crushed red pepper
- 1 small head escarole, inner leaves only, chopped (4 cups)

One 6-ounce can Italian tuna in olive oil, drained and flaked (see Note)
- ¾ cup grated Parmesan cheese

FARFALLE WITH BACON AND ENDIVES

STIR-FRIED CHINESE NOODLES WITH ROAST PORK

I. In a large pot of boiling salted water, cook the penne until al dente. Drain, reserving 1 cup of the cooking water.
2. Meanwhile, in a large skillet, heat the oil until shimmering. Add the red peppers, garlic and crushed red pepper and cook over moderately high heat until the peppers are softened, 6 minutes. Add the escarole and cook, stirring, until wilted, 3 minutes. Stir in the tuna.
3. Add the pasta, the reserved cooking water and ½ cup of the Parmesan to the skillet and cook, tossing, until the liquid is nearly absorbed, 2 minutes. Transfer to bowls, sprinkle with the remaining ¼ cup of Parmesan and serve. —*Grace Parisi*
NOTE Canned Italian tuna packed in oil has an incomparable taste to domestic brands. It's available at supermarkets.
WINE Light, dry Soave or similar white.

Stir-Fried Chinese Noodles with Roast Pork

TOTAL: 30 MIN

4 SERVINGS ● ●

1 pound thin Chinese yellow or egg noodles
½ cup chicken stock or low-sodium broth
2 tablespoons oyster sauce
2 tablespoons soy sauce
2 teaspoons sugar
¼ teaspoon chili oil
Kosher salt
2 tablespoons vegetable oil
2 large eggs, lightly beaten
1 large carrot, julienned
1 large celery rib, julienned
½ pound Chinese roast pork, cut into thin strips
1 scallion, white and green parts, thinly sliced

I. In a saucepan of boiling water, cook the noodles, stirring, until al dente, about 3 minutes. Drain; return to the pan. Fill the pan with cold water, swish the noodles and drain; repeat. Lift the noodles with your fingers occasionally to dry.
2. In a small bowl, blend the stock with the oyster sauce, soy sauce, sugar, chili oil and 1 teaspoon of salt.
3. In a wok, heat 1 tablespoon of the vegetable oil. Add the eggs and cook over moderate heat, stirring, until set, 1 minute. Transfer to a plate and break them up. Add the remaining 1 tablespoon of vegetable oil to the wok and heat until hot. Add the carrot and celery and stir-fry until softened, about 3 minutes. Add the pork, noodles and sauce; toss. Season with salt, add the scallion and eggs, toss and serve. —*Jean-Georges Vongerichten*
WINE Complex, silky red Burgundy.

pasta

Stir-Fried Noodles and Pork

TOTAL: 35 MIN

6 SERVINGS ● ●

In Japan, this dish is called *yakisoba*. *Yaki* refers to the method of cooking— grilling, broiling or pan-frying—while *soba* refers to *chuka soba,* the long, thin yellow noodles that are stir-fried here. This recipe features pork, but beef or skinless, boneless chicken can easily be substituted. Fresh shiso leaves are an innovation; this recipe uses them as an aromatic ingredient that imparts a mintlike flavor to the dish. Shiso is a relative of basil, and the leaves are often used in Japanese cooking.

- ½ cup chicken stock or low-sodium broth
- ¼ cup plus 2 tablespoons soy sauce
- 1 tablespoon Dijon mustard
- 1 tablespoon unseasoned rice vinegar
- 1 teaspoon Asian sesame oil
- ½ teaspoon chili oil
- 1 medium carrot, cut into matchsticks
- 1 pound thin dried *chuka soba* noodles or egg noodles
- 2 tablespoons vegetable oil
- ¾ pound boneless pork, preferably shoulder or butt, thinly sliced across the grain

Salt and freshly ground pepper

- 3 tablespoons finely slivered fresh ginger
- 1 small green bell pepper, cut into matchsticks
- 4 shiso leaves, thinly sliced crosswise (optional)
- 2 scallions, cut into matchsticks
- 1 cup mung bean sprouts

1. In a small bowl, combine the stock, soy sauce, mustard, vinegar, sesame oil and chili oil.

2. In a large pot of boiling water, blanch the carrot for 1 minute. Using a slotted spoon, transfer the carrot to a plate. Add the noodles to the pot and cook, stirring, until they are al dente, about 5 minutes. Drain the noodles and return them to the pot. Fill the pot with cold water and swish the noodles to cool them. Drain and repeat. Transfer the cooled noodles to a colander and lift them occasionally with your fingers to help dry them out.

3. Meanwhile, in a deep skillet, heat the vegetable oil until shimmering. Add the pork slices in a single layer, season them with salt and pepper and cook over high heat, without stirring, until browned on the bottoms, about 2 minutes. Stir a few times, then add the ginger and stir-fry over moderately high heat until fragrant, about 2 minutes. Add the bell pepper and carrot and stir-fry for 1 minute.

4. Add the noodles to the skillet and toss until well combined. Add the soy sauce mixture, shiso, scallions and bean sprouts; toss until all of the ingredients are heated through. Transfer to a large, shallow bowl and serve. —*Marcia Kiesel*

WINE Dry, crisp sparkling wine.

Grandma's Lasagna

ACTIVE: 45 MIN; TOTAL: 2 HR

10 TO 12 SERVINGS ●

This definitive lasagna has tomato sauce, chunks of meat, shredded mozzarella and creamy ricotta cheese.

- ¼ cup extra-virgin olive oil
- ½ pound ground beef chuck
- ½ pound ground sirloin
- 4 teaspoons very finely chopped garlic
- ½ teaspoon dried oregano, crumbled
- ¼ teaspoon crushed red pepper
- 2 tablespoons tomato paste

Two 28-ounce cans Italian peeled tomatoes, finely chopped, juices reserved

One 28-ounce can tomato puree

- 2 cups chicken stock or low-sodium broth
- 2 bay leaves
- 6 thyme sprigs, tied together with kitchen string

Pinch of sugar

Salt and freshly ground pepper

- 1½ pounds sweet Italian sausage, casings removed
- 2 pounds fresh ricotta
- ¼ cup very finely chopped flat-leaf parsley
- 2 tablespoons finely chopped basil
- ½ cup freshly grated Parmesan cheese
- 1 pound packaged whole milk mozzarella, shredded (3 cups)
- 1 large egg, beaten
- 12 dried lasagna noodles

1. In a large enameled cast-iron casserole, heat the olive oil over high heat until shimmering. Add the chuck and sirloin and cook over moderately high heat, breaking up the meat into large chunks, until no pink remains.

2. Add the garlic, oregano and crushed red pepper and cook until fragrant. Stir in the tomato paste and cook until the meat is coated. Add the tomatoes and their juices and the tomato puree along with the chicken stock, bay leaves, thyme and sugar. Season with salt and pepper and bring to a boil. Simmer over moderate heat, stirring occasionally, until thickened and reduced to 8 cups, about 1½ hours. Remove the bay leaves and thyme sprigs.

3. Meanwhile, heat a large skillet. Add the sausage meat in large pieces and cook over moderately high heat until browned and just cooked through, about 10 minutes. Drain the sausage and break it into ½-inch pieces.

4. In a large bowl, combine the ricotta with the parsley, basil and ¼ cup of the Parmesan. Add two-thirds of the shredded mozzarella and season with salt and pepper. Beat in the egg.

5. In a large pot of boiling salted water, cook the lasagna noodles, stirring occasionally, until al dente. Drain and rinse under cold water. Dry the noodles between layers of paper towels.

6. Preheat the oven to 375°. Spread 1 cup of the sauce in the bottom of a 9-by-13-inch glass baking dish. Line the dish with 4 overlapping noodles. Spread one-half of the ricotta mixture over the noodles, then top with one-half of the sausage, 1½ cups of the sauce and another 4 noodles. Repeat the layering with the remaining ricotta mixture, sausage and another 1½ cups of sauce. Top with 4 noodles and cover with 1½ cups of sauce. Toss the remaining 1 cup of mozzarella with the remaining ¼ cup of Parmesan and sprinkle over the lasagna.

7. Bake the lasagna for about 45 minutes, or until the top is golden and crisp around the edges and the filling is bubbling. Let the lasagna rest for 20 minutes before serving. —*Grace Parisi*

MAKE AHEAD The lasagna can be prepared through Step 5 and refrigerated overnight, or it can be baked ahead and then reheated in a 325° oven.

WINE Intense, berry-flavored Zinfandel.

Simple Tomato Sauce

ACTIVE: 8 MIN; TOTAL: 25 MIN
MAKES ABOUT 3 CUPS ● ● ●

- 1 tablespoon extra-virgin olive oil
- 2 large garlic cloves, very thinly sliced
- 1 teaspoon finely chopped rosemary
- One 28-ounce can Italian whole tomatoes, finely chopped, juices reserved
- 1 tablespoon tomato paste
- Salt and freshly ground pepper

1. Heat the olive oil in a medium nonreactive saucepan. Add the garlic and rosemary and cook over low heat until the garlic is golden, about 3 minutes.
2. Add the chopped tomatoes with their juices and the tomato paste to the saucepan. Season the mixture with salt and pepper. Simmer over low heat, stirring occasionally with a wooden spoon, until the sauce has thickened, about 10 minutes. Season the sauce again with salt and pepper and serve. —*Sophie Braimbridge*

PORCINI VARIATION Soak ¾ cup of dried porcini mushrooms (¾ ounce) in ¾ cup of boiling water until softened, about 20 minutes. Rub the porcini to remove any grit and coarsely chop them. Reserve the soaking liquid. Add the chopped porcini to the saucepan when the garlic is golden and cook for 1 minute. When the sauce is done, add the reserved porcini soaking liquid, stopping when you reach the grit, and cook the sauce until thickened, about 10 minutes.

SPICY VARIATION Add 1 large dried chile when you cook the garlic. Discard the chile before serving the sauce.

ANCHOVY VARIATION Add 4 finely chopped oil-packed anchovy fillets when you cook the garlic.

MAKE AHEAD The tomato sauces can be refrigerated for up to 1 week or frozen for up to 1 month.

Ed Giobbi's Marinara Sauce

ACTIVE: 50 MIN; TOTAL: 3 HR 45 MIN
MAKES ABOUT 3½ CUPS ● ●

- ¼ cup extra-virgin olive oil
- 2 garlic cloves, minced
- 1 large onion, coarsely chopped
- 1 medium carrot, thinly sliced
- 4 cups Home-Canned Tomatoes (recipe follows)
- Salt and freshly ground pepper
- 2 tablespoons unsalted butter
- 1 tablespoon chopped basil
- 1 teaspoon dried oregano

1. Heat the olive oil in a large skillet. Add the garlic, onion and carrot and cook over moderate heat for 5 minutes.
2. Pass the tomatoes and their juices through a food mill. Add the tomatoes to the skillet and season with salt and pepper. Cover partially and simmer over low heat for 15 minutes. Pass the sauce through a food mill and return it to the skillet. Add the butter, basil and oregano, cover partially and simmer for 30 minutes longer. —*Eugenia Bone*

Home-Canned Tomatoes

ACTIVE: 30 MIN; TOTAL: 2 HR 35 MIN
MAKES 4 PINTS ● ●

- 4 pounds tomatoes
- 8 basil leaves
- ¼ cup fresh lemon juice
- 2 teaspoons kosher salt

In a large saucepan of boiling water, blanch the tomatoes just until the skins loosen, about 30 seconds. Using a slotted spoon, transfer them to a large rimmed platter to cool. Slip off the skins. Halve them crosswise and squeeze out the seeds. Quarter any large tomatoes and pack into 4 hot sterilized 1-pint jars, stopping ½ inch from the top. Bury 2 basil leaves in each and add 1 tablespoon of lemon juice and ½ teaspoon of salt. Release air pockets with a knife. Wipe the rims and close the jars. Set them in a water bath and bring to a boil. Boil for 1 hour and 25 minutes. —*E.B.*

CHICKEN WITH RIESLING, P. 113

poultry

Golden Roast Chicken 98

Roast Chicken 98

Pan-Roasted Chicken and Leeks 99

Clay-Roasted Chicken Stuffed with Serrano Ham and Olives 99

Roast Chicken with Grapes, Chestnuts and Tarragon Butter 100

Chicken with Tarragon Sauce 100

Chicken Simmered in Spiced Yogurt 100

Chicken Pot-au-Feu 101

Chicken Breasts with Red Wine and Mustard Sauce 101

Sautéed Chicken Breasts with Cucumber Salad 102

Chicken Stuffed with Fontina, Prosciutto and Basil 102

Chicken Stuffed with Spinach 102

Parmesan-Crusted Chicken with Arugula Salad 103

Citrus Chicken with Habanero Honey 103

Chicken-Almond Curry with Apricots 104

Chicken with Fresh Apricots, Ginger and Cracked Almonds 105

Grilled Chicken Paillards with Cilantro-Mint Dressing 105

Chile-Glazed Chicken Wings 105

Spicy Southern Barbecued Chicken 106

Buttermilk Fried Chicken 106

Fried Chicken with Tomato Gravy 106

Fried Chicken Littles 108

Sweet Crunchy Mustard Chicken 108

Ginger-Sesame Chicken with Bok Choy and Mushrooms 108

Crisp Indian-Spiced Chicken with Cucumber-Tomato Raita 109

Crispy Garlic Chicken with Dipping Salt 111

Jamaican Jerk Chicken 111

Asian-Style Orange Chicken 111

Asian-Style Chicken Breasts and Bacon 112

Thai Chicken with Mushrooms, Green Beans and Basil 112

Chicken Skewers with Fresh Herb Vinaigrette and Feta 112

Chicken Tikka Masala 113

Chicken with Riesling 113

Chicken Stew with Chile 114

Mediterranean-Style Chicken and Bean Stew 114

Chicken Tagine with Sweet Tomato Sauce 115

Chicken and Sun-Dried-Tomato Meatballs 115

Chicken-Vegetable Potpie 116

Chicken and Leek Yakitori 116

Chicken and Citrus Slaw Tostadas 117

Chicken Chilaquiles 118

Chipotle Chicken and Bell Pepper Casserole 118

Herb-Roasted Game Hens 119

Grilled Quail with Green Papaya Salad 119

Capons with Garlic Gravy 119

Roasted Capons with Herb Butter and Mushroom-Madeira Sauce 120

Madeira-Braised Turkey with Fried Sage Stuffing 121

Turkey Stew with Prunes and Pearl Onions 123

Turkey Breast Escabeche with Onions and Poblanos 123

Roast Turkey Breast and Potatoes with Lemon-Soy Jus 124

Rich Turkey Stock 125

Smoky Turkey Chili 126

Chile-Roasted Turkey with Chorizo–Corn Bread Stuffing 126

Turkey with Apple-Chestnut Stuffing and Cider Gravy 127

Oaxacan Turkey Burgers with Chipotle Salsa 128

Chilled Duck with Zinfandel Sauce 129

Ancho-Chipotle-Spiced Duck Breasts with Mango Salsa 129

GOLDEN ROAST CHICKEN

PAN-ROASTED CHICKEN AND LEEKS

Golden Roast Chicken

TOTAL: 1 HR 10 MIN

4 SERVINGS

3 tablespoons unsalted butter
One 3½-pound chicken
Salt and freshly ground pepper
⅓ cup water

1. Preheat the oven to 425°. Put the butter in a small roasting pan and melt in the oven, about 30 seconds. Season the chicken inside and out with salt and pepper. Fold the wing tips under the body for a neat appearance.

2. Set the chicken in the pan and carefully roll it around to coat it with butter. Turn the chicken on its side and roast for 15 minutes; turn it on the other side and roast for 15 minutes longer. Turn the chicken on its back and roast, basting with the pan juices every 5 minutes, until the skin is browned and crisp and the cavity juices run clear, 25 minutes. Transfer to a platter; let rest for 10 minutes.

3. Meanwhile, set the roasting pan over high heat; when the juices sizzle, add the water. Boil for 2 minutes, scraping up the browned bits from the bottom of the pan. Pour the pan juices into a glass measuring cup and skim the fat from the surface. Carve the chicken and season with salt. Serve with the pan juices. —*Jacques Pépin*

WINE Light, fruity Beaujolais.

Roast Chicken

ACTIVE: 15 MIN; TOTAL: 1 HR 20 MIN

4 TO 6 SERVINGS

Bruising fresh bay leaves by holding both ends and twisting in opposite directions makes them more potent. If fresh bay leaves are unavailable, use fresh sprigs of thyme or marjoram.

Two 3-pound chickens, preferably
    free-range
24 fresh bay leaves, bruised, plus bay
    branches, for garnish
4 garlic cloves, thinly sliced
3 tablespoons extra-virgin olive oil
Salt and freshly ground pepper

1. Preheat the oven to 450°. Bend back the chicken-wing tips and tuck them under their first joints. Using your fingertips, carefully loosen the chicken skin without tearing it, working your hand under the skin all the way up the breast and down into the thighs.

2. Tuck 2 bay leaves in the cavity of each bird. Tuck the remaining leaves under the loosened skin: 2 on each thigh and 3 on each side of each breast. Distribute the garlic evenly under the skin. Tie the legs together with kitchen string for a neat appearance.

3. Set the chickens in a large roasting pan. Rub all over with the olive oil and season with salt and pepper. Roast for 55 to 65 minutes, or until the chickens are browned and the juices run clear; rotate the pan halfway through.

4. Remove the chickens from the oven and let stand in a warm place for 10 minutes. Transfer to a platter and garnish with the bay branches. Remove and discard the bay leaves from under the skin before carving the chickens. —*Jerry Traunfeld*

WINE Complex, savory Chianti Classico.

Pan-Roasted Chicken and Leeks

ACTIVE: 30 MIN; TOTAL: 55 MIN

4 SERVINGS

Roasting the chicken on a bed of leeks infuses them with flavor. You can leave the dark green parts on the leeks, but they'll be too tough to eat.

- 2 tablespoons unsalted butter
- 2 tablespoons extra-virgin olive oil
- 10 medium leeks (3 pounds)— trimmed, slit and rinsed

Salt and freshly ground pepper

One 4-pound chicken, cut into 8 pieces

- 3 rosemary sprigs, halved

1. Preheat the oven to 450°. In a skillet, melt 1 tablespoon of the butter in 1 tablespoon of the oil. Add the leeks; cook over moderately high heat, turning, until browned in spots, 6 minutes. Transfer to a 9-by-13-inch baking dish, season with salt and pepper and roast for 10 minutes, or until beginning to soften.

2. Wipe out the skillet. Melt the remaining 1 tablespoon of butter in the remaining 1 tablespoon of oil. Season the chicken with salt and pepper. Add the chicken and rosemary to the skillet; cook over moderate heat until browned, about 10 minutes. Set the chicken on the leeks, skin side up, add the rosemary and roast for about 20 minutes, or until the chicken is cooked through and the leeks are very tender. Serve hot. —*Barbara Damrosch*

WINE Light, fruity Pinot Noir.

Clay-Roasted Chicken Stuffed with Serrano Ham and Olives

ACTIVE: 45 MIN; TOTAL: 2 HR 10 MIN

4 SERVINGS ●

Roasting chicken in an unglazed red clay pot with a lid produces crisp skin and tender, succulent meat. One of the best clay cookers on the market is the Römertopf, which must be presoaked before use. The clay, which is unglazed on the interior, releases the water as it bakes, keeping food deliciously moist. The average model holds about 3 quarts, with just enough room for a large chicken. Römertopfs are available from Reco (800-221-5336 or www.reco.com).

Alternatively, you can cook the chicken in a roasting pan at 375° until an instant-read thermometer inserted in an inner thigh registers 175°.

One 3½-pound organic chicken, liver and neck reserved

Salt and freshly ground pepper

- 2 tablespoons extra-virgin olive oil
- 1 medium onion, very finely chopped
- 1 large garlic clove, minced
- 3 ounces thinly sliced Serrano ham, cut into thin strips
- ⅓ cup Picholine olives (2 ounces), pitted and coarsely chopped
- 1 cup crustless stale bread cubes (½ inch)
- ¼ cup coarsely chopped flat-leaf parsley

Freshly grated nutmeg

- 1 large egg, lightly beaten
- 2 medium celery ribs, thinly sliced crosswise
- 1 medium carrot, thinly sliced crosswise
- 1 medium leek, white and tender green parts only, thinly sliced crosswise
- 1 tablespoon brandy
- 1 tablespoon sherry vinegar
- 2 tablespoons water

1. Remove the wing tips from the chicken. Cut the wing tips and neck into 1-inch pieces. Cut the chicken liver into 6 pieces. Season the inside of the chicken with salt and pepper.

2. Heat the olive oil in a medium skillet. Add the chopped onion and garlic and cook over moderate heat until softened, about 7 minutes. Add the chicken liver, Serrano ham and chopped olives and cook, stirring frequently, for 2 minutes. Stir in the bread and parsley, season with pepper and nutmeg and cook until the bread becomes golden brown, about 2 minutes. Transfer to a bowl and let cool to room temperature.

3. Soak an unglazed red clay pot (the bottom and lid), such as a Römertopf, in water for 15 minutes, then drain. Stir the egg into the stuffing mixture and stuff the chicken cavity. Scatter the celery, carrot, leek and the reserved wing tips and neck over the bottom of the pot. Add the brandy, sherry vinegar and water and set the stuffed chicken on top. Season the chicken with salt and pepper, cover with the lid and place in the upper third of a cold oven. Turn the oven to 475° and bake the chicken for 45 minutes, or until an instant-read thermometer inserted in the thickest part of a thigh registers 155°.

4. Transfer the chicken to a carving board. Strain the contents of the pot into a small saucepan, pressing on the solids to release the juices. Skim off the fat. Return the chicken to the pot and bake, uncovered, for 30 minutes longer, or until the skin is brown and crisp. Let the chicken stand for 10 minutes.

5. Boil the cooking juices over moderately high heat until reduced to ¼ cup, about 3 minutes. Carve the chicken and serve with the stuffing and pan juices. —*Paula Wolfert*

MAKE AHEAD The uncooked stuffing can be refrigerated overnight.

WINE Round, rich Sauvignon Blanc.

poultry

Roast Chicken with Grapes, Chestnuts and Tarragon Butter

ACTIVE: 30 MIN; TOTAL: 2 HR

6 SERVINGS ●

- 1   stick plus 2 tablespoons unsalted butter, softened
- 3   tablespoons coarsely chopped tarragon
- Salt and freshly ground pepper
- One 4-pound chicken
- 1   thyme sprig
- 1   rosemary sprig
- 1   bay leaf
- 6   thick slices of lean bacon, cut into ¼-inch strips (5 ounces)
- 24 vacuum-packed whole chestnuts (7 ounces)
- 1   pound black or red grapes, stemmed

1. Preheat the oven to 350°. In a small bowl, blend 1 stick of the butter with 2 tablespoons of the tarragon; season with salt and pepper. Loosen the skin of the chicken over the breasts and legs and spread the butter under the skin. Put the thyme, rosemary and bay leaf in the chicken cavity and season with salt and pepper. Season the outside of the chicken with salt and pepper. Roast the chicken in a roasting pan for about 1½ hours, turning the pan a few times. The bird is done when the juices from the thigh run almost clear.

FOOD SAFETY TIP

chicken prep

TO AVOID SALMONELLA contamination, thaw poultry in the refrigerator, under cold running water or in the microwave—never at room temperature. Use separate utensils and a plastic cutting board, and wash everything with hot soapy water when finished. Cook the meat thoroughly; there should be no traces of pink.

2. Meanwhile, in a large skillet, cook the bacon over moderate heat until browned and lightly crisp, 5 minutes. Drain on paper towels; discard the fat. In the same skillet, melt the remaining 2 tablespoons of butter. Add the chestnuts, season with salt and cook over moderate heat until glazed, 3 minutes. Add the grapes and the remaining 1 tablespoon of tarragon and cook until the grapes are about to burst, 4 minutes. Add the bacon. Season with salt and pepper.

3. Transfer the chicken to a carving board and cover loosely with foil. Pour the pan juices into a glass measuring cup and skim off the fat. Pour the pan juices into a small saucepan and simmer over moderately high heat until reduced to ⅓ cup, about 2 minutes. Carve the chicken and serve with the grapes and chestnuts; pass the pan juices. —*Christophe Côte*

WINE Subtle, complex white Burgundy.

Chicken with Tarragon Sauce

ACTIVE: 30 MIN; TOTAL: 1 HR 15 MIN

4 SERVINGS ●

- 2   tablespoons unsalted butter, softened
- 2   bone-in chicken breast halves
- 2   whole chicken legs
- Salt and freshly ground pepper
- ½   cup dry but fruity white wine, such as Mâcon
- ½   cup chicken stock, preferably homemade
- Bouquet garni, made with 2 bay leaves, 2 thyme sprigs and 2 parsley sprigs tied in a bundle with kitchen string
- 1   small onion, halved
- 1   tablespoon all-purpose flour
- 1   cup heavy cream
- 1   tablespoon minced tarragon

1. In a large skillet, melt 1 tablespoon of the butter. Add the chicken, skin side down, and season with salt and pepper. Cook over moderate heat until lightly browned, about 10 minutes. Turn the

chicken and pour off all but 2 tablespoons of fat. Add the wine, stock, bouquet garni and onion; bring to a boil. Cover and simmer over low heat, turning the chicken a few times, until the breasts are barely done, about 20 minutes. Transfer the breasts to a plate and cover loosely with foil. Cover and simmer the legs until just cooked through, about 10 minutes longer. Transfer the legs to the plate.

2. Discard the onion and bouquet garni and boil the cooking liquid over moderately high heat until reduced to ¾ cup, about 4 minutes. Meanwhile, in a small bowl, blend the remaining 1 tablespoon of butter with the flour. Whisk the paste into the reduced cooking liquid until smooth and bring to a simmer. Add the cream and simmer the sauce over low heat for 6 minutes, whisking occasionally.

3. Stir in the tarragon. Return the chicken to the pan and turn to coat with sauce. Cover and simmer until heated through, turning a few times, about 5 minutes. Season with salt and pepper. Transfer the chicken to a platter, pour the tarragon sauce on top and serve.

—*Jacques Pépin*

MAKE AHEAD The chicken can be prepared earlier in the day. Reheat gently before serving.

SERVE WITH Steamed white rice.

WINE Subtle, complex white Burgundy.

Chicken Simmered in Spiced Yogurt

TOTAL: 1 HR 30 MIN

4 SERVINGS ● ●

Many of the spices are left whole in this recipe, so push them to the side of the plate as you find them.

- ½   cup roasted cashews
- 2   tablespoons vegetable oil
- 6   cardamom pods
- 1   cinnamon stick, broken
- 1   bay leaf
- 1   teaspoon black peppercorns

2 tablespoons Ginger Paste
  (recipe follows)
2 tablespoons Garlic Paste
  (recipe follows)
½ cup Onion Paste (recipe follows)
1 long hot green chile, seeded and
  cut into ½-inch dice
1 medium tomato, chopped
4 whole chicken legs, separated
  into drumsticks and thighs and
  skinned
2 teaspoons garam masala
⅛ teaspoon saffron threads
Salt and freshly ground pepper
2 cups plain low-fat yogurt

1. In a mini food processor, finely grind the cashews. Heat the oil in a large skillet. Add the cardamom, cinnamon, bay leaf and peppercorns and cook over moderate heat until sizzling, about 2 minutes. Add the Ginger Paste and Garlic Paste and cook, stirring, for 1 minute. Add the Onion Paste, green chile and cashews and cook for 1 minute. Add the tomato and cook until the liquid evaporates, 2 minutes.

2. Add the chicken, garam masala and saffron and season with salt and pepper. Cook, stirring occasionally, until the chicken turns white, about 3 minutes. Add the yogurt and bring to a simmer, then cover and cook over low heat until the chicken is cooked through, about 50 minutes. Season generously with salt and freshly ground pepper and serve. —*Anupam Gulati*

MAKE AHEAD The chicken can be refrigerated overnight.

WINE Lively, assertive Sauvignon Blanc.

Ginger Paste

TOTAL: 10 MIN
MAKES 1 CUP ● ● ●

¼ pound ginger, peeled and
  coarsely chopped
½ cup water

Puree the ginger and the water in a blender until combined. —*A.G.*

Garlic Paste

TOTAL: 15 MIN
MAKES 1 CUP ● ● ●

2 heads garlic, cloves peeled
  and halved
½ cup water

Puree the garlic cloves and water in a blender until combined. —*A.G.*

Onion Paste

ACTIVE: 5 MIN; TOTAL: 20 MIN
MAKES 1 CUP ● ● ●

1 large onion, quartered
1 cup water

In a small saucepan, simmer the onion in the water over low heat until just tender, about 15 minutes. Using a slotted spoon, transfer the onion to a blender and puree. —*A.G.*

Chicken Pot-au-Feu

ACTIVE: 50 MIN; TOTAL: 2 HR 30 MIN
4 SERVINGS

3 quarts chicken stock or
  low-sodium broth
One 3½-pound chicken
2 celery ribs, coarsely chopped
1 large onion, coarsely chopped
1 medium carrot, coarsely chopped
6 garlic cloves
10 whole black peppercorns
10 thyme sprigs, plus 1 teaspoon
  chopped thyme
12 baby carrots
½ pound turnips, peeled and
  cut into 1-inch cubes
1 cup frozen peas
¼ cup grainy mustard
Salt and freshly ground pepper
1 medium zucchini (½ pound), cut
  into thin 1½-inch sticks
1 small shallot, thinly sliced
Comté Polenta (recipe, p. 250)

1. In a large pot, combine the stock, chicken, celery, onion, chopped carrot, garlic, peppercorns and thyme sprigs. Simmer over low heat, turning the chicken once, until cooked through,

about 1½ hours. Transfer the chicken to a platter to cool.

2. Strain the broth and return it to the pot. Boil the broth over high heat, skimming occasionally, until reduced to 6 cups, about 12 minutes. Cover and keep hot. Remove the meat from the chicken and tear it into large pieces.

3. In a small saucepan of boiling water, cook the baby carrots until tender, about 5 minutes; using a slotted spoon, transfer them to a plate. Repeat with the turnips, cooking them for 4 minutes, and the peas, cooking them for 1 minute.

4. In a skillet, combine the chicken, baby carrots and 1 cup of the broth. Cover and rewarm, then remove from the heat. Stir the mustard into the remaining broth; season with salt and pepper. Spoon the chicken and vegetables, including the raw zucchini, into large, shallow bowls. Sprinkle the chopped thyme and sliced shallot over the top, then ladle in enough hot broth to cover. Add 2 pieces of the Comté Polenta to each bowl and serve. —*Dale Levitski*

MAKE AHEAD The recipe can be prepared through Step 3 up to 2 days ahead. Refrigerate the chicken, stock and vegetables separately.

WINE Soft, earthy Rioja.

Chicken Breasts with Red Wine and Mustard Sauce

ACTIVE: 20 MIN; TOTAL: 1 HR 40 MIN
4 SERVINGS ●

2 unpeeled medium Vidalia
  onions, halved
1 pound small red potatoes
1 bottle (750 ml) dry red wine
2 tablespoons extra-virgin olive oil
2 bay leaves
Salt and freshly ground pepper
¼ cup grainy mustard
2 tablespoons unsulfured molasses
Four 6-ounce skinless, boneless
  chicken breast halves
¼ cup chopped parsley

poultry

1. Preheat the oven to 325°. On half of a heavy-duty 2-by-1½-foot sheet of foil, mound the onions and potatoes. Add ¼ cup of the wine, the olive oil and bay leaves and season with salt and pepper. Fold the foil over the vegetables; seal the edges. Transfer to a rimmed baking sheet and bake for about 1 hour and 20 minutes, or until the vegetables are tender. Peel and slice the onions.

2. Meanwhile, in a medium saucepan, simmer the remaining 3 cups of wine with the mustard and molasses over moderately low heat, stirring, until reduced to ½ cup, about 35 minutes. Season with salt and pepper.

3. Season the chicken with salt and pepper. Put in a steamer basket, cover and steam over moderate heat for 8 minutes.

4. Reheat the sauce. Spoon the vegetables onto plates, discarding the bay leaves. Set the chicken breasts alongside and spoon the sauce over them. Sprinkle with the parsley and serve.
—*Colin Alevras*

WINE Light, fruity Beaujolais.

Sautéed Chicken Breasts with Cucumber Salad

TOTAL: 25 MIN

4 SERVINGS ● ●

- 1   teaspoon cumin seeds
- 2   medium cucumbers (1¼ pounds)—peeled, seeded, quartered lengthwise and cut into ¼-inch-thick slices
- 1   cup roasted cashews (4½ ounces), halved lengthwise or coarsely chopped
- 2   scallions, thinly sliced
- 2   teaspoons fresh lemon juice
- ¼   cup plus 2 tablespoons extra-virgin olive oil
- ¼   cup coarsely chopped flat-leaf parsley

Salt and freshly ground pepper
Four 6-ounce skinless, boneless chicken breast halves

1. In a small skillet, cook the cumin seeds over moderate heat until fragrant, about 1 minute. Transfer to a work surface and let cool, then coarsely chop. In a large bowl, combine the cumin seeds with the cucumbers, cashews, scallions, lemon juice, ¼ cup of the olive oil and the parsley; season with salt and pepper.

2. In a large skillet, heat the remaining 2 tablespoons of olive oil. Season the chicken breasts with salt and pepper and cook over moderately high heat until lightly browned, about 3 minutes. Reduce the heat to moderately low and continue cooking for 3 minutes. Turn and cook the chicken until browned on the other side and just cooked through, about 6 minutes longer. Thickly slice each chicken breast crosswise, mound the cucumber salad on top and serve.
—*Marcia Kiesel*

VARIATIONS Use the cucumber salad as an accompaniment for salmon or bluefish, or mix it with plain yogurt for a version of Indian raita.

WINE Fruity, low-oak Chardonnay.

Chicken Stuffed with Fontina, Prosciutto and Basil

TOTAL: 25 MIN

4 SERVINGS ● ●

Four 6-ounce skinless, boneless chicken breast halves, tenders removed and reserved for another use
Salt and freshly ground pepper
- 1   ounce Fontina, Manchego or fresh Pecorino Romano cheese, shaved with a vegetable peeler
- 1   ounce thinly sliced prosciutto (about 4 slices), trimmed of all fat
- 4   basil leaves
- 1   tablespoon extra-virgin olive oil
- 1   small shallot, minced
- 1½ cups grape tomatoes, halved
- 2   tablespoons balsamic vinegar
- ¼   cup chicken stock or canned low-sodium broth

1. Using a knife, cut into the side of each chicken breast half to create a pocket; do not cut all the way through. Season the pockets with salt and pepper and stuff them with the Fontina, prosciutto and basil leaves. Close the chicken pockets, tucking in any filling. Pound with a meat pounder to flatten slightly.

2. In a large nonstick skillet, heat 2 teaspoons of the olive oil until shimmering. Season the chicken with salt and pepper and cook over moderately high heat, turning once, until golden and cooked through and the cheese is beginning to melt, about 12 minutes. Transfer to plates, cover loosely and keep warm.

3. Add the remaining 1 teaspoon of olive oil to the skillet along with the shallot and cook over moderate heat until softened. Add the tomatoes and cook, tossing, until heated through, about 2 minutes. Add the vinegar and cook until nearly evaporated, about 30 seconds. Add the stock, season with salt and pepper and simmer until slightly reduced, about 2 minutes. Spoon the tomato sauce over the chicken and serve at once. —*Grace Parisi*

WINE Tart, low-tannin Barbera.

Chicken Stuffed with Spinach

TOTAL: 20 MIN

4 SERVINGS ●

- 5   ounces frozen chopped spinach, thawed and squeezed dry
- 1   scallion, finely chopped
- ¼   cup grated Parmesan cheese

Salt and freshly ground pepper
- 2   slices of thick-cut bacon, cut crosswise into ¼-inch strips
- 4   thin chicken cutlets (1½ pounds)
- 2   tablespoons red wine vinegar
- 2   tablespoons unsalted butter

1. In a bowl, combine the spinach, scallion and Parmesan; season with salt and pepper. In a large skillet, cook the bacon over moderately high heat until crisp, 4 minutes. Transfer to the bowl.

2. Season the cutlets with salt and pepper. Spread the spinach on the cutlets, fold in half and press to close. Heat the skillet with the bacon fat until sizzling. Add the chicken and cook over high heat, turning once, until cooked through, 6 minutes; transfer to a platter and keep warm. Add the vinegar to the skillet; cook for 30 seconds. Off the heat, swirl in the butter until melted. Spoon the sauce over the chicken; serve. —*Grace Parisi*

WINE Tart, low-tannin Barbera.

Parmesan-Crusted Chicken with Arugula Salad

TOTAL: 30 MIN

4 SERVINGS ● ● ●

- 1 tablespoon Dijon mustard
- 1 tablespoon extra-virgin olive oil
- ½ teaspoon chopped thyme

Four 6-ounce skinless, boneless chicken breast halves

Salt and freshly ground pepper

- ½ cup freshly grated Parmesan cheese (1½ ounces)
- 4 cups packed arugula leaves
- 1 cup cherry tomatoes, halved

1. Preheat the oven to 475°. In a small bowl, combine 2 teaspoons of the mustard with 2 teaspoons of the olive oil and the thyme. Season the chicken breasts with salt and pepper, then brush them all over with the mustard mixture. Pat 2 tablespoons of the Parmesan all over each breast. Transfer the chicken breasts to a rimmed baking sheet. Bake the chicken on the top shelf of the oven for about 15 minutes, or until just cooked through and nicely browned.

2. Meanwhile, in a medium bowl, combine the remaining 1 teaspoon each of mustard and olive oil; stir in ½ teaspoon of water. Add the arugula and tomatoes, season with salt and pepper and toss well. Spoon the salad onto plates, top with the chicken and serve.
—*Marcia Kiesel*

WINE Light, zesty, fruity Dolcetto.

Citrus Chicken with Habanero Honey

ACTIVE: 25 MIN; TOTAL: 45 MIN

4 SERVINGS ●

- 2 oranges
- 2 pink grapefruits
- 1 tablespoon extra-virgin olive oil

Four 6-ounce skinless, boneless chicken breast halves

Salt and freshly ground pepper

- 2 tablespoons honey
- ½ large habanero chile, seeded and minced

Fresh lemon juice, for serving

1. Preheat the oven to 450°. Finely grate ½ teaspoon of zest from 1 of the oranges. Using a small, sharp knife, peel all of the oranges and grapefruits, removing and discarding all of the bitter white pith. Working over a bowl, cut in between the membranes to release the orange and grapefruit sections into the bowl. Squeeze the juice from the membranes into a glass measuring cup; you should have 1 cup.

2. In a medium ovenproof skillet, heat the olive oil until shimmering. Add the chicken breasts, season with salt and pepper and cook over moderately high heat until browned, about 2 minutes per side. Transfer the skillet to the oven and roast the chicken for 4 to 5 minutes, or until just cooked through.

3. Transfer the chicken to a warmed platter and cover loosely with foil. Add the ½ teaspoon of orange zest and the citrus juices to the skillet and simmer over high heat until reduced by one-third, about 4 minutes. Add the honey and habanero and simmer over moderate heat for 2 minutes. Stir in the orange and grapefruit sections and season with salt and pepper. Return the chicken breasts and any accumulated juices to the skillet and warm over low heat for 1 minute. Season with lemon juice. Spoon the chicken breasts, citrus sections and sauce onto plates and serve at once. —*Eberhard Müller*

WINE Soft, off-dry Riesling.

TASTE TEST · canned chicken broth

Only 17 percent of the respondents to a recent F&W/AOL poll told us they wish they had time to make chicken stock from scratch—which suggests most people are happy to use canned broth instead. We tested supermarket brands and picked our three favorites.

PRODUCT	F&W COMMENT	INTERESTING BITE
College Inn Chicken Broth	"Well-seasoned, with a rich chicken flavor."	The brand began as a line of canned foods from a Chicago hotel whose chef loved cooking with broth.
Health Valley Fat-Free Chicken Broth	"Nice aroma and a natural, clean taste."	Consistent with its all-natural philosophy, Health Valley prints its labels with soy ink.
Swanson Natural Goodness Chicken Broth	"Tastes like chicken and not much else—which is great."	The company, created in 1899, was named after 23-year-old Swedish cofounder Carl Swanson.

CHICKEN-ALMOND CURRY WITH APRICOTS

CHICKEN WITH FRESH APRICOTS, GINGER AND ALMONDS

Chicken-Almond Curry with Apricots

ACTIVE: 25 MIN; TOTAL: 40 MIN

4 SERVINGS ●

- ⅓ cup whole almonds
- 12 dried apricots (3 ounces)
- Boiling water
- 1½ tablespoons vegetable oil
- Four 6-ounce skinless, boneless chicken breast halves
- Salt and freshly ground pepper
- 2 tablespoons finely grated fresh ginger
- 2 large garlic cloves, minced
- 1 large onion, finely chopped
- 1½ tablespoons curry powder
- ¼ teaspoon cayenne pepper
- 2 cups chicken stock or low-sodium broth
- 2 tablespoons plain low-fat yogurt
- 2 scallions, sliced on the diagonal

I. In a mini food processor, grind the almonds to a powder. In a small heat-proof bowl, soak the apricots in boiling water until plump, 20 minutes; drain.

2. In a large nonstick skillet, heat 1 tablespoon of the oil. Add the chicken breasts, season with salt and pepper and cook over moderately high heat until browned, about 3 minutes per side. Transfer to a large plate.

3. Add the ginger, garlic, onion and the remaining ½ tablespoon of oil to the skillet and cook over low heat, stirring, until softened, about 10 minutes. Add the curry powder and cayenne and stir until fragrant, about 3 minutes. Add the ground almonds and stock and bring to a simmer. Return the chicken breasts to the skillet and add the apricots. Simmer over low heat for 5 minutes.

4. Transfer the chicken to a platter. Boil the sauce over moderate heat until thickened, about 8 minutes. Stir in the yogurt; season with salt and pepper. Pour the sauce over the chicken, scatter the scallions on top and serve. —*Priscilla Martel*
WINE Spicy New World Gewürztraminer.

Chicken with Fresh Apricots, Ginger and Cracked Almonds

TOTAL: 30 MIN

4 SERVINGS ● ● ●

16 whole blanched almonds
(2 ounces)

2 teaspoons unsalted butter

4 ripe apricots, pitted and quartered

1 tablespoon extra-virgin olive oil

Four 6-ounce skinless, boneless
chicken breast halves

Salt and freshly ground pepper

1 teaspoon finely grated
fresh ginger

1 scallion, white and green parts
thinly sliced separately

½ teaspoon very finely grated
lime zest

½ Scotch bonnet or habanero chile,
seeded and thinly sliced

½ cup dry white wine

2 tablespoons pure maple syrup

1. Preheat the oven to 350°. Put the almonds in a pie plate and bake for 8 minutes, or until fragrant and browned; let cool. Crack the almonds coarsely with the side of a large knife.

2. In a large skillet, melt the butter. Add the apricots, cut side down, and cook over moderate heat until lightly browned, about 3 minutes. Turn the apricots and cook for 1 minute longer. Transfer to a plate.

3. Add the olive oil to the skillet and heat until shimmering. Season the chicken breasts with salt and pepper and add to the skillet. Cook over moderately high heat until browned, about 3 minutes. Turn the breasts and cook over moderately low heat until just white throughout, about 7 minutes longer. Transfer the chicken to the plate with the apricots.

4. Add the ginger, scallion whites, lime zest and chile to the skillet and cook, stirring, for 30 seconds. Add the wine and simmer over moderately high heat, scraping up the browned bits from the bottom of the skillet. Add the maple syrup, apricots and chicken and simmer just until heated through; season with salt and pepper.

5. Transfer the chicken to plates and spoon the sauce on top. Sprinkle with the cracked almonds and scallion greens and serve. —*Marcia Kiesel*

WINE Bright, citrusy Riesling.

Grilled Chicken Paillards with Cilantro-Mint Dressing

TOTAL: 25 MIN

4 SERVINGS ● ●

1 cup lightly packed cilantro leaves

¼ cup lightly packed mint leaves

1 garlic clove, smashed

1 Jalapeño, sliced (with seeds)

1 tablespoon sugar

¼ cup water

3 tablespoons fresh lime juice

2 tablespoons grapeseed or
canola oil

Kosher salt and freshly ground pepper

Four 6-ounce skinless, boneless
chicken breast halves, tenders
removed and reserved for
another use

1. Light a grill or preheat a cast-iron grill pan. In a blender or food processor, combine the cilantro, mint, garlic, jalapeño and sugar and pulse until chopped. Add the water, lime juice and 1½ tablespoons of the grapeseed oil and process until fairly smooth; season with salt and pepper.

2. Lightly pound the breasts to an even ½-inch thickness. Brush the chicken with the remaining ½ tablespoon of grapeseed oil and season with salt and pepper. Grill over a moderately hot fire, turning once, until lightly charred and cooked through, about 6 minutes. Transfer the chicken to plates, spoon some of the dressing on top and serve, passing extra dressing on the side.
—*Grace Parisi*

SERVE WITH Couscous or rice.

WINE Dry, rich Champagne.

Chile-Glazed Chicken Wings

TOTAL: 35 MIN

4 SERVINGS ● ●

Vegetable oil spray

5 pounds chicken wings, tips
discarded, wings cut in half
at the joint

Kosher salt and freshly ground pepper

½ cup sake

½ cup fresh orange juice

½ cup dark brown sugar

¼ cup low-sodium soy sauce

2 tablespoons Asian sesame oil

1 tablespoon finely chopped
lemongrass or 1 teaspoon finely
grated lemon zest

1 tablespoon finely grated
fresh ginger

3 large garlic cloves, finely chopped

¾ teaspoon crushed red pepper

2 tablespoons fresh lime juice

1. Preheat the oven to 500°. Spray 2 large rimmed baking sheets with vegetable oil spray. Spread the chicken wings on the baking sheets; season with salt and pepper. Bake for 20 minutes, or until the wings are cooked through and lightly browned.

2. Meanwhile, in a medium saucepan, combine the sake, orange juice, brown sugar, soy sauce, sesame oil, lemongrass, ginger, garlic and crushed red pepper. Boil over moderate heat, stirring occasionally, until the glaze is reduced to 1 cup, about 10 minutes. Stir in the lime juice. Pour half of the glaze into a small serving bowl.

3. Preheat the broiler. Transfer the wings to a large bowl and toss with the remaining glaze. Spread the wings on 1 of the baking sheets and broil on the middle rack of the oven for 10 minutes, turning once, until browned. Transfer to a platter. Serve with the remaining glaze.
—*Megan Moore*

MAKE AHEAD The wings can be kept at room temperature for up to 3 hours.

WINE Dry, fruity sparkling wine.

● **FAST** ● **HEALTHY** ● **MAKE AHEAD** ● **STAFF FAVORITE**

poultry

Spicy Southern Barbecued Chicken

ACTIVE: 1 HR 15 MIN; TOTAL: 2 HR 45 MIN

4 SERVINGS

Kosher salt

2 quarts cold water

One 3½-pound chicken, cut into 8 pieces

4 tablespoons unsalted butter

½ cup minced onion

2 large garlic cloves, minced

1½ teaspoons sweet paprika

1½ teaspoons ancho chile powder

½ teaspoon crushed red pepper

½ cup packed dark brown sugar

½ cup cider vinegar

½ cup tomato paste

2 tablespoons unsulfured molasses

1. In a large bowl, dissolve ¼ cup of kosher salt in the cold water. Add the chicken and refrigerate for 2 hours.

2. Melt the butter in a saucepan. Add the onion and garlic and cook over low heat until softened. Add the paprika, ancho powder and crushed red pepper; cook, stirring, for 1 minute. Add 1 cup of water, the brown sugar and vinegar and bring to a simmer. Stir in the tomato paste and molasses and simmer over low heat, stirring, until the sauce is thickened, about 10 minutes. Season with salt and let cool.

3. Light a grill or preheat the oven to 500°. Drain the chicken; pat dry. Grill over a moderately low fire, turning, until just cooked through (25 minutes for the white meat, 35 minutes for the dark). Or roast the chicken, skin side up, on a rimmed baking sheet until just cooked through (25 minutes for white meat, 35 to 40 minutes for dark).

4. Set aside half of the sauce; brush the remaining sauce on the chicken. Continue grilling or roasting the chicken for 10 minutes, or until nicely glazed. Serve with the reserved sauce. —*Scott Peacock*

MAKE AHEAD The barbecue sauce can be refrigerated for up to 1 week.

WINE Spicy New World Gewürztraminer.

Buttermilk Fried Chicken

TOTAL: 4 HR 30 MIN

6 TO 8 SERVINGS ● ◐

A sugar-and-salt-spiked whole milk brine makes this chicken sweet and juicy; a mixture of buttermilk, flour, baking powder and baking soda yields an extra crisp crust.

1 quart whole milk

Kosher salt

½ cup sugar

Two 4-pound chickens, each cut into 8 pieces

2 cups buttermilk

2 large eggs, lightly beaten

1 teaspoon sweet paprika

1 teaspoon hot sauce

½ teaspoon freshly ground pepper

2 teaspoons baking powder

1½ teaspoons baking soda

About 5 cups all-purpose flour

1 quart vegetable oil, for frying

1. In a small saucepan, combine 1 cup of the milk with ¾ cup of kosher salt and the sugar and stir over moderate heat just until the sugar and salt dissolve, about 2 minutes. Transfer to a large, deep bowl and add the remaining 3 cups of milk. Add the chicken pieces and refrigerate for 4 hours. Drain the chicken and pat thoroughly dry.

2. In a bowl, mix the buttermilk, eggs, 2 tablespoons of salt, the paprika, hot sauce and pepper. Whisk in the baking powder and baking soda. Put half of the flour in a large bowl. Working with a few pieces at a time, dredge the chicken in the flour, tapping off any excess. Dip the chicken in the buttermilk mixture, letting the excess drip off; return the chicken to the flour and turn to coat. Transfer to a rack. Repeat with the remaining chicken, adding more flour as needed. If the flour becomes too lumpy, sift it.

3. Heat the oil in 2 large, deep skillets until shimmering. Working in batches, add the coated chicken to the skillets in a single layer, without crowding. Fry the chicken pieces over moderate heat, turning occasionally with tongs, until deep golden and cooked all the way through, 18 to 20 minutes; an instant-read thermometer inserted near the bone should register 160°. Drain the chicken on wire racks lined with paper towels. Follow the same procedure to fry the remaining pieces. Serve hot or warm. —*Dave Arnold*

MAKE AHEAD The chicken can be fried up to 4 hours ahead and reheated.

WINE Ripe, creamy-textured Chardonnay.

Fried Chicken with Tomato Gravy

ACTIVE: 1 HR 30 MIN; TOTAL: 9 HR 30 MIN

4 SERVINGS

This chicken is tenderized by a nice long soak in tangy buttermilk and served with a generous amount of tomato gravy. Serve any leftover gravy with homemade biscuits such as the Angel Biscuits on page 280.

½ cup kosher salt

2 quarts cold water

One 3½-pound chicken, cut into 8 pieces

3 cups buttermilk

1½ cups all-purpose flour

¼ cup cornstarch

2 tablespoons potato starch (optional)

Fine sea salt and freshly ground pepper

1 pound lard or solid vegetable shortening, for frying

1 stick (4 ounces) unsalted butter

¼ pound sliced bacon

1 small onion, finely chopped (about ½ cup)

1 garlic clove, minced

4 cups drained canned diced tomatoes (from three 14-ounce cans)

2 teaspoons dried thyme

2 cups heavy cream

1½ cups whole milk

1. In a large bowl, dissolve the kosher salt in the cold water. Add the chicken, cover and refrigerate for 4 hours. Drain and rinse the chicken. Put the chicken in a large bowl, add the buttermilk and turn the pieces to coat. Cover and refrigerate for 4 hours.

2. In a large, sturdy plastic bag, combine the flour, cornstarch, potato starch, 1½ teaspoons of sea salt and ½ teaspoon of pepper and shake. Set aside ½ cup of the flour mixture for the gravy. Lift the chicken out of the buttermilk, wipe off any excess and set the pieces on a wire rack; let dry for 5 minutes. Add the chicken, a few pieces at a time, to the flour mixture in the bag; shake to coat. Dry the rack. Shake off any excess flour and return the chicken to the rack.

3. Meanwhile, in a large cast-iron skillet, melt the lard and butter. Add the bacon and cook over moderate heat until crisp, about 5 minutes; reserve the bacon for another use. Add the chicken, in batches if necessary, and cook over moderate heat, turning, until golden, crisp and cooked through, about 30 minutes. Lower the heat if necessary. Set the chicken on a clean wire rack to drain.

4. Transfer ¼ cup of the chicken cooking fat to a large saucepan. Add the onion and garlic and cook over moderate heat, stirring occasionally, until the onion is golden, about 5 minutes. Add the reserved ½ cup of seasoned flour and cook, whisking, for 2 minutes. Add the tomatoes and thyme and stir constantly until blended. Whisk in the cream and milk until the sauce is smooth. Season with sea salt and pepper and cook over moderate heat, stirring occasionally, until thickened and no floury taste remains, about 10 minutes.

5. Transfer the fried chicken to a platter. Pour the tomato gravy into a gravy boat and serve alongside the chicken.
—Scott Peacock
WINE Soft, earthy Rioja.

BUTTERMILK FRIED CHICKEN

SPICY SOUTHERN BARBECUED CHICKEN

poultry

Fried Chicken Littles

ACTIVE: 30 MIN; TOTAL: 1 HR

4 TO 6 SERVINGS

The secret ingredient in the batter for these chicken drumettes is self-rising flour, which makes the coating as crisp and airy as a good fritter. Drumettes are what supermarkets label their precut chicken wing parts (you might also see the name wingettes).

- 1 cup mayonnaise
- ¼ cup fresh lime juice
- 1 tablespoon minced onion
- 1½ teaspoons minced garlic
- 1 tablespoon *harissa* (see Note)
- 1 tablespoon pure ancho chile powder

Kosher salt and freshly ground white pepper

Sweet paprika

- 1 teaspoon cayenne pepper
- 1½ cups plus 2 tablespoons all-purpose flour
- ½ cup self-rising flour, or
   - ½ cup all-purpose flour plus
   - ½ teaspoon baking powder and a pinch of salt
- ½ teaspoon baking powder
- 1¾ cups water

Vegetable oil, for frying

- 4 pounds chicken drumettes

1. In a medium bowl, whisk the mayonnaise with the lime juice, onion, garlic, *harissa* and ancho chile powder. Stir in 1½ teaspoons each of salt, white pepper and paprika and the cayenne. Refrigerate until chilled.

2. In another medium bowl, combine the all-purpose and self-rising flours with the baking powder and ½ teaspoon of salt. Add the water. Using an electric mixer, beat the batter at medium speed until smooth, about 5 minutes.

3. In a large saucepan, heat 3 inches of vegetable oil to 350°. In a large, sturdy, resealable plastic bag, combine 1 teaspoon each of salt, white pepper and paprika. Add the chicken, seal the bag and shake until the drumettes are evenly coated.

4. Dip 10 of the drumettes into the prepared batter, then carefully slide them one by one into the hot oil, letting any excess batter drip back into the bowl. Fry the drumettes until golden and risen to the surface, about 12 minutes. Using a slotted spoon, drain the drumettes on a paper towel–lined wire rack. Dip and fry the remaining drumettes in batches. Serve the chicken with the chile mayonnaise.

—*Leonard Schwartz and Michael Rosen*

NOTE *Harissa,* a spicy Tunisian pepper paste, is available at specialty food shops.

MAKE AHEAD The mayonnaise can be refrigerated overnight.

WINE Dry, mineral-flavored Chenin Blanc.

Sweet Crunchy Mustard Chicken

ACTIVE: 5 MIN; TOTAL: 30 MIN

4 SERVINGS ● ●

- 3 tablespoons fine dry bread crumbs
- 2 teaspoons light brown sugar
- 1 teaspoon dried tarragon or basil
- 1 teaspoon kosher salt
- ½ teaspoon freshly ground pepper
- 2 tablespoons Dijon mustard

Four ½-pound bone-in chicken breast halves, with skin

Lemon wedges, for serving

Preheat the oven to 500°. In a small bowl, mix the bread crumbs, light brown sugar, tarragon or basil, kosher salt and pepper. Spread the mustard all over the chicken breast skin and sprinkle with the crumb mixture. Set the breasts, skin side up, in a 9-by-13-inch glass or ceramic baking dish and roast in the upper third of the oven for about 25 minutes, or until they are cooked through and crisp. Serve the chicken breasts hot, with lemon wedges.

—*Sally Sampson*

WINE Light, fruity Beaujolais.

Ginger-Sesame Chicken with Bok Choy and Mushrooms

TOTAL: 30 MIN

4 SERVINGS ● ●

- ½ cup chicken stock or canned low-sodium broth
- 3 tablespoons low-sodium soy sauce
- 1 tablespoon sherry
- 1 tablespoon sugar
- 1 teaspoon cornstarch dissolved in 1 tablespoon water
- ½ teaspoon unseasoned rice vinegar
- ½ teaspoon Asian sesame oil
- ½ teaspoon crushed red pepper
- 3 tablespoons canola oil
- ¾ pound oyster mushrooms, thickly sliced

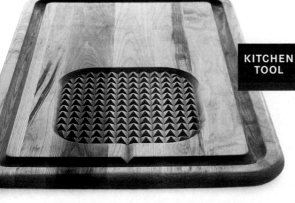

¾ pound skinless, boneless chicken breasts, cut into 1-inch pieces

Salt and freshly ground pepper

¾ pound bok choy, thickly sliced crosswise

1 small red bell pepper, cut into ¾-inch pieces

2 tablespoons finely chopped fresh ginger

1 medium garlic clove, very finely chopped

1. In a small jar, combine the chicken stock, soy sauce, sherry, sugar, cornstarch, rice vinegar, sesame oil and red pepper; shake well.

2. In a large nonstick skillet, heat 2 teaspoons of the canola oil until shimmering. Add the oyster mushrooms and cook over high heat, stirring occasionally, until browned and tender, about 6 minutes. Transfer the mushrooms to a large plate.

3. Add another 2 teaspoons of canola oil to the skillet. Season the chicken breast pieces generously with salt and pepper, add them to the skillet and cook over high heat, stirring, until they are golden and just barely cooked through, about 4 minutes. Transfer the chicken pieces to the plate with the oyster mushrooms.

4. Add 1 tablespoon of canola oil to the skillet along with the bok choy and red bell pepper and cook over high heat, stirring occasionally, until crisp-tender, about 3 minutes. Transfer the vegetables to the plate.

5. Add the remaining 2 teaspoons of canola oil to the skillet along with the ginger and garlic and cook, stirring, for 1 minute. Return the chicken and vegetables to the skillet. Shake the sauce and add it to the skillet. Bring to a boil and simmer, stirring, until it is slightly thickened, about 1 minute. Transfer the chicken and vegetables to a bowl and serve. —*Grace Parisi*

SERVE WITH Steamed rice.

WINE Spicy Alsace Gewürztraminer.

Crisp Indian-Spiced Chicken with Cucumber-Tomato Raita

TOTAL: 30 MIN

4 SERVINGS ●

It's amazing how flavorful and crispy a store-bought rotisserie chicken can become when basted with butter and a few Indian spices. It's especially delicious served with a cooling raita, the popular Indian yogurt condiment. (Be sure to salt the vegetables for the raita before you start preparing the chicken: They can be draining while you cook the rest of the dish.)

One 3½-pound plain rotisserie chicken

1 stick (4 ounces) unsalted butter, cut into tablespoons

2 teaspoons ground cumin

2 teaspoons ground cinnamon

2 teaspoons sugar

1 teaspoon ground coriander

½ teaspoon ground cardamom

½ teaspoon turmeric

½ teaspoon kosher salt

¼ teaspoon ground cloves

¼ teaspoon cayenne pepper

Cucumber-Tomato Raita (recipe follows)

1. Preheat the broiler. Using poultry shears, cut along each side of the chicken backbone and remove it. Spread the chicken, skin side up, in a medium roasting pan. Reserve any accumulated chicken juices.

2. In a small saucepan, melt the butter with the reserved chicken juices over moderately low heat. Stir in the ground cumin and cinnamon, the sugar, the ground coriander and cardamom, the turmeric, salt, cloves and cayenne and cook over low heat, stirring, until fragrant, about 3 minutes.

3. Brush half of the Indian-spiced melted butter all over the chicken's skin. Broil the chicken 6 inches from the heat for 5 minutes, or until the skin is crisp and the meat is warmed through (shift the roasting pan occasionally, turning the front to the back as necessary to prevent the skin from charring).

4. Stir the rest of the Indian-spiced butter and generously brush it all over the crisp chicken skin. Cut the chicken into quarters, then transfer the pieces to large dinner plates. Serve the spiced chicken immediately, passing the Cucumber-Tomato Raita at the table. —*David Rosengarten*

SERVE WITH Sautéed spinach and warm nan or pita bread.

WINE Round, supple, fruity Syrah.

Cucumber-Tomato Raita

ACTIVE: 10 MIN; TOTAL: 25 MIN

MAKES ABOUT 1¼ CUPS ● ● ●

1 medium cucumber—peeled, halved, seeded and coarsely shredded

1 small tomato—halved, seeded and finely diced

Kosher salt

¾ cup plain whole milk yogurt

¼ cup sour cream

1 small jalapeño, seeded and minced

2 tablespoons chopped mint, plus more for garnish

1 tablespoon fresh lemon juice

¼ teaspoon ground cumin

1. Place the shredded cucumber and diced tomato in a fine strainer set over a bowl and sprinkle with ¼ teaspoon of kosher salt. Let the vegetables stand and drain for 20 minutes.

2. Lightly press the cucumber-tomato mixture to release any excess liquid; transfer the cucumber-tomato mixture to a serving bowl. Discard the liquid. Stir in the yogurt, sour cream, minced jalapeño, 2 tablespoons of chopped mint and the lemon juice and cumin. Season the raita with salt, garnish with chopped mint and serve. —*D.R.*

MAKE AHEAD The raita can be refrigerated for up to 2 days.

CRISPY GARLIC CHICKEN WITH DIPPING SALT

Crispy Garlic Chicken with Dipping Salt

ACTIVE: 30 MIN; TOTAL: 14 HR 30 MIN

4 SERVINGS ●

One of the reasons this supermoist Hong Kong–style chicken is so good is that the chicken is fried whole in a wok, yet it doesn't taste remotely oily. The other reason is that the chicken is rubbed with aromatic five-spice powder and salt 4 hours before being basted with a vinegar and brown sugar syrup, then marinated overnight; plan accordingly.

Kosher salt

- 1 teaspoon five-spice powder
- 1 chicken bouillon cube (12 grams)

One 3½-pound chicken

- 2 cups distilled white vinegar
- 1 cup water
- 1 cup light brown sugar
- 1 teaspoon baking powder
- 3¼ cups vegetable oil
- 1 tablespoon Sichuan peppercorns
- 8 large garlic cloves, very finely chopped

I. Set a fine sieve over a small bowl. Add 2 tablespoons of kosher salt and the five-spice powder and bouillon cube; rub them through the sieve. Set the chicken on a platter. Rub the spice blend all over the chicken inside and out and refrigerate it for 4 hours.

2. In a saucepan, combine the vinegar, water, brown sugar and baking powder and cook over moderately high heat, stirring, until the sugar has dissolved. Transfer the syrup to a large bowl and let cool to room temperature. Stand the chicken in the syrup and ladle the syrup over it several times. Transfer the chicken to a rack set over a plate and refrigerate overnight. Bring to room temperature before cooking.

3. Pat the chicken dry inside and out. In a large wok, heat 3 cups of the oil to 375° over moderately high heat. Carefully lower the chicken into the hot oil, breast side up, and cook until the skin is deeply browned on the bottom, about 20 minutes. Insert a large fork into the chicken cavity and carefully transfer to a plate. Turn the chicken over and lower it into the hot oil, breast side down. Fry the chicken until deeply browned on the breast side, about 20 minutes longer.

4. Meanwhile, in a small skillet, toast the Sichuan peppercorns over moderate heat until fragrant, about 3 minutes. Transfer to a spice grinder and let cool. Add 3 tablespoons of kosher salt and grind to a fine powder.

5. In a small skillet, heat the remaining ¼ cup of oil. Add the garlic and cook over low heat until golden, about 4 minutes. Pour the garlic and oil into a small bowl.

6. Transfer the chicken to a carving board, breast side up, and let rest for 10 minutes. Carve and arrange the pieces on a platter. Scatter the garlic and oil all over the chicken and serve with the dipping salt. —*Jean-Georges Vongerichten*

MAKE AHEAD The dipping salt can be made up to 2 weeks ahead.

WINE Medium-bodied, round Pinot Blanc.

Jamaican Jerk Chicken

ACTIVE: 30 MIN; TOTAL: 9 HR

8 SERVINGS

For maximum flavor, let the chicken marinate overnight.

- 1 medium onion, coarsely chopped
- 3 medium scallions, chopped
- 2 Scotch bonnet chiles, chopped
- 2 garlic cloves, chopped
- 1 tablespoon five-spice powder
- 1 tablespoon allspice berries, coarsely ground
- 1 tablespoon coarsely ground pepper
- 1 teaspoon dried thyme, crumbled
- 1 teaspoon freshly grated nutmeg
- 1 teaspoon salt
- ½ cup soy sauce
- 1 tablespoon vegetable oil

Two 3½- to 4-pound chickens, quartered

I. In a food processor, combine the onion, scallions, chiles, garlic, five-spice powder, allspice, pepper, thyme, nutmeg and salt; process to a coarse paste. With the machine on, add the soy sauce and oil in a steady stream. Pour the marinade into a large, shallow dish, add the chicken and turn to coat. Cover and refrigerate overnight. Bring the chicken to room temperature before proceeding.

2. Light a grill. Grill the chicken over a medium-hot fire, turning occasionally, until well browned and cooked through, 35 to 40 minutes. (Cover the grill for a smokier flavor.) Transfer the chicken to a platter and serve. —*Paul Chung*

WINE Light, soft Chenin Blanc.

Asian-Style Orange Chicken

ACTIVE: 10 MIN; TOTAL: 35 MIN

4 SERVINGS ● ●

- 2 tablespoons soy sauce
- 2 tablespoons brown sugar
- 2 tablespoons thawed orange juice concentrate
- 2 garlic cloves, minced
- 1 teaspoon finely grated orange zest
- 1 teaspoon minced fresh ginger
- 1 teaspoon kosher salt
- ½ teaspoon freshly ground pepper

Four ½-pound bone-in chicken breast halves, with skin

I. Preheat the oven to 500°. In a medium bowl, combine the soy sauce with the brown sugar, orange juice concentrate, garlic, orange zest, ginger, salt and pepper. Add the chicken breasts and turn to coat. Transfer the chicken to a baking dish, skin side up.

2. Roast the chicken in the center of the oven for 25 minutes, basting with the sauce 4 times, until the chicken is just cooked through and nicely glazed. Turn on the broiler and broil the chicken until browned all over, about 2 minutes. —*Sally Sampson*

WINE Bright, citrusy Riesling.

poultry

Asian-Style Chicken Breasts and Bacon

TOTAL: 50 MIN

4 SERVINGS

- ¾ cup chicken or beef stock
- ¼ teaspoon Chinese five-spice powder
- 2 tablespoons peanut oil
- ½ pound lean slab bacon, cut into 1½-inch pieces
- 4 large garlic cloves, cut into ⅛-inch-thick slices
- ½ pound skinless, boneless chicken breasts, cut into 1½-inch pieces

Salt and freshly ground pepper

- ½ pound white mushrooms, stems discarded, caps quartered
- ½ cup dry white wine
- 1 tablespoon soy sauce
- 2 scallions, cut into 1-inch lengths

1. In a saucepan, combine the stock and five-spice powder and simmer over low heat for 3 minutes. Set the stock aside.

2. In a skillet, heat 1 tablespoon of the oil. Add the bacon and cook over low heat, turning, until the fat is rendered, 15 minutes. Transfer the bacon to a plate.

3. Add the garlic to the fat in the skillet and cook over low heat until golden, 5 minutes. Add the garlic to the bacon. Add the chicken pieces to the skillet, season with salt and pepper and cook over moderate heat until browned and just cooked through, about 8 minutes. Transfer the chicken to the plate.

4. Heat the remaining 1 tablespoon of oil in the skillet. Add the mushrooms and cook over moderate heat until all of their liquid has evaporated and they start to brown, about 8 minutes. Transfer the mushrooms to the plate. Add the wine to the skillet and simmer until reduced by half, about 4 minutes. Add the soy sauce, spiced stock, bacon, garlic, chicken and mushrooms to the skillet and cook, stirring, until heated through. Add the scallions and serve. *—Marcia Kiesel*

SERVE WITH Steamed rice.

WINE Soft, off-dry Riesling.

Thai Chicken with Mushrooms, Green Beans and Basil

TOTAL: 25 MIN

4 SERVINGS ● ●

- 1½ tablespoons oyster sauce
- 1 tablespoon Asian fish sauce
- 1 teaspoon sugar
- 2½ tablespoons vegetable oil
- ½ pound green beans, cut into 2-inch lengths
- 3 scallions, white and light green parts only, cut into 1-inch lengths
- 2 large garlic cloves, minced
- ½ teaspoon salt
- ¾ pound skinless, boneless chicken breasts, pounded thin and cut into strips
- ¼ pound small mushrooms, stemmed and quartered
- ½ cup drained canned baby corn, cut into 1-inch lengths
- 2 large jalapeños—halved, seeded and thickly sliced lengthwise
- 1 cup torn basil leaves

1. In a small bowl, mix the oyster sauce with the fish sauce and sugar.

2. In a wok, heat ½ tablespoon of the oil over high heat. Add the beans and cook, stirring occasionally, until crisp-tender, about 5 minutes. Transfer to a plate.

3. Add the remaining 2 tablespoons of oil to the wok and heat until smoking.

Add the scallions, garlic and salt and stir-fry for 45 seconds. Add the chicken in 3 batches, waiting a few seconds between additions, and stir-fry until it barely turns white, about 2 minutes. Add the mushrooms, corn, jalapeños and green beans and stir-fry until the vegetables are crisp-tender, 2 to 3 minutes. Add the oyster sauce mixture and stir-fry until the chicken is just cooked through, about 2 minutes longer. Stir in the basil, transfer to a platter and serve. *—Joyce Jue*

WINE Light, spicy Pinot Grigio.

Chicken Skewers with Fresh Herb Vinaigrette and Feta

TOTAL: 30 MIN

4 SERVINGS ● ●

- 1¼ pounds skinless, boneless chicken breasts, cut into 1½-inch pieces
- 16 yellow baby pattypan squash
- 1 large red onion, cut into 1½-inch pieces
- 8 small tomatillos, halved
- 3 tablespoons extra-virgin olive oil

Salt and freshly ground pepper

- 3 tablespoons chopped mint
- 2 tablespoons chopped parsley
- 1 garlic clove, minced
- 1 tablespoon red wine vinegar
- 1 ounce crumbled feta cheese

1. Preheat a grill or grill pan. On four 14-inch skewers, thread the chicken, squash, onion and tomatillos. Brush with 1 tablespoon of the olive oil and season with salt and pepper.

2. Grill the skewers over a medium-hot fire, turning, until the chicken is cooked through and the vegetables are lightly charred, about 12 minutes.

3. Combine the mint, parsley, garlic, vinegar and remaining 2 tablespoons olive oil; season with salt and pepper.

4. Put the chicken and vegetables on plates. Spoon the vinaigrette on top and sprinkle with the feta. *—Marcia Kiesel*

WINE Dry, medium-bodied Pinot Gris.

COOKING TIP

chicken paillard

SUPERMARKETS SELL THIN boneless chicken breasts, but you can pound your own if they're unavailable. Place boneless, skinless breasts between sheets of wax paper or plastic wrap and pound with the flat side of a meat tenderizer or a cleaver until they are the desired thickness.

Chicken Tikka Masala

ACTIVE: 45 MIN; TOTAL: 9 HR 30 MIN

4 SERVINGS ● ●

Chicken Tikka Masala is often the first dish people try when exploring Indian food. This classic version is easy to prepare, and its slightly spicy tomato cream sauce is addictive. The chicken needs to marinate overnight, so plan accordingly.

MASALA MARINADE

- 1 cup plain low-fat yogurt
- 2 garlic cloves, minced
- 1 tablespoon finely grated fresh ginger
- 1½ teaspoons ground cumin
- 1½ teaspoons ground coriander
- ¼ teaspoon ground cardamom
- ¼ teaspoon cayenne pepper
- ¼ teaspoon ground turmeric

Salt and freshly ground pepper

CHICKEN

- 2½ pounds skinless, boneless chicken thighs, fat trimmed

Salt and freshly ground pepper

- 2 tablespoons plus 1 teaspoon vegetable oil
- ¼ cup blanched whole almonds
- 1 large onion, finely chopped
- 2 garlic cloves, minced
- 1 teaspoon minced fresh ginger
- 1½ tablespoons garam masala
- 1½ teaspoons pure chile powder
- ½ teaspoon cayenne pepper

One 35-ounce can peeled tomatoes, finely chopped, juices reserved

Pinch of sugar

- 1 cup heavy cream

I. MAKE THE MASALA MARINADE: In a large glass or stainless steel bowl, combine the plain yogurt, garlic, ginger, cumin, coriander, cardamom, cayenne and turmeric. Season with salt and pepper and mix well.

2. PREPARE THE CHICKEN: Using a sharp knife, make several shallow slashes in each piece of chicken. Add the chicken to the marinade, turn to coat and refrigerate overnight.

3. Preheat the broiler and position a rack about 8 inches from the heat. Remove the chicken from the marinade; scrape off as much of the marinade as possible. Season the chicken with salt and pepper and spread the pieces on a baking sheet. Broil the chicken, turning once or twice, until just cooked through and browned in spots, about 12 minutes. Transfer to a cutting board and cut it into 2-inch pieces.

4. Meanwhile, in a small skillet, heat 1 teaspoon of the oil. Add the almonds and cook over moderate heat, stirring constantly, until golden, about 5 minutes. Transfer the almonds to a plate and let cool completely. In a food processor, pulse the almonds until finely ground.

5. In a large enameled cast-iron casserole, heat the remaining 2 tablespoons of oil until shimmering. Add the onion, garlic and ginger and cook over moderate heat, stirring occasionally, until tender and golden, about 8 minutes. Add the garam masala, chile powder and cayenne and cook, stirring, for 1 minute. Add the tomatoes with their juices and the sugar and season with salt and pepper. Cover partially and cook over moderate heat, stirring occasionally, until the sauce is slightly thickened, about 20 minutes. Add the cream and ground almonds and cook over low heat, stirring occasionally, until thickened, about 10 minutes longer. Stir in the chicken; simmer gently for 10 minutes, stirring frequently, and serve.

—*Grace Parisi*

VARIATION The marinade and sauce here are also delicious with shrimp, lamb and vegetables.

MAKE AHEAD The Chicken Tikka Masala can be refrigerated for up to 3 days. Reheat gently before serving.

SERVE WITH Steamed basmati rice, rice pilaf or warm nan.

WINE Bright, fruity rosé.

Chicken with Riesling

ACTIVE: 30 MIN; TOTAL: 1 HR 10 MIN

4 SERVINGS ● ●

- 5 tablespoons unsalted butter

One 3½-pound chicken, quartered

Salt and freshly ground pepper

- 1 large shallot, minced
- 2 tablespoons Cognac
- 1 cup dry Riesling
- 6 ounces white mushrooms, cut into ¼-inch-thick slices
- 1 tablespoon all-purpose flour
- ⅓ cup heavy cream

I. Melt 2 tablespoons of the butter in a skillet. Add the chicken, season with salt and pepper and cook over moderate heat until slightly browned, about 4 minutes per side. Add the shallot and cook, stirring, for 1 minute. Add the Cognac and carefully ignite it with a long match. When the flames subside, add the Riesling, cover and simmer over low heat until the chicken breasts are just cooked, about 25 minutes. Transfer to a large plate and cover with foil. Cover and simmer the legs until cooked through, about 10 minutes longer. Transfer to the plate.

2. In another skillet, melt 2 tablespoons of the butter. Add the mushrooms and season with salt and pepper. Cook over low heat until the liquid evaporates, about 7 minutes. Increase the heat to moderate and cook until browned, 3 minutes.

3. In a bowl, blend the flour and the remaining 1 tablespoon of butter. Stir the cream into the large skillet; bring to a simmer. Gradually whisk the flour paste into the cooking liquid and simmer, whisking, until no floury taste remains, 3 minutes. Season with salt and pepper. Return the chicken to the skillet, add the mushrooms and briefly reheat.

—*Jean-Georges Vongerichten*

MAKE AHEAD The chicken can be refrigerated overnight.

SERVE WITH Noodles, spaetzle, rice or boiled potatoes.

WINE Dry, full-flavored Alsace Riesling.

poultry

Chicken Stew with Chile

ACTIVE: 40 MIN; TOTAL: 2 HR

6 SERVINGS ●

Ají (made with chiles and tomatoes) is Ecuador's all-purpose condiment. While some versions are smooth purees, this chunky *ají* is more like a relish. If you would prefer a more fiery *ají,* include the seeds of the jalapeño.

AJÍ

- 1 large red onion, sliced paper-thin

Kosher salt

- 1 cup boiling water
- 1 plum tomato, seeded and chopped
- 1 large jalapeño or serrano chile, seeded and minced
- ¼ cup fresh lime juice
- 1½ tablespoons chopped cilantro

Freshly ground pepper

CHICKEN STEW

One 14½-ounce can whole plum tomatoes, drained

- 6 garlic cloves, coarsely chopped
- 1 large red onion, coarsely chopped
- 1½ teaspoons ground cumin

- ¾ cup chopped cilantro

Kosher salt

- 2 tablespoons Annatto Oil (recipe follows) or corn oil
- 4 pounds chicken drumsticks and thighs, excess fat trimmed

Freshly ground pepper

One 12-ounce bottle full-flavored beer, such as Dos Equis or Corona

1. MAKE THE AJÍ: In a heatproof bowl, toss the onion with 2 teaspoons of salt; let stand for 5 minutes. Add the boiling water and let stand for 10 minutes longer. Transfer to a colander to drain. Rinse under cold water and drain well; pat dry.

2. Dry the bowl and return the onion to it. Stir in the tomato, jalapeño, lime juice and cilantro; season with salt and pepper. Cover and let stand for 30 minutes.

3. PREPARE THE CHICKEN STEW: In a food processor, coarsely puree the tomatoes, garlic, onion, cumin, ½ cup of the cilantro and 1 teaspoon of salt.

4. Heat the Annatto Oil in an enameled cast-iron casserole. Season the chicken with salt and pepper. Working in 2 batches, cook the chicken over moderate heat, turning once, until golden, about 7 minutes per batch. Transfer to a plate. Pour off all but 1 tablespoon of the oil.

5. Add the tomato puree to the casserole and bring to a simmer over moderate heat. Return the chicken and its juices to the casserole and add the beer. Cover and simmer over low heat until the chicken is cooked through, about 30 minutes.

6. Transfer the chicken to a plate. Cook the sauce over moderate heat until thickened, about 15 minutes. Return the chicken to the sauce and bring to a simmer. Season with salt and pepper. Spoon the chicken onto a platter and garnish with the remaining ¼ cup of cilantro. Pass the *ají* at the table. —*Maricel Presilla*

MAKE AHEAD The *ají* can be refrigerated for up to 1 week. The stew can be refrigerated for up to 2 days and reheated.

WINE Spicy New World Gewürztraminer.

Annatto Oil

ACTIVE: 5 MIN; TOTAL: 35 MIN

MAKES ABOUT 1 CUP ● ●

Annatto seeds, also known as achiote seeds, are used throughout Latin America to add a distinctive red color to sautéed foods, especially chicken and seafood, as well as to rice pilaf. Annatto seeds are available at Latin American markets and in the Latin section of many supermarkets.

- 1 cup corn oil
- ¼ cup annatto seeds

In a small saucepan, combine the oil and annatto seeds and bring to a simmer over low heat. Remove the pan from the heat, cover and let the oil cool completely, about 30 minutes. Strain the Annatto Oil into a jar. —*M.P.*

MAKE AHEAD The Annatto Oil can be refrigerated in a tightly sealed jar for up to 2 months.

Mediterranean-Style Chicken and Bean Stew

ACTIVE: 35 MIN; TOTAL: 1 HR 15 MIN

4 SERVINGS ● ●

- 3 tablespoons extra-virgin olive oil
- 4 skinless whole chicken legs
- 1 fennel bulb—quartered, cored and thinly sliced crosswise
- 1 small onion, thinly sliced
- 2 large garlic cloves, thinly sliced

One 15-ounce can Roman or pinto beans, preferably Goya, drained and rinsed

One 12-ounce can whole tomatoes, finely chopped, juice reserved

- 12 oil-cured black olives, pitted and quartered lengthwise
- 6 sun-dried tomatoes, thinly sliced
- 1 tablespoon tomato paste
- 2 teaspoons coarsely chopped rosemary
- 1 large dried red chile (optional)

Salt and freshly ground pepper

- ½ cup water

1. Heat the olive oil in a large skillet. Add the chicken and cook over moderate heat until lightly browned, 4 minutes per side. Transfer to a platter.

2. Add the fennel, onion and garlic to the skillet and cook over moderately low heat, stirring occasionally, until softened, about 10 minutes. Stir in the beans to coat them with the oil, then add the chopped tomatoes with their juice, olives, sun-dried tomatoes, tomato paste, rosemary and chile. Season with salt and pepper and bring to a simmer. Cook over low heat until the juices thicken slightly, about 4 minutes. Add the chicken and water, cover and simmer until the chicken is tender, about 40 minutes; turn the chicken halfway through. Season the stew with salt and pepper and serve. —*Sophie Braimbridge*

MAKE AHEAD The chicken stew can be refrigerated for up to 2 days.

WINE Round, supple, fruity Syrah.

Chicken Tagine with Sweet Tomato Sauce

ACTIVE: 45 MIN; TOTAL: 1 HR 30 MIN

4 SERVINGS ●

This is a great dish for a buffet because it can be made ahead and served warm or at room temperature.

- 4 pounds plum tomatoes—peeled, seeded and coarsely chopped
- ¾ cup vegetable oil
- 6 cinnamon sticks
- ¼ teaspoon ground cinnamon

Salt

- ⅔ cup plus 3 tablespoons sugar
- ¼ cup water
- 1 teaspoon ground ginger
- 1 teaspoon salt
- ½ teaspoon freshly ground white pepper
- ½ teaspoon freshly ground black pepper
- 1 large pinch saffron threads, crumbled

One 3½-pound chicken, quartered

- 1 small bunch flat leaf parsley
- 1 small bunch cilantro
- 1 tablespoon sesame seeds

1. In a heavy medium saucepan, combine the tomatoes with ¼ cup of the oil, 2 cinnamon sticks, the ground cinnamon and a generous pinch of salt. Bring to a simmer and cook over moderate heat for 30 minutes, stirring occasionally. Add ⅔ cup of the sugar and simmer over low heat, stirring frequently, until the tomato sauce is glossy and thick, about 30 minutes longer.

2. Meanwhile, in a large enameled cast-iron casserole, mix the water with the remaining ½ cup of oil, 4 cinnamon sticks and 3 tablespoons of sugar. Add the ginger, salt, white and black pepper and saffron. Add the chicken, turn to coat and bring to a boil. Cook over moderately low heat for 25 minutes, turning occasionally. Tie the parsley and cilantro into a bundle and add it to the casserole. Cover and simmer until the chicken is cooked through, about 15 minutes longer.

3. In a small skillet, toast the sesame seeds over moderate heat, stirring, until lightly browned, about 3 minutes.

4. Using tongs, transfer the chicken to a platter and spoon the tomato sauce on top. Garnish with the sesame seeds and serve. —*Hajja Halima*

MAKE AHEAD The sauce and chicken can be prepared through Step 2 and refrigerated separately for up to 2 days. Rewarm before garnishing and serving.

WINE Soft, earthy Rioja.

Chicken and Sun-Dried-Tomato Meatballs

TOTAL: 30 MIN

4 SERVINGS ● ● ●

- 4 oil-packed sun-dried tomato halves, drained (see Note)
- 2 garlic cloves
- 1 large jalapeño—halved, seeded and coarsely chopped

Kosher salt and freshly ground pepper

- ¼ cup fine dry bread crumbs
- 1 pound ground chicken breast
- 1 large egg, lightly beaten
- 1 tablespoon fat-free milk
- ¼ cup all-purpose flour, for dusting

One 14½-ounce can peeled whole tomatoes with their juices

- ½ teaspoon dried oregano
- 2 tablespoons extra-virgin olive oil
- 1 tablespoon chopped parsley

1. In a food processor, pulse the sun-dried tomatoes, 1 garlic clove, half of the jalapeño, ½ teaspoon of salt and ⅛ teaspoon of pepper until finely chopped. Add the bread crumbs and pulse to combine. Transfer the mixture to a large bowl and stir in the chicken, egg and milk. Using moistened hands, roll the mixture into 20 meatballs, a scant 1½ tablespoons each. Dust the meatballs with flour, tapping off any excess.

2. Wipe out the food processor and add the remaining garlic clove and jalapeño half; pulse until chopped. Add the tomatoes and their juices and the oregano and process until smooth.

3. In a 9-inch cast-iron skillet, heat the olive oil until shimmering. Add the meatballs and cook over moderate heat, turning, until golden but not quite cooked through, 5 to 6 minutes. Transfer to a plate. Add the tomato sauce to the skillet; simmer until slightly thickened, 2 minutes. Return the meatballs to the skillet and simmer, turning, until just cooked through, about 2 minutes longer. Transfer to a bowl, sprinkle with the parsley and serve. —*Grace Parisi*

NOTE Sun-dried tomatoes come either packed in oil or dry-packed in cellophane. The oil-packed variety tends to be more consistent in quality—tender, juicy and full of flavor.

MAKE AHEAD The meatballs can be refrigerated overnight.

SERVE WITH Pasta or crusty bread.

WINE Simple, fruity Chianti.

poultry

Chicken-Vegetable Potpie

ACTIVE: 1 HR 30 MIN; TOTAL: 3 HR

4 SERVINGS

- 1 whole 1½-pound bone-in chicken breast, split, or 1½ pounds whole chicken legs
- 6 cups water

Salt

- 5 tablespoons unsalted butter, softened
- 4 tablespoons all-purpose flour, plus more for dusting
- 1 cup heavy cream

Freshly ground pepper

- ¼ pound pearl onions, peeled
- 1 large carrot, cut crosswise into ½-inch-thick slices
- 1 large celery rib, cut crosswise into ½-inch-thick slices
- 1 large leek, white and tender green parts only, halved lengthwise and cut crosswise into ½-inch-thick slices
- ½ pound white or cremini mushrooms, stems trimmed, quartered
- ½ cup frozen peas
- 9 ounces chilled all-butter puff pastry
- 1 large egg, lightly beaten

1. In a saucepan, cover the chicken with the water, add a pinch of salt and bring to a boil. Reduce the heat and simmer, skimming the surface occasionally, until the chicken is just cooked through, 25 minutes. Transfer to a plate and let cool. Skim the fat from the stock; boil until reduced to 2 cups, 25 minutes. Cut the chicken into ¾-inch pieces. Discard the skin and bones.

2. In a bowl, blend 4 tablespoons of the butter and the 4 tablespoons of flour into a paste. Whisk the paste into the reduced chicken stock until smooth, then bring to a boil over moderate heat. Add the cream and simmer over low heat, whisking, for 3 minutes. Season the velouté with salt and pepper.

3. Preheat the oven to 400°. In a medium saucepan of boiling salted water, cook the pearl onions until tender, about 8 minutes. With a slotted spoon, transfer the onions to a bowl. Repeat with the carrot, celery and leek, cooking them for 15 minutes, 10 minutes and 6 minutes, respectively.

4. In a medium skillet, melt the remaining 1 tablespoon of butter. Add the mushrooms, season with salt and pepper and cook over low heat until the liquid they release evaporates, about 5 minutes. Cook, stirring, until browned, about 3 minutes longer. Stir the cooked vegetables, frozen peas and chicken into the velouté and pour into a 1½-quart or 9-by-6-by-2½-inch glass or ceramic baking dish.

5. On a lightly floured work surface, roll the puff pastry out to an 8-by-11½-inch rectangle 1/16 inch thick. Brush the inner and outer rim of the baking dish with some of the egg wash. Drape the pastry over the baking dish so there is a 1½-inch overhang on all sides and the center rests on the filling; seal by pressing the overhang against the outer rim of the dish. Brush the top of the pastry with the remaining egg wash. Using a sharp paring knife, make 3 shallow diagonal slits at each end of the pastry, without cutting all the way through. Using the tip of the knife, poke three ¼-inch vents in the center, spacing them ½ inch apart.

6. Set the baking dish on a baking sheet and bake the potpie for 20 minutes. Reduce the oven temperature to 375° and bake 15 minutes longer, or until the filling is bubbling and the crust is golden brown. Let the potpie stand for at least 10 or for up to 20 minutes before serving. —*Jacques Pépin*

MAKE AHEAD The recipe can be prepared through Step 4 and refrigerated for up to 3 days. Bring to room temperature before baking.

WINE Light, fruity Beaujolais.

Chicken and Leek Yakitori

ACTIVE: 30 MIN; TOTAL: 1 HR

4 SERVINGS ● ●

Leeks make a delicious substitute here for the traditional scallions in yakitori, the classic Japanese dish of skewered grilled poultry.

- ⅓ cup sake
- ¼ cup mirin
- 3 tablespoons yellow miso paste
- 3 tablespoons soy sauce
- 2 tablespoons sugar
- 1½ teaspoons finely grated fresh ginger
- 2 pounds boneless chicken thighs— skinned, trimmed and cut into 1-inch pieces
- 1 small green bell pepper, cut into ¾-inch squares
- 1 leek, white part only, halved lengthwise and cut crosswise into ¾-inch pieces

1. In a small saucepan, combine the sake, mirin, miso, soy sauce, sugar and ginger. Simmer the sauce over moderately low heat until it is thick and shiny, about 15 minutes.

2. Meanwhile, thread the chicken, bell pepper and leek onto twelve 8-inch wooden skewers, alternating the ingredients and beginning and ending with chicken. Set the skewers on a foil-lined rimmed baking sheet.

3. Preheat the broiler and set a rack 4 inches from the heat. Cover the exposed ends of the skewers with foil and brush the skewers on both sides with the sauce. Broil the skewers for 4 to 5 minutes on each side, basting when you turn them, until the chicken is cooked through and browned at the edges. Serve the chicken yakitori hot or at room temperature. —*Jeannie Chen*

MAKE AHEAD The recipe can be prepared through Step 2 up to 1 day ahead; refrigerate the skewers and sauce separately.

WINE Full-bodied, fragrant Viognier.

CHICKEN AND LEEK YAKITORI

CHICKEN-VEGETABLE POTPIE

Chicken and Citrus Slaw Tostadas

TOTAL: 45 MIN

6 SERVINGS ●

Chipotle and fresh cilantro spice up a chicken salad served on a creamy red-and-green cabbage slaw and a crispy tortilla—a main-course tostada, Texas-style. Surprisingly, firm tofu fills in for mayonnaise in the dressing, providing creaminess without fat.

½ cup vegetable oil

Six 6-inch corn tortillas

3 ounces firm tofu, cut into 1-inch dice (½ cup)

¼ cup fresh lime juice

1 tablespoon honey

1 tablespoon Dijon mustard

1 canned chipotle chile in adobo

1 teaspoon finely grated orange zest

½ teaspoon finely grated lime zest

Salt and freshly ground pepper

½ small green cabbage, finely shredded (3 cups)

¼ small red cabbage, finely shredded (1½ cups)

1 small red onion, thinly sliced

1 large carrot, coarsely grated

3 tablespoons finely chopped cilantro

3½ cups shredded roast chicken (from 1 medium roast chicken, skin removed)

Lime wedges, for serving

1. In a small skillet, heat ¼ cup of vegetable oil over moderate heat. Add 1 tortilla and fry until nicely golden and crisp, turning once with tongs, about 2 minutes. Transfer the tostada to paper towels to drain. Repeat the procedure with the remaining tortillas. Let the tortillas sit on the paper towels to dry.

2. In a food processor or blender, mix together the diced tofu with the lime juice, honey, mustard and chipotle and process until smooth. Add the remaining ¼ cup of oil in a thin stream and process until creamy. Transfer the dressing to a bowl. Stir in the orange and lime zests and season the dressing with salt and pepper.

3. In a large bowl, toss the cabbages, onion, carrot and cilantro until thoroughly mixed; season with salt and pepper. Add all but 3 tablespoons of the dressing and toss well. Set the tostadas on plates and mound the slaw on top. Add the chicken to the bowl, toss with the reserved 3 tablespoons of dressing and mound on top of the slaw. Garnish with lime wedges and serve.
—*Paula Disbrowe*

WINE Dry, mineral-flavored Chenin Blanc.

● FAST   ● HEALTHY   ● MAKE AHEAD   ● STAFF FAVORITE

poultry

Chicken Chilaquiles

TOTAL: 35 MIN

4 TO 6 SERVINGS ● ●

Chilaquiles is a Mexican dish originally created to use up leftovers. It's traditionally made with corn tortillas, chiles, cheese and meat that are either tossed together and sautéed or layered like lasagna and baked.

1½ pounds fresh tomatillos—husked, rinsed and halved

2 large garlic cloves

1 large jalapeño—halved lengthwise, stemmed and seeded

¼ cup packed cilantro

2 tablespoons vegetable oil

1 teaspoon ground cumin

½ teaspoon coriander

Salt and freshly ground pepper

1 pound shredded cooked chicken (3 cups), at room temperature

1½ cups shredded Pepper Jack cheese (6 ounces)

½ cup farmer cheese (4 ounces)

1 scallion, sliced

One 6-ounce bag tortilla chips (8 cups)

¼ cup sour cream

1. Preheat the oven to 450°. In a blender or food processor, puree the tomatillos, garlic, jalapeño and cilantro until smooth. In a large saucepan, heat the oil until shimmering. Add the cumin and coriander and cook over high heat until fragrant, about 30 seconds. Add the tomatillo puree, bring to a boil and cook until the sauce loses its bright green color, about 3 minutes. Season the sauce with salt and pepper.

2. In a medium bowl, toss the chicken with ¾ cup of the Pepper Jack, the farmer cheese, scallion and half of the tomatillo sauce; season with salt and pepper. In another bowl, toss the tortilla chips with the remaining sauce.

3. Spread half of the tortilla chips in an 8-by-11-inch baking dish; top with the shredded chicken and cover with the remaining tortilla chips. Do not pack the chips down. Dollop the sour cream over the chips and sprinkle with the remaining ¾ cup of Pepper Jack cheese. Bake for 15 minutes, or until the cheese is browned. Serve at once.
—*Grace Parisi*

WINE Intense, berry-flavored Zinfandel.

Chipotle Chicken and Bell Pepper Casserole

ACTIVE: 1 HR 30 MIN; TOTAL: 10 HR

12 SERVINGS

The chicken has to marinate overnight, so plan accordingly.

One 7-ounce can chipotle chiles in adobo, chiles stemmed and seeded, adobo reserved

12 whole chicken legs

Salt and freshly ground pepper

3 tablespoons vegetable oil

4 tablespoons unsalted butter

1 large onion, cut into ½-inch dice

1 green bell pepper, cut into ½-inch dice

2 red bell peppers

1½ cups chicken stock or canned low-sodium broth

1 pound tomatillos—husked, washed and coarsely chopped

1 large tomato, coarsely chopped

2 large garlic cloves, minced

¼ teaspoon cayenne pepper

6 scallions, thinly sliced

1 cup finely chopped cilantro leaves

1. In a food processor, puree the chipotles and adobo until smooth. Put the chicken legs on a large rimmed baking sheet and season with salt and pepper. Coat the legs thoroughly with the puree. Cover and refrigerate overnight.

2. Preheat the oven to 350°. In a large skillet, heat 1 tablespoon of the oil until shimmering. Add 4 of the chicken legs to the skillet, skin side down, and brown over moderate heat, about 4 minutes per side. Transfer to a large rimmed baking sheet. Wipe out the skillet and repeat with the remaining oil and chicken legs. Wipe out the skillet again.

3. Melt the butter in the large skillet. Add the onion and green pepper and cook over moderately low heat until lightly browned, about 15 minutes.

4. Meanwhile, roast the red peppers directly over a gas burner or under a preheated broiler, turning occasionally, until charred all over. Transfer the peppers to a plate and let stand for 10 minutes. Discard the charred skin, stems and seeds and cut the red peppers into ½-inch dice.

5. Add the chicken stock to the onion and green pepper and simmer over moderate heat for 5 minutes. Add the tomatillos, tomato, garlic, cayenne and the roasted red peppers and simmer over moderate heat for 10 minutes. Season the sauce with salt and pepper and pour into 2 large baking dishes. Set the chicken legs on top of the sauce, skin side up. Bake for about 25 minutes, or until the chicken is deeply browned and cooked through. Scatter the scallions and cilantro over the chicken and serve. —*Ken Oringer*

MAKE AHEAD The chicken can marinate in the refrigerator for up to 2 days. The onion and pepper sauce can be refrigerated for up to 2 days.

SERVE WITH Baked Tomato Risotto (recipe, page 250).

WINE Rich, velvety Merlot.

poultry options

GAME HENS (also known as Rock Cornish hens) are young chickens weighing 1 to 2 pounds. They cook quickly and yield very tender, mostly white meat.

CAPONS are young castrated roosters. They weigh 4 to 10 pounds and have juicy, flavorful, mostly white meat.

Herb-Roasted Game Hens

ACTIVE: 45 MIN; TOTAL: 1 HR 45 MIN

4 SERVINGS ●

- 2 tablespoons chopped thyme, plus 8 thyme sprigs
- 1 tablespoon chopped rosemary, plus 2 rosemary sprigs, cut in half
- 2 tablespoons chopped parsley
- 3 tablespoons extra-virgin olive oil

Salt and freshly ground pepper

Four 1½-pound game hens, wing tips and excess fat trimmed

- 1 small onion, quartered
- 8 medium garlic cloves, smashed
- 4 tablespoons unsalted butter

1. Preheat the oven to 400°. In a small bowl, combine the chopped thyme, chopped rosemary and parsley. Stir in 1 tablespoon of the olive oil and season with salt and pepper.

2. Using your fingers, gently loosen the skin over the breasts and thighs of the game hens. Stuff 1 heaping tablespoon of the herb mixture under the skin of each bird, pushing the skin around to help distribute the herbs evenly. Season the cavities with salt, then stuff each hen with 2 thyme sprigs, 1 rosemary sprig half, 1 onion quarter and 2 smashed garlic cloves. Tie the legs of the hens together with kitchen string. Season the outside of the hens with salt and pepper.

3. In a very large ovenproof skillet, cook the butter over high heat until browned, 2 minutes. Swirl in the remaining 2 tablespoons of olive oil. Add the hens to the skillet, breast down, and cook until golden brown, 5 minutes. Turn the birds and continue to cook until golden brown all over, 15 minutes longer.

4. Transfer the hens to the oven and roast, breast up, for 1 hour, or until the juices run clear when a thigh is pierced. Remove the strings. Let the hens rest for 5 minutes. Transfer to a platter and serve. —*Maria Helm Sinskey*

WINE Rich, earthy Pinot Noir.

Grilled Quail with Green Papaya Salad

ACTIVE: 30 MIN; TOTAL: 6 HR 30 MIN

4 SERVINGS

- ½ cup dry red wine
- ½ cup canola oil
- ¼ cup Asian red chili sauce, such as *sambal oelek*
- 2 tablespoons minced fresh ginger
- 2 tablespoons minced garlic
- 8 partially boned quail (about 4 pounds)
- 1 small red onion, finely diced
- 1 tablespoon fresh lime juice
- 2 teaspoons Asian fish sauce
- 1½ pounds green papaya or underripe honeydew melon—peeled, seeded and cut into ½-inch dice

Salt and freshly ground pepper

1. In a shallow glass dish, mix the wine, canola oil, chili sauce, ginger and garlic. Add the quail and coat well. Cover and refrigerate for at least 6 hours or overnight.

2. In a medium bowl, combine the onion, lime juice and fish sauce. Fold in the green papaya and season with salt and pepper. Cover and refrigerate.

3. Light a grill or preheat a grill pan. Remove the quail from the marinade and season with salt and pepper. Grill the quail over a hot fire or high heat until lightly charred and just cooked through, about 3 minutes per side. Transfer 2 quail to each plate, spoon the papaya salad alongside and serve. —*Ming Tsai*

WINE Lively, assertive Sauvignon Blanc.

Capons with Garlic Gravy

ACTIVE: 30 MIN; TOTAL: 2 HR 25 MIN

12 SERVINGS

Two 8- to 9-pound fresh capons

Salt and freshly ground pepper

- 4 thyme sprigs
- 4 rosemary sprigs
- 1 stick (4 ounces) unsalted butter
- 1 quart chicken stock
- 4 heads garlic, halved crosswise
- 3 tablespoons all-purpose flour

1. Preheat the oven to 475°. Season the capon cavities with salt and pepper; stuff each with 2 sprigs each of thyme and rosemary and 4 tablespoons of butter. Tie the legs of each capon together with string. Season the outside with salt and pepper; fold the wing tips under. Place each capon in a separate roasting pan (the 2 pans should fit on the same oven shelf).

2. Add 1 cup of stock to each pan and roast the capons for 20 minutes. Baste the capons and arrange 2 halved heads of garlic in each pan, cut side down. Lower the oven temperature to 350° and roast for about 1 hour and 20 minutes longer, basting the capons 2 more times all over until an instant-read thermometer inserted into the thigh registers 170°.

3. Lift the capons from the roasting pans, tilting them to allow the cavity juices to run into the pans. Transfer the capons to a board and cover with foil. Set the garlic aside. Strain the pan juices into a glass measuring cup. Skim 1½ tablespoons of fat from the surface and put in small bowl. Discard the remaining fat. Whisk the flour into the reserved fat to make a paste. Set each roasting pan over moderate heat and when sizzling, pour 1 cup of the remaining stock into each. Simmer, scraping up any browned bits, for 4 minutes; add to the pan juices.

4. Transfer the juices to a saucepan. Squeeze the garlic into the juices and bring to a simmer over moderate heat. With an immersion blender, puree the garlic until the sauce is thickened. Whisk about ½ cup of the gravy into the flour paste until smooth, then whisk it into the saucepan; bring to a boil. Simmer, whisking, until no floury taste remains, about 5 minutes. Season with salt and pepper.

5. Carve the capons and serve, passing the gravy at the table. —*Tom Valenti*

SERVE WITH Autumn Fruit Compote (recipe follows).

WINE Subtle, complex white Burgundy.

poultry

Autumn Fruit Compote

ACTIVE: 20 MIN; TOTAL: 1 HR

MAKES 5 CUPS ● ●

This chunky, mixed-fruit compote is a great accompaniment to the Capons with Garlic Gravy and other savory Thanksgiving dishes.

1¼   cups dry white wine
1   cup fresh orange juice
Two 2-inch strips of orange zest
½   cinnamon stick
½   teaspoon allspice berries, crushed
½   cup dried apricots, cut into ½-inch dice
¼   cup golden raisins
½   cup corn syrup
2   Granny Smith apples—peeled, cored and cut into 1-inch pieces
2   Bosc pears—peeled, cored and cut into 1-inch pieces
6   pitted prunes, halved
½   cup fresh cranberries
¼   cup distilled white vinegar

1. In a large saucepan or medium enameled cast-iron casserole, combine the wine with the orange juice and zest. Put the cinnamon and allspice in a double layer of cheesecloth, tie into a bundle and add to the pan, then bring to a boil, cover and simmer over low heat for 15 minutes. Add the apricots and raisins, cover and simmer until almost tender, about 5 minutes. Add the corn syrup, apples and pears and simmer over moderate heat until barely tender, about 5 minutes. Add the prunes, cranberries and vinegar and simmer until the cranberries are tender, about 4 minutes.

2. Strain the fruit over a bowl and return the cooking liquid to the pan along with the spice bundle. Boil the liquid until reduced to 1 cup. Discard the spice bundle. Add the fruit to the bowl and pour the liquid over it. Stir to combine. Let cool to room temperature; serve. —*T.V.*

MAKE AHEAD The compote can be refrigerated for up to 1 week. Bring to room temperature before serving.

Roasted Capons with Herb Butter and Mushroom-Madeira Sauce

ACTIVE: 1 HR; TOTAL: 2 HR 30 MIN

12 SERVINGS

Two 7- to 8-pound capons, necks and gizzards reserved for the sauce
1   pound shiitake mushrooms, stems reserved, caps thickly sliced
½   ounce dried porcini mushrooms
6   cups chicken stock
Salt and freshly ground pepper
1½   sticks plus 2 tablespoons unsalted butter, softened
¼   cup snipped chives
¼   cup finely chopped parsley
1½   teaspoons minced garlic
1   teaspoon fresh lemon juice
3   tablespoons extra-virgin olive oil
2   large shallots, minced (½ cup)
2   tablespoons all-purpose flour
½   cup dry Madeira
½   cup water

1. In a medium saucepan, combine the reserved capon necks and gizzards with the shiitake stems, dried porcini and chicken stock and bring to a boil. Reduce the heat to moderate and simmer until reduced to 2 cups, about 1 hour and 15 minutes. Strain the stock into a heatproof bowl, pressing hard on the solids. Season lightly with salt and pepper.

2. Meanwhile, preheat the oven to 350°. In a food processor, puree 1½ sticks of the butter with the chives, parsley, garlic, lemon juice and ½ teaspoon of salt. Using your fingers and starting at the neck, gently loosen the capon skin from the breasts and legs. Rub all but 2 tablespoons of the herb butter under the skin of the birds; press gently on the skin to evenly distribute the butter.

3. Set the capons on 2 racks in 1 large or 2 medium roasting pans. Rub with 1 tablespoon of the olive oil and season generously with salt and pepper. Roast the capons for about 1 hour and 40 minutes, or until golden and an instant-read thermometer inserted in the inner thigh of each capon registers 170°. The juices in the cavity will still be slightly pink. Transfer the birds to a carving board, cover loosely with foil and let stand for at least 10 minutes or for up to 30 minutes.

4. Meanwhile, in a large, deep nonstick skillet, heat the remaining 2 tablespoons of olive oil. Add the shiitake, season with salt and pepper and cook over moderately high heat until browned, 8 minutes. Add the remaining 2 tablespoons of unsalted butter and cook, stirring, until melted. Add the shallots and cook, stirring occasionally, until golden, about 6 minutes.

5. Add the flour to the mushrooms and cook, stirring, for 2 minutes. Add the Madeira and bring to a boil, stirring constantly, for 1 minute longer. Add the strained stock and bring to a boil, stirring. Reduce the heat to moderately low and simmer for 30 minutes. Whisk in the remaining 2 tablespoons of herb butter and season with salt and pepper; keep warm.

6. Pour the juices from the roasting pan into a heatproof bowl and skim off the fat. Set the roasting pan over 2 burners on high heat, add the water and scrape to release any browned bits from the bottom; add to the pan juices in the bowl. Strain the pan juices into the Madeira sauce, along with any drippings from the capons; stir and season with salt and pepper. Carve the birds; serve them with the sauce on the side. —*David Waltuck*

MAKE AHEAD Make the stock and butter the capons up to 1 day ahead. Bring the capons to room temperature before roasting; finish the sauce while the birds rest before carving.

WINE Light, fruity Pinot Noir.

Madeira-Braised Turkey with Fried Sage Stuffing

ACTIVE: 1 HR 30 MIN; TOTAL: 5 HR, PLUS
4 HR IF MAKING HOMEMADE STOCK
12 SERVINGS PLUS LEFTOVERS

About 4 baguettes (1½ pounds total), cut into ½-inch dice
2¼ cups plus 1 tablespoon Malmsey Madeira
¼ cup dried currants
1 stick plus 1 tablespoon unsalted butter, softened
½ cup fresh sage leaves
¼ cup extra-virgin olive oil
6 large garlic cloves, thinly sliced
4 ounces thinly sliced prosciutto, cut into thin strips
3 medium red onions, minced
Salt and freshly ground pepper
3 Bosc pears, peeled and cut into ½-inch dice
3 large eggs, lightly beaten
9 cups Rich Turkey Stock (recipe, p. 125) or low-sodium broth
1 fresh 18-pound turkey, at room temperature
½ cup all-purpose flour

1. Preheat the oven to 350°. Spread the diced bread on 3 rimmed baking sheets and bake in the oven just until crisp but not browned, about 15 minutes. Let cool, then transfer the bread cubes to a very large bowl.

2. In a small saucepan, bring ¼ cup of the Madeira to a simmer over low heat. Add the currants, remove from the heat and let cool.

3. In a large skillet, melt 2 tablespoons of the butter. Add the sage leaves in a single layer and cook over moderate heat, undisturbed, until lightly browned on the bottoms, about 2 minutes. Using tongs, turn each sage leaf and cook until crisp and brown, about 1 minute longer. Transfer the sage to a plate to cool, then crumble coarsely. Add to the bowl with the bread cubes.

4. In the same skillet, melt 2 tablespoons of the butter in 2 tablespoons of the olive oil. Add the garlic slices and cook over low heat, shaking the skillet a few times, until golden brown, about 3 minutes. Add the prosciutto and cook over moderate heat, stirring, until just starting to brown, about 2 minutes. Scrape into the bowl with the bread.

5. Melt 1 tablespoon of the butter in the remaining 2 tablespoons of olive oil. Add the onions, season with salt and pepper and cook over moderately high heat for 3 minutes. Reduce the heat to low; cook until softened, 20 minutes. Scrape the onions and fat into the bowl with the bread. Add the pears and the currants with their soaking liquid. Season with salt and pepper and stir well.

6. In a medium bowl, beat the eggs with 3 cups of the stock; add to the stuffing and stir well. Loosely fill the main turkey cavity with about 8 cups of the stuffing. Fill the neck cavity with about 2 cups of the stuffing and tuck the extra skin underneath or secure with toothpicks. Spread the remaining stuffing in a buttered large baking dish and refrigerate.

7. Preheat the oven to 425°. Set the turkey in a large roasting pan. Rub the turkey all over with the remaining 4 tablespoons of butter and season with salt and pepper. Fold the wing tips under so that the turkey sits upright. Add 2 cups of the Madeira and 1 cup of the stock to the roasting pan and roast the turkey for 30 minutes.

8. Baste the turkey and reduce the oven temperature to 350°. Roast the turkey for 1 hour, basting it after 30 minutes. Cover the turkey loosely with foil and roast for 1 hour longer, basting after 30 minutes. Reduce the oven temperature to 325° and roast for about 1 hour longer, or until an instant-read thermometer inserted in an inner thigh registers 170° and the stuffing registers 165°. Transfer the bird to a carving board and cover loosely with foil.

9. Increase the oven temperature to 400° and bake the stuffing in the baking dish for 20 minutes in the upper third of the oven, or until heated through and crisp on top.

10. Meanwhile, pour the juices from the roasting pan into a large glass measuring cup. Skim off the fat; add 3 tablespoons of the fat to a medium bowl and whisk in the flour. Pour the pan juices into a medium saucepan; add the remaining 5 cups of stock. Whisk 1 cup of the stock mixture into the flour paste, then whisk the mixture into the saucepan. Bring to a boil over moderately high heat, whisking constantly until thickened. Simmer over low heat, whisking occasionally, until no floury taste remains, about 10 minutes. Add the remaining 1 tablespoon of Madeira. Season the gravy with salt and pepper; transfer to a gravy boat. Carve the turkey and serve with the stuffing and gravy. —*Marcia Kiesel*

MAKE AHEAD The uncooked stuffing can be refrigerated overnight. Stuff the turkey just before roasting.

WINE Tannic, complex Cabernet.

TURKEY STEW WITH PRUNES AND PEARL ONIONS

Turkey Stew with Prunes and Pearl Onions

ACTIVE: 50 MIN; TOTAL: 3 HR 30 MIN

4 SERVINGS ● ●

- 1 tablespoon plus 1 teaspoon extra-virgin olive oil
- 4 turkey drumsticks (about 14 ounces each)

Salt and freshly ground pepper

- 1½ cups dry white wine
- 4 thyme sprigs
- 2 rosemary sprigs
- 3 cups turkey stock or low-sodium chicken broth
- 1 cup pitted prunes (6 ounces)
- ½ cup brandy
- 1 cup white pearl onions (¼ pound)

1. Preheat the oven to 325°. Heat 1 tablespoon of the olive oil in a large enameled cast-iron casserole. Add 2 of the turkey drumsticks to the casserole, season with salt and pepper and cook over moderately high heat until browned all over, about 8 minutes; transfer to a plate. Reduce the heat to moderate and repeat with the remaining 2 drumsticks and salt and pepper. Discard the fat.

2. Add the wine to the casserole and cook, scraping up the browned bits on the bottom, until it has reduced to ½ cup, about 10 minutes. Tie the thyme and rosemary into a bundle and add to the casserole along with the drumsticks and stock and bring to a simmer. Cover and braise in the oven for 1½ hours, turning the drumsticks occasionally.

3. In a bowl, soak the prunes in the brandy until plump, about 30 minutes. Bring a small saucepan of water to a boil. Add the pearl onions and blanch for 2 minutes, then drain and let cool slightly. Trim the root ends of the onions and slip off the skins. Heat the remaining 1 teaspoon of olive oil in a small skillet. Add the pearl onions and cook over moderately high heat until lightly browned, about 5 minutes.

4. Add the onions, prunes and any remaining brandy to the casserole. Cover and braise for 1 hour longer, or until the turkey drumsticks are tender.

5. Using a slotted spoon, transfer the turkey, prunes and pearl onions to a platter. Discard the herb bundle. Skim the fat off the cooking liquid, then simmer the liquid over moderate heat until reduced to 1½ cups, about 30 minutes. Return the turkey, prunes and onions to the casserole, simmer until hot and serve. Discard the turkey skin before eating. —*Grace Parisi*

MAKE AHEAD The stew can be refrigerated for up to 3 days.

SERVE WITH Boiled noodles, steamed rice or boiled potatoes.

WINE Light, fruity Beaujolais.

Turkey Breast Escabeche with Onions and Poblanos

ACTIVE: 50 MIN; TOTAL: 3 HR

6 SERVINGS

Escabeche—loosely defined as pickling—is a classic Spanish cooking preparation brought to Mexico's Yucatán by the conquistadors. Prepared with partridge in Spain, in Mexico it is often made with chicken or small turkeys.

- ½ **tablespoon dried oregano**
- ½ **tablespoon cumin seeds**
- ¾ **teaspoon whole black peppercorns**
- 4 **whole cloves**
- 8 **garlic cloves, minced**

Kosher salt

- 1 **cup plus 1½ tablespoons cider vinegar**

One 5-pound whole boneless turkey breast with skin, halved lengthwise, tenderloins reserved for another use

- 4 **medium onions, thinly sliced**
- 1 **quart water**
- 4 **poblano or banana chiles**

Vegetable oil, for brushing

Chile-Herb White Rice (recipe, p. 241)

1. In a spice grinder, grind the oregano, cumin, peppercorns and cloves to a fine powder. On a work surface, using the side of a heavy knife, mash the minced garlic with 2 teaspoons of salt and transfer to a small bowl. Stir in the 1½ tablespoons of vinegar and the ground spices.

2. Rub 1 tablespoon of the spice paste onto the meaty side of each turkey breast half and ½ tablespoon of the paste onto the skin side. Let stand at room temperature for 1 hour.

3. Meanwhile, put the onions in a large bowl and add the 1 cup of vinegar. Toss well and let stand for 1 hour.

4. In a large enameled cast-iron casserole, bring the water to a boil. Stir in the remaining spice paste and add the turkey breast halves, skin side down. Cover partially and simmer over moderately low heat for 30 minutes. Turn the breasts over and simmer until just cooked through and tender, about 30 minutes longer.

5. Meanwhile, roast the poblano chiles directly over an open flame or under a preheated broiler, turning frequently, until blackened all over. Transfer the poblanos to a small bowl, cover with plastic wrap and let stand for 5 minutes. Discard the blackened skin, the stems and seeds and cut the poblanos into thin strips.

6. Transfer the turkey breasts, skin side up, to a baking sheet and let cool until warm. Cover with plastic so the meat doesn't dry out.

7. Drain the onions and add to the cooking liquid in the casserole. Cover the pan and simmer over moderate heat, stirring occasionally, until the onions are tender, about 12 minutes. Uncover and simmer over moderately high heat for 3 minutes. Add the poblano strips and simmer until heated through, about 3 minutes. Season the cooking liquid with salt.

8. Preheat the broiler. Brush the skin with oil and broil the turkey breasts about 6 inches from the heat for about 2 minutes, until browned and crisp, rotating the pan as needed. Transfer the turkey to a carving board and let rest for a few minutes. Slice the turkey about ⅓ inch thick and arrange the slices on a platter. Spoon the onion-and-poblano cooking liquid over the turkey breasts and serve with Chile-Herb White Rice. —*Patricia Quintana*

MAKE AHEAD The spice rub and the roasted poblanos can be refrigerated overnight.

WINE Light, spicy Pinot Grigio.

Roast Turkey Breast and Potatoes with Lemon-Soy Jus

ACTIVE: 30 MIN; TOTAL: 3 HR

12 SERVINGS PLUS LEFTOVERS

Roasting an unstuffed turkey is one way to speed the cooking process. But an even quicker method is to roast just the breast—it takes only 1 hour and 45 minutes. Surround the meat with potatoes and you'll end up with a crisp and flavorful side dish that's as delicious as any traditional stuffing. Consider serving the turkey with Instant Spiced Apple Cider—Cranberry Sauce (recipe follows), which makes a terrific, tangy accompaniment.

- 1 fresh 10-pound bone-in turkey breast, at room temperature
- 1 stick (4 ounces) unsalted butter, melted

Salt and freshly ground pepper

- 1 small lemon, halved lengthwise and seeded
- 3 tablespoons extra-virgin olive oil
- 6 pounds medium Yukon Gold potatoes, peeled and halved (see Note)
- 2 tablespoons soy sauce
- 3½ cups home-style store-bought turkey stock or chicken broth
- 2½ tablespoons cornstarch

1. Preheat the oven to 400°. Put the turkey breast in a very large roasting pan. Brush the melted butter all over the turkey breast and season it with salt and pepper. Add the lemon halves to the pan, cut side down. Roast the turkey for about 45 minutes, or until the lemon halves are browned on the cut side. Transfer the lemon halves to a plate and baste the turkey.

2. Add the olive oil to the pan. Push the turkey to one side and add the potatoes. Turn the potatoes in the fat until coated all over and arrange them, cut side down, around the turkey. Season with salt and pepper.

3. Roast the turkey for 1 hour longer, basting the turkey and potatoes every 20 minutes. The breast is done when an instant-read thermometer inserted in the thickest part (but not touching the bone) registers 160°.

4. Increase the oven temperature to 500°. Transfer the turkey to a carving board and cover loosely with aluminum foil. Transfer the potatoes to a bowl. Pour the pan juices into a large glass measuring cup and skim off the fat. Add ¼ cup of the fat to the roasting pan; reserve the remaining fat. Return the potatoes to the roasting pan, cut side down, and roast in the bottom third of the oven for about 30 minutes longer, or until deeply browned. Using a metal spatula, transfer the potatoes to a warmed bowl.

5. Meanwhile, in a medium saucepan, heat 2 teaspoons of the reserved roasting fat. Add the lemon halves, cut side down, and the soy sauce and cook over moderately high heat for 1 minute. Stir in 3 cups of the stock and bring to a boil, then reduce the heat to moderately low and simmer for 5 minutes. Remove the lemon halves, and when cool enough to handle, squeeze the juice into the saucepan. Add the reserved pan juices.

6. In a small bowl, whisk the remaining ½ cup of stock with the cornstarch until smooth. Whisk the slurry into the saucepan and bring to a boil over moderately high heat. Simmer until the jus is slightly thickened, about 1 minute. Season the jus with salt and pepper and transfer to a warmed gravy boat.

7. Carve the turkey breast and serve with the roasted potatoes, passing the lemon-soy jus. —*Marcia Kiesel*

NOTE The Yukon Gold is a yellow-fleshed potato with a moderate starch content. It's a terrific jack-of-all-trades potato, great for roasting, steaming or boiling. If you find baby Yukon Gold potatoes, you can roast them whole in this recipe. You can also substitute the Yellow Finn potato, a close cousin to the Yukon Gold that is slightly starchier. In a pinch you can use the basic all-purpose, or boiling, potato.

WINE Light, fruity Beaujolais.

Instant Spiced Apple Cider—Cranberry Sauce

ACTIVE: 5 MIN; TOTAL: 15 MIN

MAKES ABOUT 4 CUPS ● ● ●

- Two 12-ounce bags fresh or frozen cranberries (6 cups)
- 2 cups apple cider
- ½ teaspoon cinnamon
- ¼ teaspoon ground cloves
- ¼ teaspoon freshly grated nutmeg
- ¼ teaspoon ground cardamom

1. In a large saucepan, combine the cranberries and apple cider with the cinnamon, cloves, nutmeg and cardamom and bring to a boil.

2. Cook the sauce over moderately high heat, coarsely mashing the berries with a wooden spoon, until the sauce is softened and jamlike, about 5 minutes. Serve warm, at room temperature or chilled. —*Grace Parisi*

MAKE AHEAD The cranberry sauce can be refrigerated for up to 1 week.

Q+A
perfect gravy

Q: I wish I could figure out how to get drippings for gravy when I cook a turkey. I always roast my bird at a high heat to finish it faster and brown the outside, but I end up with hardly any drippings.

A: If you roast your bird at more than 375° without adding any stock to the pan, you may find yourself with some delicious caramelized juices that are virtually welded on, as well as some fat, but no drippings to speak of. A few years back in the F&W Test Kitchen, we tested a recipe that called for roasting the turkey, with some stock, at 350°. It's quite amazing, because you end up with incredibly tasty drippings. For a gorgeously browned bird, you can always hike up the oven temperature at the last minute.

Q: Thanks for the advice—this time I got lots of drippings. I made gravy with them, but I came away frustrated because it was too thin. How do I fix that?

A: The consistency of gravy is easy to correct. If your gravy is thin, simply make a smooth paste with equal amounts of all-purpose flour and unsalted butter, bring your gravy to a boil and gradually whisk in bits of the paste until you get the thickness you desire. Be sure to cook the gravy for at least 5 minutes after you've added the paste in order to eliminate any raw flour flavor. As a general guideline, for 2 cups of liquid, 3 tablespoons each of butter and flour will yield a lightly thickened gravy; 4 tablespoons each will yield a medium-thick one.

Q: I made gravy again, and the consistency was perfect. But I used canned chicken broth and the flavor was pretty dull. Is there anything I could have done to make my gravy taste better?

A: The good news is that you can dress up a humdrum gravy with anything from mushrooms, caramelized shallots, chopped fresh herbs and olives to sausage, country ham, giblets and cider, sherry or Madeira. You can even add a touch of cream or crème fraîche. And don't forget to add salt and freshly ground pepper; proper seasoning can make the difference between a flat sauce and a lively one. But nothing can duplicate the flavor of using homemade stock. Even if you usually wouldn't consider making stock, try to do so at Thanksgiving. The recipe here is one that the F&W Test Kitchen has relied on for years.

Rich Turkey Stock

ACTIVE: 20 MIN; TOTAL: 4 HR 30 MIN
MAKES ABOUT 3 QUARTS ● ●

Because there are never enough drippings to make as much gravy as you need—at least 1/3 cup per person—you should prepare stock in advance to have on hand when you need it.

- 7 pounds turkey parts, such as wings, thighs and drumsticks
- 4 quarts water
- 1 large onion, thickly sliced
- 1 large carrot, thickly sliced
- 1 large celery rib, thickly sliced
- 2 garlic cloves, smashed
- 1 teaspoon kosher salt

Freshly ground pepper

1. Preheat the oven to 400°. In a large roasting pan, roast the turkey parts for 1½ hours, or until well browned; transfer to a large pot.

2. Set the roasting pan over 2 burners. Add 4 cups of the water and bring to a boil, scraping up the browned bits from the bottom. Add the liquid to the pot.

3. Add the onion, carrot, celery, garlic, salt and several pinches of pepper to the pot along with the remaining 3 quarts of water and bring to a boil. Reduce the heat to moderately low, cover partially and simmer the stock for about 2½ hours. Strain the stock and skim the fat before using or freezing.
—*Food & Wine Test Kitchen*

MAKE AHEAD The stock can be refrigerated for 3 days or frozen for 1 month.

poultry

Smoky Turkey Chili

ACTIVE: 1 HR; TOTAL: 3 HR 30 MIN

8 SERVINGS ● ●

- 2 tablespoons vegetable oil
- 5 pounds turkey legs with skin

Salt and freshly ground pepper

- 6 large garlic cloves, finely chopped
- 2 large onions, finely chopped
- 3 tablespoons ancho chile powder
- 2 tablespoons chipotle chile powder
- 4 teaspoons ground cumin
- ½ teaspoon ground cloves

One 28-ounce can crushed tomatoes

- 1 quart water

One 2-pound butternut squash, peeled
and cut into 1-inch dice

Two 15-ounce cans black beans, drained

- 4 large poblano chiles—roasted,
peeled and cut into ½-inch pieces
- ¼ cup tomato paste

1. In an enameled casserole, heat the
oil. Season the turkey with salt and pepper, add to the casserole and cook over
moderate heat until browned, 15 minutes. Transfer to a plate. Add the garlic and
onions to the casserole and cook over
low heat, stirring, until softened, 10 minutes. Stir in the chile powders, cumin and
cloves and cook for 5 minutes. Add the
tomatoes and water; bring to a simmer.
2. Return the turkey to the casserole;
bring to a boil. Cover and simmer over
low heat until tender, about 2 hours.
Transfer the turkey to a plate and let
cool slightly. Discard the bones and skin
and cut the meat into bite-size pieces.
3. Skim the fat from the chili. Add the
squash and turkey. Simmer over low heat
until the squash is tender, 15 minutes.
Add the beans and poblanos. Season
with salt and pepper. Ladle 1 cup of chili
into a bowl. Stir in the tomato paste until
dissolved, then stir the chili back into the
casserole. Simmer for 5 minutes, then
serve in mugs or bowls. —*Marcia Kiesel*
SERVE WITH Cilantro leaves, low-fat sour
cream and corn bread.
WINE Light, zesty, fruity Dolcetto.

Chile-Roasted Turkey with Chorizo—Corn Bread Stuffing

**ACTIVE: 2 HR; TOTAL: 4 HR 30 MIN, PLUS
4 HR IF MAKING HOMEMADE STOCK**

12 SERVINGS PLUS LEFTOVERS

CORN BREAD STUFFING

- 4 ears of corn, husked
- ½ pound chorizo, peeled and
thickly sliced (see Note)
- 1½ sticks (6 ounces) unsalted
butter, 1 stick melted
- 1 sweet onion, minced (2 cups)
- 3 celery ribs, finely diced (1½ cups)
- 3 large garlic cloves, minced
- 2 large poblano chiles or 3 large
jalapeños, seeded and finely diced
- 1½ tablespoons chopped thyme

Crispy Skillet Corn Bread
(recipe, p. 263), coarsely
crumbled (13 cups)

- 2 cups Rich Turkey Stock
(recipe, p. 125) or low-sodium
chicken broth

Salt and freshly ground pepper

TURKEY

- 3 ancho chiles, seeded
- 3 large garlic cloves, smashed
- 3 tablespoons unsalted butter

Salt and freshly ground pepper

- 1 fresh 18-pound turkey, at room
temperature
- 5 cups Rich Turkey Stock
(recipe, p. 125) or low-sodium
chicken broth
- ¼ cup all-purpose flour

1. MAKE THE CORN BREAD STUFF-
ING: Preheat the broiler and position a
rack 8 inches from the heat. Broil the
corn, turning, until lightly charred,
about 7 minutes. Let cool slightly, then
cut the kernels from the cobs.
2. In a food processor, chop the chorizo
into ½-inch pieces. In a large skillet,
cook the chorizo over moderately high
heat, stirring occasionally, until the fat
is rendered, about 5 minutes. Drain
the chorizo and transfer to a paper
towel—lined plate; discard the fat.

3. Wipe out the skillet and melt the
4 tablespoons of solid butter in it. Add
the onion, celery, garlic, poblanos and
thyme and cook over moderate heat,
stirring occasionally, until softened,
about 10 minutes. Scrape into a large
bowl. Add the chorizo, corn kernels,
corn bread, melted butter and stock.
Season with salt and pepper and stir
well. Let cool.
4. MEANWHILE, PREPARE THE TURKEY:
Preheat the oven to 450°. Put the
anchos in a medium bowl and cover
with hot water. Let soak until softened,
about 30 minutes. Drain well. In a food
processor, puree the anchos with the
garlic and butter until smooth. Season
with salt and pepper. Rub 2 tablespoons
of the ancho paste in the main turkey
cavity. Loosen the skin at the neck and
carefully extend your hands all the way
to the thigh and leg. Rub the remaining ancho paste under the skin.
5. Loosely fill the main turkey cavity
with 5 cups of the stuffing and tie the
legs together with kitchen string.
Spoon 1 cup of the stuffing into the
neck cavity and tuck the extra skin
underneath or secure with toothpicks.
Spoon the remaining stuffing into a
buttered 3-quart baking dish and drizzle with 1 cup of the stock.
6. Set the turkey in a very large roasting pan and season it with salt and
pepper. Roast the turkey for 30 minutes,
then reduce the heat to 375°. Add
1 cup of the stock to the roasting pan
and roast the turkey for 3 hours longer,
or until an instant-read thermometer
inserted in an inner thigh registers
180° and the stuffing registers 165°.
Cover the turkey loosely with foil if the
skin browns quickly. Transfer the turkey
to a cutting board, cover with foil and
let rest for 30 minutes.
7. Bake the stuffing in the baking dish
for about 30 minutes, or until heated
through and crisp on top.

SMOKY TURKEY CHILI

CHILE-ROASTED TURKEY

8. Meanwhile, pour the roasting pan juices into a large glass measuring cup. Skim off the fat. In a small cup, whisk ½ cup of the Rich Turkey Stock with the flour and set aside.

9. Set the roasting pan over 2 burners on high heat. Add the remaining 2½ cups of stock and bring to a simmer. Using a wooden spoon, scrape up any browned bits from the bottom and sides of the pan. Add the reserved pan juices to the roasting pan, then strain all the liquid through a fine sieve into a medium saucepan. Boil the juices over high heat until reduced to 3 cups, about 10 minutes. Whisk in the flour mixture and boil until thickened, about 5 minutes. Season the gravy with salt and pepper and transfer to a warmed gravy boat.

10. Carve the turkey and serve with the gravy. Spoon the corn bread stuffing from the turkey and serve it with the stuffing from the baking dish alongside the turkey. —*Grace Parisi*

NOTE Chorizo is a coarsely ground pork sausage that is flavored with garlic, chili powder and other highly aromatic seasonings, and is widely used in Spanish and Mexican cooking. The casing is always removed before cooking. You can purchase chorizo at specialty markets, delicatessens and some supermarkets.

MAKE AHEAD The uncooked corn bread stuffing can be covered in a casserole or in a bowl with plastic wrap and refrigerated overnight. Stuff the turkey just before roasting.

WINE Powerful, spicy Syrah.

Turkey with Apple-Chestnut Stuffing and Cider Gravy

ACTIVE: 1 HR 30 MIN; TOTAL: 4 HR 30 MIN, PLUS 2 DAYS FOR BRINING AND 4 HR IF MAKING HOMEMADE STOCK

12 SERVINGS PLUS LEFTOVERS

Brining turkey by soaking it in salt water virtually guarantees a juicy bird.

5½ gallons cold water

Kosher salt

1 fresh 18-pound turkey

Freshly ground pepper

Apple-Chestnut Stuffing, prepared through Step 2 (recipe, p. 266)

3 cups Rich Turkey Stock (recipe, p. 125) or low-sodium broth

6 tablespoons unsalted butter

2 cups apple cider

½ cup all-purpose flour

¼ cup Calvados or Cognac

poultry

1. In a very large stockpot, combine the water with ¼ cup of kosher salt and stir until the salt dissolves. Add the turkey, breast down; refrigerate for 2 days. Remove the turkey from the brine and dry it inside and out with paper towels. Bring the bird to room temperature and season all over with salt and pepper.

2. Preheat the oven to 425°. Loosely fill the main and neck cavities of the turkey with about 10 cups of the Apple-Chestnut Stuffing. Spread the remaining stuffing in a buttered large, shallow glass or porcelain baking dish; cover with plastic wrap and refrigerate.

3. Pour 1 cup of the stock into a large roasting pan and set the turkey in the pan. Add the butter to the pan and roast the turkey for 30 minutes. Baste with the pan juices. Reduce the oven temperature to 350° and roast for 45 minutes. Add the apple cider to the pan, baste the turkey and roast for about 1 hour and 15 minutes, or until the skin is richly browned; if the skin on the legs browns too quickly, cover them with foil. Baste again and cover the whole bird with foil. Roast the turkey for about 1 hour and 20 minutes longer, or until an instant-read thermometer inserted in a thigh registers 170° and the stuffing registers 165°. Transfer the turkey to a carving board and cover the bird loosely with foil.

duck breasts

THE SKIN ON A DUCK BREAST adds flavor and crunch when prepared correctly. First, trim off any overhanging skin and fat from each duck breast half. Using a paring knife, score the remaining skin diagonally three or four times (or in a crosshatch). This lets the fat melt during cooking.

4. Increase the oven temperature to 400°. Bake the stuffing in the baking dish for 20 minutes, or until cooked through and crisp on top.

5. Meanwhile, pour the juices from the roasting pan into a 1-quart glass measuring cup; skim off the fat and reserve. Set the roasting pan over 2 burners on moderately high heat. Add the remaining 2 cups of stock to the pan and bring to a simmer, scraping up the browned bits from the sides and bottom with a wooden spoon. Reduce the heat to moderate and cook for 4 minutes. Add the stock in the roasting pan to the juices in the measuring cup.

6. Strain the pan juices into a medium saucepan. Spoon ¼ cup of the reserved turkey fat into a small bowl; whisk in the flour. Whisk 1 cup of the pan juices into the flour mixture until smooth. Whisk the mixture into the pan juices in the saucepan and bring to a boil over moderately high heat, whisking often. Add the Calvados and simmer, whisking occasionally, until no floury taste remains, about 5 minutes. Season the gravy with salt and pepper and transfer to a gravy boat. Carve the turkey and serve with the stuffing and gravy. —*Marcia Kiesel*

MAKE AHEAD The uncooked stuffing can be refrigerated overnight. Stuff the turkey just before roasting.

WINE Ripe, creamy-textured Chardonnay.

Oaxacan Turkey Burgers with Chipotle Salsa

TOTAL: 1 HR

4 SERVINGS ●

- 1½ pounds ground turkey
- 3 tablespoons chopped cilantro
- 1 scallion, finely chopped
- 1 garlic clove, minced
- 1 teaspoon pure ancho chile powder
- 1 teaspoon kosher salt
- ½ teaspoon freshly ground pepper
- ½ teaspoon ground cumin
- ½ teaspoon ground coriander

Pinch of ground cinnamon
Vegetable oil, for brushing
- 4 English muffins, toasted
- ½ ripe Hass avocado, sliced
- 3 tablespoons toasted shelled pumpkin seeds *(pepitas)*
Chipotle Salsa (recipe follows)

1. In a large bowl, lightly knead the turkey with the cilantro, scallion, garlic, ancho powder, salt, pepper, cumin, coriander and cinnamon. Shape the meat into 4 patties about ¾ inch thick and set them on a plate lined with plastic wrap.

2. Light a grill. When the fire is medium hot, brush the burgers and the grate lightly with oil. Grill the turkey burgers for 13 minutes, turning once, for medium meat. Set the burgers on the muffins; top with the avocado, pumpkin seeds and Chipotle Salsa. Close the muffins and serve with the remaining salsa. —*Steven Raichlen*

WINE Bright, fruity rosé.

Chipotle Salsa

TOTAL: 20 MIN

MAKES 2 CUPS ● ● ●

- 5 large garlic cloves
- 6 small tomatillos, husked
- 4 plum tomatoes
- ¼ large onion
- 1 to 3 canned chipotle chiles in adobo, seeded and chopped
- 3 tablespoons chopped cilantro
- ½ teaspoon sugar

Kosher salt

Light a grill. Skewer the garlic cloves on a 4-inch bamboo skewer. Grill the garlic, tomatillos, tomatoes and onion over a medium-hot fire for 8 to 10 minutes, turning, until charred and softened. Let cool. Transfer to a food processor and pulse until finely chopped. Add the chipotles, 2 teaspoons of the adobo sauce, the cilantro and sugar and pulse until combined. Season with salt. —*S.R.*

MAKE AHEAD The salsa can be refrigerated for up to 2 days.

Chilled Duck with Zinfandel Sauce

ACTIVE: 20 MIN; TOTAL: 7 HR 30 MIN

4 SERVINGS ●

Make sure to use Japanese soy sauce, not Chinese, since it has a lighter flavor and won't overwhelm the Zinfandel in the marinade. Look for Kikkoman or Yamasa.

- 1   cup Zinfandel
- ½   cup soy sauce
- ½   cup mirin
- 4   large scallions, green parts only, coarsely chopped
- 2   large garlic cloves, very thinly sliced

One 1-inch piece of fresh ginger, thinly sliced

Two 1-pound Muscovy duck breasts, fat trimmed

- 2   cups small arugula leaves (2 ounces)

I. In a medium saucepan, boil the Zinfandel over high heat until reduced by half, about 5 minutes. Let cool to room temperature.

2. Bring a large pot of water to a boil. In a large, sturdy, resealable plastic freezer bag, combine the soy sauce, mirin, scallions, garlic, ginger and Zinfandel reduction.

3. Gather 10 bamboo skewers in your hand and puncture the duck skin all over, through to the meat. Alternatively, use the tip of a very sharp knife to poke the duck skin all over.

4. Heat a skillet over high heat. Add the duck breasts, skin side down, and cook over moderate heat until browned, about 8 minutes. Turn the duck over and cook until browned on the other side, about 3 minutes. Transfer the duck breasts to the bag with the marinade and seal it. Place the sealed bag inside a double layer of sturdy plastic bags, sealing each bag. Carefully lower the duck breasts into the boiling water. Cover, turn off the heat and let stand for 10 minutes.

5. Prepare a large bowl of ice water. Plunge the bags with the duck into the ice bath and let stand for 45 minutes, or until completely chilled. Refrigerate the duck in the bags for at least 6 hours or overnight.

6. Remove the duck breasts from the marinade and pat them dry with paper towels. Strain the Zinfandel marinade into a medium saucepan and boil over high heat until it has thickened, about 7 minutes. Using a thin, sharp knife, thinly slice the duck breasts crosswise. Drizzle each dinner plate with some of the reduced Zinfandel marinade and arrange the sliced duck breasts on top. Mound the arugula leaves on the plates and serve. —*Nobuo Fukuda*

MAKE AHEAD The recipe can be prepared up to 3 days ahead; refrigerate the Zinfandel marinade and the cooked duck separately.

WINE Intense, berry-flavored Zinfandel.

Ancho-Chipotle-Spiced Duck Breasts with Mango Salsa

ACTIVE: 35 MIN, TOTAL: 2 HR 45 MIN

4 SERVINGS ●

Pure chile powders are traditionally made by toasting chiles and grinding them—a time-consuming process. Fortunately, it is easier than ever to find high-quality, single-chile, additive-free powders at stores, and savvy cooks have come to rely on them as quick rubs for hearty meats like beef, pork and duck.

Salt

- ¾   teaspoon sugar

Four ½-pound magret duck breast halves, skin and fat removed

- 1   tablespoon pure ancho chile powder
- 1   teaspoon pure chipotle chile powder
- 1   large ripe mango, diced
- ¼   cup chopped cilantro
- 3   tablespoons fresh lime juice
- 1   large sweet onion, cut into ¼-inch-thick slices, the slices kept intact
- 3   tablespoons extra-virgin olive oil

Freshly ground pepper

I. In a small bowl, mix 1¼ teaspoons of salt with ¼ teaspoon of the sugar. Sprinkle evenly over both sides of the duck breasts. Cover the duck with plastic wrap and let stand at room temperature for 2 hours, or for up to 4 hours in the refrigerator. In another small bowl, mix the ancho and chipotle powders.

2. Meanwhile, in another small bowl, toss the mango with the cilantro, lime juice, a pinch of salt and the remaining ½ teaspoon of sugar. Cover and refrigerate.

3. Preheat the broiler and line a broiler pan with foil. Brush the onion slices with 2 tablespoons of the olive oil and arrange on the pan. Broil the onions 6 inches from the heat for 12 minutes, turning once and brushing with the oil in the pan, until softened and lightly charred in spots. Transfer the onions to a bowl, separating the rings. Season with salt and pepper.

4. Pat the duck breasts dry with paper towels and sprinkle each of them on each side with 1 teaspoon of the ground chile mixture. Heat the remaining 1 tablespoon of olive oil in a large nonstick skillet. Add the duck breasts and cook, turning once, until browned outside but still pink inside, 6 to 8 minutes; lower the heat if the chile rub begins to brown too quickly. Transfer the duck breasts to a cutting board and let rest for 5 minutes, then thickly slice on the diagonal.

5. To serve, mound the onion slices on large plates. Arrange the duck breast slices on top. Spoon the mango salsa over the duck and serve immediately. —*Sally Schneider*

MAKE AHEAD The mango salsa can be refrigerated overnight.

WINE Round, supple, fruity Syrah.

ROSY RACK OF LAMB WITH GARLIC, P. 150

● FAST

● HEALTHY

● MAKE AHEAD

● STAFF FAVORITE

beef, lamb + game

STEAK BORDELAISE

GRILLED CHILI-RUBBED FLANK STEAK

Steak Bordelaise

ACTIVE: 25 MIN; TOTAL: 1 HR 50 MIN

4 SERVINGS

The sauce here keeps well and is just as good served with lamb, venison or poached eggs.

- 1 cup plus 1 tablespoon grapeseed oil
- 4 large shallots, unpeeled, plus 1 small shallot, chopped
- 3 cups dry red wine
- 3 cups red wine vinegar
- 3 cups veal stock (see Note)
- 1 tablespoon cold unsalted butter

Salt and freshly ground pepper

Four 10-ounce boneless strip steaks, about ½ inch thick

- 2 tablespoons coarsely chopped flat-leaf parsley

Fleur de sel (French sea salt; see Note)

I. In a small saucepan, combine 1 cup of the grapeseed oil with the unpeeled shallots and bring to a boil. Simmer over low heat until the shallots are very tender, about 1 hour.

2. Meanwhile, in a medium saucepan, combine the red wine, vinegar and chopped shallot and bring to a boil. Simmer over moderately high heat until reduced to 3 tablespoons, 1 hour. Add the veal stock and simmer over moderate heat until reduced to 1½ cups, about 30 minutes. Strain through a fine sieve set over a small saucepan. Whisk in the butter over low heat and season with salt and pepper. Keep warm.

3. In a large skillet, heat the remaining 1 tablespoon of grapeseed oil until almost smoking. Season the steaks with salt and pepper and add them to the skillet. Cook over high heat until

richly browned on the bottoms, about 3 minutes. Turn and cook the steaks for about 2 minutes for medium rare. While the steaks cook, reheat the shallots in their oil until hot, then drain and, using a serrated knife, cut the shallots in half. Transfer the steaks to plates. Spoon ¼ cup of the sauce over each steak and place the shallots alongside the steaks. Sprinkle with the parsley and fleur de sel and serve.

—*Christophe Gerard*

NOTE Veal stock and fleur de sel are available at specialty food stores and some supermarkets.

MAKE AHEAD The sauce can be refrigerated for up to 1 week. Reheat gently. The cooked shallots can be removed from the oil and kept for 6 hours, then reheated; save the shallot oil for frying.

WINE Tannic, complex Cabernet.

Grilled Chili-Rubbed Flank Steak

TOTAL: 30 MIN

4 SERVINGS ●

- 1 large garlic clove
- 1 tablespoon chopped red onion
- 1 tablespoon fresh lime juice
- 2 teaspoons chili powder
- 2 teaspoons salt
- 1 teaspoon ground cumin
- 2 tablespoons olive oil
- One 1½-pound flank steak
- 10 lime wedges
- 3½ ounces Monterey Jack cheese, shredded (1 cup)
- 2 tablespoons chopped cilantro
- Twelve 6-inch corn tortillas, warmed

1. In a processor, pulse the garlic with the onion, lime juice, chili powder, salt and cumin. With the machine on, slowly drizzle in the olive oil until a wet paste forms. Rub the paste all over the steak.

2. Light a grill or preheat a grill pan. Grill the steak over a medium high fire for 10 minutes, turning once, until an instant-read thermometer inserted in the thickest part registers 125° to 130° for medium rare. Transfer the steak to a cutting board and let rest for 5 minutes.

3. Cut the steak across the grain into ¼-inch-thick slices and transfer to a platter. Squeeze 2 lime wedges over the slices, then top with the cheese and cilantro. Serve with the warm tortillas and remaining lime. —*Bruce Aidells*

WINE Intense, berry-flavored Zinfandel.

Peppered Rib-Eye Steaks with Pan-Fried Watercress

TOTAL: 15 MIN

4 SERVINGS ●

- Two 10- to 12-ounce rib-eye steaks, cut 1 inch thick
- 1 tablespoon coarsely ground pepper
- Salt
- ¼ cup dry red wine
- 2 tablespoons unsalted butter
- 2 bunches watercress, stemmed

1. Season the steaks on both sides with the coarsely ground pepper, patting it lightly to adhere.

2. Set a large cast-iron skillet over moderately high heat. Season the steaks with salt, add them to the skillet and cook until they are brown and crusty on one side, about 4 minutes. Turn and cook on the other side for 4 minutes longer for medium-rare meat. Transfer the steaks to a platter. Pour off the fat from the skillet, add the wine and cook until reduced by half, about 30 seconds. Pour the sauce over the steaks.

3. Wipe out the skillet and add the butter. Add the watercress and cook over high heat, tossing, until wilted, about 1 minute. Season with salt. Cut the steaks in half, transfer to plates and serve with the watercress. —*Jim Fobel*

WINE Intense, berry-flavored Zinfandel.

Latin-Spiced Rib Eye with Sautéed Onions and Cilantro

TOTAL: 35 MIN

4 SERVINGS ●

Known as *bistec encebollado* throughout the Caribbean, this dish is particularly popular in Puerto Rico. Since the meat cooks so quickly, it's best to use a tender cut, like rib eye or strip steak; filet mignon works too, if you feel like splurging. To save some time, have your butcher cut the steak and pound it.

- 1 teaspoon ground cumin
- 1 teaspoon dried oregano
- 1 teaspoon garlic powder
- 1 teaspoon onion powder
- Kosher salt and freshly ground pepper
- 1½ pounds rib-eye steak or 1 pound New York strip or tenderloin, cut into 8 pieces and pounded ⅓ inch thick
- 2 large garlic cloves, minced and smashed to a puree
- 2 tablespoons extra-virgin olive oil
- 2 medium sweet onions, cut crosswise into ⅛-inch-thick slices
- 1 cup beef stock or low-sodium broth
- 1 tablespoon plus 1 teaspoon distilled white vinegar
- 2 tablespoons unsalted butter, at room temperature
- ¾ cup cilantro leaves

1. In a small bowl, combine the cumin and oregano with the garlic and onion powders. Stir in 1 teaspoon of salt and ½ teaspoon of pepper until well combined. Season the steaks on both sides with the spice mixture and rub them with the garlic puree.

2. In a large skillet, heat 1 tablespoon of the olive oil until shimmering. Add 4 of the steaks and cook over high heat until browned, 1 minute per side; transfer to a plate. Repeat with the remaining olive oil and meat.

3. Reduce the heat to moderate and add the onions to the skillet, stirring until coated with oil. Cover and cook until just softened, about 5 minutes, stirring halfway through. Using a slotted spoon, transfer the onions to a shallow bowl and cover with foil.

4. Add the stock to the skillet and bring to a simmer over moderately high heat. Simmer for 1 minute, scraping up any browned bits from the bottom of the pan with a wooden spoon. Stir in the vinegar and butter and cook until the butter is completely melted and smoothly incorporated into the sauce.

5. Return the meat, any of its accumulated juices and the onions to the pan and turn to coat with the sauce and to gently heat through. Transfer the meat and sauce to serving plates, garnish with the cilantro leaves and serve at once. —*David Rosengarten*

MAKE AHEAD The beef can marinate in the refrigerator for up to 4 hours. Let stand at room temperature for 20 minutes before cooking.

SERVE WITH Crispy fried potatoes.

WINE Assertive, heady Grenache.

beef, lamb + game

Spicy Beef and Broccoli Salad with Kimchi

TOTAL: 20 MIN

4 SERVINGS ● ●

Kimchi, added here for heat, is a Korean condiment that is also commonly eaten in Japan. It is made from a variety of vegetables, but brined napa cabbage with hot red peppers and garlic is the most familiar. Kimchi is sold at many supermarkets and Asian food shops.

- 1 tablespoon sesame seeds
- 3 cups water
- ¾ pound broccoli, cut into 1-inch florets, stalks peeled and cut into ½-inch-thick slices
- 1 pound trimmed beef rib eye, cut into ¼-inch-thick slices

Salt and freshly ground pepper

- 1 tablespoon soy sauce (see Note)
- 1 tablespoon unseasoned rice vinegar
- 1 teaspoon Asian sesame oil
- ¾ cup thinly sliced kimchi

1. In a small skillet, toast the sesame seeds over moderate heat until fragrant, about 2 minutes. Transfer the sesame seeds to a plate to cool.

2. In a medium saucepan, bring the water to a boil. Add the broccoli florets and stems and cook until they are bright green, about 2 minutes. Using a slotted spoon, transfer the broccoli pieces to a colander and refresh under cold running water. Gently pat the broccoli dry with paper towels.

3. Add the sliced rib eye to the boiling water and cook until medium rare, about 40 seconds. Using a slotted spoon, transfer the beef to a plate. Spread the beef slices in an even layer and season them generously with salt and pepper.

4. In a large bowl, combine 3 tablespoons of the cooking water with the soy sauce, rice vinegar and sesame oil. Add the broccoli, sliced beef, kimchi and sesame seeds to the bowl and toss the salad well to coat all the ingredients with the dressing. Transfer the beef and broccoli salad to serving dishes and serve at once. —*Marcia Kiesel*

NOTE For this recipe, opt for Japanese soy sauce *(shoyu),* which is sweeter and less salty than Chinese soy sauce. It is available at most supermarkets, specialty markets and at Asian markets.

WINE Bright, fruity rosé.

Ropa Vieja with Capers

ACTIVE: 1 HR 40 MIN; TOTAL: 3 HR

4 SERVINGS PLUS LEFTOVERS FOR 4 ADDITIONAL SERVINGS ●

This classic Cuban beef stew is called *ropa vieja*— "old clothes"—because the juicy beef is shredded like rags. The version here is the ideal recipe for a lazy Sunday afternoon: It is long-simmered and makes enough for two meals. On Sunday night, serve the meat with rice and beans. Later in the week, reheat it gently in a large pot, covered, for 15 minutes, then wrap it in warm tortillas with avocado slices, chopped red onion, hot sauce and cilantro and add a squeeze of fresh lime juice.

- ¼ cup plus 1 tablespoon extra-virgin olive oil
- 4 pounds flank steak, cut with the grain into 6 pieces

Kosher salt and freshly ground pepper

- 8 cups water
- 2 bay leaves
- 2 medium onions, thinly sliced
- 2 medium red bell peppers, thinly sliced
- 2 medium green bell peppers, thinly sliced
- 14 medium garlic cloves, minced (about ⅓ cup)
- 8 whole cloves
- 2 cinnamon sticks

One 28-ounce can peeled tomatoes in puree, drained and coarsely chopped (4 cups)

- ¼ cup capers, drained and rinsed

1. In a large enameled cast-iron casserole, heat 1 tablespoon of the olive oil until shimmering. Blot the flank steak dry with paper towels and season it generously with salt and pepper. Working in 2 batches, add the meat to the casserole and brown it on all sides over high heat, about 10 minutes. Transfer the browned steak to a plate and repeat with the remaining meat. Return all of the meat to the casserole. Add the water and 1 bay leaf; bring to a boil. Reduce the heat to low, cover and simmer until the meat is very tender, 1½ to 2 hours.

2. Transfer the stewed meat to a large bowl and cover with aluminum foil; reserve 3 cups of the cooking liquid. Discard the bay leaf.

3. In the same casserole, heat the remaining ¼ cup of olive oil. Add the onions and red and green bell peppers to the casserole and cook over high heat, stirring frequently, until the onions are softened and golden, about 10 minutes. Add the garlic and cook, stirring, until fragrant, about 2 minutes.

4. Lay the cloves, cinnamon sticks and the remaining bay leaf on a square of cheesecloth. Gather the edges of the cheesecloth and tie them in a bundle with kitchen string; add the spice bag to the casserole. Stir in the chopped tomatoes, the capers and the reserved 3 cups of cooking liquid. Bring the mixture to a boil, then simmer over moderately low heat until the sauce thickens, about 15 minutes. Season with salt and pepper. Discard the spice bag.

5. Meanwhile, using 2 forks, pull the meat into long shreds. Add the meat to the sauce and simmer over low heat until warmed through, then serve.

—*David Rosengarten*

MAKE AHEAD The beef stew can be refrigerated for up to 4 days.

SERVE WITH Steamed white rice and black or pinto beans.

WINE Rich, smoky-plummy Shiraz.

Steak with Shallots and Lyonnaise Potatoes

TOTAL: 30 MIN

4 SERVINGS ●

- 3 tablespoons extra-virgin olive oil
- 3 large Yukon Gold potatoes (1¼ pounds), peeled and cut into ¼-inch-thick slices
- 1 large Vidalia onion, halved lengthwise and sliced crosswise

Kosher salt and freshly ground pepper

- 2 tablespoons red wine vinegar

Four 7-ounce sirloin steaks (1 inch thick)

- 2 tablespoons unsalted butter
- 4 large shallots, very thinly sliced
- ½ cup dry red wine
- 2 tablespoons minced parsley

1. In a very large nonstick skillet, heat 2 tablespoons of the olive oil until shimmering. Add the potatoes in a slightly overlapping layer and cook over moderately high heat, stirring occasionally, until golden, about 8 minutes. Add the onion, season with salt and pepper and cook, stirring, until tender, about 5 minutes longer. Add ½ tablespoon of the vinegar and toss. Cover and keep warm.

2. In another skillet, heat the remaining 1 tablespoon of olive oil. Season the steaks with salt and pepper and cook over moderately high heat, turning, until crusty, 8 to 10 minutes for medium rare. Keep warm on a platter.

3. Add 1 tablespoon of the butter and the shallots to the skillet and cook over moderate heat for about 5 minutes. Add the remaining 1½ tablespoons of vinegar and cook until evaporated, about 30 seconds. Add the wine and cook until reduced, about 2 minutes. Remove from the heat and swirl in the remaining 1 tablespoon of butter. Add the parsley and any meat juices, season with salt and pepper and spoon over the meat. Serve with the Lyonnaise potatoes. —*Daniel Boulud*

WINE Powerful, spicy Syrah.

SPICY BEEF AND BROCCOLI SALAD WITH KIMCHI

ROPA VIEJA WITH CAPERS

beef, lamb + game

Beef Sirloin with Piquillo Peppers and Capers

TOTAL: 30 MIN

4 SERVINGS ● ○

- 2 teaspoons sweet paprika
- 1 teaspoon dark brown sugar

Kosher salt and freshly ground pepper

- 1½ pounds sirloin steak (1¼ inches thick)
- ¼ cup olive oil
- 3 garlic cloves, thinly sliced
- 2 medium shallots, thinly sliced
- 1 tablespoon drained capers
- 1 teaspoon chopped fresh sage
- 8 piquillo peppers (Spanish roasted peppers), seeded and chopped
- 1 teaspoon Dijon mustard
- ½ teaspoon Worcestershire sauce

1. In a small bowl, mix the paprika with the brown sugar, 2 teaspoons of kosher salt and 1 teaspoon of pepper. Pat the mixture all over the meat.

2. In a small skillet, heat the oil over moderate heat. Add the garlic, shallots and capers and cook until the garlic and shallot are softened, about 3 minutes. Stir in the chopped sage and cook for 1 minute. Add the piquillo peppers, mustard and Worcestershire sauce; simmer over moderate heat for 15 minutes, stirring occasionally.

3. Meanwhile, light a grill or preheat a grill pan. Grill the steak over a moderately high fire for 12 minutes, turning once, until a thermometer inserted in the thickest part registers 125° to 130° for medium-rare meat. Let the steak rest for 5 minutes, then slice and serve with the piquillo-pepper sauce. *Bruce Aidells*

WINE Round, supple, fruity Syrah.

Tea-Spiced Beef Short Ribs

ACTIVE: 50 MIN; TOTAL: 2 HR 20 MIN

4 SERVINGS ●

The Riesling in this dish adds a slight sweetness that balances the smoky Lapsang Souchong tea and spicy chiles in the rub on the ribs.

RUB

- 1 tablespoon Lapsang Souchong tea (from 3 tea bags)
- 1 tablespoon light brown sugar
- 1½ teaspoons chipotle chile powder
- ½ teaspoon crushed red pepper

RIBS

- 8 beef short ribs (about 5 pounds)

Salt and freshly ground pepper

- ¼ cup vegetable oil
- 3 medium onions, chopped
- 8 garlic cloves, minced

Four ¼-inch-thick slices of fresh ginger

- 1 bottle (750 ml) Riesling, such as a Spätlese
- ½ cup soy sauce
- ½ cup light brown sugar
- 1 bay leaf

About 1 quart water

White rice, for serving

1. MAKE THE RUB: In a small bowl, mix all of the ingredients.

2. PREPARE THE RIBS: Season the ribs with salt and pepper and rub them all over with the spice rub. In a large enameled cast-iron casserole, heat 1 tablespoon of the oil until it is shimmering. Add half of the ribs and cook over moderately high heat, turning once, until deeply browned on both sides, about 6 minutes total. Transfer to a large

plate. Add 1 tablespoon of oil to the casserole and sear the remaining ribs.

3. Pour off the fat from the casserole and wipe it out. Add the remaining 2 tablespoons of oil to the casserole and heat over moderate heat. Add the onions, garlic and ginger and cook until softened, about 7 minutes. Add the wine and boil over high heat until reduced by half, about 6 minutes. Add the soy sauce, brown sugar, bay leaf and the short ribs. Pour in just enough water to cover the ribs and bring to a boil. Cover and simmer over low heat, stirring occasionally, until the ribs are very tender, about 1½ hours.

4. Transfer the ribs to a large plate and discard the bay leaf and ginger. Boil the sauce over high heat, skimming a few times, until very flavorful, about 10 minutes. Using an immersion blender, puree the sauce; season with salt and pepper. Return the short ribs to the casserole and simmer gently to reheat them. Place 2 short ribs on each plate, spoon the sauce on top and serve with white rice. —*Ming Tsai*

MAKE AHEAD The cooked ribs can be refrigerated for up to 2 days.

WINE Rich, velvety Merlot.

Korean Barbecued Short Ribs with Sesame Salt

ACTIVE: 1 HR; TOTAL: 4 HR

6 SERVINGS

We especially love this recipe because the ribs are cut across the bone and cook for only 10 minutes. They taste just like juicy seared steak, but they're more fun to eat.

RIBS

- 4 pounds meaty kalbi or flanken-style short ribs (see Note)
- ½ cup soy sauce
- ¼ cup Korean rice wine or mirin (see Note)
- ¼ cup pineapple juice
- 2 tablespoons sugar

2 tablespoons Sesame Salt
(recipe follows)

3 tablespoons very finely
chopped garlic

¼ cup chopped scallions

¼ cup minced onion

1 tablespoon finely grated
fresh ginger

1 small Asian pear, cut into
1-inch chunks

3 tablespoons Asian sesame oil

2 teaspoons coarsely ground
Korean red chile
(*gocho karu;* see Note)

2 teaspoons freshly ground
black pepper

ACCOMPANIMENTS

1 head red-leaf lettuce,
leaves separated

4 large garlic cloves,
very thinly sliced

Sesame Salt (recipe follows)

Scallion Salad (recipe follows)

Korean Chili Sauce (recipe follows)

I. MAKE THE RIBS: Put the short ribs in a large bowl. Combine all of the remaining ribs ingredients in a food processor and puree. Add to the short ribs, turn to coat and let marinate at room temperature for at least 3 hours, or refrigerate overnight.

2. Light a grill or preheat the broiler. Remove the ribs from the marinade and shake off any excess. Grill or broil the ribs, turning once, until cooked through, about 5 minutes per side. Serve the short ribs with the accompaniments in separate bowls and let everyone season and wrap their own meat.
—*Anya von Bremzen*

NOTE These ingredients are available at Korean markets. The ribs are also available at a good butcher. Kalbi, or Korean short ribs, is available precut, both on and off the bone. Flanken-style, or L.A. cut, short ribs are sliced ½ inch thick across 3 ribs.

WINE Powerful, spicy Syrah.

Sesame Salt

TOTAL: 10 MIN

MAKES ABOUT ½ CUP ● ●

½ cup sesame seeds

2 teaspoons coarse salt

In a skillet, toast the sesame seeds over moderate heat, stirring, until fragrant and lightly browned, 3 to 4 minutes. Transfer to a spice grinder to cool completely. Grind the sesame seeds with the salt to a coarse powder. —*A.v.B.*

MAKE AHEAD The Sesame Salt can be refrigerated for up to 1 month.

Scallion Salad

ACTIVE: 10 MIN; TOTAL: 1 HR 10 MIN

6 SERVINGS ●

1 large bunch scallions, white and green parts, cut crosswise into 4-inch lengths, then lengthwise into thin strips

2 tablespoons unseasoned rice vinegar

2 teaspoons sugar

1 tablespoon Asian sesame oil

½ teaspoon coarsely ground Korean chile (*gocho karu;* see Note at left)

Large pinch of coarse salt

Submerge the scallion strips in a bowl of ice water until curled, about 1 hour. Drain well and pat dry. Transfer the scallions to a bowl and toss with the remaining ingredients. —*A.v.B.*

Korean Chili Sauce

TOTAL: 5 MIN

MAKES A SCANT ½ CUP ● ●

3 tablespoons Korean sweet-spicy chili paste (*kochujang;* see Note at left)

2½ tablespoons water

1 tablespoon Asian sesame oil

1 teaspoon sugar

In a small bowl, whisk all of the ingredients together until blended. —*A.v.B.*

MAKE AHEAD The chili sauce can be refrigerated for up to 1 week.

Beef with Red and Yellow Bell Peppers

ACTIVE: 40 MIN; TOTAL: 2 HR 40 MIN

4 SERVINGS ●

2 large garlic cloves, cut into very thin slices

2 tablespoons low-sodium soy sauce

2 tablespoons dry sherry

1 teaspoon sugar

½ teaspoon freshly ground pepper

1 tablespoon plus 2 teaspoons vegetable oil

1 pound beef eye of round, halved lengthwise and cut crosswise into 1⁄16-inch-thick slices

1 cup chicken stock or canned low-sodium broth

2 tablespoons oyster sauce

1 teaspoon cornstarch

1 red onion, cut into ½-inch-thick slices

2 yellow bell peppers, cut into 2-inch squares

1 red bell pepper, cut into 2-inch squares

1 teaspoon Chinese chili-garlic paste

½ teaspoon Asian sesame oil

¼ cup coarsely chopped basil

I. In a bowl, mix the garlic, soy sauce, sherry, sugar, pepper and 1 teaspoon of the oil. Add the beef eye of round and coat well. Cover and let stand at room temperature for 2 hours, or refrigerate overnight.

2. In a small bowl, mix the stock, oyster sauce and cornstarch.

3. In a large skillet, heat ½ tablespoon of the oil. Add half of the meat and cook over high heat until browned on one side, about 1 minute. Transfer to a plate. Repeat with ½ tablespoon of the oil and the remaining meat.

4. Add the onion and the remaining 1 teaspoon of oil to the skillet and cook over moderate heat, stirring, until softened, about 3 minutes. Add the bell peppers and lower the heat. Cook the

GRILLED STEAK TACOS

peppers over moderately low heat, stirring, until crisp-tender, about 6 minutes. Stir the stock mixture, then pour it into the skillet and simmer over moderate heat, stirring, until it starts to thicken, about 2 minutes. Return the meat to the skillet and simmer until heated through. Remove from the heat. Stir in the chili-garlic paste, sesame oil and basil and serve. —*Marcia Kiesel*

SERVE WITH Steamed rice.

WINE Tannic, complex Cabernet.

Pancetta-Wrapped Beef Tenderloin

ACTIVE: 45 MIN; TOTAL: 1 HR 30 MIN

6 SERVINGS

- 2 ounces dried porcini mushrooms
- 2 cups boiling water
- 3 tablespoons unsalted butter
- 3 large shallots, minced
- 2 garlic cloves, minced
- 4 scallions, minced

Salt and freshly ground pepper

One 3-pound center-cut trimmed beef tenderloin

- 3½ tablespoons vegetable oil
- 7 ounces thinly sliced pancetta, chilled

I. Preheat the oven to 450°. Soak the porcini in the boiling water for 20 minutes. Rub the porcini in the soaking liquid to remove any grit; pat dry and coarsely chop. Transfer the porcini to a mini food processor and puree.

2. Melt the butter in a medium skillet. Add the shallots and cook over moderately low heat until softened. Add the garlic and cook for 2 minutes. Add the scallions and cook until softened, 2 minutes. Stir in the porcini puree. Season with salt and pepper. Let cool.

3. Season the roast with salt and pepper. Heat 2 tablespoons of the oil in a large skillet. Sear the roast over moderately high heat until browned all over; let cool.

4. On a work suface, slightly overlap three 16-inch-square pieces of wax

paper. Arrange the pancetta on the paper in 4 overlapping rows to form a rectangle the length of the tenderloin. Spread the porcini puree over the pancetta. Set the tenderloin on the bottom edge of the pancetta. Using the wax paper as a guide, tightly roll up the roast in the pancetta, pressing to adhere. Carefully peel off the wax paper. Tie the roast with kitchen string at 1-inch intervals. Transfer to a rimmed baking sheet and brush with the remaining 1½ tablespoons of oil.

5. Roast the beef for 25 minutes, or until the pancetta is crisp and an instant-read thermometer inserted in the center of the meat registers 120°. Let rest for 10 minutes. Cut off the strings and remove. Thickly slice the roast with a serrated knife and serve. —*Marcia Kiesel*

SERVE WITH Sautéed broccoli rabe and roasted potatoes.

WINE Rich, earthy Pinot Noir.

Grilled Steak Tacos

ACTIVE: 50 MIN; TOTAL: 1 HR 30 MIN

6 SERVINGS

- 2 cups all-purpose flour

Kosher salt

- 4 tablespoons unsalted butter, cut into small pieces and chilled
- ⅔ cup warm water

One 3-pound sirloin steak, cut 2 inches thick

- 1 tablespoon extra-virgin olive oil

Freshly ground pepper

Pico de Gallo (recipe follows)

Chunky Guacamole with Cumin (recipe, p. 12)

Mango-Cucumber Salsa (recipe follows)

Simple Black Beans (recipe, p. 259)

I. Preheat the oven to 350°. In a large bowl, whisk the flour with 1 teaspoon of kosher salt. Using a pastry blender or 2 knives, cut in the cold butter until the mixture resembles coarse meal. Add the water and stir with a wooden spoon until a stiff dough forms.

2. Scrape the dough out onto a floured work surface and knead until smooth. If the dough is more than slightly tacky, knead in a few more tablespoons of flour. Shape the dough into a disk, wrap in plastic and refrigerate for 30 minutes.

3. On a floured work surface, cut the chilled dough into quarters. Cut each quarter into 3 equal pieces. Using a rolling pin, roll each piece into a disk, cover with plastic wrap and let rest for 15 minutes. Roll each disk into a very thin 7-inch tortilla.

4. Light a grill. Heat a cast-iron skillet. Lightly oil the skillet and cook each tortilla over moderately high heat until speckled with brown, about 1 minute per side. Transfer the tortilla to a large sheet of foil. Repeat with the remaining tortillas and wrap them in the foil.

5. Rub the steak with the olive oil and season with salt and pepper. Grill the steak over a medium-hot fire until medium rare, 12 to 14 minutes per side, depending on the thickness. Transfer the steak to a carving board and let rest for 10 minutes. Thinly slice the steak across the grain.

6. Heat the tortillas in the oven for about 5 minutes. Serve the steak and tortillas with the Pico de Gallo, Chunky Guacamole, Mango-Cucumber Salsa and Simple Black Beans. —*Fanny Singer*

WINE Intense, berry-flavored Zinfandel.

Pico de Gallo

TOTAL: 15 MIN

MAKES 2½ CUPS ● ● ●

- 1 pint cherry tomatoes, quartered
- ¼ cup minced red onion
- 3 tablespoons chopped cilantro
- 1 jalapeño, seeded and minced
- 1 tablespoon fresh lime juice

Salt

In a bowl, combine the cherry tomatoes with the red onion, cilantro, jalapeño and lime juice. Season with salt and toss well. —*F.S.*

beef, lamb + game

Mango-Cucumber Salsa

TOTAL: 15 MIN

MAKES 2½ CUPS ● ● ●

- 1 firm mango, peeled and cut into ½-inch dice
- 1 medium cucumber—peeled, seeded and cut into ½-inch dice
- ¼ cup chopped cilantro
- 2 tablespoons fresh lime juice
- 1 jalapeño, seeded and very finely chopped

Salt

In a bowl, combine the mango with the cucumber, cilantro, lime juice and jalapeño. Season with salt. —*F.S.*

Stir-Fried Beef with Oven-Fried Potatoes

ACTIVE: 40 MIN; TOTAL: 1 HR 30 MIN

6 SERVINGS

- 2 pounds beef tenderloin, cut into ¼-inch-thick slices, then ¼-inch-wide strips
- 1 teaspoon freshly ground pepper
- 1 teaspoon ground cumin
- ¼ cup soy sauce
- 2 tablespoons corn oil
- 3 large garlic cloves, very finely chopped
- 2 medium red onions, halved lengthwise and cut crosswise into ½-inch-thick slices
- 4 jalapeños, seeded and thinly sliced
- 1½ pounds plum tomatoes—halved, seeded and cut into eighths
- ¼ cup dry red wine
- ¼ cup beef stock or low-sodium broth
- 2 tablespoons chopped cilantro

Oven-Fried Potatoes (recipe follows)

1. In a large bowl, toss the beef tenderloin with the pepper, cumin and 1 tablespoon of the soy sauce. In a large skillet or wok, heat the oil until shimmering. Working in batches, add the beef strips and stir-fry over high heat until lightly browned, about 3 minutes per batch. Transfer the beef to a bowl with a slotted spoon.

2. Add the garlic to the skillet and cook over moderate heat, stirring, until golden, 30 seconds. Add the onions and stir-fry until softened, about 5 minutes. Add the jalapeños and cook, stirring, for 1 minute. Using a slotted spoon, add the vegetables to the beef in the bowl. Add the tomatoes to the skillet and cook, stirring occasionally, until slightly softened, about 2 minutes.

3. Increase the heat to high and return the beef and vegetables to the skillet. Add the wine, stock and the remaining 3 tablespoons of soy sauce and stir-fry for 3 minutes. Add the cilantro and Oven-Fried Potatoes and toss gently to combine. Transfer to a platter and serve. —*Maricel Presilla*

WINE Round, supple, fruity Syrah.

Oven-Fried Potatoes

ACTIVE: 20 MIN; TOTAL: 1 HR 15 MIN

6 SERVINGS

In South America, fried potatoes are more than just a side dish; they are an integral part of many main dishes.

- 2 pounds russet potatoes, peeled and cut lengthwise into ¼-inch strips
- ¼ cup corn oil

Kosher salt

1. Preheat the oven to 450°. In a large bowl, cover the potatoes with cold water and let stand for 20 minutes.

2. Heat 2 large rimmed baking sheets in the oven for 5 minutes. Drain the potatoes and pat dry with paper towels. Return the potatoes to a dry bowl, add the oil and toss to coat.

3. Spread the oiled potatoes on the hot baking sheets and bake for about 35 minutes, or until they are golden brown and crisp, stirring every 10 minutes. If the edges start to darken, stir them more often. Season the potatoes with salt and serve. —*M.P.*

Roast Beef Tenderloin with Morel Cream Sauce

ACTIVE: 25 MIN; TOTAL: 1 HR

6 SERVINGS ●

- 2 ounces dried morels (2 cups)
- 1½ cups boiling water
- One 3¼-pound trimmed and tied beef tenderloin roast

Salt and freshly ground pepper

- 3 tablespoons unsalted butter
- 1 tablespoon vegetable oil
- 2 large shallots, minced
- 1¼ cups heavy cream

1. Preheat the oven to 375°. In a large heatproof bowl, soak the morels in the boiling water until softened, 20 minutes. Reserving the soaking liquid, rub the morels under running water to remove any grit; coarsely chop any large ones.

2. Season the roast with salt and pepper. In a very large, ovenproof skillet, melt 2 tablespoons of the butter in the oil. Add the roast and brown over moderately high heat on 3 sides for 4 minutes per side. Turn the roast on the fourth side and roast for about 35 minutes, or until an instant-read thermometer inserted in the center registers 125° for rare. Transfer the roast to a carving board, cover loosely with foil and let rest.

3. Discard any fat from the skillet and set over high heat. Pour in the mushroom liquid, stopping when you reach the grit. Boil the liquid, scraping up the browned bits on the bottom of the pan, until reduced to ½ cup, 3 minutes. Strain through a fine sieve over a bowl.

4. Wipe out the skillet and add the remaining 1 tablespoon of butter. Add the shallots and cook over moderate heat until softened, about 4 minutes. Stir in the morels. Add the heavy cream and the reserved mushroom liquid and simmer until thickened, about 7 minutes. Season with salt and pepper. Cut the roast into ½-inch-thick slices and serve with the sauce. —*Christophe Côte*

WINE Tannic, complex Cabernet.

Roast Beef with Spicy Yogurt-Walnut Sauce

TOTAL: 30 MIN

4 SERVINGS ●

One 2-pound beef eye of round roast
2 tablespoons soy sauce
1½ tablespoons extra-virgin olive oil
Salt and freshly ground pepper
1 cup walnut halves (3 ounces)
2 medium Italian frying peppers, cut into small dice
1 teaspoon ground cumin
1 teaspoon ground coriander
¼ teaspoon cayenne pepper
2 cups plain whole milk yogurt
2 small garlic cloves, minced
2 plum tomatoes, diced

1. Preheat the oven to 450°. Heat a large ovenproof skillet until very hot. On a plate, rub the roast all over with the soy sauce and then with 1 tablespoon of the olive oil; season with salt and pepper. Add the roast to the skillet, fat side down, along with any extra oil from the plate. Cook over moderately high heat, turning, until browned all over, 4 minutes. Turn the roast fat side up and roast in the oven for 25 minutes, or until an instant-read thermometer inserted in the thickest part registers 115° for rare. Transfer to a carving board to rest.

2. Meanwhile, toast the walnuts on a baking sheet until lightly browned, about 5 minutes; let cool. Coarsely chop.

3. In a medium skillet, heat the remaining ½ tablespoon of olive oil. Add the frying peppers, cumin, coriander and cayenne, cover and cook over moderately low heat until the peppers are barely softened, about 5 minutes. Let cool.

4. In a medium bowl, combine the yogurt, garlic, walnuts, frying peppers and tomatoes and season with salt and pepper. Thinly slice the roast and serve with the walnut sauce. —*Marcia Kiesel*

VARIATIONS Use the spicy walnut sauce on chicken or lamb, or serve as a dip.

WINE Assertive, heady Grenache.

Tomato and Beef Ragù

ACTIVE: 30 MIN; TOTAL: 45 MIN

MAKES 4 CUPS ● ●

2 tablespoons extra-virgin olive oil
1 medium carrot, finely chopped
1 small celery rib, finely chopped
1 small onion, finely chopped
1 pound beef eye of round or top round, finely chopped
Salt and freshly ground pepper
2 garlic cloves, minced
1 bay leaf
1 teaspoon dried oregano
Pinch of freshly grated nutmeg
One 28-ounce can whole tomatoes, finely chopped, juice reserved
1 tablespoon tomato paste
½ cup dry red wine

Heat the olive oil in a large skillet. Add the carrot, celery and onion and cook over low heat, stirring occasionally, until softened, about 10 minutes. Add the meat, season with salt and pepper and cook over moderate heat, stirring, until no pink remains, about 4 minutes. Add the garlic, bay leaf, oregano and nutmeg and cook, stirring, until fragrant, about 1 minute. Stir in the chopped tomatoes with their juice and the tomato paste and simmer over low heat, stirring occasionally, until thickened, about 10 minutes. Add the wine, cover and simmer for 10 minutes longer. Remove from the heat and season with salt and pepper and serve. —*Sophie Braimbridge*

MAKE AHEAD The ragù can be refrigerated overnight.

WINE Tart, low-tannin Barbera.

Braised Meat-and-Potato Pie

ACTIVE: 30 MIN; TOTAL: 1 HR 30 MIN

6 SERVINGS

2 pounds Yukon Gold potatoes, peeled and cut into 2-inch chunks
Salt
1 tablespoon unsalted butter
2 tablespoons vegetable oil
1 pound onions, thinly sliced
2 garlic cloves, minced
1 tablespoon all-purpose flour
2 cups beef or chicken stock or low-sodium broth
1½ pounds leftover braised beef or lamb, cut into ¼-inch slices, or thickly sliced delicatessen roast beef
⅓ cup chopped flat-leaf parsley
Freshly ground pepper
1 cup milk
3 large eggs
½ cup shredded Gruyère cheese

1. Preheat the oven to 400°. Butter a 3-quart glass or ceramic baking dish.

2. In a large saucepan, cover the potatoes with water and add a large pinch of salt. Bring to a boil, then simmer over moderate heat until tender, about 25 minutes. In another large saucepan, melt the butter in the oil. Add the onions and cook over moderately high heat until just wilted and golden, about 7 minutes. Stir in the garlic and flour, then add the stock and bring to a boil, stirring constantly. Add the meat and simmer over low heat until the sauce is slightly thickened, about 15 minutes. Stir in the parsley; season with salt and pepper. Transfer to the prepared baking dish.

3. Drain the potatoes; return them to the saucepan. Shake the potatoes over moderate heat until completely dry; remove from the heat and mash. Whisk in the milk and season with salt and pepper. Whisk in the eggs, 1 at a time.

4. Spread the potatoes over the meat and sprinkle the Gruyère on top. Bake in the upper third of the oven for 30 minutes, or until the sauce is bubbling and the potato topping is golden brown. Let the gratin rest for at least 10 minutes and for up to 20 minutes before serving. —*Jacques Pépin*

MAKE AHEAD The meat filling can be refrigerated for up to 2 days. Bring to room temperature before proceeding.

WINE Rich, smoky-plummy Shiraz.

beef, lamb + game

Beef Brisket with Mustard and Rye Crumbs

ACTIVE: 1 HR; TOTAL: 13 HR

12 SERVINGS

The brisket has to be refrigerated overnight, so plan accordingly.

BRISKET

One 10-pound beef brisket,
  trimmed of excess fat

Salt

Four 12-ounce bottles amber beer

2   cups water

4   celery ribs, coarsely chopped

4   medium onions, coarsely chopped

3   carrots, coarsely chopped

4   bay leaves

1   bunch thyme

1   bunch flat-leaf parsley

6   large garlic cloves, chopped

One 1-inch piece of fresh ginger,
  thinly sliced

2   teaspoons coriander seeds

2   teaspoons mustard seeds

1   teaspoon fennel seeds

1   teaspoon black peppercorns

CRUMB TOPPING

One 1-pound loaf rye bread with seeds,
  crusts removed, bread
  cut into 1-inch pieces

1   stick (4 ounces) unsalted
  butter, softened

1   tablespoon sugar

Salt

6   tablespoons Dijon mustard

I. MAKE THE BRISKET: Season the brisket all over with salt and let stand at room temperature for at least 30 minutes or for up to 4 hours.

2. Preheat the oven to 325°. Set a large roasting pan over 2 burners and add all of the remaining brisket ingredients. Nestle the brisket in the braising liquid and bring to a boil over high heat. Cover with foil and braise in the oven for about 3 hours, or until the brisket is very tender. Let the brisket cool in the braising liquid, then cover and refrigerate the meat overnight.

3. MAKE THE CRUMB TOPPING: Preheat the oven to 300°. In a food processor, process the rye bread to coarse crumbs. Add the butter and sugar; pulse until evenly coated. Spread the crumbs on a large rimmed baking sheet and bake for about 20 minutes, stirring occasionally, until they start to dry out. Increase the oven temperature to 350°, season the crumbs with salt and bake for about 12 minutes longer, stirring occasionally, until golden brown and crisp. Let cool completely.

4. Skim the fat from the surface of the braising liquid and let the brisket return to room temperature. Lower the oven temperature to 325°. Cover the brisket and bake for about 1 hour, or until heated through. Transfer the brisket to a carving board and cover with foil. Strain the braising liquid into a medium saucepan, reserving the vegetables. Skim the fat from the braising liquid and boil over high heat until reduced to 6 cups, about 20 minutes. Season with salt and pepper.

5. Increase the oven temperature to 350°. Trim any fat from the surface of the brisket and cut it into 12 pieces. Transfer the brisket pieces back to the roasting pan. Pour in enough of the hot braising liquid to reach halfway up the meat. Spread ½ tablespoon of mustard over the top of each piece. Return the braised vegetables to the roasting pan. Cover the brisket and vegetables with foil and bake for about 15 minutes, or until heated through.

6. To serve, pour ½ cup of the hot braising liquid into each of 12 shallow serving bowls and add some of the braised vegetables. Place a piece of brisket in each bowl, top with ¼ cup each of the crisp rye bread crumbs and serve immediately.
—*Ken Oringer*

MAKE AHEAD The recipe can be prepared through Step 4 and then refrigerated overnight. Bring the braised brisket and vegetables to room temperature before reheating. The rye bread crumbs can be stored in an airtight container at room temperature for up to 2 days.

SERVE WITH Boiled or steamed potatoes.

WINE Tannic, full-bodied Barbaresco.

Brisket with Onion-and-Chile Jam

ACTIVE: 40 MIN; TOTAL: 5 HR 30 MIN

6 SERVINGS ●

Letting the brisket rest in the pan juices for a half hour makes it especially moist.

2   tablespoons pure olive oil

11 medium onions, 7 minced,
  4 coarsely chopped

2   Thai chiles, with some
  seeds, minced

Salt

5   large carrots, coarsely chopped

1   bunch celery, coarsely chopped

Freshly ground pepper

One 5-pound beef brisket, fat trimmed
  to a thin layer

2   quarts hot chicken stock or
  low-sodium broth

½   teaspoon soy sauce

I. Heat the pure olive oil in a large skillet. Add the minced onions and the Thai chiles and season with salt. Cook over low heat, stirring occasionally, until the onions are very soft, about 25 minutes. Increase the heat to moderately low and cook, stirring, until the onions are deeply browned, about 10 minutes longer.

2. Preheat the oven to 325°. Spread the carrots, celery and coarsely chopped onions in an even layer in a roasting pan and season them with salt and pepper. Season the brisket with salt and pepper and set it on top of the vegetables, fat side up. Spread the onion-and-chile jam in an even layer over the top of the brisket and pour the hot stock into the pan around the meat. Cover the roasting pan and braise the brisket for about 4½ hours, or until it is very tender, basting every 30 minutes.

BEEF BRISKET WITH MUSTARD AND RYE CRUMBS

beef, lamb + game

3. Let the brisket rest in the pan juices for 30 minutes, then transfer it to a carving board. Strain the pan juices into a saucepan, pressing on the vegetables, then skim off the fat. Add the soy sauce, season with pepper and bring to a simmer. Thinly slice the brisket across the grain and serve with the pan juices.

—*Jean-Georges Vongerichten*

MAKE AHEAD The recipe can be prepared through Step 2 and refrigerated for up to 2 days. Reheat before proceeding.

SERVE WITH Boiled egg noodles.

WINE Rich, velvety Merlot.

Beef Stew

ACTIVE: 1 HR; TOTAL: 11 HR 15 MIN

6 SERVINGS ●

This beef stew gives you everything you want in comfort food—it's hearty and satisfying—but what makes it stand out is its subtle, sophisticated use of coriander and fenugreek seeds. The cooked meat needs to be refrigerated overnight, so plan accordingly.

3½ pounds well-marbled beef chuck, trimmed of excess fat, cut into 2-inch pieces

Salt and freshly ground pepper

2 tablespoons vegetable oil

6 garlic cloves, minced

1 large Spanish onion, very coarsely chopped

2 cups soft, dry red wine, such as Merlot

INGREDIENT TIP

marbled beef

CUTS OF MARBLED BEEF—meat that's got some fat running through it—are more tender and flavorful than lean cuts. The front of the animal generally has more marbled meat (shoulder, ribs) than the back. For stews, opt for beef chuck, which comes from the shoulder.

---

4 thyme sprigs

4 plum tomatoes, coarsely chopped

4 medium carrots, cut into 1-inch pieces

1 bay leaf

1 teaspoon coriander seeds and ¼ teaspoon fenugreek seeds, tied in cheesecloth

1 quart beef stock or low-sodium broth

2 tablespoons unsalted butter

1 pound white mushrooms, quartered

1 cup water

1 pound turnips, peeled and cut into 1-inch dice

2 tablespoons all-purpose flour

2 tablespoons chopped flat-leaf parsley

1. Season the meat with salt and pepper. In a large enameled cast-iron casserole, heat 1 tablespoon of the vegetable oil until shimmering. Add half of the beef and cook over moderately high heat until the meat is browned all over, about 12 minutes. Transfer the meat to a large, shallow bowl. Repeat with the remaining vegetable oil and meat.

2. Add the garlic and onion to the casserole and cook over low heat, stirring occasionally, until softened, about 8 minutes. Return the meat and any accumulated juices to the casserole. Add the wine and bring to a boil, then reduce the heat and simmer for 2 minutes. Add the thyme, tomatoes, carrots, bay leaf, spice bag and stock and bring to a boil. Cover partially and simmer over low heat until the meat is tender, about 1½ hours. Let the stew cool, then refrigerate overnight.

3. Cover the stew and rewarm it over low heat. Meanwhile, melt the butter in a large skillet. Add the quartered mushrooms, season with salt and pepper and cook over moderately low heat until they release their liquid, about 6 minutes. Pour 2 tablespoons of the liquid into a

small bowl and let cool. Cook the mushrooms over moderate heat, stirring occasionally, until they are browned, about 6 minutes longer. Add the mushrooms to the stew.

4. Return the large skillet to moderate heat. Add the water and turnips and season with salt. Cover the skillet and cook the turnips over moderate heat until they are just fork-tender, about 5 minutes. Add the turnips to the stew. Discard the thyme sprigs, bay leaf and the spice bag.

5. Whisk the flour into the reserved mushroom liquid to form a paste. When the stew comes to a simmer, stir ½ cup of the sauce into the paste until blended. Stir the paste into the stew and bring to a boil. Simmer the stew over moderate heat, stirring frequently, until the sauce thickens, about 2 minutes. Season the stew with salt and pepper, stir in the parsley and serve at once.

—*Marcia Kiesel*

MAKE AHEAD The beef stew can be covered and refrigerated for up to 2 days. Bring the stew to room temperature and reheat gently before serving.

SERVE WITH Buttered noodles.

WINE Rich, velvety Merlot.

Beef Stew with Red Currant Jelly and Cream

ACTIVE: 35 MIN; TOTAL: 10 HR 35 MIN

6 SERVINGS ●

In classic French cuisine, when the sauce for wine-braised boar or venison is flavored with red currant jelly and cream, the dish is called *grand veneur*. Beef and pork are delicious prepared in *grand veneur* style, too.

4 pounds well-trimmed beef chuck, cut into 1-inch cubes

3 celery ribs, coarsely chopped

2 large carrots, coarsely chopped

2 medium onions, coarsely chopped

1½ cups dry red wine

2 bay leaves

1½ tablespoons juniper berries
1 tablespoon chopped rosemary
1 tablespoon chopped thyme
¼ cup peanut oil
¼ cup all-purpose flour
¼ cup red wine vinegar
¼ cup tomato paste
1 quart chicken stock
  or low-sodium broth
¾ cup red currant jelly
Salt and freshly ground pepper
½ cup heavy cream

1. In a large bowl, toss the beef with the celery, carrots, onions, wine, bay leaves, juniper berries, rosemary and thyme. Cover and refrigerate overnight, stirring a few times.

2. Drain the meat and vegetables in a colander set over a bowl. Pick out the juniper berries and discard them; reserve the marinade. In a large enameled cast-iron casserole, heat 2 tablespoons of the oil until shimmering. Add half of the meat and vegetables and cook over moderately high heat until lightly browned on the bottom, about 3 minutes. Stir and cook until lightly browned all over, about 2 minutes longer. Transfer the mixture to a bowl. Repeat with the remaining 2 tablespoons of oil and the remaining meat and vegetables.

3. Return the meat and vegetables to the casserole. Stir in the flour and cook, stirring, for about 2 minutes. Add the vinegar and stir to scrape up any browned bits from the bottom of the casserole. Add the reserved marinade and the tomato paste and simmer, stirring, for 2 minutes. Add the stock and 6 tablespoons of the currant jelly, season with salt and pepper and bring to a boil. Reduce the heat to low and simmer, stirring occasionally, until the meat is very tender, 2 to 2½ hours.

4. Drain the stew in a colander set over a bowl. Transfer the pieces of meat to a platter. Press on the solids in the colander to extract as much liquid as possible. Pour the liquid back into the casserole and return the meat to the pot. Stir in the cream and bring to a simmer. Season the stew with salt and pepper.

5. Place the remaining 6 tablespoons of red currant jelly in a saucepan and cook over moderate heat until it is completely melted. Ladle the stew into large, shallow bowls. Drizzle the warm jelly over the stew and serve. —*Wolfgang Puck*

MAKE AHEAD The recipe can be prepared through Step 3 and refrigerated overnight. Reheat before proceeding.

SERVE WITH Spaetzle with Gruyère and Caramelized Onions (recipe, p. 83).

WINE Rich, smoky-plummy Shiraz.

Beef Kefta with Coriander and Cumin

TOTAL: 55 MIN

8 SERVINGS ●

Moroccan cooks like to knead their finely ground and spiced beef or lamb so that their kefta (meatballs or patties) will be smooth.

2 pounds lean ground beef
1 tablespoon ground coriander
1 tablespoon ground cumin
1 teaspoon salt
1 teaspoon sweet paprika
¼ cup extra-virgin olive oil
Homemade Harissa (recipe follows)

1. In a large bowl, mix the ground beef with the coriander, cumin, salt, paprika and 3 tablespoons of the olive oil. Form the meat into sixteen 3-inch patties.

2. In a large skillet, heat the remaining 1 tablespoon of olive oil. Cook the kefta in 2 batches over moderately high heat, turning once, until just cooked through, 5 to 6 minutes. Drain on paper towels and serve warm or at room temperature with the Homemade Harissa. —*Hajja Halima*

MAKE AHEAD The kefta can be kept at room temperature for up to 2 hours.

WINE Bright, fruity rosé.

Homemade Harissa

TOTAL: 30 MIN

MAKES ⅔ CUP ● ● ●

The ultimate hot sauce from North Africa, *harissa* is the traditional condiment served with couscous. It is easy to prepare.

⅔ pound fresh red chiles
  (about 5 inches long),
  stemmed and cut into pieces
¼ cup water
1 teaspoon salt
⅓ cup extra-virgin olive oil

1. In a blender, puree the chiles with the water and salt until as smooth as possible; the seeds will remain whole.

2. Heat the olive oil in a medium saucepan. Add the chile puree and cook over moderately low heat, stirring occasionally, until the liquid is evaporated and the oil separates, about 25 minutes. Let cool, then transfer to a jar. —*H.H.*

MAKE AHEAD The *harissa* can be refrigerated for up to 2 weeks.

Classic Beef Burgers

TOTAL: 30 MIN

4 SERVINGS ●

Many restaurants claim to be the birthplace of the hamburger. Louis' Lunch, in New Haven, Connecticut, is a leading contender. Since 1900, the Lassen family has been grinding its beef daily, hand-shaping the patties to order and grilling the burgers in antique cast-iron broilers over an open flame. The ground beef formula uses five different parts of the chuck; a combination of chuck and sirloin makes a similarly meaty, juicy burger. The Louis' Lunch classic is topped with just onion and tomato, though the Lassens do offer a Cheddar cheese sauce. The version of that sauce here is spiked with beer.

½ pound Colby cheese or mild
  yellow Cheddar,
  shredded (about 2 cups)
2 teaspoons cornstarch

beef, lamb + game

1 garlic clove, halved

1 cup lager

2 teaspoons Dijon mustard

Salt and freshly ground pepper

¾ pound ground sirloin, at room temperature

¾ pound ground chuck, at room temperature

4 hamburger buns

2 tablespoons unsalted butter, melted

Vegetable oil, for brushing

4 Boston lettuce leaves

4 thin tomato slices

1. In a small bowl, toss the cheese with the cornstarch. Rub the garlic all over the inside of a medium saucepan, then add the clove to the pan with the lager and bring to a boil. Add the cheese mixture in large handfuls, stirring until melted, and bring to a boil. Add the mustard, season with salt and pepper and simmer over moderate heat until thickened, about 3 minutes; keep warm over low heat.

2. In a medium bowl, lightly knead the sirloin with the chuck and loosely form into 4 patties about ¾ inch thick. Season the burgers very generously with salt and pepper and transfer to a plate lined with plastic wrap. Brush the cut sides of the buns with the melted butter.

3. Light a grill. When the fire is medium hot, oil the grate. Grill the burgers for 10 minutes, turning once, for medium meat. Move the burgers away from the heat and grill the cut sides of the buns for about 1 minute, until toasted.

4. Set a lettuce leaf and a tomato slice on the bottom half of each bun. Top each with a burger and a generous spoonful of cheese sauce. Cover with the top half of a bun and serve, passing the remaining cheese sauce on the side. —*Steven Raichlen*

MAKE AHEAD The cheese sauce can be refrigerated overnight. Rewarm gently.

WINE Intense berry-flavored Zinfandel.

Pepper Jack Cheeseburgers with Jalapeño-Cumin Sauce

TOTAL: 30 MIN

4 SERVINGS ●

The cheeseburger is an American icon; this one acquires Tex-Mex overtones, thanks to jalapeño-laced Pepper Jack cheese. Mixing the cheese right into the ground beef keeps the burgers incredibly moist, even when they're cooked to medium. Be sure to oil the grate well before cooking so the burgers won't stick to the grill.

3 large fresh jalapeños, seeded and coarsely chopped

½ cup plus 3 tablespoons coarsely chopped cilantro

3 large garlic cloves, smashed

2 tablespoons fresh lime juice

2 tablespoons water

1 teaspoon ground cumin

Kosher salt

1½ pounds ground sirloin, at room temperature

4 ounces Pepper Jack cheese, shredded (about 1 cup)

Freshly ground pepper

4 hamburger buns

Olive oil, for brushing

About ¼ cup mayonnaise

1 cup shredded iceberg lettuce

4 thin tomato slices

Pickled sliced jalapeños, for serving

1. In a blender, combine the fresh jalapeños with ½ cup of the cilantro, the garlic, lime juice, water, ½ teaspoon of the ground cumin and a generous pinch of salt. Puree the jalapeño-cumin sauce until smooth.

2. In a medium bowl, lightly knead the sirloin with the Pepper Jack cheese and the remaining 3 tablespoons of cilantro and ½ teaspoon of cumin. Loosely shape the meat into 4 patties about ¾ inch thick; tuck any large pieces of cheese into the burgers. Season very generously with salt and pepper and transfer the burgers to a plate lined with plastic wrap. Brush the cut sides of the buns with olive oil.

3. Light a grill. When the fire is medium hot, brush the grate with olive oil. Grill the cheeseburgers for about 10 minutes, turning once, for medium meat. Move the cheeseburgers away from the heat and grill the cut sides of the buns until they are toasted, about 1 minute.

4. Spread a thin layer of mayonnaise on the cut sides of the buns. Set the cheeseburgers on the bottom halves and top with the lettuce, tomato and pickled jalapeños. Spoon some of the jalapeño sauce on the burgers, top with the buns and serve right away, passing the remaining sauce on the side.

—*Steven Raichlen*

WINE Intense berry-flavored Zinfandel.

New Mexican Chile-Sirloin Burgers with Salsa Verde

ACTIVE: 1 HR; TOTAL: 1 HR 30 MIN

4 SERVINGS

These hamburgers get their kick from roasted green chiles—both as *rajas* (roasted chile strips) that are spooned on the burgers and in the salsa verde topping. The chiles of choice are the long, slender, mild green New Mexico variety, also known as Anaheim; for a bit more heat, substitute poblanos.

Olive oil, for brushing

4 unpeeled garlic cloves

1½ pounds New Mexico or poblano chiles

2 tablespoons finely chopped cilantro

2 teaspoons fresh lime juice

½ teaspoon ground cumin

½ teaspoon dried oregano, crumbled

¼ cup water

Kosher salt and freshly ground pepper

4 ounces sharp white Cheddar cheese, shredded (about 1 cup)

1½ pounds ground sirloin, at room temperature

4 hamburger buns

1. Light a grill. When the fire reaches medium hot, brush the grate with oil. Skewer the garlic cloves on a 4-inch bamboo skewer. Grill the chiles and garlic, turning occasionally, until blackened all over, about 6 minutes for the garlic and 15 to 20 minutes for the chiles. Transfer the chiles and garlic to a medium bowl, cover with plastic wrap and let cool. Peel, core and seed the chiles and cut them into ¼-inch strips. Peel the garlic cloves.

2. Transfer the garlic and two-thirds of the chiles to a blender. Add the cilantro, lime juice, cumin, oregano and water and puree until smooth. Season the sauce with salt and pepper and transfer to a small saucepan. Simmer over moderate heat, stirring, until the sauce is slightly thickened, about 5 minutes. In a small bowl, combine the remaining roasted chiles with the cheese.

3. Shape the meat into 4 patties about ¾ inch thick and season very generously with salt and pepper. Grill the burgers over a medium-hot fire for about 10 minutes, turning once, for medium-rare meat. Move the burgers away from the heat. Brush the cut sides of the buns with oil and grill until lightly toasted, about 1 minute.

4. Set the grilled burgers on the bottom halves of the buns. Top the burgers with the chile-cheese mixture and a spoonful of the salsa verde. Cover the green-chile burgers with the buns and serve right away, passing the remaining salsa verde on the side. —*Steven Raichlen*

WINE Assertive, heady Grenache.

Melted Edam with Beef

ACTIVE: 35 MIN; TOTAL: I HR

6 TO 8 SERVINGS

In the Yucatán, a whole aged cheese is often stuffed with ground meat and steamed, then served with two sauces: tomato-chile and creamy white. The Edam we get in the United States has a less sturdy rind, so it's easier to shred and bake the cheese, then top it with the ground meat, as done here.

- ¼ cup pure olive oil
- 6 garlic cloves, minced
- 2 Anaheim chiles, coarsely chopped
- 1 white onion, coarsely chopped
- 1 large tomato, coarsely chopped
- 1 pound ground beef

Salt and freshly ground pepper

- ¾ cup pitted green olives, chopped
- ¾ cup golden raisins (4 ounces)
- ¼ cup drained capers
- 2 large hard-cooked egg yolks, finely chopped
- ¾ pound Edam cheese, shredded

1. Preheat the oven to 400°. In a medium skillet, heat the oil. Add the garlic, chiles and onion and cook over moderate heat, stirring, until lightly browned and softened, about 12 minutes. Add the tomato and cook for 1 minute, then push the mixture to one side. Add the ground beef to the skillet. Break it up with a wooden spoon and cook over moderately high heat, stirring, until starting to brown, 4 minutes. Stir in the sauce, season with salt and pepper and cook over moderate heat until the meat is cooked through, about 4 minutes. Add the olives, raisins and capers and cook, stirring, until heated through, about 3 minutes. Add the egg yolks, season with salt and pepper and keep warm.

2. Spread the cheese in a large, shallow baking dish. Cover with aluminum foil and bake until just melted, 10 minutes. Spoon the beef mixture on top and serve hot. —*Patricia Quintana*

SERVE WITH Warm corn tortillas and Yucatán Table Sauce (recipe, p. 171).

WINE Soft, earthy Rioja.

TASTE TEST # bottled barbecue sauce

To find the zippiest and most delicious barbecue sauce available on supermarket shelves, the F&W staff tasted 27 nationally sold brands stocked by grocery stores. These four barbecue sauces won out.

PRODUCT	F&W COMMENT	INTERESTING BITE
Bone Suckin' Sauce Hot	"Tangy and smoky, with a real kick."	The company president's grandmother used to suck the sauce off ribs and chicken bones, hence the name.
Napa Valley Barbecue Co.'s Johnny's Original	"Nice heat and not too sweet."	This recipe was invented by company founder Johnny McIntosh, who once owned a barbecue restaurant.
Texas Best Original Rib Style Barbecue Sauce	"Great for brushing on meat and poultry; a little fruity and a little spicy."	The original recipe dates back to 1933; in 2001, the company lightened and sweetened it.
Hay Day Country Market Memphis BBQ Sauce	"Hot, with a pleasing lemony flavor."	Tomato-based Memphis-style sauces get their spice from black pepper; this one uses cayenne, too.

● FAST ● HEALTHY ● MAKE AHEAD ● STAFF FAVORITE

SUMMER VEGETABLE STEW WITH BRAISED RABBIT

Summary Vegetable Stew with Braised Rabbit

ACTIVE: 1 HR 30 MIN; TOTAL: 3 HR 15 MIN

4 SERVINGS ●

RABBIT

- 2 tablespoons unsalted butter
- 2 rabbit legs (1 pound)

Kosher salt and freshly ground pepper

- 1 medium onion, finely chopped
- 2 carrots, finely chopped
- 2 celery ribs, finely chopped
- 6 medium garlic cloves, lightly smashed
- 1 tomato, coarsely chopped
- 3 cups chicken stock or canned low-sodium broth
- 1 cup dry white wine
- 2 bay leaves
- 1 sprig of summer savory (optional)

VEGETABLES

- 5 ounces sugar snap peas (1½ cups)
- ¾ pound fingerling potatoes
- 3 tablespoons extra-virgin olive oil
- ¼ pound shiitake mushrooms, stems discarded, caps quartered
- 12 baby zucchini or yellow squash, halved lengthwise
- 8 small radishes, quartered
- ½ medium red onion, very thinly sliced

Salt and freshly ground pepper

- 1½ teaspoons very finely chopped garlic
- 1 tomato—peeled, seeded and finely chopped
- ¼ cup finely chopped flat-leaf parsley
- 4 tablespoons unsalted butter, cut into tablespoons
- 2 tablespoons sherry vinegar

Grilled peasant bread, for serving

1. MAKE THE RABBIT: In a large, heavy, heatproof casserole, heat 1 tablespoon of the butter. Season the rabbit with salt and pepper and cook over moderate heat until golden all over, about 10 minutes. Transfer the rabbit to a plate. Add the remaining 1 tablespoon of butter to the casserole along with the onion, carrots, celery and garlic. Cover and cook over moderate heat, stirring occasionally, until softened, about 5 minutes. Add the tomato and cook, stirring, just until softened. Add the chicken stock, wine, bay leaves and summer savory and bring to a boil.

2. Return the rabbit to the casserole and cook, uncovered, over moderately low heat until it is just tender, about 1½ hours. Let the rabbit cool in the broth for 30 minutes, then transfer to a plate to cool completely.

3. Pull the meat from the bones and tear it into large shreds. Cover the meat with plastic wrap. Strain the broth, pressing hard on the vegetables to extract as much liquid as possible; discard the vegetables.

4. MAKE THE VEGETABLES: Bring a medium saucepan of water to a boil. Add the sugar snaps and cook until crisp-tender, 1 minute. Using a slotted spoon, transfer the sugar snaps to a cutting board and let cool. Return the water to a boil. Add the potatoes and cook over moderate heat until tender, about 25 minutes; drain. Cut the potatoes into ½-inch slices and the sugar snaps into ½-inch lengths.

5. In a large skillet, heat 2 teaspoons of the olive oil until shimmering. Add the shiitake mushrooms and cook over moderately high heat until tender and lightly browned, about 5 minutes. Transfer the mushrooms to a large plate and cover loosely; keep warm. Add another 2 teaspoons of olive oil to the skillet. Add the zucchini and cook until tender and lightly browned, about 3 minutes. Transfer to the plate with the mushrooms. Add another 2 teaspoons of olive oil to the skillet. Add the potatoes and cook until lightly browned, about 3 minutes. Transfer to the plate. Add the radishes and onion to the skillet and cook until crisp-tender and lightly browned, about 3 minutes. Return all of the vegetables to the skillet and season with salt and pepper; keep warm.

6. In a large saucepan, heat the remaining 1 tablespoon of olive oil until shimmering. Add the rabbit meat and garlic, season with salt and pepper and cook over moderate heat until fragrant, 2 minutes. Add the tomato and cook until softened, 3 minutes. Add the reserved rabbit broth and the parsley and bring to a simmer. Whisk in the butter, a piece at a time. Add the vinegar and season with salt and pepper. Spoon the vegetables into bowls, ladle the rabbit stew on top and serve with grilled peasant bread. —*Stuart Brioza*

MAKE AHEAD The recipe can be prepared through Step 3 up to 2 days ahead.

WINE Complex, silky red Burgundy.

Grilled Lamb with Radicchio and Black-Olive Oil

TOTAL: 45 MIN

4 SERVINGS

- ½ cup Calamata olives, pitted
- ⅓ cup plus ¼ cup extra-virgin olive oil, plus more if needed
- 1 teaspoon minced garlic
- ½ teaspoon finely chopped rosemary
- 1 teaspoon finely grated lemon zest
- 1 teaspoon sherry vinegar
- 1 large head radicchio, quartered
- 1 tablespoon minced shallot
- ¼ teaspoon finely chopped thyme

Salt and coarsely cracked pepper

- 2 teaspoons ground cumin
- 2 teaspoons sweet paprika
- 1¼ pounds boneless leg of lamb, cut into 1-inch cubes

1. In a blender, combine the olives with ⅓ cup of the olive oil and puree. Add the garlic, rosemary, lemon zest and vinegar and puree. If the black-olive oil is too thick, add a little more olive oil.

beef, lamb + game

2. Preheat a grill or grill pan. Brush the radicchio quarters with 1 tablespoon of the remaining oil and grill them over high heat until they are wilted, about 5 minutes. Toss with 2 tablespoons of the oil, the shallot and thyme. Season with salt and pepper; keep warm.

3. In a bowl, mix the cumin, paprika and the remaining 1 tablespoon of oil. Add the lamb; turn to coat. Season with salt and pepper. Grill over high heat until medium rare, about 2 minutes per side. Thread each lamb cube onto a small skewer. Arrange the radicchio on a platter, top with the lamb and serve with the black-olive oil. —*Sang Yoon*
WINE Assertive, heady Grenache.

Grilled Lamb Sirloin with Greek Salad
TOTAL: 25 MIN
4 SERVINGS ●

- 2 tablespoons fresh lemon juice
- 2 teaspoons grated lemon zest
- 1½ teaspoons chopped rosemary
- 1 garlic clove, chopped
- Freshly ground pepper
- ¼ cup plus 1 tablespoon olive oil
- Two 8-ounce lamb sirloins, butterflied
- Salt
- 1 pint grape tomatoes
- 1 medium cucumber—peeled, seeded and thinly sliced
- ⅓ cup pitted black olives
- ⅓ cup crumbled feta cheese

buying lamb
INGREDIENT TIP

THERE ARE FIVE USDA GRADES of lamb, based on the ratio of fat to lean meat. Starting with the best, they are Prime, Choice, Good, Utility and Cull. The color of the meat indicates the age of the animal—the darkest comes from the oldest, the palest from the youngest.

1. In a food processor, combine the lemon juice with the lemon zest, rosemary, garlic and 1 teaspoon of pepper and pulse to blend. With the machine on, slowly pour in 1 tablespoon of the olive oil until a paste forms. Spread 1 tablespoon of the lemon paste all over the lamb and refrigerate for 10 minutes.
2. Light a grill or preheat a grill pan. Season the lamb with salt and grill over a medium-high fire for 8 minutes, turning once, until an instant-read thermometer inserted in the thickest part of the meat registers 125° to 130° for medium rare. Transfer the lamb to a platter and let rest for 5 minutes.
3. Meanwhile, in a medium bowl, toss the tomatoes with the cucumber, olives and feta cheese. In a small bowl, whisk the remaining lemon paste with the remaining ¼ cup of olive oil and season with salt and pepper. Toss the salad with the dressing and mound on plates. Carve the lamb across the grain into 1-inch slices and serve with the salad. —*Bruce Aidells*
WINE Tart, low-tannin Barbera.

Rosy Rack of Lamb with Garlic
ACTIVE: 20 MIN; TOTAL: 3 HR
2 SERVINGS
A meat thermometer is essential for testing the rack for doneness. You'll want to take the rack out at 130° for rare and 140° for medium; the internal temperature will rise about 5° as the lamb rests before carving.

- 2 medium garlic cloves, finely chopped
- 1 teaspoon finely chopped rosemary
- 1 teaspoon finely chopped thyme
- ¼ cup plus 3 tablespoons finely chopped parsley
- One 1½-pound trimmed rack of lamb, frenched
- Coarse salt and freshly ground pepper
- 2 teaspoons extra-virgin olive oil
- 3 tablespoons minced onion

1. Mix the garlic, rosemary, thyme and ¼ cup of the parsley and rub the herbs over the meaty side of the lamb. Let stand at room temperature for 2 hours.
2. Wipe off the marinade from the lamb and season with salt and pepper. In a medium ovenproof skillet, heat the olive oil until shimmering. Add the lamb and cook over moderately high heat until browned all over, about 5 minutes. Remove from the heat and let rest for 15 minutes.
3. Preheat the oven to 300°. Bake the rack of lamb in the skillet for about 25 minutes for rare, or until an instant-read thermometer inserted in the thickest part of the meat registers 130°. Transfer the lamb to a carving board and let rest for 10 minutes.
4. Carve the rack into 8 chops and arrange on 2 plates. Scatter the onion and the remaining 3 tablespoons of chopped parsley over the chops and serve. —*Paula Wolfert*
WINE Tannic, complex Cabernet.

Pancetta-Wrapped Roast Leg of Lamb
ACTIVE: 40 MIN; TOTAL: 2 HR 30 MIN
4 TO 6 SERVINGS
The potent garlic-herb paste helps the pancetta hug the lamb and flavors both as they roast.

- 6 anchovy fillets, drained
- 3 large garlic cloves
- 2 tablespoons thyme leaves
- 2 tablespoons rosemary leaves
- Finely grated zest of 1 orange
- ¼ cup extra-virgin olive oil
- Salt and freshly ground pepper
- 1 small leg of lamb with the aitchbone removed (about 5 pounds)
- 1 pound thinly sliced pancetta
- 1 large onion, coarsely chopped
- 1 large carrot, coarsely chopped
- 1 celery rib, cut into 1-inch pieces
- 2 cups dry white wine

1. Preheat the oven to 375°. In a food processor, combine the anchovies with the garlic, thyme, rosemary, orange zest and olive oil and process to a smooth paste. Season with salt and pepper. Using a small paring knife, make 1½-inch-deep slits all over the lamb. Spread the herb paste all over the lamb, working it into the slits; season the lamb with salt and pepper.

2. On a large sheet of plastic wrap or wax paper, overlap the pancetta slices to form a 12-by-15-inch rectangle. Set the lamb on the pancetta and wrap the plastic around the leg, pressing to help the pancetta adhere. Peel off the plastic and reposition any slices of pancetta. Using 7 or 8 long pieces of kitchen string, tie the roast at 1-inch intervals.

3. Set the lamb in a roasting pan and scatter the onion, carrot and celery around it. Roast for about 2¼ hours, or until the pancetta is golden and an instant-read thermometer inserted in the thickest part of the meat registers 140°. Transfer the lamb to a cutting board and let rest for 20 minutes.

4. Meanwhile, set the roasting pan over high heat. Add the wine and bring to a boil, scraping up any browned bits from the bottom of the pan. Strain the wine into a small saucepan and simmer until reduced to 1 cup, about 20 minutes. Skim the fat from the sauce and transfer to a gravy boat. Remove the kitchen string from the lamb and thinly slice the meat. Serve at once with the sauce.

—*Michael White*

WINE Tannic, full-bodied Barbaresco.

Lavender-Marinated Leg of Lamb

ACTIVE: 30 MIN; TOTAL: 9 HR 20 MIN

8 SERVINGS

Try to butterfly the lamb so it's about the same thickness all over and will cook evenly on the grill, or have the butcher do it for you. The lamb is marinated overnight, so plan accordingly.

One 5½-pound butterflied leg
  of lamb, trimmed
4 anchovy fillets, cut crosswise
  into 24 pieces
2 garlic cloves, each cut into
  6 slices and halved lengthwise
2 teaspoons minced rosemary
¼ cup extra-virgin olive oil,
  plus more for serving
¼ cup dry white wine
1 tablespoon dried lavender
  (see Note)
Salt and freshly ground pepper
Lemon wedges, for serving

1. Using a small knife, make 24 incisions all over the lamb. Stuff each with a piece of anchovy and garlic and a pinch of rosemary. In a roasting pan, combine the ¼ cup of olive oil with the wine and lavender. Add the lamb; coat well. Cover and refrigerate overnight.

2. Light a grill. Bring the lamb to room temperature and season with salt and pepper. Grill the lamb over a moderately low fire for about 40 minutes, or until lightly charred and an instant-read thermometer inserted in the thickest part registers 125° for medium rare. Transfer the lamb to a carving board, cover with foil and let rest for 10 minutes before thinly slicing it. Serve with lemon wedges and additional olive oil.

—*Michael Tusk*

NOTE Dried lavender is available at specialty food stores and from Dean & DeLuca, 800-221-7714.

SERVE WITH Roasted tomato halves.

WINE Deep, pungent, tannic Barolo.

Indian-Spiced Butterflied Leg of Lamb

ACTIVE: 20 MIN; TOTAL: 9 HR

8 SERVINGS

This easy Indian-inspired lamb dish uses a cornucopia of fragrant spices. The spice-rubbed meat needs to be refrigerated for at least 6 hours, so plan accordingly.

3 tablespoons coriander seeds
2 tablespoons cumin seeds
2 teaspoons yellow mustard seeds
2 small dried red chiles
1 teaspoon black peppercorns
1 tablespoon ground turmeric
1 tablespoon ground fenugreek
1 teaspoon ground cardamom
½ teaspoon ground ginger
One 5-pound butterflied leg of lamb
¼ cup extra-virgin olive oil
Salt

1. In a medium skillet, combine the coriander, cumin and mustard seeds with the chiles and peppercorns. Toast the spices over moderate heat, shaking the pan, until fragrant, about 1 minute. Transfer to a spice grinder to cool completely, then grind to a powder. Transfer the spices to a bowl and stir in the turmeric, fenugreek, cardamom and ginger.

2. Spread the lamb on a large baking sheet and rub it all over with the spices. Cover with plastic wrap and refrigerate for at least 6 hours or overnight.

3. Preheat the oven to 400°. Scrape most of the spices off the lamb. Rub the meat with 3 tablespoons of the olive oil and season with salt.

4. In a large roasting pan set over 2 burners, heat the remaining 1 tablespoon of olive oil until shimmering. Add the lamb, fat side down, and cook over moderate heat until deeply browned, about 5 minutes. Turn the lamb over and cook the other side over moderate heat until golden, about 3 minutes. Transfer the lamb to the oven and roast for 25 minutes, or until an instant-read thermometer inserted in the thickest part registers 120° for medium rare.

5. Transfer the lamb to a carving board and let stand for 10 minutes. Carve the meat into thick slices and serve.

—*Gail Monaghan*

MAKE AHEAD The spice-rubbed lamb can be refrigerated for up to 24 hours.

WINE Powerful, spicy Syrah.

ROAST LEG OF LAMB PROVENÇAL

GRILLED LAMB CHOPS WITH TAHINI SAUCE

Roast Leg of Lamb Provençal

ACTIVE: 25 MIN; TOTAL: 1 HR 45 MIN

8 SERVINGS

One 4-pound trimmed boneless
    leg of lamb, rolled and tied with
    kitchen string in 4 places
2 tablespoons unsalted
    butter, softened
Salt and freshly ground pepper
4 slices of white bread, cut into
    quarters
1 cup flat-leaf parsley leaves
2 garlic cloves, chopped
2 medium shallots, chopped
2 tablespoons extra-virgin
    olive oil

1. Preheat the oven to 425°. Set the lamb in a roasting pan, fat side up; rub it all over with the butter. Season generously with salt and pepper. Roast in the oven for 20 minutes.

2. Meanwhile, in a food processor, process the bread into fine crumbs. Transfer the crumbs to a small bowl. Add the parsley, garlic, shallots and olive oil to the food processor; process to make a paste. Mix the paste with the bread crumbs.

3. Baste the lamb with the rendered fat in the pan. Pat the parslied crumbs over the top and sides of the roast. Reduce the oven to 400°; roast the lamb for 45 minutes, or until an instant-read thermometer inserted in the thickest part of the meat registers 125° for medium-rare meat. Transfer to a cutting board; let rest for 15 minutes.

4. Carefully cut and remove the string from the roast. With a serrated knife, carve the lamb into thick slices and serve. —*Jacques Pépin*

WINE Powerful, spicy Syrah.

Lamb Chops with Spicy Thai Peanut Sauce

TOTAL: 25 MIN

4 SERVINGS ● ●

2 large garlic cloves
⅓ cup cilantro leaves
⅓ cup unsalted natural peanut butter
2 tablespoons peanut oil
2 tablespoons ketchup
1 tablespoon Thai green curry paste
1 tablespoon fresh lime juice
1 tablespoon Asian fish sauce
1 tablespoon soy sauce
1 teaspoon sugar
Eight 1-inch-thick loin lamb chops
    (about 2 pounds)

1. In a food processor, pulse the garlic and cilantro until finely chopped. Add all of the remaining ingredients except the lamb; pulse until a paste forms. Spread ¼ cup of the paste over the lamb chops.

2. In a saucepan, whisk remaining paste with ⅓ cup of water. Warm the sauce over low heat; it should be pourable.

3. Light a grill or preheat a grill pan. Grill the chops over a medium-high fire for 4 minutes per side, or until an instant-read thermometer inserted in the thickest part of a chop registers 125° to 130° for medium rare. Transfer the chops to a platter. Spoon some warm peanut sauce over the lamb chops and serve, passing the extra sauce on the side.

—*Bruce Aidells*

WINE Round, supple, fruity Syrah.

Grilled Lamb Chops with Tahini Sauce

TOTAL: 25 MIN

4 SERVINGS ●

- ½ cup loosely packed cilantro leaves, plus 1 tablespoon chopped cilantro, for garnish
- 2 small garlic cloves
- 10 large mint leaves
- ⅓ cup plus 2 tablespoons fresh lemon juice
- 2½ tablespoons olive oil
- 2 teaspoons sweet paprika
- 1 teaspoon freshly ground black pepper
- 1 teaspoon ground cumin
- 1 teaspoon ground turmeric
- 1 teaspoon ground fennel seeds
- ¼ teaspoon cayenne pepper

Pinch of cinnamon

Kosher salt

- 8 lamb chops, ½ to ¾ inch thick (2¼ pounds)
- 1 tablespoon tahini paste
- 2 tablespoons hot water

1. In a food processor, combine the ½ cup of cilantro leaves with the garlic and mint and pulse until just coarsely chopped. Add ⅓ cup of the lemon juice, 1 tablespoon of olive oil, the paprika, black pepper, cumin, turmeric, fennel seeds, cayenne and cinnamon. Stir in 1 teaspoon of kosher salt to combine.

Process the mixture until a paste forms. Put the chops in a baking dish, pour the spice-paste marinade over them and turn them to coat.

2. Light a grill or preheat a grill pan. Grill the lamb chops over a medium-high fire for 8 minutes, turning once with tongs, until an instant-read thermometer inserted in the thickest part of a chop registers 125° to 130° for medium rare. Transfer the chops to a platter and let rest for 5 minutes.

3. Meanwhile, in a small bowl, whisk the tahini and water with the remaining 2 tablespoons of lemon juice and 1½ tablespoons of olive oil until smooth. Garnish the chops with the chopped cilantro and serve with the tahini sauce.

—*Bruce Aidells*

WINE Complex, savory Chianti Classico.

Spice-Dusted Lamb Chops with Cherry Tomatoes

TOTAL: 30 MIN

4 SERVINGS ●

- 1½ tablespoons ground coriander
- 1¼ teaspoons ground ginger
- 1 teaspoon ground turmeric
- 1 teaspoon freshly ground black pepper
- ½ teaspoon ground cumin
- ½ teaspoon ground cinnamon
- ¼ teaspoon ground cloves
- ¼ teaspoon cayenne pepper

Eight 12-ounce lamb loin chops, about 1½ inches thick

Salt

Vegetable oil, for brushing

- 2 pints cherry tomatoes, halved
- 1 tablespoon unsalted butter

1. Light a grill or preheat a grill pan. In a small bowl, combine all of the spices. Season the lamb chops with salt, rubbing it into the meat. Rub each chop all over with a scant teaspoon of the spice dust. Let the chops stand for 10 minutes.

2. Brush the chops all over with enough vegetable oil to coat and then grill over

a medium-hot fire or in the grill pan over moderate heat, turning once with tongs, until crusty and medium rare, about 6 minutes per side. Transfer the chops to a serving platter and let rest for about 5 minutes.

3. Meanwhile, in a large bowl, toss the cherry tomatoes with the remaining spice dust. In a large skillet, melt the butter. Add the cherry tomatoes to the skillet, sprinkle with salt and cook over moderately high heat, tossing, until just hot, about 1 minute. Transfer to the platter with the chops and serve at once.

—*Marcia Kiesel*

VARIATIONS Use the savory spice dust on chicken or pork before grilling or broiling, or sprinkle it on sautéed vegetables and toss well.

WINE Assertive, heady Grenache.

COOKING TIP

jalapeño-mint jelly

Mint jelly and lamb are a mouthwatering match. This version of jelly gets an extra kick from fresh chiles. Crush together 3½ cups sugar and 1 cup small mint sprigs in a large saucepan. Add 1 cup water and ½ cup apple cider vinegar and bring to a boil over high heat, stirring. Boil until the sugar melts, about 2 minutes. Add 2 jalapeños, seeded and minced, and boil hard for 2 minutes. Add one 3-ounce pouch liquid pectin and 1 drop green food coloring and boil for 30 seconds. Strain the jalapeño-mint jelly through a fine sieve, then pour into 4 hot sterilized ½-pint jars without creating many bubbles; stop ¼ inch from the top. Wipe the glass rims and close the jars. Set in a water bath and boil for 10 minutes. —*Eugenia Bone*

beef, lamb + game

Lamb Steaks with Shallot-Anchovy Relish

TOTAL: 25 MIN

4 SERVINGS ● ●

- 5 tablespoons extra-virgin olive oil
- 4 large shallots, thinly sliced
- ¼ cup very coarsely chopped flat-leaf parsley
- 3 large anchovy fillets, very finely chopped
- 1 teaspoon coriander seeds, crushed
- 1 teaspoon minced rosemary

Salt and freshly ground pepper

4 bone-in lamb leg steaks (6 to 7 ounces each), cut ½ inch thick (see Note)

1. Heat 1 tablespoon of the olive oil in a large skillet. Add the shallots and cook over high heat, stirring, until just softened, about 1 minute; transfer to a small bowl. Stir in 3 tablespoons of the olive oil and the parsley, anchovies, coriander seeds and rosemary. Season the shallot relish with salt and pepper.

2. In the same skillet, heat the remaining 1 tablespoon of olive oil. Season the lamb steaks with salt and pepper. When the oil is almost smoking, add the lamb steaks and cook over high heat until well browned on the bottoms, about 3 minutes. Turn the steaks and cook just until the lamb is medium rare, about 1 minute longer. Transfer the lamb steaks to a platter, top with the shallot relish and serve. —*Marcia Kiesel*

NOTE Lamb leg steaks are center slices from the sirloin and leg sections of the lamb. Ask a butcher to cut them for you if you don't see them in the market.

MAKE AHEAD The shallot-anchovy relish can be refrigerated for up to 1 day. Bring to room temperature before serving.

WINE Intense, berry-flavored Zinfandel.

White Wine—Braised Lamb Shoulder with Red Wine Jus

ACTIVE: 15 MIN; TOTAL: 3 HR 10 MIN

8 SERVINGS ●

In this rustic but elegant recipe, Adolfo Muñoz braises a boneless lamb shoulder in a dry white wine, which will not overshadow the meat's flavor the way a red might. After the lamb is cooked, though, he adds a red wine reduction to the braising liquid to deepen the flavor of the jus.

One 6-pound boneless lamb shoulder roast, tied with kitchen string at 1-inch intervals

Salt and freshly ground pepper

- ¼ cup plus 2 tablespoons extra-virgin olive oil
- 2 bottles (750 ml each) light, dry white wine, such as Pinot Grigio or Muscadet
- 1 quart water
- 2 large rosemary sprigs
- 2 large thyme sprigs
- 2 large marjoram sprigs
- 2 large sage sprigs
- 1½ cups dry red wine, such as Syrah

1. Preheat the oven to 325°. Season the lamb shoulder generously with salt and pepper. In a large roasting pan set over 2 burners, heat ¼ cup of the olive oil until shimmering. Add the lamb shoulder to the pan and cook it over moderate heat, using tongs to turn it on 4 sides, until browned all over, about 7 minutes per side. Transfer the lamb shoulder to a large plate and pour off the fat from the roasting pan.

2. Return the lamb to the roasting pan. Pour in the white wine and water and bring to a boil over high heat. Add the rosemary, thyme, marjoram and sage sprigs. Cover the lamb with parchment paper, then cover the roasting pan with foil. Braise the lamb in the oven for about 2½ hours, or until very tender, turning it halfway through.

3. Transfer the lamb to a cutting board and cover it with foil. Pour the braising liquid into a large saucepan and skim off the fat. Boil the liquid over high heat, skimming the surface occasionally with a metal spoon, until reduced to 4 cups, about 30 minutes.

4. Meanwhile, in a medium saucepan, boil the red wine over high heat until reduced to approximately ⅔ cup, about 7 minutes. Strain the reduced lamb-braising liquid into the warm red wine reduction. Add the remaining 2 tablespoons of the olive oil and bring to a boil. Boil over high heat until the jus is reduced to 2½ cups, 10 to 15 minutes. Season with salt and pepper.

5. Cut the strings from the lamb roast and discard. Using a carving knife, cut the lamb into ½-inch-thick slices and transfer to serving plates. Ladle the warm jus over the lamb slices and serve right away. —*Adolfo Muñoz*

MAKE AHEAD The lamb roast and jus can be refrigerated separately overnight. Thickly slice the lamb while it is still cold, arrange the meat in a roasting pan and cover it with the jus. Cover the roasting pan with foil and bake in a 350° oven until heated through.

SERVE WITH Cherry tomatoes sautéed in olive oil and dusted with *pimentón*, the Spanish smoked paprika.

WINE Powerful, spicy Syrah.

COOKING TIP

tenderizing meat

THERE ARE A FEW WAYS TO make tough meat more tender. Use a meat pounder (a mallet sold at kitchenware shops) to break down tendons and fibers in boneless cuts. Marinades that contain salt, an acidic ingredient (like lemon juice or vinegar) or even milk can also help. Braising and stewing, a method of simmering meat in a liquid over a long period of time, can tenderize meat as well.

Cumin Lamb Kebabs with Fresh Mango Chutney

ACTIVE: 1 HR; TOTAL: 2 HR

4 SERVINGS

A blend of zesty spices and herbs gives lots of flavor to these lamb shish kebabs. When using wooden skewers for kebabs, be sure to soak them in water for about an hour beforehand to prevent them from burning on the grill.

- 1 tablespoon cumin seeds
- 2 teaspoons black peppercorns
- Cardamom seeds from 2 pods (scant ⅛ teaspoon)
- 2 whole cloves
- 1 dried red chile, crumbled
- ¼ cup cashews, coarsely chopped
- 2 tablespoons dry red wine
- ⅛ teaspoon ground mace or nutmeg
- 2 cups plain low-fat yogurt
- Juice of 2 lemons
- Salt
- 2 pounds boneless leg of lamb, cut into 1½-inch pieces
- 1 large mango, peeled, fruit cut off the pit (see Note)
- 2 cups cilantro leaves
- 1 cup mint leaves
- 2 teaspoons chopped shallot
- ½ teaspoon chopped garlic
- Vegetable oil, for brushing

I. In a small skillet, combine the cumin, peppercorns, cardamom, cloves and chile and toast over moderate heat for 1 minute. Transfer to a spice grinder and let cool. Grind to a powder and transfer to a large bowl. Finely grind the cashews. In the bowl, mix the spices with the cashews, wine, mace, 1 cup of the yogurt and the juice of 1 lemon. Season with salt. Stir in the lamb and refrigerate for 1 to 2 hours.

2. Cut half of the mango into ⅓-inch dice and coarsely chop the rest. In a food processor, coarsely puree the cilantro, mint, shallot, garlic and coarsely chopped mango with the remaining yogurt and lemon juice. Transfer the chutney to a bowl. Stir in the diced mango and season the chutney with salt.

3. Light a grill. Thread the lamb onto eight 8-inch skewers. Brush with oil and grill over a hot fire until medium rare, about 3 minutes per side. Serve at once with the mango chutney. —*Thomas John*

NOTE Follow this easy method for slicing a mango. First remove the skin with a vegetable peeler or paring knife. Place the peeled mango on its narrow side and slice off as much flesh as possible, lengthwise and parallel to the pit. Now slice the flesh crosswise.

WINE Rich, smoky-plummy Shiraz.

Lamb Shanks Osso Buco—Style

ACTIVE: 40 MIN; TOTAL: 4 HR

8 SERVINGS ●

Full-flavored lamb substitutes for the usual mild veal in this classic Italian stew with tomatoes, onions and carrots. The shank is an affordable, lean cut that is perfect for braising and stewing. If you want to get the best, ask your butcher to include about an inch of the arm chop and arm bone.

- ¼ cup vegetable oil
- 8 lamb shanks (1¼ pounds each), fat trimmed
- Salt and freshly ground pepper
- 3 tablespoons extra-virgin olive oil
- 12 garlic cloves, very finely chopped
- 4 medium onions, coarsely chopped
- 4 medium carrots, halved lengthwise and cut into 1-inch pieces
- 2 large celery ribs, cut into ½-inch dice
- 1 bottle (750 ml) dry red wine
- One 28-ounce can crushed tomatoes
- 2½ cups chicken stock or low-sodium broth
- Three 3-inch-long strips of orange zest
- 2 teaspoons dried oregano
- ¼ cup coarsely chopped flat-leaf parsley

I. Preheat the oven to 325°. In a very large skillet, heat 2 tablespoons of the vegetable oil. Add 4 of the lamb shanks, season with salt and pepper and cook over moderate heat until well browned all over, about 10 minutes. Transfer the shanks to a large roasting pan. Repeat with the remaining vegetable oil and shanks. Pour off the fat.

2. Heat the olive oil in the same skillet. Add the garlic, onions, carrots and celery and cook over moderate heat until softened, about 10 minutes. Add the wine, bring to a boil over moderately high heat and simmer for 3 minutes. Add the tomatoes, stock, orange zest, oregano and 2 tablespoons of the parsley and bring to a boil. Pour the mixture over the lamb and cover with foil. Braise in the oven for about 3 hours, or until the lamb shanks are very tender.

3. Increase the oven temperature to 350°. Transfer the lamb shanks to a large, deep baking dish, cover with aluminum foil and keep warm. Pour the sauce and vegetables into a large saucepan; discard the strips of orange zest. Simmer the sauce over moderate heat, skimming the surface occasionally, until it is richly flavored, about 15 minutes. Season with salt and pepper and pour over the lamb shanks.

4. Cover the dish of lamb shanks with foil and bake for about 10 minutes, or until they are heated through. Set a lamb shank on each plate and spoon some of the sauce over and alongside. Garnish with the remaining 2 tablespoons of parsley and serve. —*Joshua Wesson*

MAKE AHEAD The recipe can be prepared through Step 3 and refrigerated overnight. Spoon the cold fat from the surface and bring the lamb shanks to room temperature before reheating them in a 325° oven for about 45 minutes.

SERVE WITH Rutabaga Mash (recipe, p. 230), boiled noodles, potatoes or rice.

WINE Deep, pungent, tannic Barolo.

beef, lamb + game

Lamb Tagine with Toasted Almonds and Prunes

ACTIVE: 40 MIN; TOTAL: 2 HR 30 MIN

6 SERVINGS ●

Tagine is the Moroccan word for both a stew and the conical earthenware dish it traditionally cooks in. If you don't have the classic pot, use an enameled cast iron casserole. The caramelized prunes in this luscious lamb stew add a mild sweetness to the dish, making it a perfect partner for fluffy couscous or crusty bread.

- 1 pound pitted prunes
- 2 tablespoons unsalted butter
- 3 large garlic cloves, minced
- 1 teaspoon kosher salt
- 1½ teaspoons ground cinnamon
- ¾ teaspoon ground ginger
- ¾ teaspoon ground turmeric
- ¾ teaspoon freshly ground pepper
- ¼ teaspoon freshly grated nutmeg

Pinch of saffron threads

- 3 pounds trimmed boneless lamb shoulder, cut into 2-inch pieces
- 2 cups water
- 1 cup whole blanched almonds
- 1 tablespoon sesame seeds
- 2 tablespoons sugar
- 1 tablespoon orange flower water

1. In a medium bowl, cover the prunes with warm water and let stand for 1 hour, or until softened. Drain well.

2. Meanwhile, add the butter to a large tagine set over a metal heat diffuser on low heat for 10 minutes. Increase the heat to moderate. Using the side of a heavy knife, mash the garlic with the salt and add to the tagine. Add ½ teaspoon of the cinnamon and the ginger, turmeric, pepper, nutmeg and saffron. Cook over low heat until sizzling. Add the lamb and cook over moderate heat, stirring, until the spices are fragrant and have coated the meat, 5 minutes. Add the water and bring to a boil. Cover with the tagine lid or with a piece of parchment paper and a large metal lid; simmer over moderate heat, stirring occasionally, until the lamb is tender, about 2 hours.

3. While the lamb is cooking, preheat the oven to 350°. Spread the almonds on a baking sheet and toast for 5 minutes, or until golden. Transfer to a plate to cool. Spread the sesame seeds on the baking sheet and toast for 3 minutes, until golden. Transfer to the plate.

4. Pour ½ cup of the lamb cooking juices into a large skillet. Add the prunes, the remaining 1 teaspoon of cinnamon, the sugar and the orange flower water. Cook over low heat, stirring occasionally, until the prunes are lightly caramelized, about 25 minutes. Transfer the prunes to the tagine, leaving the syrup in the skillet.

5. Transfer the lamb to a plate. Working in 2 batches, brown the lamb in the skillet with the prune syrup over moderate heat, stirring, for about 5 minutes. Return the lamb to the tagine.

6. Skim the fat from the stew and reheat, stirring a few times. Sprinkle the almonds and the sesame seeds on top and serve. —*Paula Wolfert*

MAKE AHEAD The lamb tagine can be refrigerated for up to 3 days.

WINE Bright, fruity rosé.

Lamb Tagine with Artichokes and Peas

ACTIVE: 45 MIN; TOTAL: 1 HR 30 MIN

8 SERVINGS ●

- ¼ cup vegetable oil
- 1 teaspoon salt
- 1 teaspoon ground ginger
- ½ teaspoon freshly ground white pepper
- ½ teaspoon freshly ground black pepper
- 1 large pinch of saffron threads
- ¼ teaspoon ground turmeric
- 8 lamb blade chops, cut ¾ inch thick
- 1 small onion, finely chopped
- 1 small bunch flat-leaf parsley
- 1 small bunch cilantro
- 1 cup water
- ½ preserved lemon, pulp discarded, rind cut into thin strips (see Note)
- 1 lemon, halved
- 8 small artichokes (¼ pound each)

One 10-ounce box frozen baby peas, thawed

1. In a large enameled cast-iron casserole, mix the oil with the salt, ginger, white and black pepper, saffron and turmeric. Add 4 of the blade chops in a layer; cook over moderate heat, turning once, until lightly browned, about 15 minutes. Transfer to a plate. Lightly brown the remaining 4 chops. Return the first 4 chops to the casserole and sprinkle the onion over the top. Tie the parsley and cilantro into a bundle and add it to the casserole along with the water and preserved lemon. Cover and bring the stew to a boil, then reduce the heat to moderate and cook until the lamb is just tender, about 30 minutes.

2. Meanwhile, squeeze the lemon halves into a large bowl of cold water; add the halves. Working with 1 artichoke at a time, snap off the outer green leaves. Using a sharp knife, trim the stem to ½ inch and cut off the top two-thirds of the leaves. Peel the bottom and stem. Scrape out the hairy choke, then drop the artichoke into the lemon water.

3. Drain the artichokes and add them to the casserole, tucking them under and between the lamb chops, then add the peas. Cover and cook until the lamb and artichokes are very tender, about 20 minutes. Transfer the lamb, artichokes and peas to a platter and strain the juices into a small saucepan. Skim off the fat, then boil the juices until reduced, about 10 minutes. Pour the juices over the lamb and serve. —*Hajja Halima*

NOTE Preserved lemons are pickled in salted lemon juice. They can be mail-ordered from Kalustyan's, 212-685-3451.

MAKE AHEAD The tagine can be refrigerated for up to 3 days.

WINE Light, fruity Pinot Noir.

LAMB TAGINE WITH ARTICHOKES AND PEAS

LAMB AND SWEET POTATO SHEPHERD'S PIE

HEARTY LAMB RAGÙ WITH RIGATONI

Greek-Style Lamb Burgers with Yogurt-Cucumber Sauce

TOTAL: 45 MIN

4 SERVINGS

In Greece (and in much of the Middle East and Asia), the meat of choice for grilling is lamb—either whole pieces or patties and sausages.

1½ pounds ground lamb
1 small onion, minced
1 garlic clove, minced
3 tablespoons very finely
   chopped mint
3 tablespoons finely chopped
   flat-leaf parsley
Kosher salt and freshly ground pepper
Olive oil, for brushing
4 pocketless pita breads or nan,
   about 8 inches in diameter
4 romaine lettuce leaves
4 thin tomato slices
4 paper-thin red onion slices
Yogurt-Cucumber Sauce
   (recipe follows)

1. In a medium bowl, lightly knead the ground lamb with the onion, garlic, mint, and parsley. Season with 1 scant teaspoon each of salt and pepper. Shape the meat mixture into 4 long, oval patties about ½ inch thick. Transfer the patties to a plate lined with plastic wrap. Brush the burgers with enough olive oil to coat them lightly.

2. Light a grill. When the fire is medium hot, brush the grate with olive oil. Grill the lamb burgers for about 12 minutes, turning once, for medium meat. Move the burgers away from the heat and grill the pita breads, turning once, until just lightly toasted on both sides, about 1 minute total.

3. Set the burgers on the pita breads and top them with the lettuce, tomato, onion and a generous spoonful of the Yogurt-Cucumber Sauce. Fold the pita breads over the burgers and serve them right away, passing a bowl of the remaining Yogurt-Cucumber Sauce alongside.
—*Steven Raichlen*

WINE Light, zesty, fruity Dolcetto.

Yogurt-Cucumber Sauce

TOTAL: 10 MIN

MAKES ABOUT 1½ CUPS ● ● ●

½ seedless cucumber, peeled and
   halved lengthwise
1 garlic clove, minced
½ teaspoon kosher salt
1 cup plain whole milk yogurt
2 tablespoons extra-virgin olive oil
1 tablespoon very finely chopped
   fresh mint
Freshly ground pepper

1. Using a melon baller or small spoon, scoop out the seedy center of the cucumber. Coarsely shred the cucumber flesh. Gently squeeze the excess liquid from the shredded cucumber without mashing it.

2. In a small bowl, using the back of a spoon, mash the garlic with the salt to a paste. Stir in the yogurt, olive oil and mint. Add the shredded cucumber, season with pepper and serve. —S.R.

MAKE AHEAD The sauce can be refrigerated overnight.

Lamb and Sweet Potato Shepherd's Pies

ACTIVE: 40 MIN; TOTAL: 2 HR 30 MIN

4 SERVINGS

This shepherd's pie combines the earthy flavor of lamb with exotic spices and sweet potatoes.

- 3 tablespoons extra-virgin olive oil
- 2 pounds boneless lamb shoulder, cut into ½-inch pieces

Salt and freshly ground pepper

- 4 garlic cloves, minced
- 1 medium onion, finely chopped
- 2 carrots, cut into ½-inch dice
- 1¼ teaspoons ground cumin
- 1¼ teaspoons hot paprika
- ½ teaspoon ground allspice
- ¼ teaspoon turmeric
- 1½ tablespoons all-purpose flour
- 3½ cups water
- 5 cups baby spinach (3 ounces)
- 2 pounds sweet potatoes, baked and peeled
- 1½ ounces soft goat cheese
- ½ cup milk
- 1 tablespoon unsalted butter

1. In a large enameled cast-iron casserole, heat 2 tablespoons of the olive oil until shimmering. Working in batches if necessary, add the lamb and season with salt and pepper. Cook over moderately high heat until browned all over, about 6 minutes. Transfer the lamb to a shallow bowl.

2. Add the garlic, onion and the remaining 1 tablespoon of olive oil to the casserole and cook over moderate heat until softened. Add the carrots and spices and cook, stirring constantly, until fragrant, about 2 minutes. Stir in the flour until incorporated. Add the lamb and water. Bring to a boil, stirring with a wooden spoon to scrape up any browned bits from the bottom of the casserole. Reduce the heat to low and simmer uncovered, stirring the stew occasionally, until the lamb is very tender and the sauce is thickened, about 1½ hours.

3. Raise the heat to moderately high and stir in the spinach until wilted. Season with salt and pepper. Spoon the lamb stew into 4 shallow 2½-cup glass or ceramic baking dishes.

4. Meanwhile, preheat the oven to 425°. In a medium saucepan, mash and stir the sweet potatoes over high heat until warmed through. Mash in the goat cheese, milk and butter and season with salt and pepper.

5. Spread the mashed sweet potatoes over the lamb stew and bake for about 10 minutes, or until hot and bubbling at the edges. Preheat the broiler. Broil the topping 4 inches from the heat until golden, about 1 minute. Serve at once. —Marcia Kiesel

WINE Rich, velvety Merlot.

Hearty Lamb Ragù with Rigatoni

ACTIVE: 45 MIN; TOTAL: 2 HR 15 MIN

4 TO 6 SERVINGS ●

- ¼ cup plus 2 tablespoons extra-virgin olive oil
- 2 large carrots, finely chopped
- 1 large onion, finely chopped
- 1 medium red bell pepper, finely chopped
- 4 ounces thickly sliced pancetta, cut into ¼-inch dice
- 1 pound boneless lamb shoulder, cut into ½-inch dice
- ¾ cup dry red wine

One 28-ounce can peeled Italian tomatoes, coarsely chopped, juices reserved

- 1 cup chicken stock or canned low-sodium broth
- 1 bay leaf
- ½ teaspoon crushed red pepper

Salt and freshly ground black pepper

- 1 pound rigatoni

Freshly grated Pecorino Romano cheese, for serving

1. In a medium enameled cast-iron casserole, heat ¼ cup of the olive oil until shimmering. Add the carrots, onion and red bell pepper and cook over moderate heat, stirring occasionally, until softened and just beginning to brown, about 12 minutes. Using a slotted spoon, transfer the vegetables to a plate.

2. Heat the remaining 2 tablespoons of oil in the casserole. Add the pancetta and stir once or twice over moderately high heat until sizzling. Add the lamb and cook, stirring occasionally, until the liquid has evaporated and the meat is browned, 10 minutes. Return the vegetables to the casserole. Add the red wine and simmer until evaporated, scraping up any browned bits from the bottom of the casserole. Add the tomatoes and their juices, the chicken stock, bay leaf and crushed red pepper. Season with salt and black pepper and bring to a boil. Reduce the heat to moderately low, cover partially and simmer, stirring occasionally, until the lamb is very tender, 1½ hours. Discard the bay leaf.

3. In a large pot of boiling salted water, cook the rigatoni until al dente. Drain the rigatoni and toss with half of the lamb ragù. Serve the pasta in large bowls, passing the remaining lamb ragù and the Pecorino cheese at the table. —Michael White

MAKE AHEAD The lamb ragù can be refrigerated for up to 5 days or frozen for up to 1 month.

WINE Tannic, full-bodied Barbaresco.

SPICY KOREAN GLAZED PORK RIBS, P. 171

pork + veal

CRISPY PORK TENDERLOIN WITH APPLE RINGS

PORK TENDERLOIN WITH COMPOTE

Crispy Pork Tenderloin with Fried Apple Rings

TOTAL: 35 MIN

4 SERVINGS ● ●

- ¼ cup all-purpose flour
- 2 large eggs, beaten
- 2¼ cups *panko* (Japanese bread crumbs) or dry bread crumbs

Kosher salt and freshly ground pepper

Two 12-ounce pork tenderloins, each sliced in half lengthwise and pounded ⅛ inch thick

- 1 large Granny Smith apple, cored and cut into 8 rings
- 1⅓ cups peanut oil, for frying
- 1 lemon, cut into 4 wedges

I. Preheat the oven to 250°. Put the flour, eggs and *panko* in 3 dishes. Season each with salt and pepper. Season the pork generously with salt and pepper. Dredge each piece of pork in the flour, shaking off any excess. Dip the pork in the egg, letting any excess drip back into the dish, then roll it in the *panko* to coat. Set the pork on a baking sheet. Repeat to coat the apple rings.

2. In a large skillet, heat 1 cup of the peanut oil until a pinch of *panko* dropped in bubbles rapidly. Add 2 pieces of pork and fry, turning once, until golden brown all over, about 7 minutes. Transfer to paper towels to drain. Repeat with the remaining 2 pieces of pork. Transfer the pork to a rack set over a baking sheet and keep warm in the oven.

3. Add the remaining ⅓ cup of oil to the skillet. When the oil is hot, add the apple and fry until golden, 2 minutes per side. Drain on paper towels. Place the crispy pork and apple rings on a platter, garnish with the lemon and serve. —*Bruce Aidells*

WINE Dry, full-flavored Alsace Riesling.

Pork Tenderloin with Rhubarb-Shallot Compote

ACTIVE: 20 MIN; TOTAL: 35 MIN

4 SERVINGS ● ● ●

- 1 pound rhubarb, stalks only, cut into ½-inch-thick slices
- ½ cup shallots, halved lengthwise and thinly sliced crosswise
- 1½ tablespoons unsalted butter, melted
- ⅓ cup sugar
- 1 teaspoon minced thyme plus twelve 2-inch thyme sprigs

Kosher salt and freshly ground pepper

- 2 pork tenderloins (¾ pound each), cut into 6 pieces each

I. Light a grill. In a medium bowl, toss the rhubarb and shallots with the butter to coat. Stir in the sugar and minced thyme and season generously with salt and pepper.

2. Tear off four 16-inch-long sheets of extra-heavy duty foil. Mound half of the rhubarb mixture in the center of each of 2 foil sheets. Gently pound the thicker pieces of pork about 1 inch thick. Season with salt and pepper and press a thyme sprig onto each piece. Arrange the pieces of pork in a layer on the rhubarb. Cover with the 2 remaining sheets of foil; fold up the edges all around to seal.

3. Grill the hobo packs over a very hot fire for about 12 minutes, or until sizzling and puffed. Using oven mitts, transfer the packs to a rimmed platter. Open the packs carefully, transfer the pork and rhubarb to plates and serve at once.
—Grace Parisi

WINE Light, fruity Pinot Noir.

Pork Tenderloin with Wild Mushrooms, Ginger and Scallions

TOTAL: 30 MIN

4 SERVINGS ● ●

- ½ cup chicken stock or canned low-sodium broth
- 2 tablespoons soy sauce
- 1 tablespoon Chinese cooking wine (Shao-Hsing) or dry sherry
- 1½ tablespoons ketchup
- 1 tablespoon sugar
- 1½ teaspoons chile-garlic paste or hot sauce
- 1 teaspoon rice vinegar or distilled white vinegar
- 2 teaspoons cornstarch
- 1 pound pork tenderloin, thinly sliced crosswise

Salt

- ¼ cup peanut oil
- 1 tablespoon very finely chopped fresh ginger
- 1 large garlic clove, minced
- ¾ pound mixed wild mushrooms, such as oyster and shiitake, stemmed and thickly sliced
- 4 large scallions, cut into 1-inch lengths

1. In a small bowl, whisk the stock with the soy sauce, cooking wine, ketchup, sugar, chile-garlic paste, rice vinegar and 1 teaspoon of the cornstarch. In another medium bowl, season the pork with salt and toss with the remaining 1 teaspoon of cornstarch.

2. In a large nonstick skillet, heat 2 tablespoons of the peanut oil until shimmering. Add the pork in a single layer and fry over high heat, undisturbed, until nearly cooked but still pink in the center, about 1½ minutes. Add the ginger and garlic and cook, stirring, just until fragrant, about 1 minute. Transfer the pork to a plate.

3. Add the remaining 2 tablespoons of peanut oil to the skillet and heat until just smoking. Add the mushrooms and scallions, season with salt and cook over high heat, stirring occasionally, until lightly browned, about 5 minutes. Return the pork and any accumulated juices to the skillet and toss with the mushrooms and scallions. Stir the sauce, add it to the skillet and bring to a boil. Cook until thickened, about 30 seconds. Serve at once.
—Grace Parisi

SERVE WITH Steamed rice.
WINE Rich, earthy Pinot Noir.

Herbed Pork Tenderloin with Strawberry Salsa

ACTIVE: 25 MIN; TOTAL: 1 HR

4 SERVINGS ●

Two ¾-pound pork tenderloins
Kosher salt and freshly ground pepper

- ⅓ cup chopped flat-leaf parsley
- 1 tablespoon minced sage
- 1 tablespoon minced rosemary
- 1 tablespoon plus 1 teaspoon extra-virgin olive oil
- 1 pint strawberries, cut into ⅓-inch dice
- 1 cup diced papaya (6 ounces)
- 2 tablespoons chopped cilantro
- 2 tablespoons minced red onion
- 1 tablespoon fresh lime juice

1. Preheat the oven to 400°. Rub each tenderloin with ½ teaspoon of salt and ¼ teaspoon of pepper. On a plate, mix the parsley, sage and rosemary; add the pork and pat to coat. Cover and refrigerate for at least 20 minutes.

2. Heat 1 tablespoon of the olive oil in a large ovenproof skillet. Add the tenderloins and brown over moderate heat, about 4 minutes per side. Transfer the skillet to the oven and roast the pork until an instant-read thermometer inserted in the thickest part registers 145° to 150°, about 15 minutes. Transfer to a carving board to rest for 10 minutes.

3. In a medium bowl, mix the strawberries, papaya, cilantro, onion, lime juice and the remaining 1 teaspoon of olive oil. Season with salt. Carve the meat and serve with the strawberry salsa.
—Janie Hibler

WINE Dry, rich Champagne.

Spiced Pork Tenderloin with Wilted Arugula

TOTAL: 35 MIN

4 SERVINGS ● ● ●

- 3 tablespoons vegetable oil
- 3 tablespoons fresh orange juice
- 2 tablespoons low-sodium soy sauce
- 1½ teaspoons chili-garlic paste
- 1½ teaspoons Asian sesame oil
- 1 teaspoon finely grated orange zest
- 2 medium garlic cloves, very finely chopped
- 2 bunches arugula (½ pound)

Kosher salt and freshly ground pepper

- 1 pound pork tenderloin, cut into ½-inch-thick slices
- 2 tablespoons minced cilantro

1. In a bowl, combine 1 tablespoon of the vegetable oil with the orange juice, soy sauce, chili paste, sesame oil, zest and garlic. Transfer 2 tablespoons of the marinade to a bowl, add the arugula and toss. Season with salt and pepper. Add the pork to the remaining marinade; let stand for 15 minutes.

pork + veal

2. In a large skillet, heat the remaining 2 tablespoons of vegetable oil until shimmering. Drain the pork, scrape off the marinade and season with salt. Cook over high heat, turning once, until browned, 4 minutes. Transfer to a plate.

3. Add the arugula to the skillet and cook, tossing frequently, until wilted, about 1 minute. Transfer the arugula to plates and top with the pork. Garnish with the minced cilantro and serve. —*Megan Moore*

MAKE AHEAD The pork and arugula can be kept at room temperature for 2 hours.

WINE Tannic, complex Cabernet.

Pork with Sweet Riesling Sauce and Toasted Almonds

TOTAL: 25 MIN

4 SERVINGS ●

- 2 tablespoons slivered almonds
- 1¼ pounds pork tenderloin, cut into 1-inch-thick medallions
- Kosher salt and freshly ground pepper
- 2 tablespoons all-purpose flour
- 3½ tablespoons unsalted butter
- 1 tablespoon olive oil
- 1 medium onion, very thinly sliced
- 1 teaspoon minced garlic
- ½ cup late-harvest Riesling
- ½ cup chicken stock or broth
- ⅓ cup golden raisins
- 3 tablespoons white balsamic vinegar
- 1½ teaspoons chopped thyme

INGREDIENT TIP

microwaving nuts

INSTEAD OF TOASTING whole or sliced almonds (and other nuts like cashews, pecans and walnuts) in a small skillet or a toaster oven, microwave them for about 2 minutes on high power. This creates the same toasty nut flavor in less than half the time—and with minimal effort and cleanup.

1. In a small skillet, toast the slivered almonds over moderately high heat, tossing occasionally, until they are golden, about 2 minutes; let cool.

2. Season the pork medallions with salt and pepper, then coat in the flour. In a large skillet, melt 2 tablespoons of the butter in the olive oil. Add the medallions and cook over moderately high heat until lightly browned on both sides and just cooked through, about 4 minutes. Transfer to a plate.

3. Add the onion to the skillet and cook over moderate heat until softened and just beginning to brown, about 4 minutes. Add the garlic and cook until fragrant, about 1 minute. Add the Riesling, stock, raisins, vinegar and thyme and bring to a boil. Cook over high heat, scraping up any browned bits from the bottom of the pan, until the liquid has reduced slightly, about 2 minutes.

4. Return the meat to the skillet and simmer until heated through, about 1 minute. Transfer to a platter. Add the remaining 1½ tablespoons of butter to the sauce and cook over moderate heat, swirling, just until melted. Pour the sauce over the pork, garnish with the almonds and serve. —*Bruce Aidells*

WINE Dry, full-flavored Alsace Riesling.

Pork Medallions with Prosciutto, Arugula and Tomatoes

TOTAL: 30 MIN

4 SERVINGS ●

- 2 tablespoons olive oil
- 5 ounces thinly sliced prosciutto, finely chopped
- 2 large garlic cloves, very finely chopped
- 1½ pounds pork tenderloin, cut into 1-inch-thick slices
- Salt and freshly ground pepper
- 2 tablespoons balsamic vinegar
- 1 pound arugula, large stems discarded, leaves chopped
- 1 pound plum tomatoes, chopped

1. In a very large skillet, heat the olive oil. Add the prosciutto and garlic and cook over moderate heat, stirring, until the garlic is golden, about 4 minutes. Transfer the prosciutto and garlic to a plate.

2. Season the pork slices with salt and pepper and add to the skillet. Cook over high heat until browned and medium done, 3 to 4 minutes per side. Transfer to a platter and keep warm.

3. Add the vinegar to the skillet and cook, scraping up any browned bits, until evaporated. Add the arugula and toss for 2 minutes. Add the tomatoes, prosciutto and garlic and cook over high heat for 2 minutes, stirring; season with salt and pepper. Spoon the mixture over the pork and serve. —*Nancy Verde Barr*

WINE Tannic, full-bodied Barbaresco.

Savory Cabbage and Mushroom Pancakes with Pork and Shrimp

TOTAL: 40 MIN

4 SERVINGS ●

- 6 tablespoons all-purpose flour
- 2 large eggs, lightly beaten
- 4 cups shredded green cabbage
- 3 shiitake mushrooms, stems discarded, caps thinly sliced
- Salt
- 1 tablespoon drained pickled ginger, plus more for garnish
- 1 tablespoon bonito flakes, plus more for garnish (see Note)
- ¼ pound pork tenderloin, sliced crosswise and cut into ¼-inch-thick matchsticks
- ¼ pound small shrimp, shelled and deveined
- Freshly ground pepper
- ¼ cup mirin
- 2 tablespoons low-sodium soy sauce
- 2 tablespoons Worcestershire sauce
- 2 tablespoons ketchup
- 2 tablespoons vegetable oil
- Nori flakes, for garnish (see Note)
- Mayonnaise, for serving

1. In a large bowl, whisk the flour into the eggs until a smooth batter forms. Add the shredded cabbage, sliced shiitake, ¾ teaspoon of salt and 1 tablespoon each of the pickled ginger and bonito flakes. Mix until thoroughly combined. In a small bowl, combine the pork and shrimp and season lightly with salt and pepper.

2. In a small saucepan, whisk together the mirin, soy sauce, Worcestershire sauce and ketchup. Bring the sauce just to a boil, then simmer over moderately low heat until thickened slightly, about 5 minutes. Remove the saucepan from the heat.

3. In a 12-inch nonstick skillet, heat the vegetable oil. Stir the pancake mixture. Spoon four 1-cup portions of the pancake mixture into the skillet and flatten each into a 5-inch pancake about ½ inch thick. Cook the pancakes over moderate heat until they are golden brown on the bottom, 5 to 7 minutes. If the pancakes brown too quickly, lower the heat slightly.

4. Make a slight indentation in the top of each pancake and top each with one-fourth of the pork and shrimp, pressing down slightly. Carefully turn over the pancakes; if necessary, use 2 spatulas to hold the pancakes together. Cook the pancakes until they are golden brown on the second side and the pork and shrimp are cooked through, about 6 minutes.

5. Transfer the pancakes to a platter, pork and shrimp side up. Brush the pancakes with some of the sauce and top each of them with a little pickled ginger and some bonito and nori flakes. Serve the pancakes hot, with the remaining sauce and mayonnaise on the side.
—Jeannie Chen

NOTE Bonito flakes and nori flakes are available at Japanese or Asian markets.
SERVE WITH Plain stir-fried noodles.
WINE Flinty, high-acid Chablis.

Crispy Pork Cutlets with Citrus Sauce
TOTAL: 45 MIN
4 SERVINGS

Regular dry bread crumbs can be used to coat the pork slices here, but the coarser *panko* (Japanese bread crumbs) make a crisper crust.

- 1 tablespoon soy sauce
- 2 teaspoons Dijon mustard
- ¼ cup fresh orange juice
- ½ cup all-purpose flour
- 2 large eggs
- 2 tablespoons water
- 2½ cups Japanese *panko*
- 1 pound pork tenderloin, cut into twelve ½-inch-thick slices and pounded ⅛ inch thick
- Salt and freshly ground pepper
- Vegetable oil, for frying
- ½ cup coarsely chopped fresh orange or tangerine sections

1. In a small bowl, stir the soy sauce with the mustard and the orange juice until combined. Set the sauce aside.

2. Put the flour in a shallow bowl. In another shallow bowl, beat the eggs with the water. Spread the bread crumbs in a third shallow bowl. Season the pork slices with salt and pepper, then dredge them in the flour, shaking off the excess. Dip the slices in the beaten egg and then coat them completely with the *panko* bread crumbs.

3. In a large skillet, heat ¼ inch of vegetable oil until shimmering. Working in batches, fry the pork slices over high heat until they are browned and crisp, about 2 minutes per side; if the pork browns too quickly, lower the heat. Transfer the fried pork to paper towels to drain, then keep the slices warm in a low oven while you fry the rest.

4. Arrange the pork slices on plates. Top the pork slices with the chopped orange sections and serve, passing the citrus sauce at the table. —Marcia Kiesel

WINE Dry, mineral-flavored Chenin Blanc.

Pot-Roasted Pork and Apples
ACTIVE: 30 MIN; TOTAL: 50 MIN
4 SERVINGS ●

- 3 tablespoons extra-virgin olive oil
- Two ¾-pound pork tenderloins
- 1 pound medium shallots, peeled
- 1 medium parsnip (½ pound), halved lengthwise and cut on the diagonal into ½-inch-thick slices
- 2 garlic cloves, coarsely chopped
- 4 baking apples (about 2 pounds)—peeled and cut into 8 wedges each (see Note)
- 2 cups apple cider
- 3 large thyme sprigs
- Salt and freshly ground pepper

1. Heat 1 tablespoon of the oil in a large enameled cast-iron casserole. Add the pork and brown over moderately high heat; transfer to a platter.

2. Heat another tablespoon of the olive oil in the casserole. Add the shallots and parsnip and cook until lightly browned, about 8 minutes; add to the platter. Heat the remaining 1 tablespoon of olive oil in the pot. Add the garlic and cook for 1 minute. Add the apples and cook until lightly browned, about 5 minutes.

3. Add the cider and thyme to the pot and simmer, stirring to scrape up all the browned bits from the bottom. Add the pork and vegetables and season with salt and pepper. Cover and simmer over low heat until the meat is barely rosy within, about 25 minutes. Remove the pork. Simmer the apples and vegetables over moderately high heat until tender, about 5 minutes. Carve the pork and serve with the apples and vegetables.
—Jane Sigal

NOTE With so many good apples to choose from these days, it's fun to cook with some new varieties. Any one of the following would work well in this dish: Bracburn, Empire, Granny Smith, Idared, Jonagold, Jonathan, Northern Spy, Stayman or Winesap.

WINE Bright, citrusy Riesling.

PORK CHOPS WITH VEGETABLE FRICASSEE

SWEET AND SALTY PORK CHOPS

Herbed Pork Involtini

TOTAL: 30 MIN

4 SERVINGS ● ●

Classically, *involtini* are thin slices of veal that are stuffed and rolled. This version uses slices of pork tenderloin.

One 1½-pound boneless pork tenderloin, cut on the extreme diagonal into 12 slices

Salt and freshly ground pepper

¼ cup freshly grated Pecorino Romano cheese

1½ teaspoons finely chopped sage

1 teaspoon finely chopped rosemary

1 teaspoon minced garlic

¼ cup all-purpose flour

3 tablespoons extra-virgin olive oil

1 cup dry white wine

1. Lightly pound the pork slices a scant ¼ inch thick. Season with salt and pepper. In a bowl, combine the Pecorino, sage, rosemary and garlic. Sprinkle 1 teaspoon of the mixture over each slice and roll into a cylinder; secure with toothpicks. Season with salt and pepper.
2. Spread the flour in a pie plate. Coat the *involtini* with flour, tapping off the excess. In a large skillet, heat the oil until shimmering. Add the *involtini* and cook over moderately high heat until browned all over, about 3 minutes. Add the wine, cover and simmer until the *involtini* are cooked through, 3 minutes longer. Transfer the *involtini* to a plate and cover loosely with foil.
3. Boil the cooking liquid until reduced to a thick sauce, about 2 minutes. Return the *involtini* to the skillet and shake the pan to coat them with sauce. Transfer the *involtini* to plates and serve.
—*Michael White*

WINE Soft, earthy Rioja.

Korean Barbecued Pork

ACTIVE: 50 MIN; TOTAL: 10 HR

4 TO 6 SERVINGS

In Korea, this recipe, known as *toejigogi kui,* is made with pork belly, but it's equally delicious—and much leaner—when prepared with pork loin. To save time, have your butcher slice and pound the pork cutlets.

⅓ cup mirin

2 tablespoons soy sauce

2 tablespoons Asian sesame oil

1 tablespoon sesame seeds, lightly toasted and finely ground

2 tablespoons minced garlic

2 scallions, white and light green parts only, chopped

2 tablespoons minced fresh ginger

1 tablespoon Asian chili-garlic paste

¼ teaspoon freshly ground black pepper

⅛ teaspoon crushed red pepper

2 pounds boneless center-cut pork loin, cut into ½-inch-thick slices and pounded ⅓ inch thick

Vegetable oil, for the grill

1 large head red-leaf or green-leaf lettuce, leaves separated

Miso, red pepper paste, chili-garlic paste and sliced hot green chiles plus thinly sliced scallions or kimchi, for serving

1. In a large glass baking dish, combine the mirin, soy sauce, sesame oil, sesame seeds, garlic, scallions, ginger, chili-garlic paste, black pepper and crushed red pepper. Add the slices of pork loin and turn to coat. Cover and refrigerate the pork for 8 to 24 hours.

2. Light a grill. Lightly brush the grate with vegetable oil. Grill the marinated pork over a medium-hot fire until it is golden brown and just cooked through, about 2 minutes per side. Transfer the grilled pork to one end of a platter and arrange the lettuce leaves on the other end. Serve the pork with the suggested condiments. —*David Rosengarten*

SERVE WITH Steamed white rice or white sticky rice.

WINE Assertive, heady Grenache.

Peppered Pork Chops with Vegetable Fricassee

TOTAL: 35 MIN

4 SERVINGS ●

Four 10-ounce pork rib chops (1 inch thick)

Kosher salt

2 tablespoons plus 2 teaspoons Dijon mustard

Coarsely and finely ground black pepper

6 tablespoons extra-virgin olive oil

½ cup finely chopped shallots

2 tablespoons red wine vinegar

½ cup dry white wine

1 cup heavy cream

1½ tablespoons finely chopped flat-leaf parsley

½ pound sugar snap peas

¼ pound white mushrooms, thickly sliced

4 scallions, white and tender green parts, thinly sliced

½ cup frozen baby peas, thawed

1. Preheat the oven to 400°. Season the pork chops on both sides with salt. Brush each chop with 1 teaspoon of the mustard; generously sprinkle all over with coarsely ground black pepper.

2. In a large skillet, heat 2 tablespoons of the olive oil until shimmering. Add the pork chops and cook over moderate heat, turning once, until golden, about 6 minutes. Transfer the chops to a baking sheet and roast for 12 minutes, until cooked through; keep warm.

3. Meanwhile, pour off the fat from the skillet. Add ¼ cup of water and cook over high heat for 1 minute, scraping up any browned bits from the bottom of the pan. Pour the pan juices into a cup and wipe out the skillet.

4. Heat 2 tablespoons of the olive oil in the skillet. Add all but 1 tablespoon of the shallots and cook over moderately high heat until softened, 3 minutes. Add the vinegar and cook until nearly evaporated, about 30 seconds. Add the wine and cook until nearly evaporated, about 2 minutes. Add the cream and cook over moderately high heat until slightly reduced, about 2 minutes. Add the remaining 4 teaspoons of mustard, the reserved pan juices and half of the parsley. Season the sauce with salt and finely ground black pepper; keep warm.

5. Heat the remaining 2 tablespoons of olive oil in another large skillet. Add the sugar snap peas, sliced mushrooms, sliced scallions and the reserved 1 tablespoon of shallots and cook over moderately high heat, stirring occasionally, until the sugar snaps are crisp-tender and the mushrooms are tender and lightly browned, about 5 minutes.

6. Stir in the baby peas and the remaining chopped parsley and season with salt and finely ground pepper. Pour the cream sauce onto plates and top with the warm pork chops. Spoon the vegetables alongside the chops and serve. —*Daniel Boulud*

WINE Deep, pungent, tannic Barolo.

Sweet and Salty Pork Chops with Beef Jerky

ACTIVE: 1 HR; TOTAL: 9 HR 30 MIN

12 SERVINGS

These pork chops were inspired by the seasonings used in Vietnamese cuisine: lemongrass, ginger, garlic, fish sauce and more. The chops have to marinate overnight, so plan accordingly.

PORK CHOPS

¼ cup coarsely chopped cilantro leaves

8 garlic cloves, halved

3 tablespoons soy sauce

3 tablespoons Asian fish sauce

3 tablespoons sugar

2 stalks of fresh lemongrass, lower third only, chopped

1 teaspoon freshly ground pepper

¼ cup plus 1 tablespoon vegetable oil

Twelve 6-ounce boneless pork chops

SAUCE

1 cup sugar

¼ cup water

2 stalks of fresh lemongrass, lower third only, minced

One 1-inch piece of fresh ginger, peeled and minced

3 tablespoons white wine vinegar

½ cup Asian fish sauce

½ teaspoon freshly ground black pepper

¼ cup vegetable oil

12 large garlic cloves, thinly sliced

½ cup roasted unsalted peanuts, chopped

½ cup chopped chives

½ cup finely shredded beef jerky (1 ounce), for garnish

pork + veal

1. MARINATE THE PORK CHOPS: In a mini food processor, combine the cilantro, garlic, soy sauce, fish sauce, sugar, lemongrass, pepper and 1 tablespoon of the oil and process to a paste. Put the pork chops in a large, shallow dish and coat with the marinade. Cover and refrigerate overnight.

2. MAKE THE SAUCE: In a small saucepan, combine the sugar and water and bring to a simmer over moderate heat to dissolve the sugar. Simmer, without stirring, until an amber caramel forms, about 8 minutes. Add the lemongrass and ginger and slowly pour in the vinegar and fish sauce, stirring, until the sauce is clear. Add the pepper and remove from the heat.

3. Heat the ¼ cup of oil in a small skillet. Add the garlic and cook over low heat, stirring occasionally, until golden, about 4 minutes. Transfer the garlic and oil to a small bowl.

4. COOK THE PORK CHOPS: Preheat the oven to 400°. In each of 2 large skillets, heat 2 tablespoons of oil until shimmering. Scrape some of the marinade off the pork chops. Add 6 chops to each skillet and cook over high heat until browned, about 4 minutes per side.

KITCHEN TOOL

thermometer

Oxo's thermometer has a needle-thin probe, so less juice leaks out when meat is tested ($15; 800-545-4411).

Transfer the chops to a rimmed baking sheet. Bake the chops for 10 minutes, or until barely pink in the center. Transfer the chops to a large platter and spoon the caramel sauce on top. Drain the fried garlic and scatter it over the chops, along with the peanuts and chives. Garnish with the jerky and serve at once.

—Ken Oringer

MAKE AHEAD The recipe can be prepared through Step 3 and refrigerated overnight. Reheat the sauce and garlic before serving.

SERVE WITH Steamed bok choy.

WINE Round-textured Sémillon.

Pork Chops with Mustard Cream

TOTAL: 1 HR 20 MIN

4 SERVINGS

- 4 teaspoons coarsely cracked black peppercorns
- 4 teaspoons thyme leaves
- 2 tablespoons extra-virgin olive oil
- Four ¾-pound pork rib chops, cut 1¼ inches thick
- ½ cup veal stock or chicken stock
- 1½ teaspoons pure olive oil
- 1 medium shallot, minced
- 1 garlic clove, smashed
- 1½ teaspoons Dijon mustard
- 1 tablespoon whole-grain mustard
- ½ cup brandy
- 1 cup dry white wine
- 1 cup heavy cream
- 1½ teaspoons Worcestershire sauce
- Kosher salt and freshly ground white pepper

1. In a large glass baking dish, combine the peppercorns with the thyme and extra-virgin olive oil. Add the pork chops and turn to coat. Let stand at room temperature for at least 1 hour and for up to 4 hours or refrigerate overnight.

2. Meanwhile, in a small saucepan, boil the veal stock until reduced to 1 tablespoon, about 15 minutes.

3. In a saucepan, heat the pure olive oil until shimmering. Add the shallot and

garlic and cook over moderate heat, stirring, until softened, about 4 minutes. Stir in the Dijon mustard and half of the whole-grain mustard. Add the brandy and cook until nearly evaporated, about 3 minutes. Add the wine; simmer until reduced by half, about 10 minutes. Add the cream, Worcestershire sauce and reduced veal stock and simmer until thickened, about 15 minutes. Strain the mustard sauce into a heatproof bowl. Whisk in the remaining whole-grain mustard; season with salt and white pepper. Cover and keep warm.

4. Preheat the oven to 450°. Season the pork chops with salt. Heat a large ovenproof skillet. Add the chops and cook over moderate heat for 2 minutes. Transfer the skillet to the oven and roast for about 6 minutes, or until the chops are golden on the bottom. Turn the chops and continue roasting until just cooked through, about 7 minutes.

5. Transfer the pork chops to plates. Strain the pan juices into the mustard sauce and simmer in a saucepan, stirring frequently, until heated through. Spoon the mustard cream sauce alongside.

—Lee Hefter

MAKE AHEAD The mustard cream sauce can be refrigerated overnight.

SERVE WITH Alsatian Cabbage (recipe, p. 231).

WINE Light, fruity Beaujolais.

Garam Masala—Rubbed Pork Chops

ACTIVE: 20 MIN; TOTAL: 35 MIN

4 SERVINGS ●

Garam masala, a warm, slightly sweet Indian spice blend that is traditionally sprinkled on curries and cooked vegetables, fish and meat, can also be used as a rub for pork or shrimp. To balance commercial blends with overly assertive cinnamon or cardamom aromas, add half a teaspoon of curry powder for every tablespoon of garam masala.

1 cup plain whole milk yogurt

1 teaspoon finely grated lime zest

1 tablespoon garam masala

1¼ teaspoons salt

Four 1-inch-thick bone-in pork rib chops

1 tablespoon unsalted butter

1 tablespoon extra-virgin olive oil

¼ cup apricot or peach chutney

½ cup coarsely chopped cilantro leaves

I. Preheat the oven to 400°. In a small bowl, mix the yogurt and lime zest; cover and set aside.

2. Mix the garam masala with the salt; sprinkle on both sides of the pork chops. In a large nonstick ovenproof skillet, melt the butter in the olive oil. Add the pork chops and cook over moderately high heat until browned, 2 to 3 minutes per side. Transfer the skillet to the oven and roast the chops for 5 minutes longer, or until cooked through. Remove from the oven and let rest for 10 minutes.

3. Spoon ¼ cup of the lime yogurt onto each of 4 plates. Top with the chutney. Set the chops next to the yogurt, sprinkle with the cilantro and serve.

—*Sally Schneider*

WINE Spicy New World Gewürztraminer.

Grilled Pork Chops with Corn Salad and Lavender Peach Sauce

ACTIVE: 1 HR 20 MIN; TOTAL: 2 HR 20 MIN

4 SERVINGS

Dried lavender buds are available at organic markets and specialty food shops, and by mail order from Dean & DeLuca (800-221-7714). Make sure they are food grade and that they haven't been treated with oils for potpourri.

½ cup honey

1 tablespoon dried lavender buds

3 whole cloves

3 tablespoons sherry vinegar

3 tablespoons unsalted butter

¼ cup packed light brown sugar

1 tablespoon fresh lemon juice

6 firm, ripe peaches— 4 peeled and halved, 2 peeled and finely chopped

4 ears of corn, husked

1 Vidalia onion, cut crosswise into ½-inch-thick slices

3 tablespoons extra-virgin olive oil

Kosher salt and freshly ground pepper

4 thick-cut slices of bacon, cut crosswise into ¼-inch pieces

1 tablespoon finely chopped parsley

1 teaspoon *piment d'Espelette* or ½ teaspoon cayenne pepper (see Note)

Four 12-ounce pork rib chops (1 inch thick)

⅓ cup Riesling

I. Preheat the oven to 375°. In a small saucepan, combine the honey with the lavender and the whole cloves and cook over moderate heat, undisturbed, for 6 minutes. Remove the honey from the heat and stir in 2 tablespoons of the sherry vinegar. Let the honey cool for 10 minutes, then strain the lavender-infused honey through a fine sieve into a small heatproof bowl.

2. Add 2 tablespoons of the butter to the saucepan along with the brown sugar and lemon juice and cook just until melted. Stir in half of the lavender-infused honey. Arrange the halved peaches in a small baking dish in a single layer and spoon the brown sugar mixture over them. Bake the peaches for 1 hour, turning once and basting every 10 minutes, until soft and lightly caramelized. Transfer the peaches to a plate and pour the pan juices into a heatproof cup.

3. Meanwhile, light a grill or preheat a grill pan. Brush the ears of corn and the onion slices all over with 1 tablespoon of the olive oil and season generously with salt and pepper. Grill over high heat until charred and tender, 8 to 10 minutes. Let cool slightly, then cut the corn kernels from the cobs and coarsely chop the onion.

4. In a large, deep skillet, heat 1 tablespoon of the olive oil. Add the bacon and cook over moderate heat until it is golden and crisp, about 4 minutes. Using a slotted spoon, transfer the bacon to a plate. Add the corn and onion to the skillet and cook just until heated through, about 3 minutes. Add the parsley, *piment d'Espelette*, the remaining 1 tablespoon of vinegar and the reserved bacon. Season the corn salad with salt and pepper and cover with foil to keep warm.

5. Brush the pork chops with the remaining 1 tablespoon of olive oil and season with salt and pepper. Grill over moderately high heat, turning once, until an instant-read thermometer registers 138° when inserted near the bone, about 12 minutes. Transfer the chops to a plate and brush liberally with the remaining lavender-infused honey.

6. Meanwhile, heat a large, heavy skillet until very hot. Add the finely chopped peaches and cook without stirring for 1 minute. Add the Riesling and cook until it is reduced by two-thirds, about 1 minute. Add the reserved peach pan juices and bring to a boil, then simmer until thickened, about 2 minutes. Swirl in the remaining 1 tablespoon of butter and season the peach sauce with salt and pepper.

7. Spoon the corn salad onto plates and arrange the roasted peach halves alongside. Put the chops on the plates, spoon the peach sauce over the chops and serve. —*Bruce Sherman*

NOTE *Piment d'Espelette* is a sweet and mildly spicy seasoning made from a pepper native to the Basque country. It is available at specialty food shops and by mail order from Piperade (415-391-2555 or www.piperade.com).

MAKE AHEAD The recipe can be prepared through Step 3 and refrigerated overnight.

WINE Dry, mineral-flavored Chenin Blanc.

pork + veal

Chili-Dusted Pork Chops

ACTIVE: 12 MIN; TOTAL: 25 MIN

4 SERVINGS ●

- 1 teaspoon chili powder
- 1 teaspoon ground cumin
- 1 teaspoon kosher salt
- ½ teaspoon freshly ground pepper
- Four ½-pound boneless pork loin chops, cut 1¼ inches thick
- 1 tablespoon extra-virgin olive oil
- 2 garlic cloves, very finely chopped
- Finely grated zest and juice of 1 lime
- 3 tablespoons finely chopped cilantro leaves

1. Preheat the oven to 400°. In a small bowl, mix the chili powder with the cumin, salt and pepper. Rub the spice mixture all over the pork chops.

2. In a large ovenproof skillet, heat the olive oil until shimmering. Add the pork chops and cook over high heat, turning once, until browned, about 1 minute per side. Add the garlic, lime zest, lime juice and cilantro to the skillet.

3. Transfer the skillet to the center of the oven and roast the chops until rosy throughout, about 10 minutes. Transfer the chops to plates and serve at once.
—*Sally Sampson*

WINE Spicy Alsace Gewürztraminer.

Garlic-Rubbed Spareribs

ACTIVE: 1 HR 45 MIN; TOTAL: 10 HR

6 SERVINGS

Mexico City chef Patricia Quintana loves to roast meat and fish in banana leaves, which add flavor and keep food moist. She cooks pork spareribs that way, then serves them with warm tortillas and bowls of garnishes alongside. You can also shred the sparerib meat, mix it with the onions roasted with it and the pan juices and use the combination as a filling for the tortillas.

- ¼ cup plus 2 tablespoons annatto (achiote) seeds
- 16 garlic cloves, 10 halved
- 1 medium onion, coarsely chopped
- 2 tablespoons dried oregano, preferably Mexican
- 2 tablespoons freshly ground pepper
- ½ cup fresh grapefruit juice
- ½ cup fresh orange juice
- ½ cup vegetable oil
- 3 racks large pork spareribs (about 3½ pounds each), trimmed of excess fat
- Kosher salt
- 6 banana leaves, about 12 by 18 inches each (optional; see Note), thawed and patted dry
- 18 bay leaves
- 3 small red onions, cut into very thin slices
- Two dozen 6-inch corn tortillas
- Pickled Red Onions (recipe follows)
- Yucatán Table Sauce (recipe follows)

1. In a small saucepan, cover the annatto seeds with water, bring to a boil and simmer over moderate heat for 3 minutes. Remove from the heat and let stand for 2 hours. Drain the seeds and pat dry with paper towels. Transfer to a spice grinder and grind to a paste.

2. Preheat the oven to 500°. Put the 6 whole garlic cloves in a pie plate and roast on the top rack of the oven for about 10 minutes, or until blackened on top. In a food processor, puree the roasted garlic with the halved garlic cloves and the onion. Add the annatto paste, oregano, pepper, grapefruit and orange juices and vegetable oil and process until blended.

3. Rub the spareribs with 2 tablespoons of kosher salt. Set 1 of the racks in a large roasting pan and coat with one-third of the annatto marinade. Repeat with the remaining ribs and marinade, stacking the racks on top of each other. Cover with plastic wrap and refrigerate for at least 4 hours or overnight.

4. Preheat the oven to 350°. Line each of 3 large rimmed baking sheets with a banana leaf. Set a rack of ribs on each leaf, meaty side up. Arrange 6 bay leaves and one-third of the red onion slices on each rack and cover with a second banana leaf. Cover each pan tightly with foil and bake for about 2½ hours, or until the ribs are very tender; shift the pans halfway through cooking. Remove the spareribs from the oven and let cool, covered, for 15 minutes. Meanwhile, wrap the tortillas in foil and warm in the oven for about 10 minutes.

5. Preheat the broiler. Uncover the ribs and discard the banana leaves, onions and bay leaves. Broil the ribs, 1 rack at a time, 8 inches from the heat, for about 4 minutes, until crispy; baste occasionally with the pan juices.

6. Cut the racks into ribs and serve with the warm tortillas and bowls of Pickled Red Onions and Yucatán Table Sauce.
—*Patricia Quintana*

NOTE Banana leaves are available in the freezer section of Latin and Asian markets and in the fresh produce section of some supermarkets.

MAKE AHEAD The recipe can be prepared through Step 3; refrigerate overnight.

WINE Assertive, heady Grenache.

Pickled Red Onions

TOTAL: 30 MIN

MAKES ABOUT 1 QUART ● ●

This simple, piquant condiment is wonderful with grilled or baked meat or seafood, including Garlic-Rubbed Spareribs.

- Kosher salt
- 2½ quarts water
- 5 medium red onions, cut into very thin slices
- ½ cup extra-virgin olive oil
- 10 bay leaves
- 10 allspice berries
- 6 marjoram sprigs
- 1½ tablespoons dried oregano, preferably Mexican
- 1 teaspoon freshly ground pepper
- ½ cup cider vinegar

1. In a large bowl, dissolve 2 tablespoons of kosher salt in the water. Add the onion slices, let soak for 10 minutes and drain well.

2. Heat the olive oil in a large skillet. Add the onions, bay leaves, allspice, marjoram, oregano and pepper and cook over moderately high heat, stirring occasionally, until the onions are tender, about 10 minutes. Remove from the heat and stir in the vinegar. Season the mixture with salt and let cool. Discard the allspice, marjoram and bay leaves before serving. —P.Q.

MAKE AHEAD The pickled onions can be refrigerated for up to 1 week.

Yucatán Table Sauce

TOTAL: 25 MIN

MAKES ABOUT 1 CUP ● ●

This all-purpose hot sauce is called *xnipek,* or dog's nose, because it's so spicy it makes your nose as moist as a dog's. It is prepared with two kinds of chiles, including fiery habaneros.

- 2 jalapeños
- 4 scallions, cut crosswise into very thin slices
- 3 habanero or Scotch bonnet chiles, seeded and thinly sliced
- ½ cup coarsely chopped cilantro leaves
- ½ cup fresh grapefruit juice
- ¼ cup fresh orange juice
- ¼ cup fresh lime juice

Salt

1. Roast the jalapeños directly over an open flame or under a preheated broiler, turning, until blackened all over. Put the jalapeños in a small bowl, cover with plastic wrap and let stand for 5 minutes. Discard the blackened skins, stems and seeds; cut the jalapeños into thin strips.

2. Mix the jalapeños, scallions, habaneros, cilantro and grapefruit, orange and lime juices; season with salt. —P.Q.

MAKE AHEAD The sauce can be refrigerated for up to 1 week.

Maple-Roasted Pork Spareribs

ACTIVE: 15 MIN; TOTAL: 2 HR 10 MIN

4 TO 6 SERVINGS ●

- ½ cup pure maple syrup
- ¼ cup tomato sauce
- ¼ cup red wine vinegar
- ¼ cup fresh lemon juice
- 2 tablespoons light brown sugar
- 1 tablespoon minced garlic
- ½ teaspoon ground ginger

Salt and freshly ground pepper

Two 3-pound racks pork spareribs

1. Preheat the oven to 350°. In a saucepan, combine the maple syrup, tomato sauce, vinegar, lemon juice, brown sugar, garlic, ginger and 1 teaspoon each of salt and pepper; bring to a boil. Simmer over low heat for 15 minutes.

2. Meanwhile, set each rack of ribs on a large rimmed baking sheet, meaty side up, and season all over with salt and pepper. Roast the ribs for 30 minutes, shifting the pans from top to bottom halfway through cooking.

3. Brush the ribs with some of the sauce and roast for about 1½ hours longer, brushing with the sauce every 15 minutes and shifting the pans occasionally. If the pan juices begin to burn, add a few tablespoons of water to the pans and scrape up any caramelized drippings; baste the ribs with the drippings. Remove from the oven.

4. Preheat the broiler and position a rack 8 inches from the heat source. Put both racks of ribs on 1 baking sheet, meaty side down, and brush with the sauce. Broil the ribs for 2 to 3 minutes, until glazed and lightly crusty. Turn the ribs, brush with any remaining sauce and broil for about 3 minutes, or until glazed and crusty; transfer to a work surface. Cut in between the bones, mound the ribs on a platter and serve. —Alexandra Anglo

MAKE AHEAD The ribs can be refrigerated for 2 days. Reheat in a 325° oven.

WINE Ripe, creamy-textured Chardonnay.

Spicy Korean Glazed Pork Ribs

ACTIVE: 20 MIN; TOTAL: 1 HR 5 MIN

4 SERVINGS ●

- 5 pounds pork baby back ribs, trimmed of excess fat
- 2 quarts water
- 4 ounces unpeeled fresh ginger, thinly sliced (about 1 cup)
- ½ cup packed light brown sugar
- 8 large garlic cloves, very finely chopped
- 1½ cups soy sauce
- 3 tablespoons Asian sesame oil
- 3 tablespoons Korean red pepper flakes or 2 tablespoons crushed red pepper

1. In a large roasting pan set over 2 burners, cover the ribs with cold water and bring to a boil over moderately high heat. Boil for 5 minutes. Transfer the ribs to a large plate; discard the water.

2. Return the pan to the 2 burners and add the 2 quarts of water. Add the ribs and ginger; bring to a boil. Add the sugar, garlic, soy sauce, sesame oil and red pepper flakes. Cover with foil and boil over moderately high heat for 7 minutes. Simmer over moderately low heat, turning the ribs a few times, until tender, about 20 minutes.

3. Preheat the broiler. Transfer the ribs to a large rimmed baking sheet, meaty side down. Boil the braising liquid until thickened and intensely flavored, about 10 minutes. Strain the liquid; you should have about 2 cups.

4. Generously brush the ribs with the braising liquid and broil 4 inches from the heat, rotating the pan, until glazed and lightly charred, about 3 minutes. Turn the ribs meaty side up and brush again with the braising liquid. Broil, brushing occasionally and rotating the pan, until the ribs are glazed, about 4 minutes. Let rest for 5 minutes, then cut between the ribs, mound on a platter and serve. —Jenny Kwak

WINE Fruity, low-oak Chardonnay.

pork + veal

Pork Scallopine with Spicy Cherry-Pepper Sauce

TOTAL: 30 MIN

4 SERVINGS ●

1½ teaspoons kosher salt
1 teaspoon freshly ground
   black pepper
1 teaspoon dried sage
Eight ½-inch-thick boneless pork
   chops, pounded ¼ inch thick
3 tablespoons olive oil
3 large garlic cloves, very finely
   chopped
½ cup dry white wine
4 to 6 jarred hot cherry peppers—
   stemmed, quartered and seeded,
   plus 2 teaspoons vinegar
   from the jar (see Note)
One 12-ounce jar fire-roasted red or
   yellow bell peppers, drained and
   cut into 1-inch pieces
1 scallion, white and light green
   parts only, very finely chopped

1. In a bowl, combine the salt, pepper and sage; sprinkle all over the pork.
2. In a large skillet, heat 1½ tablespoons of the olive oil. Add 4 of the scallopine and cook over high heat until lightly browned, about 2 minutes per side. Transfer to a plate. Repeat with the remaining olive oil and pork.
3. Pour off all but 1 tablespoon of fat from the skillet. Add the garlic and cook over moderate heat for 1 minute. Add the wine and the cherry-pepper vinegar and bring to a boil, scraping up any browned bits from the bottom of the pan. Cook the sauce until it just begins to thicken, about 1 minute. Add the cherry peppers and roasted peppers and cook until warmed through. Add the pork and any accumulated juices and cook until hot, 1 minute longer. Transfer to plates, sprinkle with the scallion and serve.

—*Bruce Aidells*

NOTE These pickled peppers are sold in jars at the supermarket.

WINE Round-textured Sémillon.

South Carolina Barbecue Pork Burgers

TOTAL: 50 MIN

4 SERVINGS

These succulent burgers were inspired by Carolina pulled pork (shredded slow-cooked pork shoulder). Instead of crisp bits of roasted pork skin, browned bacon bits give a smoky flavor to the ground pork. In the tradition of South Carolina, the burger topping is a honey-mustard sauce.

4 slices of smoky bacon, cut into
   ¼-inch pieces
1 small onion, finely chopped
4 tablespoons unsalted
   butter, melted
⅓ cup honey
⅓ cup Dijon mustard
¼ cup cider vinegar
Salt and freshly ground pepper
1 teaspoon sweet paprika
1 teaspoon dark brown sugar
½ teaspoon onion powder
½ teaspoon garlic powder
¼ teaspoon celery seed
1½ pounds lean ground pork,
   at room temperature
1 teaspoon liquid smoke (optional)
8 thick-cut slices of sandwich bread
Vegetable oil, for brushing
1 cup shredded green cabbage

1. In a small saucepan, cook half of the bacon and the onion in 1 tablespoon of the melted butter over moderate heat until the onion is golden, 5 to 6 minutes. Add the honey, mustard and vinegar and simmer until the sauce is thickened and slightly reduced, about 8 minutes. Season with salt and pepper.
2. Meanwhile, in a small, heavy skillet, cook the remaining pieces of bacon until crisp. Transfer the bacon to paper towels to drain. Let cool thoroughly. In a bowl, combine the paprika, brown sugar, onion powder, garlic powder and celery seed with 1 teaspoon each of salt and pepper.

3. In a medium bowl, gently knead the pork with the crisp bacon and liquid smoke. Loosely form the meat into 4 patties about ¾ inch thick and set them on a plate lined with plastic wrap. Sprinkle the spice mixture all over the burgers, patting to help it adhere. Brush the burgers and both sides of the bread with the remaining 3 tablespoons of butter.
4. Light a grill. When the fire is medium hot, brush the grate with oil. Grill the burgers for 12 minutes, turning once, until just cooked through. Move the burgers away from the heat and grill the bread on both sides until toasted, about 2 minutes.
5. Set the burgers on 4 of the toast slices and top with the cabbage and a generous spoonful of the honey-mustard sauce. Cover with the remaining toasted bread and serve right away, passing the extra sauce separately.

—*Steven Raichlen*

MAKE AHEAD The honey-mustard sauce can be refrigerated overnight. Rewarm gently before serving.

WINE Light, fruity Beaujolais.

Sweet and Spicy Pork Noodles

ACTIVE: 25 MIN; TOTAL: 40 MIN

4 TO 6 SERVINGS

3 tablespoons vegetable oil
1 pound ground pork
2 Thai chiles, minced
1 medium red onion, finely chopped
1 tablespoon minced fresh ginger
1 tablespoon minced garlic
1 tablespoon Chinese fermented
   black beans, rinsed and chopped
⅓ cup hoisin sauce
½ cup Shao-Hsing rice wine
   or dry sherry
1 cup chicken stock or
   low-sodium broth
1 large scallion, thinly sliced
Salt and freshly ground pepper
1 pound fresh or dried Chinese
   egg noodles

1. In a large, deep skillet, heat the oil. Add the ground pork and cook over high heat, breaking up the meat, until it is browned, about 5 minutes. With a slotted spoon, transfer the cooked pork to a plate. Add the chiles, onion, ginger, garlic and black beans to the skillet and cook over moderately high heat, stirring, until softened, about 5 minutes. Add the hoisin sauce and cook, stirring, for 1 minute. Add the rice wine and simmer until reduced by half, about 2 minutes. Add the stock and pork and simmer until thickened, about 4 minutes. Add the scallion and season with salt and pepper.

2. Meanwhile, in a large pot of boiling salted water, cook the noodles until tender, 5 to 8 minutes, depending on the thickness. Drain the noodles. Add them to the skillet and toss well to thoroughly coat them with the sauce. Transfer to a large, shallow bowl and serve.
—*Ming Tsai*

MAKE AHEAD The sauce can be refrigerated overnight.

WINE Spicy New World Gewürztraminer.

Tofu with Spicy Meat Sauce
ACTIVE: 15 MIN; TOTAL: 25 MIN

4 SERVINGS ● ●

This updated version of the classic Sichuan dish *ma po tofu* was developed by cookbook author Joyce Jue. It makes converts of those people who claim to dislike tofu.

- ¾ cup small tree ear mushrooms
- 2 tablespoons soy sauce
- 1 tablespoon dry sherry or dry rice wine
- 1 teaspoon Asian sesame oil
- 1 tablespoon plus 1 teaspoon cornstarch
- ½ pound ground pork
- 1½ tablespoons water
- 1½ tablespoons vegetable oil
- 1 tablespoon Chinese chili-bean sauce

SOUTH CAROLINA BARBECUE PORK BURGERS

PORK SCALLOPINE WITH CHERRY-PEPPER SAUCE

pork + veal

2 garlic cloves, minced

2 teaspoons very finely chopped
fresh ginger

6 fresh water chestnuts,
peeled and chopped

4 scallions, white and light green
parts only, chopped

¾ teaspoon freshly ground
white pepper

½ teaspoon sugar

1 pound firm tofu, drained
and cut into ½-inch dice

¾ cup chicken stock or
low-sodium broth

½ cup frozen baby peas, thawed

1. In a small bowl, cover the tree ears with water and let soak for 15 minutes; drain and coarsely chop.

2. In a medium bowl, mix 1 tablespoon of the soy sauce with the sherry, sesame oil and 1 teaspoon of the cornstarch. Stir in the pork. In a small bowl, mix the remaining 1 tablespoon of cornstarch with the 1½ tablespoons of water.

3. In a wok, heat the oil until smoking. Add the chili-bean sauce, garlic and ginger and cook over high heat until fragrant, about 20 seconds. Add the water chestnuts and chopped mushrooms and stir-fry for 15 seconds. Add the pork and stir-fry for 2 minutes, breaking up any large clumps. Stir in the scallions, white pepper and sugar. Gently stir in the tofu, broth, peas and

the remaining 1 tablespoon of soy sauce and bring to a boil. Add the cornstarch slurry and stir-fry until the sauce thickens, about 15 seconds. Transfer to a platter and serve. —Joyce Jue

WINE Light, soft Chenin Blanc.

Crispy Slow-Roasted Pork Shoulder with Apricot Chutney

ACTIVE: 20 MIN; TOTAL: 7 HR

12 SERVINGS

One 7- to 8-pound pork shoulder
on the bone

2 tablespoons extra-virgin olive oil

½ cup plus 1 tablespoon
white wine vinegar

1 tablespoon minced garlic

One 1½-inch piece of fresh
ginger, finely grated,
plus 1 tablespoon minced

1 tablespoon crushed red pepper

Kosher salt and freshly ground
black pepper

2½ cups dried apricots
(14 ounces), chopped

2½ cups water

3 tablespoons yellow mustard seeds

1 cup (½ pound) golden raisins

1. Preheat the oven to 500°. Set the pork in a large roasting pan, fat side up. In a small bowl, combine the olive oil with 2 tablespoons of the vinegar, the garlic, minced ginger, crushed red pepper and 2 teaspoons each of salt and black pepper. Spread the rub all over the pork and roast for 25 minutes. Reduce the oven temperature to 250° and continue roasting for 5 to 6 hours, or until the meat is well browned and almost falling off the bone. Let the meat rest for 20 minutes.

2. Meanwhile, put the apricots in a large bowl, cover with the water and let stand for 4 hours.

3. In a medium saucepan, toast the mustard seeds over moderately high heat, shaking the pan until the seeds begin to pop and are lightly browned,

about 1½ minutes. Add the raisins, the remaining 7 tablespoons of vinegar and the finely grated ginger. Stir in the apricots and their soaking liquid and bring to a boil. Simmer over moderate heat, stirring occasionally, for 10 minutes. Season the apricot chutney with salt and pepper and transfer to a bowl.

4. Thickly slice the pork and serve warm or at room temperature on plates with the chutney. —Elisabeth Prueitt

MAKE AHEAD The apricot chutney can be refrigerated for up to 5 days. Bring to room temperature before serving.

WINE Spicy Alsace Gewürztraminer.

Pork Chili with Beans and Hominy

ACTIVE: 30 MIN; TOTAL: 1 HR

6 SERVINGS ●

You'll need a pressure cooker for this recipe (see Cooking Tip at left). If guajillo chiles are hard to find, pasilla, ancho or New Mexico chiles are almost as good.

½ cup dried pink beans, picked
over and rinsed

8 cups water, 4 cups very hot

6 dried guajillo chiles, stemmed

2 dried chipotle chiles, stemmed

4 large garlic cloves, smashed

1 medium onion, coarsely chopped

1 teaspoon ground cumin

½ teaspoon dried oregano,
preferably Mexican

½ teaspoon ground coriander

One 28-ounce can peeled Italian
tomatoes

3 tablespoons extra-virgin olive oil

2½ pounds trimmed boneless pork
shoulder, cut into 1-inch pieces

Salt and freshly ground pepper

2 cups chicken stock or broth

2 bay leaves

One 15-ounce can white or yellow
hominy, drained and rinsed

Rice, sour cream, cilantro and Cheddar
cheese, for serving

1. Put the pink beans and 4 cups of water in a pressure cooker. Close the lid and bring to high pressure over high heat. Reduce the heat to low or just enough to maintain pressure and cook for 5 minutes. Remove from the heat; let stand for 10 minutes, then carefully release the steam valve and drain. The beans should be barely tender with a hard core.

2. Meanwhile, in a medium bowl, soak the guajillo and chipotle chiles in the 4 cups of very hot water until softened, about 15 minutes. Drain, reserving ¼ cup of the liquid. Transfer the chiles and the reserved liquid to a blender and add the garlic, onion, cumin, oregano and coriander. Blend until fairly smooth. Add the tomatoes and their juices and puree until smooth. Strain into a bowl through a fine sieve, pressing hard on the solids.

3. Wipe out the pressure cooker with a paper towel. Add the olive oil and heat until shimmering. Season the pork with salt and pepper and add half of it to the pressure cooker. Cook the pork over moderately high heat until browned all over, about 10 minutes. Using a slotted spoon, transfer the meat to a plate. Brown the remaining meat. Return all of the meat to the pot and add the tomato puree, stock, bay leaves and drained beans. Close the lid and bring to high pressure over high heat. Reduce the heat to low or just enough to maintain high pressure and cook for 30 minutes.

4. Remove the pressure cooker from the heat and let stand for 10 minutes, then carefully release the steam valve. Stir in the hominy and cook uncovered over moderately high heat, stirring occasionally, until the hominy is heated through, about 5 minutes. Discard the bay leaves. Season the chili with salt and pepper. Serve with rice, sour cream, cilantro and cheese. —*Grace Parisi*

WINE Intense, berry-flavored Zinfandel.

Sweet Sausage, Onion and Pepper Skewers

ACTIVE: 45 MIN; TOTAL: 1 HR
10 SERVINGS

The sausages in this recipe are really wonderful with the intense, dark red condiment *harissa* (at right) to heat things up and a minty yogurt sauce (following page) to cool things down. Almost any sausages can be used, but the classic sweet Italian pork sausages are a great match.

- 10 sweet Italian sausages (about 1¾ pounds)
- 2 large red bell peppers, cut into 1-inch pieces
- 1 large red onion, cut into ¾-inch wedges, layers separated
- California Harissa (recipe follows)
- Mint Yogurt Sauce (recipe follows)

1. Light a grill or preheat the broiler. In a large saucepan of boiling water, cook the sausages over moderate heat just until firm, 2 to 3 minutes. Drain them and let them cool slightly. Using a very sharp knife, slice each sausage diagonally into 4 equal pieces.

2. Thread the sausages and peppers onto 10 long bamboo skewers with 1 or 2 onion pieces each, alternating the ingredients and beginning and ending with the sausage. Arrange the skewers on a large platter and brush with ¼ cup of the *harissa*.

3. Grill the sausage skewers over a medium-hot fire or broil in the oven for about 8 minutes, turning occasionally, until the sausage is cooked through and the peppers and onion are nice and tender and slightly charred. Serve the sausage skewers right away with bowls of the remaining *harissa* and the Mint Yogurt Sauce. —*Suzanne Goin*

MAKE AHEAD The uncooked skewers can be refrigerated overnight. Keep on a small baking sheet or in a baking dish, covered with plastic wrap.

WINE Complex, savory Chianti Classico.

California Harissa

ACTIVE: 5 MIN; TOTAL: 25 MIN
MAKES ABOUT 1½ CUPS ● ● ●

This spicy-hot Tunisian sauce is traditionally served alongside couscous, but it can be paired with most poultry, meat and hearty fish. *Harissa* can be found in cans and jars at Middle Eastern markets, but nothing beats the piquant flavor of the homemade version.

- 5 dried ancho chiles (2 ounces), stemmed and seeded
- 2 cups boiling water
- 1 large garlic clove
- ¾ cup plus 2 tablespoons extra-virgin olive oil
- 2½ teaspoons kosher salt
- 1 plum tomato, halved and seeded
- 1 tablespoon plus 1 teaspoon *pimentón* (Spanish smoked paprika) or sweet paprika (see Note)
- 1 teaspoon sherry vinegar
- 1 teaspoon fresh lemon juice
- ¾ teaspoon cayenne pepper
- ½ teaspoon ground cumin

1. In a small heatproof bowl, cover the ancho chiles with the boiling water and let stand until nice and softened, about 20 minutes. Drain the chiles. Transfer half of the softened ancho chiles to a food processor along with the garlic clove, olive oil and kosher salt and puree until completely smooth. Add the plum tomato, *pimentón,* sherry vinegar, lemon juice, cayenne pepper and cumin and puree the mixture again until it is completely smooth.

2. Finely chop the remaining softened anchos. Add them to the food processor and pulse 2 or 3 times, just until combined. Transfer the *harissa* to a small bowl. —*S.G.*

NOTE *Pimentón* is available at specialty food stores.

MAKE AHEAD The *harissa* can be refrigerated for up to 1 week. Keep in a covered jar.

SPICY PINEAPPLE-GLAZED HAM

Mint Yogurt Sauce

ACTIVE: 5 MIN; TOTAL: 15 MIN

MAKES ABOUT 1 ½ CUPS ● ● ●

- ½ European seedless cucumber— peeled, seeded and finely diced
- 2 tablespoons fresh lime juice
- 1 tablespoon finely chopped mint

Pinch of sugar

Kosher salt and freshly ground pepper

- 1½ cups whole milk yogurt

In a medium bowl, combine the cucumber with the lime juice, mint and sugar and season with salt and pepper. Let stand for 10 minutes. Add the yogurt and refrigerate until chilled. —*S.G.*

MAKE AHEAD The sauce can be refrigerated for up to 6 hours.

Italian Sausage Heroes with Peppers and Onions

TOTAL: 40 MIN

4 SERVINGS

The big and messy sausage-and-pepper hero is a staple of every Italian-American street fair. This neater version—made with smaller rolls and sausage halves— is perfect for a quick weeknight dinner at home and requires little cleanup.

- ¼ cup plus 1 tablespoon extra-virgin olive oil, plus more for drizzling
- 2 large onions, cut into very thin slices
- 1 teaspoon sweet paprika
- ½ teaspoon sugar
- 2 large bell peppers (1 red and 1 green), cut into thin strips
- ¼ cup water
- 1½ teaspoons dried oregano, crumbled

Kosher salt and freshly ground pepper

- 4 sweet or hot Italian sausages
- 4 hoagie or small submarine sandwich rolls

1. In a large skillet, heat ¼ cup of the olive oil. Add the onion slices and cook over high heat, stirring frequently, until golden, 10 minutes.

2. Stir in the paprika, sugar and red and green bell peppers. Reduce the heat to moderate and cook, stirring occasionally, until the peppers are softened, about 12 minutes. Stir in the water and oregano. Season with salt and pepper, cover and keep warm.

3. Meanwhile, heat the remaining 1 tablespoon of olive oil in a medium skillet. Prick the sausages all over, add them to the skillet and cook over moderately high heat, turning frequently, until browned all over, about 5 minutes.

4. Transfer the sausages to a cutting board and halve lengthwise. Return the halves to the skillet and cook over moderately high heat, turning occasionally, until no trace of pink remains within, about 5 minutes. Transfer to a plate.

5. Halve each roll (keep it hinged). Pull out some of the bread within. Toast the rolls.

6. Drizzle the cut sides of the rolls with olive oil and set 2 sausage halves on each roll. Top with the sautéed onions and peppers, close the sandwiches and serve immediately. —*David Rosengarten*

SERVE WITH Arugula salad with Parmesan.

WINE Intense, berry-flavored Zinfandel.

Spicy Pineapple-Glazed Ham

ACTIVE: 40 MIN; TOTAL: 4 HR 15 MIN

12 SERVINGS ● ●

One 16- to 18-pound smoked ham on the bone, with skin (see Note)

One 4½-pound pineapple—peeled, halved crosswise and cored, 1 half cut crosswise into ⅓-inch-thick slices, 1 half coarsely chopped

- 2 medium onions, cut into very thin slices
- 2 bay leaves
- 2 cups dry Marsala
- 2 cups dry Riesling
- 2 cups water
- ½ teaspoon freshly grated nutmeg
- ¼ cup whole-grain mustard
- 2 tablespoons Dijon mustard
- 2 large jalapeños, cut crosswise into ⅛-inch-thick slices, stems and seeds discarded

1. Preheat the oven to 450°. Cut off the ham skin, leaving a thick layer of fat. Using a very sharp knife, lightly score the fat layer in a diamond pattern. Arrange the pineapple rings all over the bottom of a large roasting pan. Add the onions, bay leaves, Marsala, Riesling, water and nutmeg. Set the ham on top, fat side up. Cover the ham with parchment paper, then tightly cover the whole pan with foil. Bake the ham for 40 minutes.

2. Turn the oven to 325° and bake the ham for 2 hours and 30 minutes longer, or until an instant-read thermometer inserted in the thickest part without touching the bone registers 120°.

3. Meanwhile, in a food processor, puree the chopped pineapple, then blend with the mustards.

4. Remove the ham from the oven. Turn the oven to 400°. Spread the prepared pineapple mustard all over the ham and arrange the jalapeño rings on top in even rows. Bake the ham for 15 minutes, or until nicely browned. Transfer the ham to a cutting board and let it rest for about 20 minutes.

5. Meanwhile, strain the pan juices into a medium saucepan and boil them over high heat until the liquid is reduced to 3 cups, about 20 minutes. Using a metal spoon, skim off the fat and pour the juices into a warmed gravy boat.

6. Carve the ham into thin slices and arrange on a serving platter or dinner plates. Serve warm with the pan juices. —*Marcia Kiesel*

NOTE Most American hams are smoked, and traditional slow-smoked varieties are the best. Two excellent mail-order sources for ham are Dakin Farm (www.dakinfarm.com) and Karl Ehmer (www.karlehmer.com). Always look for a bone-in ham because it is the most flavorful. Plus, you can use the bone to flavor soup, stew or a bean dish.

WINE Soft, off-dry Riesling.

pork + veal

Veal Blanquette

ACTIVE: 45 MIN; TOTAL: 10 HR 40 MIN

4 SERVINGS ●

Soaking the veal in milk overnight makes the meat especially tender and moist.

- 1½ pounds trimmed veal shoulder, cut into 1½-inch cubes
- 1 cup milk
- 4 thyme sprigs
- 2 bay leaves
- 4 tablespoons unsalted butter
- 1 tablespoon vegetable oil
- Salt and freshly ground pepper
- 1 medium onion, chopped
- 1 small carrot, chopped
- 1 small celery rib, chopped
- ½ cup Cognac
- 1 cup dry white wine
- 1 cup heavy cream
- 1 cup water
- 1 large parsley sprig, plus 2 tablespoons chopped parsley
- 1 pound button mushrooms, stems trimmed and reserved
- 1 pint pearl onions
- 4 large egg yolks
- 1 tablespoon fresh lemon juice

1. Combine the veal, milk, thyme and bay leaves in a dish; cover and refrigerate.

2. Remove the veal from the milk and pat dry with paper towels. Reserve the thyme and bay leaves. In a large saucepan or pot, melt 1 tablespoon of the butter in ½ tablespoon of the oil over moderately high heat. Add half of the veal, season with salt and pepper and cook until browned, about 3 minutes per side. Transfer the veal to a large plate. Repeat with 1 tablespoon of the remaining butter, the remaining ½ tablespoon of oil and the remaining veal.

3. Add the onion, carrot and celery to the same pan and cook over moderate heat until softened, about 5 minutes. Return the veal and any juices to the pan. Add the Cognac and simmer over moderately high heat, scraping up the browned bits from the bottom, about 1 minute. Add the wine and simmer until reduced by half, about 4 minutes. Add the cream and ¾ cup of the water and bring to a simmer. Tie the reserved thyme and bay leaves and the parsley sprig into a bundle and add to the stew along with the mushroom stems. Cover and simmer gently over low heat until the veal is tender, about 1¼ hours.

4. Meanwhile, in a medium saucepan of boiling water, cook the pearl onions in their skins over moderate heat until tender, about 5 minutes. Drain and peel the onions, leaving them whole.

5. In a large skillet, melt the remaining 2 tablespoons of butter over moderate heat. Add the mushroom caps and season with salt and pepper. Cover and cook for 5 minutes. Uncover and cook, stirring occasionally, until browned, about 5 minutes. Transfer to a shallow bowl. Add the remaining ¼ cup of water to the skillet and simmer for 30 seconds, scraping up the browned bits from the bottom of the skillet. Pour the mushroom liquid into the stew.

6. Using a slotted spoon, transfer the veal to a bowl. Strain the sauce, pressing on the solids to extract as much liquid as possible. Return the sauce to the pan. Put the egg yolks in a small heatproof bowl and whisk in ¼ cup of the hot sauce, then whisk in 1 cup of the sauce. Whisk the egg yolk mixture into the sauce in the saucepan and cook over moderately low heat, whisking constantly, until just thickened, about 5 minutes; do not boil. Whisk in the lemon juice. Stir in the veal, pearl onions and mushroom caps and season with salt and pepper.

7. Rewarm the stew over low heat, stirring gently; do not let it come to a boil. Spoon the stew into serving bowls, sprinkle with the chopped parsley and serve. —*David Pratt*

MAKE AHEAD The recipe can be prepared through Step 5 a day ahead. Cool and refrigerate the stew. Refrigerate the pearl onions and mushrooms separately.

SERVE WITH Boiled potatoes or noodles or steamed rice.

WINE Complex, silky red Burgundy.

Roasted Veal Chops with Red Grapes

TOTAL: 25 MIN

4 SERVINGS ●

- 1 pound seedless red grapes
- 3 tablespoons sherry vinegar
- 2½ tablespoons unsalted butter, softened
- ½ teaspoon sugar
- Salt and freshly ground pepper
- Four 1-inch-thick veal rib chops (about ½ pound each)

1. Preheat the oven to 500°. On a sturdy rimmed baking sheet, toss the grapes with the vinegar, 1½ tablespoons of the butter and the sugar; season with salt and pepper. Roast for about 10 minutes, shaking the baking sheet halfway through, until the grapes are hot and the pan is sizzling.

2. Rub the veal chops with the remaining 1 tablespoon of butter and season with salt and pepper. Push the grapes to one

---

side of the baking sheet. Add the veal chops and roast for about 5 minutes, or until sizzling underneath. Turn the chops and roast for 5 minutes longer for medium-rare meat. Transfer the veal chops to a platter, scrape the grapes and juices on top and serve. —*Melissa Clark*
WINE Rich, velvety Merlot.

Pot-Roasted Veal

ACTIVE: 20 MIN; TOTAL: 2 HR 15 MIN
6 SERVINGS

One 3-pound boneless veal
    shoulder roast, tied
  1 garlic clove, cut into 12 slivers
Salt and freshly ground pepper
  1 tablespoon unsalted butter
  1 tablespoon pure olive oil
  1 medium onion, cut into
    ½-inch-thick slices
  ½ teaspoon herbes de Provence
  ½ cup water

1. With a small, sharp knife, pierce the top and sides of the veal roast in 12 evenly spaced places and insert the garlic slivers. Season the roast with salt and pepper.

2. In a medium enameled cast-iron casserole, melt the butter in the olive oil until sizzling. Add the veal roast to the casserole and cook over moderate heat until browned all over, about 3 minutes per side. Scatter the onion and the herbes de Provence around the roast. Add the water and bring to a boil. Cover the casserole partially and gently simmer the roast over low heat, turning once, until an instant-read thermometer inserted in the thickest part of the meat registers 165°, about 1 hour and 45 minutes. Remove from the heat and let the veal roast rest in the casserole for 15 minutes.

3. Transfer the veal roast to a carving board and discard the strings. Strain the pan juices into a glass measuring cup and skim the fat from the surface. Season the pan juices with salt and

pepper. Carve the veal roast into ½-inch-thick slices and serve with the pan juices. —*Jacques Pépin*
MAKE AHEAD The garlic-studded veal roast can be refrigerated overnight, unseasoned. Bring to room temperature and season it before proceeding.
WINE Rich, earthy Pinot Noir.

Roasted Veal Loin

ACTIVE: 1 HR 20 MIN; TOTAL: 10 HR
8 SERVINGS

  ¼ cup plus 2 tablespoons
    extra-virgin olive oil
Juice of 2 limes
  1 medium onion, thinly sliced
  3 tablespoons thyme leaves
Two 1¾-pound veal loin roasts,
    trimmed and tied at 2-inch
    intervals with kitchen string
Freshly ground pepper
Salt
Sweet-and-Sour Vegetable Caponatina
    (recipe, page 231), for serving

1. In a large, sturdy, resealable plastic bag, combine the ¼ cup of olive oil, the lime juice, onion and thyme. Season the veal with pepper, add it to the bag and seal. Turn to coat the veal with the marinade. Refrigerate for at least 8 hours or for up to 12 hours. Bring to room temperature before roasting.

2. Preheat the oven to 350°. Remove the veal from the marinade and pat dry with paper towels. Season with salt and pepper. Heat the remaining 2 tablespoons of olive oil in 2 large skillets until shimmering. Add the veal loins and cook over moderately high heat until browned all over, about 5 minutes. Transfer the loins to a large roasting pan, leaving as much room between them as possible, and roast for 1 hour, or until an instant-read thermometer inserted in the thickest part of each roast registers 140°. Transfer to a carving board, cover loosely with foil and let rest for 10 minutes.

3. Cut the string from the roasts and discard. Carve into ¼-inch-thick slices and serve with the Sweet-and-Sour Vegetable Caponatina. —*Sergio Sigala*
WINE Rich, earthy Pinot Noir.

Osso Buco with Asian Flavors

ACTIVE: 40 MIN; TOTAL: 3 HR 40 MIN
4 SERVINGS ●

  ¼ cup vegetable oil
Four 1-pound pieces of veal shank
Salt and freshly ground pepper
  4 garlic cloves, smashed
  2 tablespoons sugar
  1 medium onion, very finely
    chopped
  ¼ cup chopped fresh ginger, plus
    2 tablespoons finely slivered
 20 cilantro sprigs with roots, plus
    cilantro leaves for garnish
  4 star anise pods
  2 tablespoons Sichuan peppercorns
  1 teaspoon crushed red pepper
  3 cups water
  1 cup dry sherry
  ½ cup soy sauce
  2 large scallions, thinly sliced

1. Preheat the oven to 325°. Heat 2 tablespoons of the oil in an enameled cast-iron casserole. Add the veal shanks, season with salt and pepper and cook over moderately high heat until browned, about 4 minutes per side. Transfer the shanks to a plate and discard the oil.

2. Add the remaining 2 tablespoons of oil and the smashed garlic, sugar, chopped onion and chopped ginger to the casserole and cook over low heat, stirring occasionally, until the onion is deeply browned, about 7 minutes. Add the cilantro sprigs, star anise, Sichuan peppercorns and crushed red pepper and cook for 1 minute. Add the water, sherry and soy sauce and bring to a simmer. Return the veal shanks to the casserole and bring to a simmer. Cover and braise in the oven for about 3 hours, or until the veal is very tender.

pork + veal

3. Transfer the veal shanks to a platter and cover with foil. Strain the sauce and return it to the casserole. Simmer gently over low heat until very flavorful, about 5 minutes. Add the slivered ginger and the veal shanks, season with salt and pepper and bring to a simmer. Transfer the shanks to shallow serving bowls and spoon the sauce on top. Sprinkle with the sliced scallions and cilantro leaves and serve.

—Jean-Georges Vongerichten

WINE Complex, silky red Burgundy.

Veal Scallops with Scotch Whisky Pan Sauce

TOTAL: 30 MIN

4 SERVINGS ●

- 1 large garlic clove, finely chopped
- ½ teaspoon dried thyme
- ½ teaspoon dried tarragon, crumbled
- ½ teaspoon sweet paprika

Kosher salt and freshly ground pepper

- 1½ pounds thin veal scallops (see Note)
- 2 tablespoons unsalted butter
- 2 tablespoons extra-virgin olive oil
- ½ pound white mushrooms, thinly sliced

- 1 scallion, white and tender green parts, finely chopped
- ¼ cup Scotch whisky
- ¾ cup chicken stock or canned low-sodium broth
- 2 tablespoons heavy cream

1. In a small bowl, combine the garlic with the thyme, tarragon, paprika, 1 teaspoon of salt and ½ teaspoon of pepper until thoroughly mixed. Rub the mixture all over the veal.

2. In a large skillet, melt 1 tablespoon of butter in 1 tablespoon of olive oil. Add half of the veal and cook over high heat until lightly browned and nearly cooked through, about 1½ minutes per side. Transfer to a large platter. Repeat with the remaining 1 tablespoon of butter, 1 tablespoon of olive oil and veal. Lower the heat if the pan juices start to darken.

3. Add the mushrooms and scallion to the skillet and cook over high heat, stirring occasionally, until just softened and beginning to brown, about 3 minutes. Carefully add the whisky and ignite with a long match. Cook until the flames subside. Add the stock and cook until reduced by half, scraping up any browned bits from the bottom of the pan, about 5 minutes. Add the cream and simmer just until slightly thickened, 1 to 2 minutes longer; season with salt and pepper. Add the veal, turning to coat. Transfer to the platter and serve.

—Bruce Aidells

NOTE Veal scallops, scallopini and cutlets are all names for the same thing.

WINE Dry, light, crisp Champagne.

Veal Stew with Rosemary and Lemon

ACTIVE: 30 MIN; TOTAL: 2 HR 20 MIN

6 SERVINGS ●

- 3 tablespoons pure olive oil
- 3 pounds boneless veal shoulder, cut into 1½-inch pieces

Salt and freshly ground pepper

- 1 tablespoon unsalted butter
- 2 celery ribs, finely chopped
- 1 large onion, finely chopped
- 1 large carrot, finely chopped
- 2 cups dry white wine
- 1 cup tomato sauce
- 1 tablespoon coarsely chopped rosemary
- 2 tablespoons coarsely chopped flat-leaf parsley
- 1 teaspoon finely grated lemon zest

Baked Polenta with Parmesan (recipe, p. 251), for serving

1. In a large enameled cast-iron casserole, heat 1 tablespoon of the olive oil. Add half of the veal pieces, season with salt and pepper and cook over moderately high heat until browned all over, about 8 minutes. Transfer the veal to a plate. Repeat with another 1 tablespoon of olive oil and the remaining pieces of veal. Pour off the oil from the casserole and discard.

2. In the casserole, melt the butter in the remaining 1 tablespoon of olive oil. Add the celery, onion and carrot and cook over low heat, stirring occasionally, until they are softened and golden, about 12 minutes. Add the white wine and boil over moderately high heat until almost evaporated, about 12 minutes. Stir in the tomato sauce, chopped rosemary and seared veal, along with any accumulated juices. Cover and simmer over low heat, stirring once or twice, until the veal is very tender, about 1 hour and 15 minutes.

3. Stir the chopped parsley and lemon zest into the stew and season it generously with salt and pepper. Spoon the Baked Polenta with Parmesan into shallow serving bowls, top with a mound of the veal stew and serve at once.

—Marika Seguso

MAKE AHEAD The stew can be refrigerated for up to 3 days.

WINE Light, fruity Pinot Noir.

Veal Tournedos with Cellophane Noodles, Chanterelles and Coconut-Corn Sauce

ACTIVE: 1 HR 30 MIN; TOTAL: 5 HR

8 SERVINGS

- 2 tablespoons grapeseed or vegetable oil
- 2½ pounds veal bones and trimmings
- 1 pound chanterelle mushrooms— cleaned, stems trimmed and reserved, caps thickly sliced
- 1 bottle (750 ml) Cabernet Sauvignon, preferably Silver Oak
- 2½ cups chicken stock or low-sodium broth
- 1 tablespoon cornstarch dissolved in 1 tablespoon water

Salt and freshly ground pepper

- 4 cups rich veal stock (see Note)
- 2 cups dried unsweetened shredded coconut (6 ounces)
- 3 small dried red chiles
- 2 large ears of corn, husked
- 2 tablespoons water
- 7 tablespoons unsalted butter
- 2 tablespoons fresh lime juice
- ¼ pound chorizo, peeled and cut into 1-by-¼-inch matchsticks
- 4 ounces cellophane noodles
- 2 tablespoons soy sauce
- ¼ cup snipped chives

Eight 5-ounce veal medallions (tournedos), tied with string

1. In a stockpot, heat 1 tablespoon of the grapeseed oil until shimmering. Add the veal bones and trimmings and cook over moderately high heat, stirring occasionally, until browned all over. Stir in the chanterelle stems. Add the red wine and cook over moderate heat, scraping up any browned bits from the bottom of the pot, until reduced by about half, about 30 minutes. Add 2 cups of the chicken stock, bring to a boil and simmer over moderate heat until reduced to about 1½ cups, about 30 minutes. Strain the liquid into a small saucepan; discard the solids. Stir the cornstarch, then whisk it into the sauce and boil until slightly thickened, about 1 minute. Season the wine reduction generously with salt and pepper.

2. Meanwhile, in a medium saucepan, stir the veal stock with the shredded coconut and dried chiles and simmer over moderately low heat for 45 minutes. Strain the coconut stock into a clean saucepan, pressing hard on the solids; you should have about 3 cups. Discard the solids.

3. Cut the kernels from the corn and scrape the cobs to extract the milk and pulp. Transfer all of the corn to a blender, add the water and puree. Strain the corn puree through a fine sieve, pressing hard to extract as much of the liquid as possible. Add the corn liquid and 2 tablespoons of the butter to the coconut stock and simmer over moderate heat until reduced to just under 1 cup, about 25 minutes. Transfer the coconut-corn sauce to a blender and blend for 1 minute. Transfer the sauce to a small saucepan and stir in 1 tablespoon of lime juice. Season the coconut-corn sauce lightly with salt and pepper.

4. In a large skillet, melt 1 tablespoon of the butter. Add the chanterelle caps and cook over high heat, stirring occasionally, until they begin to brown, about 8 minutes. Stir in the remaining 1 tablespoon of lime juice and season the chanterelles with salt and pepper. Transfer the chanterelles to a bowl. Return the skillet to high heat. Add the chorizo matchsticks and cook, stirring constantly, until they are browned and crisp and the fat has been rendered, about 4 minutes. Transfer the chorizo to a paper towel–lined plate to drain. Wipe out the skillet with a paper towel. Return the chorizo matchsticks and chanterelles to the skillet and reserve.

5. In a large bowl, cover the cellophane noodles with hot tap water and let soak for 15 minutes; drain.

6. Meanwhile, bring a large saucepan of water to a boil. Add the noodles to the boiling water and cook until softened and glassy, about 1 minute. Drain well, shaking off any excess water. Add the remaining ½ cup of chicken stock and 4 tablespoons of butter and the soy sauce to the saucepan and bring to a boil. Off the heat, add the noodles and let stand, stirring occasionally, until the liquid is absorbed, about 10 minutes. Stir in the chives.

7. Preheat the oven to 350° and set a wire rack on a baking sheet. In a large skillet, heat the remaining 1 tablespoon of grapeseed oil. Season the veal medallions with salt and pepper, add them to the skillet and cook over high heat, turning occasionally, until lightly browned on 4 sides, about 5 minutes total; transfer to a plate. Using tongs, dip each medallion into the wine reduction, letting any excess drip back into the saucepan, and set them on the wire rack. Roast the veal for about 17 minutes, or until an instant-read thermometer inserted in the center of a medallion registers 130°. Let the meat rest for 10 minutes, then cut off and discard the strings.

8. Meanwhile, gently rewarm the wine reduction, coconut-corn sauce, chanterelles and chorizo and cellophane noodles. Pour some of the coconut-corn sauce into the center of each of 8 warmed dinner plates and swirl to coat. Mound the noodles in the center and top with the veal medallions. Garnish with the chanterelles and chorizo, drizzle with the wine reduction and serve. —*Laurent Gras*

NOTE Rich veal stock is available frozen at most supermarkets.

MAKE AHEAD The wine reduction and coconut-corn sauce can be refrigerated overnight. The chanterelles and chorizo can be prepared several hours ahead and gently rewarmed.

WINE Tannic, complex Cabernet.

BROILED BACON-BASTED SALMON WITH MUSHROOM-OYSTER SAUCE, P. 186

● FAST

● HEALTHY

● MAKE AHEAD

● STAFF FAVORITE

fish

ROASTED SALMON WITH SPAGHETTI-SQUASH SALAD

SALMON STEAK WITH GRAPE TOMATOES AND MINT

Roasted Salmon with Spaghetti-Squash Salad

TOTAL: 30 MIN

4 SERVINGS ● ● ●

One 3½-pound spaghetti squash,
    halved lengthwise

2 tablespoons vegetable oil, plus
    more for brushing

2 tablespoons fresh lime juice

2 tablespoons fresh orange juice

2 small garlic cloves, minced

1 small red chile, minced

½ teaspoon finely grated orange zest

¼ teaspoon finely grated lime zest

Salt and freshly ground pepper

1½ pounds skinless center-cut
    salmon fillet, cut into strips

2 large kirby cucumbers—halved
    lengthwise, seeded and cut into
    thin half-moons

2 tablespoons shredded mint

1. Preheat the oven to 500°. In a large pot of boiling salted water, cook the squash until al dente, about 12 minutes.
2. Meanwhile, combine the 2 tablespoons of oil with the lime and orange juices, garlic, chile and orange and lime zests. Season with salt and pepper.
3. Carefully transfer the squash halves to a large bowl and let cool. Using a fork, scrape up the strands. Pat dry.
4. Spread the salmon fillet strips on a rimmed baking sheet. Brush lightly with oil and season with salt and pepper. Roast the salmon for about 3 minutes, or until barely cooked through.
5. In a medium bowl, toss the cucumber slices, mint and dressing with the squash strands. Mound the salad on plates, top with the salmon and serve.
—*Marcia Kiesel*

WINE Dry, fruity sparkling wine.

Salmon Fillet Baked in Fig Leaves with Garlicky Potatoes

ACTIVE: 25 MIN; TOTAL: 1 HR

6 SERVINGS ●

Fig leaves lend the fish a smoky, fruity flavor, but Swiss chard leaves are okay in a pinch. Either way, the baked leaves taste like the best vegetable chips ever.

2½ pounds medium Yukon Gold
    potatoes

3 tablespoons extra-virgin olive oil,
    plus more for brushing

15 fig leaves or 6 large Swiss chard
    leaves, ribs removed

Salt and freshly ground pepper

One 2½-pound center-cut piece of
    salmon fillet, skinned

¼ cup chopped parsley

1 large garlic clove, minced

1. Preheat the oven to 400°. In a large saucepan, cover the potatoes with water and bring to a boil. Cook over moderately high heat until barely tender, about 12 minutes. Drain and cool, then cut the potatoes into 1-inch dice.

2. Brush a large rimmed baking sheet with olive oil. Overlap the leaves on the baking sheet to form an oval 4 inches larger than the salmon fillet. Season with salt and pepper. Set the salmon on the leaves, brush with olive oil and season with salt and pepper. Fold the leaves over the top of the salmon and cover with more leaves if needed. Brush the leaves with more olive oil and season with salt and pepper. Bake the salmon for about 20 minutes, until the fish is just cooked through and the leaves are crisp.

3. Meanwhile, in a large skillet, heat the remaining 3 tablespoons of olive oil. Add the potatoes and cook over moderately high heat until browned on the bottoms, about 4 minutes. Stir and cook until browned all over, about 6 minutes longer. Season with salt and pepper and toss with the parsley and garlic. Cut the wrapped salmon into 6 portions and serve with the potatoes. —*Fanny Singer*
WINE Subtle, complex white Burgundy.

Salmon Steaks with Grape Tomatoes and Mint

TOTAL: 20 MIN
4 SERVINGS ● ●

¾ pound grape tomatoes, quartered
⅓ cup finely diced red onion
3 tablespoons chopped mint
Salt and freshly ground pepper
Four 8- to 10-ounce salmon steaks, cut 1 inch thick
1 tablespoon extra-virgin olive oil
¼ cup fresh lemon juice

1. Preheat the oven to 425°. In a bowl, toss the tomatoes with the onion and mint; season with salt and pepper.

2. Season the salmon with salt and pepper. In a large ovenproof skillet, heat the olive oil until shimmering. Add the salmon and cook for 1½ minutes

per side. Transfer the skillet to the oven. Roast the salmon for 7 minutes, or until barely cooked through. Transfer to plates. Pour off the fat from the skillet and stir in the lemon juice. Pour the mixture over the salmon, spoon the salad on top and serve. —*Sally Sampson*
WINE High-acid, savory Vermentino.

Salt-Baked Salmon with Prosecco Butter Sauce

ACTIVE: 35 MIN; TOTAL: 1 HR 25 MIN
8 SERVINGS

This recipe calls for a salmon roast—a large chunk cut from the widest end of the fish (right behind the head). You will need to special-order it from your fishmonger. When you pack the salmon in the salt, be sure to note where the thickest part of the fish is, so you will know where to insert the thermometer to test for doneness.

8 large egg whites
3½ pounds kosher salt
One 4½- to 5-pound salmon roast (with skin and bones), cut from the head end of the fish
Sea salt and freshly ground black pepper
1¼ cups Prosecco
3 scallions, white and green parts minced separately
1 stick plus 2 tablespoons (5 ounces) unsalted butter, cut into 5 chunks and chilled

1. Preheat the oven to 375°. Line a large rimmed baking sheet with parchment paper. In a very large bowl, thoroughly blend the egg whites and kosher salt. On the baking sheet, form part of the salt mixture into a rectangular bed 1 inch larger than the piece of salmon and 1 inch deep. Set the salmon in the center of the salt mixture and season it inside with sea salt and black pepper. Pack the remaining salt around the salmon, pressing the salt against the fish so it adheres all over.

2. Bake the salmon for 50 minutes, or until an instant-read thermometer inserted into the thickest part of the fish registers 125° for rare, or 130° for medium. Remove the salmon from the oven and let it rest for 15 minutes.

3. Meanwhile, in a small saucepan, simmer the Prosecco and scallion whites over moderately high heat until the liquid is reduced to 2 tablespoons, about 15 minutes. Reduce the heat to low and whisk in the butter, 1 chunk at a time, making sure it is fully incorporated before adding more; do not boil. Stir in the scallion greens and season with sea salt and pepper.

4. Using the back of a serrated knife, knock along the edge of the salt crust to crack it, then insert the knife blade to loosen the crust; carefully lift off the pieces. With 2 large forks, peel off the salmon skin and scrape off the dark flesh. Lift the fish from the bones and transfer to plates. Spoon the sauce over the salmon and serve. —*Paul Bertolli*
WINE Flinty, high-acid Chablis.

Salmon with Arugula Cream and Soy-Braised Beets

ACTIVE: 30 MIN; TOTAL: 1 HR 30 MIN
4 SERVINGS

24 baby or 12 small golden or red beets or a combination
⅓ cup balsamic vinegar
⅓ cup soy sauce
½ cup chicken stock
⅓ cup plus 3 tablespoons extra-virgin olive oil
¼ cup dry white wine
¾ cup heavy cream
1½ cups finely chopped arugula leaves (from a medium bunch)
Salt and freshly ground pepper
Four 6-ounce salmon fillets, with skin

1. Preheat the oven to 400°. In a medium enameled cast-iron casserole, combine the beets, vinegar, soy sauce, stock and ⅓ cup of the oil. Bring to a

fish

simmer. Cover and braise in the oven for about 1 hour, or until the beets are tender. Remove from the oven and let cool slightly. Peel the beets, cut them in wedges and return them to the braising liquid; keep warm. Leave the oven on.

2. In a small saucepan, bring the wine to a boil. Add the cream and return to a boil. Reduce the heat to moderate and cook until reduced by half. Remove from the heat and stir in the arugula. Season with salt and pepper and keep warm.

3. Heat the remaining 3 tablespoons of oil in a large ovenproof skillet. Season the salmon with salt and pepper and sear, skin side down, over high heat until the skin is crisp, about 1 minute. Turn over the salmon fillets carefully and sear 1 minute.

4. Transfer the salmon to the oven and roast for about 3 minutes, or until it is medium rare and still bright pink in the center. Transfer to serving plates and spoon the arugula cream on top. Spoon the beets alongside, drizzled with some of their cooking liquid, and serve at once. —*Eric Czerwinski*

WINE Light, fruity Pinot Noir.

salmon

TIP When cooking salmon fillets or steaks in a pan or on the grill, wait until they're well browned to turn; that way they'll release easily, without flaking, when you flip them with a spatula.

VITAL STATS Omega-3 fatty acids have a vaguely science-fiction-y name, but don't let that put you off. These fats, found in large quantities in salmon as well as other fatty fish, protect the heart in several ways—by preventing blood clots and steadying heart rhythm, for instance. They may even alleviate depression.

Tandoori-Style Salmon with Cilantro Gremolata

ACTIVE: 20 MIN; TOTAL: 12 HR 30 MIN

8 SERVINGS ●

The spiced yogurt marinade needs to be refrigerated overnight, so plan accordingly.

- 1 cup plain whole milk yogurt
- ¼ cup tandoori paste (see Note)
- 1 large garlic clove, minced
- 1 tablespoon plus ¼ teaspoon finely grated peeled fresh ginger

Salt and freshly ground pepper

Eight 6-ounce skinless salmon fillets

- 1 small shallot, minced
- 1 jalapeño, seeded and very finely chopped

Finely grated zest of 1 small lime

- ¼ cup finely chopped cilantro
- ¼ cup finely chopped mint

1. In a medium bowl, mix the yogurt with the tandoori paste, garlic, 1 tablespoon of the ginger and ⅛ teaspoon each of salt and pepper. Cover and refrigerate overnight.

2. Arrange the salmon fillets in a single layer in a large glass baking dish and pour the marinade on top, spreading it to completely coat the fish. Cover with plastic wrap and refrigerate for at least 4 hours and for up to 8 hours.

3. In a small bowl, combine the shallot, jalapeño, lime zest, cilantro, mint and the remaining ¼ teaspoon of grated ginger. Season with salt.

4. Preheat the oven to 500°. Transfer the salmon fillets to a large, lightly oiled baking sheet, skinned side down, leaving a thick coating of the marinade on the fish. Season with salt and pepper. Bake in the upper third of the oven for 10 minutes, or until just cooked through. Transfer the salmon to a platter, scatter the cilantro gremolata on top and serve. —*Gail Monaghan*

NOTE Tandoori paste is available at specialty food stores and Indian markets.

WINE Spicy Alsace Gewürztraminer.

Broiled Bacon-Basted Salmon with Mushroom-Oyster Sauce

TOTAL: 50 MIN

6 SERVINGS

Two 1¼-pound skinless salmon fillets, about 1 inch thick

Kosher salt and freshly ground pepper

- 10 slices of bacon, 4 slices cut into 1-inch pieces
- ¾ pound mixed mushrooms, such as oyster and cremini, thinly sliced
- ¼ cup finely minced parsley
- ¼ cup finely chopped chives
- 2 teaspoons minced garlic
- ½ cup hot water
- ¼ cup Chinese oyster sauce

Pinch of freshly grated nutmeg

- 2 tablespoons cold unsalted butter, cut into tablespoons

1. Preheat the broiler. Lightly season the salmon fillets with salt and pepper. Wrap 3 slices of the bacon crosswise around each salmon fillet, spacing the slices 1 inch apart. Place the salmon fillets in a medium roasting pan and broil the fish 6 inches from the heat for about 13 minutes, shifting the pan halfway through, or until the salmon fillets are just cooked through.

2. Meanwhile, in a large skillet, cook the bacon pieces over high heat, stirring occasionally, until lightly browned and slightly crisp, about 4 minutes. Pour off all but 2 teaspoons of the bacon fat and reduce the heat to moderately high. Add the mushrooms to the skillet and sauté them until they are golden brown, about 3 minutes. Reduce the heat to moderate and stir in the minced parsley, 2 tablespoons of the chopped chives and the minced garlic. Cook until the garlic is fragrant, about 1 minute.

3. In a small bowl, whisk the hot water with the oyster sauce until blended. Add to the mushrooms and cook over moderately high heat, stirring, until the sauce

thickens slightly, about 1 minute. Stir in the nutmeg, then whisk in the butter and cook until just melted. Remove the mushroom sauce from the heat.

4. Remove the strips of bacon from the salmon fillets and cut each fillet into 3 pieces. Save the broiled bacon slices for another use. Transfer the salmon to a platter. Spoon the mushroom sauce over the fish, garnish with the remaining chives and serve. —*David Rosengarten*
WINE Complex, silky red Burgundy.

Papillotes of Sea Bass in Red Curry Sauce

ACTIVE: 30 MIN; TOTAL: 45 MIN
4 SERVINGS

Thai red curry paste made from chiles, lemongrass and galangal imparts a distinctly pungent flavor to dishes. Its intense heat is usually mellowed by another Southeast Asian staple, coconut milk. The coconut milk blends with the fish juices here to make an instant creamy sauce.

- 1 tablespoon unsalted butter
- 2 medium shallots, finely chopped
- ½ cup dry white wine
- ¾ cup unsweetened coconut milk
- 1 tablespoon Asian fish sauce
- 2 teaspoons fresh lime juice
- 1½ teaspoons Thai red curry paste
- 1 teaspoon sugar
- Four 6-ounce skinless white-fleshed fish fillets, such as sea bass, grouper or halibut
- Salt and freshly ground pepper
- 4 basil sprigs

1. Preheat the oven to 450°. Melt the butter in a medium saucepan. Add the shallots, cover and cook over low heat, stirring occasionally, until golden, 5 minutes. Add the wine and simmer until almost evaporated, about 3 minutes. Whisk in the coconut milk, fish sauce, lime juice, red curry paste and sugar and simmer until slightly thickened, about 5 minutes; you should have

¾ cup of sauce. Remove from the heat.
2. Cut four 20-inch sheets of heavy-duty aluminum foil or parchment paper. Set 1 sheet on a work surface and turn up the edges slightly so the curry sauce can be contained. Spoon 1 tablespoon of the sauce on one side of the sheet and set a fish fillet on top; season with salt and pepper and spoon 2 more tablespoons of the sauce on the fish. Top with a basil sprig. Fold the foil over the fish and, starting at one corner, fold the edge over itself in neat pleats, folding each successive pleat so it slightly overlaps the previous one to make a tight seal all around. Repeat with the remaining curry sauce, fish fillets and basil.
3. Slide the papillotes onto a cookie sheet and bake them on the bottom rack of the oven for 12 to 14 minutes, or until puffed. Remove from the oven and let stand for 2 minutes.
4. Transfer the papillotes to large, shallow soup bowls. Carefully cut the foil or paper around the pleats. Fold back the flaps to expose the fish and serve immediately. —*Sally Schneider*
WINE Soft, off-dry Riesling.

Steamed Bass with Caramelized Onion, Ginger and Scallion

ACTIVE: 15 MIN; TOTAL: 45 MIN
2 SERVINGS ●

- 2 tablespoons peanut oil
- 1 small onion, thinly sliced
- Salt
- One 1½-inch piece of fresh ginger, peeled and julienned (3 tablespoons)
- One 2½-pound whole black sea bass, cleaned and scaled
- Soy sauce, for drizzling
- 1 teaspoon Asian sesame oil
- 2 tablespoons chopped cilantro
- 1 scallion, cut into 2-inch julienne strips

1. Heat 1 tablespoon of the peanut oil in a small skillet. Add the onion and a pinch

of salt and cook over high heat, stirring once or twice, until browned, about 2 minutes. Transfer to a small bowl and stir in the ginger.
2. In a large wok, set a round rack that will sit at least 3 inches above the bottom. Add 2 inches of water and bring to a boil. Set the fish on a heatproof plate that will fit in the wok and sprinkle the onion and ginger on top. Set the plate on the rack, cover the wok and steam the fish over moderate heat until just cooked through, about 20 minutes.
3. Drizzle the fish with soy sauce. In a small skillet, warm the remaining 1 tablespoon of peanut oil with the sesame oil over moderately high heat, then pour it over the fish. Sprinkle with the cilantro and scallion and serve.
—*Jean-Georges Vongerichten*
WINE Full-bodied, fragrant Viognier.

Swordfish Sicilian-Style

TOTAL: 20 MIN
4 TO 6 SERVINGS ● ● ●

- 2 tablespoons fresh lemon juice
- 2 teaspoons table salt
- 2 teaspoons chopped fresh oregano
- ¼ cup extra-virgin olive oil
- Freshly ground pepper
- 2 pounds swordfish steaks, cut ½ inch thick

1. Light a grill or preheat the broiler. In a small bowl, mix the lemon juice with the salt until the salt dissolves. Stir in the oregano. Slowly whisk in the olive oil until emulsified and season generously with pepper.
2. Grill the swordfish steaks over high heat (as close to the heat as possible), turning once, until cooked through, 6 to 7 minutes. Transfer the fish to a platter. Prick each fish steak in several places with a fork to allow the sauce to penetrate. Using a spoon, beat the sauce, then drizzle it over the fish. Serve at once. —*Marcella Hazan*
WINE Round-textured Semillon.

WHOLE ROASTED SEA BASS WITH POTATOES AND OLIVES

Whole Roasted Sea Bass with Potatoes and Olives

ACTIVE: 30 MIN; TOTAL: 1 HR 35 MIN

6 SERVINGS ●

1½ pounds baking potatoes, peeled and cut into ⅛-inch-thick slices

¼ cup plus 1 tablespoon extra-virgin olive oil

¼ cup coarsely chopped flat-leaf parsley, plus 2 parsley sprigs

1 tablespoon finely chopped rosemary

Salt and freshly ground pepper

20 cherry or grape tomatoes, halved

1 cup Gaeta olives (5 ounces)

One 6-pound whole black sea bass or red snapper, cleaned and scaled

2 thyme sprigs

1 cup dry white wine

1. Preheat the oven to 400°. In a large roasting pan, toss the potatoes with 2 tablespoons of the olive oil, the chopped parsley and the rosemary; season with salt and pepper. Spread the potatoes in an even layer in the pan. Scatter the tomatoes and olives over the potatoes and drizzle with 2 more tablespoons of the olive oil.

2. Season the cavity of the fish with salt and pepper and stuff the parsley and thyme sprigs into it. Lay the fish on the potatoes and pour the wine over it. Rub the surface of the fish with the remaining 1 tablespoon of olive oil and season with salt and pepper. Cover the roasting pan with foil and bake the fish for 50 minutes, or until almost cooked through. Discard the foil and baste the fish with the pan juices. Bake the fish for about 20 minutes longer, or until it is cooked through and the potatoes are tender.

3. To serve, transfer the fish to a work surface. Transfer the potatoes, tomatoes and olives to a platter. Fillet the fish and set the fillets on top of the potatoes. Pour the pan juices over the fish and serve. —*Marika Seguso*

WINE Dry, mineral-flavored Chenin Blanc.

Sole Meunière

ACTIVE: 25 MIN; TOTAL: 45 MIN

4 SERVINGS ●

Meunière means "miller's wife" and refers to the dusting of flour on the fish.

2 teaspoons fennel seeds

1 cup all-purpose flour

1 tablespoon kosher salt

1 teaspoon freshly ground white pepper

¼ cup heavy cream

¼ cup dry white wine

Four 6-ounce sole fillets

2 tablespoons canola oil

2 tablespoons extra-virgin olive oil

4 tablespoons unsalted butter

1 tablespoon drained capers

1 tablespoon red wine vinegar

1 tablespoon minced parsley

1. In a small skillet, toast the fennel seeds over moderately high heat until fragrant, about 30 seconds. Transfer the fennel seeds to a spice grinder and let cool, then grind them to a powder. Scrape the powder into a shallow bowl and whisk in the flour, salt and white pepper. In another shallow bowl, combine the heavy cream and white wine. Dip the sole fillets in the cream, then dredge them in the flour mixture.

2. In each of 2 large skillets, heat 1 tablespoon each of the canola and olive oils until they are shimmering. Add 2 sole fillets to each skillet and cook the fish fillets over high heat until they are golden brown on the bottoms, about 3 minutes. Carefully turn the fillets and cook until golden brown on the outside and white throughout, 1 to 2 minutes; transfer the fish fillets to plates.

3. Wipe out 1 skillet and add the butter. Cook over moderate heat, shaking the skillet often, until lightly browned, about 3 minutes. Add the capers and shake the pan, then add the vinegar. Spoon the sauce over the fish, sprinkle with the parsley and serve. —*Rob Larman*

WINE Subtle, complex white Burgundy.

Mushroom-Crusted Flounder with Creamed Spinach

TOTAL: 30 MIN

4 SERVINGS ●

4 tablespoons unsalted butter

2 garlic cloves, minced

1 medium shallot, minced

Two 5-ounce bags baby spinach

½ cup heavy cream

Pinch of cayenne pepper

Kosher salt and freshly ground pepper

¼ pound shiitake mushrooms, stems discarded, caps thinly sliced

2 tablespoons fine dry bread crumbs

Vegetable oil, for brushing

Four 6-ounce flounder fillets

1 tablespoon minced parsley

1. Preheat the broiler and position a rack 8 inches from the heat. In a large skillet, melt 1 tablespoon of the butter. Add half of the garlic and shallot and cook over moderately high heat until fragrant, about 1 minute. Add the spinach and cook, tossing, until wilted. Add the cream and cayenne and cook over moderately high heat until thickened, about 7 minutes. Season with salt and pepper; keep warm.

2. Meanwhile, in a medium skillet, melt 1 tablespoon of the butter. Add the remaining garlic and shallot and cook over moderate heat until fragrant, about 2 minutes. Add the shiitake, season with salt and pepper and cook, stirring occasionally, until tender, about 4 minutes. Remove the pan from the heat. Stir in the remaining 2 tablespoons of butter and the bread crumbs.

3. Lightly brush a large baking sheet with oil. Set the flounder fillets on the sheet and pat the mushroom mixture onto each fillet. Broil the fish for 4 to 5 minutes, or until cooked through. Transfer the fish to plates and spoon the creamed spinach alongside. Sprinkle with parsley and serve. —*Daniel Boulud*

WINE Subtle, complex white Burgundy.

fish

Halibut with Fried Capers and Lemon

TOTAL: 35 MIN

4 SERVINGS ●

- 1 cup large salt-packed capers (5 ounces), rinsed
- ¼ cup plus 2 tablespoons extra-virgin olive oil
- Zest of 1 lemon, cut into fine julienne
- ½ cup all-purpose flour
- Four 6- to 8-ounce skinless halibut fillets, about ¾ inch thick
- Salt and freshly ground pepper
- ½ cup dry white wine
- 2 tablespoons fresh lemon juice
- 2 tablespoons unsalted butter

1. In a medium saucepan, bring 1 quart of water to a boil. Add the capers and simmer over moderately high heat for 5 minutes. Spread out the capers in an even layer on paper towels and pat dry thoroughly.

2. In a large skillet, heat ¼ cup of the olive oil. Add the lemon zest and cook over moderately high heat, stirring, until starting to brown, about 40 seconds. With a slotted spoon, transfer the zest to paper towels to drain.

3. Dredge the capers in the flour and shake off any excess. Reheat the olive oil. Add the capers and fry over moderately high heat, stirring, until crisp, about 3 minutes. With a slotted spoon, transfer the capers to paper towels to drain. Wipe out the skillet.

4. Add the remaining 2 tablespoons of olive oil to the skillet and heat until shimmering. Season the halibut with salt and pepper, add it to the skillet and cook over high heat until browned and crisp on the bottoms, about 4 minutes. Turn the fillets and cook over moderate heat until just white throughout, about 4 minutes longer. Transfer the fish to plates and tent with aluminum foil to keep warm.

5. Add the wine to the skillet and cook over moderately high heat until it is reduced by half, about 3 minutes. Add the lemon juice and remove from the heat. Swirl in the butter until melted and season the sauce with salt and pepper. Drizzle the sauce over the halibut, top with the fried lemon zest and capers and serve. —*Marcia Kiesel*

VARIATIONS Serve the fried capers and lemon zest on pizza, grilled chicken, in salads or in an omelet.

WINE Flinty, high-acid Chablis.

Halibut with Corn Pops and Basil Broth

ACTIVE: 40 MIN; TOTAL: 1 HR 25 MIN

4 SERVINGS

- 6 tablespoons unsalted butter, softened
- 2½ tablespoons Corn Pops cereal, finely chopped
- 2½ tablespoons fine dry bread crumbs
- Scant ½ teaspoon mild curry powder
- ¼ teaspoon salt
- Pinch of cayenne pepper
- 2½ cups whole milk
- 1 bay leaf
- 1 star anise pod
- 2 ears of corn, husked and halved
- ⅓ cup crème fraîche or sour cream
- 1 tablespoon grapeseed oil
- Four 6-ounce skinless halibut fillets
- Kosher salt and freshly ground pepper
- ¼ cup coarsely chopped basil, plus sprigs for garnish

1. In a bowl, stir the butter with the Corn Pops, bread crumbs, curry powder, salt and cayenne. Form it into a 3-inch-long cylinder in plastic wrap; refrigerate.

2. Meanwhile, in a medium saucepan, combine the milk with the bay leaf and star anise. Add the corn and simmer over moderately low heat until tender, about 40 minutes. Let cool slightly, then discard the bay leaf and star anise. Cut the kernels from the cobs and transfer them to a blender. Add ½ cup of the milk and blend at low speed until pureed. Increase the speed to high, gradually add the remaining milk and puree. Add the crème fraîche; puree.

3. Preheat the oven to 250°. Cut the Corn Pops butter into 4 pieces. In a large nonstick skillet, heat the oil until shimmering. Season the halibut with salt and pepper and cook over high heat, turning once, until golden, about 6 minutes. Transfer to a baking dish and top each fillet with a slice of the Corn Pops butter. Bake for 2 minutes.

4. Add the basil to the blender and puree with the soup; season with salt. Transfer the halibut to shallow bowls. Pour the soup around, garnish with basil sprigs and serve. —*Cornelius Gallagher*

MAKE AHEAD The recipe can be prepared through Step 2 and refrigerated overnight. Rewarm the soup before pureeing with the basil.

WINE Light, soft Chenin Blanc.

KITCHEN TOOL

seafood knife

Kyocera's KT-300-HIP Sashimi Knife is made of ceramic, which is both lighter and stronger than metal. It glides effortlessly through everything from raw fish to steak ($800 for an 8.25" blade; www. kyoceratycom.com).

Halibut Roasted in Grape Leaves with Lemon Vinaigrette

TOTAL: 35 MIN

4 SERVINGS ● ● ●

12 large brined grape leaves, rinsed, stems trimmed

¼ cup plus 4 teaspoons extra-virgin olive oil

2 teaspoons chopped thyme

Kosher salt and freshly ground white pepper

Four 6-ounce skinless halibut fillets, about 1 inch thick

3 tablespoons fresh lemon juice

1 teaspoon Dijon mustard

I. Preheat the oven to 400°. Lightly oil a baking dish. On a work surface, overlap 3 of the grape leaves, vein side up, to create a 7- to 8-inch round. Repeat with the remaining grape leaves for a total of 4 rounds. Drizzle 1 teaspoon of the olive oil into the center of each round; sprinkle 1 teaspoon of the thyme over all of the rounds. Season with salt and white pepper. Set the halibut on the seasoned oil and fold the grape leaves around the fish. Arrange the fish packets, seam side down, in the baking dish. Roast for about 20 minutes, or until the grape leaves are crisp.

2. In a small bowl, whisk the lemon juice with the mustard and the remaining ¼ cup of olive oil and 1 teaspoon of thyme. Season with salt and pepper.

3. Transfer the fish packets to a platter. Peel back the grape leaves. Spoon the vinaigrette over the fish and serve hot or at room temperature. —*Megan Moore*

WINE Aromatic, zesty Albariño.

Lemony Halibut Skewers with Charmoula

ACTIVE: 1 HR 10 MIN; TOTAL: 1 HR 30 MIN

10 SERVINGS ●

CHARMOULA

2 tablespoons cumin seeds

3 garlic cloves

2½ cups coarsely chopped cilantro

1 cup flat-leaf parsley leaves

1 tablespoon sweet paprika

1 teaspoon cayenne pepper

1 teaspoon kosher salt

1¼ cups extra-virgin olive oil

1 tablespoon fresh lemon juice

1½ teaspoons rice vinegar

SKEWERS

3 pounds skinless halibut fillets, cut into 1½-inch cubes (40 pieces)

1 large lemon, halved lengthwise and cut into ¼-inch-thick slices

30 fresh bay leaves, or dried bay leaves soaked in warm water for 30 minutes and drained

Vegetable oil, for brushing

Kosher salt

California Harissa (recipe, page 175)

Mint Yogurt Sauce (recipe, page 177)

I. MAKE THE CHARMOULA: Toast the cumin seeds over moderate heat until fragrant, about 2 minutes. Transfer to a spice grinder to cool, then grind.

2. In a food processor, finely chop the garlic. Add the cilantro and parsley and finely chop. Add the ground cumin, paprika, cayenne, salt and olive oil and mix. Pour 6 tablespoons of the *charmoula* into a large bowl; transfer the remaining *charmoula* to a bowl and stir in the lemon juice and vinegar.

3. PREPARE THE SKEWERS: Light a grill or preheat the broiler. Add the halibut to the *charmoula* in the large bowl and toss. Cut the lemon slices in half. Thread the halibut, bay leaves and lemon onto 10 long bamboo skewers, beginning and ending with fish.

4. Brush the grate with oil. Season the skewers with salt. Grill or broil, turning occasionally, until the fish is just cooked through, 8 to 11 minutes. Transfer to a platter and serve with the extra *charmoula,* the California Harissa and the Mint Yogurt Sauce. —*Suzanne Goin*

MAKE AHEAD The *charmoula* can be refrigerated for up to 4 days.

WINE Light, dry Soave or similar white.

Smoked Trout Hash with Potatoes and Corn

TOTAL: 35 MIN

4 SERVINGS ● ●

1 tablespoon canola oil

1 pound baking potatoes, peeled and cut into ½-inch dice

3 scallions, thinly sliced

⅓ cup chopped red onion

One 10-ounce package frozen corn kernels, thawed (2 cups)

1 pound smoked trout fillets, skinned and torn into large flakes

Salt and freshly ground pepper

4 large eggs

I. Heat the oil in a large skillet. Add the potatoes and cook over moderate heat until tender, 5 to 6 minutes. Add the scallions and onion and cook until softened. Stir in the corn and trout until warm. Season with salt and pepper.

2. In a pan of simmering water, poach the eggs until medium-cooked, about 3 minutes. Drain on paper towels. Mound the hash on plates, top with the eggs and serve. —*Jason Knibb*

WINE Soft, off-dry Riesling.

COOKING TIP

grilling in foil

WRAP RAW INGREDIENTS in a foil packet and cook them on the grill, and what you've got is a hobo pack. This technique combines steaming with the intense flavor of grilling, since the high heat caramelizes the food on the bottom. Lightly oil the foil to prevent food from sticking. Add vegetables or fruit, then layer seafood, chicken or meat and flavorings (such as herbs, olives or onions). The trick is to choose quick-cooking ingredients; cut up the larger ones so that everything in the pack finishes simultaneously.

● FAST ● HEALTHY ● MAKE AHEAD ● STAFF FAVORITE

CRISPY COD WITH LIMA BEANS, CRAB AND CORN

SMOKED TROUT AND APPLE SALAD

Smoked Trout and Apple Salad

TOTAL: 20 MIN

6 SERVINGS ● ●

- 3 tablespoons buttermilk
- 3 tablespoons mayonnaise
- 3 tablespoons prepared horseradish, drained
- 3 tablespoons snipped chives
- 1½ tablespoons extra-virgin olive oil

Kosher salt and freshly ground pepper

One 5-ounce bunch baby arugula, thick stems discarded

- 1 large Granny Smith apple, cut into thin matchsticks
- 1 whole smoked trout (about 10 ounces)—boned, skinned and flaked (5 ounces)

1. In a small bowl, whisk the buttermilk with the mayonnaise, horseradish, snipped chives and olive oil; season with salt and pepper.

2. In a large bowl, toss the arugula and apple with two-thirds of the dressing and transfer to a large platter. Add the trout to the bowl and toss with the remaining dressing; season with pepper. Mound the trout on the arugula salad and serve. —*Melissa Clark*

WINE Bright, citrusy Riesling.

Crispy Cod with Lima Beans, Crab and Corn

ACTIVE: 50 MIN; TOTAL: 1 HR

4 SERVINGS

- 1 stick (4 ounces) unsalted butter, 4 tablespoons softened
- 2 tablespoons very finely chopped flat-leaf parsley
- 1½ tablespoons minced tarragon
- 2½ teaspoons very finely chopped chives

Salt

- 2 cups frozen baby lima beans (10 ounces)
- 1 small onion, halved
- 1 thyme sprig
- 2 beefsteak tomatoes (1 pound), coarsely chopped
- 1 small shallot, minced
- ½ cup fresh corn kernels (from 1 ear)
- ¼ cup finely diced smoked ham

Pinch of Old Bay seasoning

- 1 cup Champagne
- 1 medium tomato, seeded and cut into ¼-inch dice
- 2 tablespoons vegetable oil

Four 6-ounce black cod fillets, skin scored

Freshly ground pepper

- ¼ pound lump crabmeat, picked over

1. In a food processor, combine the 4 tablespoons softened butter with the parsley, ½ tablespoon of the tarragon and the chives. Season with salt. Transfer the butter to a piece of plastic wrap, form into a cylinder and refrigerate.

2. In a medium saucepan of boiling water, cook the lima beans with the onion, thyme sprig and a pinch of salt over moderate heat until the lima beans are tender, about 10 minutes. Drain and discard the onion and thyme.

3. In a food processor, puree the beefsteak tomatoes. Strain the puree into a medium bowl; you should have about 1½ cups of tomato puree.

4. In a large skillet, melt 2 tablespoons of the butter. Add the shallot and cook over moderate heat until softened, 2 minutes. Add the corn, ham and Old Bay seasoning and cook, stirring, for 2 minutes. Add the Champagne and simmer over moderately high heat until reduced by half, 3 minutes. Add the diced tomato, lima beans and tomato puree. Simmer over moderate heat until the stew is flavorful and the liquid has thickened slightly, 4 minutes. Remove from the heat.

5. In a large skillet, heat the oil until nearly smoking. Season the cod with salt and pepper and cook, skin side down, over high heat until the skin is browned and crisp, about 4 minutes. Turn the fish, reduce the heat to moderately low and cook until just opaque throughout, about 3 minutes longer.

6. Stir the crabmeat and the remaining 1 tablespoon of tarragon into the stew; simmer for 1 minute to heat through. Off the heat, swirl in the remaining 2 tablespoons of butter; season with salt and pepper. Spoon the stew into bowls and set a cod fillet in each. Top each fillet with a pat of the herb butter and serve. —*Bryan Moscatello*

MAKE AHEAD The lima bean stew can be prepared through Step 4 and refrigerated overnight. Reheat gently before proceeding with the recipe.

WINE Dry, light, crisp Champagne.

Warm Cured-Cod Salad with Orange and Basil

ACTIVE: 40 MIN; TOTAL: 1 HR 10 MIN

8 SERVINGS ●

The best way to replicate high-quality salt cod is to cure fresh cod in sea salt, then rinse it and poach it in olive oil.

- 1 pound center-cut skinless cod fillet
- 1 tablespoon coarse sea salt
- 4 medium navel oranges
- 6 tablespoons extra-virgin olive oil

Salt and freshly ground pepper

- 2 ounces mesclun (4 cups)
- ½ cup small basil leaves
- 1 small sweet onion, thinly sliced
- ½ small red bell pepper, minced
- ½ small green bell pepper, minced

1. Put the cod in a shallow baking dish and pat the sea salt all over it. Cover and refrigerate for 1 hour.

2. Meanwhile, peel the oranges with a sharp knife, removing all the bitter white pith. Working over a bowl, cut in between the membranes to release the orange sections into the bowl. Squeeze the juice from the membranes into the bowl.

3. Transfer ¼ cup of juice to a bowl. Stir in 2 tablespoons of oil. Season the dressing with salt and pepper. Drain the orange sections; discard any remaining juice.

4. Rinse the cod under cold water and pat dry. In a skillet, heat the remaining ¼ cup of oil. Add the cod and cook over moderately low heat, turning once and shaking the pan, until the cod is just cooked through and separates into large flakes, 10 minutes. Transfer to a plate.

5. In a large bowl, combine the mesclun and basil leaves and toss with 2 tablespoons of the dressing. Transfer to plates and top with the orange sections and cod, separating the flakes slightly. Scatter the onion and red and green bell peppers over the salads, drizzle with the remaining dressing and serve. —*Adolfo Muñoz*

WINE Lively, assertive Sauvignon Blanc.

Cod with Creamy Nut Sauce

TOTAL: 25 MIN

4 SERVINGS ● ●

- 2 slices of peasant bread (2 ounces), crusts removed, bread diced
- ½ cup water
- ⅓ cup whole almonds
- 3 tablespoons red wine vinegar
- 2 large garlic cloves, minced
- ¼ cup extra-virgin olive oil, plus more for brushing
- 2 tablespoons chopped parsley

Salt and freshly ground pepper

Four 6-ounce cod fillets

- 1 small lemon, sliced paper-thin

1. Soak the bread in the water, then squeeze dry; reserve ¼ cup of the water.

2. In a mini food processor, grind the almonds to a powder. Add the soaked bread, reserved water, vinegar, garlic and ¼ cup of olive oil and process to a thick sauce. Scrape into a bowl, stir in the parsley and season with salt and pepper.

3. Preheat the broiler. On a broiler pan, brush the cod fillets with olive oil and season with salt and pepper. Arrange a few lemon slices on each fillet and broil for 4 to 5 minutes, or until browned and just cooked through. Transfer the fillets to plates, top each with 2 tablespoons of the sauce and serve. —*Priscilla Martel*

WINE Dry, medium-bodied Pinot Gris.

Miso-Glazed Cod with Napa Cabbage

ACTIVE: 30 MIN; TOTAL: 1 HR 35 MIN

4 SERVINGS ●

The cod marinates anywhere from one hour to overnight, so plan accordingly.

MARINADE

- 1½ cups water
- 2 tablespoons sugar
- 2 tablespoons sake
- ¼ cup yellow miso paste

FISH

Four ½-pound skinless cod fillets, ¾ inch thick, rinsed and patted dry

fish

½ cup mirin

¼ cup sake

5 tablespoons slivered fresh ginger

2 tablespoons water

2 tablespoons yellow miso paste

2 tablespoons sugar

Vegetable oil, for frying

One 1-pound head napa cabbage,
cut crosswise into ¼-inch
strips (5 cups)

Salt

I. MAKE THE MARINADE: In a small saucepan, combine the water with the sugar and sake and cook over moderately low heat until the sugar dissolves. Whisk the miso paste into the marinade until smooth. Let the marinade cool completely.

2. PREPARE THE FISH: Put the cod fillets in a baking dish large enough to hold them in a single layer and pour the marinade over them. Cover with plastic wrap and refrigerate for at least 1 hour or overnight.

3. Meanwhile, in a small saucepan, combine the mirin with the sake and 1 tablespoon of the ginger and bring to a simmer over moderately low heat. Cook for 5 minutes. In a small bowl, combine the water, miso and sugar and add to the sauce. Cook over low heat until the sauce is reduced to ⅔ cup, about 25 minutes; keep warm.

4. In another small saucepan, heat ½ inch of vegetable oil over moderate heat until shimmering. Add the remaining ¼ cup of slivered ginger and fry until golden, about 30 seconds. Using a slotted spoon, quickly transfer the fried ginger to paper towels to drain; reserve the ginger cooking oil.

5. Preheat the broiler and arrange an oven rack 4 inches from the heat source. In a large, deep skillet or wok, heat 2 tablespoons of the ginger oil. Add the napa cabbage and cook over moderately high heat, stirring frequently, until softened slightly and

nicely browned on the edges, about 5 minutes; season the cabbage generously with salt.

6. Remove the cod from the marinade and pat dry. Set the fillets on a rack set over a baking sheet and broil for about 7 minutes, or until just cooked through. Spoon the cabbage onto plates and set the cod on top. Spoon a few tablespoons of sauce over the fish, garnish with the fried ginger and serve.

—*Jeannie Chen*

SERVE WITH Steamed white rice.

WINE Dry, mineral-flavored Chenin Blanc.

Thai Tuna Burgers with Ginger-Lemon Mayonnaise
ACTIVE: 30 MIN; TOTAL: 1 HR

4 SERVINGS ● ●

Use sushi-quality tuna so that you can serve the burgers medium rare.

2 kirby cucumbers, thinly sliced

¼ medium red onion, thinly sliced

3 tablespoons rice vinegar

1 tablespoon plus 1 teaspoon sugar

Kosher salt and freshly ground pepper

2 teaspoons finely grated
fresh ginger

1 garlic clove, smashed

1 Thai or serrano chile,
seeded and minced

2 tablespoons Asian fish sauce

2 tablespoons finely
chopped cilantro

1 tablespoon finely chopped basil

1½ pounds sushi-quality tuna

1½ tablespoons vegetable oil

1½ teaspoons Asian sesame oil

4 hamburger buns

Ginger-Lemon Mayonnaise
(recipe follows)

2 tablespoons finely chopped
dry-roasted peanuts

I. In a medium bowl, toss the cucumbers, onion, vinegar, 1 tablespoon of the sugar and 1 teaspoon of salt. Season with pepper and let stand for 1 hour at room temperature.

2. In a mortar or medium bowl, mash the ginger with the garlic, chile and remaining 1 teaspoon of sugar to a paste. Stir in the fish sauce, cilantro and basil. Thinly slice the tuna. Stack the slices and cut into matchsticks. Cut the matchsticks into rough cubes, then chop until the pieces are ⅛ inch. Add the tuna to the ginger paste and stir to combine.

3. Using lightly moistened hands, shape the tuna mixture into 4 patties about 1 inch thick. Set on a plate lined with plastic wrap. Refrigerate for 20 minutes.

4. Light a grill. In a bowl, combine the vegetable and sesame oils. Lightly brush the burgers and the cut sides of the buns with the oil. Brush the grate with oil. Grill the burgers for 6 minutes, turning once, for medium rare. Grill the cut sides of the buns until toasted, 1 minute.

5. Drain the cucumber salad. Spread the Ginger-Lemon Mayonnaise on the cut sides of the buns and set the tuna burgers on the bottoms. Top with the cucumber salad and peanuts. Cover the burgers with the buns and serve.

—*Steven Raichlen*

WINE Soft, off-dry Riesling.

Ginger-Lemon Mayonnaise
TOTAL: 10 MIN

MAKES 1 CUP ● ●

1 cup mayonnaise

2 tablespoons soy sauce

2 tablespoons minced cilantro

2 tablespoons finely chopped
scallion greens

1 tablespoon black sesame seeds
or toasted sesame seeds

2 teaspoons finely grated
fresh ginger

Finely grated zest of 1 lemon

2 teaspoons fresh lemon juice

Freshly ground pepper

In a medium bowl, combine all of the ingredients. —*S.R.*

MAKE AHEAD The mayonnaise can be refrigerated for up to 3 days.

THAI TUNA BURGER WITH GINGER-LEMON MAYONNAISE

fish

Seafood Stew in Saffron Broth

TOTAL: 1 HR

12 SERVINGS

- 1 teaspoon saffron threads
- 2 cups dry white wine
- 2 tablespoons extra-virgin olive oil
- 1 Spanish onion, coarsely chopped
- 3 carrots, cut crosswise into
  ¼-inch-thick slices
- 3 celery ribs, cut crosswise into
  ¼-inch-thick slices
- 8 garlic cloves, coarsely chopped

One 28-ounce can whole tomatoes,
  drained and coarsely chopped
- 5 cups fish stock or 2½ cups water
  plus 2½ cups bottled clam juice

Kosher salt and freshly ground pepper
- 1½ pounds monkfish fillets, cut
  into 1-inch cubes
- 1½ pounds tilapia fillets, cut
  into 1-inch cubes
- 1 pound sea scallops, quartered
- 1 pound rock shrimp,
  shelled and deveined
- 4 dozen mussels, cleaned and
  debearded
- ½ cup heavy cream
- 1 bunch flat-leaf parsley,
  very finely chopped

I. In a small bowl, add the saffron to ½ cup of the white wine and let it infuse for 20 minutes.

2. In a large, wide pot, heat the olive oil. Add the onion, carrots, celery and garlic and cook over moderately high heat, stirring, until softened, 8 minutes. Add the remaining 1½ cups of wine and the tomatoes and cook until reduced by half, about 10 minutes. Add the fish stock and saffron mixture and season with salt and pepper. Bring to a boil, then reduce the heat to moderately low and simmer for 5 minutes.

3. Add the monkfish, tilapia, scallops and shrimp to the broth and cook over moderate heat, stirring occasionally, for 3 minutes. Add the mussels, cover the pot and cook until the fish and scallops are just cooked through, the shrimp are pink and the mussels have opened, about 3 minutes; discard any mussels that do not open.

4. Stir the cream and parsley into the seafood stew and season with salt and pepper. Ladle into bowls and serve.
—*Jesse Browner*

WINE Aromatic, zesty Albariño.

Fisherman's Stew

TOTAL: 1 HR 30 MIN

8 SERVINGS ● ●

- ½ cup extra-virgin olive oil
- 1 medium onion, coarsely chopped
- 5 garlic cloves, coarsely chopped
- 1 celery rib, coarsely chopped
- ½ teaspoon crushed red pepper
- 1 cup dry white wine

One 14.5-ounce can peeled
  whole tomatoes, drained and
  coarsely chopped
- 3 bay leaves

Salt and freshly ground pepper
- 4 pounds thick, firm white fish
  fillets, such as snapper, bass,
  halibut, swordfish or monkfish,
  cut into 2-inch pieces
- 6 cups Classic Fish Stock
  (recipe follows)
- ½ pound medium shrimp, shelled
  and deveined

Heat the olive oil in a large pot. Add the coarsely chopped onion, garlic and celery and the crushed red pepper and cook over moderately low heat, stirring frequently, until the vegetables are softened, about 10 minutes. Add the white wine and cook over moderately high heat until the wine is reduced to ¼ cup, about 10 minutes. Stir in the peeled tomatoes and the bay leaves and season with salt and pepper, then gently stir in the pieces of fish fillet. Add the Classic Fish Stock and bring the stew to a boil, then simmer over moderate heat until the fish is tender, about 12 minutes. Add the shrimp and cook until pink, about 2 minutes longer. Season the fish stew with salt and pepper and discard the bay leaves. Serve the stew in shallow soup bowls. —*Gianfranco Becchina*

MAKE AHEAD The Fisherman's Stew can be refrigerated overnight. Return to room temperature before rewarming.

SERVE WITH Slices of garlic-rubbed toasted peasant bread.

WINE Ripe, creamy-textured Chardonnay.

Classic Fish Stock

ACTIVE: 15 MIN; TOTAL: 45 MIN

MAKES 6 CUPS ● ●

Ask your fishmonger for the bones and heads of freshly filleted fish for this stock, staying away from oily fish like salmon. You can also include a few small squid or a handful of shrimp shells. The greater the variety of seafood, the more delicious the stock will be.

- 2 pounds fish bones
  and heads, rinsed
- 6 cups water
- 1 cup dry white wine
- 1 medium leek, cut into thin slices
- 1 medium onion, cut into thin slices
- 1 medium celery rib, cut into
  thin slices
- 1 medium garlic clove,
  coarsely chopped
- 3 bay leaves
- 1 teaspoon whole black
  peppercorns
- 1 teaspoon sea salt

In a large pot, combine the fish bones and fish heads with the water, white wine, sliced leek, onion and celery and the chopped garlic, bay leaves, peppercorns and sea salt. Bring the fish stock to a gentle simmer over moderately low heat. Simmer the stock for 30 minutes. Strain the fish stock through a sieve lined with several layers of moistened cheesecloth. —*G.B.*

MAKE AHEAD The fish stock can be refrigerated overnight or frozen for up to 1 month.

Spicy Fish and Vegetable Stew

ACTIVE: 40 MIN; TOTAL: 1 HR 5 MIN

4 SERVINGS ●

3½ cups water
½ cup chicken stock or
low-sodium broth
¾ pound Yukon Gold potatoes,
peeled and cut into ¼-inch dice
1 small onion, thinly sliced
12 baby carrots (6 ounces)
2 celery ribs, cut crosswise into
¼-inch-thick slices
1 jalapeño, seeded and thinly sliced
2 medium tomatoes, seeded
and chopped
8 heads baby bok choy
(10 ounces), halved lengthwise
Four 5-ounce skinless black bass fillets
Salt and freshly ground pepper
½ cup thinly sliced basil leaves

1. In a medium saucepan, bring the water and stock to a boil. Add the potatoes and onion, cover and simmer over low heat for 10 minutes. Add the carrots, celery and jalapeño, cover and simmer for 8 minutes. Stir in the tomatoes and bok choy.

2. Season the fish fillets with salt and pepper and lay them on the vegetables. Cover and simmer for 2 minutes. Carefully turn the fish fillets and simmer uncovered until just cooked through, 1 to 2 minutes longer. Using a slotted spatula, carefully transfer the fish fillets to shallow bowls. Season the stew with salt and pepper and add the basil. Ladle the stew over the fish and serve.
—*Eberhard Müller*

WINE Dry, full-flavored Alsace Riesling.

Monkfish Stew with Fried Garlic Sauce

TOTAL: 1 HR 30 MIN

4 SERVINGS ●

Make this stew in a *cazuela,* a partially glazed shallow pot from Spain (available at the Spanish Table, 505-986-0243). Alternatively, use a heavy-bottomed skillet. To achieve the proper thick and creamy consistency of the *picada*—a blend of almonds, croutons, fried garlic, cayenne and sherry that gets stirred into the stew at the end—use a mortar or an electric mixer.

1½ pounds cleaned monkfish,
about 1 inch thick, rinsed
and cut into 12 pieces
Salt
¼ cup extra-virgin olive oil
12 blanched almonds
1 cup crustless stale bread cubes
(½-inch cubes)
10 large garlic cloves, cut into
thick slices
2 tablespoons dry oloroso sherry
2 tablespoons water
2 teaspoons finely chopped
flat-leaf parsley
Cayenne pepper
2 plum tomatoes, coarsely grated
on a box grater
2 cups fish stock or 1 cup
bottled clam juice blended with
1 cup water
¾ pound Yukon Gold potatoes,
peeled and cut into ½-inch dice
1 pound littleneck or Manila clams
or cockles, scrubbed
8 cherry tomatoes, halved
Freshly ground pepper

1. Season the monkfish with salt and refrigerate until ready to cook.

2. Pour the olive oil into a large *cazuela* or cast-iron skillet set over a metal heat diffuser (see Note) on low heat for 10 minutes. Increase the heat to moderate, add the blanched almonds and cook over moderate heat, stirring occasionally, until golden, about 3 minutes. Using a slotted spoon, transfer the almonds to a work surface and let cool.

3. Add the bread cubes to the *cazuela* and cook, stirring occasionally, until golden brown and crisp, about 3 minutes. Using a slotted spoon, transfer the bread cubes to a blender. Add the garlic to the *cazuela* and spread in an even layer. Cook the garlic over low heat, without stirring, until it is deeply browned, about 15 minutes. Meanwhile, smash the almonds with the side of a large knife and transfer them to the blender. Using a slotted spoon, transfer the garlic to the blender. Reserve the oil in the *cazuela*.

4. Add the sherry, the water, 1 teaspoon of the chopped parsley and a pinch of cayenne pepper to the blender and puree until smooth. Scrape the *picada* into a bowl.

5. Add the grated plum tomatoes to the *cazuela* and cook over moderate heat, stirring a few times, until they are thickened and slightly scorched, about 10 minutes. Stir in the fish stock and bring to a boil. Add the diced potatoes. Simmer the stew over moderate heat until the potatoes are almost tender, about 6 minutes. Stir in the *picada* and simmer over low heat for 2 minutes.

6. Add the seasoned monkfish to the *cazuela* and cook over moderate heat for 6 minutes. Turn the monkfish over, then add the clams and cherry tomatoes. Cover the stew with a large piece of parchment paper and a large metal lid and simmer until the monkfish is cooked all the way through and the clams open, about 8 minutes. Discard any clams that don't open.

7. Season the monkfish stew with salt, black pepper and cayenne pepper. Spoon the stew into shallow serving bowls, sprinkle with the remaining teaspoon of chopped parsley and serve at once. —*Paula Wolfert*

NOTE Metal heat diffusers are metal mats that shield pots and their contents from direct heat. They are available at kitchen supply stores.

MAKE AHEAD The almond-garlic *picada* can be refrigerated, covered, for up to 2 days.

WINE Aromatic, zesty Albariño.

MAINE LOBSTER ROLLS, P. 206

shellfish

CURRY-ROASTED SHRIMP

SHRIMP AND SAUSAGE GUMBO

Curry-Roasted Shrimp with Chutney and Yogurt

ACTIVE: 15 MIN; TOTAL: 20 MIN

4 SERVINGS ● ●

¼ cup mango or peach chutney, finely chopped

2 tablespoons finely chopped cilantro

2 tablespoons finely chopped basil

¼ cup plain low-fat yogurt

1½ pounds shelled and deveined large shrimp

1 tablespoon extra-virgin olive oil

1 tablespoon Madras curry powder

1 teaspoon kosher salt

½ teaspoon freshly ground pepper

Lime wedges, for serving

1. Preheat the oven to 500°. In a bowl, mix the chutney, cilantro and basil. In a small bowl, mix half of the herbed chutney into the yogurt.

2. Heat a large rimmed baking sheet in the oven for 5 minutes. In a large bowl, toss the shrimp with the olive oil, curry powder, salt and pepper. Spread the shrimp in an even layer on the heated baking sheet and roast in the upper third of the oven for about 5 minutes, or until just pink and curled. Toss the cooked shrimp with the remaining herbed chutney and mix well. Transfer to serving plates and serve with the chutney-yogurt sauce and lime wedges.
—*Sally Sampson*

WINE Dry, fruity sparkling wine.

Shrimp and Sausage Gumbo

TOTAL: 25 MIN

4 SERVINGS ●

2 tablespoons vegetable oil

1 red bell pepper, cut into ¾-inch pieces

1 medium onion, cut into ½-inch pieces

1 medium celery rib, cut into ½-inch pieces

2 medium garlic cloves, very finely chopped

¼ teaspoon cayenne pepper

Salt and freshly ground pepper

½ pound andouille sausage or spicy kielbasa, halved lengthwise and cut crosswise into ½-inch-thick slices

2 tablespoons all-purpose flour

4 cups chicken stock or canned low-sodium broth

2 thyme sprigs

¾ pound shelled and deveined medium shrimp

1 scallion, thinly sliced

1 tablespoon finely chopped flat-leaf parsley

1. In a large saucepan, heat the vegetable oil until shimmering. Add the red bell pepper, chopped onion, celery, chopped garlic and cayenne. Season the vegetables with salt and pepper and cook them over moderately high heat until they are softened, about 2 minutes. Add the sausage to the vegetables and cook, stirring occasionally, until lightly browned, about 5 minutes. Sprinkle the flour on top of the sausage and vegetables and stir until evenly coated. Add the chicken stock and thyme sprigs and simmer over moderate heat for 10 minutes.

2. Add the shrimp and scallion to the saucepan, season lightly with salt and simmer, stirring, until the shrimp are opaque and cooked through, about 2 minutes longer. Discard the thyme sprigs. Stir the parsley into the gumbo and serve at once. —*Grace Parisi*
SERVE WITH Rice or crusty bread.
WINE Soft, off-dry Riesling.

Shrimp and Avocado Salad with Citrus Dressing

TOTAL: 30 MIN
6 SERVINGS ● ●

- 2 pounds large shrimp, shelled and deveined
- ¼ cup fresh grapefruit juice
- 1 tablespoon fresh lime juice
- 1 tablespoon cider vinegar
- ¼ teaspoon dried oregano, preferably Mexican
- Salt and freshly ground pepper
- 6 medium tomatoes, thinly sliced
- 2 ripe Hass avocados—halved, peeled and cut crosswise into ¼-inch-thick slices
- 1 medium red onion, thinly sliced
- Extra-virgin olive oil, for drizzling

1. In a large saucepan of boiling salted water, cook the shrimp until loosely curled and just cooked through, about 2 minutes. Drain well; transfer to a large bowl and let cool slightly.

2. In a small bowl, combine the grapefruit and lime juices, vinegar and oregano and season with salt and pepper.

3. Add 2 tablespoons of the citrus dressing to the shrimp, toss well and season with salt and pepper. Season the tomatoes and avocado slices with salt and pepper and arrange on a platter with the onion, alternating and overlapping the slices. Spoon the remaining citrus dressing over the salad and top with the shrimp. Drizzle olive oil over all and serve immediately. —*Patricia Quintana*
WINE Lively, assertive Sauvignon Blanc.

Caribbean Mango and Steamed Shrimp Salad

ACTIVE: 50 MIN; TOTAL: 1 HR 45 MIN
4 SERVINGS ●

- 1 stalk of fresh lemongrass, tender inside only
- 3 tablespoons canola oil
- 2 garlic cloves, thinly sliced
- 1 shallot, thinly sliced
- 1 tablespoon chopped fresh ginger
- 1½ pounds large shrimp, shelled and deveined, shells reserved
- 1 tablespoon tomato paste
- ½ cup dry white wine
- 3 cups water
- 2 tablespoons fresh lime juice
- Salt and freshly ground black pepper
- Cayenne pepper
- 1½ teaspoons minced tarragon
- 3 mangoes (about 14 ounces each), peeled and cut into ½-inch dice

1. Thinly slice the bottom 4 inches of the stalk of lemongrass. Heat 1 tablespoon of the oil in a medium saucepan. Add the garlic, shallot, lemongrass and ginger and cook over low heat until softened, about 5 minutes. Add the shrimp shells and cook, stirring, until bright pink, about 3 minutes. Add the tomato paste and cook, stirring, until glossy, about 2 minutes. Add the white wine and bring to a boil. Add the water and simmer over low heat for 30 minutes.

Remove the shrimp stock from the heat and let stand for 10 minutes.

2. Strain the stock, pressing hard on the solids. Return the stock to the saucepan and boil until reduced to ⅓ cup, about 20 minutes; let cool. Whisk in the lime juice and the remaining 2 tablespoons of oil and season with salt and black pepper.

3. Season the shrimp with salt, black pepper and cayenne and steam until just opaque throughout, 3 to 5 minutes.

4. Stir the tarragon into the dressing. In a large bowl, toss the mangoes with ¼ cup of the dressing and mound on plates. Top with the shrimp, drizzle on the remaining ¼ cup of dressing and serve. —*Eric Ripert*
WINE Bright, citrusy Riesling.

Shrimp and Feta Salad with Minty Almond Pesto

TOTAL: 30 MIN
4 SERVINGS ●

- 1 cup extra-virgin olive oil
- ¼ cup fresh lemon juice
- 3 large garlic cloves, 1 clove minced
- ½ teaspoon finely chopped oregano
- Salt and freshly ground pepper
- 1 pound shelled and deveined large shrimp
- ¼ cup roasted salted almonds
- 1 cup flat-leaf parsley leaves
- 1 cup mint leaves
- 1 bunch watercress, thick stems discarded
- 1 fennel bulb—trimmed, cored and thinly sliced
- ¼ pound feta cheese (preferably French), thinly sliced

1. In a small bowl, combine ¼ cup of the olive oil with 2 tablespoons of the lemon juice, the minced garlic and the oregano. Season with salt and pepper and add the shrimp; toss to coat.

2. In a food processor, finely chop the roasted almonds with the 2 whole garlic cloves, parsley leaves and mint leaves.

shellfish

With the machine on, pour in ½ cup of the oil, scraping the bowl. Season with salt and pepper; transfer the pesto to a bowl. **3.** In a large bowl, combine the remaining ¼ cup of olive oil with the remaining 2 tablespoons of lemon juice. Season with salt and pepper. Add the watercress and fennel and toss. Add three-fourths of the feta. Transfer to plates. **4.** Preheat a grill pan or cast-iron skillet. When the pan is hot, add the shrimp and cook over high heat, turning once, until browned in spots, 4 to 5 minutes. Place the shrimp on the salad and top with the remaining feta. Spoon some pesto on top and serve. —*Laura Chenel*
WINE High-acid, savory Vermentino.

Fragrant Butterflied Shrimp

ACTIVE: 25 MIN; TOTAL: 1 HR 15 MIN
4 SERVINGS ●

- 2 tablespoons chickpea flour (see Note)
- 1 tablespoon Garlic Paste (recipe, page 101)
- 1 tablespoon Ginger Paste (recipe, page 101)
- 1 tablespoon fresh lemon juice
- 1 tablespoon vegetable oil
- Salt
- 1½ pounds large shrimp—shelled, deveined and butterflied
- ½ cup plain low-fat yogurt
- 2 teaspoons finely grated lime zest
- 2 teaspoons finely grated lemon zest
- 1 teaspoon garam masala (see Note)
- ½ teaspoon freshly ground pepper
- ¼ teaspoon cayenne pepper
- ¼ teaspoon ground turmeric

1. In a small skillet, toast the chickpea flour, stirring, until golden, about 2 minutes. Scrape onto a plate and let cool. **2.** In a shallow dish, combine the Garlic Paste, Ginger Paste, lemon juice, oil and a pinch of salt. Add the shrimp, turn to coat and refrigerate for 10 minutes. In a bowl, mix the yogurt, lime and lemon zests, garam masala, pepper, cayenne,

turmeric and chickpea flour. Add the shrimp and refrigerate for 45 minutes. **3.** Preheat the broiler. Thread the shrimp onto four 10-inch skewers. Broil about 3 inches from the heat, rotating the pan, for 3 minutes, or until the shrimp are just cooked through. —*Anupam Gulati*
NOTE Chickpea flour, or *besan,* is available at Indian and Italian groceries and at health food markets. Garam masala is a spice blend that's available at many supermarkets and at Indian markets.
WINE Full-bodied, fragrant Viognier.

Coconut Shrimp with Crispy Shallot, Basil and Sesame Sprinkle

TOTAL: 30 MIN
4 SERVINGS ●

- 2 large shallots, thinly sliced crosswise
- 2 tablespoons vegetable oil
- ¾ cup shredded sweetened coconut (2 ounces)
- 2 tablespoons sesame seeds
- 1 cup chopped basil
- 3 tablespoons minced candied ginger
- 2 red or green chiles with seeds, such as Thai chiles or jalapeños, thinly sliced
- 1 cup unsweetened coconut milk
- 1½ pounds shelled and deveined medium shrimp
- 2 tablespoons fresh lemon juice
- Salt and freshly ground pepper

1. Preheat the oven to 450°. On a large rimmed baking sheet, separate the sliced shallot into rings and toss with the oil. Spread the shallots on the baking sheet and bake for 10 minutes, stirring once, until most of the rings are deeply browned. Transfer to a medium bowl. **2.** Meanwhile, in a medium skillet, toast the coconut over moderately high heat, stirring, until lightly browned, about 2 minutes. Transfer to the bowl with the shallots and wipe out the skillet. Add

the sesame seeds and toast over moderately high heat, shaking the pan, until golden, about 30 seconds. Transfer to the bowl with the shallots and coconut. Stir in the basil, ginger and chiles. **3.** Add the coconut milk to the skillet; bring to a boil over moderately high heat. Add the shrimp and simmer them over moderate heat, stirring frequently, until the shrimp are just cooked through, about 3 minutes. Stir in the lemon juice. Season with salt and pepper. Spoon the coconut shrimp into bowls, top with the shallot, basil and sesame seed sprinkle and serve. —*Marcia Kiesel*
SERVE WITH Steamed rice.
WINE Dry, full-flavored Alsace Riesling.

Bahia-Style Shrimp in Coconut Sauce

ACTIVE: 45 MIN; TOTAL: 1 HR 10 MIN
6 SERVINGS ●

The rich coconut sauce in this rustic seafood dish is typical of recipes from Brazil's tropical seaside state of Bahia.

- 2 pounds large shrimp, shelled and deveined, tails left on
- 3 garlic cloves, minced
- Juice of 1 lime
- Kosher salt
- 2 tablespoons Annatto Oil (recipe, page 114) or corn oil
- 1 small onion, minced
- 6 scallions, white and light green parts, minced
- ½ medium red bell pepper, minced
- ½ medium green bell pepper, minced
- 6 plum tomatoes, minced
- ¼ cup tomato sauce
- ½ cup unsweetened coconut milk
- 1 Scotch bonnet or habanero chile, halved and seeded
- 1 tablespoon minced cilantro
- Lime wedges, for serving

1. Toss the shrimp with the garlic, lime juice and 1 teaspoon of salt. Marinate at room temperature for 30 minutes.

2. In a large skillet, heat the Annatto Oil. Add the onion, scallions and red and green bell peppers and cook over moderately high heat, stirring, until softened, about 4 minutes. Add the minced tomatoes and cook for 5 minutes. Add the tomato sauce, coconut milk, chile and 1 teaspoon of salt and simmer over moderately low heat until reduced by one-fourth, about 10 minutes. Increase the heat, stir in the shrimp and cook until they are opaque, about 5 minutes. Transfer to a dish, discard the chile and garnish with the cilantro and lime. —*Maricel Presilla*

WINE Light, soft Chenin Blanc.

Shrimp with Coconut-Curry Tomato Sauce

TOTAL: 30 MIN

4 SERVINGS ●

- 3 tablespoons peanut or canola oil
- 1 medium onion, thinly sliced
- 1 garlic clove, minced
- 1 jalapeño, seeded and minced
- ½ tablespoon minced fresh ginger
- 1½ tablespoons mild curry powder

One 28-ounce can Italian peeled tomatoes, drained and chopped, juices reserved

One 14-ounce can unsweetened coconut milk

- 1 teaspoon sugar

Salt and freshly ground pepper

- 1¼ pounds shelled and deveined large shrimp
- ¼ cup coarsely chopped cilantro

1. In a saucepan, heat 2 tablespoons of the peanut oil. Add the onion, garlic, jalapeño and ginger and cook over moderately high heat, stirring, until softened, about 5 minutes. Add the curry powder and cook until fragrant. Add the tomatoes and their juices, the coconut milk and sugar; season with salt and pepper. Bring to a boil, then simmer over moderate heat, stirring occasionally, until slightly thickened, 15 minutes.

2. In a large skillet, heat the remaining 1 tablespoon of peanut oil until almost smoking. Spread the shrimp in the pan in 1 layer and cook over moderately high heat, turning once, until browned, about 2 minutes. Stir in the coconut-curry sauce and simmer until thick and the shrimp are just cooked through, 3 to 4 minutes. Stir in the chopped cilantro and serve. —*Grace Parisi*

WINE High-acid, savory Vermentino.

Sweet Shrimp with Creamy Semolina

TOTAL: 40 MIN

6 SERVINGS ● ●

- 2 pounds small shrimp
- 1 quart water
- 1 cup semolina flour (6 ounces)
- 2 tablespoons unsalted butter

Salt

- 2 teaspoons extra-virgin olive oil
- 2 small garlic cloves, minced
- 2 tablespoons coarsely chopped flat-leaf parsley

Freshly ground pepper

Fruity extra-virgin olive oil, for serving

1. Bring a saucepan of salted water to a boil. Add the shrimp and cook until opaque, about 2 minutes. Drain and let cool, then peel and transfer to a bowl.

2. In a medium saucepan, bring the 1 quart of water to a boil over moderate heat. Slowly whisk in the semolina flour until smooth. Reduce the heat to low and whisk the semolina until thickened, about 4 minutes. Remove from the heat. Whisk in the butter and season with salt.

3. Toss the shrimp with the extra-virgin olive oil, the garlic and the parsley and season with salt and pepper. Spoon the warm semolina into shallow bowls. Top the semolina with the shrimp and serve at once, passing the fruity extra-virgin olive oil for drizzling at the table. —*Marika Seguso*

WINE Light, dry Soave or similar white.

Creamy Shrimp Casserole with Buttery Crumbs

ACTIVE: 45 MIN; TOTAL: 1 HR 40 MIN

12 SERVINGS ● ●

- 2 pounds medium shrimp, shelled and deveined, shells reserved
- 3 cups heavy cream
- ¼ cup dry sherry

Salt

- 5 tablespoons unsalted butter, 4 tablespoons melted
- 6 medium scallions, white and tender green parts, minced
- 2 teaspoons fresh lemon juice
- 1 teaspoon Worcestershire sauce

Freshly ground pepper

Hot sauce

- 4 cups small oyster crackers
- ¼ teaspoon sweet paprika

1. Butter a 3½-quart shallow glass baking dish. Arrange the shrimp in 1 layer. Cover with plastic and refrigerate.

2. In a saucepan, combine the cream, sherry, shrimp shells and a pinch of salt. Bring to a boil, then simmer for 25 minutes. Strain through a coarse sieve.

3. Preheat the oven to 400°. Melt the 1 tablespoon of solid butter in a skillet. Add the scallions and cook, stirring, for 3 minutes. Add the shrimp cream and simmer until reduced to 2 cups, about 5 minutes. Pour into a bowl and stir in the lemon juice and Worcestershire sauce; season with salt, pepper and hot sauce. Let cool slightly. Season the shrimp with salt and pepper; pour the cream on top.

4. Using a rolling pin, crush the oyster crackers in a sturdy, resealable plastic bag. Transfer the crumbs to a bowl. Stir in the melted butter and paprika to coat.

5. Smooth the crumbs over the casserole. Bake in the center of the oven for 25 minutes, or until the edges are bubbling, then broil for 30 seconds, until browned. Let stand for 5 to 10 minutes before serving. —*Marcia Kiesel*

WINE Tangy, crisp Vernaccia.

shellfish

Sautéed Jumbo Shrimp with Passion Fruit Dressing

ACTIVE: 40 MIN; TOTAL: 1 HR 15 MIN

8 SERVINGS ●

Jumbo shrimp are a fine substitute for the beautiful, bright red Spanish shrimp Adolfo Muñoz uses in this salad.

6 ripe passion fruit, halved (see Note)

½ cup plus 1 tablespoon extra-virgin olive oil

Salt and freshly ground pepper

8 baby carrots, peeled

8 asparagus spears

2 medium red bell peppers, quartered

1 large fennel bulb, cut through the core into eighths

8 shiitake mushroom caps, stems discarded (about ½ pound)

2 large Belgian endives, quartered lengthwise

8 jumbo shrimp, shelled and deveined (about ¾ pound)

1. Preheat the oven to 350°. Set a small strainer over a small bowl. Using a small spoon, scrape the passion fruit seeds and pulp into the strainer. With the spoon, press firmly on the passion fruit seeds to extract the juice; discard any stringy clumps attached to the seeds. Add the seeds to the passion fruit juice and stir in 2 tablespoons of the olive oil until well blended. Season the passion fruit dressing generously with salt and pepper; set aside.

2. In a large skillet of boiling salted water, cook the baby carrots, asparagus spears and red bell peppers over moderately high heat until tender, about 4 minutes for the asparagus and 10 minutes for the carrots and peppers. Using a slotted spoon, transfer the vegetables to a paper towel–lined baking sheet to drain. Peel the red bell peppers.

3. Add the fennel pieces to the skillet and cook until tender, about 10 minutes. Transfer the fennel pieces to the baking sheet with the other vegetables. Pat all of the vegetables dry and discard the paper towels.

4. Drain the skillet and wipe it dry. Heat 2 tablespoons of the olive oil in the skillet. Add the baby carrots, asparagus spears and fennel pieces and season them with salt and pepper. Cook the vegetables over high heat, turning once, until they are lightly browned, about 2 minutes per side. Transfer the vegetables back to the baking sheet.

5. Add 1 tablespoon of the olive oil to the skillet and add the peeled red bell peppers. Season the peppers with salt and pepper and cook them over moderately high heat, turning once, until they are lightly browned, about 2 minutes per side; transfer to the baking sheet. Repeat the procedure with 2 tablespoons of the olive oil and the shiitake mushroom caps and the endives. Transfer the baking sheet to the oven to keep the vegetables warm.

6. Wipe out the skillet. Add the remaining 2 tablespoons of olive oil to the skillet and heat until shimmering. Add the jumbo shrimp, season them with salt and pepper and cook them over moderately high heat, turning once, until they are golden brown and just cooked through, 3 to 4 minutes per side.

7. Transfer the vegetables to shallow bowls and top with the warm shrimp. Drizzle the passion fruit dressing over the vegetables and serve immediately.
—*Adolfo Muñoz*

NOTE The color of a passion fruit's skin doesn't indicate its ripeness. Whether green or purple, look for thin-skinned fruit with plenty of wrinkles. Avoid those with smooth, thick skins—these will not be ripe.

MAKE AHEAD The recipe can be prepared through Step 3 and refrigerated overnight. Bring the vegetables to room temperature before proceeding.

WINE Aromatic, zesty Albariño.

Herb-Poached Shrimp with Cauliflower Couscous and Brown Butter

TOTAL: 2 HR

8 SERVINGS

6 ounces daikon radish, peeled and cut into ½-inch dice (2 cups)

½ cup unseasoned rice vinegar

¼ cup sugar

½ tablespoon Madras curry powder

Salt

½ teaspoon coriander seeds

1 small star anise pod

½ cinnamon stick

½ teaspoon black peppercorns

2 cups extra-virgin olive oil

12 thyme sprigs, tied with string

2 bay leaves

1 head garlic, cut in half horizontally

Freshly ground pepper

24 large shrimp (about 1 pound), shelled and deveined

1 large head cauliflower (about 3 pounds)

1 apricot, finely diced

2 tablespoons finely chopped basil

2 tablespoons coarsely chopped toasted pistachios

2 small plum tomatoes—peeled, seeded and finely diced

1 stick plus 2 tablespoons unsalted butter

⅓ cup snipped chives

1. Bring a saucepan of water to a boil. Add the daikon and cook over high heat just until tender, about 5 minutes; drain. Rinse out the saucepan and add the vinegar, sugar, curry powder and ½ teaspoon of salt. Tie the coriander seeds, star anise, cinnamon stick and peppercorns in a small piece of cheesecloth, add them to the saucepan and simmer, stirring just until the sugar is dissolved. Cover and let the mixture steep for 15 minutes. Transfer the pickling liquid to a large heatproof bowl, add the blanched daikon and let stand at room temperature until cool, or refrigerate for up to 6 hours or overnight.

2. In another medium saucepan, gently heat the olive oil with the thyme, bay leaves, garlic and a pinch each of salt and pepper over low heat just until warm to the touch. Add the shrimp and cook over very low heat, stirring occasionally, until firm and white throughout, about 9 minutes. Using a slotted spoon, gently transfer the shrimp to a plate. Strain the shrimp oil and reserve.

3. Meanwhile, trim the cauliflower leaves and stem; discard. Using a serrated knife, shave about 1 inch off the cauliflower, leaving the inner stems, core and some inner florets (reserve these for another use). Transfer the cauliflower trimmings to a food processor and pulse until they resemble coarse couscous.

4. Bring a large saucepan of lightly salted water to a boil. Add the cauliflower and cook just until tender, 2 to 3 minutes. Drain the cauliflower in a fine sieve, pressing hard to extract as much of the water as possible. Wipe out the saucepan and return the cauliflower to it. Add the apricot, basil, pistachios, half of the tomatoes and 2 tablespoons of the reserved shrimp oil. Season the cauliflower couscous with salt and pepper and keep warm over very low heat.

5. Drain the pickled daikon, reserving ¼ cup of the pickling liquid. In a small saucepan, cook the butter over moderate heat until browned, 5 minutes. Off the heat, add the reserved ¼ cup of daikon pickling liquid, the chives and the remaining diced tomato. Season the mixture with salt and pepper.

6. Mound the cauliflower couscous in the center of 8 plates and arrange the shrimp on top. Scatter the pickled daikon around the cauliflower, drizzle the brown butter mixture around the plate and serve. —*Cornelius Gallagher*

MAKE AHEAD The daikon can be refrigerated in its pickling liquid overnight.

WINE Dry, mineral-flavored Chenin Blanc.

SAUTÉED JUMBO SHRIMP

HERB-POACHED SHRIMP

shellfish

Maine Lobster Rolls

ACTIVE: 30 MIN; TOTAL: 2 HR

4 SERVINGS

In Maine you're likely to find lobster rolls served two ways. Innovators prefer a crunchy, tangy and slightly spicy version of the lobster salad that includes celery, lettuce, lemon juice and a pinch of cayenne. Purists leave out those ingredients because they believe nothing should interfere with the mix of sweet, tender summer lobster and mayonnaise.

Four 1- to 1¼-pound lobsters

¼ **cup plus 2 tablespoons mayonnaise**

Salt and freshly ground pepper

¼ **cup finely diced celery**

2 **tablespoons fresh lemon juice**

Pinch of cayenne pepper

4 **top-split hot dog buns**

2 **tablespoons unsalted butter, melted**

½ **cup shredded Boston lettuce**

1. Prepare a large ice-water bath. In a very large pot of boiling salted water, cook the lobsters until they turn bright red, about 10 minutes. Using tongs, plunge the lobsters into the ice-water bath for 2 minutes, then drain.

2. Twist off the lobster tails and claws and remove the meat. Remove and discard the intestinal vein that runs the length of each lobster tail. Cut the lobster meat into ½-inch pieces and pat dry, then transfer to a strainer set over a bowl and refrigerate until very cold, at least 1 hour.

3. In a large bowl, mix the lobster meat with the mayonnaise and season with salt and pepper. Fold in the diced celery, lemon juice and cayenne pepper until well blended.

4. Heat a large skillet. Brush the sides of the hot dog buns with the melted butter and toast them over moderate heat until golden brown on both sides. Transfer the hot dog buns to plates, fill them with the shredded lettuce and the lobster salad and serve immediately.
—*Sam Hayward*

WINE Ripe, creamy-textured Chardonnay.

Lobster Capellini with Leek-Tarragon Cream Sauce

TOTAL: 50 MIN

6 SERVINGS

1 **stick (4 ounces) unsalted butter**

4 **large leeks, white and tender green parts, halved lengthwise and thinly sliced crosswise**

¼ **cup dry white wine**

1 **tablespoon finely chopped tarragon, plus ¼ cup leaves**

1 **cup heavy cream**

Salt and freshly ground pepper

1 **medium beet, peeled and coarsely shredded**

1 **teaspoon fresh lemon juice**

2 **tablespoons water**

1 **pound cooked lobster meat (from three 1½-pound lobsters)**

1 **pound capellini**

1. In a large saucepan, melt 3 tablespoons of the butter. Add the leeks and cook over moderate heat, stirring occasionally, until just tender, about 5 minutes. Add the wine and chopped tarragon and cook until the wine evaporates, 2 to 3 minutes. Add the cream and season with salt and pepper. Cover partially and cook over low heat until the cream is slightly reduced, about 10 minutes. Scrape the mixture into a blender and puree until smooth. Return the creamy leek sauce to the saucepan and season with salt and pepper. Cover and keep warm.

2. Melt 1 tablespoon of the butter in a small skillet. Add the shredded beet, season with salt and pepper and cook over moderately high heat, stirring constantly, until tender, about 8 minutes. Stir in the lemon juice.

3. In a medium saucepan, melt the remaining 4 tablespoons of butter in the water over moderately low heat, whisking constantly. Add the lobster meat and cook just until heated through, 1 to 2 minutes. Keep warm.

4. Meanwhile, cook the pasta in a large pot of boiling salted water until barely al dente. Drain, reserving 1 cup of the pasta cooking water. Return the pasta to the pot and add the leek sauce, reserved pasta water and the butter from the lobster; season with salt and pepper and toss. Transfer to shallow bowls and top with the lobster meat. Garnish with the beets and tarragon leaves and serve. —*Alexandra Angle*

WINE Fruity, low-oak Chardonnay.

Scallops with Avocado Salsa

TOTAL: 30 MIN

4 SERVINGS ● ●

¼ **cup finely shredded basil leaves**

2 **tablespoons fresh lime juice**

1 **tablespoon extra-virgin olive oil**

1 **small onion, minced**

1 **jalapeño—halved, seeded and thinly sliced**

1 **small garlic clove, minced**

2 **Hass avocados (10 ounces each)—peeled, pitted and cut into ½-inch dice**

Salt and freshly ground pepper

2 **tablespoons vegetable oil**

2 **pounds sea scallops**

¼ **cup water**

4 plum tomatoes, cut into
½-inch dice

1 tablespoon balsamic vinegar

1. In a bowl, combine the basil, lime juice, olive oil, onion, jalapeño and garlic. With a rubber spatula, fold in the avocados; season with salt and pepper.

2. In a large skillet, heat the vegetable oil until shimmering. Season the scallops with salt and pepper and cook over high heat until browned outside but still rare in the centers, about 2 minutes per side. Transfer the scallops to a warmed platter.

3. Add the water and tomatoes to the skillet and cook over moderately high heat, scraping up any browned bits from the bottom, until the water has reduced to 2 tablespoons, about 2 minutes. Remove from the heat. Stir in the balsamic vinegar and season with salt and pepper. Pour the pan sauce over the scallops and serve the avocado salsa on the side. —*Marcia Kiesel*

VARIATIONS Use the avocado salsa on steak, with boiled shrimp, in a chicken sandwich or with tortilla chips.

WINE Fruity, low-oak Chardonnay.

Scallops with Saffron Cream and Turnip Greens

TOTAL: 35 MIN

4 SERVINGS ●

1 small pinch of saffron threads

⅔ cup heavy cream

¼ cup extra-virgin olive oil

1 pound baby turnip greens, stems and thick ribs discarded, leaves coarsely chopped

24 large sea scallops (about 1¼ pounds)

Salt and freshly ground pepper

1 tablespoon unsalted butter

2 tablespoons minced shallot

¼ cup dry vermouth

1. In a bowl, crumble the saffron into the heavy cream. In a large skillet, heat 2 tablespoons of the olive oil until shimmering. Add the turnip greens and cook over moderately high heat, tossing, until wilted, 3 minutes. Transfer to a bowl; keep warm. Wipe out the skillet.

2. Heat the remaining 2 tablespoons of olive oil in the skillet until shimmering. Season the scallops with salt and pepper and add them to the skillet in a single layer. Cook over high heat until browned on the bottoms, 3 to 4 minutes. Turn and cook until lightly browned and opaque throughout, about 2 minutes longer. Transfer the scallops to a plate and pour off any oil in the skillet.

3. Melt the butter in the skillet. Add the minced shallot and cook over moderately high heat, stirring, until softened, about 1½ minutes. Add the vermouth and cook, scraping up any browned bits from the bottom of the pan, until nearly evaporated. Add the saffron cream and simmer until thickened and slightly reduced, 3 to 4 minutes. Season the sauce with salt and pepper. Mound the turnip greens on plates, top with the scallops and sauce and serve. —*John Hikade*

WINE Dry, medium-bodied Pinot Gris.

Scallops with Endives and Lemongrass Glaze

ACTIVE: 35 MIN; TOTAL: 1 HR 45 MIN

6 SERVINGS

Sautéing the scallops on skewers makes a dramatic presentation, but they could be cooked loose in a skillet, too.

2 cups water

¼ cup sugar

4 tablespoons unsalted butter

6 Belgian endives, cored

Salt and freshly ground pepper

¼ cup chopped flat-leaf parsley

2 garlic cloves, thinly sliced

1 medium shallot, thinly sliced

1 lemongrass stalk, bottom half only, thinly sliced

1 cup rich veal stock (see Note)

24 sea scallops (about 2¼ pounds)

1 tablespoon vegetable oil

1. In a skillet that will hold the endives snugly, combine the water with the sugar and 1 tablespoon of the butter and bring to a simmer. Add the endives and season with salt and pepper. Simmer over moderately low heat, turning occasionally, until tender, about 1 hour.

2. Drain off the cooking liquid and add 1 tablespoon of the butter to the skillet. Sauté the endives over moderate heat, turning occasionally, until browned, about 8 minutes.

3. Melt 1 tablespoon of the butter in a small saucepan. Add the chopped parsley, sliced garlic, shallot and lemongrass and cook over low heat for 4 minutes. Add the veal stock and simmer over moderate heat until reduced by half, about 5 minutes. Strain the stock and return it to the saucepan. Boil over high heat until reduced to ¼ cup, about 3 minutes. Season with salt and pepper.

4. Thread 4 scallops onto a parallel pair of 6-inch bamboo skewers. Repeat with the remaining scallops. Season with salt and pepper.

5. In a large skillet, melt ½ tablespoon of the butter in ½ tablespoon of the oil. Add half of the scallops and cook over high heat until deeply browned on the bottoms, about 2 minutes. Turn and cook until browned on the other side but barely cooked through, about 1 minute longer; transfer to a platter. Repeat with the remaining butter, oil and scallops. Set an endive on each plate and top with a scallop skewer. Drizzle the lemongrass glaze over the scallops and serve them immediately. —*Christophe Côte*

NOTE Rich veal stock is available in the freezer sections of specialty food stores and supermarkets. Perfect Addition is an excellent brand.

MAKE AHEAD The glaze can be refrigerated for up to 2 days. The endives can be cooked up to 4 hours ahead.

WINE Dry, medium-bodied Pinot Gris.

SCALLOP SALAD WITH ASPARAGUS

SPICY SCALLOPS WITH CAPELLINI

Seared Scallop Salad with Asparagus and Scallions

TOTAL: 40 MIN

8 SERVINGS ●

- 1 pound large whole scallions
- 1¼ pounds asparagus, tough stems discarded, stalks peeled
- ¼ cup plus 2 tablespoons extra-virgin olive oil

Salt and freshly ground pepper

- 1¾ pounds sea scallops
- 1 teaspoon chopped thyme
- 1 medium shallot, minced
- ¼ cup balsamic vinegar

1. In a pot of boiling salted water, blanch the scallions just until tender, 3 minutes. Using a slotted spoon, transfer to paper towels. Repeat with the asparagus.

2. In a large skillet, heat 2 tablespoons of the olive oil. Add the scallions and asparagus and season with salt and pepper. Cook over moderately high heat, gently tossing occasionally, just until golden, about 5 minutes. Keep warm.

3. Pat the scallops dry; season with salt and pepper. In another large skillet, heat 2 tablespoons of the oil until shimmering. Working in batches, sear the scallops over moderately high heat until golden, 2 minutes per side. Transfer to warmed plates. Wipe out the skillet.

4. Heat 1 tablespoon of the remaining oil in the same skillet. Add the thyme and shallot and cook over moderately high heat, stirring, until the shallot is slightly softened, about 1 minute. Remove from the heat. Add the vinegar and the remaining 1 tablespoon of olive oil; stir with a wooden spoon, scraping up any browned bits from the pan.

5. Garnish the scallops with the warm asparagus spears and scallions. Drizzle the scallop salad with the warm shallot vinaigrette and serve immediately.

—Sergio Sigala

WINE Round, rich Sauvignon Blanc.

Spicy Scallops with Capellini

TOTAL: 25 MIN

4 SERVINGS ● ●

- 1 pound sea scallops, quartered if large
- 6 tablespoons extra-virgin olive oil
- ¼ cup dry white wine
- 2 tablespoons coarsely chopped flat-leaf parsley
- 1 tablespoon very finely chopped garlic
- 1 small dried chipotle chile with seeds, stemmed and chopped

Fine sea salt

- ½ pound capellini

1. Preheat the oven to 400°. In a large, shallow glass or ceramic baking dish, toss the scallops with the oil, wine, parsley, garlic and chipotle. Season with salt and bake for about 15 minutes, or until the oil is sizzling and the scallops are firm.

2. Meanwhile, in a large pot of boiling salted water, cook the capellini until just al dente, about 3 minutes. Drain; transfer to a serving bowl. Add the scallops and their juices, toss well and serve immediately. —*Ruth Van Waerebeek*

WINE Full-bodied, fragrant Viognier.

Sea Scallops with Peas, Bacon and Carrots

TOTAL: 35 MIN

4 SERVINGS ●

- 4 slices of thick-cut bacon, cut into ¼-inch matchsticks
- 3 tablespoons unsalted butter
- ½ small Vidalia or other sweet onion, cut into ½-inch pieces
- 1 medium carrot, thinly sliced on the diagonal
- ½ cup frozen baby peas, thawed
- ¼ cup chicken stock or low-sodium broth
- 1 cup packed shredded Boston lettuce (6 leaves)
- 1 teaspoon fresh lemon juice
- 2 tablespoons finely chopped flat-leaf parsley

Kosher salt and freshly ground pepper

- 1 tablespoon extra-virgin olive oil
- 16 large sea scallops (about 1½ pounds)

1. In a large skillet, cook the bacon over moderate heat until browned and crisp, about 4 minutes. Using a slotted spoon, transfer the bacon pieces to paper towels to drain.

2. Pour off all but 1 tablespoon of the bacon fat from the skillet and add 2 tablespoons of the butter. Add the onion and carrot and cook over moderate heat, stirring, until the carrot is just crisp-tender, about 5 minutes.

Add the peas and cook just until heated through. Add the chicken stock, cover and simmer until the carrot is tender, about 3 minutes. Stir in the shredded lettuce, lemon juice, parsley and bacon and cook just until the lettuce wilts. Season the vegetables generously with salt and pepper and keep warm.

3. In another large skillet, melt the remaining 1 tablespoon of butter in the olive oil. Season the sea scallops with salt and pepper and cook over moderately high heat, turning once, until browned, 5 to 6 minutes. Transfer the vegetables to warmed plates, top with the seared scallops and serve at once. —*Daniel Boulud*

WINE Flinty, high-acid Chablis.

Portuguese Clam and Chorizo Stew

ACTIVE: 25 MIN; TOTAL: 35 MIN

6 FIRST-COURSE SERVINGS ● ●

Piquillo peppers add a spicy, bittersweet edge to this classic seafood stew. Roasted red bell peppers and a pinch of cayenne pepper may be substituted. The recipe serves six as a first course, or you can serve it as a main dish for four people.

- ½ pound chorizo—peeled, halved and cut into ½-inch pieces
- 1½ cups chicken stock or low-sodium broth
- 6 thick slices of peasant bread
- ¼ cup extra-virgin olive oil, plus more for brushing
- 3 large garlic cloves, peeled, 2 minced
- ¼ pound thickly sliced bacon, cut crosswise into ½-inch pieces
- 1 very large onion, thinly sliced

One 8-ounce can or jar piquillo peppers, liquid reserved, peppers cut into ½-inch strips

- 4 dozen littleneck clams, scrubbed

1. Preheat the oven to 350°. Put the chorizo in a small saucepan with 1 cup

of the stock and simmer until softened, about 15 minutes. Drain the chorizo and discard the broth.

2. Meanwhile, brush the bread with olive oil and toast for about 10 minutes, until golden. Rub the toasts with the peeled whole garlic clove and transfer each slice to a deep soup bowl.

3. In a large enameled cast-iron casserole, heat 2 tablespoons of the olive oil until shimmering. Add the bacon and cook over moderate heat, stirring, until crisp, 7 to 8 minutes. Using a slotted spoon, transfer the bacon to a plate and reserve it for another use.

4. Add the onion and minced garlic to the casserole and cook over low heat for 5 minutes. Add the peppers and their liquid; cook for 1 minute. Add the chorizo and the remaining ½ cup of stock; bring to a boil. Add the clams, cover and cook over high heat until they've opened, 10 minutes. Discard any unopened clams. Spoon the stew and the remaining 2 tablespoons of olive oil over the garlic toasts. —*Grace Parisi*

WINE Aromatic, zesty Albariño.

INGREDIENT TIP

cleaning shellfish

BECAUSE MUSSELS AND CLAMS live on the bottom of the sea, they usually have sand and sometimes seaweed trapped in their shells. To clean them, scrub them with a stiff brush while holding them under cold running water. Then soak them in salted water for several minutes, drain, and repeat to remove any remaining sand. To debeard clams and mussels, grasp the black fibrous material on the outside of the shell and pull off. Mussels die soon after they are debearded, so use immediately.

shellfish

Rosé-Steamed Mussels

ACTIVE: 25 MIN; TOTAL: 35 MIN

8 SERVINGS ● ●

- 2 tablespoons extra-virgin olive oil
- 2 garlic cloves, minced
- 2 shallots, minced
- ½ teaspoon crushed red pepper
- 1 cup rosé wine
- 6 pounds mussels, scrubbed and debearded
- 3 tablespoons unsalted butter

Salt and freshly ground pepper

- 2 tablespoons coarsely chopped flat-leaf parsley

I. Heat the olive oil in a large pot. Add the garlic, shallots and crushed red pepper and cook over low heat until fragrant, about 4 minutes. Add the wine and bring to a boil over high heat. Add the mussels, cover and cook, shaking the pot a few times, until the mussels open, about 5 minutes.

2. Using a slotted spoon, transfer the mussels to 8 shallow bowls. Add the butter to the cooking liquid in the pot, swirl to melt and season with salt and pepper. Pour the sauce over the mussels, stopping before you reach the grit at the bottom of the pot. Garnish with the chopped parsley and serve.

—Joshua Wesson

SERVE WITH Crusty bread.

WINE Bright, fruity rosé.

Spicy Crab Cakes with Mango Puree

ACTIVE: 45 MIN; TOTAL: 1 HR 5 MIN

4 SERVINGS

When making crab cakes, it's customary to keep the crabmeat in chunks. Here, it's best to break up some of the meat to keep the patties together.

- 1 pound lump crabmeat, well drained and picked over
- ¼ cup mayonnaise
- 3 tablespoons minced chives
- 2 teaspoons fresh lime juice
- ½ teaspoon honey
- 4 teaspoons Asian red chili sauce, such as *sambal oelek*

Salt and freshly ground pepper

- 1 ripe mango, peeled and cut into chunks
- ¼ cup plus 3 tablespoons vegetable oil

All-purpose flour, for dredging

- 3 large eggs, beaten
- 2 cups *panko* (Japanese bread crumbs) or other dry bread crumbs
- 1 cup packed micro greens or mesclun

I. In a large bowl, combine the crabmeat with the mayonnaise, chives, lime juice, honey and 1 tablespoon of the chili sauce; season with salt and pepper. Stir well to break up some of the crabmeat. Form the mixture into 8 crab cakes, packing them firmly. Put the crab cakes on a baking sheet and refrigerate until firm, about 25 minutes.

2. Meanwhile, in a blender, puree the mango with 1 tablespoon of the oil and the remaining 1 teaspoon of chili sauce until smooth. Scrape the mango puree into a small bowl and season with salt and pepper.

3. Put a handful of flour into a medium, shallow bowl. Put the eggs in another shallow bowl and the *panko* in a third bowl. Take a crab cake in your hand and carefully dust it all over with flour, shaking off any excess. Dip the crab cake in the beaten egg and then coat it well with the *panko*. Repeat with the remaining crab cakes.

4. In a medium skillet, heat 3 tablespoons of the vegetable oil until shimmering. Add 4 of the crab cakes to the skillet and cook them over moderately high heat until they are browned and crisp, about 3 minutes per side. Drain the crab cakes on a wire rack set over a baking sheet. Repeat with the remaining 3 tablespoons of vegetable oil and 4 crab cakes.

5. Drizzle the mango puree on 4 dinner plates and set 2 crab cakes on each plate. Mound the micro greens alongside each serving and serve right away.

—Ming Tsai

MAKE AHEAD The formed crab cakes and the mango puree can be refrigerated overnight. Bring the mango puree to room temperature before serving.

WINE Light, soft Chenin Blanc.

Crab Cakes with Bloody Mary Gazpacho

ACTIVE: 1 HR 20 MIN; TOTAL: 2 HR 20 MIN

4 SERVINGS ●

GAZPACHO

- ¼ teaspoon celery seed
- 2 large tomatoes (1 pound), seeded and cut into ¼-inch dice
- 2 kirby cucumbers (½ pound), seeded and cut into ¼-inch dice
- 2 jalapeños, seeded and very finely chopped
- 1 yellow bell pepper, cut into ¼-inch dice
- 1 celery rib, peeled and cut into ¼-inch dice
- 1 small red onion, very finely chopped
- 1 cup tomato juice
- 1 teaspoon Worcestershire sauce
- ½ teaspoon hot sauce
- ½ teaspoon finely grated lime zest
- 2 tablespoons drained horseradish
- 2 tablespoons fresh lime juice
- ½ cup coarsely chopped cilantro leaves

Salt

AVOCADO MOUSSE

- 1 Hass avocado, very coarsely chopped
- 3 tablespoons fresh lime juice

Salt

CRAB CAKES

- 1 tablespoon vegetable oil, plus more for frying
- 4 large scallions, finely chopped

ROSÉ-STEAMED MUSSELS

SPICY CRAB CAKES WITH MANGO PUREE

1 small red onion, finely chopped
Salt and freshly ground pepper
1 large egg
2 tablespoons whole-grain mustard
2 teaspoons fresh lime juice
1 teaspoon Worcestershire sauce
¼ teaspoon hot sauce
1 pound jumbo lump crabmeat, picked over
1½ cups fresh bread crumbs

I. MAKE THE GAZPACHO: In a small skillet, toast the celery seed over moderate heat, shaking the pan, until fragrant, about 30 seconds; let cool. In a large bowl, combine the toasted celery seed with the tomatoes, cucumbers, jalapeños, yellow bell pepper, celery, red onion, tomato juice, Worcestershire sauce, hot sauce and lime zest. Refrigerate the gazpacho for at least 1 hour or for up to 2 hours.

2. MAKE THE AVOCADO MOUSSE: In a food processor, puree the avocado and lime juice. Scrape the mousse into a bowl and season with salt. Cover and refrigerate.

3. MAKE THE CRAB CAKES: In a medium skillet, heat 1 tablespoon of oil. Add the scallions and red onion, season with salt and pepper and cook over low heat until softened, about 8 minutes. Transfer the scallions and red onion to a medium bowl and let cool to room temperature. Beat in the egg with a fork, then mix in the mustard, lime juice, Worcestershire sauce and hot sauce. With a spatula, gently fold in the crabmeat, then fold in the bread crumbs and season with salt and pepper. Form the mixture into 8 crab cakes and transfer to a platter. Refrigerate until firm, about 20 minutes.

4. Preheat the oven to 300°. In a medium saucepan, heat 2 inches of vegetable oil to 350°. Set a wire rack over a rimmed baking sheet. When the oil is hot, add 4 crab cakes at a time and fry them until golden brown, about 2 minutes per side. With a slotted spoon, transfer the crab cakes to the wire rack and keep them warm in the oven while you fry the rest.

5. Just before serving, stir the horseradish, lime juice and cilantro into the gazpacho and season with salt. Ladle the gazpacho into large, shallow bowls. Add 2 hot crab cakes and a dollop of avocado mousse to each bowl and serve immediately. —*David Bull*

MAKE AHEAD The avocado mousse and the uncooked crab cakes can be refrigerated overnight.

WINE Dry, crisp sparkling wine.

SOFT-SHELL CRAB AND BACON SANDWICH

Crab Cakes with Lemongrass Mayonnaise

ACTIVE: 1 HR; TOTAL: 1 HR 30 MIN

4 SERVINGS

MAYONNAISE

1 cup canola oil

One 2-inch piece of peeled fresh ginger, thinly sliced

1 stalk of fresh lemongrass, bottom 4 inches only, thinly sliced

1 tablespoon mirin

1 tablespoon rice vinegar

1½ teaspoons dry mustard

2 large egg yolks

Salt and freshly ground white pepper

PICKLED MELON

2 cups water

½ cup sugar

½ cup white wine vinegar

1 teaspoon coriander seeds

½ teaspoon mustard seeds

¼ teaspoon crushed red pepper

1 bay leaf

2½ cups honeydew melon balls

CRAB CAKES

3 tablespoons minced scallions

1 tablespoon finely chopped basil

1 tablespoon finely chopped cilantro

1½ cups *panko* or coarse dry bread crumbs, plus more for coating

1 pound lump crabmeat, picked over

Salt and freshly ground white pepper

2 tablespoons unsalted butter

2 tablespoons extra-virgin olive oil

I. MAKE THE MAYONNAISE: In a saucepan, combine the canola oil, ginger and lemongrass. Cook over moderately low heat until small bubbles appear around the side, 10 minutes. Let cool, then strain. In a blender or mini food processor, process the mirin, rice vinegar, dry mustard and egg yolks until smooth. With the machine on, add the infused oil in a thin stream and process until emulsified. Season with salt and white pepper.

2. MAKE THE PICKLED MELON: In a saucepan, combine the water, sugar, vinegar, coriander seeds, mustard seeds, crushed red pepper and bay leaf and simmer until the sugar has dissolved. In a heatproof bowl, carefully toss the melon balls with the brine and let cool.

3. MAKE THE CRAB CAKES: In a bowl, mix ¾ cup of the lemongrass mayonnaise, the scallions, basil, cilantro and the 1½ cups of bread crumbs. Add the crab and season with salt and white pepper. Pat the mixture into 8 cakes about ¾ inch thick; coat with bread crumbs. Set the crab cakes on a wax paper–lined plate.

4. In a nonstick skillet, melt 1 tablespoon of the butter in 1 tablespoon of the oil. Add half of the crab cakes and cook over moderately high heat, turning once, until golden, 6 minutes; drain on paper towels. Repeat with the remaining butter, oil and crab cakes. Set 2 crab cakes on each dinner plate and add a dollop of the mayonnaise. Discard the bay leaf from the melon balls and serve the melon alongside in small bowls. —*Hans Röckenwagner*

WINE Medium-bodied, round Pinot Blanc.

Pan-Fried Crab Cakes

TOTAL: 35 MIN

4 SERVINGS ●

These small crab cakes have the ideal ratio of crisp coating to creamy crab.

¼ cup mayonnaise

¼ cup minced onion

2 large eggs, lightly beaten

½ teaspoon Worcestershire sauce

½ teaspoon dry mustard

¼ teaspoon salt

¼ teaspoon cayenne pepper

1 pound lump crabmeat, picked over

1 cup finely crushed soda crackers

2 tablespoons unsalted butter

¼ cup vegetable oil

Lemon wedges, for serving

I. In a medium bowl, combine the mayonnaise, onion, eggs, Worcestershire sauce, dry mustard, salt and cayenne.

Fold in the crabmeat and ¼ cup of the cracker crumbs. Shape the mixture into 16 cakes about 1 inch thick. Coat the crab cakes with the remaining cracker crumbs and transfer to a baking sheet lined with wax paper.

2. In a large skillet, melt 1 tablespoon of the butter in 2 tablespoons of the oil. When the foam subsides, add half of the crab cakes and cook over moderate heat until golden and crisp, 2 to 3 minutes per side. Drain the crab cakes on paper towels and keep them warm in a low oven. Cook the remaining crab cakes in the remaining 1 tablespoon of butter and 2 tablespoons of oil. Serve the crab cakes at once with lemon wedges. —*Tom Kee*

WINE Spicy Alsace Gewürztraminer.

Soft-Shell Crab and Bacon Sandwiches

ACTIVE: 45 MIN; TOTAL: 1 HR

10 SERVINGS ●

As a Baltimore native, David Lentz feels strongly about the proper way to cook soft-shells: pan-frying.

½ cup red wine vinegar

2 teaspoons honey

½ small head green cabbage, cored and shredded

½ small red onion, thinly sliced lengthwise

1 small carrot, coarsely shredded

Salt and freshly ground black pepper

¼ cup mayonnaise

3 tablespoons grainy mustard

2 tablespoons minced chives

2 tablespoons coarsely chopped flat-leaf parsley

⅛ teaspoon cayenne pepper

1 tablespoon crème fraîche

1 pound thickly sliced bacon

About ⅓ cup all-purpose flour

8 medium soft-shell crabs, cleaned

1 long baguette, split lengthwise

Lemon wedges, for serving

shellfish

1. In a small saucepan, boil the vinegar over moderately high heat until reduced by half. Transfer to a large heatproof bowl and let cool, then stir in the honey until dissolved. Add the cabbage, onion and carrot, season with salt and black pepper and toss well. Let the slaw stand at room temperature for 15 minutes, stirring occasionally. Stir in the mayonnaise, 2 tablespoons of the mustard, the chives, parsley and cayenne until thoroughly combined and season again with salt and black pepper.

2. In a small bowl, combine the remaining 1 tablespoon of mustard with the crème fraîche.

3. In 2 large skillets, cook the bacon over moderately high heat until crisp, about 6 minutes. Transfer to paper towels to drain. Reserve the bacon fat in the skillets.

4. Spread the flour on a large plate. Lightly dust the crabs with the flour. Warm the bacon fat over moderately high heat until shimmering. Add the crabs to the skillets and cook, turning once, until golden, about 8 minutes total. Transfer to paper towels to drain and season lightly with salt.

5. Arrange the bacon on the bottom half of the baguette and mound the slaw on top. Arrange the fried crabs on the

INGREDIENT TIP
buying crabmeat

CRABMEAT IS AVAILABLE IN lump, flaked or claw meat. Lump meat, which consists of larger, choice pieces from the body of the crab, is the most expensive. Flaked meat is made up of smaller pieces from the rest of the body. Claw meat tends to be darker and a bit sweeter than lump or flaked. Always try to buy fresh crabmeat rather than canned, as the flavor can be inconsistent.

sandwich as close together as possible and drizzle with the mustard crème fraîche. Close the sandwich and carefully cut it crosswise with a serrated knife into 10 pieces. Serve the sandwiches immediately, with lemon wedges for seasoning. —*David Lentz*

WINE Ripe, creamy-textured Chardonnay.

Curried Crab and Watermelon Salad with Arugula
TOTAL: 35 MIN

4 SERVINGS ● ● ●

- 3 tablespoons extra-virgin olive oil
- 2 tablespoons finely chopped Granny Smith apple
- 1 tablespoon finely chopped onion
- 1½ teaspoons mild curry powder
- Pinch of saffron threads, crumbled (optional)
- 1 teaspoon water
- ½ cup mayonnaise
- 1 tablespoon finely chopped cilantro
- 1 tablespoon finely chopped fresh mint leaves
- Salt and freshly ground pepper
- 1 pound jumbo lump crabmeat, picked over
- Four ½-inch-thick half-round watermelon slices from a large watermelon, rind removed
- 2 tablespoons plus 1 teaspoon fresh lime juice
- 1 bunch arugula (5 ounces), large stems discarded

1. In a small saucepan, heat 1 tablespoon of the olive oil until shimmering. Add the apple, onion, curry and saffron and cook over moderate heat until the onion is softened, about 5 minutes. Remove from the heat and stir in the water; let cool.

2. Scrape the curry mixture into a mini food processor. Add the mayonnaise and process until smooth. Transfer the curried mayonnaise to a medium bowl. Add the cilantro and mint and season

with salt and pepper. Gently fold the lump crabmeat into the curried mayonnaise until thoroughly mixed.

3. Cut each slice of watermelon into 2 triangles and transfer to plates. Season the watermelon with salt and pepper and sprinkle each serving with 1 teaspoon of lime juice. Mound the crab salad on the watermelon.

4. In another bowl, toss the arugula with the remaining 1 tablespoon of lime juice and the remaining 2 tablespoons of olive oil and season with salt and pepper. Arrange the arugula around the watermelon and crab on the plates and serve. —*Daniel Boulud*

WINE Dry, light, crisp Champagne.

Grilled Seafood Paella
ACTIVE: 1 HR 30 MIN; TOTAL: 2 HR

6 SERVINGS ●

Traditionally made over an outdoor fire, paella doesn't get any better than this grilled seafood version. The quick broth made here from shrimp shells adds a distinctly rich flavor, but you can substitute fish stock or three parts bottled clam juice diluted with one part water. After adding the broth, don't stir the paella again; this will allow a delicious crisp bottom crust to form. It's important to have all the ingredients and two heavy-duty oven mitts ready grillside before you start.

BROTH

- 2 tablespoons vegetable oil
- Reserved shrimp shells (see below)
- 1 medium onion, thinly sliced
- 1 small carrot, thinly sliced
- 3 tablespoons tomato paste
- ¼ cup dry sherry
- 2 quarts water
- 6 large garlic cloves, chopped
- 4 thyme sprigs
- 2 bay leaves
- 1 large chipotle chile in adobo
- Large pinch of saffron threads
- Salt

PAELLA

- 2 tablespoons extra-virgin olive oil
- 4 scallions, white and green parts, cut into 1-inch lengths
- 1 small onion, finely chopped
- 1 large poblano chile—stemmed, seeded and cut into ½-inch dice
- 1¾ cups short-grain Spanish rice, such as Valencia or Bomba
- 2 medium tomatoes, chopped
- 1 cup fresh corn kernels
- ½ pound green beans, preferably flat Romano, cut into 1-inch lengths
- 1 teaspoon kosher salt

Large handful of woody herb sprigs, such as rosemary or thyme

- 1½ pounds medium shrimp, shelled and deveined, shells reserved
- 1½ pounds small mussels, scrubbed and debearded

1. MAKE THE BROTH: In a large saucepan, heat the oil. Add the shrimp shells and cook over moderate heat, stirring, until they are browned, about 5 minutes. Add the onion and carrot and cook, stirring, until the onion begins to brown, about 5 minutes longer. Stir in the tomato paste and cook for 2 minutes to incorporate. Add the sherry and boil for 1 minute, then add the water and return the liquid to a boil. Stir in the garlic, thyme, bay leaves, chipotle and saffron and simmer over low heat for 25 minutes.

2. Strain the broth through a sieve into a saucepan, pressing hard on the solids; you should have 6 cups. Season the broth with salt. Cover and keep warm over low heat.

3. MAKE THE PAELLA: Light a grill. If using charcoal, build a large fire that will last at least 30 minutes. Start more coals in a chimney starter to have ready to feed the fire when necessary. If using a gas grill, set the center burner on high heat and the side or front and back burners on low.

4. Place a 14- to 16-inch paella pan or a 14-inch stainless steel roasting pan over a medium-hot fire. Add the olive oil and heat until sizzling. Add the scallions, onion and poblano. If using charcoal, move the pan over to the cooler side of the grill; if using gas, reduce the heat to low. Cook the vegetables, stirring them with a large wooden paddle or spoon, until they soften, about 5 minutes. Add the rice and cook, stirring, for 2 minutes. Stir in the tomatoes, corn, green beans and kosher salt.

5. Add the warm broth to the rice; shake the pan to distribute the rice evenly, but don't stir. Move the pan to the hotter part of a charcoal grill or increase the heat to moderately low on a gas grill. If using charcoal, scatter the herbs over the coals. If using a gas grill, place the herbs in the smoker box or scatter over the heat bars.

6. Cover the grill and let the paella cook, shaking the pan once or twice, until the broth has been absorbed and the rice is almost tender, about 20 minutes. Don't stir. The rice should cook at a steady simmer; add hot coals to the fire if it starts to fade.

7. Scatter the shrimp over the rice and nestle the mussels in the paella, hinge side down. Cover the grill; cook until the shrimp are pink and the mussels open, about 5 minutes. Discard any mussels that do not open. Using a large wooden paddle or spoon, transfer the seafood paella to dinner plates, scraping up the crusty rice from the bottom of the pan as you dish it out. Serve immediately. —*Marcia Kiesel*

WINE Bright, fruity rosé.

Jerk Seafood Packs

ACTIVE: 30 MIN; TOTAL: 35 MIN

4 SERVINGS ● ●

- ¼ cup coarsely chopped cilantro
- 4 scallions, white and green parts, cut into 1½-inch lengths
- 2 large garlic cloves, smashed
- 1 tablespoon finely chopped thyme
- 2 teaspoons finely grated fresh ginger
- ¼ Scotch bonnet chile or 1 tablespoon Scotch bonnet sauce

Pinch of ground allspice

Pinch of freshly grated nutmeg

- 2 tablespoons extra-virgin olive oil
- 1½ tablespoons tomato paste
- 1½ teaspoons distilled white vinegar

Salt and freshly ground pepper

- 2 pounds mussels, scrubbed and debearded
- 2 pounds cockles, scrubbed
- 3 tomatoes, seeded and cut into ½-inch pieces
- 1 pound large shrimp, shelled and deveined

1. Light a grill. In a food processor, pulse the cilantro with the scallions, garlic, thyme, ginger, chile, allspice and nutmeg until coarsely pureed. Blend in the olive oil, tomato paste and vinegar. Season with salt and pepper.

2. Transfer 6 tablespoons of the spice puree to a large bowl. Add the mussels, cockles and tomatoes and toss to coat thoroughly. Tear off four 20-inch-long sheets of extra-heavy-duty foil. Mound half of the mussel and cockle mixture in the center of each of 2 foil sheets. Add the shrimp to the bowl and toss with the remaining spice puree. Arrange the shrimp in a layer on the seafood. Cover with the 2 remaining sheets of foil; fold up the edges and crimp all around to seal.

3. Grill the hobo packs over a hot fire for about 6 minutes, or until sizzling and puffed. Using oven mitts, transfer the hobo packs to a large rimmed platter. Open the aluminum foil carefully. Pour the seafood into individual shallow serving bowls and serve immediately. —*Grace Parisi*

SERVE WITH Grilled garlic bread.

WINE Light, spicy Pinot Grigio.

BRUSSELS SPROUTS WITH ONION AND BACON, P. 229

vegetables

MARINATED MUSHROOMS

CRISPY CELERY ROOT CUTLETS

Marinated Mushrooms

TOTAL: 20 MIN

4 SERVINGS ● ● ●

1¼ pounds white or cremini
   mushrooms—stems trimmed,
   large mushrooms quartered and
   medium mushrooms halved

3 tablespoons extra-virgin olive oil

2 tablespoons fresh lemon juice

1 bay leaf

1 teaspoon black peppercorns

1 teaspoon salt

1 medium onion, quartered,
   layers separated

½ cup dry white wine

½ teaspoon thyme leaves

½ teaspoon coriander seeds

In a medium saucepan, combine all of
the ingredients and bring them to a boil
over high heat. Cover the saucepan and
boil for 6 minutes, stirring once or twice.

Transfer the contents of the saucepan to
a heatproof bowl and let cool to room
temperature. The marinated mushrooms
can be served at once or covered with
plastic wrap and refrigerated.
—*Jacques Pépin*

MAKE AHEAD The marinated mushrooms
can be refrigerated for up to 4 days.
Bring to room temperature and discard
the bay leaf before serving.

Baked Apples with Oyster Mushrooms

ACTIVE: 25 MIN; TOTAL: 1 HR 5 MIN

4 SERVINGS ●

Vegetable oil cooking spray

4 baking apples
   (about ½ pound each)

½ lemon

1 tablespoon extra-virgin olive oil

2 garlic cloves, finely chopped

½ pound oyster mushrooms, cut
   into ¼-inch-thick slices

Salt and freshly ground pepper

½ cup coarsely chopped mixed
   herbs, such as parsley, basil,
   tarragon and chives

½ cup apple cider

1. Preheat the oven to 350°. Spray a
small, shallow baking dish just large
enough to hold the apples with vegetable oil cooking spray. Cut a thin
slice off the top of each apple. Using a
small spoon, scrape out the apple flesh,
leaving a ¼-inch-thick shell. Rub and
moisten the apple cups with the lemon
to discourage browning. Discard the
skin from the apple tops and the seeds
from the apple cores and finely chop
the apple flesh.

2. Heat the olive oil in a large nonstick
skillet. Add the garlic and cook until

fragrant, about 1 minute. Add the chopped apple and the oyster mushrooms and season with salt and pepper. Cook the mixture over moderately high heat until the liquid evaporates, about 5 minutes. Stir in the herbs.

3. Season the apple cups with salt and pepper. Spoon the mushroom mixture into the cups, mounding it slightly. Set the apples in the prepared baking dish and pour the cider around them. Bake in the oven for 45 minutes to 1 hour, or until the apples are tender; if they begin to brown during cooking, cover them with foil. Serve hot. —*Jane Sigal*

MAKE AHEAD The apples can be stuffed and refrigerated for up to 1 hour.

SERVE WITH Pork, veal, pheasant or mild sausages.

Cheese-Stuffed Portobello Burgers

ACTIVE: 35 MIN; TOTAL: 1 HR

4 SERVINGS

These Gouda-stuffed Portobellos have more smoky flavor than most commercially available veggie burgers.

- 6 large Portobello mushrooms (6 ounces each), stemmed, the stems reserved
- 2 tablespoons extra-virgin olive oil, plus more for brushing
- 1 yellow bell pepper, finely chopped
- 2 medium shallots, minced
- 2 garlic cloves, minced
- ⅓ cup coarsely chopped roasted salted cashews
- ¼ cup finely chopped dill or basil
- 4 ounces aged Gouda or Cheddar cheese, shredded (1 cup), plus 4 thin slices aged Gouda or Cheddar
- Kosher salt
- Cayenne pepper
- ½ cup mayonnaise
- Freshly ground black pepper
- 4 kaiser rolls, split
- 1 small bunch arugula
- 4 thin tomato slices

1. Brush the underside of 4 of the Portobello mushrooms with olive oil. Cut the stems and the remaining 2 mushroom caps into ½-inch dice. Transfer the diced mushrooms to a food processor and pulse just until finely chopped.

2. In a large skillet, heat the 2 tablespoons of olive oil until shimmering. Add the bell pepper, shallots and half of the garlic and cook over moderate heat, stirring, until softened and beginning to brown, about 5 minutes. Add the chopped mushrooms and cook over high heat, stirring, until softened and all of the liquid has evaporated, about 5 minutes longer. Add the cashews and half of the dill and transfer to a bowl to cool. Stir in the shredded cheese and season with salt and cayenne.

3. In a small bowl, combine the mayonnaise with the remaining minced garlic and dill and season with black pepper.

4. Light a grill. When the fire is medium hot, brush the grate with oil. Grill the mushrooms, stemmed side down, for 7 to 8 minutes, or until browned. Brush the tops with olive oil and transfer to a platter, stemmed side up. Pack the filling into the caps in a slightly flattened mound. Top with the cheese.

5. Return the mushrooms to the grill, filling side up. Cover and grill until the cheese is melted and the Portobello bottoms are browned and cooked through, 5 minutes. Grill the cut sides of the rolls until toasted. Spread 2 tablespoons of the mayonnaise on the rolls' cut sides. Set the mushrooms on the bottom halves, top with the arugula and tomatoes and serve, with the roll tops alongside. —*Steven Raichlen*

Crispy Celery Root Cutlets

TOTAL: 25 MIN

4 SERVINGS ● ●

Buttery bread crumbs enhance the nutty flavor of the celery root in this simple, clever vegetarian dish.

Two ¾-pound celery roots—peeled, halved and cut into ½-inch-thick slices
- 1 large egg
- 1 cup fine dry bread crumbs
- Salt and freshly ground pepper
- 4 tablespoons unsalted butter
- 2 tablespoons extra-virgin olive oil
- 1 tablespoon finely chopped parsley
- Lemon wedges, for serving

1. Put the celery root slices in a medium saucepan of salted water and bring to a boil. Cook until just tender, about 8 minutes. Drain and pat dry.

2. Beat the egg in a shallow bowl. In another shallow bowl, season the bread crumbs with salt and pepper. Dip the celery root slices in the egg and then in the seasoned crumbs, pressing to coat.

3. In a large skillet, melt the butter in the oil. Add the slices in a single layer and cook over moderately high heat, turning occasionally, until golden and crisp, 6 to 7 minutes. Transfer to paper towels to drain. Sprinkle with salt and parsley and serve with lemon wedges. —*Barbara Damrosch*

MAKE AHEAD The cutlets can be fried up to 6 hours ahead; reheat at 375°.

INGREDIENT TIP

mushroom prep

1. To prep button mushrooms, trim the stems. No need to wash them; they're clean enough.

2. Wash gritty varieties like fresh porcini or morels just before using them. Swish them in a large bowl of cold water until no sandy residue remains in the bowl.

3. To get porcini to soak up less oil and butter, add a pinch of salt when cooking them. Cover the mushrooms until they start to exude their liquid, then uncover them and let the liquid evaporate.

vegetables

Roasted Asparagus with Almonds and Asiago

TOTAL: 20 MIN

6 SERVINGS ● ● ●

1½ pounds pencil-thin asparagus (see Note)

3 tablespoons extra-virgin olive oil

Salt and freshly ground pepper

⅓ cup sliced almonds

1 tablespoon fresh lemon juice, plus lemon wedges for serving

2 ounces Asiago cheese, shaved (1 cup)

I. Preheat the oven to 450°. On a large rimmed baking sheet, toss the asparagus with 2 tablespoons of the olive oil. Season with salt and pepper and roast for 15 minutes, until tender. Meanwhile, put the almonds in a pie plate and toast in the oven for 5 minutes, until golden.

2. Transfer the asparagus to a platter and drizzle with the lemon juice and the remaining 1 tablespoon of olive oil. Season with salt and pepper. Scatter the Asiago over the asparagus, sprinkle with the almonds and serve with lemon wedges. —*Grace Parisi*

NOTE If you prefer to serve thicker asparagus spears, add about 10 minutes to the roasting time.

carrots + health

Carrots are an extraordinary source of beta-carotene, an antioxidant that may help prevent heart disease and some kinds of cancer. Carrots are also an excellent source of fiber, minerals and vitamin C, and deliver some vitamin E as well. One medium carrot provides over 5 mg of vitamin A (more than twice the recommended daily requirement), which helps maintain good eyesight, fight infection and support bone growth.

Asparagus Baked in Parchment Paper

ACTIVE: 25 MIN; TOTAL: 2 HR 25 MIN

4 SERVINGS

24 thick asparagus spears (about 1½ pounds), tough ends trimmed, stalks peeled

⅓ cup extra-virgin olive oil

¼ teaspoon sugar

Salt

1 tarragon sprig

12 salted capers

2 tablespoons mayonnaise

2 tablespoons heavy cream

I. Preheat the oven to 175°. Spread a 2-foot-long sheet of parchment paper on a baking sheet. Arrange the asparagus in a neat, even pile on top. Drizzle the oil over the asparagus; sprinkle with the sugar, season with salt and top with the tarragon sprig. Fold the paper over the spears and tuck the ends under to form a tight package; secure with string.

2. Bake the asparagus for 1½ to 2 hours, or until it feels very tender when pressed through the parchment.

3. Soak the capers in water for 1 to 2 hours. Pat dry and coarsely chop. In a small bowl, blend the mayonnaise, heavy cream and capers; season with salt.

4. Cut the parchment package open; transfer the asparagus to a plate. Mix the juices into the sauce; pour over the asparagus and serve. —*Paula Wolfert*

Glazed Carrots with Green Olives

ACTIVE: 25 MIN; TOTAL: 1 HR 50 MIN

2 TO 4 SERVINGS ● ●

1 pound large carrots, peeled

2 tablespoons unsalted butter

2 tablespoons water

1 large garlic clove, thinly sliced

1 tablespoon finely chopped parsley

1 teaspoon finely chopped thyme

½ cup Picholine olives—pitted, chopped and rinsed

Salt and freshly ground pepper

3 tablespoons heavy cream

I. Preheat the oven to 300°. Cut each carrot in half crosswise, then halve or quarter the carrot halves lengthwise so the pieces are of equal thickness.

2. In a large ovenproof skillet, melt 1 tablespoon of the butter. Add the carrots and the water. Cover with a round of parchment paper and a tight-fitting lid and bake until the carrots are very tender, about 1 hour and 15 minutes.

3. Transfer the carrots to a plate and let stand for 5 minutes. Add the remaining 1 tablespoon of butter to the skillet and melt over moderate heat. Add the garlic, parsley and thyme and cook until fragrant. Add the carrots and olives, season with salt and pepper and cook, stirring gently, until coated with butter. Add the cream, cover and cook over low heat, shaking the pan, until the carrots are nicely glazed, about 2 minutes. Transfer to plates and serve. —*Paula Wolfert*

Carrot-Cranberry Gratin

ACTIVE: 25 MIN; TOTAL: 1 HR 5 MIN

4 SERVINGS ●

Despite its sweetness, this is a side dish, not a dessert. It would be good with pork, turkey, duck or game.

1¼ pounds carrots, coarsely shredded

1 Fuji apple, peeled and coarsely shredded

1 cup fresh cranberries

½ cup apple juice

1 tablespoon honey

2 tablespoons unsalted butter, softened

I. Preheat the oven to 400°. Butter a 9-inch square glass baking dish. In a medium bowl, toss the carrots, apple, cranberries, apple juice and honey. Pack the mixture into the dish, smoothing the surface. Spread the butter over the top.

2. Bake in the upper third of the oven for about 40 minutes, or until the carrots are tender and the top is browned. Serve the gratin at once. —*Andrew J. Powning*

Whisky-Glazed Parsnips and Carrots

TOTAL: 35 MIN

12 SERVINGS ● ● ●

- 4 tablespoons unsalted butter
- ½ cup whisky
- ¼ cup light brown sugar
- 2 pounds carrots, peeled and cut into 2-by-½-inch sticks
- 1 pound tender young parsnips, peeled and cut into 2-by-½-inch sticks

Salt and freshly ground pepper

In a large, deep skillet, melt the butter with the whisky and brown sugar. Stir in the carrots and parsnips. Press a round of parchment paper directly onto the vegetables. Cover with a tight-fitting lid and cook over moderate heat until the vegetables are tender and the liquid is almost evaporated, 15 minutes. Uncover and cook, tossing, until the vegetables are coated in a thick syrup, 1 to 2 minutes. Season the vegetables with salt and pepper and serve. —*Grace Parisi*

Glazed Caramelized Carrots

ACTIVE: 25 MIN; TOTAL: 1 HR

12 SERVINGS ●

- 3 pounds carrots, peeled and cut diagonally into 1½-inch pieces
- 1 tablespoon unsalted butter
- ½ cup chicken stock or broth

Salt and freshly ground pepper

- 1 teaspoon chopped thyme

1. In a saucepan of boiling salted water, cook the carrots for 7 minutes. Drain.

2. In a large skillet, melt the butter in the chicken stock. Add the blanched carrots and season lightly with salt. Cover and cook over moderately low heat, stirring occasionally, until tender, 25 minutes.

3. Uncover the carrots and cook, without stirring, until golden brown on the bottom, about 4 minutes. Season the carrots with salt and pepper. Transfer them to a shallow bowl. Sprinkle with the thyme and serve. —*Tom Valenti*

ASPARAGUS BAKED IN PARCHMENT PAPER

CARROT-CRANBERRY GRATIN

SWEET WINTER SQUASH SALAD

GRILLED ZUCCHINI KEBABS WITH ZUCCHINI DIP

Seared Zucchini Salad with Cinnamon

TOTAL: 20 MIN

8 SERVINGS ● ● ●

1½ tablespoons sugar

1 tablespoon distilled white vinegar

½ teaspoon cinnamon

Salt

¼ cup extra-virgin olive oil

2 pounds small zucchini, cut crosswise into ⅓-inch-thick slices

1. In a small bowl, mix the sugar, vinegar, cinnamon and a pinch of salt.

2. Heat the olive oil in a large skillet. Add the zucchini, season with salt and cook over moderately high heat, stirring occasionally, until tender and browned, about 10 minutes. Add the dressing and cook, tossing, for 1 minute longer. Serve warm or at room temperature. —*Hajja Halima*

Zucchini Tagine

ACTIVE: 15 MIN; TOTAL: 50 MIN

4 SERVINGS ● ●

2 tablespoons extra-virgin olive oil

3 garlic cloves, thinly sliced

1 small onion, thinly sliced

1½ pounds small zucchini, cut into ½-inch dice

7 saffron threads

½ teaspoon ground cumin

Pinch of ground turmeric

Salt and freshly ground white pepper

1½ tablespoons fresh lemon juice

1 tablespoon chopped mint

Heat the oil in a large saucepan. Add the garlic and onion and cook over moderate heat, stirring, until softened, about 4 minutes. Add the zucchini, saffron, cumin and turmeric; season with salt and pepper. Cook, stirring, until barely tender, about 8 minutes. Transfer to a bowl and refrigerate for 20 minutes. Stir in the lemon juice; season with salt and pepper and the mint. Serve chilled or at room temperature. —*Eric Ripert*

Sweet Winter Squash Salad with Sesame Seeds

ACTIVE: 20 MIN; TOTAL: 45 MIN

8 SERVINGS ● ●

Several spiced or sweetened vegetable salads, such as this one, are served at the beginning of a Moroccan meal.

1 medium butternut squash (about 2 pounds)—peeled, seeded and cut into 1-inch chunks

4 cinnamon sticks

1 cup water

½ cup sugar

¼ cup vegetable oil

Salt

2 teaspoons sesame seeds

1. In a large saucepan, combine the squash, cinnamon, water, sugar and oil. Season with salt and bring to a boil. Cook over moderate heat, stirring once or twice, until the squash is tender and the liquid nearly absorbed, 20 minutes. Transfer to a bowl and let cool slightly.

2. In a small skillet, toast the sesame seeds over moderate heat, stirring, until golden, about 3 minutes. Sprinkle the sesame seeds over the squash and serve warm or at room temperature. —*Hajja Halima*

MAKE AHEAD The cooked squash can be refrigerated for up to 2 days. Return to room temperature and sprinkle with sesame seeds before serving.

Grilled Zucchini Kebabs with Zucchini Dip

ACTIVE: 35 MIN; TOTAL: 1 HR 30 MIN

4 SERVINGS ●

KEBABS

- 2 round zucchini (10 ounces each), each cut into six $1/3$-inch-thick rounds
- 2 tablespoons extra-virgin olive oil
- 2 garlic cloves, minced
- 1 tablespoon chopped parsley

Salt and freshly ground white pepper

DIP

- 2 tablespoons extra-virgin olive oil
- 2 zucchini ($3/4$ pound), chopped
- 2 garlic cloves, minced
- $1/2$ small onion, coarsely chopped

Salt and freshly ground pepper

- $1/2$ cup packed basil leaves
- 1 teaspoon fresh lemon juice

1. **MAKE THE KEBABS:** Push one 8-inch skewer horizontally through 2 zucchini slices; keeping another skewer parallel, push it through the slices to secure. Repeat to form 6 kebabs. Brush with the olive oil and transfer to a dish. Sprinkle with the garlic and parsley, season with salt and white pepper and let marinate at room temperature for 30 minutes. Light a grill.

2. **MEANWHILE, MAKE THE DIP:** Heat 1 tablespoon of the olive oil in a medium skillet. Add the zucchini, garlic and onion and cook over moderately low heat, stirring occasionally, until tender, about 8 minutes. Season with salt and pepper, transfer to a platter and refrigerate until chilled, about 20 minutes.

3. Scrape the mixture into a blender, add the basil and the remaining 1 tablespoon of oil and blend until smooth. Scrape into a bowl. Stir in the lemon juice and season with salt and pepper.

4. Scrape the garlic off the kebabs and grill over a hot fire for about 2 minutes per side, or until lightly charred and just tender. Serve the kebabs with the dip. —*Eric Ripert*

Braised Summer Squash

ACTIVE: 20 MIN; TOTAL: 1 HR

4 SERVINGS ● ●

- 3 tablespoons extra-virgin olive oil
- $1 1/2$ pounds zucchini, cut into $3/4$-inch-thick slices
- $1/2$ pound Yukon Gold potatoes— peeled, halved and cut into $1/3$-inch-thick slices
- 1 medium tomato—peeled, seeded and coarsely chopped
- 1 medium red onion, thinly sliced
- 2 tablespoons coarsely chopped celery leaves
- $1/2$ tablespoon finely chopped basil
- $1/4$ teaspoon crushed red pepper

Sea salt

- $1/4$ cup boiling water

Freshly grated Parmesan cheese

1. Heat the olive oil in a medium saucepan or deep skillet. Add the zucchini, potatoes, tomato, onion, celery leaves, basil and crushed red pepper and season with sea salt. Cover and cook the vegetables over moderate heat until they are barely tender when pierced with a fork, about 25 minutes.

2. Add the boiling water, cover and cook until the vegetables are tender, about 12 minutes longer. Season the vegetables with salt and serve hot or at room temperature. Pass extra Parmesan cheese alongside at the table. —*Gianfranco Becchina*

MAKE AHEAD The braised vegetables can be refrigerated overnight. Rewarm gently before serving.

Roasted Butternut Squash with Onions, Brown Butter and Sage

ACTIVE: 30 MIN; TOTAL: 1 HR 30 MIN

4 SERVINGS

- One $3 1/2$-pound butternut squash— peeled, halved, seeded and cut into $1/2$-inch pieces
- 2 medium onions, cut into $1/2$-inch pieces
- 2 tablespoons extra-virgin olive oil
- 2 tablespoons packed dark brown sugar

Salt and freshly ground pepper

- 4 tablespoons unsalted butter
- 32 fresh sage leaves (see Note)

1. Preheat the oven to 400°. In a large bowl, toss the butternut squash with the onions, olive oil and brown sugar; season with salt and pepper. Spread the squash in an even layer on a baking sheet. Roast for 1 hour, or until the squash and onions are very tender and browned on the edges. Transfer the vegetables to a serving bowl.

2. Set a small skillet over moderately high heat. When it is hot, add the butter and cook until melted and bubbling, about 3 minutes. Add the sage leaves in 1 layer and cook for about 2 minutes, until the butter is a pleasant golden brown color and the sage leaves are crisp. Season the browned butter and sage with salt, pour over the squash and onions and serve at once. —*Maria Helm Sinskey*

NOTE Bunches of fresh sage are available year-round at produce markets and most supermarkets. Do not substitute dried sage in this recipe.

vegetables

Roasted Butternut Squash with Cilantro Cream

ACTIVE: 1 HR; TOTAL: 1 HR 15 MIN

12 SERVINGS ● ● ●

- ½ cup unsalted pumpkin seeds
- 8 pounds butternut squash— peeled, seeded and cut into ¾-inch pieces
- ¼ cup plus 2 tablespoons vegetable oil

Salt and freshly ground pepper

- 6 large garlic cloves, minced
- 2 large red onions, finely diced
- 4 large scallions, coarsely chopped
- 1½ teaspoons ground cumin
- ½ teaspoon hot paprika
- ¼ teaspoon cinnamon
- ¾ cup drained canned whole tomatoes, finely diced, ¼ cup juices reserved
- ½ cup sour cream
- ¼ cup milk
- ¼ cup finely chopped cilantro
- 2 teaspoons fresh lime juice

1. Preheat the oven to 425°. Toast the pumpkin seeds on a pie plate in the oven until browned, 3 to 4 minutes. Transfer to a plate and let cool. Leave the oven on.

2. Spread the squash on 3 large rimmed baking sheets. Drizzle 1 tablespoon of olive oil over the squash on each sheet, season with salt and pepper, and toss to coat. Bake the squash for 40 minutes, or until just tender and browned; rotate the baking sheets for even browning.

3. Meanwhile, in a large skillet, heat the remaining 3 tablespoons of olive oil. Add the garlic and onions and cook over moderately high heat until sizzling, about 3 minutes. Season with salt and pepper, reduce the heat to moderate and cook, stirring occasionally, until the onions are very soft, about 15 minutes. Add the scallions and cook, stirring occasionally, until they are browned, about 12 minutes. Stir in the cumin, paprika and cinnamon; cook, stirring, until fragrant, about 4 minutes. Add the tomatoes and their juices and simmer for 1 minute. Season with salt. Spoon the sauce over the squash and toss.

4. In a bowl, blend the sour cream with the milk, cilantro and lime juice; season with salt and pepper. Drizzle the cilantro cream over the squash, sprinkle with the pumpkin seeds and serve. —*Marcia Kiesel*

MAKE AHEAD The squash and cilantro cream can be refrigerated separately overnight. The toasted pumpkin seeds can be stored in an airtight container. Bring the squash to room temperature and transfer to 2 oiled baking dishes. Reheat in a 350° oven.

Butternut Squash Gratin

ACTIVE: 15 MIN; TOTAL: 1 HR 25 MIN

6 SERVINGS ●

What's so unusual about this terrific gratin is that the squash is cooked and mashed before it's baked with cream.

- 2 tablespoons unsalted butter
- 3 pounds butternut squash— peeled, seeded and cut into cubes
- 1 cup water
- 1 garlic clove, minced
- 1 cup crème fraîche

Salt and freshly ground pepper

- 6 large egg yolks
- 1 cup shredded Gruyère cheese

1. Preheat the oven to 350°. Butter a deep 2-quart baking dish. Melt the 2 tablespoons of butter in a large skillet. Add the squash and stir to coat. Add the water, cover and cook over moderate heat until the squash is tender, about 10 minutes. Uncover and cook over high heat until the water has evaporated, about 3 minutes. Transfer the squash to a large bowl, mash it and let cool to room temperature.

2. Add the garlic and crème fraîche to the squash and season with salt and pepper, then whisk in the egg yolks. Spread the squash in the baking dish and scatter the cheese over the top.

3. Cover the squash with foil and bake for about 40 minutes, or until almost set. Increase the oven temperature to 425°. Uncover the squash and bake in the upper third of the oven for about 12 minutes, or until the cheese is browned. Remove the gratin from the oven and let stand for 10 minutes before serving. —*Christophe Côte*

squash varieties

Squashes to try, clockwise from top: EIGHT BALL is dark green and perfect for stuffing. GOLDBAR is a yellow version of the common rod-shaped green zucchini. SUNBURST has yellow skin and is shaped like a flying saucer; it's excellent for sautéing, steaming or stuffing. YELLOW CROOKNECK is an old standard that is especially good for roasting. RONDE DE NICE has striped, light green skin. PATTYPAN, also called CYMLING, is the shape of a scalloped bowl; it's very pale green, with firm flesh.

Broccoli with Brown Butter Crumbs

ACTIVE: 20 MIN; TOTAL: 35 MIN

12 SERVINGS ●

- 5 pounds broccoli, cut into 1½-inch florets
- 1½ sticks (6 ounces) unsalted butter, ½ stick melted

Salt and freshly ground pepper

- ¾ cup dry bread crumbs or *panko* (Japanese bread crumbs)
- 2 medium garlic cloves, very finely chopped
- 2 hard-cooked large egg yolks
- ¼ cup minced flat-leaf parsley

1. Preheat the oven to 375°. In a large pot, blanch the broccoli in boiling salted water for 4 minutes. Drain, pat dry and transfer to a large baking dish. Toss the broccoli with the melted butter, season with salt and pepper and bake for 15 minutes.

2. Meanwhile, in a medium skillet, melt the remaining stick of butter. Add the bread crumbs and cook over moderate heat, stirring, until golden, about 4 minutes. Add the garlic and cook, stirring, until fragrant and the crumbs are crisp, about 3 minutes; season with salt and pepper. Spoon the crumbs over the broccoli. Press the egg yolks through a fine sieve over the broccoli. Garnish with the parsley and serve.
—David Waltuck

Garlicky Roasted Broccoli

ACTIVE: 15 MIN; TOTAL: 25 MIN

4 SERVINGS ● ●

- 1½ pounds broccoli, cut into long spears
- 2 tablespoons extra-virgin olive oil
- 1 tablespoon very finely chopped garlic
- 1 teaspoon finely chopped fresh ginger
- ½ teaspoon kosher salt
- ½ teaspoon crushed red pepper

Lemon wedges, for serving

Preheat the oven to 450°. In a large bowl, toss the broccoli with the olive oil, garlic, ginger, salt and crushed red pepper. Spread the broccoli on a rimmed baking sheet and roast in the upper third of the oven for 20 minutes, stirring occasionally, until crisp-tender and browned in spots. Serve with lemon wedges. —Sally Sampson

Broccoli and Cauliflower Gratin with Cheddar Cheese

TOTAL: 35 MIN

4 TO 6 SERVINGS ●

- 4 cups broccoli florets (from 2 small heads)
- 4 cups cauliflower florets (from 1 small head)
- ¼ cup extra-virgin olive oil
- 2 large garlic cloves, minced
- ⅛ teaspoon crushed red pepper
- ½ pound sharp Cheddar cheese, coarsely shredded (2 cups)
- ¼ cup pitted oil-cured green or black olives, coarsely chopped
- 1 cup coarse plain dry bread crumbs

Salt and freshly ground pepper

1. Preheat the oven to 400°. Butter a 2-inch-deep 2-quart baking dish. Bring a saucepan of salted water to a boil, add the broccoli and cauliflower and cook for 3 minutes. Drain thoroughly.

2. In a large skillet, heat 2 tablespoons of the oil over moderate heat. Add the garlic and crushed red pepper and cook just until fragrant. Off the heat, add the broccoli and cauliflower and toss. Add half of the cheese and the olives. Transfer to the baking dish and sprinkle with the remaining cheese.

3. In a small bowl, toss the bread crumbs with the remaining 2 table-spoons of olive oil; season with salt and pepper. Sprinkle the crumbs on top of the cheese. Bake in the upper third of the oven for 12 minutes, or until the cheese is bubbling and the crumbs are golden. Serve hot. —Laura Chenel

Spanish-Style Carrots and Cauliflower

ACTIVE: 25 MIN; TOTAL: 40 MIN

4 SERVINGS ●

- 2 large red bell peppers
- 1 ounce spicy chorizo, peeled and minced
- 3 tablespoons almond butter (see Note)
- 2 garlic cloves, minced
- ¼ teaspoon ground cumin
- 1 cup plus 1 tablespoon water

Salt and freshly ground pepper

- 2 large carrots, cut into ¼-inch-thick slices
- 1 head cauliflower (2 pounds), florets cut into ⅓-inch-thick slices

Cilantro leaves, for garnish

1. Roast the bell peppers directly over a gas flame or under the broiler until charred all over. Transfer to a plate to cool. Peel, core and seed the peppers, then coarsely chop them.

2. In a small skillet, cook the chorizo over moderate heat until crisp, about 4 minutes. Drain on paper towels.

3. In a mini food processor, puree the roasted peppers with the almond butter, garlic, cumin and the 1 tablespoon of water. Scrape the sauce into a bowl and season with salt and pepper.

4. In a large skillet, cover the carrots with ½ cup of the water and add a pinch of salt. Cover and cook over moderate heat for 5 minutes. Add the sliced cauliflower and the remaining ½ cup of water, cover and cook until just tender, about 5 minutes longer; drain.

5. Transfer the vegetables to a platter and drizzle with some of the almond sauce. Top with the chorizo and cilantro and serve with the extra sauce.
—Priscilla Martel

NOTE Almond butter is made from roasted almonds that have been finely ground. It can replace any nut butter, and is widely available at health food stores and most supermarkets.

● FAST ● HEALTHY ● MAKE AHEAD ● STAFF FAVORITE

vegetables

Indian-Spiced Stuffed Cauliflower

ACTIVE: 25 MIN; TOTAL: 1 HR 40 MIN

4 SERVINGS ●

A head of cauliflower, stuffed with nuts and spices and then slathered with a spicy paste and browned in the oven, makes a great vegetarian main dish.

- 1 tablespoon ground turmeric

Salt

- One 3-pound head cauliflower, core trimmed
- 2 tablespoons chickpea flour
- 1 cup plain low-fat yogurt
- 2 tablespoons Ginger Paste (recipe, page 101)
- 2 tablespoons Garlic Paste (recipe, page 101)
- 2 tablespoons vegetable oil
- ¼ cup roasted cashews, chopped
- ⅓ cup finely chopped green beans
- 1 small carrot, finely chopped
- ¼ teaspoon garam masala
- ¼ teaspoon ground cumin
- ⅛ teaspoon cayenne pepper
- ⅛ teaspoon ground fenugreek
- 1 cup cottage cheese
- ¼ cup shredded Cheddar cheese
- 2 tablespoons dried currants

Freshly ground pepper

1. Preheat the oven to 425°. Bring a pot of water to a boil. Stir in the turmeric and 1 tablespoon of salt, add the cauliflower and cook until barely tender, 15 minutes. Drain in a colander and let cool.

2. In a skillet, toast the chickpea flour over moderate heat, stirring, until golden brown, about 2 minutes. Scrape the flour into a bowl and let cool, then stir in the yogurt, Ginger Paste, Garlic Paste and 1 tablespoon of the oil; season with salt.

3. In a mini food processor, finely grind the cashews. In the skillet, heat the remaining 1 tablespoon of oil. Add the green beans and carrot and cook over low heat, stirring, until crisp-tender, about 5 minutes. Add the garam masala, cumin, cayenne and fenugreek and

cook, stirring, until fragrant, about 1 minute. Scrape the mixture into a medium bowl; let cool, then stir in the cottage cheese, Cheddar, currants and cashews; season with salt and pepper.

4. Carefully stuff the head of cauliflower, packing small amounts of the vegetable mixture in between the florets and in the crannies on the underside of the head. Set the stuffed cauliflower in a baking dish, right side up, and spoon the yogurt topping all over the head. Bake the cauliflower for about 1 hour, or until richly browned. Let cool for about 5 minutes before serving. —*Anupam Gulati*

Cauliflower Masala

ACTIVE: 15 MIN; TOTAL: 1 HR 10 MIN

4 SERVINGS ● ●

- 1 head cauliflower, cored and cut into 2-inch florets
- 2 tablespoons canola oil

Salt

- 1 teaspoon cumin seeds
- 2 garlic cloves, minced
- 2 teaspoons minced peeled ginger
- 1 small shallot, minced
- 4 plum tomatoes, cut into ½-inch dice
- 1 teaspoon turmeric
- ½ teaspoon Aleppo pepper or Korean red pepper flakes
- ½ cup water

1. Preheat the oven to 350°. In a 9-by-13-inch glass or ceramic baking dish, toss the cauliflower florets with 1 tablespoon of the oil. Season with salt and bake for about 45 minutes, or until just tender and lightly browned.

2. Meanwhile, in a large skillet, heat the remaining 1 tablespoon of oil. Add the cumin seeds and cook over moderate heat until fragrant. Add the garlic, ginger and shallot and cook, stirring, until softened. Add the diced tomatoes, turmeric and red pepper flakes and cook, stirring occasionally, until the tomatoes soften, about 4 minutes.

3. Stir the water into the skillet and bring the sauce to a boil. Add the baked cauliflower and simmer, stirring, until the florets are evenly coated in a slightly thickened sauce, about 2 minutes. Season with salt and serve hot, warm or at room temperature. —*Floyd Cardoz*

Sautéed Leeks with Chestnuts

ACTIVE: 30 MIN; TOTAL: 1 HR

12 SERVINGS ●

- 1 tablespoon unsalted butter
- 1 cup whole cooked chestnuts, coarsely chopped

Salt and freshly ground pepper

- 2 tablespoons extra-virgin olive oil
- 3 medium garlic cloves, very finely chopped
- 1 large anchovy fillet, very finely chopped
- ½ cup dry white wine
- 6 large leeks, white and tender green parts only—halved lengthwise, cut into 1½-inch lengths and julienned
- 1 large carrot, shredded
- ¾ cup Rich Turkey Stock (recipe, p. 125) or chicken broth
- 2 tablespoons heavy cream

1. Melt the butter in a deep skillet. Add the chestnuts, season with salt and pepper and cook over moderately high heat, undisturbed, until browned on the bottoms, 4 minutes. Transfer to a bowl.

2. Heat the oil in the skillet. Add the garlic and anchovy and cook over moderately low heat, stirring, for 4 minutes. Add the wine and cook over moderate heat for 1 minute. Stir in the leeks and carrot, add the stock and bring to a simmer. Cover and cook, stirring occasionally, until tender, about 15 minutes.

3. Stir the heavy cream into the leeks and season with salt and pepper. Fold in the chestnuts and serve. —*Marcia Kiesel*

MAKE AHEAD The recipe can be prepared ahead through Step 2. Refrigerate the chestnuts and leeks separately.

Q+A
cooking corn

choosing corn

Q: I love corn on the cob, but I'm hopeless at picking good ears! When I'm at the market, I know I'm not supposed to strip the husks to peek at the kernels. What can I do?

A: Tips for selecting perfect ears of corn aren't as foolproof as those for choosing a bunch of arugula (taste a leaf) or a basket of strawberries (take a whiff), but there are a few telltale signs of freshness. At the market, reach for ears from the bottom of the heap, where the temperature is coolest. Check the ends of the ears—they should look like they were just cut from the stalk, not withered or dry. The ears should be tightly encased in their husks, and intact. If possible, avoid buying husked supermarket corn, the kind that's had the tops lopped off and been wrapped in plastic. The ears should feel heavy for their size and have husks that are green and fresh, kernels that feel plump and tight and silk that's shiny and golden. There's one problem that's very hard to avoid, unfortunately: worms. They're wily creatures and sometimes burrow their way into a tasty cob without leaving a trail. Simply cut out the invaded part and throw it away.

grilling corn

Q: I love the smoky-roasted flavor of grilled corn, but every recipe I consult suggests a different grilling method. Can you help?

A: It comes down to two things: how much time you want to spend, and how you plan to enjoy the cooked corn. If you're in a hurry and want to make a roasted-corn salsa or succotash, dishes that don't need a lot of corn, you can take a shortcut. Simply cut the kernels from the cobs and pan-roast them in a well-seasoned cast-iron skillet over moderate heat until they're browned or charred to your liking. If, on the other hand, it's all about corn on the cob, you'll need to fire up the grill. To prepare the ears for grilling, peel back the husks layer by layer, pull off the silk and re-form the husks, tying them at the top with a strip of husk if necessary. Grill covered over moderate heat, turning the ears, until the husks are charred all around, about 15 minutes. For a less intense smoky flavor, leave the silk on and grill uncovered. Either way, soak the ears at least briefly before grilling. To eat, pull back the charred husks and use them as a handle.

baking corn

Q: I made corn pudding and ended up with a curdled mess. Thoughts?

A: Perhaps the dish was too deep, so the pudding's edges overcooked before it set in the center; or maybe the heat was too high. Try again with this lovely recipe. It's adapted from *The Gift of Southern Cooking* by Edna Lewis and Scott Peacock.

Summer Corn Pudding
ACTIVE: 10 MIN; TOTAL: 1 HR
6 SERVINGS

- 4 ears of corn, shucked
- ⅓ cup sugar
- 2 tablespoons all-purpose flour
- 1 teaspoon salt
- 2 large eggs, beaten
- 1 cup milk
- 1 cup heavy cream
- 1 tablespoon unsalted butter, melted
- Pinch of freshly grated nutmeg

1. Preheat the oven to 350°. Butter an 8-inch glass baking dish. Cut the kernels off the corn. In a bowl, toss the corn kernels, sugar, flour and salt.
2. In a bowl, mix the eggs, milk and cream. Stir into the corn until blended. Stir in the butter. Pour the pudding into the baking dish. Set the dish in a hot-water bath. Bake on the top shelf of the oven until just set, about 40 minutes. Let cool for 10 minutes before serving.

YOUNG GREEN BEAN, ANCHOVY AND POTATO SALAD

Green Beans with Mustard-Seed Butter

TOTAL: 40 MIN

12 SERVINGS ●

- 2 tablespoons yellow mustard seeds
- 4 medium shallots, very thinly sliced
- 2/3 cup sherry vinegar
- 1/4 cup water
- 1/2 cup heavy cream
- 1 stick (4 ounces) unsalted butter, softened
- 1/4 cup whole-grain mustard

Salt and freshly ground pepper

4 1/2 pounds green beans, trimmed

1. In a large skillet, toast the mustard seeds over moderately high heat, shaking the pan frequently, until they pop and start to brown, about 30 seconds. Transfer to a plate and let cool.

2. Add the shallot slices, sherry vinegar and water to the skillet and simmer over moderately low heat, stirring occasionally, until the liquid is reduced to 1 tablespoon, about 12 minutes. Add the heavy cream and simmer over moderate heat until the liquid has thickened, about 5 minutes. Pour the sauce into a bowl and let cool to room temperature, then stir in the butter, mustard and toasted mustard seeds. Season with salt and pepper.

3. In a large pot of boiling salted water, cook the green beans until crisp-tender, about 8 minutes. Drain the beans, pat dry and transfer to a large bowl. Add the mustard-seed butter, season with salt and pepper, toss and serve. —*Marcia Kiesel*

MAKE AHEAD The mustard-seed butter can be refrigerated for up to 3 days or frozen for up to 1 month; wrap well in plastic wrap and foil. Let the butter return to room temperature before using. The cooked green beans can be refrigerated overnight. To reheat, quickly blanch in boiling water or steam until just heated through.

Young Green Bean, Anchovy and Potato Salad

TOTAL: 45 MIN

4 SERVINGS ●

- 1 pound young green beans, cut into 2-inch lengths

Salt

- 1 pound medium Yukon Gold potatoes, peeled and cut into 1/4-inch-thick slices
- 1/4 cup plus 2 tablespoons extra-virgin olive oil
- 2 medium tomatoes, seeded and coarsely chopped
- 1/2 cup brine-cured black olives, such as Calamata, Gaeta or Niçoise, pitted
- 1 medium red onion, halved lengthwise and thinly sliced crosswise
- 2 tablespoons fresh lemon juice
- 1/2 teaspoon dried oregano, crumbled

Freshly ground pepper

- 4 large hard-cooked eggs, halved
- 6 large anchovy fillets (see Note)

1. Bring a large saucepan of water to a boil. Add the green beans and 1 tablespoon of salt and cook until the beans are tender, about 5 minutes. Using a slotted spoon, transfer the beans to a colander and rinse under cold water. Drain, pat dry and transfer to a large serving bowl.

2. Return the water to a boil. Add the potatoes and cook until tender, about 7 minutes. Drain and shake dry, then add to the beans in the bowl. Add 1/4 cup of the olive oil and gently toss to coat. Scatter the tomatoes, olives and onion slices over the top.

3. In a small bowl, combine the remaining 2 tablespoons of olive oil with the lemon juice and oregano and season with salt and pepper. Drizzle the dressing over the bean and potato salad. Alternate the halved eggs and the anchovies around the edge and serve. —*Gianfranco Becchina*

NOTE Salted anchovies taste best in this salad; they are easily cleaned by pulling apart the 2 fillets (discarding the backbone) and rinsing them quickly under running water. If you can't find salted anchovies, look for large, plump fillets packed in olive oil in a jar.

MAKE AHEAD The green bean salad can be made through Step 2 and kept at room temperature for up to 2 hours.

Brussels Sprouts with Onion and Bacon

ACTIVE: 20 MIN; TOTAL: 40 MIN

12 SERVINGS

- 1/2 pound thickly sliced lean bacon, cut crosswise into thin strips
- 1 Spanish onion, thinly sliced
- 8 garlic cloves, halved lengthwise
- 4 cups chicken stock or low-sodium broth

Coarse salt and freshly ground pepper

Sugar (optional)

- 4 pounds brussels sprouts, trimmed

1. In a large, deep skillet, cook the bacon over moderately high heat until browned, about 8 minutes. Add the onion and garlic, reduce the heat to moderate and cook, stirring, until softened, about 5 minutes. Add the stock, season with salt, pepper and a pinch of sugar and cook until the liquid has reduced to 1 cup, about 12 minutes.

2. Meanwhile, in a large pot of boiling salted water, blanch the brussels sprouts until barely tender when pierced with a fork, about 3 minutes.

3. Add the brussels sprouts to the skillet. Simmer gently over moderate heat, stirring occasionally, until tender throughout, about 10 minutes; season with salt and pepper. Using a slotted spoon, transfer the brussels sprouts to a bowl. Boil the liquid in the skillet over moderately high heat until reduced to 1/2 cup. Pour the sauce over the brussels sprouts and serve at once. —*Tom Valenti*

vegetables

Rutabaga Mash

ACTIVE: 25 MIN; TOTAL: 1 HR 30 MIN

8 SERVINGS ●

A pungent cross between Savoy cabbage and turnips, rutabagas have long been dismissed as cattle fodder. But when these large roots are mashed with potatoes, butter and cream, they are absolutely delicious.

- 5 pounds rutabagas—quartered, peeled and cut into 2-inch chunks
- 1½ pounds baking potatoes, peeled and cut into 2-inch chunks

Salt

- ¾ cup warm milk
- ¾ cup warm heavy cream
- 4½ tablespoons unsalted butter

Freshly ground pepper

1. In a large pot, cover the rutabagas and potatoes with 2 inches of water and bring to a boil. Add a large pinch of salt and boil over moderately high heat until the vegetables are tender, about 50 minutes. Drain the rutabagas and potatoes and return them to the pot.

2. Shake the pot over high heat for about 2 minutes to dry the rutabagas and potatoes. Mash with a potato masher, then mash in the milk, cream and butter until a coarse puree forms. Season the puree with salt and pepper and serve hot. —*Marcia Kiesel*

MAKE AHEAD The recipe can be prepared up to 4 hours ahead.

---

cleaning leeks

LEEKS MUST BE CLEANED thoroughly, as a lot of dirt and sand gets trapped between their layers as they grow. Trim the top and root of the leek, then remove and discard the outer leaves. Slit the leek lengthwise and hold it under cold running water, fanning out the leaves, until all the dirt is gone.

Fennel and Leek Ragout with Pecorino

TOTAL: 40 MIN

4 SERVINGS ●

- 4 tablespoons unsalted butter
- 1 small onion, finely chopped
- 4 small fennel bulbs (¾ pound each)—halved, cored and thinly sliced
- 3 plump leeks, white and tender green parts only, thinly sliced
- ½ cup dry white wine
- ½ cup shredded Pecorino Sardo or Pecorino Toscano cheese
- 1 tablespoon minced dill

Salt and freshly ground pepper

Melt the butter in a large skillet. Add the onion and cook over moderate heat, stirring occasionally, until softened, about 4 minutes. Add the fennel and leeks and cook over moderately high heat, stirring frequently, until the vegetables are sizzling and lightly browned, 13 to 15 minutes. Add the wine and cook, stirring, until nearly evaporated. Remove from the heat and stir in the cheese until melted. Add the dill, season with salt and pepper and serve. —*Chip Angell*

MAKE AHEAD The ragout can be refrigerated overnight. Rewarm and add the dill just before serving.

Baked Endives with Bacon and Mascarpone

ACTIVE: 35 MIN; TOTAL: 45 MIN

4 TO 6 SERVINGS ●

- ¼ pound thick-sliced bacon, cut into ½-inch matchsticks
- 1 cup mascarpone (8 ounces)
- 2 tablespoons finely chopped flat-leaf parsley
- 1 teaspoon thyme leaves

Salt and freshly ground pepper

- 12 baby Belgian endives (1¾ pounds), halved lengthwise
- 1 tablespoon extra-virgin olive oil
- 2 tablespoons fine dry bread crumbs

1. Preheat the oven to 500°. Lightly oil a large glass or ceramic baking dish.

2. In a small saucepan, cook the bacon over moderate heat until crisp; drain on paper towels. In a small bowl, mix the bacon, mascarpone, parsley and thyme and season with salt and pepper.

3. Using a small melon baller or spoon, scoop a little of the core from each endive half, leaving a shallow bowl. Rub the endives lightly with the olive oil. Spread 2 teaspoons of the mascarpone mixture on the cut side of each endive half, smearing it between the leaves. Arrange the filled endives in the baking dish and sprinkle with the bread crumbs. Bake for about 8 minutes, or until the filling is bubbling and the endives are just tender.

4. Preheat the broiler. Broil the endives for about 1 minute, or until the bread crumbs are toasted. Serve hot. —*Eric Czerwinski*

MAKE AHEAD The endives can be baked ahead and broiled just before serving.

Butter-Braised Radishes with Sorrel

ACTIVE: 25 MIN; TOTAL: 40 MIN

6 SERVINGS ●

Not too many people think of eating warm radishes, but they are simply delectable, like turnips with a little bite.

- 1 cup vegetable stock or water
- 1 tablespoon unsalted butter
- 2 pounds radishes with their greens, radishes quartered and greens reserved

Salt and freshly ground pepper

- ½ ounce sorrel leaves, stemmed and thickly sliced (1 packed cup)

In a large skillet, bring the stock and butter to a boil over moderate heat. Add the radishes and cook, stirring occasionally, until crisp-tender and the liquid has thickened, about 15 minutes. Season with salt and pepper and transfer to a shallow bowl. Scatter the sorrel over the top and serve. —*Tony Maws*

Savory Escarole with Anchovies

TOTAL: 20 MIN

4 SERVINGS ●

- ¼ cup extra-virgin olive oil
- ¼ pound thickly sliced pancetta, cut into ¼-inch dice
- 3 garlic cloves, thinly sliced
- 5 small anchovy fillets, minced

Pinch of crushed red pepper

- 1 large head escarole, chopped
- ½ cup chicken stock or broth

Salt and freshly ground pepper

In a deep skillet, heat the olive oil until shimmering. Add the pancetta and cook over moderately high heat, stirring, until golden, 4 to 5 minutes. Add the garlic, anchovies and crushed red pepper and cook until the garlic is softened, about 2 minutes. Add the escarole in large handfuls, tossing until wilted, 1 to 2 minutes. Add the chicken stock, cover and cook for 1 minute. Uncover and cook until the liquid is nearly evaporated and the escarole is tender, 2 to 3 minutes. Season with salt and pepper and serve. —*Michael White*

Alsatian Cabbage

ACTIVE: 20 MIN; TOTAL: 50 MIN

6 SERVINGS ●

- 1 tablespoon unsalted butter
- 1 small onion, finely chopped
- 4 ounces slab bacon, cut into ¼-inch dice
- 1 medium green cabbage (about 2½ pounds)—halved, cored and cut into 1-inch pieces
- 1½ teaspoons caraway seeds

Salt and freshly ground white pepper

Melt the butter in an enameled casserole. Add the onion and cook over moderate heat until softened, 2 minutes. Add the bacon and cook until golden and the fat is rendered, 4 minutes. Add the cabbage and caraway seeds, cover and cook over moderately low heat, stirring, until tender, 30 minutes. Season with salt and pepper and serve. —*Lee Hefter*

Roasted Radicchio

TOTAL: 25 MIN

6 SERVINGS ● ●

In Italy, this side dish is traditionally made with radicchio di Treviso, which has long, bright purplish leaves. If you can find Treviso, buy 2½ pounds and slice in half lengthwise before roasting.

- 3 large heads radicchio (about ¾ pound each), cored and cut into 8 wedges each
- ¼ cup extra-virgin olive oil

Salt and freshly ground pepper

Preheat the oven to 500°. Lay the radicchio wedges on a large rimmed baking sheet and brush with the olive oil. Season with salt and pepper. Roast for 20 minutes, or until crisp on the edges and just tender. Serve. —*Marika Seguso*

Steamed Artichokes with Red Wine Aioli

ACTIVE: 15 MIN; TOTAL: 1 HR 50 MIN

4 SERVINGS ● ●

- 1½ cups dry red wine
- 4 garlic cloves, 3 halved, 1 minced
- ½ cup low-fat mayonnaise
- ½ cup low-fat yogurt
- ¼ teaspoon ground cumin

Pinch of cayenne pepper

Salt and freshly ground pepper

- 4 large artichokes, stems trimmed

1. In a medium saucepan, boil the wine and halved garlic cloves until reduced to ¼ cup, about 8 minutes. Transfer to a medium bowl and mash the garlic with a fork. Let cool to room temperature. Stir in the mayonnaise, yogurt, minced garlic, cumin and cayenne and season with salt and pepper. Cover and refrigerate for at least 1 hour.

2. Meanwhile, put the artichokes in a steamer basket, cover and steam over moderate heat until the bottoms are very tender, about 40 minutes. Remove from the pot and let cool. Transfer the artichokes to a platter and serve with the red wine aioli. —*Colin Alevras*

Sweet-and-Sour Vegetable Caponatina

TOTAL: 1 HR 15 MIN

6 SERVINGS ● ●

- 2 tablespoons pine nuts
- ½ cup white wine vinegar
- 2 tablespoons sugar
- 2 tablespoons extra-virgin olive oil
- 2 medium onions, finely chopped
- 2 celery ribs, finely chopped

Two 1-pound eggplants, cut into ¼-inch dice

- 1 large red bell pepper, cut into ¼-inch dice
- 1 large yellow bell pepper, cut into ¼-inch dice
- 2 medium zucchini, cut into ¼-inch dice
- 2 tomatoes, seeded and chopped

Salt and freshly ground pepper

- 2 tablespoons capers, rinsed and finely chopped
- 8 black olives, such as Gaeta or Calamata, pitted and chopped
- 5 large basil leaves, shredded

1. In a small skillet, toast the pine nuts over moderate heat, shaking the skillet frequently, until golden, about 5 minutes. Transfer to a plate and let cool.

2. In a small saucepan, combine the vinegar and sugar and boil, then cook over high heat until reduced by half, about 6 minutes. Let cool.

3. Heat the olive oil in a large saucepan. Add the onions and celery and cook over moderate heat until slightly softened, about 5 minutes. Stir in the eggplants and cook for 5 minutes. Add the red and yellow bell peppers and cook for 3 minutes, then stir in the zucchini and tomatoes and cook for 3 minutes longer. Gradually stir in the reduced vinegar; season with salt and pepper. Cook, stirring often, until the vegetables are tender, about 10 minutes. Stir in the capers, olives, pine nuts and basil. Season with salt and pepper and serve. —*Sergio Sigala*

WINTER VEGETABLE JALFREZI

ROOT VEGETABLE PAN ROAST

Winter Vegetable Jalfrezi

TOTAL: 1 HR

4 SERVINGS ●

All the ingredients for this traditional Indian vegetable dish can be found at the supermarket. *Jalfrezi,* a sort of stir-fry or sauté, is one of those dishes that lends itself to interpretation; try substituting or adding other vegetables as they come into season. Chiles, cumin, coriander and turmeric give the dish its complexity.

- 6 ounces green beans
- 2 large carrots, cut into 2-by-¼-inch sticks
- 1 red or green bell pepper, cut into ¼-inch strips
- 4 medium red potatoes (10 ounces), peeled
- 2 tablespoons vegetable oil
- 2 garlic cloves, sliced paper-thin
- 1 tablespoon finely julienned fresh ginger
- 1 long, hot green chile, seeded and cut into ¼-inch dice
- 1 teaspoon cumin seeds
- 2 medium scallions, cut into 1-inch lengths
- 1 medium onion, coarsely chopped
- 1 medium tomato, coarsely chopped

Salt

- 1½ teaspoons ground coriander
- ½ teaspoon freshly ground pepper
- ¼ teaspoon ground turmeric

1. In a medium saucepan of boiling salted water, cook the green beans until crisp-tender, about 3 minutes. Using a slotted spoon, transfer the green beans to a colander and rinse under cold water. Drain well. Repeat with the carrots, cooking them until barely tender, about 5 minutes, then drain. Repeat with the bell pepper, cooking it for about 1 minute, then drain. Add the red potatoes to the saucepan and boil until tender when pierced with a fork, about 10 minutes. Drain the potatoes well and then cut them into 1-inch chunks.

2. Heat the oil in a large skillet. Add the garlic, ginger, green chile and cumin seeds and cook over low heat until fragrant, about 3 minutes. Add the scallions and onion and cook until softened, about 5 minutes. Add the tomato, season with salt and cook over moderate heat until the liquid evaporates, about 2 minutes. Add the vegetables, coriander, pepper and turmeric and season with salt. Cook, stirring, until the vegetables are heated through, about 3 minutes. Serve hot. —*Anupam Gulati*

vegetables

Root Vegetable Pan Roast with Chestnuts and Apples

ACTIVE: 25 MIN; TOTAL: 1 HR 10 MIN

6 SERVINGS ● ●

- ½ cup cider vinegar
- ½ cup chicken or vegetable stock or canned low-sodium broth
- 2 tablespoons unsalted butter
- 1 tablespoon pure maple syrup
- 2 large sweet potatoes, peeled and cut into 2-inch chunks
- 2 medium red onions, each cut into 8 wedges through the core
- 1 cup (6 ounces) vacuum-packed whole chestnuts (see Note)
- ¼ cup extra-virgin olive oil
- 1 tablespoon thyme leaves
- Salt and freshly ground pepper
- 2 medium beets, peeled and cut into 2-inch chunks
- 2 large tart apples, such as Granny Smith, cored and cut into eighths

1. Preheat the oven to 400°. In a small saucepan, combine the cider vinegar, chicken stock, butter and maple syrup and bring to a boil. Cook over moderately high heat until reduced by half, about 15 minutes.

2. Meanwhile, in a large shallow roasting pan, toss the sweet potatoes, onions and chestnuts with the olive oil and thyme; season with salt and pepper. Tuck the beets among the other vegetables and roast for 20 minutes. Gently turn the vegetables, add the apples and roast for 20 minutes longer, or until all of the vegetables and the apples are tender and lightly browned. Add the maple sauce and toss all of the ingredients gently. Transfer to a large platter and serve.
—*Alexandra Angle*

NOTE Whole chestnuts, most of which are imported, are available in vacuum-sealed jars or cellophane packages at specialty food stores and some well-stocked supermarkets.

Beet Tartare with Horseradish and Caraway

ACTIVE: 25 MIN; TOTAL: 2 HR 50 MIN

4 SERVINGS ● ●

- 1½ pounds medium beets
- 2 teaspoons caraway seeds
- ⅓ cup minced red onion
- 2 tablespoons extra-virgin olive oil
- 2 tablespoons finely grated fresh horseradish or drained prepared horseradish
- 2 anchovy fillets, finely chopped
- 1 tablespoon sherry vinegar
- 1 tablespoon finely chopped capers
- Salt and freshly ground pepper
- 2 teaspoons minced chives
- 2 teaspoons minced parsley
- ½ teaspoon fresh lemon juice

1. Preheat the oven to 400°. Put the beets in a baking dish, cover with foil and bake for about 1 hour, or until tender. When the beets are cool enough to handle, peel and coarsely grate them.

2. Meanwhile, in a small skillet, toast the caraway seeds over moderate heat for 1 minute. Transfer to a work surface to cool, then finely chop.

3. In a medium bowl, combine the red onion with the olive oil, horseradish, anchovies, vinegar, capers and caraway seeds. Fold in the beets and season with salt and pepper. Cover and refrigerate for 1 hour. Stir in the chives, parsley and lemon juice and serve.
—*Eberhard Müller*

Swiss Chard Gratin with Toasted Bread Crumbs

ACTIVE: 45 MIN; TOTAL: 2 HR

12 SERVINGS ●

- 2 pounds Swiss chard (about 3 bunches), stems and large ribs removed and chopped, leaves cut into 1-inch ribbons
- 1 stick (4 ounces) unsalted butter
- 1 medium onion, finely chopped
- 4 medium garlic cloves, very finely chopped
- ¼ cup plus 2 tablespoons all-purpose flour
- 1 teaspoon freshly grated nutmeg
- 3 cups half-and-half
- 2 tablespoons fresh lemon juice
- Kosher salt and freshly ground pepper
- 6 slices of country bread, ground into coarse crumbs in a food processor (about 3 cups)
- ¼ cup extra-virgin olive oil
- ¼ cup chopped flat-leaf parsley
- 2 teaspoons minced thyme

1. Preheat the oven to 350°. In a large pot of boiling salted water, cook the chard stems and ribs until almost tender, about 8 minutes. Add the chard leaves; cook until just wilted, about 2 minutes. Drain the chard, let cool slightly and squeeze dry. Working in batches, pulse the chard in a food processor until coarsely chopped. Transfer to a bowl.

2. Melt the butter in a medium saucepan. Add the onion and garlic and cook over moderate heat until softened, 6 minutes. Add the flour and nutmeg and cook, stirring, until smooth. Whisk in the half-and-half and bring to a boil, whisking until slightly thickened. Pour over the chard and mix well. Add the lemon juice; season with salt and pepper.

3. Transfer the creamed chard to a deep 8-by-12-inch baking dish and bake in the middle of the oven for 22 minutes, or until hot and bubbling.

4. Meanwhile, spread the bread crumbs on a rimmed baking sheet and toast on the bottom of the oven for 10 minutes, or until golden and crisp. Transfer to a bowl and toss with the olive oil, parsley and thyme. Season with salt and pepper.

5. Sprinkle the toasted bread crumbs over the gratin and serve warm.
—*Elisabeth Prueitt*

MAKE AHEAD The recipe can be prepared through Step 4 early in the day; refrigerate the gratin and leave the bread crumbs at room temperature. Reheat the gratin and top with the crumbs.

vegetables

Sautéed Chard with Pancetta

TOTAL: 40 MIN

4 SERVINGS

Rainbow Swiss chard (also known as Bright Lights) has green leaves, but its stems and ribs range from yellow to red. It's available at some supermarkets. Plain, all-green Swiss chard can be substituted for the more colorful variety.

- ¼ **pound pancetta, sliced ¼ inch thick and cut into ½-inch-wide matchsticks**
- 1½ **pounds red or Rainbow Swiss chard, thick stems trimmed**
- 2 **large garlic cloves, thinly sliced**

Salt and freshly ground pepper

I. In a large skillet, cook the pancetta over moderate heat until crisp. Meanwhile, cut the chard stems from the leaves where the leaf meets the stem. Slice the leaves into 1-inch-wide strips and the stems into ¼-inch pieces. Wash the leaves and stems and lightly dry.

2. Add the garlic to the pancetta in the skillet and cook until golden, about 2 minutes. Increase the heat to moderately high; add the chard in 3 batches, allowing each batch to wilt slightly before adding the next. Reduce the heat to moderate and continue to cook until the liquid is almost evaporated and the stems are tender, about 15 minutes. If the skillet seems dry, add 3 tablespoons of water. Season with salt and pepper and serve. —*Maria Helm Sinskey*

COOKING TIP

milder collards

COLLARD GREENS ARE BITTER when raw. Some cooking methods, such as steaming, only intensify the bitterness. For tender, milder greens, opt for a technique such as sautéing or braising. These stronger cooking methods cook down the collards more, cutting the bitterness.

Swiss Chard and Leek Panade

ACTIVE: 50 MIN; TOTAL: 3 HR

8 SERVINGS ●

A *panade* is a Mediterranean winter soup that is as thick and silky as a bread pudding. Onions, greens and toasted bread (ideally from a stale, good chewy loaf with a soft crust) get layered with milk, stewed leeks and cheese and slowly bake until they meld and the top bubbles and turns golden brown. This recipe works well in a deep earthenware baking dish, a glazed stoneware *poêlon* or a porcelain soufflé dish.

- 1 **pound stale, chewy peasant bread, cut into 1-inch cubes**
- ¼ **cup extra-virgin olive oil**
- 3 **large leeks, white and tender green parts only, coarsely chopped**
- 1 **medium red onion, chopped**
- 8 **large garlic cloves, very thinly sliced**

Kosher salt

- 2 **pounds Swiss chard, tough stems and ribs discarded, leaves cut crosswise into ½-inch strips**
- ½ **pound arugula**
- 1½ **tablespoons fresh lemon juice**

Freshly ground pepper

Freshly grated nutmeg

- 3 **cups whole milk**
- ½ **pound Cantal or Gruyère cheese, shredded**

I. Preheat the oven to 350°. Oil a 9-by-13-inch earthenware baking dish. Spread the bread on 2 large rimmed baking sheets and bake for 15 minutes, or until golden and crisp. Let cool. Reduce the oven temperature to 300°.

2. In a large, heavy pot, heat the olive oil. Add the leeks, onion and garlic and cook over moderate heat, stirring occasionally, until softened, about 10 minutes. Add 1 teaspoon of salt and cook for 5 minutes. Add the chard and arugula, cover and cook over low heat, stirring occasionally, until the vegetables are very tender, about 45 minutes. Uncover and boil away any excess liquid. Let the vegetables cool to room temperature. Stir in the lemon juice and season with pepper and nutmeg.

3. In a medium saucepan, bring the milk to a simmer over moderate heat. Meanwhile, spread one-third of the toasted bread in the prepared baking dish and top with half of the vegetables. Repeat the layering and top with the remaining bread; pat lightly to even the surface. Slowly pour the milk over the bread and scatter the cheese on top.

4. Cover the *panade* with foil and bake for 45 minutes, or until set. Increase the oven temperature to 425°. Uncover and bake the *panade* for 12 minutes longer, or until the top is browned. Let stand for 10 minutes before serving with freshly ground pepper.
—*Paula Wolfert*

MAKE AHEAD The recipe can be prepared through the first baking in Step 4 up to 1 day ahead. Continue with the remainder of the recipe to brown the *panade* before serving.

Spinach with Fried Ginger

ACTIVE: 50 MIN; TOTAL: 1 HR 25 MIN

6 SERVINGS ●

- 3 **pounds spinach leaves, stemmed**

One 4-inch piece of fresh ginger, peeled and coarsely chopped

- 2 **tablespoons chili oil**
- ½ **cup peanut oil**
- 3 **tablespoons soy sauce**
- 1 **tablespoon plain rice vinegar**

Large pinch of sugar

I. In a large pot of boiling water, blanch the spinach for barely 1 minute. Drain the spinach in a colander and rinse it well in cold water. Squeeze dry, coarsely chop and transfer to a large, shallow dish.

2. In a mini food processor, finely chop the ginger and mix with the chili oil. Let stand for 10 minutes.

3. Heat the peanut oil in a medium skillet. Add the ginger and fry over moderate heat until golden, about 4 minutes. Pour through a fine sieve and drain the ginger on paper towels.

4. In a small bowl, whisk the soy sauce with the rice vinegar and the pinch of sugar. Drizzle this dressing over the chopped spinach and stir lightly until thoroughly incorporated. Refrigerate the spinach for 20 minutes. Sprinkle the fried ginger on top and serve chilled. —*Jean-Georges Vongerichten*

MAKE AHEAD The recipe can be prepared through Step 3 up to 1 day ahead. Refrigerate the spinach and keep the ginger covered at room temperature.

Chipotle and Tamarind—Braised Collard Greens

ACTIVE: 45 MIN; TOTAL: 1 HR 30 MIN

12 SERVINGS ● ● ●

- 3 large dried chipotle chiles, stemmed and seeded
- ½ cup extra-virgin olive oil
- 1 medium sweet onion, very thinly sliced
- 4 large garlic cloves, thinly sliced
- 6 cups Rich Turkey Stock (recipe, p. 125) or low-sodium chicken broth
- 6 pounds collard greens, stems and inner ribs discarded, leaves cut into 1-inch ribbons (about 28 cups)

Salt and freshly ground pepper

- 3 tablespoons tamarind concentrate or ¼ cup fresh lime juice

I. Using kitchen shears, cut the chiles into very thin strips. In a stockpot, heat the olive oil until shimmering. Add the onion, garlic and chiles and cook over high heat until the garlic is just beginning to brown, about 7 minutes.

2. Add the stock to the stockpot and bring to a boil. Add the collard greens by large handfuls and stir to wilt each batch before adding more. Season with salt and pepper and bring to a simmer. Cover and cook over moderately low heat until the collard greens are extremely tender, about 40 minutes.

3. Transfer ½ cup of the cooking liquid to a small bowl and stir in the tamarind concentrate, then stir this mixture into the collards. Season with salt and pepper. Transfer the collards and their liquid to a large bowl and serve. —*Grace Parisi*

MAKE AHEAD The greens can be refrigerated overnight.

Vegetable Hobo Packs with Goat Cheese

ACTIVE: 20 MIN; TOTAL: 35 MIN

4 SERVINGS ● ●

- 3 medium leeks (1¼ pounds), white and tender green parts only, halved lengthwise and cut crosswise into ½-inch-thick slices
- 1 pound small zucchini, halved lengthwise and cut into ½-inch-thick slices
- ½ pound thin asparagus, cut into 1½-inch lengths
- 2 tablespoons extra-virgin olive oil
- 1 tablespoon very finely chopped dill

Kosher salt and freshly ground black pepper

- 2 tablespoons soft goat cheese, crumbled (1 ounce)

I. Light a grill. In a large bowl, toss the leeks with the zucchini, asparagus, olive oil and dill. Season with salt and pepper and toss again.

2. Tear off four 14-inch-long sheets of extra-heavy-duty foil. Mound half of the vegetables in the center of each of 2 foil sheets. Cover the vegetables with the 2 remaining sheets of foil; fold up the edges all around to seal.

3. Grill the packs over a very hot fire for about 16 minutes, or until sizzling and puffed. Using oven mitts, transfer the packs to a large platter. Open carefully and transfer the vegetables to the platter. Top with the goat cheese and serve. —*Grace Parisi*

Sliced Tomatoes Tonnato

TOTAL: 20 MIN

6 SERVINGS ● ●

In a recipe title, "tonnato" indicates that the dish is prepared with tuna.

- ¼ cup extra-virgin olive oil
- 2 tablespoons tightly packed flat-leaf parsley leaves

Kosher salt

One 3-ounce can imported tuna packed in olive oil, drained and flaked

- ¼ cup mayonnaise
- 1 tablespoon water
- 1½ teaspoons drained small capers
- 1 teaspoon fresh lemon juice
- 2 anchovy fillets
- 1 garlic clove, smashed

Freshly ground pepper

- 2 pounds large ripe tomatoes, cut into ⅓- to ½-inch-thick slices

Thickly sliced country bread, for serving

I. In a blender, combine 3 tablespoons of the olive oil with the parsley and process until smooth. Season lightly with salt. Transfer 2 tablespoons of the parsley oil to a small bowl. Add the flaked tuna, the mayonnaise, water, capers, lemon juice, anchovies, garlic and the remaining 1 tablespoon of olive oil to the blender and puree until creamy. Season the tonnato sauce with salt and pepper.

2. Spoon some of the tonnato sauce onto 6 plates and arrange the tomato slices on top. Season the tomatoes with salt and pepper. Spoon the remaining sauce on the tomatoes, then drizzle the reserved parsley oil on top. Serve the tomatoes with bread. —*Melissa Clark*

MAKE AHEAD The tonnato sauce can be refrigerated overnight.

ROASTED BUTTERNUT SQUASH AND LENTIL SALAD, P. 254

potatoes, grains + more

BAKED POTATO WITH SHALLOT-CORN BUTTER

WINE-ROASTED FINGERLING POTATOES

Baked Potatoes with Shallot-Corn Butter

TOTAL: 30 MIN

4 SERVINGS ● ●

- 4 large Idaho potatoes, scrubbed
- 1½ cups fresh corn kernels (from about 3 ears)
- 1 stick (4 ounces) unsalted butter, softened
- 2 tablespoons chopped shallots
- 1 teaspoon fresh lime juice
- 2 tablespoons minced chives

Salt and freshly ground pepper

I. Preheat the oven to 400°. Using a fork, poke the potatoes all over. Cook the potatoes in a microwave oven at high power for 10 minutes. Transfer the potatoes to the preheated oven and bake for 15 minutes longer.

2. Meanwhile, in a saucepan of boiling water, cook the corn kernels until just tender, about 3 minutes. Drain; let cool.

3. In a food processor, combine the butter, shallots, lime juice and 1 cup of the corn kernels and puree. Scrape the butter into a bowl, fold in the chives and the remaining ½ cup of corn kernels and season with salt and pepper. Split the baked potatoes, fill with a dollop of the corn butter and serve. —*Marcia Kiesel*

VARIATIONS Use the butter on roasted baby potatoes, pasta or grilled seafood.

All-American Potato Salad

ACTIVE: 20 MIN; TOTAL: 1 HR

4 TO 6 SERVINGS ●

- 2½ pounds medium baking potatoes

Kosher salt

- ⅔ cup mayonnaise
- 1 tablespoon Dijon mustard
- ¼ cup finely chopped onion
- ¼ cup sweet pickle relish
- 2 tablespoons minced dill pickle
- 1 tablespoon minced flat-leaf parsley
- ⅛ teaspoon celery seed

Freshly ground pepper

- ½ cup finely diced celery
- 2 hard-cooked eggs, finely chopped

I. Put the potatoes in a large saucepan, cover with water and bring to a boil. Add a large pinch of salt and simmer until the potatoes are tender, about 35 minutes. Let cool slightly, then peel the potatoes and cut them into 1-inch dice.

2. Meanwhile, in a bowl, combine the mayonnaise, mustard, onion, relish, dill pickle, parsley and celery seed. Season with salt and pepper. Fold in the potatoes, celery and eggs and let cool; refrigerate until chilled and serve cold.

—*Leonard Schwartz and Michael Rosen*

MAKE AHEAD The potato salad can be refrigerated for 2 days.

Warm Potato Salad with Smoked Sausage and Blue Cheese

TOTAL: 35 MIN

4 SERVINGS ● ●

- 1½ pounds small Yukon Gold potatoes, cut into ¼-inch-thick slices
- ¼ cup plus 1 tablespoon extra-virgin olive oil
- Salt and freshly ground pepper
- 2 cooked smoked sausages (about 3 ounces each), such as andouille
- 1½ tablespoons red wine vinegar
- 1 tablespoon minced shallot
- 2 teaspoons Dijon mustard
- 1 small bunch arugula, trimmed
- 1 scallion, white and tender green parts only, thinly sliced
- ¼ pound blue cheese, such as Maytag, crumbled (½ cup)

1. Preheat the oven to 400°. Position a rack in the upper third. On a large rimmed baking sheet, toss the potatoes with 1 tablespoon of the olive oil and season with salt and pepper. Spread the potatoes in a single layer and roast for 12 minutes, turning once, until barely cooked. Add the sausages and roast for about 10 minutes longer, turning them once, until the potatoes are tender and the sausages are lightly browned and heated through. Blot the potatoes and sausages dry with paper towels and cut the sausages into ⅓-inch-thick slices. Transfer to a bowl.

2. Meanwhile, in a small bowl, whisk the vinegar, shallot and mustard. Slowly whisk in the remaining ¼ cup of olive oil and season with salt and pepper. In a medium bowl, toss the arugula with 1 tablespoon of the dressing and a pinch each of salt and pepper. Transfer to a platter. Add the rest of the dressing to the potatoes and sausages, then toss in the scallion. Add the blue cheese and toss quickly. Mound the potato salad over the arugula and serve.
—*Laura Chenel*

Potato, Green Bean and Venison Sausage Salad

ACTIVE: 30 MIN; TOTAL: 1 HR 45 MIN

6 SERVINGS ●

For this salad, try a smoky venison sausage from Broken Arrow Ranch in Ingram, Texas (800-962-4263). A mild andouille or kielbasa sausage would be delicious as well.

- 1 tablespoon pure olive oil
- ½ teaspoon dried thyme
- Kosher salt
- 6 medium plum tomatoes, halved lengthwise
- 3 pounds medium new potatoes, scrubbed
- 1½ tablespoons sherry vinegar
- 1 pound *haricots verts*
- 1 garlic clove, chopped
- ¼ cup mayonnaise
- 2 tablespoons extra-virgin olive oil
- Freshly ground pepper
- ½ pound smoked venison sausage, cut into ⅓-inch-thick slices
- ¼ cup coarsely chopped basil

1. Preheat the oven to 250°. Drizzle the pure olive oil on a rimmed baking sheet and sprinkle with the thyme and a pinch of salt. Arrange the tomatoes, cut side down, on the sheet and roast for 1 hour. Pull off the skins. Turn the tomatoes and roast for 30 minutes longer, until slightly dried. Let cool, then chop.

2. Meanwhile, in a large pot of cold water, bring the potatoes to a boil. Cook over moderately high heat until tender, about 20 minutes. Drain and let cool. Peel the potatoes and quarter them. Transfer the potatoes to a large bowl and toss with 1 tablespoon of vinegar.

3. Bring a saucepan of salted water to a boil. Add the *haricots verts* and boil until tender, about 5 minutes. Drain and rinse under cold water; pat dry.

4. On a work surface, mash the garlic to a paste with a pinch of salt. Transfer the garlic paste to a mini food processor along with the mayonnaise and the remaining ½ tablespoon of vinegar and puree until smooth. Add the extra-virgin olive oil in a thin stream and process until blended. Add the tomatoes and pulse several times, stopping while the dressing is still slightly chunky. Season with salt and pepper.

5. Set a medium skillet over high heat. Add the sausage and cook, turning once, until browned and crisp, about 2 minutes. Using a slotted spoon, transfer the sausage to the potatoes. Add the beans, basil and tomato dressing, season with salt and pepper and toss well. Transfer to a bowl and serve.
—*Paula Disbrowe*

Wine-Roasted Fingerling Potatoes with Onions and Olives

ACTIVE: 30 MIN; TOTAL: 2 HR

8 SERVINGS ●

California chef Michael Tusk cooks these potatoes with spring garlic heads, which have not yet formed a papery skin and are very juicy and delicate. If you can find them, add up to 1 cup of thin slices to the potatoes in place of the garlic cloves in the recipe.

- 4 pounds medium fingerling potatoes, peeled
- 1 medium red onion, thinly sliced
- 1 cup Niçoise olives (6 ounces)
- ½ cup extra-virgin olive oil
- ¼ cup dry white wine
- 4 bay leaves
- 2 large garlic cloves, thinly sliced
- Kosher or sea salt

Preheat the oven to 375°. In a roasting pan, toss the potatoes with the onion, olives, oil, wine, bay leaves and garlic; season with salt. Cover with foil and bake until just tender, 1 hour. Uncover, stir well and bake for 30 minutes longer, or until the potatoes are very tender and glazed. Discard the bay leaves. Season with salt and serve. —*Michael Tusk*
MAKE AHEAD The potatoes can be peeled early and held in cold water.

potatoes, grains + more

Spicy Potatoes and Corn with Fried Cheese

ACTIVE: 15 MIN; TOTAL: 40 MIN

6 SERVINGS

- 3 jalapeños, seeded and coarsely chopped
- 6 medium plum tomatoes, seeded and coarsely chopped
- 2 tablespoons cilantro leaves, chopped
- ¼ cup water
- 1 small white onion, coarsely chopped
- 2 tablespoons chopped mint

Kosher salt

- 2 pounds medium Yukon Gold potatoes
- 6 ears of *choclo* (white Andean corn; see Note) or yellow corn
- 1 cup frozen lima beans
- 2 teaspoons corn oil
- 1 pound *queso blanco para freir* (frying cheese), cut into ¼-inch-thick slices (see Note)

I. In a food processor, coarsely chop the jalapeños with the tomatoes and cilantro leaves. Add the water and pulse until the consistency of a smooth salsa. Transfer to a medium bowl. Stir in the onion and mint and season with salt. Let stand for 30 minutes.

2. Meanwhile, in a large pot of boiling water, cook the potatoes until almost tender, about 10 minutes. Add the corn and cook for 10 minutes longer. Add the lima beans and cook for 5 minutes more. Drain all of the vegetables and set them aside.

3. Heat the oil in a medium nonstick skillet until shimmering. Add the frying cheese in several batches and cook over moderately low heat until golden brown, about 40 seconds per side.

4. Transfer the potatoes to a plate and cut them in half. To serve, arrange 1 ear of corn, 1 halved potato, about ½ cup of lima beans and 2 slices of cheese on each serving plate. Top the potato with about 2 tablespoons of the salsa and serve, passing the remaining salsa at the table. —*Maricel Presilla*

NOTE *Queso blanco* and frozen *choclo* are both available at Latin markets.

SERVE WITH Grilled skirt steak.

Rich and Creamy Potato Gratin

ACTIVE: 45 MIN; TOTAL: 3 HR

12 SERVINGS ●

To save time and effort, use a mandoline or food processor to slice the potatoes.

- 3 cups heavy cream
- 15 garlic cloves, smashed
- 4 large thyme sprigs
- 2 bay leaves
- 1 teaspoon freshly grated nutmeg
- ½ teaspoon black peppercorns

Salt and freshly ground pepper

- 4 pounds baking potatoes, peeled and cut into ⅛-inch-thick slices

I. In a medium saucepan, combine the heavy cream, garlic, thyme, bay leaves, nutmeg and peppercorns and bring to a boil. Remove from the heat, cover and let stand for 1 hour. Strain the cream. Season with salt and pepper.

2. Preheat the oven to 375°. Butter a 3-inch-deep 3-quart oval baking dish. Spread one-fourth of the potatoes in the dish. Season with salt and pepper and drizzle with one-fourth of the cream. Repeat the layering and seasoning twice more. Arrange the last layer in concentric circles. Drizzle with the remaining cream. Press the potatoes down to submerge in the cream. Press a sheet of lightly buttered parchment paper onto the potatoes. Cover the dish with foil.

3. Bake the gratin for 45 minutes, or until the potatoes are barely tender when pierced with a sharp knife. Remove the foil and parchment paper and bake for 40 minutes longer, or until the potatoes are tender, the cream is absorbed and the top is golden brown. Let stand for 10 minutes; serve.
—*Tom Valenti*

MAKE AHEAD The gratin can be made early in the day; reheat in a 325° oven.

Potato and Fennel Gratin

ACTIVE: 25 MIN; TOTAL: 2 HR

4 SERVINGS ●

Use a shallow ceramic baking dish, a *cazuela* (a partially glazed shallow pot from Spain) or an enameled cast-iron gratin dish to make this gratin of thinly sliced potato and fennel. The melted cheese on top of the gratin will develop an ultracrisp crust.

- 4 large red potatoes (1½ pounds), peeled and sliced paper-thin on a mandoline
- 2 medium fennel bulbs—halved, cored and sliced paper-thin on a mandoline
- 2 tablespoons all-purpose flour

Kosher salt and freshly ground pepper

- 2 cups whole milk
- 3 ounces semihard cheese, such as Gruyère, shredded (about 1 cup)

I. Preheat the oven to 375°. Butter a medium *cazuela* or a 7-by-10-inch ceramic baking dish. Rinse the potato slices under cold water and shake dry. Transfer the potato and fennel slices to a large bowl. Sprinkle the flour over the vegetables, season generously with salt and pepper and toss until they are well coated.

2. Arrange the potato and fennel slices in the prepared baking dish in slightly overlapping layers. Pour the milk evenly over the vegetables. Bake the gratin for 1 hour, or until the vegetables are just tender when pierced with a knife.

3. Scatter the cheese over the top and bake the gratin on the top shelf of the oven for 30 minutes longer, or until it is golden brown. Let stand for 10 minutes before serving. —*Paula Wolfert*

MAKE AHEAD The gratin can stand at room temperature for up to 3 hours. Reheat in a 375° oven.

Maple Whipped Sweet Potatoes

ACTIVE: 25 MIN; TOTAL: 1 HR 15 MIN

12 SERVINGS ● ●

- 6 pounds sweet potatoes, peeled and cut into 2-inch chunks
- 6 cups apple cider
- 4 cups water
- 1 stick (4 ounces) unsalted butter
- ⅔ cup pure maple syrup

Salt

1. In a large saucepan, combine the sweet potatoes with the cider and water and bring to a boil. Simmer over moderate heat until the sweet potatoes are just tender, about 35 minutes. Drain in a colander and shake dry.

2. In the same large saucepan, bring the butter and maple syrup to a boil. Add the sweet potato chunks and toss. Working in batches, puree the sweet potatoes in a food processor; do not overprocess. Season with salt.

3. Return the whipped sweet potatoes to the saucepan and heat gently over moderate heat, stirring occasionally, until thoroughly warmed through, about 10 minutes. —*Grace Parisi*

MAKE AHEAD The whipped potatoes can be refrigerated overnight and reheated in a buttered baking dish in a 350° oven for 25 minutes or in a saucepan over moderate heat on the stovetop for about 10 minutes.

Roasted Sweet Potatoes with Caramelized Onions

ACTIVE: 20 MIN; TOTAL: 45 MIN

4 SERVINGS ● ●

- 4 small orange sweet potatoes (6 ounces each)
- 1 tablespoon extra-virgin olive oil
- 1 medium red onion, thinly sliced
- 2 teaspoons balsamic vinegar

Salt and freshly ground pepper

- ¼ cup low-fat plain yogurt
- 2 garlic cloves, minced

1. Preheat the oven to 350°. Put the sweet potatoes on a baking sheet and roast for 40 minutes, or until tender.

2. Meanwhile, heat the olive oil in a medium skillet. Add the red onion, cover and cook over low heat, stirring a few times, until caramelized, about 15 minutes. Remove from the heat and stir in the vinegar; season with salt and pepper.

3. In a small bowl, mix the yogurt with the garlic and season with salt and pepper.

4. Split the sweet potatoes, leaving them attached at the bottoms. Season the insides with salt and pepper. Spoon 1 tablespoon of the garlicky yogurt into each potato, then fill with the caramelized onion. Serve, or gently close the sweet potatoes and wrap them in foil for packing. —*Marcia Kiesel*

MAKE AHEAD The potatoes can be wrapped for up to 4 hours.

Cilantro Rice Salad with Olives

ACTIVE: 15 MIN; TOTAL: 30 MIN

8 SERVINGS ● ●

Salt

- 2 cups basmati rice
- ¼ cup plus 1 tablespoon extra-virgin olive oil
- ¼ cup white wine vinegar

Freshly ground pepper

- 2 tomatoes, cut into ½-inch dice
- 1 medium red onion, minced
- 1 cup chopped cilantro
- ½ cup Calamata olives, pitted and finely chopped

1. Bring a pot of water to a boil and add salt. Stir in the rice and boil over moderately high heat until just tender, about 15 minutes. Drain the rice thoroughly and transfer to a large bowl. Toss the rice with a rubber spatula from time to time to cool it to room temperature.

2. In a small bowl, mix the olive oil and vinegar and season with salt and pepper. Gently fold the tomatoes, onion, cilantro and olives into the rice. Add the vinaigrette and toss well. Season with salt and pepper and serve. —*Marcia Kiesel*

MAKE AHEAD The rice salad can stand at room temperature for up to 1 hour.

Chile-Herb White Rice

ACTIVE: 15 MIN; TOTAL: 1 HR 10 MIN

6 SERVINGS ●

- 1 small onion, coarsely chopped
- 3 garlic cloves, halved
- 3 tablespoons vegetable oil
- 2 cups long-grain rice
- 3 cups water
- 2 teaspoons kosher salt
- 6 flat-leaf parsley sprigs, plus 2 tablespoons chopped parsley
- 1 large jalapeño, 1 half cut into 6 slices, 1 half minced

1. In a mini processor, puree the onion and garlic. In a medium saucepan, heat the oil. Add the puree and cook over moderately high heat, stirring, for 1 minute. Add the rice and cook, stirring, for 1 minute. Add the water and salt, stir well and bring to a boil. Add the parsley sprigs and jalapeño slices, cover and cook over low heat for 25 minutes.

2. Remove the pan from the heat and let stand, covered, for 30 minutes. Uncover the rice and immediately move the lid away so the condensation does not drip into the rice. Discard the parsley sprigs and jalapeño slices and fluff the rice. Transfer the rice to a bowl and garnish with the chopped parsley and minced jalapeño. Serve right away.

—*Patricia Quintana*

potatoes, grains + more

Sardinian Rice Salad

TOTAL: 40 MIN

6 SERVINGS ● ●

You can also try adding shaved carrots or radishes to this salad.

- 2 cups Texmati or basmati rice (14 ounces)

Kosher salt

- ⅓ cup fresh lemon juice
- ¼ cup extra-virgin olive oil
- 8 small scallions, very thinly sliced crosswise
- ⅓ cup cornichons, cut into very thin slices
- ⅓ cup pitted Calamata olives, coarsely chopped
- ¼ cup very finely chopped flat-leaf parsley
- 2 large celery ribs, very thinly sliced crosswise
- 2 tablespoons drained capers
- 1 teaspoon finely grated lemon zest

Two 6-ounce cans imported tuna packed in olive oil, drained and left in chunks

- 2 hard-cooked eggs, cut into thin slices

Freshly ground pepper

1. In a large saucepan, bring 6 cups of water to a boil. Add the Texmati rice and 1 teaspoon of salt and cook over moderately high heat, uncovered, until tender, about 12 minutes. Drain the rice, shaking off the excess water. Let the rice cool slightly.

2. Meanwhile, in a large bowl, whisk the lemon juice with the olive oil. Stir in the scallions, cornichons, olives, parsley, celery, capers and lemon zest. Add the cooked rice, tuna and eggs and toss gently to combine. Season the salad with salt and pepper, transfer to a serving bowl and serve warm or at room temperature. —*Paula Disbrowe*

MAKE AHEAD The rice salad can be kept, covered, at room temperature for up to 4 hours.

Wild Rice and Chickpea Salad with Ham

ACTIVE: 20 MIN; TOTAL: 1 HR

6 SERVINGS ● ●

To turn this into a vegetarian salad, replace the smoked ham with toasted sliced almonds.

- 1½ cups wild rice (10 ounces)

Kosher salt

- 2½ tablespoons fresh lemon juice
- 2 tablespoons red wine vinegar
- 2 tablespoons Dijon mustard
- 1 tablespoon honey
- 1 teaspoon curry powder
- 1 teaspoon ground cumin

Pinch of cayenne pepper

- ¼ cup extra-virgin olive oil

One 19-ounce can chickpeas, drained and rinsed

- ¼ pound smoked ham, cut into ½-inch dice
- 4 small scallions, white and light green parts, thinly sliced
- ¼ cup golden raisins

Freshly ground pepper

Hot sauce

1. Fill a large saucepan three-quarters full of water and bring to a boil. Add the wild rice and 1 tablespoon of salt and simmer over moderate heat until the rice is very tender and most of the grains have just split, 50 minutes. Drain and rinse the rice thoroughly under cold running water, then drain again in a colander and let sit.

2. Meanwhile, in a large bowl, whisk the lemon juice, wine vinegar, mustard, honey, curry powder, cumin and cayenne. Add the olive oil and whisk until combined. Toss in the chickpeas, ham, scallions, raisins and wild rice. Season the wild rice salad with salt, pepper and hot sauce, transfer to a serving bowl and serve. —*Paula Disbrowe*

MAKE AHEAD The salad can be covered and refrigerated overnight. Bring to room temperature and toss the salad thoroughly before serving.

Korean-Style Rice Bowl

TOTAL: 35 MIN

4 SERVINGS ● ●

- 2 tablespoons yellow miso
- 1 tablespoon tomato paste
- 1 teaspoon chili-garlic paste, plus more for serving

Salt

- ¼ pound firm tofu, cut into ½-inch dice
- 1½ tablespoons vegetable oil
- 2 large eggs
- ¼ pound snow peas
- 1 carrot, coarsely shredded
- 1 large scallion, halved lengthwise and cut crosswise into 2-inch lengths
- ½ cup bean sprouts
- 1½ cups sushi rice, or Japanese short-grain white rice
- 2 cups water
- 2 tablespoons toasted sesame seeds

Seasoned or plain nori (Japanese seaweed), cut into 3-inch squares, for serving

1. In a small bowl, combine the miso, tomato paste, chili-garlic paste and a pinch of salt; add the tofu and toss thoroughly to coat.

2. Heat ½ tablespoon of the oil in a 10-inch cast-iron skillet. Crack the eggs into the skillet and cook over high heat until the whites are lightly browned around the edges and the yolks are barely set, 1 to 2 minutes. Transfer the eggs to a plate.

3. Add the remaining 1 tablespoon of oil to the skillet and heat until shimmering. Add the snow peas, shredded carrot and scallion pieces, season with salt and stir-fry over high heat until crisp-tender, 2 to 3 minutes. Add the bean sprouts and cook for 30 seconds. Transfer the vegetables to a bowl, cover and keep warm.

4. Add the rice and water to the skillet along with a generous pinch of salt and

WILD RICE AND CHICKPEA SALAD WITH HAM

KOREAN-STYLE RICE BOWL

bring to a boil. Cover with foil and a tight-fitting lid and simmer over low heat until tender, about 15 minutes. Spoon the tofu and sauce over the rice, cover and cook for 5 minutes longer. Stir in the vegetables and top with the eggs and sesame seeds. Mix everything together and serve with seasoned nori and chili-garlic paste. —*Grace Parisi*

Fried Chicken Rice Bowl with Egg

TOTAL: 1 HR

4 SERVINGS ●

Donburi is a Japanese dish consisting of a bowl of rice topped with various combinations of meat, seafood, eggs and vegetables. This particular meal-in-a-bowl is known as *oyako donburi,* or parent and child rice bowl, because it uses both chicken and eggs.

2½ cups Japanese short-grain white rice

3 cups water

5 tablespoons soy sauce

3 tablespoons mirin

2 tablespoons sake

1½ teaspoons finely grated fresh ginger

1 pound skinless, boneless chicken breasts, cut crosswise into ¼-inch-thick slices

3 tablespoons vegetable oil

½ cup all-purpose flour

1¼ cups low-sodium chicken broth

1 tablespoon unseasoned rice vinegar

1 medium onion, halved lengthwise and cut crosswise into ¼-inch-thick slices

1 small red bell pepper, thinly sliced

4 large eggs, lightly beaten

2 scallions, thinly sliced on the diagonal

Nori strips, for garnish

1. Put the rice in a medium saucepan and rinse under cold running water, rubbing the rice with your fingers until the water runs clear. Transfer the rice to a colander and let drain for 30 minutes.

2. Transfer the rice back to the saucepan, then cover with the 3 cups of water. Cover the saucepan and bring the rice to a simmer over high heat. Reduce the heat to low and cook the rice for 15 minutes. Remove the pan from the heat and let the rice steam with the lid on for 5 minutes, until tender. Stir the rice gently with a fork to separate the grains, then cover the saucepan and keep the rice warm until serving.

3. Meanwhile, place 3 tablespoons of the soy sauce in a medium bowl.

● FAST ● HEALTHY ● MAKE AHEAD ● STAFF FAVORITE

243

CHICKEN BIRYANI

Add 1 tablespoon of the mirin, 1 table-spoon of the sake and the ginger. Add the chicken to the bowl, stir to coat and let marinate for 15 minutes.

4. In a large nonstick skillet, heat the vegetable oil. Coat the chicken slices lightly with the flour and add to the skil-let in a single layer. Stir-fry the chicken over moderately high heat until golden brown, about 4 minutes. Transfer the chicken to a plate and keep warm. Wipe out the skillet.

5. Add the chicken broth, the remain-ing 2 tablespoons of soy sauce, 2 table-spoons of mirin, 1 tablespoon of sake and the rice vinegar to the skillet. Bring the sauce to a simmer over moderately low heat and cook for 5 minutes. Add the onion slices and simmer over mod-erate heat, stirring occasionally, until softened, about 5 minutes. Add the bell pepper and cook until softened, about 3 minutes.

6. Spread the onion and bell pepper slices out in an even layer in the skillet and pour the beaten eggs on top of the vegetables. Spread the cooked chicken over the egg mixture and then top it with half of the scallions. Cook over moderately low heat until the eggs are almost set, 6 to 8 minutes.

7. Spoon the rice into serving bowls and top with the fried chicken and eggs. Garnish the chicken with the remaining scallion slices and the nori strips and serve immediately. —*Jeannie Chen*

Chicken Biryani

ACTIVE: 30 MIN; TOTAL: 1 HR 15 MIN

4 SERVINGS ●

Though some of the fat has been cut from this version of the elaborate rice pilaf called biryani, the saffron-infused milk and the drizzle of melted butter over the top make it a dish fit for Shah Jahan, the creator of the Taj Mahal. The rice is cooked with whole spices, which are not meant to be eaten.

2 tablespoons warm milk
⅛ teaspoon saffron threads, crumbled
3 tablespoons vegetable oil
6 white or green cardamom pods
1 cinnamon stick, broken
1 bay leaf
1 teaspoon whole black peppercorns
2 cups basmati rice (¾ pound)
3 cups water
Salt
2 medium onions, 1 finely chopped, 1 thinly sliced
1 large tomato, coarsely chopped
2 tablespoons Garlic Paste (recipe, p. 101)
2 tablespoons Ginger Paste (recipe, p. 101)
2 teaspoons garam masala (see Note)
½ teaspoon cayenne pepper
½ teaspoon ground turmeric
¼ teaspoon ground cloves
¼ teaspoon ground mace
¼ teaspoon ground cardamom
¼ teaspoon ground cinnamon
1½ pounds skinless, boneless chicken thighs, cut into 1-inch pieces
½ cup coarsely chopped cilantro leaves
Freshly ground pepper
1 tablespoon unsalted butter, melted
2 tablespoons coarsely chopped mint leaves
1 tablespoon finely julienned fresh ginger

1. Preheat the oven to 350°. In a small bowl, combine the warm milk with the saffron threads; let the mixture steep for at least 10 minutes.

2. Heat 1 tablespoon of the oil in a medium saucepan until shimmering. Add the cardamom pods, cinnamon stick, bay leaf and black peppercorns and cook over moderate heat until sizzling, about 3 minutes. Add the rice and stir to coat with the oil, about 1 minute. Add the water and 1 teaspoon of salt and bring to a boil. Cover and cook over low heat until the rice is ten-der and the water has been absorbed, about 12 minutes. Let stand, covered, for 5 minutes, then fluff the rice with a fork. Season with salt.

3. Meanwhile, heat 1 tablespoon of the oil in a large skillet. Add the chopped onion and cook over moderate heat, stirring occasionally, until browned, about 5 minutes. Add the tomato and cook for 1 minute. Add the Garlic Paste, Ginger Paste, garam masala, cayenne, turmeric, cloves, mace, cardamom and ground cinnamon and cook, stirring fre-quently, until fragrant, about 2 minutes. Stir in the chicken, cover and cook over low heat, stirring occasionally, until the chicken is white throughout, about 12 minutes. Stir in the cilantro and sea-son with salt and pepper.

4. Spread half of the rice in a medium enameled cast-iron casserole. Top with the chicken mixture, then cover with the remaining rice. Drizzle the saffron milk evenly over the rice, followed by the melted butter. Cover and bake the biryani for 30 minutes.

5. Meanwhile, heat the remaining 1 tablespoon of vegetable oil in a large skillet until shimmering. Add the sliced onion and cook over moderate heat, stirring once or twice, until nicely browned, about 6 minutes. Using a slot-ted spoon, transfer the onion slices to paper towels to drain. Sprinkle the biryani with the chopped mint, julienned ginger and fried onions. Serve at once. —*Anupam Gulati*

NOTE Garam masala, a blend of as many as 12 spices, is available at Indian markets and specialty food stores.

MAKE AHEAD The chicken can be cooked, covered and refrigerated for up to 2 days. Reheat it gently before assembling the dish.

potatoes, grains + more

Curried Chicken and Jasmine Rice

ACTIVE: 25 MIN; TOTAL: 1 HR

4 SERVINGS

This Asian variation of *arroz con pollo,* or rice with chicken, calls for soft Thai jasmine rice and a fragrant Indian curry paste.

One 3½-pound chicken, cut into
    8 pieces and patted dry
Salt and freshly ground pepper
  2 tablespoons extra-virgin olive oil
  3 medium onions, finely chopped
One 14-ounce box jasmine rice,
    rinsed and drained
  ⅓ cup mild Indian curry paste
3¾ cups low-sodium chicken broth
About 1 tablespoon dark brown sugar
  1 cup plain whole milk yogurt
  ½ cup very coarsely
    chopped cilantro

1. Season the chicken with salt and pepper. Heat the olive oil in a large skillet. Add the chicken and cook over moderately high heat, turning once with tongs, until nicely browned, 10 minutes. Transfer to a plate.

2. Pour off all but 2 tablespoons of the fat from the skillet. Add the onions and cook over moderately low heat, stirring occasionally, until they are tender and golden, about 3 minutes. Add the rice and cook, stirring, for 1 minute. Stir in the curry paste and cook for 1 minute. Add the chicken broth and brown sugar. Nestle the chicken into the rice; bring to a simmer. Cover and cook the chicken over low heat until the breasts are white throughout, about 20 minutes. Transfer the breasts to a platter, cover with foil and keep warm.

3. Continue simmering the curry until the legs and thighs are almost cooked through, about 5 minutes. Remove from the heat and let stand, covered, until the rice is tender and the chicken legs and thighs are cooked through, about 5 minutes longer.

4. In a small bowl, mix the yogurt and cilantro. Add the legs and thighs to the chicken breasts. Season the rice with salt and pepper and add a little more brown sugar if the curry is too sharp. Spoon the rice alongside the chicken and serve, passing the yogurt at the table. —*Sally Schneider*

Garlic Risotto with Calamari and Parmesan Crisps

TOTAL: 2 HR

4 SERVINGS ●

  2 heads garlic, cloves peeled
  ½ cup extra-virgin olive oil
1½ cups heavy cream
Kosher salt and freshly ground
    white pepper
  ¼ cup grapeseed oil
  1 tablespoon fresh lime juice
  1 tablespoon finely chopped
    flat-leaf parsley
  ¾ cup freshly grated Parmesan
    cheese (2½ ounces)
1½ cups arborio rice (10 ounces)
  4 ounces daikon, peeled and cut
    into 3-by-¼-inch matchsticks
  1 pound cleaned baby calamari,
    bodies cut lengthwise into
    ¼-inch strips

1. Bring a medium saucepan of water to a boil. Add all but 1 small garlic clove to the water and blanch for 1 minute; drain. In a small saucepan, simmer the blanched garlic cloves in the olive oil over moderately low heat until the oil is fragrant, 10 minutes. Drain, reserving the garlic cloves and oil separately.

2. Return the garlic to the saucepan. Add the cream and simmer over moderately low heat for 10 minutes. Transfer the garlic and cream to a blender and let cool slightly, then puree until smooth. With the machine on, pour in ¼ cup plus 2 tablespoons of the garlic oil and blend until slightly thickened and frothy. Season the garlic cream with salt and white pepper. Transfer the garlic

cream to a bowl; rinse out the blender.

3. Add the uncooked garlic clove to the blender with the grapeseed oil, lime juice and parsley; blend until smooth. Transfer the parsley vinaigrette to a bowl and season with salt and white pepper.

4. Heat a nonstick skillet over moderate heat. Add 3 tablespoons of the Parmesan in a 4-inch round and cook until golden and bubbling, 3 to 4 minutes. Using a thin spatula, transfer the Parmesan crisp to a rack to cool. Wipe the skillet and repeat with the remaining Parmesan to make 3 more crisps.

5. Bring a large saucepan of salted water to a boil. Add the rice and cook for 9 minutes, stirring occasionally. Drain well and return the barely cooked rice to the saucepan. Add ½ cup of the garlic cream and cook over moderate heat, stirring constantly, until absorbed. Add the remaining garlic cream, ½ cup at a time, cooking and stirring until the rice is al dente and a creamy sauce has formed, about 10 minutes total. If the rice seems very thick, stir in up to ½ cup of very hot water. Season with salt and white pepper and keep warm.

6. In a large, heavy skillet, heat 1 tablespoon of the garlic oil. Add the daikon and cook over high heat until golden and crisp-tender, about 2 minutes. Transfer to a plate. Return the skillet to high heat for 1 minute. Add the remaining 1 tablespoon of garlic oil and heat until nearly smoking. Add the calamari and cook over high heat until tender and browned in spots, about 2 minutes; season with salt and pepper. Mound the risotto on 4 plates; top with the daikon and squid. Drizzle the parsley vinaigrette on top, garnish with the Parmesan crisp and serve. —*Angel Palacios*

MAKE AHEAD The garlic cream can be refrigerated overnight; rewarm before proceeding. The crisps can be kept in an airtight container overnight; recrisp before serving.

GARLIC RISOTTO WITH CALAMARI AND PARMESAN CRISP

CARAMELIZED-ONION RISOTTO WITH BACON

MUSHROOM RISOTTO

Caramelized-Onion Risotto with Bacon

ACTIVE: 35 MIN; TOTAL: 1 HR 15 MIN

4 SERVINGS

When cooks make risotto, they typically sauté onions until translucent before adding raw rice. Here the onions are browned, then stirred into the finished dish to keep their flavor distinct.

- ½ **pound thickly sliced meaty bacon**
- ¼ **cup extra-virgin olive oil**
- 2 **large onions, halved lengthwise and thinly sliced crosswise**
- 2 **quarts chicken stock or low-sodium broth**
- 2 **garlic cloves, minced**
- 2 **cups arborio rice**
- 1 **teaspoon coarsely chopped thyme**
- ½ **cup freshly grated Parmesan cheese, plus more for serving**

Salt and freshly ground pepper

1. In a large skillet, cook the bacon over moderate heat until crisp, about 8 minutes. Transfer to paper towels to drain, then crumble.

2. In a large saucepan, heat 3 tablespoons of the olive oil. Add the onions and cook over moderately high heat until lightly browned, about 4 minutes. Reduce the heat to low and cook, stirring occasionally, until the onions are very soft and browned, about 20 minutes. Transfer the onions to a plate. Rinse out the saucepan.

3. Bring the chicken stock to a boil in a medium saucepan. Cover and keep the stock hot over low heat. Heat the remaining 1 tablespoon of olive oil in the large saucepan. Add the minced garlic and cook over moderate heat until fragrant, about 1 minute. Add the rice and cook, stirring, for 2 minutes. Add enough hot chicken stock to cover the rice, about 1½ cups, and stir constantly over moderate heat until the stock has been absorbed. Continue adding stock, about 1½ cups at a time, and cook, stirring constantly, until the stock has been completely absorbed before adding more. The rice is done when the grains are just tender and the sauce is creamy, about 20 minutes.

4. Remove the pan from the heat and stir in the onions, bacon, thyme and ½ cup of Parmesan. Season the risotto with salt and pepper. Spoon the risotto into shallow bowls and serve, passing additional Parmesan cheese at the table.

—*Joshua Wesson*

MAKE AHEAD The recipe can be prepared through Step 2 up to 4 hours ahead. The bacon and onions can be kept, separately, at room temperature.

Mushroom Risotto

ACTIVE: 40 MIN; TOTAL: 1 HR 20 MIN

4 SERVINGS

The perfectly creamy texture and the intense mushroomy flavor in this dish make it a model risotto, but the crispy fried enoki mushroom topping adds a unique touch.

- ¾ ounce dried porcini mushrooms
- 1 cup hot water
- 3 tablespoons unsalted butter

One 3-ounce package enoki mushrooms

Salt and freshly ground pepper

- 1½ tablespoons extra-virgin olive oil
- ½ pound shiitake mushrooms, stems discarded, caps cut into ¼-inch-thick slices
- 4½ cups chicken stock or low-sodium broth
- 1 small onion, minced
- 1 garlic clove, minced
- 1 teaspoon thyme leaves
- 1 cup arborio rice (7 ounces)
- ¼ cup dry white wine
- 2 tablespoons freshly grated Parmesan cheese, plus more for serving
- 1 tablespoon finely chopped flat-leaf parsley

1. In a heatproof bowl, cover the dried porcini with the hot water and let the mushrooms soak until they are softened, about 20 minutes. Lift the porcini from the soaking liquid, then rinse and coarsely chop them. Slowly pour the porcini soaking liquid into a measuring cup, stopping just before you reach the grit at the bottom.

2. Melt 2 tablespoons of the unsalted butter in a medium skillet. Add the enoki mushrooms in an even layer, season with salt and pepper and cook over moderate heat, without stirring, until the mushrooms are golden brown, about 4 minutes. Stir the enoki and cook until evenly browned and crisp, about 1 minute longer. Using a slotted spoon,

transfer the enoki mushrooms to a paper towel to drain.

3. Add ½ tablespoon of the olive oil to the medium skillet. Add the shiitake mushrooms and season with salt and pepper. Cover and cook the mushrooms over moderate heat until golden, about 4 minutes. Uncover and cook, stirring, until the mushrooms are browned all over, about 2 minutes longer. Cover and set aside.

4. In a medium saucepan, bring the chicken stock and the porcini soaking liquid to a boil. Cover the stock and reduce the heat to low.

5. In a large, heavy saucepan, heat the remaining 1 tablespoon of olive oil. Add the minced onion and garlic and the thyme and cook over moderate heat until the onion is golden, about 4 minutes. Add the rice and cook, stirring, until coated with oil. Add the wine and simmer until almost evaporated, about 1 minute. Add enough hot stock to cover the rice and cook, stirring constantly, until it is absorbed. Continue to add the stock, 1 cup at a time, stirring constantly until it is absorbed between additions. The risotto is done when the rice is just tender and very creamy, about 25 minutes total.

6. Stir in the reserved porcini and shiitake mushrooms, the remaining 1 tablespoon of butter and the 2 tablespoons of Parmesan cheese. Season with salt and pepper.

7. Add the enoki to the shiitake skillet. Cook over high heat, stirring, until hot. Spoon the mushroom risotto into shallow bowls. Top the risotto with the fried enoki mushrooms and chopped parsley and serve with more Parmesan cheese. —*Marcia Kiesel*

MAKE AHEAD The shiitake and enoki mushrooms can be prepared through Step 3 early in the day. Keep separately in lightly covered nonreactive bowls at room temperature.

Risotto with Asparagus and Buffalo Mozzarella

ACTIVE: 45 MIN; TOTAL: 55 MIN

6 SERVINGS ●

- 7 cups light chicken stock or low-sodium broth
- ½ pound thin asparagus
- ¼ cup extra-virgin olive oil, plus more for drizzling
- 1 medium onion, finely diced
- 1 medium leek, white and tender green parts only, finely diced
- 1 teaspoon thyme leaves
- 2 cups arborio rice (11 ounces)
- ½ cup dry white wine
- 4 cups lightly packed baby spinach leaves (3 ounces)

Salt and freshly ground pepper

- 6 ounces buffalo mozzarella, cut into 6 slices, at room temperature

Balsamic vinegar, for drizzling

1. Bring the stock to a simmer in a medium saucepan. Add the asparagus and cook over moderately high heat until barely tender, about 3 minutes. Using a slotted spoon, transfer the asparagus to a plate to cool. Cut the asparagus into 1-inch lengths. Cover the stock and keep at a bare simmer.

2. Heat the ¼ cup of oil in a saucepan. Add the onion, leek and thyme and cook over moderate heat, stirring, until softened, about 6 minutes. Add the rice and cook, stirring, until golden, 1 minute. Add enough hot stock to cover the rice and simmer, stirring constantly, until almost evaporated. Add the wine and enough stock to cover and simmer, stirring, until absorbed. Continue adding more stock and stirring until absorbed. The risotto is done when it is still a little loose and the rice is tender but slightly firm, about 25 minutes total. Stir in the spinach and asparagus. Season with salt and pepper.

3. Spoon the risotto into bowls and top each with the mozzarella. Drizzle with vinegar and oil and serve. —*Fanny Singer*

potatoes, grains + more

Baked Tomato Risotto

ACTIVE: 45 MIN; TOTAL: 2 HR

12 SERVINGS ● ● ●

- 9 cups chicken stock or canned low-sodium broth
- ¼ cup extra-virgin olive oil
- 2 large garlic cloves, minced
- 1 large onion, finely chopped
- 2 large tomatoes—peeled, seeded and finely chopped
- 1 pound arborio rice

Salt and freshly ground pepper

- ¼ cup finely chopped flat-leaf parsley

1. Preheat the oven to 500°. Butter a 9-by-12-inch glass baking dish. In a medium saucepan, bring the stock to a bare simmer; cover and keep warm over low heat.

2. Heat the olive oil in a large saucepan. Add the garlic and onion and cook over moderately low heat until softened, about 6 minutes. Add the tomatoes and cook over moderate heat until softened, about 8 minutes. Stir in the rice. Add about 2 cups of the hot stock, or enough to just cover the rice, and cook, stirring constantly, until the stock has been absorbed. Continue to add the stock, 2 cups at a time, stirring briskly, until the rice is tender and the sauce is creamy, about 30 minutes total. Season with salt and pepper and stir in the parsley. Transfer the rice to the prepared baking dish.

3. Bake the rice for 1 hour, uncovered, until richly browned on top. Serve at once or let stand for up to 20 minutes before serving. —*Ken Oringer*

MAKE AHEAD The baked risotto can be refrigerated overnight. Bring to room temperature before reheating.

Risi e Bisi with Pancetta

ACTIVE: 15 MIN; TOTAL: 50 MIN

6 SERVINGS ●

Risi e bisi (rice and peas) is a famous Venetian dish. The proportions are what make it so unusual—for each grain of rice there should be a pea.

- 2 tablespoons extra-virgin olive oil
- 1 medium onion, finely chopped
- 2 ounces pancetta, coarsely chopped (½ cup)
- ¼ cup coarsely chopped flat-leaf parsley
- 2½ quarts light chicken stock

Two 10-ounce packages frozen peas

- 1 pound arborio or vialone nano rice
- 1 cup freshly grated Parmesan cheese, plus more for serving
- 2 tablespoons unsalted butter

Salt and freshly ground pepper

1. In a medium enameled cast-iron casserole, heat the olive oil until shimmering. Add the onion and cook over low heat until softened, about 7 minutes. Add the pancetta and 2 tablespoons of the parsley and cook for 5 minutes. Add the stock, peas and rice and bring to a simmer over moderately high heat.

2. Cover and cook over moderately low heat until the rice is tender and most of the liquid is absorbed, about 20 minutes. Stir in the 1 cup of Parmesan, the butter and the remaining 2 tablespoons of parsley and season with salt and pepper. Ladle the rice and peas into bowls and serve at once, passing more Parmesan at the table. —*Marika Seguso*

MAKE AHEAD The *risi e bisi* can be refrigerated overnight. Reheat gently, adding more stock as necessary to achieve a stewlike consistency.

Comté Polenta

ACTIVE: 25 MIN; TOTAL: 2 HR 25 MIN

4 SERVINGS ●

Comté is a cooked, pressed French cheese made with unpasteurized cow's milk. And, yes, the French eat polenta, too, not just the Italians; it's a staple of the alpine Savoie region near Italy.

- 3 cups water
- 1 cup fine cornmeal, preferably white (5 ounces)
- 3 ounces Comté or Gruyère cheese, shredded (1 cup)
- 1 tablespoon unsalted butter

Salt and freshly ground pepper

- 3 tablespoons canola oil

1. Grease a 9-inch square baking dish. Bring the water to a boil in a medium saucepan. Slowly add the cornmeal, whisking constantly, and bring to a boil over moderately high heat. Reduce the heat to low and cook, stirring often with a wooden spoon, until the polenta is very thick, about 15 minutes. Stir in the cheese and butter and season with salt and pepper. Scrape the polenta into the prepared dish and smooth the top, using a rubber spatula. Press a piece of plastic wrap directly on the polenta and chill until firm, at least 2 hours.

2. Cut the polenta into 8 rectangles. Heat the oil in a large nonstick skillet. Add the polenta pieces and fry over moderate heat until golden, about 5 minutes per side. Drain the polenta on paper towels and serve at once.

—*Dale Levitski*

MAKE AHEAD The cooked polenta can be refrigerated for up to 2 days before it is fried.

Baked Polenta with Parmesan

TOTAL: 1 HR 40 MIN

6 SERVINGS

True polenta can take up to an hour to make and requires constant stirring. This oven-baked version yields the same rich result but with much less effort.

- 2 quarts water
- Kosher salt
- 2½ cups stone-ground cornmeal
- 6 tablespoons unsalted butter
- ½ cup freshly grated Parmesan cheese, plus more for serving
- Freshly ground pepper

Preheat the oven to 450°. In a medium ovenproof saucepan, bring the water to a boil over high heat. Add 2 teaspoons of salt and reduce to a gentle simmer. Slowly whisk in the cornmeal until smooth and bring to a simmer, whisking constantly, over low heat; cover and transfer to the oven. Bake for 1½ hours, stirring vigorously every 15 minutes, until thick and no longer gritty. Stir in the butter and ½ cup of Parmesan cheese, season with salt and pepper and serve, passing more Parmesan at the table.
—*Marika Seguso*

Polenta Squares with Sautéed Broccoli Rabe and Pancetta

ACTIVE: 45 MIN; TOTAL: 1 HR 30 MIN

6 SERVINGS

- 2 cups chicken stock or canned low-sodium broth
- 2¼ cups water
- Salt
- 1⅓ cups cornmeal (about 7 ounces)
- ¼ cup extra-virgin olive oil
- 6 ounces thickly sliced pancetta, cut into ¼-inch dice (1¼ cups)
- 1 large onion, thinly sliced
- 2 large garlic cloves, thinly sliced
- ½ teaspoon crushed red pepper
- 2 pounds broccoli rabe, chopped
- Freshly ground pepper
- ½ cup freshly grated Pecorino Romano cheese (2 ounces)

1. Preheat the oven to 425°. Lightly oil an 8-by-11½-inch or 9-by-13-inch baking dish. In a medium saucepan, bring the chicken stock and 2 cups of water to a boil. Add 1 teaspoon of salt. Gradually whisk in the cornmeal until smooth. Cook over moderate heat, stirring with a wooden spoon, until thickened, about 10 minutes. Pour the polenta into the baking dish and smooth the top; brush with 1 tablespoon of olive oil. Bake for 1 hour and 15 minutes, until the top and bottom are golden and crusty.

2. Meanwhile, in a large, deep skillet, heat the remaining 3 tablespoons of olive oil until shimmering. Add the pancetta and cook over moderately high heat until golden, 4 to 5 minutes. Add the onion, garlic and crushed red pepper and cook until the onion softens. Add the broccoli rabe and the remaining ¼ cup of water, season with salt and pepper and toss gently. Cover and cook until softened, 5 minutes. Uncover and cook, stirring occasionally, until the water has evaporated and the broccoli rabe is tender, 2 minutes longer.

3. Cut the polenta into 6 pieces and place on serving plates. Stir half of the Pecorino into the broccoli rabe and spoon it over the polenta. Sprinkle with the remaining Pecorino and serve.
—*Michael White*

MAKE AHEAD The unbaked polenta and the cooked broccoli rabe can be refrigerated overnight.

White Polenta with Wild Mushrooms and Robiola Cheese

ACTIVE: 1 HR 10 MIN; TOTAL: 10 HR ●

12 SERVINGS ●

- 4 tablespoons unsalted butter
- 2 tablespoons extra-virgin olive oil
- 2½ pounds assorted mushrooms, such as chanterelles, shiitake, oysters and creminis, stems trimmed, shiitake stemmed and large mushrooms quartered
- Kosher salt and freshly ground pepper
- 6½ cups milk
- 3 garlic cloves, minced
- 1½ cups fine white cornmeal
- 5 ounces aged Robiola cheese, rind removed, cheese cut into ¼-inch-thick slices

1. Butter a 10-by-14-inch baking dish. In a large skillet, melt 1 tablespoon of the butter in the olive oil. Add the mushrooms, season lightly with salt and pepper and cook over moderately high heat until the mushrooms start to exude their liquid, about 3 minutes. Reduce the heat to moderate and continue to cook, stirring occasionally, until the liquid has evaporated and the mushrooms are browned, about 20 minutes. Season with salt and pepper. Transfer half of the mushrooms to the prepared baking dish and the other half to a medium bowl. Cover the mushrooms in the bowl with plastic wrap and refrigerate.

2. In a medium saucepan, combine the milk and garlic with the remaining 3 tablespoons of butter and 2 teaspoons of salt and bring to a boil. Slowly whisk in the cornmeal over moderate heat. Reduce the heat to moderately low and cook, stirring often with a wooden spoon, until thickened, about 15 minutes. Season with salt and pepper. Pour the polenta over the mushrooms in the baking dish and smooth the surface. Place a piece of plastic wrap directly on the polenta and let cool to room temperature. Refrigerate overnight.

3. Preheat the oven to 350°. Bring the polenta to room temperature. Top with the Robiola and bake in the upper third of the oven until the cheese is melted and golden brown, about 45 minutes. Let the polenta rest for 10 minutes.

4. Meanwhile, in a medium skillet, reheat the reserved mushrooms over moderately high heat until sizzling. Spoon the mushrooms on top of the polenta and serve. —*Tom Valenti*

potatoes, grains + more

Quinoa Pilaf with Carrot and Zucchini

ACTIVE: 15 MIN; TOTAL: 30 MIN

4 SERVINGS ● ● ●

- 1 tablespoon extra-virgin olive oil
- 1 medium onion, very finely chopped
- ½ teaspoon ground turmeric
- ½ teaspoon pure chile powder
- 1 carrot, cut into ¼-inch dice
- 1 zucchini, cut into ½-inch dice
- 1 tomato, cut into ½-inch dice

Salt

- 1 cup quinoa, rinsed and drained several times
- ½ cup chicken stock
- 1 bay leaf
- ¼ cup chopped mint
- ¼ cup finely chopped flat-leaf parsley

Freshly ground pepper

Heat the olive oil in a medium saucepan. Add the onion and cook over moderate heat, stirring, until softened, about 2 minutes. Stir in the turmeric and chile powder, then add the carrot, zucchini, tomato and 1 teaspoon of salt and cook, stirring, for 1 minute. Add the quinoa, stock and bay leaf and bring to a simmer. Reduce the heat to low, cover and cook until the quinoa is al dente, about 12 minutes. Discard the bay leaf. Fold in the mint and parsley, season with salt and pepper and serve. —*Jeannie Chen*

MAKE AHEAD The quinoa pilaf can be refrigerated overnight.

Toasted Onion-Barley Pilaf

ACTIVE: 20 MIN; TOTAL: 1 HR 10 MIN

12 SERVINGS ●

- 1 tablespoon unsalted butter
- 2 tablespoons extra-virgin olive oil
- 3 cups pearl barley
- 1 large onion, chopped
- 9½ cups chicken stock or low-sodium broth
- 2 small bay leaves

Salt and freshly ground pepper

1. In a large saucepan, melt the butter in the olive oil. Add the barley and cook over moderate heat, stirring, until evenly toasted, about 12 minutes. Add the onion and cook, stirring, for 2 minutes. Add the stock, bay leaves and 2 teaspoons each of salt and pepper and bring to a boil. Reduce the heat to low and simmer, stirring occasionally, until the barley is tender but still a little chewy and the stock has been absorbed, about 50 minutes.

2. Discard the bay leaves and season the pilaf with salt and pepper. Transfer to a bowl and serve. —*David Waltuck*

Bulgur Salad with Cucumbers, Olives and Feta

TOTAL: 25 MIN

6 SERVINGS ● ●

- 1 cup fine bulgur

Kosher salt

- 1¼ cups very hot tap water
- ¼ cup finely diced red onion
- 3 tablespoons fresh lemon juice
- 2 tablespoons finely chopped oregano
- 1 tablespoon drained small capers, finely chopped
- 1 garlic clove, minced
- ¼ cup extra-virgin olive oil
- 1 medium cucumber—peeled, seeded and cut into ¼-inch dice
- ¼ cup chopped pitted mixed olives
- 3 large romaine lettuce leaves, coarsely chopped

Freshly ground pepper

- 3 ounces feta cheese, crumbled (½ cup)

1. In a medium bowl, toss the bulgur with 1 teaspoon of salt. Stir in the water, cover with plastic wrap and let stand until the water is absorbed and the bulgur is tender, about 20 minutes.

2. Meanwhile, in a large serving bowl, combine the red onion with the lemon juice, oregano, capers and garlic and let stand for 5 minutes. Whisk in the olive oil and then add the cucumber and olives. Fluff the bulgur with a fork and add it to the dressing. Add the lettuce, season with salt and pepper and toss well. Top the bulgur salad with the crumbled feta and serve right away.
—*Melissa Clark*

Tangy Tabbouleh Salad

ACTIVE: 25 MIN; TOTAL: 45 MIN

6 SERVINGS ● ●

In this contemporary version of the Middle Eastern salad, there are plenty of greens and lots of lemon juice to make it tangy.

- 1 cup medium bulgur (6 ounces), rinsed

Hot water

- ¼ cup fresh lemon juice
- ¼ cup extra-virgin olive oil
- 1 pound plum tomatoes—halved, seeded and coarsely chopped (2 cups)
- 4 scallions, white and tender green parts only, cut crosswise into thin slices (½ cup)
- ⅓ cup finely chopped flat-leaf parsley, plus ⅓ cup whole leaves
- ⅓ cup finely chopped mint

Salt and freshly ground pepper

1. In a large bowl, cover the bulgur with 2 inches of hot water and let soak for 20 minutes. Drain the bulgur in a fine sieve, pressing hard to release any excess water. Wipe out the bowl with a paper towel.

2. In the large bowl, whisk the lemon juice with the olive oil. Add the bulgur, chopped tomatoes, sliced scallions, chopped parsley and whole parsley leaves and mint. Season the salad generously with salt and pepper and toss to thoroughly combine. Let the tabbouleh stand for 10 minutes before serving. —*Grace Parisi*

MAKE AHEAD The tabbouleh can be made about 8 hours before serving. Keep covered at room temperature.

Provençal Wheat Berry Salad with Smoked Turkey

ACTIVE: 20 MIN; TOTAL: 1 HR 10 MIN

6 SERVINGS ● ●

- 2 cups (14 ounces) hard red wheat berries (see Note)
- ⅔ cup low-fat plain yogurt
- ¼ cup Champagne or white wine vinegar
- 2 tablespoons Dijon mustard
- 2 garlic cloves, minced
- 1 serrano chile, seeded and minced
- ¼ cup extra-virgin olive oil

Kosher salt and freshly ground pepper

- 6 ounces smoked turkey, cut into matchsticks
- 1 pint grape or cherry tomatoes, halved
- ⅓ cup oil-cured olives, pitted and coarsely chopped
- ¼ cup coarsely chopped basil
- 2 tablespoons finely chopped mint

1. In a large saucepan, cover the wheat berries with 3 inches of cold water and bring to a boil. Simmer over moderate heat until tender, 1 hour. Drain and rinse under cold water. Drain and let cool.

2. Meanwhile, line a small strainer with a coffee filter or a moistened paper towel. Spoon the yogurt into the filter and let drain for 15 minutes. Discard the liquid. Transfer the yogurt to a bowl; whisk in the vinegar, mustard, garlic and chile. Whisk in the oil and season with salt and pepper. Add the turkey, tomatoes, olives, basil, mint and wheat berries and toss. Season the salad with salt and pepper and serve. —*Paula Disbrowe*

NOTE Hard red wheat berries are whole, unprocessed, reddish brown kernels of wheat that have been husked. Wheat referred to as hard is high-protein and grown in colder climates. Look for the berries at health food stores and in the organic section of the supermarket.

MAKE AHEAD The salad can be refrigerated overnight. Bring to room temperature before serving.

TANGY TABBOULEH SALAD

PROVENÇAL WHEAT BERRY SALAD

potatoes, grains + more

Lentil Salad with Roast Beets and Carrots

ACTIVE: 25 MIN; TOTAL: 2 HR

8 SERVINGS ● ●

- 2½ pounds large beets
- 2 pounds baby carrots, peeled
- 2 teaspoons sugar
- ½ cup plus 2 tablespoons extra-virgin olive oil

Salt and freshly ground pepper

- 1 pound black or French green lentils (see Note)
- 6 cups water
- 1 medium onion, halved
- 2 teaspoons ground coriander
- 1 bay leaf
- 4 garlic cloves, 2 minced
- 3 tablespoons minced preserved lemon peel (see Note)

Finely grated zest of 1 lemon

Juice of 1 lemon

- ½ cup chopped mint leaves
- 1 large shallot, minced
- 1 tablespoon balsamic vinegar
- 2 tablespoons coarsely chopped cilantro leaves
- 3 scallions, thinly sliced

I. Preheat the oven to 400°. Wrap each beet individually in aluminum foil, place directly on an oven rack and bake for 1½ hours, or until tender. Let the beets cool, then peel them and cut them into ½-inch wedges.

2. Meanwhile, in a large baking dish, toss the baby carrots with the sugar and 2 tablespoons of the olive oil. Season with salt and pepper. Roast the carrots for about 45 minutes, tossing occasionally, until they are quite tender and browned in spots.

3. Meanwhile, in a large saucepan, combine the black lentils with the water, onion, coriander, bay leaf and 2 whole garlic cloves and bring to a boil over moderately high heat. Reduce the heat to moderate and cook until the lentils are barely tender, about 20 minutes. Add 2 teaspoons of salt and cook until the lentils are tender, about 5 minutes longer. Drain in a colander; discard the onion, garlic cloves and bay leaf.

4. Transfer the lentils to a large bowl. Stir in the minced garlic, preserved lemon peel, lemon zest, lemon juice, mint, shallot and the remaining ½ cup of olive oil. Season with salt and pepper.

5. In another large bowl, toss the beets and carrots with the balsamic vinegar and arrange on the lentils. Sprinkle the chopped cilantro and sliced scallions on top and serve the salad warm or at room temperature. —*Gail Monaghan*

NOTE Black lentils are available at Indian and Middle Eastern markets. Jarred preserved lemons are available at specialty shops and Middle Eastern markets.

MAKE AHEAD The lentil salad can be kept at room temperature for up to 4 hours.

Roasted Butternut Squash and Lentil Salad

ACTIVE: 35 MIN; TOTAL: 1 HR 15 MIN

4 SERVINGS ●

- 1½ teaspoons cumin seeds
- 1 butternut squash (about 2¼ pounds), peeled and cut into ½-inch dice
- 1 parsnip—peeled, halved lengthwise and cut into ¼-inch-thick slices
- 2 medium onions, coarsely chopped
- 1½ teaspoons ground cardamom
- 1 teaspoon grated fresh ginger

Pinch of freshly grated nutmeg

- ¼ cup extra-virgin olive oil

Salt and freshly ground pepper

- ¼ cup green lentils
- 1 cup water
- 1 small shallot, peeled
- 1 bay leaf
- ¾ cup walnuts (about ¼ pound)
- ½ cup coarsely chopped cilantro leaves
- 2 tablespoons fresh lemon juice

I. Preheat the oven to 425°. In a small skillet, toast the cumin seeds over moderate heat until fragrant, about 2 minutes. Transfer to a spice grinder and let cool, then finely grind. On a large rimmed baking sheet, toss the butternut squash with the parsnip, onions, ground cumin, cardamom, ginger, nutmeg and 2 tablespoons of the olive oil. Season with salt and pepper. Roast for about 35 minutes, stirring once, or until the squash and parsnip are tender and lightly browned. Leave the oven on.

2. Meanwhile, in a small saucepan, combine the lentils with the water, shallot and bay leaf and bring to a boil. Reduce the heat to low and simmer until tender, about 25 minutes. Drain off any liquid; discard the bay leaf and shallot and season the lentils with salt and pepper.

3. In a pie plate, toast the walnuts in the oven for 5 to 7 minutes, or until fragrant. Let cool, then coarsely chop. In a small bowl, mix the cilantro with the lemon juice and the remaining 2 tablespoons of olive oil. Season with salt and pepper.

4. In a large bowl, toss the roasted vegetables with the lentils, walnuts and dressing and serve. —*Jeannie Chen*

COOKING TIP

lentil know-how

BEFORE COOKING LENTILS, always sort through them carefully to remove any tiny stones, debris and damaged ones. Then place them in a sieve and rinse thoroughly with cold water. Unlike beans, lentils do not need to soak before cooking. To cook, combine 1 part lentils to 3 parts water and bring to a simmer. Cook the lentils until tender, about 45 minutes to an hour. Don't add salt until the end, as it will toughen the lentils.

Chickpea Stew with Spinach and Potatoes

ACTIVE: 1 HR; TOTAL: 11 HR

8 SERVINGS ● ●

- ¾ pound dried chickpeas (2¼ cups)—rinsed, soaked overnight and drained
- 4 garlic cloves, 1 minced
- 2 large thyme sprigs
- 1 bay leaf

Kosher salt

- 2 tablespoons extra-virgin olive oil
- 1 medium onion, coarsely chopped
- 2 ounces lean bacon, finely diced
- 2 medium Yukon Gold potatoes (¾ pound), peeled and cut into ½-inch dice
- 2 cups chicken stock

Pinch of crushed red pepper

Pinch of saffron, crumbled

Freshly ground black pepper

- 1 pound spinach, stemmed, leaves coarsely chopped

1. In a large saucepan, combine the chickpeas with the 3 whole garlic cloves, the thyme and the bay leaf. Cover with 4 inches of water and bring to a boil. Simmer over moderate heat until just tender, 1¾ to 2 hours; add more water as needed to keep the chickpeas submerged. Season with salt and simmer 10 minutes longer. Drain the chickpeas, reserving 1 cup of the cooking liquid. Discard the garlic, thyme and bay leaf. **2.** Heat the oil in a heavy casserole. Add the onion, bacon and minced garlic; cook over moderate heat, stirring, until the onion is softened, 5 minutes. Add the potatoes and cook, stirring, until crisp-tender, about 8 minutes. Add the stock, reserved cooking liquid, chickpeas, crushed red pepper, saffron and black pepper and bring to a boil. Simmer over moderate heat until the potatoes are tender, 10 to 15 minutes. Add the spinach and cook for 5 minutes. Season with salt and pepper. Ladle the soup into bowls and serve. —*Grace Parisi*

Couscous Salad with Plums and Smoked Duck

TOTAL: 30 MIN

6 SERVINGS ● ○

- One 10-ounce box instant couscous (about 1⅔ cups)

Kosher salt

- 1⅔ cups very hot tap water
- ¼ cup plus 2 tablespoons fresh lemon juice
- 2½ teaspoons ground cumin
- 1½ teaspoons minced garlic
- 1½ teaspoons finely grated lemon zest
- ½ cup plus 2 tablespoons extra-virgin olive oil

Freshly ground pepper

- 1 tablespoon finely chopped rosemary
- 3 ripe purple or red plums, cut into ½-inch dice
- ¼ pound mesclun (6 cups)
- 1 large smoked duck breast half (14 ounces), skinned and thinly sliced crosswise (see Note)

1. In a large bowl, toss the couscous with 1 teaspoon of salt. Stir in the water, cover with foil and let stand until the water is absorbed, about 15 minutes. **2.** Meanwhile, in a small bowl, whisk the lemon juice with the cumin, garlic and lemon zest. Gradually whisk in the olive oil and season with salt and pepper. **3.** Fluff the couscous with a fork. Add three-fourths of the dressing and the rosemary and let stand for 5 minutes. Stir in the plums. **4.** In a large bowl, toss the mesclun with 2 tablespoons of the dressing. Transfer to a large platter. Mound the couscous on the mesclun and top with the sliced duck. Drizzle with the remaining dressing and serve right away. —*Melissa Clark*

NOTE Smoked duck is available at specialty food stores and some well-stocked supermarkets, or by mail order from D'Artagnan (800-327-8246 or www.dartagnan.com).

White Bean and Squid Salad with Marjoram

ACTIVE: 30 MIN; TOTAL: 9 HR 30 MIN

6 SERVINGS ●

- 2 cups dried cannellini beans, soaked overnight and drained
- 4 whole cloves
- 1 small onion
- 2 garlic cloves, lightly smashed
- 2 bay leaves

Kosher salt

- ¼ cup fresh lemon juice
- 1 teaspoon finely grated lemon zest
- ¼ cup plus 1 tablespoon extra-virgin olive oil
- ½ small red onion, thinly sliced
- 2 tablespoons minced marjoram

Freshly ground pepper

- 1½ pounds cleaned small squid
- ½ teaspoon crushed red pepper

1. In a large saucepan, cover the beans with 4 inches of cold water. Stick the cloves into the onion and add it to the saucepan, along with the garlic and bay leaves, and bring to a boil. Reduce the heat to moderate and cook until the beans are tender, about 45 minutes. Add 1 tablespoon of salt and simmer for 5 minutes longer. Let the beans cool in the liquid for 30 minutes, then drain. Discard the onion, bay leaves and garlic. **2.** In a large bowl, whisk the lemon juice and lemon zest with ¼ cup of the olive oil. Add the beans, red onion and marjoram and season with salt and pepper. **3.** Meanwhile, light a grill. In a bowl, toss the squid with the remaining 1 tablespoon of olive oil and the crushed red pepper. Grill the squid over high heat until charred, about 3 minutes. Transfer the squid to a work surface. Cut the bodies into ½-inch rings and the tentacles in half. Add the squid to the beans, toss and serve. —*Paula Disbrowe*

MAKE AHEAD The recipe can be prepared through Step 2 and refrigerated overnight. Bring to room temperature before adding the squid.

potatoes, grains + more

Sweet-and-Smoky Beans

TOTAL: 25 MIN

6 SERVINGS ● ● ●

¼ pound thick-cut bacon

1 small onion, minced

1 large garlic clove, very finely chopped

2 tablespoons cider vinegar

¾ cup smoky barbecue sauce

¼ cup water

2 tablespoons brown sugar

1½ teaspoons Dijon mustard

1 teaspoon hot sauce

Two 15-ounce cans small white, pink, cranberry or pinto beans, drained and rinsed

I. In a large, deep skillet, cook the bacon over moderately high heat until crisp, 5 to 6 minutes. Transfer to a plate. Pour off all but 1 tablespoon of the bacon fat.

2. Add the onion and garlic to the skillet and cook over moderate heat, stirring occasionally, until softened, about 5 minutes. Add the vinegar and cook until nearly evaporated. Crumble the bacon into the skillet and stir to combine. Stir in the barbecue sauce, water, sugar, mustard and hot sauce and bring to a boil. Stir in the beans and cook over moderate heat until the sauce is thickened, about 10 minutes. Transfer the beans to a bowl and serve at once.

—Grace Parisi

Cranberry Bean and Pumpkin Stew with Grated Corn

ACTIVE: 45 MIN; TOTAL: 10 HR

6 TO 8 MAIN-COURSE SERVINGS ● ●

This hearty recipe is a cross between a soup and a stew. The grated fresh corn that's added at the end gives the dish body and a wonderfully fresh flavor. The beans need to soak overnight, so plan accordingly.

1 pound dried cranberry or pinto beans, soaked overnight and drained

2 tablespoons vegetable oil

½ pound smoky bacon, sliced ¼ inch thick and cut into ¼-inch dice

4 large garlic cloves, minced

1 large white onion, cut into ½-inch dice

1 green bell pepper, cut into ½-inch dice

1 *ají cristal* chile (see Note) or jalapeño, seeded and minced

2 teaspoons ground cumin

1 teaspoon dried oregano, crumbled

1 teaspoon sweet paprika

Kosher salt and freshly ground pepper

4 plum tomatoes, coarsely chopped

6 cups chicken stock or low-sodium broth

½ pound peeled and seeded pumpkin or butternut squash, cut into 1-inch chunks

6 ears of fresh corn, shucked

2 tablespoons coarsely chopped basil

I. In a large saucepan, add the beans and enough cold water to cover and bring to a boil. Reduce the heat to moderate and simmer until the beans are just tender, about 45 minutes. Drain the beans.

2. In a large cast-iron casserole, heat the oil until shimmering. Add the bacon and cook over moderate heat, stirring occasionally with a wooden spoon, until golden, about 5 minutes. Add the garlic and cook until fragrant, about 1 minute. Stir in the onion, bell pepper, chile, cumin, oregano, paprika, 1 tablespoon of salt and 1 teaspoon of pepper. Cook, stirring, until the vegetables soften, about 5 minutes. Add the tomatoes and cook, stirring, until the tomatoes begin to break down, about 2 minutes.

3. Add the beans and chicken stock to the vegetables and bring to a boil over high heat. Cover partially and cook over moderate heat for 45 minutes, stirring occasionally. Add the pumpkin and cook until tender, about 15 minutes.

4. Meanwhile, grate the corn on the large holes of a box grater set in a shallow bowl; you should have about 1¼ cups. Add the corn and its juices to the stew along with the basil and simmer over moderate heat until thickened, about 10 minutes longer. Season with salt and pepper and serve.

—Maricel Presilla

NOTE The *ají cristal* chile is a medium-hot yellow pepper native to Chile.

MAKE AHEAD The stew can be refrigerated for up to 4 days.

Homey Borlotti Bean Stew

ACTIVE: 30 MIN; TOTAL: 10 HR 45 MIN

6 SERVINGS ● ●

The traditional beans for this stew are *fagioli di Lamon,* a dried cranberry type from Lamon, a town in Veneto, Italy. Dried borlotti, or cranberry, beans make a fine substitute.

2 tablespoons extra-virgin olive oil

1 medium onion, coarsely chopped

1 celery rib, coarsely chopped

1 carrot, coarsely chopped

1 pound dried borlotti, or cranberry, beans, soaked in water overnight and drained

¼ pound prosciutto, in 1 piece

1 cup dry red wine

½ cup chopped flat-leaf parsley

1 quart vegetable stock or water

Salt and freshly ground pepper

I. In a large saucepan, heat the olive oil. Add the onion, celery and carrot and cook over moderately low heat, stirring occasionally, until lightly browned, about 20 minutes. Add the beans and prosciutto and cook until sizzling, about 4 minutes. Add the red wine and simmer over moderately high heat until almost evaporated, about 10 minutes.

2. Add the parsley and stock to the beans and bring to a boil. Cover partially and simmer over low heat, stirring occasionally, until the beans are almost tender, about 1½ hours.

3. Uncover the saucepan and simmer the stew over moderate heat until thick, about 30 minutes longer. Discard the prosciutto, season with salt and pepper and serve. —*Marika Seguso*

MAKE AHEAD The bean stew can be refrigerated for up to 3 days.

Orinoco Red Beans and Rice

ACTIVE: 55 MIN; TOTAL: 1 HR 10 MIN

6 TO 8 SERVINGS ●

This is a great all-purpose side dish for meat, poultry or seafood stews. The fresh, mild, lantern-shaped *ají dulce* chile peppers used here are widely available at Latin markets, where they are often labeled *ají cachucha*. (Italian frying peppers can be substituted.)

- 1 tablespoon extra-virgin olive oil
- ¼ pound bacon, finely chopped
- 8 medium garlic cloves, very finely chopped
- 1 small onion, finely chopped
- 1 small red bell pepper, finely chopped
- 12 *ají dulce* chile peppers or 3 Italian frying peppers, seeded and finely chopped
- 4 scallions, white and light green parts, finely chopped
- 1 medium leek, white and light green parts, finely chopped
- 1 celery rib with leaves, finely chopped
- 1 tablespoon chopped cilantro, plus 3 cilantro sprigs
- 1 tablespoon chopped flat-leaf parsley
- One 15½-ounce can red kidney beans, drained and rinsed
- 2 cups long-grain rice, rinsed well and drained
- 4 cups water

Kosher salt

I. In a very large, deep skillet, heat the olive oil. Add the chopped bacon and cook over moderate heat, stirring, until golden brown. Add the garlic and cook, stirring, until golden. Add the onion, bell pepper, chile peppers, scallions, leek, celery, chopped cilantro and parsley and cook, stirring frequently, until the vegetables soften. Add the beans and cook, stirring gently, for 2 minutes. Add the rice, water, cilantro sprigs and 2 teaspoons of salt and bring to a boil. Reduce the heat to moderately low and simmer until the liquid is almost completely absorbed, about 6 minutes.

2. Fluff the rice with a fork. Reduce the heat to very low, cover and cook until the rice is firm-tender, about 25 minutes. Fluff the rice, season with salt and serve. —*Maricel Presilla*

Cuban Home-Style Red Beans with Pork

ACTIVE: 25 MIN; TOTAL: 2 HR 20 MIN

8 SERVINGS ● ●

- 7 cups cold water
- 3 medium carrots, cut into 1-inch chunks
- 3 bay leaves
- 3 medium onions, coarsely chopped (1½ cups)
- 1 pound dried red kidney beans, picked over and rinsed
- ¼ cup canola oil
- 2 pounds meaty spareribs or pork chops, or a combination, trimmed of all visible fat, spareribs cut into individual ribs

Salt and freshly ground pepper

One 8-ounce can tomato sauce (1 cup)

- ½ cup coarsely chopped cilantro leaves
- 1 tablespoon fresh lemon juice
- 1 tablespoon minced garlic
- ½ teaspoon minced rosemary

Hot sauce, for serving

I. In a large enameled cast-iron casserole, combine the water, carrots, bay leaves, half of the chopped onions and the beans and bring to a boil over high heat. Reduce the heat to low. Cover the casserole and simmer the beans gently until they are just tender, about 1 hour and 15 minutes.

2. Meanwhile, heat the oil in a large skillet. Add the spareribs and/or pork chops, season generously with salt and pepper and cook over moderate heat, turning once, until well browned, about 5 minutes per side. Add the remaining ¾ cup of chopped onions to the skillet and cook, stirring occasionally, until the onions are softened, about 5 minutes. Add the tomato sauce, cilantro, lemon juice, garlic and rosemary to the skillet and stir with a wooden spoon, scraping up any browned bits from the bottom of the pan.

3. When the beans are tender, add the spareribs and their sauce to the casserole and stir gently to mix well. Bring to a boil over moderately high heat. Reduce the heat to low, cover and simmer until the meat is tender, about 50 minutes.

4. Discard the bay leaves. Using a large fork or tongs, remove the meat from the casserole and discard all of the bones. Return the meat to the casserole and stir it into the beans. Season generously with salt and pepper. Serve in shallow bowls, with hot sauce for sprinkling. —*Gloria Pépin*

MAKE AHEAD The cooked beans with pork can be refrigerated for up to 3 days. Reheat gently.

SERVE WITH White rice.

LATIN BEAN STEW WITH BACON AND ONIONS

Latin Bean Stew with Bacon and Onions

ACTIVE: 30 MIN; TOTAL: 1 HR 10 MIN

4 SERVINGS ●

This bean stew can be served Mexican-style with warm tortillas, cilantro and sour cream, or Mediterranean-style with garlicky toasts brushed with olive oil.

- ½ pound thickly sliced bacon, cut into ½-inch matchsticks
- 3 medium onions, thinly sliced

Salt

- Three 15½-ounce cans Roman or small red beans, rinsed and drained
- 1½ cups low-sodium chicken broth
- 1 tablespoon balsamic vinegar
- 2 bay leaves
- 1 teaspoon sugar

Freshly ground pepper

Warm tortillas, chopped cilantro, sour cream and lime wedges, for serving

1. Put the bacon in a large nonstick skillet, cover and cook over moderate heat until crisp, about 7 minutes. Using a slotted spoon, transfer the bacon to paper towels to drain. Pour off all but 2 teaspoons of the fat from the skillet.

2. Add the sliced onions to the skillet, cover and cook over moderate heat until the onions soften and release their liquid, about 5 minutes. Add ½ teaspoon of salt and cook, uncovered, stirring frequently, until the onions are golden brown, about 20 minutes. Transfer half of the caramelized onions to a bowl and reserve at room temperature.

3. Add the bacon, beans, chicken broth, balsamic vinegar, bay leaves and sugar to the onions in the skillet and bring to a simmer over moderate heat. Reduce the heat to low and cook, stirring frequently, until thick and stewlike, about 20 minutes. Discard the bay leaves and season with salt and a generous amount of pepper. Spoon the beans into shallow soup bowls, top with the reserved caramelized onions and serve with warm tortillas, lime wedges, chopped cilantro and sour cream.
—*Sally Schneider*

MAKE AHEAD The bean stew can be refrigerated in an airtight container for up to 2 days. Reheat gently.

Black Bean and Hominy Stew

TOTAL: 25 MIN

4 TO 6 SERVINGS ● ●

- 2 tablespoons extra-virgin olive oil
- 1 green bell pepper, coarsely chopped
- 1 medium onion, coarsely chopped
- 1 large garlic clove, minced
- ½ pound smoked ham, sliced ½ inch thick and cut into ½-inch dice
- ½ teaspoon ground cumin
- ½ teaspoon coriander
- 1 canned chipotle chile in adobo, minced (about 1 teaspoon)
- Two 15-ounce cans black beans, drained
- One 15-ounce can hominy, drained
- 1½ cups chicken stock or canned low-sodium broth
- ¼ cup finely chopped cilantro

Salt and freshly ground pepper

- ½ cup shredded Cheddar cheese

1. In a large saucepan, heat the olive oil until shimmering. Add the bell pepper, onion and garlic and cook over moderately high heat until the vegetables are just beginning to brown, about 4 minutes. Add the ham, cumin, coriander and chipotle and cook until the ham is lightly browned, about 3 minutes longer. Add the black beans, hominy and stock and bring to a boil. Simmer the stew over moderate heat until slightly thickened, about 10 minutes.

2. Add the cilantro and season the stew with salt and pepper. Spoon the stew into deep bowls, sprinkle with the Cheddar and serve. —*Grace Parisi*

MAKE AHEAD The stew can be refrigerated overnight.

Simple Black Beans

TOTAL: 9 HR 40 MIN

6 SERVINGS ● ●

- 1 pound dried black beans, rinsed and soaked overnight
- 1 medium red onion, quartered
- ¼ pound fresh pork fat, unrendered bacon fat or fatty bacon

Salt and freshly ground pepper

1. Drain the black beans and put them in a large saucepan. Add the red onion and pork fat, cover with 2 inches of water and bring to a boil. Simmer the black beans over low heat, stirring occasionally, until the beans are tender, about 1½ hours.

2. Set a colander over a large heatproof bowl and drain the black beans. Discard the onion and pork. Return the black beans to the saucepan and add about half of the cooking liquid to moisten them. Season the beans with salt and pepper and serve. —*Fanny Singer*

MAKE AHEAD The beans can be refrigerated for 2 days.

Fava Bean Salad

TOTAL: 45 MIN

4 SERVINGS ●

- 2 pounds fresh fava beans, shelled
- 1 tablespoon plus 1 teaspoon extra-virgin olive oil
- 1 tablespoon fresh lemon juice
- 1 garlic clove, minced

Pinch of crushed red pepper

Salt and freshly ground black pepper

- 4 tender escarole leaves, chopped
- 8 small mint leaves
- ¼ cup grated Pecorino Romano

1. In a medium saucepan of boiling water, blanch the fava beans until barely tender, about 2 minutes. Drain and let cool slightly, then peel the beans.

2. In a bowl, combine the oil, lemon juice, garlic and red pepper; season with salt and black pepper. Add the favas, escarole and mint; toss. Sprinkle with the Pecorino, toss and serve. —*Jody Williams*

ITALIAN TUNA SALAD SANDWICH WITH BLACK-OLIVE DRESSING, P. 273

breads, pizzas + sandwiches

CARROT-WALNUT BREAD

CYPRIOT OLIVE BREAD

Carrot-Walnut Bread

ACTIVE: 15 MIN; TOTAL: 1 HR 30 MIN
MAKES ONE 9-BY-5-INCH LOAF;
8 SERVINGS ● ●

Vegetable oil cooking spray
  3 medium carrots (7 ounces),
     thickly sliced
  ½ cup walnut halves
1½ cups all-purpose flour
  1 teaspoon baking soda
  1 teaspoon freshly grated nutmeg
  1 teaspoon cinnamon
  ½ teaspoon salt
  2 large eggs
  1 cup sugar
  ¼ cup vegetable oil
  ¼ cup low-fat buttermilk

I. Preheat the oven to 350°. Spray a 9-by-5-inch loaf pan with cooking spray. Bring a medium saucepan of water to a boil. Add the carrots and boil over moderately high heat until tender, about 15 minutes. Drain and mash the carrots with a potato masher. Let cool.

2. In a pie plate, toast the walnuts for about 7 minutes, or until lightly browned. Let cool, then coarsely chop.

3. Sift the flour with the baking soda, nutmeg, cinnamon and salt. In a large bowl, whisk the eggs with the sugar until pale yellow. Whisk in the oil and buttermilk. Stir in the carrots and walnuts, then stir in the flour mixture until blended.

4. Pour the batter into the prepared pan and bake for 50 minutes, or until a cake tester inserted in the center comes out clean. Let the loaf cool in the pan for 10 minutes, then turn it out onto a rack to cool completely. *—Andrew J. Powning*
MAKE AHEAD The loaf can be wrapped in plastic and stored for up to 3 days or frozen for up to 1 month.

Cypriot Olive Bread

ACTIVE: 25 MIN; TOTAL: 7 HR
MAKES ONE 1½-POUND LOAF ●
A red clay pot with a lid produces a great crust, but the bread can also be baked directly on a pizza stone.

  2 cups bread flour, sifted
1½ teaspoons rapid-rise yeast
  ½ teaspoon sugar
  ⅓ cup extra-virgin olive oil, plus
     more for coating
  ⅔ cup warm water
  ¾ cup finely chopped cilantro
  ½ cup very finely chopped onion
  ½ cup oil-cured black olives
     (3 ounces), pitted
  2 teaspoons sesame seeds

I. In a food processor, pulse the bread flour with the yeast and sugar. Pulse in ⅓ cup of the olive oil until fine crumbs form. Add the water and process for

20 seconds, or until a smooth dough forms. Gently pulse in the cilantro, onion and black olives. Transfer the dough to a work surface and knead it lightly until completely smooth.

2. Coat a large bowl with olive oil. Put the dough in the bowl and turn to coat. Cover the bowl with plastic wrap and let stand in a warm place until the dough has almost doubled in volume, about 1 hour and 30 minutes.

3. Transfer the dough to a work surface. With lightly oiled hands, punch it down and shape into an oval. Let stand for 15 minutes. Meanwhile, soak the lid and the bottom of a medium unglazed red clay pot in water for 15 minutes. Drain and pat dry. Lightly oil the inside of the pot.

4. Carefully transfer the dough to the pot. Using a sharp knife, slash the dough on the diagonal at 2-inch intervals. Sprinkle the loaf with the sesame seeds and cover with the lid. Put the pot in a cold oven and turn the oven to 475°. Bake for 45 minutes. Uncover the bread and bake for 10 minutes longer, or until the top is golden brown. Turn the bread out onto a wire rack and let cool for at least 4 hours before slicing. —*Paula Wolfert*

MAKE AHEAD The bread can be stored at room temperature, wrapped in plastic, for up to 4 days.

Hearty Multigrain Bread
ACTIVE: 45 MIN; TOTAL: 12 HR
MAKES TWO 11-INCH ROUND LOAVES ● ●
The bread starter has to sit overnight, so plan accordingly.

- 1⅔ cups plus 1½ cups unbleached flour
- 2½ teaspoons active dry yeast
- 1½ cups boiling water
- 3 cups seven-grain cereal
- 3¼ cups whole wheat flour
- 2 tablespoons honey
- 1 tablespoon plus 2 teaspoons kosher salt

1. In a medium bowl, combine 1⅔ cups of the unbleached flour with ½ cup of warm water and ¼ teaspoon of the yeast and stir until a shaggy dough forms. Cover with plastic wrap and let stand overnight at room temperature.

2. In a large bowl, pour the boiling water over the cereal; stir until moistened. Let stand at room temperature until cool.

3. Meanwhile, in a large bowl, combine the remaining 2¼ teaspoons of yeast with ¼ cup of lukewarm water (90° to 110°) and let stand until the yeast is dissolved, about 5 minutes. Add the starter to the bowl along with the remaining 1½ cups unbleached flour, the whole wheat flour, honey and salt. Add 2¼ cups of lukewarm water and stir until a soft, sticky dough forms. Turn the dough out onto an unfloured work surface and, alternating between using a dough scraper and your hands, knead, pull and stretch the sticky dough until smooth, about 5 minutes. Do not add more flour. Return the dough to the bowl and let rest for 15 minutes.

4. Knead the dough 4 times in the bowl and let rest for 15 minutes. Knead the dough again 4 times and let rest for 15 minutes. Turn the dough out onto an unfloured work surface and knead in the cooled cereal until evenly incorporated and the dough is firm and smooth, about 5 minutes. Form the dough into a large ball and return it to the bowl. Cover and let rise until billowy and doubled in bulk, about 1 hour.

5. Punch down the dough and let rest for 30 minutes. Turn the dough out onto a lightly floured work surface. Divide it in half and form each half into a smooth ball. Transfer each ball to a lightly floured baking sheet and cover with an inverted large bowl. Let the dough rise in a warm, draft-free spot until nearly doubled in bulk, about 45 minutes.

6. Meanwhile, set a pizza stone on the bottom shelf of the oven and preheat to 500°, allowing 45 minutes for the stone to heat. Slide both loaves onto the stone and bake for 10 minutes. Lower the oven temperature to 425° and bake for 35 minutes longer, or until the loaves are deep brown and sound hollow when tapped on the bottoms. Alternatively, bake the loaves directly on the baking sheets. Transfer the bread to a wire rack and let it cool overnight. —*David Norman*

MAKE AHEAD The loaves can be frozen in an airtight plastic bag for up to 2 months; thaw in the bag.

Crispy Skillet Corn Bread
ACTIVE: 10 MIN; TOTAL: 30 MIN
MAKES TWO 9-INCH ROUND CORN BREADS ● ●

- 3 tablespoons vegetable oil
- 1½ cups all-purpose flour
- ¼ cup plus 2 tablespoons sugar
- 2 tablespoons baking powder
- 2 teaspoons salt
- 2½ cups cornmeal, preferably stone-ground
- 2 cups milk
- 4 large eggs, lightly beaten
- 6 tablespoons unsalted butter, melted

1. Preheat the oven to 425°. Warm two 9-inch cast-iron skillets over moderate heat. Add 1½ tablespoons of the oil to each and heat.

2. Meanwhile, in a bowl, sift the flour with the sugar, baking powder and salt. Stir in the cornmeal. Add the milk and eggs and stir lightly. Stir in the melted butter just until blended. Scrape the batter into the hot skillets; the oil should bubble. Transfer the skillets to the oven and bake the corn breads for about 18 minutes, or until the centers spring back when gently pressed. Turn the corn breads out onto a wire rack to cool. —*F&W Test Kitchen*

MAKE AHEAD The breads can be stored at room temperature for up to 2 days.

breads, pizzas + sandwiches

Anadama Bread

ACTIVE: 20 MIN; TOTAL: 3 HR 20 MIN
MAKES TWO 8½-BY-4½-INCH
LOAVES ●

1½ cups water
1 cup whole milk
½ cup yellow cornmeal
3 tablespoons unsalted butter
½ cup molasses
1 teaspoon salt
1 teaspoon sugar
1 tablespoon active dry yeast
6½ to 7 cups all-purpose flour

1. In a medium saucepan, heat the water with ¾ cup of the milk just until lukewarm. Add the cornmeal and cook over low heat, stirring constantly, just until small bubbles appear around the edge. Remove from the heat. Stir in the butter, molasses and salt; transfer to a large bowl and let cool.

2. In a saucepan, heat the remaining ¼ cup of milk and sugar until lukewarm. Remove from the heat. Sprinkle in the yeast and let stand until foamy, about 10 minutes. Stir the yeast mixture into the cornmeal mixture. Stir in 6½ cups of the flour until a stiff dough forms.

3. Turn the dough out onto a floured surface; knead until smooth, adding the remaining ½ cup of flour as needed. Form the dough into a ball and place in a buttered bowl. Cover the bowl with plastic wrap and let rise in a warm, draft-free spot until doubled, about 1 hour.

4. Lightly butter two 8½-by-4½-inch loaf pans. Punch down the dough and divide in half. Form each into a loaf; place in the pans. Flour the tops, cover with a towel and let rise in a warm, draft-free spot until nearly doubled, about 1 hour.

5. Preheat the oven to 350°. Bake the loaves for 50 minutes, or until the tops are brown and the bottoms sound hollow when tapped; carefully turn out onto a rack. Let cool. —*Alexandra Angle*

MAKE AHEAD The bread can be stored at room temperature for up to 4 days.

Mom's Dinner Rolls

ACTIVE: 1 HR; TOTAL: 4 HR
MAKES ABOUT 2½ DOZEN ROLLS ●
This recipe makes plenty of sweet, buttery rolls; they're great the next day, and they can also be frozen for 1 month.

2 envelopes active dry yeast
½ cup sugar
2 cups warm water
1 large egg, lightly beaten
2 teaspoons salt
About 6 cups all-purpose flour, plus more for rolling
2 sticks plus 2 tablespoons (9 ounces) unsalted butter, 1 stick softened

1. In a bowl, mix the yeast, a pinch of the sugar and ½ cup of the water and let stand until foamy. Stir in the egg, salt and the remaining sugar and 1½ cups of water. Add 5 cups of the flour and stir to form a soft, sticky dough. Stir in the stick of softened butter. Add the remaining 1 cup of flour and stir. Scrape out the dough onto a work surface and knead until smooth; add a few tablespoons of flour to prevent sticking. Transfer the dough to a buttered bowl, cover with plastic wrap and let rise in a draft-free place until doubled, 1 hour.

2. Punch down the dough and knead 2 or 3 times; cover and let rest for 15 minutes. On a very lightly floured surface, roll out the dough ³⁄₈ inch thick. Using a 2¾-inch round cutter dipped in flour, stamp out 24 rounds as close together as possible; if necessary, reroll and cut out the scraps.

3. Melt the remaining 10 tablespoons of butter in a small saucepan; set aside 2 tablespoons. Dip both sides of each round in the remaining butter, letting any excess drip into the pan. Fold the rounds in half and set, folded side down, in a 9-by-13-inch glass baking dish. Cover with plastic wrap and let the rolls rise in a draft-free spot until they are nearly doubled in bulk, about 1 hour.

4. Preheat the oven to 425°. Remove the plastic and bake the rolls for 30 minutes, or until golden, shifting the pans halfway through baking.

5. Remove the rolls from the oven and brush the tops with the reserved 2 tablespoons of butter. Let cool for 10 minutes. Invert the rolls onto a wire rack, set a platter on top and invert again. Serve warm or at room temperature. —*Sandy Carpenter*

Steamed Buns with Cured Ham

ACTIVE: 30 MIN; TOTAL: 3 HR 40 MIN
MAKES 16 BUNS ●
These fluffy buns need two risings.

¾ cup plus 2 tablespoons warm water
2 tablespoons sugar
2 teaspoons active dry yeast
3 cups all-purpose flour
1 tablespoon solid vegetable shortening
2 teaspoons baking powder
Asian sesame oil, for brushing
1 pound sliced ham or Chinese roast pork, or 1½ Chinese roast ducks, cut crosswise into ⅓-inch-thick slices
2 large scallions, julienned
Hoisin sauce (optional)

1. In a medium bowl, combine the water with the sugar and yeast and let stand until foamy, about 5 minutes.

2. Meanwhile, sift the flour into a large bowl. Using a pastry blender, cut in the shortening. Add the baking powder to the yeast mixture, then stir it into the flour. Scrape the dough out onto a work surface and knead until smooth and elastic. Return the dough to the bowl, cover with plastic wrap and let rise until tripled in bulk, about 2 hours.

3. Lightly oil a large baking sheet. Punch down the dough and divide it in half. Cover half with plastic wrap. Roll the other half into a cylinder about 1 inch in diameter; slice into 8 equal pieces.

Q+A
gougères

Q: I had the most amazing gougères at Alain Ducasse at the Essex House in New York City. Are they hard to make?

A: Gougères are simply *choux* pastry (the dough used for eclairs, cream puffs and profiteroles) flavored with cheese. In Burgundy, they're the classic accompaniment to the local wine cocktail, the Kir (Aligoté wine and crème de cassis). They are indeed delicious!

Q: I tried making the gougères and they were tasty, but so dense—not the light, airy puffs I was expecting. What did I do wrong?

A: Gougères puff up in part because of the magic of the eggs; perhaps you beat your eggs into the dough when it was too hot or didn't mix them in thoroughly. When you begin to stir, the dough does separate into slippery clumps and seems like it will never come together, but eventually it does.

Q: Another problem! This time, I made the dough correctly, piped it onto two baking sheets and cooked the gougères on the same rack in the oven. Those on one sheet burned and the others came out beautifully. What happened?

A: Your oven may heat unevenly, or maybe one of your baking sheets is heavier or sturdier than the other. Unless you have great sheets, consider investing in a pair of Silpats, reusable silicone pan liners. You can buy them at kitchenware shops, or for $26 each from Williams-Sonoma (877-812-6235).

People also run into trouble when they use two racks in the oven; the food on the lower rack (the one closest to the heat source) tends to cook more quickly on the bottom, and the food on the top rack cooks faster on the surface. Always switch baking sheets or pans from top to bottom and also from front to back halfway through cooking. This trick will usually compensate for the idiosyncrasies of most conventional ovens.

Q: When I tried the recipe again, I got distracted and ended up doubling the amount of cheese called for. Undeterred, I spread the dough in a 9-by-13-inch glass baking dish and baked it into an amazing cheese pastry in 25 minutes at 400°. It was perfect topped with ham.

A: It sounds easier than making individual gougères! That's how many recipes are born—happy accidents.

Alain Ducasse's Gougères

ACTIVE: 15 MIN; TOTAL: 45 MIN
MAKES ABOUT 28 GOUGÈRES ●

- ½ cup water
- ½ cup milk
- 1 stick (4 ounces) unsalted butter, cut into tablespoons
- Large pinch of coarse salt
- 1 cup all-purpose flour
- 4 large eggs
- 3½ ounces shredded Gruyère cheese (1 cup), plus more for sprinkling
- Freshly ground pepper
- Freshly grated nutmeg

1. Preheat the oven to 400°. Line 2 baking sheets with parchment paper. In a medium saucepan, combine the water, milk, butter and salt and bring to a boil. Add the flour and stir it in with a wooden spoon until a smooth dough forms; stir over low heat until it dries out and pulls away from the pan, about 2 minutes.

2. Scrape the dough into a bowl; let cool for 1 minute. Beat the eggs into the dough, 1 at a time, beating thoroughly between each one. Add the cheese and a pinch each of pepper and nutmeg.

3. Transfer the dough to a pastry bag fitted with a ½-inch round tip and pipe tablespoon-size mounds onto the baking sheets, 2 inches apart. Sprinkle with cheese and bake for 22 minutes, or until puffed and golden brown. Serve hot, or let cool and refrigerate or freeze. Reheat in a 350° oven until piping hot.

breads, pizzas + sandwiches

Roll each piece into a ball. Using a rolling pin, roll each ball into a 4-inch round about ⅛ inch thick. Brush the rounds with sesame oil, fold in half and transfer to the baking sheet. Repeat with the remaining dough. Cover the baking sheet loosely with plastic wrap and let the buns rise until doubled in bulk, about 1 hour.

4. Generously oil the bottom of a triple-tiered bamboo steamer. Bring 2 inches of water to a boil in a wok. Arrange the buns in the steamer without crowding, set over the boiling water and steam until puffy and cooked, about 5 minutes. Alternatively, oil the basket of a single-layer metal steamer and steam the buns in batches. Immediately transfer the buns to a platter and cover with a tea towel. Serve hot. Let your guests split the buns and fill them with the meat and scallions at the table. Pass the hoisin sauce separately. —*Jean-Georges Vongerichten*

MAKE AHEAD The buns can be brushed with sesame oil, folded and frozen for up to 2 months. Let thaw and rise a second time before steaming.

KITCHEN TOOL scale

Guzzini's ultra-stylish "Grammy" can handle up to 4½ pounds of ingredients ($65; 212-252-9560).

Butternut Squash Bread Pudding

ACTIVE: 40 MIN; TOTAL: 2 HR 30 MIN

12 SERVINGS ● ●

1½ pounds butternut squash, halved lengthwise and seeded
Kosher salt and freshly ground pepper
One 1½-pound loaf of sourdough bread, ends trimmed, loaf cut into 1-inch cubes
2 tablespoons unsalted butter
2 medium leeks, white and tender green parts only, chopped
2 garlic cloves, minced
15 large eggs, lightly beaten
3 cups milk
3 cups heavy cream
2 teaspoons chopped thyme
¼ teaspoon freshly grated nutmeg

1. Preheat the oven to 400°. Butter a shallow 10-by-15-inch baking dish. Season the squash with salt and pepper and set the halves on a rimmed baking sheet, cut side down. Bake the squash for 35 minutes, or until just tender. Let cool slightly, then peel and cut into ½-inch dice.

2. On 2 large rimmed baking sheets, toast the bread until dry and just crisp, about 10 minutes. Let cool completely. Reduce the oven temperature to 350°.

3. Meanwhile, melt the butter in a medium skillet. Add the leeks and garlic and cook over moderately high heat for 2 minutes. Reduce the heat to moderately low and cook, stirring occasionally, until softened, about 20 minutes.

4. In a large bowl, whisk the eggs, milk, cream, thyme, nutmeg, 1½ teaspoons of salt and 1 teaspoon of pepper. Add the bread cubes and let stand for 15 minutes. Fold in the squash and leeks and transfer to the prepared dish. Bake for 1 hour, or until browned and just set. Let rest for 15 minutes before serving. —*Elisabeth Prueitt*

MAKE AHEAD The bread pudding can be prepared earlier in the day and reheated in a 350° oven.

Apple-Chestnut Stuffing

ACTIVE: 45 MIN; TOTAL: 1 HR 15 MIN

12 SERVINGS PLUS LEFTOVERS ●

2 pounds challah bread, cut into ¾-inch dice
2 cups cooked chestnuts (from one 14.8-ounce vacuum-packed jar), crumbled into ½-inch pieces
1 stick (4 ounces) unsalted butter
5 large celery ribs, peeled and cut into ½-inch dice, plus ½ cup chopped celery leaves
2 large onions, cut into ½-inch dice
½ cup chopped flat-leaf parsley
2 Empire or Jonathan apples— peeled, cored and cut into ½-inch dice
2 tablespoons chopped thyme
1 tablespoon chopped fresh sage
3 large eggs, lightly beaten
About 3 cups Rich Turkey Stock (recipe, p. 125) or low-sodium chicken broth
Kosher salt and freshly ground pepper

1. Preheat the oven to 350°. Spread the challah on 3 large rimmed baking sheets and bake for 15 minutes, or until golden brown. Let cool, then transfer to a very large bowl. Add the chestnuts to the challah. Turn the oven to 400°.

2. Meanwhile, melt the butter in a large skillet. Add the celery ribs and leaves and the onions and parsley. Cook over moderate heat, stirring occasionally, until softened, about 20 minutes. Transfer to the bowl with the challah. Add the apples, thyme and sage; toss well.

3. In a bowl, mix the eggs with 2 cups of the stock and season with 1 tablespoon of salt and ½ teaspoon of pepper. Pour over the challah; stir well. Add another ½ to 1 cup of stock; the stuffing should be moist but the bread still intact.

4. Butter 2 large, shallow glass baking dishes and spread the stuffing in them. Bake the stuffing for 20 minutes, or until heated through and crisp on top. —*Marcia Kiesel*

Sausage, Pine Nut and Oyster Stuffing

ACTIVE: 1 HR; TOTAL: 1 HR 40 MIN

12 SERVINGS ● ●

The combination of meaty sausage and briny oysters makes for a sublime stuffing for any poultry, such as turkey, capon, or Rock Cornish hen.

Two 1-pound loaves sourdough bread, crusts removed, bread cut into 1-inch dice (20 cups)

½ cup pine nuts

1½ pounds sausage meat

8 tablespoons unsalted butter, 4 tablespoons melted

6 large celery ribs, peeled and thinly sliced crosswise

2 large sweet onions, cut into ¼-inch dice

Salt and freshly ground pepper

1 cup dry white wine

2 dozen medium to large shucked oysters, halved, ½ cup liquor reserved (see Note)

2 tablespoons coarsely chopped thyme

1 tablespoon coarsely chopped marjoram

2½ to 3 cups chicken stock or low-sodium broth

I. Preheat the oven to 350°. Butter two 9-by-13-inch baking dishes. Spread the bread on 2 large rimmed baking sheets and bake for 20 minutes, stirring a few times, until crisp; let cool. Transfer to a very large mixing bowl. Meanwhile, spread the pine nuts on a baking sheet and bake for about 5 minutes, until golden brown. Increase the oven temperature to 400°.

2. In a large skillet, cook the sausage meat over moderate heat, breaking it up with a spoon, until no pink remains, about 10 minutes. Continue to cook the sausage, stirring occasionally, until it is browned, about 10 minutes longer. With a slotted spoon, add the sausage to the bread in the bowl.

3. Add the 4 tablespoons of solid butter to the sausage fat in the skillet and heat until melted. Stir in the sliced celery and diced onions, season them lightly with salt and pepper and cook over moderately high heat, stirring frequently with a wooden spoon, just until the onions begin to soften, about 5 minutes. Reduce the heat to low and cook, stirring occasionally, until the celery and onions are completely softened, about 20 minutes.

4. Add the white wine to the skillet and simmer over high heat, stirring once, until reduced by three-fourths, about 4 minutes. Remove the pan from the heat and let the vegetable mixture cool to room temperature.

5. Add the vegetable mixture and the pine nuts to the bread cubes and sausage and toss. Add the oysters and their liquor, the thyme and marjoram and enough stock so that the bread is very moist but not overly soggy; season the stuffing with salt and pepper. Divide the stuffing equally between the 2 prepared baking dishes. Evenly brush the tops of the 2 stuffings with all of the melted butter.

6. Bake the stuffing in the upper third of the oven for about 15 minutes, or until hot throughout. Preheat the broiler. Broil the stuffing 6 inches from the heat for about 2 minutes, rotating the baking dishes as needed, until the stuffing is nicely browned on top. Serve right away. —*Tom Valenti*

NOTE Shucked oysters in their liquor are available in 8-ounce containers in the refrigerated sections at many supermarkets and at fish markets. Each plastic container holds approximately 12 oysters.

MAKE AHEAD The sausage-and-oyster stuffing can be prepared through Step 5 up to 1 day ahead and refrigerated. Bake and crisp the tops of the stuffing just before serving.

Arugula and Gorgonzola Pizza

TOTAL: 30 MIN

4 SERVINGS ● ●

1 tablespoon extra-virgin olive oil

½ pound spring onions, white bulbs only, sliced, or 1 small white onion, thinly sliced

Salt and freshly ground pepper

½ tablespoon minced garlic

¼ cup dry white wine

¾ pound pizza dough (see Note)

Olive oil cooking spray

1 tablespoon cornmeal

1½ ounces Gorgonzola cheese, crumbled (6 tablespoons)

½ cup freshly grated Parmesan cheese (1½ ounces)

¼ pound young arugula, trimmed and coarsely chopped

¼ cup walnut pieces, toasted and coarsely chopped

I. Preheat the oven to 500°. Heat the olive oil in a large skillet. Add the sliced onions, season with salt and pepper and cook over moderate heat, stirring occasionally, until the onion is softened, about 4 minutes. Add the garlic and cook for 1 minute. Add the wine and cook until evaporated, 3 to 4 minutes. Remove the skillet from the heat.

2. On a lightly floured surface, roll out the pizza dough to a 12-inch round. Spray a baking sheet with olive oil cooking spray, sprinkle with the cornmeal and transfer the dough to the baking sheet. Spread the onion on top and sprinkle with both the Gorgonzola and ¼ cup of the Parmesan.

3. Bake the pizza for 10 to 12 minutes, or until the crust is golden. Sprinkle with the arugula, toasted walnuts and the remaining ¼ cup of Parmesan. Slice into wedges and serve. —*Annie Somerville*

NOTE Ask to purchase pizza dough from your local pizza parlor, or you can use store-bought pizza dough or bread dough, which you'll find in the refrigerated section of your supermarket.

breads, pizzas + sandwiches

Salad Pizza with Baby Greens and Herbs

ACTIVE: 1 HR 20 MIN; TOTAL: 3 HR

6 SERVINGS

FLAT BREAD DOUGH

- 2 cups warm water
- 2 teaspoons active dry yeast

Pinch of sugar

5 to 5½ cups all-purpose flour

- 1 tablespoon kosher salt
- 1 cup pure olive oil, plus more for brushing
- 4 garlic cloves, smashed
- 2 rosemary sprigs

Cornmeal (optional)

Coarse sea salt

SALAD

- 3 tablespoons fresh lemon juice
- 1½ tablespoons Dijon mustard
- 1½ tablespoons red wine vinegar
- ¼ cup plus 2 tablespoons extra-virgin olive oil

Salt and freshly ground pepper

- 1 pound mixed baby greens
- 1¼ cups mixed herbs, such as basil, mint, chervil, parsley and dill
- 4 medium scallions, thinly sliced
- 6 ounces goat cheese, crumbled

I. MAKE THE FLAT BREAD DOUGH: In a large bowl, combine ½ cup of the water with the yeast and sugar and let stand until foamy, about 5 minutes. Add the remaining 1½ cups of water, 5 cups of the flour and the kosher salt and stir until a stiff, crumbly dough forms. Scrape the dough out onto a lightly floured work surface and knead until smooth and elastic, about 5 minutes; add more flour as necessary to prevent sticking. Divide the dough into 6 pieces and form each piece into a ball. Lightly brush each ball with olive oil and transfer to an oiled baking sheet. Cover with plastic wrap and let rise until doubled in bulk, about 1 hour.

2. Meanwhile, in a small saucepan, combine the 1 cup of olive oil with the garlic and rosemary and cook over moderate heat until the garlic begins to sizzle, 2 minutes. Remove from the heat; let cool. Discard the garlic and rosemary.

3. Set a pizza stone on the bottom shelf of the oven. Preheat the oven to 500°, allowing at least 45 minutes for the stone to heat. Alternatively, lightly brush a large baking sheet with olive oil and sprinkle it with cornmeal. Punch down the balls of dough, cover with plastic and let rest for 15 minutes.

4. On a lightly floured surface, working with 1 ball of dough at a time and keeping the rest covered, stretch or roll out the dough to an 8-inch round. Transfer the dough round to a lightly floured pizza peel. Brush it lightly with garlic oil and sprinkle with sea salt. Slide the round onto the stone and bake for 5 to 6 minutes, or until golden. If using the baking sheet, transfer 2 of the rounds to the sheet and bake for 10 minutes, or until golden. Remove the baking sheet from the oven and bake the flat breads directly on the oven rack for 2 minutes longer. Transfer the flat breads to a rack and repeat with the remaining dough.

5. MAKE THE SALAD: In a large bowl, whisk the lemon juice, mustard and vinegar. Whisk in the olive oil and season with salt and pepper. Add the greens, herbs and scallions and toss to coat. Mound the salad onto the flat breads, sprinkle with the goat cheese and serve.

—*Paula Disbrowe and David Norman*

MAKE AHEAD The garlic oil can be refrigerated for up to 1 week. The flat breads can be made several hours ahead and reheated in a 325° oven for 5 minutes.

Asparagus Pizzettas with Fontina and Prosciutto

ACTIVE: 45 MIN; TOTAL: 1 HR 30 MIN

MAKES FOUR 8-INCH PIZZETTAS

Michael Tusk tops his pizzettas sparingly, as bakers in Italy do, to show off the crisp crusts. Here we've added extra topping, in keeping with American taste.

- 1 pound pizza or bread dough (see Note, p. 267)
- 2 pounds medium asparagus, tough ends discarded
- 1 large shallot, thinly sliced
- 2 tablespoons extra-virgin olive oil, plus more for brushing

Salt and freshly ground pepper

Semolina or fine cornmeal, for dusting

- 2 cups shredded Fontina cheese (6 ounces)
- 1 cup shredded fresh mozzarella (3 ounces)
- 1½ ounces prosciutto, julienned
- 4 large sorrel leaves, julienned

Fresh lemon juice

I. Set a pizza stone on the bottom, or on the bottom shelf, of the oven. Preheat the oven to 500° for 30 minutes for the stone to heat. On a lightly floured work surface, cut the dough into 4 pieces and roll each piece into a ball. Cover with plastic wrap and let rest for 10 minutes.

2. In a saucepan of boiling salted water, cook the asparagus until tender, about 4 minutes. Drain and pat dry. Cut the asparagus into ¼-inch-thick slices on the diagonal and transfer to a bowl. Add the shallot and 2 tablespoons of the olive oil and season with salt and pepper.

3. On a lightly floured surface, roll 1 ball of dough into an 8-inch round. Dust a pizza peel with semolina and set the dough round on it. Brush the dough with olive oil. Scatter ½ cup of the Fontina and ¼ cup of the mozzarella on the dough, then top with one-fourth of the asparagus and ¼ cup of the prosciutto.

4. Slide the pizzetta onto the hot stone. Bake for about 6 minutes, or until it is crisp and browned on the bottom and bubbling on top. Using a large spatula, transfer the pizzetta to a work surface and cut it into quarters. Sprinkle with the sorrel and the lemon juice and serve. As soon as 1 pizzetta is in the oven, prepare the next. Slide it into the oven when the first comes out. —*Michael Tusk*

ASPARAGUS PIZZETTA WITH FONTINA AND PROSCIUTTO

breads, pizzas + sandwiches

Grilled Pizza with Prosciutto

ACTIVE: 1 HR 15 MIN; TOTAL: 3 HR 30 MIN

MAKES SIX 8-INCH PIZZAS

The pizza dough recipe that follows is simple, with a rich wheat flavor, but store-bought pizza dough is a fine substitute; you'll need about 1½ pounds. Make sure you have all the toppings assembled grillside before starting.

- ½ pound Fontina cheese, shredded (about 2 cups loosely packed)
- ½ cup freshly grated Pecorino Romano cheese (about 1½ ounces)

Pizza Dough (recipe follows)

Extra-virgin olive oil, for brushing and drizzling

- 2 teaspoons very finely chopped garlic

Two 14-ounce cans chopped Italian tomatoes, drained

- ½ cup basil leaves, cut into thin ribbons
- 12 paper-thin slices prosciutto di Parma, torn into large pieces

1. Light a grill, preferably using hardwood charcoal. Set the grill grate 3 to 4 inches above the coals. In a medium bowl, toss the Fontina with the Pecorino Romano cheese.

2. Divide the dough into 6 equal pieces; work with 1 piece at a time and keep the rest covered with a clean towel.

On 3 lightly oiled baking sheets, flatten and stretch the dough with your hands to form six 8-inch rounds about 1/16 inch thick; do not make a lip and don't stretch the dough so thinly that it tears. Brush the rounds with olive oil.

3. When the grill is hot, working in batches if necessary, gently drape the pizza dough over the hot grate and cook until it puffs slightly, the underside firms up and grill marks appear, about 1 minute. Rotate the dough once and cook for 30 seconds.

4. Brush the tops of the pizza rounds with oil and flip them over using tongs. Scatter one-sixth of the garlic and cheese over each pizza, followed by 3 heaping tablespoons of chopped tomatoes. Then drizzle each pizza with ½ tablespoon of olive oil.

5. Slide the pizzas near the hot coals but not directly over them. Using tongs, rotate the pizzas frequently, checking often to make sure that the undersides are not charring. The pizzas are done when the cheese is melted and the tomatoes are hot, 3 to 4 minutes. Scatter one-sixth of the basil and prosciutto over each pizza and serve hot off the grill. —*Johanne Killeen and George Germon*

Pizza Dough

ACTIVE: 25 MIN; TOTAL: 2 HR 45 MIN

MAKES ENOUGH FOR SIX 8-INCH PIZZAS ●

- 1 envelope active dry yeast
- 1 cup warm water

Pinch of sugar

- 2¼ teaspoons kosher salt
- 3 tablespoons whole wheat flour

Extra-virgin olive oil

- 2½ to 3 cups unbleached all-purpose flour

1. In a large bowl, mix the yeast, water and sugar and let stand until foamy, 5 minutes. Stir in the salt, whole wheat flour and 1 tablespoon of olive oil. Gradually add 2 cups of the all-purpose flour,

stirring with a wooden spoon until the dough is fairly stiff. Turn the dough out onto a well-floured work surface and knead, gradually adding as much of the remaining all-purpose flour as necessary, until it is smooth, elastic and no longer tacky, 5 to 6 minutes.

2. Transfer the dough to a lightly oiled bowl and brush the surface with olive oil. Cover the bowl with plastic wrap and let the dough rise in a warm, draft-free place until it doubles in bulk, 1½ to 2 hours.

3. Punch down the dough and knead it lightly, then return it to the bowl. Cover the bowl and let the dough rise again until doubled in bulk, about 45 minutes. Punch down the dough again and use or refrigerate. —*I.K. and G.G.*

MAKE AHEAD The Pizza Dough can be refrigerated overnight or frozen for up to 1 month. Let the dough return to room temperature before using.

Coriander-Lamb Nan Pizzas

TOTAL: 35 MIN

MAKES THREE 7½-INCH PIZZAS ●

This pizza borrows the flavors of an old Parsi lamb dish that is typically served as a main dish with rice.

- 1 tablespoon vegetable oil
- 1 medium onion, very finely chopped
- 1 large tomato—peeled, seeded and diced
- 2 bird's eye chiles—stemmed, seeded and minced
- 1 teaspoon very finely chopped garlic
- 1 teaspoon minced fresh ginger
- ½ pound ground lamb
- 1 teaspoon ground coriander
- 1 teaspoon ground cumin
- 1 tablespoon red wine vinegar

Salt and freshly ground pepper

Three 7½-inch nan breads (see Note)

Extra-virgin olive oil, for brushing

- 1 cup very finely chopped cilantro leaves

1. Preheat the oven to 350°. Heat the oil in a large skillet. Add the onion and cook over moderately high heat, stirring, until translucent, about 3 minutes. **2.** Add the tomato, chiles, garlic and ginger to the skillet; cook for 3 minutes. Add the lamb and cook, stirring, for 6 minutes. Add the coriander, cumin and vinegar and cook over moderate heat, stirring occasionally, for 10 minutes. Season with salt and pepper. **3.** Brush the nan with olive oil and bake for 2 minutes. Spread the lamb mixture evenly on top and bake for 7 minutes. Sprinkle the cilantro over the pizzas and serve hot. —*Jehangir Mehta*

NOTE Nan is a typical Indian leavened flat bread made in a clay oven. You can buy it at Indian markets or mail-order it from Kalustyan's (800-352-3451 or www.kalustyans.com).

Zucchini and Hummus Nan Pizzas

ACTIVE: 20 MIN; TOTAL: 35 MIN
MAKES THREE 7½-INCH PIZZAS ● ●

- 3 medium zucchini, halved lengthwise and cut into ½-inch-thick slices
- 1 tablespoon extra-virgin olive oil, plus more for brushing
- 2 tablespoons fresh lemon juice
- 2 teaspoons minced garlic
- Salt and freshly ground pepper
- Three 7½-inch nan breads
- ½ cup plus 1 tablespoon Classic Hummus (recipe, p. 20)

1. Preheat the oven to 350°. In a bowl, toss the zucchini with 1 tablespoon of the olive oil, the lemon juice and garlic and season with salt and pepper. Spread the zucchini on a baking sheet and bake for about 20 minutes, or until tender. **2.** Brush the nan with olive oil and bake for 2 minutes. Spread the hummus over the nan. Top with the zucchini and bake for 7 minutes. Sprinkle with salt; serve —*Jehangir Mehta*

Grilled Cheddar Toasts with Red Onions and Peppers

TOTAL: 35 MIN
4 SERVINGS ●

- 2 large red bell peppers—halved, cored and seeded
- 2 large red onions, cut crosswise into ⅓-inch-thick slices
- 1 tablespoon extra-virgin olive oil, plus more for brushing
- Eight ½-inch-thick slices peasant bread
- ½ cup mayonnaise
- 3 tablespoons prepared pesto sauce
- 1½ teaspoons red wine vinegar
- Kosher salt and freshly ground pepper
- ½ pound sliced sharp Cheddar cheese

1. Light a charcoal grill or preheat a gas grill. Brush the peppers and onions with olive oil and grill over high heat until softened and charred in spots, 8 to 9 minutes. Transfer the peppers to a bowl, cover with plastic wrap and let cool. Peel the peppers and cut into thin strips. **2.** Lightly brush the bread on both sides with olive oil and grill until toasted, 2 to 3 minutes. Transfer to a wire rack. In a small bowl, mix the mayonnaise with the pesto sauce and spread it on the bread. Preheat the broiler. **3.** In a bowl, mix the tablespoon of olive oil with the vinegar. Add the onions and peppers, season with salt and pepper and toss to coat. Mound the peppers and onions on the toast. Cover with the cheese and broil for 1 to 2 minutes, turning the rack, until melted. Serve. —*Laura Chenel*

Turkey and Earl Grey Honey Butter Tea Sandwiches

TOTAL: 30 MIN
MAKES 32 TEA SANDWICHES ● ●
You will need a coffee grinder to grind the tea leaves used in this recipe.

- 1 stick (4 ounces) unsalted butter, softened
- 1 tablespoon honey
- 1 teaspoon Earl Grey tea (from 1 bag), finely ground
- Pinch of salt
- ½ Granny Smith apple, peeled and coarsely shredded
- 1 teaspoon fresh lemon juice
- 16 thin slices of pumpernickel bread
- ¾ pound sliced smoked turkey

1. In a mini food processor or in a bowl, blend the butter, honey, ground tea and salt. In a medium bowl, toss the apple with the lemon juice. Squeeze out any excess liquid and pulse or mix the apple into the honey butter. **2.** Spread a scant ½ tablespoon of the apple butter onto each slice of pumpernickel bread. Top half of the slices with the smoked turkey and top with the remaining bread slices to close the sandwiches. Using a sharp serrated knife, trim off the bread crusts. Cut the sandwiches into 4 triangles, transfer to a plate and serve. —*Grace Parisi*

MAKE AHEAD The uncut sandwiches can be covered with a lightly moistened paper towel and plastic wrap and then refrigerated overnight. Bring to room temperature before serving.

Smoked Salmon and Scallion Tea Sandwiches

TOTAL: 45 MIN
MAKES 32 TEA SANDWICHES ●

- ¼ cup sesame seeds
- ¾ pound sliced smoked salmon
- 1½ teaspoons wasabi powder mixed with 1½ teaspoons water
- 1 teaspoon finely grated fresh ginger
- ¼ cup crème fraîche
- ¾ pound cream cheese, at room temperature
- 4 scallions, green parts only, chopped
- ¼ cup chopped watercress leaves
- Kosher salt and freshly ground white pepper
- 24 thin slices of white sandwich bread

SWEET COPPA AND PEPPER PANINI

SMOKED SALMON SANDWICHES WITH ALMONDS

I. In a small skillet, toast the sesame seeds over moderate heat, shaking the pan, until light golden, about 2 minutes. Transfer to a plate and let cool.

2. In a food processor, combine the salmon, wasabi, ginger and crème fraîche and pulse until completely smooth. Transfer the mixture to a bowl. Wipe out the processor.

3. Add the cream cheese, scallions and watercress to the food processor and puree until smooth. Season with salt and white pepper.

4. Using a small spatula, spread a scant tablespoon of the scallion cream cheese onto each of 3 slices of the sandwich bread. Spread a scant tablespoon of the salmon mixture onto each of 2 slices of bread. Stack the bread, beginning and ending with a scallion layer; top the stack with a plain slice of bread and

press to close. Repeat the procedure with the remaining bread, scallion cream cheese and salmon mixture to form 4 sandwich stacks.

5. Using a sharp serrated knife, trim the crusts off the sandwiches. Cut each sandwich stack in half. Spread scallion cream cheese over the long side of each sandwich half, then dip the long sides into the toasted sesame seeds, pressing to coat. Cut each sandwich half into 4 smaller sandwiches, leaving 1 side coated with sesame seeds. Transfer the sandwiches to a plate and serve.
—*Grace Parisi*

MAKE AHEAD The halved sandwiches can be covered with a lightly moistened paper towel and plastic wrap and refrigerated overnight. Bring to room temperature before cutting into small sandwiches and serving.

Smoked Salmon and Chopped Egg Sandwiches

TOTAL: 20 MIN

4 SERVINGS ● ●

- 3 large eggs
- ⅓ cup mayonnaise
- 2 teaspoons horseradish, drained
- 8 slices of rye bread or pumpernickel
- 4 large radishes, thinly sliced (⅓ cup)
- ¼ cup small sprouts, such as radish or alfalfa
- 2 scallions, white and tender green parts only, thinly sliced
- ½ pound sliced smoked salmon

Salt and freshly ground pepper

I. In a small saucepan, cover the eggs with cold water and bring to a rolling boil. Cover, remove from the heat and let stand for 7 minutes. Drain the eggs and rinse them under cool running water.

Shake the pan to crack the eggshells. Drain again and pat dry, then peel and coarsely chop.

2. Meanwhile, in a small bowl, mix the mayonnaise and horseradish and spread on the bread. Arrange the radishes on 4 of the slices and top with the sprouts, scallions and salmon. Spoon the eggs on top, season with salt and pepper and close the sandwiches. Press gently, cut the sandwiches in half and serve.
—*Anne Quatrano*

Smoked Salmon Sandwiches with Curried Almonds

TOTAL: 25 MIN

4 SERVINGS ● ● ●

- 1 teaspoon vegetable oil
- ¾ cup sliced unblanched almonds
- 1 teaspoon curry powder
- ¼ cup low-fat plain yogurt
- Salt and freshly ground pepper
- Eight 1-ounce slices of whole-grain bread
- ½ pound thinly sliced smoked salmon
- 4 medium radishes, cut into ¼-inch-thick slices
- 1 Granny Smith apple—quartered, cored and cut into ¼-inch-thick slices

I. Heat the oil in a medium skillet. Add the almonds and cook over moderate heat, tossing, until golden, about 3 minutes. Sprinkle the curry powder over the almonds and toss to coat. Cook, stirring, until the almonds are fragrant, about 1 minute. Transfer to a bowl and let cool. Stir in the yogurt and season with salt and pepper.

2. Spread the curried-almond mixture evenly on half the whole-grain bread slices. Top the bread with the smoked salmon slices, radish slices and apple slices. Cover the sandwiches with the remaining bread slices to close. Pile the sandwiches on a platter and serve.
—*Marcia Kiesel*

PITA VARIATION Slice 1 inch off four 5-inch whole wheat pitas. Spread the smoked salmon on the bottom of each, then layer almonds, sliced radishes and apple slices on top.

MAKE AHEAD The sandwiches can be prepared up to 4 hours ahead. Cover with plastic wrap to prevent the bread from drying out.

Sweet Coppa and Pepper Panini

TOTAL: 30 MIN

4 SERVINGS ●

The secret to perfect panini is not over-cooking the bread, which makes it too brittle. Use a sandwich press or follow the stovetop method below using a cast-iron skillet as a weight.

- One 1-pound ciabatta loaf, 4 large ciabatta rolls or eight ½-inch-thick slices of sourdough bread
- 24 thin slices of coppa or soppressata (about 6 ounces)
- 4 pickled hot cherry peppers— stemmed, seeded and thinly sliced
- 32 small arugula leaves
- 8 teaspoons extra-virgin olive oil, plus more for drizzling
- Balsamic vinegar, for drizzling
- Salt and freshly ground pepper

I. Cut the ciabatta crosswise into 4 even pieces. Cut off a very thin layer from the top and bottom crusts. Halve each ciabatta horizontally; arrange 6 coppa slices on the bottom half of each sandwich, then top with 1 sliced cherry pepper and 8 arugula leaves. Drizzle a little oil and vinegar over the arugula; season with salt and pepper. Close up the sandwiches.

2. Heat 4 teaspoons of olive oil in each of 2 large cast-iron skillets. Add 2 of the sandwiches to each skillet and weight them down with a smaller cast-iron skillet. Cook over moderately high heat until browned and crisp, 2 minutes per side. Cut the panini in half and serve them hot. —*Jason Denton*

Italian Tuna Salad Sandwiches with Black-Olive Dressing

TOTAL: 30 MIN

MAKES 4 SANDWICHES ● ● ●

- ¾ cup chopped flat-leaf parsley
- ¾ cup black olives, such as Gaeta, Calamata or Niçoise (3½ ounces), pitted and chopped
- ½ cup extra-virgin olive oil
- 4 anchovy fillets, minced
- 3 garlic cloves, minced
- 1½ tablespoons fresh lemon juice
- 1 tablespoon chopped thyme
- Salt and freshly ground pepper
- 6 ounces snow peas
- Two 6-ounce jars or cans imported olive oil–packed tuna, drained
- 4 crusty rolls or four 6-inch lengths of baguette, halved
- 1 small red onion, thinly sliced
- 2 medium tomatoes, cut into ⅓-inch-thick slices
- 4 hard-cooked eggs, cut into ¼-inch-thick slices

I. In a medium bowl, mix the parsley, black olives, olive oil, anchovies, garlic, lemon juice and thyme. Season the dressing with salt and pepper.

2. In a small pot of boiling salted water, blanch the snow peas for 1 minute, or until they are bright green and just tender. Drain the snow peas and refresh them under cold water, then pat dry. Slice the snow peas lengthwise into ¼-inch strips and toss them with 1 tablespoon of the olive dressing.

3. In a medium bowl, lightly break up the drained tuna with a fork. Mix in 6 tablespoons of the olive dressing and toss gently.

4. Spread the cut sides of the rolls or baguette pieces with the remaining olive dressing. On the bottom halves, arrange the snow peas, followed by the red onion slices, tomato slices, tuna and sliced eggs. Place the remaining bread slices on top to close the sandwiches and serve. —*Marcia Kiesel*

breads, pizzas + sandwiches

Curried Chicken on Pita

TOTAL: 25 MIN

MAKES 4 SANDWICHES ● ●

1¼ cups plain low-fat yogurt

4 garlic cloves, very finely chopped

2 teaspoons garam masala

2 teaspoons curry powder

1 pound skinless, boneless chicken breast halves, cut crosswise into ⅓-inch strips

1 tablespoon vegetable oil

2 jalapeños, seeded and very thinly sliced

1 large red onion, halved lengthwise and thinly sliced crosswise

Salt and freshly ground pepper

Four 8-inch whole wheat pita breads

4 romaine lettuce leaves

1 large tomato, cut into thin wedges

1 medium cucumber—peeled, halved, seeded and cut into thin crescents

1. Preheat the oven to 400°. In a medium bowl, mix 1 tablespoon of the yogurt with the garlic, garam masala and curry powder. Add the chicken strips and stir until they are thoroughly coated with the yogurt-spice mixture.

2. In a large nonstick skillet, heat the vegetable oil. Add the sliced jalapeños, red onion and coated chicken strips, season with salt and pepper and cook over moderately high heat, stirring, until the chicken strips are just white throughout, about 5 minutes. Remove the skillet from the heat and let stand for 1 minute to let the chicken, jalapeños and red onion cool slightly. Fold the remaining 1 cup plus 3 tablespoons of yogurt into the chicken, jalapeños and red onion until well combined.

3. Heat the pita breads in the oven until just warm, about 30 seconds. Set the pitas on serving plates and top each one with a lettuce leaf, tomato wedges and cucumber slices. Spoon the chicken in yogurt sauce on top and serve right away.

—*Marcia Kiesel*

Chicken Sandwiches with Zucchini Slaw

TOTAL: 25 MIN

MAKES 6 SANDWICHES ●

3 tablespoons crème fraîche or sour cream

1 canned chipotle chile in adobo, seeded and minced (see Note)

2 tablespoons fresh lime juice

2 small zucchini, cut into coarse shreds

Kosher salt

One 5-ounce bunch arugula, thick stems discarded

1 tablespoon extra-virgin olive oil

Freshly ground pepper

6 small baguette rolls, split lengthwise

1 roast chicken (about 4 pounds), meat and skin shredded

1. In a small bowl, combine the crème fraîche with the chipotle chile and 1½ tablespoons of the lime juice. Add the shredded zucchini and a pinch of kosher salt; toss well to thoroughly coat the zucchini. Let the zucchini slaw stand for 5 minutes.

2. In a medium bowl, toss the arugula with the olive oil and the remaining ½ tablespoon of lime juice; season the arugula with salt and pepper.

3. Using a slotted spoon, spread the marinated zucchini on the bottom halves of the baguette rolls. Mound the shredded chicken on the zucchini and season generously with salt and pepper. Top the shredded chicken with the arugula salad. Place the remaining baguette slices on top to close the chicken sandwiches and serve them at once. —*Melissa Clark*

NOTE Chipotle chiles are dried, smoked jalapeños. They are frequently found canned and packed in adobo sauce, a dark red Mexican blend of ground chiles, herbs and vinegar. They are available at Latin grocery stores and some supermarkets.

Bacon and Cheese Melts with Garlicky Watercress

TOTAL: 40 MIN

MAKES 4 SANDWICHES

32 thin slices of lean bacon (about 1½ pounds)

¼ cup plus 2 tablespoons water

2 tablespoons extra-virgin olive oil

8 large garlic cloves, cut into ⅛-inch-thick slices

2 teaspoons Dijon mustard

2 teaspoons red wine vinegar

Salt and freshly ground pepper

8 slices of pumpernickel bread (⅓ inch thick)

¼ pound Comté or Gruyère cheese, thinly sliced

2 ounces watercress, large stems discarded (4 cups)

1. Preheat the oven to 400°. In a large skillet, cook half of the bacon over moderate heat, turning once, until crisp, about 6 minutes. Drain on paper towels. Repeat with the remaining bacon.

2. In a medium skillet, bring the water and olive oil to a simmer. Add the garlic in an even layer, cover and cook over moderate heat until the water has evaporated, about 5 minutes. Uncover and cook over moderate heat, undisturbed, until the garlic begins to turn golden, about 5 minutes longer. As the garlic colors, transfer it to a plate. Pour 1 tablespoon of the garlic oil into a medium bowl. Whisk in the mustard and vinegar and season with salt and pepper.

3. Arrange the bread on a baking sheet and top each slice with 4 slices of bacon. Cover the bacon with the cheese. Bake for 4 minutes, until the bacon is sizzling and the cheese is melted.

4. Add the watercress and the garlic slices to the dressing in the bowl and toss well. Mound the watercress on 4 of the cheese melts and close the sandwiches; cut in half and serve.

—*Marcia Kiesel*

CHICKEN SANDWICHES WITH ZUCCHINI SLAW

GOAT CHEESE AND FRESH HERB SOUFFLÉ, P. 291

● FAST

● HEALTHY

● MAKE AHEAD

● STAFF FAVORITE

breakfast + brunch

APRICOT-CORNMEAL MUFFINS

ICED CINNAMON BUN SCONES

Apricot-Cornmeal Muffins

ACTIVE: 15 MIN; TOTAL: 40 MIN

MAKES 8 MUFFINS ● ●

Vegetable oil cooking spray

- ⅓ cup finely chopped dried apricots
- ½ cup hot water
- ¾ cup all-purpose flour
- 2 tablespoons coarsely ground cornmeal
- 1 tablespoon dry milk
- ½ teaspoon baking powder
- ¼ teaspoon baking soda
- ⅛ teaspoon salt
- ¼ cup buttermilk
- 1½ tablespoons canola oil
- 1 tablespoon honey
- 1 large egg
- 1 large egg white
- ½ teaspoon finely grated orange zest

1. Preheat the oven to 400°. Lightly coat 8 muffin cups with vegetable oil cooking spray. Soak the apricots in the hot water until softened, about 20 minutes. Drain the apricots, reserving ¼ cup of the soaking liquid.

2. In a medium bowl, sift the flour with the cornmeal, dry milk, baking powder, baking soda and salt. In another bowl, mix the buttermilk with the oil, honey, whole egg, egg white, orange zest, drained apricots and the reserved apricot soaking liquid. Fold in the dry ingredients just until blended.

3. Spoon the batter into the prepared muffin cups and bake for about 14 minutes, or until golden and risen. Unmold and let cool slightly before serving.
—*Jason Knibb*

MAKE AHEAD The muffins can be made up to 1 day ahead and reheated.

Iced Cinnamon Bun Scones

ACTIVE: 20 MIN; TOTAL: 1 HR

MAKES 8 SCONES ●

- ⅔ cup light brown sugar
- 1 stick (4 ounces) cold unsalted butter, cut into ½-inch dice, plus 2 tablespoons softened
- 1¼ teaspoons cinnamon
- 3 cups all-purpose flour, plus more for dusting
- ⅓ cup granulated sugar
- 1 tablespoon baking powder
- ½ teaspoon salt
- 1 cup heavy cream
- 1 large egg
- 1 teaspoon pure vanilla extract
- ¼ cup cream cheese, softened
- 1 teaspoon fresh lemon juice
- 2 cups confectioners' sugar

1. Preheat the oven to 425°. Line a large, heavy baking sheet with parchment paper. In a food processor, pulse the light brown sugar with the 2 table-spoons of softened butter and 1 tea-spoon of the cinnamon until soft crumbs form. Transfer the brown sugar mixture to a small bowl.

2. In the processor, pulse the 3 cups of flour with the granulated sugar, baking powder and salt until combined. Add the remaining ¼ teaspoon of cinnamon and pulse to blend. Add the diced pieces of butter and pulse until the mixture resembles small peas. Scrape all of the mixture into a large bowl and make a well in the center.

3. Add the cream, egg and vanilla to the well and stir with a wooden spoon to combine. Using the wooden spoon, gradually draw in the flour mixture and stir until a firm dough forms. Using your fingers, crumble the brown sugar mixture all over the dough and gently knead it into the dough until it is just incorpo-rated, leaving some streaks.

4. Lightly dust a work surface with flour. Turn the dough out onto it and knead the dough 3 times. Pat or roll the dough into an 8-inch round, about 1 inch thick. Cut the round into 8 wedges, then trans-fer the scones to the baking sheet and refrigerate for 10 minutes. Bake the scones for 18 to 20 minutes, or until they are nicely browned. Let the scones cool slightly on the baking sheet, then transfer them to a wire rack and let them cool completely.

5. In a medium bowl, beat the cream cheese with the lemon juice. Beat in the confectioners' sugar until smooth. Spread the icing over the warm scones. Let the scones sit briefly, then serve. —*Marcy Goldman*

MAKE AHEAD The Iced Cinnamon Bun Scones can be stored in an airtight con-tainer for 2 days. Let the cream cheese icing harden completely before storing the scones, and separate them between layers of wax paper.

Candled Orange–Oat Scones

ACTIVE: 20 MIN; TOTAL: 45 MIN

MAKES 8 SCONES ●

1½ cups rolled oats (not instant)
1½ cups all-purpose flour
¼ cup granulated sugar
1½ teaspoons baking powder
Pinch of salt
1½ sticks (6 ounces) unsalted butter, cut into ½-inch pieces and chilled
¼ cup finely chopped candied orange peel (1½ ounces)
¾ cup buttermilk
1 tablespoon heavy cream
1 tablespoon demerara or turbinado sugar, for sprinkling
Softened butter and marmalade, for serving

1. Preheat the oven to 375° and position a rack in the center. In a medium skil-let, toast the oats over moderately high heat, stirring constantly, until golden and fragrant, about 5 minutes. Trans-fer to a plate to cool completely.

2. In a large bowl, combine the flour with the granulated sugar, baking pow-der and salt. Using 2 knives or a pastry blender, cut in the butter until the pieces are the size of small peas. Stir in the rolled oats and candied orange peel. Make a well in the center and pour in the buttermilk. Stir with a wooden spoon just until the dough is evenly moistened. Transfer the dough to a floured surface and pat it into an 8-inch round about ½ inch thick. Pinch together any cracks around the edges.

3. Brush the dough with the heavy cream and sprinkle it with the demerara sugar. Cut the round into 8 wedges; transfer the wedges to a baking sheet. Bake for 25 minutes, or until golden. Transfer the scones to a wire rack to cool slightly. Serve with softened but-ter and marmalade. —*Grace Parisi*

MAKE AHEAD The scones can be stored in an airtight container overnight.

Sweet Fennel-and-Tomato Scones

ACTIVE: 20 MIN; TOTAL: 30 MIN

MAKES 16 SCONES ● ●

2½ cups all-purpose flour
1 tablespoon baking powder
1 teaspoon salt
1 teaspoon ground fennel seeds plus 1 tablespoon whole seeds
½ teaspoon baking soda
4 tablespoons cold unsalted butter, cut into ½-inch pieces, plus more for serving
1 plum tomato, seeded and diced
½ cup milk
¼ cup honey, warmed
1 large egg yolk mixed with 1 tablespoon water
2 teaspoons sugar

1. Preheat the oven to 400°. In a large bowl, whisk the flour with the baking powder, salt, the ground fennel seeds and the baking soda. Using a pastry blender or 2 knives, cut in the butter until the mixture resembles coarse meal. Add the chopped tomato and toss until evenly distributed.

2. In a small bowl, mix the milk with the warmed honey. Pour the milk mixture into the flour. Using a wooden spoon, stir until a soft dough forms. Scrape the dough onto a lightly floured work surface and knead 2 or 3 times, until smooth. Pat the dough out to a ½-inch thickness. Using a 2-inch-round biscuit cutter, stamp as many rounds as possible out of the dough. Gather the scraps and stamp out more rounds. Transfer the rounds to a baking sheet and brush the tops with the egg yolk mixture. Sprinkle the scones with the whole fennel seeds and the sugar and bake for about 10 minutes, or until they are golden and puffy. Transfer the scones to a wire rack to cool slightly. Serve the scones with butter. —*Alexandra Angle*

MAKE AHEAD The scones can be stored in an airtight container overnight.

breakfast + brunch

Angel Biscuits

ACTIVE: 45 MIN; TOTAL: 11 HR

MAKES ABOUT 40 BISCUITS

These biscuits are great for novice cooks because they use two leaveners, which makes the recipe virtually foolproof. The biscuit dough needs to be refrigerated overnight, so plan accordingly.

- 1 envelope active dry yeast (2¼ teaspoons)
- ¼ cup plus 1 pinch of sugar
- 2 tablespoons lukewarm water
- 5 cups self-rising flour
- 1 cup cold solid vegetable shortening, cut into small pieces
- 2 cups buttermilk
- 6 tablespoons unsalted butter, melted

1. In a small bowl, dissolve the yeast and the pinch of sugar in the lukewarm water and let stand for 5 minutes, or until foamy. Meanwhile, in a large bowl, mix the flour with the remaining ¼ cup of sugar. Using a pastry blender, cut the shortening into the flour until pea-size pieces form. Add the yeast mixture and the buttermilk and stir until the dough just comes together.

2. Turn the dough out onto a lightly floured work surface and knead 5 times; the dough should be soft and moist. Transfer the dough to a clean bowl; cover the bowl with plastic wrap and refrigerate overnight or for up to 2 days.

3. Transfer the biscuit dough to a lightly floured surface and knead 10 times. Roll out the dough to a 16-inch round ⅓ inch thick. Using a 2¼-inch biscuit cutter, stamp out biscuits as close together as possible. Gather the dough scraps, knead 3 times and reroll, then stamp out biscuits as close together as possible. Discard remaining scraps.

4. Lightly butter 2 large baking sheets. Brush the biscuit tops with half of the melted butter. Fold the biscuits in half, brush the tops with the remaining butter and set them, unbuttered side down, on the prepared baking sheets. Cover loosely with plastic wrap and let rise in a draft-free place for 2 hours.

5. Preheat the oven to 400°. Bake the biscuits for about 15 minutes, or until browned on the bottoms and golden on top. Serve warm. —*Scott Howell*

Peach Halves in Sugar Syrup

ACTIVE: 25 MIN; TOTAL: 1 HR 25 MIN

MAKES 4 PINTS ● ●

The trick to canning peaches is packing the peach halves tightly without squashing them; a full jar is prettiest. These lovely peaches make a terrific accompaniment to scones and other breakfast breads.

- 2 pounds freestone peaches
- 3 cups water
- 2 cups sugar

1. Bring a large saucepan of water to a boil. Add the peaches and blanch just until the skins loosen, about 30 seconds. Using a slotted spoon, transfer the peaches to a rimmed baking sheet to cool slightly. Slip off the skins, halve the peaches and remove the pits.

2. In a medium saucepan, combine the water and sugar and bring to a boil over moderately low heat, stirring occasionally, until the sugar dissolves.

3. Meanwhile, pack the peach halves into 4 hot sterilized 1-pint jars without crushing them. Pour the boiling syrup over the peaches, stopping ½ inch from the top. Wipe the glass rims and close the jars. Set in a water bath and bring to a boil. Boil the jars for 25 minutes. —*Eugenia Bone*

Sweet Cherries with Basil

ACTIVE: 30 MIN; TOTAL: 1 HR 35 MIN

MAKES 4 QUARTS ●

Top your favorite muffins or scones with this scrumptious cherry compote.

- 8 pounds sweet cherries, pitted
- 3 cups sugar
- 16 basil leaves

1. In a large, heavy pot, combine the cherries and sugar. Cover and bring the mixture to a boil over low heat, stirring occasionally. Uncover and simmer until the liquid is slightly thickened and glossy and the cherries float in the liquid, about 10 minutes. Add the basil and cook for 2 minutes.

2. Pack the cherries and their juices into 4 hot sterilized 1-quart jars, stopping ½ inch from the top. Wipe the glass rims and close the jars. Set them in a water bath and bring to a boil. Boil for 20 minutes. —*Eugenia Bone*

Sour Cream–Banana Toffee Crumb Cake

ACTIVE: 20 MIN; TOTAL: 2 HR 20 MIN

MAKES ONE 10-INCH CAKE ●

CRUMB TOPPING

- ¼ cup confectioners' sugar
- ⅓ cup all-purpose flour
- 2 tablespoons unsalted butter, softened
- ¼ cup toffee bits

CAKE

- Vegetable oil cooking spray
- 2¾ cups all-purpose flour
- 2½ teaspoons baking powder
- ½ teaspoon baking soda
- ½ teaspoon salt
- 1½ sticks (6 ounces) unsalted butter, softened
- 1½ cups granulated sugar
- 3 large eggs
- 1½ teaspoons pure vanilla extract
- 1 cup sour cream
- ½ cup mashed bananas (2 medium)

1. MAKE THE CRUMB TOPPING: In a small bowl, combine the confectioners' sugar with the flour and butter and pinch to form crumbs. Stir in the toffee bits.

2. MAKE THE CAKE: Preheat the oven to 350°. Spray a 10-inch springform pan with vegetable oil cooking spray. In a medium bowl, whisk the flour, baking powder, baking soda and salt. In a large bowl, using a handheld electric mixer,

SOUR CREAM–BANANA TOFFEE CRUMB CAKE

BLUE CORN–COTTAGE CHEESE GRIDDLE CAKES

beat the butter until creamy. Add the granulated sugar and beat at medium speed until light and fluffy. Then beat in the eggs and vanilla. Add the sour cream and bananas; beat at low speed just until blended. Add the dry ingredients and beat until smooth. Scrape the batter into the prepared pan and smooth the top.

3. Sprinkle the crumbs evenly over the batter and bake for 1 hour and 10 minutes, or until the crumb cake is golden and a toothpick inserted in the center comes out with moist crumbs attached. Loosely cover the cake with foil during the last 20 minutes. Let cool in the pan for 15 minutes, then remove the ring and let cool completely before serving. —*Marcy Goldman*

MAKE AHEAD The crumb cake can be stored at room temperature in an airtight container for up to 1 week.

Blue Corn–Cottage Cheese Griddle Cakes

ACTIVE: 15 MIN; TOTAL: 45 MIN

4 SERVINGS ●

If you can't find blue cornmeal, substitute any good brand of yellow cornmeal.

- 4 large eggs
- 1 cup low-fat (1%) cottage cheese
- 3 tablespoons stone-ground blue cornmeal
- ¼ cup all-purpose flour
- 1 teaspoon sugar

Pinch of salt

- ½ cup skim milk
- 1 tablespoon unsalted butter, melted

Vegetable oil, for brushing

- 6 tablespoons pure maple syrup, warmed
- ¾ cup fresh berries

Confectioners' sugar, for dusting

1. In a food processor, blend the eggs with the cottage cheese until smooth. Scrape the mixture into a bowl. Whisk in the cornmeal, flour, sugar and salt, then stir in the milk and melted butter. Let the batter rest for 30 minutes.

2. Heat a griddle or cast-iron skillet and brush very lightly with oil. For each pancake, spoon a 3-tablespoon-size dollop of batter onto the griddle; cook until the bottom browns and bubbles appear on the surface. Flip the pancakes and cook just until browned on the second side. Transfer the pancakes to a baking sheet and keep them warm at a low temperature in the oven while you make the rest.

3. Roll up the pancakes and set 3 on each plate. Top with the maple syrup and berries, dust with confectioners' sugar and serve. —*Bob Peterson*

● FAST ● HEALTHY ● MAKE AHEAD ● STAFF FAVORITE

breakfast + brunch

Pancakes with Apricot Honey

ACTIVE: 45 MIN; TOTAL: 2 HR 15 MIN

2 TO 4 SERVINGS

Eugenia Bone adapted this recipe from *The New Joy of Cooking* (1953).

- 1¼ cups all-purpose flour
- 2 teaspoons sugar
- 2¼ teaspoons baking powder
- ½ teaspoon salt
- 1 large egg, beaten
- 1 cup milk
- 2 tablespoons unsalted butter, melted, plus softened butter for serving

Vegetable oil, for the griddle

Apricot Honey (recipe follows)

1. Preheat the oven to 300°. In a bowl, whisk the flour with the sugar, baking powder and salt. In another bowl, combine the egg with the milk and melted butter. Pour the liquid ingredients into the flour mixture and stir until the flour is just moistened; ignore the lumps.

2. Heat a large cast-iron skillet. Lightly oil the surface. Pour ¼ cup of the batter into the skillet for each pancake, spreading it slightly. Cook over moderate to moderately low heat until the edges look dry, about 3 minutes. Turn the pancakes and cook for 1 minute. Transfer the pancakes to a cookie sheet and keep them warm in the oven while making the rest. Serve the pancakes with softened butter and Apricot Honey.
—*Eugenia Bone*

Apricot Honey

ACTIVE: 30 MIN; TOTAL: 1 HR 40 MIN

MAKES 6 PINTS ●

This recipe was adapted from *Fruit Fixins of the North Fork 1882-1972*.

- 4 pounds apricots (3 quarts), pitted and coarsely chopped
- 4½ pounds sugar (10 cups)
- ½ cup fresh lemon juice

Puree the apricots in a food processor. In a large, heavy pot, mix the apricot puree with the sugar and lemon juice and bring to a boil over moderate heat, skimming as necessary. Cover and cook over low heat, stirring occasionally, until thickened, about 20 minutes. Pour the apricot honey into 6 hot sterilized 1-pint jars, stopping ¼ inch from the top. Wipe the rims and close the jars. Set them in a water bath and bring to a boil. Boil for 15 minutes. —*E.B.*

Light and Crispy Waffles

TOTAL: 35 MIN

MAKES ABOUT SEVEN 3¾-INCH SQUARE WAFFLES ●

- ¾ cup all-purpose flour
- ¼ cup cornstarch
- ½ teaspoon salt
- ½ teaspoon baking powder
- ¼ teaspoon baking soda
- ¾ cup buttermilk
- 6 tablespoons vegetable oil
- ¼ cup whole milk
- 1 large egg, separated
- 1 tablespoon sugar
- ½ teaspoon pure vanilla extract

Vegetable oil, for the waffle iron

Pure maple syrup, for serving

1. Preheat the oven to 200°. In a bowl, combine the flour, cornstarch, salt, baking powder and baking soda. In another bowl, blend the buttermilk, vegetable oil and milk. Beat in the egg yolk.

2. In a medium bowl, beat the egg white to soft peaks. Add the sugar and beat until firm and glossy. Beat in the vanilla.

3. Pour the liquid ingredients into the dry ingredients and whisk until just blended. Using a rubber spatula, gently fold in the egg white.

4. Preheat an 8-inch square waffle iron and oil it lightly. Pour about 1½ cups of the waffle batter into the waffle iron and smooth the surface with a spatula. Bake for 4 minutes, or until browned and crisp. Transfer the waffles to the oven rack to keep warm and repeat with the remaining batter. Serve at once with maple syrup. —*Pam Anderson*

Banana Waffles with Pecans

TOTAL: 1 HR

MAKES SIXTEEN 4-INCH WAFFLES ●

A good amount of butter in the batter makes these waffles extra crisp. As a general rule, adding less butter to a batter results in a fluffier waffle.

- ½ cup pecans
- 1½ cups all-purpose flour
- ½ cup yellow cornmeal
- 1 tablespoon baking powder
- ¼ teaspoon salt
- 1¼ cups milk
- 1½ sticks (6 ounces) unsalted butter, melted
- 3 large eggs, separated
- 2 large ripe bananas, quartered lengthwise and cut into ½-inch pieces
- ¼ cup sugar

Maple syrup, for serving

1. Preheat the oven to 350°. Spread the pecans in a pie plate and bake for 10 minutes, or until golden. Let cool, then coarsely chop. Lower the oven temperature to 225°.

2. Preheat an 8-inch waffle iron. In a bowl, whisk the flour, cornmeal, baking powder and salt. In a small bowl, combine the milk, melted butter and egg yolks. Stir the liquid into the dry ingredients just until moistened; lumps are okay. Fold the bananas into the batter.

3. In a clean bowl, beat the egg whites at medium speed until frothy. Increase the speed to high and beat until firm peaks form. Add the sugar and beat until the whites are stiff and glossy. Fold the whites into the batter until no streaks remain.

4. Oil or butter the waffle iron. Pour 1¼ cups of batter into the iron and bake until the waffle is golden, about 6 minutes. Transfer the waffle to the oven rack to keep warm and repeat with the remaining batter. Separate the waffles and serve with the toasted pecans and maple syrup. —*Grace Parisi*

Q+A
leftover bread

french toast

Q: I love to make challah French toast, but sometimes it's perfect and other times it turns out mushy. How can I prevent that infernal sogginess?

A: A soggy center in French toast can be caused by one of three things: You haven't used enough eggs in the custard mixture (for six 1-inch-thick slices of bread, you want 3 to 4 eggs and 1 cup of milk); you've undercooked your French toast slices; or your bread is too fresh. Assuming that you're always using the same recipe, the culprit behind your soggy toast seems to be reason number three. French toast should be fluffy and light, but if the bread's very fresh and moist before cooking, the interior of the French toast will remain custardy-soft. One- or two-day-old bread is a better bet. Don't let it get completely dried out, though, or it will disintegrate. Brioche, cinnamon-raisin bread or a white loaf from a bakery all make delicious French toast. In a pinch, you can use a sliced supermarket loaf, but don't let the pieces stand for too long after dipping in the custard mixture or they'll fall apart. Here's the recipe we like to use in the F&W test kitchen.

Classic French Toast
TOTAL: 25 MIN
MAKES 6 SLICES ●

For lots of piping hot French toast, brown the egg-soaked slices on the stove and then finish cooking them at the same time in the oven. You can finish them in the skillet, too.

3 to 4 large eggs
  1 cup milk
Six ¾- to 1-inch-thick slices of challah
  or other bread
Unsalted butter and/or vegetable oil
Confectioners' sugar
Berries and warmed pure maple syrup

I. Preheat the oven to 375°. In a medium bowl, beat the eggs with the milk. Slowly draw a slice of bread through the custard mixture once or twice and set it on a plate. Repeat with the remaining slices, stacking as you go. Let stand until the custard mixture is absorbed.
2. Heat a griddle or a large nonstick skillet and grease well. Carefully add as many slices as will fit in a single layer and cook over moderately high heat until browned on both sides, about 4 minutes. Transfer to a baking sheet and repeat with the remaining slices.
3. Bake the French toast for 4 to 5 minutes, or until puffed and just firm to the touch when lightly pressed. Dust with confectioners' sugar and serve immediately with berries and maple syrup.

croutons

Q: I always have bread that is too stale for sandwiches, but I hate to toss anything out. Suggestions?

A: The first thing to do is make croutons. They're great for topping egg dishes or tossing on salads and soups. (Or crush them up and sprinkle them on pastas, cooked vegetables and grilled chicken, beef or fish.) And you can make them from any bread. Here's a recipe from the F&W test kitchen.

Classic Croutons
Cut stale bread into cubes. Toss the cubes with olive oil, season with salt and pepper and spread them on a rimmed baking sheet in a single layer. Bake at 400° for about 8 minutes, or until browned, raking the cubes once or twice for even browning. Let the croutons cool completely before storing them in an airtight container.

For *herbed croutons,* stir fresh herbs, such as thyme, rosemary and oregano, into the olive oil. For *garlic croutons,* infuse the oil with crushed garlic cloves for at least 30 minutes and strain before using. For *cheese croutons,* sprinkle some freshly grated Parmesan or Romano cheese onto the croutons after 6 minutes, toss and bake them for about 2 minutes more.

breakfast + brunch

French Toast with Cheese

ACTIVE: 20 MIN; TOTAL: 30 MIN

4 SERVINGS ● ●

Great bread is essential here. Try a mild-flavored country bread such as ciabatta. If the loaf is too flat, slice it on the diagonal for larger slices.

- 2 large eggs, lightly beaten
- ⅔ cup low-fat (2%) milk
- ¼ teaspoon salt
- Pinch of freshly ground pepper
- Pinch of cayenne pepper
- ¾ cup plus 1½ tablespoons freshly grated Parmesan cheese
- Four ½-inch-thick slices of country bread
- 1 tablespoon canola oil or other mild oil

1. In a medium baking dish, whisk the eggs with the milk, salt, pepper and cayenne. Stir in the Parmesan. Add the bread slices and turn to coat well, then pierce them all over with a fork and let them soak for 5 minutes. Flip the bread slices, then pierce them all over with the fork again and let them soak for about 3 minutes longer. Flip and soak the bread 2 more times, or until almost all of the custard is absorbed; the cheese will form a coating on the outside of the bread.

2. Heat ¾ teaspoon of the canola oil in each of 2 medium nonstick skillets. Add 2 slices of bread to each pan and cook over moderately low heat without moving the slices until a deep brown crust forms on the bottoms, about 3 minutes. Add another ¾ teaspoon of the oil to each pan, flip the bread and cook until deeply browned on the other side, about 2 minutes longer. Serve the French toast at once. —*Sally Schneider*

SERVE WITH Frisée salad with walnuts.

French Toast with Maple Apples

TOTAL: 40 MIN

4 SERVINGS ●

- 3 large eggs
- 1 cup skim milk
- 1 teaspoon pure vanilla extract
- ½ teaspoon freshly grated nutmeg
- Eight ¾-inch-thick slices of white bread (½ pound)
- 2 tablespoons unsalted butter
- 2 Granny Smith apples (1 pound)—peeled, halved, cored and cut into ¼-inch-thick slices
- ¾ cup pure maple syrup
- ¼ teaspoon cinnamon
- 2 teaspoons vegetable oil, such as canola

1. In a shallow glass dish, beat the eggs with the skim milk, vanilla and nutmeg. Add the bread, turn to coat and let soak for 5 minutes.

2. Meanwhile, in a large skillet, melt 1 tablespoon of the butter. Add the apples and 2 tablespoons of the maple syrup and cook over high heat, stirring frequently, until softened and lightly caramelized, about 8 minutes. Add the cinnamon and the remaining ½ cup plus 2 tablespoons of maple syrup and simmer for 1 minute; keep warm.

3. Heat a large nonstick skillet over moderately high heat. Add ½ tablespoon of butter and 1 teaspoon of vegetable oil and heat until just shimmering. Add half of the bread slices and cook, turning once, until golden brown all over, about 2 minutes per side. Repeat with the remaining butter, oil and bread. Halve the slices of French toast on the diagonal and stack on plates. Top with the glazed apples and serve at once. —*Jason Knibb*

Sundance Granola

ACTIVE: 15 MIN; TOTAL: 1 HOUR 10 MIN

FOURTEEN ½-CUP SERVINGS ● ●

- ⅔ cup whole almonds
- ⅔ cup pecans
- ⅓ cup roasted unsalted sunflower seeds
- 3 cups rolled oats
- 1 cup wheat germ
- ½ teaspoon cinnamon
- ¼ cup honey
- ¼ cup pure maple syrup
- 2 tablespoons molasses
- 2 tablespoons vegetable oil
- 1½ cups raisins

1. Preheat the oven to 275°. In a large bowl, toss the almonds with the pecans, sunflower seeds, oats, wheat germ and cinnamon. In a small saucepan, combine the honey, maple syrup, molasses and oil. Warm the liquid over low heat. Add the liquid mixture to the nuts and grains and toss thoroughly.

2. Spread the granola in a single layer on a large rimmed baking sheet and bake for about 40 minutes, stirring with a wooden spoon every 10 minutes to prevent sticking and to turn the grains and nuts, until the mixture is nicely toasted. Let the granola cool.

3. Add the raisins. Toss with a wooden spoon until thoroughly incorporated. —*Jason Knibb*

MAKE AHEAD Once cooled completely, the granola can be stored in an airtight container for up to 1 month.

KITCHEN TOOL

whisks

Cuisipro's silicone-covered whisks won't scratch nonstick cookware when you stir ($14; 302-326-4802).

Scrambled Eggs with Chicken, Ham and Potatoes

ACTIVE: 50 MIN; TOTAL: 1 HR 50 MIN

6 SERVINGS

- 3 tablespoons corn oil
- 1 large onion, halved lengthwise and thinly sliced crosswise
- 1 red bell pepper, cut into ¼-inch strips
- 6 ounces roasted or poached chicken breast meat, shredded
- 6 ounces baked ham, cut into ¼-inch strips
- 12 large eggs
- ¼ cup milk

Kosher salt and freshly ground pepper

- 3 tablespoons chopped parsley

Oven-Fried Potatoes (recipe, page 140)

Hot sauce, for serving

1. Heat the oil in a skillet. Add the onion and cook over moderate heat, stirring, until browned, about 8 minutes. Add the bell pepper and cook until softened, about 5 minutes. Add the chicken and ham and cook until heated through.

2. In a bowl, beat the eggs with the milk, 1 teaspoon of kosher salt, ½ teaspoon of pepper and the parsley. Add to the skillet and cook over moderate heat, stirring frequently, until just cooked, about 5 minutes. Add half of the Oven-Fried Potatoes and toss until heated. Serve with the remaining potatoes and hot sauce. —*Maricel Presilla*

Scrambled Eggs with Goat Cheese and Shiitake Mushrooms

TOTAL: 15 MIN

4 SERVINGS ●

- 3 tablespoons unsalted butter
- 6 ounces shiitake mushrooms, stems removed, caps thinly sliced

Salt and freshly ground pepper

- 8 large eggs, well beaten
- 3 tablespoons snipped chives
- 3 ounces mild fresh goat cheese, crumbled (about ½ cup)

Toast, for serving

1. In a large nonstick skillet, melt 2 tablespoons of the butter. Add the mushrooms, season with salt and pepper and cook over moderate heat, stirring occasionally, until softened and lightly browned, about 5 minutes.

2. In a bowl, season the eggs with salt and pepper. Melt the remaining butter in the skillet with the mushrooms; add the eggs. Cook over moderately low heat without stirring until the bottom is barely set, 30 seconds. Add the chives and cook, stirring occasionally, until the eggs form large soft curds. Remove from the heat and sprinkle on the cheese; let stand until softened, 30 seconds. Gently fold the cheese into the eggs; serve with toast. —*Laura Chenel*

Baked Egg and Asparagus Gratins

TOTAL: 35 MIN

4 SERVINGS ●

- 1 cup dry bread crumbs
- 2 tablespoons unsalted butter, melted
- 1¼ pounds asparagus, cut into 2-inch lengths
- 1½ cups heavy cream
- 1 garlic clove, thinly sliced

Salt and freshly ground pepper

- 8 large eggs

1. Preheat the oven to 350°. In a pie plate, toss the bread crumbs and butter. Bake for 6 minutes, stirring once.

2. Bring a saucepan of water to a rapid boil. Add the asparagus and cook until crisp-tender, about 3 minutes. Drain and refresh under cold water, then pat dry.

3. In a saucepan, simmer the heavy cream and garlic; season with salt and pepper. Arrange the asparagus in 4 individual-size gratin dishes and season with salt and pepper. Crack 2 eggs into each dish, pour the garlic cream on top and sprinkle with the crumbs. Bake the eggs for 15 minutes, or until the whites are firm and the yolks are still runny. Serve at once. —*Anne Quatrano*

Grilled Ham and Cheese Sandwiches with Fried Eggs

TOTAL: 25 MIN

4 SERVINGS ●

- 8 slices of peasant or Tuscan bread
- 6 ounces thinly sliced Serrano ham or prosciutto
- 1½ ounces Manchego cheese, shaved (½ cup)
- 2 tablespoons unsalted butter
- 3 tablespoons extra-virgin olive oil
- 4 large eggs

Salt and freshly ground pepper

- 1 bunch arugula, stemmed
- 1 tablespoon fresh lemon juice

1. Preheat the oven to 300°. Lay the bread slices on a work surface. Arrange the pieces of ham and cheese on 4 of the bread slices, then top with the remaining 4 bread slices to close up the sandwiches.

2. In a large skillet, melt 1 tablespoon of the butter in 1 tablespoon of the oil. Brush the sandwiches on one side with some of the melted butter and oil, then add to the skillet, buttered side up. Cook the sandwiches over moderate heat, turning once, until the cheese is fully melted and the sandwiches are golden all over, about 4 minutes. Transfer the sandwiches to a baking sheet and keep warm in the oven.

3. Melt the remaining 1 tablespoon of butter in 1 tablespoon of the olive oil in the same skillet. Crack the eggs individually into the skillet and cook them over moderate heat until the whites are set and the yolks are still runny, about 2 minutes. Top each grilled sandwich with a fried egg and season with salt and pepper.

4. In a medium bowl, toss the arugula with the remaining 1 tablespoon of olive oil and the lemon juice and season generously with salt and pepper. Transfer the egg-topped sandwiches and salad to serving plates and serve immediately. —*Anne Quatrano*

HUEVOS RANCHEROS WITH SPICY HAM SOFRITO   **OPEN-FACED EGG WHITE OMELET**

Breakfast Pan-Roast with Fried Eggs and Parsley Sauce

ACTIVE: 25 MIN; TOTAL: 1 HR

4 SERVINGS

- 1 bunch flat-leaf parsley (3 ounces), stemmed and coarsely chopped
- 3 tablespoons water
- 3 tablespoons chopped shallots
- 1 teaspoon thyme leaves
- 3 tablespoons extra-virgin olive oil

Salt and freshly ground pepper

- ¾ pound lean slab bacon, cut crosswise into four 2-inch-long pieces
- 1½ pounds Yukon Gold potatoes, cut into 2-inch chunks
- 8 large eggs

I. Preheat the oven to 400°. In a blender, puree the parsley, water, shallots, thyme and 2 tablespoons of the olive oil; season with salt and pepper.

2. In a large cast-iron skillet, heat the remaining 1 tablespoon of olive oil in the oven for 10 minutes. Add the bacon to the skillet and bake for 12 minutes, or until the fat is rendered and the bacon is slightly crisp. Transfer the bacon to a plate. Add the potatoes to the skillet and turn to coat them with the fat; season with salt and pepper. Bake the potatoes for 15 minutes, or until tender and lightly browned; transfer to the plate with the bacon.

3. Set the skillet over moderately low heat. Crack 4 of the eggs into the skillet and fry for 2 minutes per side, until the whites are set and the yolks are still runny. Transfer the eggs to 2 plates. Repeat with the remaining eggs. Spoon the bacon and potatoes alongside the eggs and dollop the parsley sauce on top. Serve at once. —*Marcia Kiesel*

Huevos Rancheros with Spicy Ham Sofrito

TOTAL: 35 MIN

4 SERVINGS ● ●

- 3 tablespoons vegetable oil
- 10 ounces smoked ham, cut into 2-by-¼-inch strips
- 4 large garlic cloves, thinly sliced
- 2 medium red onions, thinly sliced
- 2 Scotch bonnet chiles or jalapeños—halved, seeded and thinly sliced crosswise
- 1 large green bell pepper, thinly sliced
- 1 teaspoon sweet paprika
- 2 medium tomatoes, coarsely chopped

Salt and freshly ground pepper

Eight 6-inch corn tortillas

- 8 large eggs

1. Preheat the oven to 475°. In a large skillet, heat ½ tablespoon of the vegetable oil. Add the smoked ham and cook over moderately high heat until browned on the bottom, about 2 minutes. Using a slotted spoon, transfer the ham to a plate. Add 1½ tablespoons of the vegetable oil to the skillet along with the garlic, onions, Scotch bonnet chiles and green bell pepper. Cover and cook over moderately low heat, stirring occasionally, until the vegetables are softened, about 12 minutes. Stir in the paprika and cook over moderately high heat for 1 minute. Add the tomatoes and cook until they release their juices, about 2 minutes. Stir in the ham and season the sofrito with salt and pepper.

2. Meanwhile, wrap the tortillas in aluminum foil and warm them in the oven. In a large cast-iron skillet, heat ½ tablespoon of the vegetable oil. Crack 4 of the eggs into the skillet, season with salt and pepper and fry sunny-side up over moderate heat until the egg whites are set and the egg yolks are still slightly runny, about 3 minutes. Transfer the eggs, yolk side up, to a plate and keep them warm by tenting them with aluminum foil. Add the remaining ½ tablespoon of vegetable oil to the skillet and fry the remaining eggs.

3. Set 2 tortillas on each plate. Top with the fried eggs, spoon the sofrito on the side and serve. —*Marcia Kiesel*

VARIATIONS Use the sofrito in cheese quesadillas or on grilled chicken, or toss with roasted new potatoes.

Black Bean Huevos Rancheros

ACTIVE: 35 MIN; TOTAL: 50 MIN

4 SERVINGS ●

If you're in a hurry, you can roll up these eggs and beans in the tortillas to make breakfast burritos you can eat on the run.

- 4 large Anaheim chiles
- 2 ounces Pepper Jack cheese, shredded (½ cup)

- 8 corn tortillas

Vegetable oil

- 2 garlic cloves, minced
- 1 cup drained canned black beans
- ½ cup chicken stock or canned low-sodium broth
- 1 teaspoon chopped chipotle chiles in adobo or chipotle chile sauce
- 1 tablespoon minced cilantro
- 4 large eggs
- ½ small avocado, cut into 4 wedges
- ¼ cup diced plum tomatoes
- 4 teaspoons finely diced red onion
- 2 teaspoons minced jalapeño

1. Preheat the broiler. Roast the Anaheim chiles under the broiler for 6 to 7 minutes, turning frequently, until charred all over. Transfer them to a bowl, cover with plastic wrap and let steam for 5 minutes. When the chiles are cool enough to handle, peel and coarsely chop them. In a bowl, mix the chiles with the cheese.

2. Turn the oven to 375°. Very lightly brush the tortillas with vegetable oil. Spread the roasted chiles and cheese on half of the tortillas and top with the remaining tortillas. Transfer the filled tortillas to a baking sheet, cover with foil and top with another baking sheet.

3. Heat 1 teaspoon of oil in a small skillet. Add the garlic and cook over moderately high heat for 1 minute. Add the beans, chicken stock and chopped chipotles and simmer for 5 minutes. Stir in the cilantro and keep warm.

4. Bake the tortillas for about 5 minutes, or until they are heated through and the cheese is melted. Meanwhile, in a lightly oiled large skillet, cook the eggs sunny-side up or over easy.

5. Transfer the filled tortillas to plates. Top with the beans and then the eggs. Garnish with the avocado wedges, diced tomatoes and onion and minced jalapeño and serve. —*Jason Knibb*

Open-Faced Egg White Omelets with Roasted Vegetables

ACTIVE: 35 MIN; TOTAL: 50 MIN

4 SERVINGS ●

This egg white omelet with goat cheese is a vegetarian's dream.

Kosher salt

- 4 small leeks, white parts only, quartered lengthwise
- 1 fennel bulb—halved, cored and cut into eighths
- 1 tablespoon extra-virgin olive oil
- 2 large plum tomatoes, quartered
- 16 large egg whites

Freshly ground pepper

- 4 ounces soft fresh goat cheese
- 4 basil sprigs, for garnish

1. Preheat the oven to 475°. Bring a medium pot of water to a boil with 2 tablespoons of salt. Add the leek and fennel slices and blanch for 2 minutes; drain and pat dry. Transfer the blanched vegetables to a large baking sheet and drizzle with 2 teaspoons of the oil. Roast in the upper third of the oven for about 15 minutes, or until nicely browned. Add the tomato quarters to the vegetables on the baking sheet and roast them for about 3 minutes, or until softened.

2. In a large bowl, whisk the egg whites with salt and pepper. Lightly rub an 8-inch nonstick ovenproof skillet with some of the remaining 1 teaspoon of oil and set it over moderate heat. Add one-fourth of the beaten egg whites to the hot pan and cook the eggs until just barely set, about 3 minutes. Top the omelet with one-fourth of the roasted vegetables and crumble one-fourth of the goat cheese over the vegetables. Bake for about 2 minutes, or until the whites are just firm. Slide the omelet onto a serving plate and repeat with the remaining oil, egg whites, roasted vegetables and goat cheese. Garnish the omelets with the basil sprigs and serve them at once. —*Jason Knibb*

breakfast + brunch

Rolled Egg White Omelet with Wild Mushrooms

TOTAL: 15 MIN

1 SERVING ●

2 tablespoons salted butter, melted

2 teaspoons minced shallot

Pinch of fresh thyme

½ cup small chanterelles or sliced wild mushrooms

Salt and freshly ground pepper

4 large egg whites

1. Preheat the broiler; set a broiler rack 5 inches from the heat. Heat 1 tablespoon of the butter in a nonstick ovenproof skillet. Add the shallot and thyme and cook over moderate heat for 30 seconds. Add the mushrooms, season with salt and pepper and cook over moderately high heat until tender and lightly browned, about 5 minutes.

2. In a medium bowl, whisk the egg whites until frothy. Season with salt and pepper and beat in the remaining 1 tablespoon of melted butter. Pour the beaten whites into the skillet and cook over moderate heat until almost opaque, drawing in the edges of the omelet with a spatula as they set and tilting the pan to allow the uncooked whites to seep underneath, about 40 seconds.

3. Transfer the skillet to the broiler and broil the omelet for 10 seconds, or until the top is just set. Run the spatula around the edge of the pan. Fold one-third of the omelet onto itself, then roll it out onto a plate in a neat shape and serve at once. —*Laurent Manrique*

Creamy Mozzarella Omelet

ACTIVE: 30 MIN; TOTAL: 1 HR 30 MIN

4 SERVINGS

This recipe calls for burrata, a smooth mozzarella cheese enclosing a center of mozzarella scraps and cream. Look for it at cheese shops and Italian food markets, or substitute 4 ounces of shredded fresh mozzarella mixed with 2 ounces of cream cheese.

2 large baking potatoes, scrubbed

1 teaspoon vegetable oil

4 tablespoons unsalted butter

Sea salt

1 dozen large eggs

4 teaspoons freshly grated Parmesan cheese

Freshly ground pepper

4 slices of burrata cheese (6 ounces)

1. Preheat the oven to 425°. Rub the potatoes with the oil. Place on the oven rack and bake for 1 hour, until tender. Let cool slightly, then cut each potato crosswise into 4 thick slices.

2. Melt 2 tablespoons of the butter in a skillet. Add the potatoes and cook over moderate heat, turning, until golden and crisp, about 8 minutes. Season the potatoes with salt and transfer to a paper towel–lined plate.

3. In a 7-inch omelet pan, melt ½ tablespoon of butter. In a bowl, beat 3 eggs, 1 teaspoon of Parmesan and a pinch each of salt and pepper and add to the omelet pan; cook until just set, 2 to 3 minutes. Flip the omelet, set a burrata slice in the center and fold the sides of the omelet over. Slide onto a plate. Repeat to make 3 more omelets and serve with the pan-fried potatoes. —*Bruce Marder*

Fresh Herb Omelet

TOTAL: 5 MIN

MAKES 1 OMELET ●

3 large eggs

1 tablespoon chopped flat-leaf parsley

1 tablespoon (total) chopped mixed chervil, tarragon and chives

Salt and freshly ground pepper

1½ teaspoons unsalted butter

1. In a medium bowl, lightly beat the eggs with a fork; beat in the parsley and the mixed herbs and a pinch each of salt and pepper.

2. In a 6- or 7-inch nonstick skillet, melt the butter over high heat. Swirl the butter in the pan, and when it foams, pour in the beaten eggs. Holding the fork parallel to the bottom of the pan, briskly stir the eggs, drawing them into the center of the pan as they cook; with your other hand, shake the skillet to distribute the eggs evenly. Stop stirring when the eggs are still moist but no longer runny, after about 10 seconds. If the omelet seems to be sticking to the skillet, shake the pan to loosen it.

3. Tilt the skillet and use the fork to fold opposite sides of the omelet into the center. Turn the omelet out onto a heated plate, seam side down, and serve immediately. —*Jacques Pépin*

Ham and Cheese Strata

ACTIVE: 10 MIN; TOTAL: 30 MIN

4 SERVINGS ●

8 large eggs

1½ cups milk

½ teaspoon salt

½ teaspoon freshly ground pepper

4 cups Italian bread cubes (1 inch)

6 ounces Virginia ham, cut into ½-inch dice (1½ cups)

6 ounces Gouda cheese, cut into ¾-inch dice (1½ cups)

½ cup julienned sun-dried tomatoes, drained

¼ cup plus 1 tablespoon snipped chives

1 cup coarsely grated Cheddar cheese (about 4 ounces)

1. Preheat the oven to 450°. Whisk the eggs, milk, salt and pepper. Stir in the bread until evenly moistened, then stir in the ham, Gouda cheese, sun-dried tomatoes and ¼ cup of the chives.

2. Butter a 9-by-12-inch baking dish and pour in the strata mixture. Sprinkle the Cheddar cheese on top. Bake for about 20 minutes, until puffed and golden. Let cool slightly, sprinkle with the remaining chives and serve. —*Diana Sturgis*

HAM AND CHEESE STRATA

breakfast + brunch

Spinach and Cheese Grits Frittatas

ACTIVE: 1 HR 30 MIN; TOTAL: 2 HR 20 MIN

12 SERVINGS ● ●

You can substitute 1½ cups of shredded Monterey Jack cheese plus 1 cup of sharp white Cheddar cheese for the Spanish tetilla, Manchego and Mahón cheeses used below.

- ¼ cup freshly grated Parmesan cheese
- 8 cups water
- Salt
- 3 cups stone-ground yellow or white grits (see Note)
- Two 5-ounce bags baby spinach
- 2 cups parsley leaves
- 6 tablespoons unsalted butter, 5 tablespoons softened and 1 tablespoon melted
- 2 large garlic cloves, minced
- Freshly ground pepper
- 3 ounces chilled tetilla cheese, coarsely shredded (1 cup)
- 3 ounces chilled Mahón cheese, coarsely shredded (1 cup)
- 1½ ounces chilled young Manchego cheese, coarsely shredded (½ cup)
- 6 large eggs, lightly beaten

1. Preheat the oven to 350°. Butter two 9-inch springform pans and dust with 2 tablespoons of the Parmesan cheese.
2. In a medium enameled cast-iron casserole, bring the water to a boil with a large pinch of salt. Whisk in the grits. Cover and simmer over low heat, whisking often, for 1 hour and 15 minutes. Transfer the grits to a large bowl and let cool, stirring occasionally, until warm.
3. Meanwhile, in a medium saucepan of boiling water, working in 2 batches, blanch the spinach for 30 seconds. Using a slotted spoon, transfer the spinach to a colander. Blanch the parsley in the boiling water until almost tender, about 4 minutes. Transfer to the colander. Lightly squeeze the greens dry and coarsely chop.
4. In a large skillet, melt 2 tablespoons of the softened butter. Add the garlic and cook over low heat until fragrant, about 2 minutes. Add the spinach and parsley and cook, stirring, for 2 minutes. Season with salt and pepper.
5. Stir the tetilla, Mahón and Manchego cheeses, the remaining 3 tablespoons of softened butter and the spinach and parsley into the grits. Season with salt and pepper and stir in the eggs. Pour half of the mixture into each of the prepared pans. Brush the frittatas with the melted butter and sprinkle with the remaining 2 tablespoons of Parmesan.
6. Bake the frittatas on the top shelf of the oven for about 40 minutes, or until golden brown and just set. Let cool in the pans for 15 minutes. Remove the pan rings. To serve, cut the frittatas into wedges with a serrated knife, wiping the knife between cuts. —*Marcia Kiesel*

NOTE Stone-ground grits are available from www.hoppinjohns.com, or call 800-828-4412.

MAKE AHEAD The frittatas can be refrigerated in the pans for up to 2 days. Bring to room temperature before reheating.

Frittata with Fresh Herbs

TOTAL: 30 MIN

4 SERVINGS ●

- 4 garlic cloves, halved
- ½ cup extra-virgin olive oil
- 3 slices of white bread, cut into ½-inch dice (¾ cup)
- 8 large eggs, beaten
- ½ cup freshly grated Parmesan cheese
- ⅓ cup heavy cream
- 1 tablespoon snipped chives
- 1 teaspoon finely chopped tarragon
- Salt and freshly ground pepper
- ⅓ cup ricotta cheese

1. Preheat the oven to 350°. In a small saucepan, simmer the garlic in the olive oil over moderate heat until soft and golden, 7 minutes; discard the garlic.

In a pie plate, toss the diced bread with 1 tablespoon of garlic oil. Bake for 6 minutes, or until crisp. Leave the oven on.
2. In a medium bowl, whisk the eggs with the Parmesan cheese, heavy cream, chives and tarragon; season the eggs with salt and pepper. Whisk in ¼ cup of the garlic oil.
3. In a 10-inch nonstick ovenproof skillet, heat the remaining garlic oil until shimmering. Whisk the eggs again, then add to the skillet and cook without stirring for 1 minute, until just set around the edge. Using a rubber spatula, lift the edge and tilt the pan so the uncooked egg seeps underneath. Continue until the eggs are mostly set, about 3 minutes. Spoon the ricotta in small dollops over the frittata; season with salt and pepper. Sprinkle with the croutons. Bake for 4 minutes, until fluffy and set. Slide onto a large plate, cut into wedges and serve. —*Anne Quatrano*

Potato, Sausage and Kale Frittata

TOTAL: 30 MIN

4 TO 6 SERVINGS ●

- 10 large eggs
- ¼ cup freshly grated Parmesan cheese
- Salt and freshly ground pepper
- 3 tablespoons plus 1 teaspoon extra-virgin olive oil
- 3 sweet Italian fennel sausages (½ pound), meat removed from the casings
- 1 small onion, cut into ¼-inch dice
- 1 pound Yukon Gold potatoes, peeled and cut into ½-inch pieces
- 3 large kale leaves, stems and inner ribs discarded, leaves coarsely chopped

1. Preheat the broiler and position the rack 8 inches from the heat. Crack the eggs into a large bowl. Add 2 tablespoons of grated Parmesan, season generously with salt and pepper and beat the eggs until blended.

2. In a large nonstick ovenproof skillet, heat 1 teaspoon of the olive oil. Add the sausage meat and onion and cook over moderately high heat, breaking the sausage up into small pieces, until browned and cooked through, about 5 minutes. Transfer to a plate. Add 2 tablespoons of the olive oil to the skillet and heat until shimmering. Add the potatoes and cook over moderately high heat, stirring occasionally, until crisp and cooked through, about 5 minutes. Add the kale, season with salt and cook, tossing, until softened, about 2 minutes longer.

3. Add the remaining 1 tablespoon of olive oil to the skillet and tilt the skillet to swirl the oil around the sides. Scatter the sausage and onion in the skillet. Stir the eggs and add them to the skillet. Cook over moderate heat for 1 minute. Gently lift the edge of the frittata and tilt the pan, allowing some of the uncooked egg to seep underneath. Cook until the bottom and sides are barely set, about 3 minutes.

4. Sprinkle the remaining 2 tablespoons of grated Parmesan cheese on top of the frittata. Broil until the eggs are set and the top of the frittata is lightly browned, 1 to 2 minutes longer. Slide the frittata onto a large plate, cut into wedges and serve hot or warm.
—*Grace Parisi*

Goat Cheese and Fresh Herb Soufflé

ACTIVE: 30 MIN; TOTAL: 1 HR 30 MIN

4 SERVINGS

- ¼ cup freshly grated Parmesan cheese
- 4 tablespoons unsalted butter
- ½ cup all-purpose flour
- 2 cups milk
- 1 bay leaf
- ½ pound fresh goat cheese, crumbled

Salt and freshly ground pepper

- 4 large eggs, separated
- 2 tablespoons snipped chives
- 1 tablespoon very finely chopped dill
- 1 tablespoon very finely chopped flat-leaf parsley
- 2 teaspoons very finely chopped tarragon

I. Preheat the oven to 375°. Butter a 2-quart soufflé dish. Add the Parmesan cheese and turn the soufflé dish to evenly coat the bottom and side of the dish. Tap out any excess cheese.

2. In a medium saucepan, melt the butter over moderate heat. Whisk in the flour until a smooth paste forms. Whisk in 1 cup of the milk until smooth, then whisk in the remaining 1 cup of milk and add the bay leaf. Bring the sauce to a boil, whisking constantly. Reduce the heat to low and cook, whisking frequently, until very thick, about 10 minutes. Scrape the sauce into a large bowl. Stir in the goat cheese and season with salt and pepper, then whisk in the egg yolks until thoroughly incorporated. Cover the cheese sauce and let cool, then stir in the herbs.

3. In a large stainless steel bowl, beat the egg whites with a pinch of salt until firm but not dry. Fold one-third of the beaten whites into the cheese sauce. Fold in the remaining whites, leaving a few white streaks.

4. Scrape the soufflé mixture into the prepared baking dish and bake in the center of the oven for 45 minutes, or until browned, puffed and still slightly jiggly in the center. Serve at once.
—*Marcia Kiesel*

MAKE AHEAD The soufflé base can be prepared through Step 2, without adding the herbs, and refrigerated overnight. Bring the soufflé base to room temperature and stir in the herbs before folding in the beaten egg whites.

TASTE TEST yogurt

The dairy aisle is stocked with dozens of yogurt brands. Never mind all the flavors and mix-ins—even choosing a plain yogurt can be daunting. We tasted 15 plain varieties; these are our four favorites.

PRODUCT	F&W COMMENT	INTERESTING BITE
Total 2%	"Full-bodied, rich, almost like crème fraîche."	This Greek yogurt is thicker than American-made yogurt because the whey is strained off.
Horizon Organic Fat Free	"Creamy, with a slightly tart, lemony flavor."	Horizon's founders lobbied to pass the Organic Standards Act, which came into effect in 2002.
Dannon Premium Lowfat	"Silky, with a pleasantly mild taste."	The company recently downsized its single-portion cups from 8 ounces to 6.
Old Chatham Sheepherding Company (made with whole milk)	"Lovely thick consistency and a sharp, tangy flavor."	Old Chatham yogurt is made with sheep's milk, which is higher in protein than cow's milk.

● FAST ● HEALTHY ● MAKE AHEAD ● STAFF FAVORITE

breakfast + brunch

Omelet Soufflé with Spinach and Goat Cheese

ACTIVE: 45 MIN; TOTAL: 1 HR 30 MIN

12 SERVINGS ●

This is a light and fluffy rolled omelet that gets sliced and served.

Vegetable oil cooking spray
- 1 stick (4 ounces) unsalted butter
- ½ cup all-purpose flour
- ¼ cup semolina flour
- 2¼ cups milk
- 2 cups heavy cream
- 8 large eggs, separated
- ¾ cup freshly grated Parmesan cheese (3 ounces)

Pinch of cayenne
Salt and freshly ground pepper
- ½ teaspoon cream of tartar

Three 5-ounce bags baby spinach
- 2 garlic cloves, minced
- ¾ cup fresh goat cheese (7 ounces)

1. Preheat the oven to 300°. Line a 12-by-17-inch rimmed baking sheet with parchment paper and spray with vegetable oil cooking spray.

2. In a saucepan, melt 7 tablespoons of the butter. Whisk in the all-purpose flour and cook over moderately high heat, whisking, until browned, 2 minutes. Add the semolina and whisk constantly for 1 minute. Off the heat, whisk in the milk and cream. Cook over moderately high heat, stirring, until thickened, 5 minutes.

3. Transfer 1 cup of the hot mixture to a large bowl and whisk in the egg yolks. Whisk in the remaining hot mixture, then whisk in the Parmesan and cayenne and season with salt and pepper.

4. In another large bowl, using an electric mixer, beat the egg whites with the cream of tartar at medium speed until frothy. Increase the speed to high and beat until soft peaks form. Beat one-fourth of the whites into the yolk mixture, then fold in the remaining whites until no streaks remain.

5. Spread the batter in the prepared baking sheet and smooth the surface. Bake for 30 minutes, or until the omelet is risen and puffed and small cracks appear on the surface. Let the omelet cool in the pan.

6. Meanwhile, heat a large skillet. Add the spinach in large handfuls and cook over high heat until wilted, allowing each batch to wilt slightly before adding the next. Transfer to a strainer and press out as much liquid as possible. Coarsely chop the spinach. Wipe out the skillet and melt the remaining 1 tablespoon of butter. Add the garlic and cook over moderate heat, stirring, until softened. Add the spinach, season with salt and pepper and cook, stirring, for 1 minute.

7. Cover the omelet with a sheet of wax paper and a clean kitchen towel. Place a cookie sheet over the omelet and invert it onto a work surface with the long side facing you. Remove the rimmed baking sheet and carefully peel off the parchment paper.

8. Arrange the spinach along the bottom edge of the omelet in a 3-inch strip. Dollop the goat cheese over the spinach. Using the kitchen towel as a guide, roll the omelet up like a jelly roll, peeling back the wax paper as you go. Carefully roll the omelet onto a long platter. Using a large spatula, tuck any omelet under that may have unrolled. Cut into slices and serve. —*Tom Valenti*

Spinach and Goat Cheese Quiche

ACTIVE: 1 HR; TOTAL: 3 HR 15 MIN

MAKES ONE 12-INCH QUICHE

For a more rustic look, crumble the goat cheese and scatter it over the filling instead of arranging the slices in the tart shell.

PASTRY
- 1¾ cups all-purpose flour

Pinch of salt
- 1 stick (4 ounces) cold unsalted butter, cut into small pieces
- 1 large egg
- 2 tablespoons ice water

FILLING
- 1 pound spinach, large stems discarded, leaves rinsed but not dried
- 1 garlic clove, minced
- 1 cup milk
- ½ cup heavy cream
- 2 large eggs
- 2 large egg yolks
- 1 teaspoon kosher salt
- ¼ teaspoon freshly ground pepper

One ½-pound goat cheese log, cut into seven ⅓-inch rounds

1. MAKE THE PASTRY: In a large bowl, whisk the flour with the salt. Using a pastry blender, cut in the butter until the mixture resembles coarse meal. Lightly beat the egg with the water and sprinkle over the flour mixture. Stir with a fork to lightly blend, then squeeze gently until a dough forms. Pat into a disk, wrap in plastic and refrigerate for at least 30 minutes.

2. Preheat the oven to 350°. On a very lightly floured surface, roll out the pastry to a 14-inch round about ⅛ inch thick. Fit the round into a 12-inch tart pan with a removable bottom and trim the overhang. Refrigerate the pastry shell for at least 20 minutes.

3. Line the tart shell with foil and fill with pie weights or rice. Bake until the pastry is firm, about 30 minutes.

Remove the foil and weights and bake for about 10 minutes longer, or until golden brown. Transfer the shell to a rack to cool.

4. MAKE THE FILLING: Heat a large skillet. Add a large handful of the spinach and cook over moderately high heat, stirring, until wilted. Transfer to a colander set over a bowl. Repeat until all of the spinach has been cooked; let cool. Squeeze the spinach dry and coarsely chop it. Toss the spinach with the garlic and spread it in the cooled pastry shell.

5. In a medium bowl, whisk the milk with the cream, eggs, egg yolks, salt and pepper. Arrange the goat cheese rounds on the spinach. Pour the custard into the shell and bake the quiche for about 40 minutes, or until just set. Transfer the quiche to a rack to cool slightly. Cut into wedges and serve. —*Christophe Côte*

Canadian Bacon and Cheddar Cheese Flan

ACTIVE: 20 MIN; TOTAL: 1 HR 25 MIN

8 SERVINGS ●

Canadian bacon is a lean, smoked meat that is more similar to ham than to bacon. It comes from the loin cut.

- 2 tablespoons unsalted butter
- ½ pound white mushrooms, stems discarded, caps thinly sliced
- 5 ounces thickly sliced Canadian bacon, cut into ½-inch dice (1 cup)
- 2 tablespoons chopped flat-leaf parsley
- 1½ teaspoons freshly ground pepper
- 10 large eggs
- 1 quart heavy cream
- 1 teaspoon kosher salt

Cayenne pepper

- 6 ounces sharp Cheddar cheese, shredded (2 cups)

I. Preheat the oven to 350°. Butter a 9-by-13-inch glass baking dish. In a large skillet, melt the 2 tablespoons of butter. Add the mushrooms and cook over moderate heat until their liquid evaporates, about 5 minutes. Raise the heat to moderately high and cook, stirring, until browned, about 3 minutes. Transfer the mushrooms to the prepared baking dish. Add the bacon, parsley and pepper to the baking dish and toss with the mushrooms, then spread the mixture in an even layer.

2. In a large bowl, whisk the eggs well. Whisk in the heavy cream, salt and a pinch of cayenne. Slowly pour the custard over the mushrooms and bacon and sprinkle the cheese over the top. Bake the custard for 50 minutes, or until the flan is just set. Transfer the flan to a rack to cool for 15 minutes, then cut into squares and serve hot or warm. —*The Grateful Palate*

Leek and Gruyère Tart

TOTAL: 35 MIN

4 SERVINGS ●

All-purpose flour, for dusting

- ½ pound frozen puff pastry, thawed
- 2 tablespoons extra-virgin olive oil
- 3 medium leeks, white and tender green—halved lengthwise, thinly sliced crosswise and rinsed well
- 1 teaspoon finely chopped thyme

Salt and freshly ground pepper

- ½ pound Gruyère cheese, coarsely shredded (2 cups)
- 3 ounces thinly sliced prosciutto

I. Preheat the oven to 475°. On a lightly floured surface, roll out the pastry to a 13-inch square. Fold the corners in and lightly roll the pastry into a rough round. Transfer to a baking sheet; refrigerate.

2. In a large skillet, heat the olive oil until shimmering. Add the leek slices and thyme, season with salt and pepper and cook over moderate heat, stirring occasionally, until the leeks are softened, about 5 minutes.

3. Sprinkle half of the cheese over the pastry, leaving a 1-inch border. Spread the leeks over the cheese. Cover with the prosciutto; sprinkle on the remaining cheese. Season with salt and pepper. Fold up the tart edge to form a rim and bake for 20 minutes, until golden and bubbling. Blot any excess fat with a paper towel. Cut the tart into wedges. —*Laura Chenel*

Swiss Chard and Two Cheese Bread Pudding

ACTIVE: 30 MIN; TOTAL: 1 HR 30 MIN

8 SERVINGS ●

- 2 tablespoons extra-virgin olive oil
- 1 onion, halved and thinly sliced
- ½ fennel bulb, cored and finely diced
- 3 garlic cloves, thinly sliced
- 1½ teaspoons thyme leaves

One 2-inch rosemary sprig

- ¼ teaspoon crushed red pepper
- 1 pound Swiss chard, stems and ribs discarded, leaves chopped

Salt and freshly ground pepper

- 2 large eggs, lightly beaten
- 1½ cups heavy cream
- ¼ cup grated Parmesan cheese
- ¼ cup mild goat cheese, softened
- 3 cups roughly torn (1-inch pieces) peasant bread, with crust

I. Preheat the oven to 350°. Butter an 8-inch-square baking dish. In a skillet, heat the oil. Add the onion, fennel, garlic, thyme, rosemary and crushed red pepper and cook over moderate heat until softened, 6 minutes. Add the Swiss chard, season with salt and pepper and cook, tossing, until wilted, 3 minutes. Transfer to a large bowl and discard the rosemary sprig.

2. In a bowl, mix the eggs, cream, Parmesan and goat cheese and add to the vegetables; season with salt and pepper. Add the bread and stir until moistened. Transfer to the baking dish. Bake for 1 hour, or until set and golden on top. Let the pudding cool for 15 minutes and then serve at once. —*Suzanne Goin*

MAKE AHEAD The bread pudding can be refrigerated overnight.

STRAWBERRY SHORTCAKE WITH STAR ANISE SAUCE, P. 310

tarts, pies + fruit desserts

BITTERSWEET CHOCOLATE TART WITH MASCARPONE

LEMON TART WITH CHOCOLATE-ALMOND CRUST

Bittersweet Chocolate Tart with Coffee Mascarpone Cream

ACTIVE: 30 MIN; TOTAL: 3 HR 30 MIN

MAKES ONE 9½-INCH TART ●

TART SHELL

1⅓ cups all-purpose flour

¾ cup confectioners' sugar

Pinch of salt

7 tablespoons unsalted butter, softened

1 large egg yolk

FILLING

¾ cup heavy cream

½ cup whole milk

½ pound bittersweet chocolate

1 large egg, beaten

TOPPING

1¼ teaspoons unflavored gelatin

2 tablespoons cold water

1½ teaspoons pure coffee extract (see Note)

1½ cups heavy cream

¼ cup plus 2 tablespoons mascarpone cheese

¼ cup sugar

1 tablespoon unsweetened cocoa powder

1. MAKE THE TART SHELL: In a food processor, pulse the flour with the confectioners' sugar and salt. Add the butter and egg yolk and process until a soft, crumbly dough forms. Transfer the dough to a 9½-inch fluted tart pan with a removable bottom. Pat the dough over the bottom and up the side of the pan in an even layer. Refrigerate until firm.

2. Preheat the oven to 350°. Line the tart shell with parchment paper and fill it with pie weights or dried beans. Bake the shell for 30 minutes, or until golden around the edge and dry in the center. Remove the parchment and weights and

cover the rim with foil. Continue to bake the shell for 15 to 20 minutes longer, or until golden and cooked through. Transfer to a rack; let cool.

3. MAKE THE FILLING: Chop the chocolate. In a small saucepan, heat the cream with the milk over moderate heat until small bubbles appear around the edge. Off the heat, add the chocolate and let stand for 1 minute, then whisk until smooth. Let cool for 5 minutes. Whisk in the egg; the mixture will thicken slightly.

4. Set the tart shell on a baking sheet and fill it with the chocolate custard. Bake for 25 minutes, or until set around the edge but still very jiggly in the center. Transfer the tart to a rack to cool, then refrigerate until chilled.

5. MAKE THE TOPPING: In a very small saucepan, sprinkle the gelatin

over the water and let stand until softened, about 5 minutes. Add the coffee
extract and cook over low heat just until
the gelatin melts; let cool slightly.

6. In a large bowl, beat the cream, mascarpone and sugar with an electric
mixer until firm peaks form. At low
speed, scrape in the gelatin and beat
to combine. Dollop the cream onto the
tart and swirl decoratively. Sift the cocoa
over the cream. Refrigerate the tart until
firm before serving. —*François Payard*
NOTE If coffee extract is unavailable, dissolve 1½ teaspoons of espresso powder
in 1½ teaspoons of water.

Lemon Tart with Chocolate-Almond Crust

ACTIVE: 45 MIN; TOTAL: 4 HR
MAKES ONE 11-INCH TART ●
The chocolate pastry recipe leaves you
with enough leftover dough to make
about 12 rolled cookies.

CHOCOLATE PASTRY
1½ **cups all-purpose flour**
¾ **cup almond flour (see Note)**
½ **cup plus 3 tablespoons sugar**
6 **tablespoons cocoa powder**
Pinch of salt
1½ **sticks (6 ounces) cold unsalted
butter, cut into cubes**
1 **large egg**

LEMON CURD
1 **cup plus 2 tablespoons sugar**
¾ **cup fresh lemon juice**
8 **large egg yolks**
1 **large egg**
1½ **sticks (6 ounces) unsalted
butter, softened**
**Bittersweet chocolate shavings,
for garnish**

I. MAKE THE CHOCOLATE PASTRY:
In a food processor, combine the all-
purpose flour, almond flour, sugar, cocoa
and salt; pulse to blend. Add the butter;
pulse until the mixture resembles coarse
meal. Add the egg; process until the
dough just comes together. Turn the

dough out onto a sheet of plastic, flatten
into a disk and chill for 30 minutes.

2. Preheat the oven to 350°. Butter an
11-inch fluted tart pan with a removable
bottom. On a lightly floured work surface, roll the pastry out to a 14-inch
round ¼ inch thick. Fit the pastry into the
tart pan. Run the rolling pin across the
rim of the pan to cut off any overhanging dough. Patch any tears in the pastry
with scraps. Line the pastry with foil and
fill with pie weights or dried beans. Bake
in the center of the oven for 30 minutes, or until the crust is nearly dry.
Remove the foil and bake the crust for
15 minutes longer, or until firm. Let cool.
Lower the oven temperature to 300°.

3. MEANWHILE, MAKE THE LEMON
CURD: Set a fine sieve over a medium
bowl. In a medium saucepan, combine
½ cup plus 1 tablespoon of the sugar
with the lemon juice and bring to a simmer, stirring until the sugar dissolves.
In another medium bowl, beat the egg
yolks with the whole egg and the
remaining ½ cup plus 1 tablespoon of
sugar. Whisk half of the hot lemon syrup
into the egg mixture; add the mixture
to the saucepan and cook over moderate heat, stirring constantly, until the
curd just comes to a boil, about 3 minutes; it should be the consistency of
sour cream. Strain the curd through the
fine sieve and let cool to room temperature, then whisk in the softened butter until the curd is light and fluffy.

4. Pour the curd into the crust and bake
for 20 minutes, or just until set. Cool
the tart on a wire rack, then refrigerate
until chilled. Unmold the tart and garnish it with chocolate shavings. Transfer
the tart to a large plate and serve.
—*Kate Zuckerman*

NOTE Almond flour is available at specialty markets. Or finely grind ¾ cup
(3 ounces) of blanched almonds.

MAKE AHEAD The baked tart can be
refrigerated overnight.

Ricotta Tart with Honey-Thyme Glaze and a Pine-Nut Crust

ACTIVE: 1 HR 15 MIN; TOTAL: 3 HR 45 MIN
MAKES ONE 11-INCH TART ●
PASTRY
¼ **cup pine nuts**
2 **cups all-purpose flour**
½ **cup sugar**
½ **vanilla bean, split lengthwise,
seeds scraped**
6 **tablespoons cold unsalted butter**
2 **large egg yolks**
1 **large egg**
FILLING
1 **cup fresh ricotta cheese**
8 **ounces cream cheese, softened**
1 **vanilla bean, split lengthwise,
seeds scraped**
½ **cup mascarpone cheese**
½ **cup crème fraîche**
¼ **cup sugar**
¼ **cup honey**
3 **large eggs**
1 **teaspoon minced thyme**
½ **teaspoon finely grated lemon zest**
Salt
GLAZE
½ **cup honey**
½ **teaspoon thyme leaves**
¼ **teaspoon finely grated lemon zest**

I. MAKE THE PASTRY: In a skillet,
toast the pine nuts over moderate heat,
shaking the pan, until golden brown,
3 minutes; let cool. In a food processor, process the flour, sugar, vanilla
seeds and pine nuts until the pine nuts
are coarsely ground. Add the butter and
process until pea-size clumps appear.
Add the egg yolks and whole egg and
process just until blended. Scrape the
dough out onto a lightly floured work
surface and knead just until it comes
together. Pat into a disk, wrap in plastic
and refrigerate until firm, about 1 hour.

2. Preheat the oven to 375°. On a
floured work surface, roll out the dough
to a 9-inch round. Transfer to an 11-inch
tart pan with a removable bottom.

tarts, pies + fruit desserts

Press the dough evenly into the pan and up the side. Trim the overhang with a sharp knife. Refrigerate the tart shell until firm, about 30 minutes.

3. Line the tart shell with aluminum foil and fill with pie weights. Bake for 25 minutes, or until dry and lightly browned around the edge. Remove the foil and weights and bake the tart shell for 20 minutes longer, until crisp and golden. Transfer to a rack to cool.

4. MAKE THE FILLING: In a large bowl, using an electric mixer, beat the ricotta, cream cheese, vanilla seeds, mascarpone and crème fraîche at moderate speed until smooth. Beat in the sugar and honey. Add the eggs, 1 at a time; beat well after each addition. Beat in the thyme, lemon zest and a pinch of salt. Pour the filling into the tart shell and bake for 30 minutes, or until just set and a little wobbly. Transfer to a rack to cool completely.

5. MAKE THE GLAZE: In a saucepan, bring the honey to a boil over moderately high heat. Remove from the heat and let cool to warm, 10 minutes. Stir in the thyme and lemon zest, then pour the glaze over the tart. Serve at room temperature or chilled. Alternatively, slice the tart and drizzle with the honey.
—*Ken Oringer*

MAKE AHEAD The unglazed tart can be refrigerated for up to 2 days.

Rustic Apple Tart
ACTIVE: 45 MIN; TOTAL: 2 HR
6 SERVINGS ●

This tart has the flakiest, easiest, best pie crust we've ever tested. The virtually fail-safe recipe is completely hassle-free: You don't even need to chill the dough before you roll it out. It can be topped with apples, but you can use almost any firm fruit in season, such as pears, peaches, apricots, plums or rhubarb. If using especially juicy fruit, add 1 tablespoon of ground nuts to the 1 tablespoon of flour and 2 tablespoons of sugar that are sprinkled over the pastry before the fruit is added.

1½ **cups plus 1 tablespoon all-purpose flour**
Pinch of salt
1½ **sticks (6 ounces) cold unsalted butter, cut into ½-inch pieces, plus 2 tablespoons melted**
⅓ **cup ice water**
3½ **tablespoons sugar**
4 **large Golden Delicious apples— peeled, cored and cut into ¼-inch-thick slices**
2 **tablespoons melted and strained apricot preserves**

I. In a food processor, pulse 1½ cups of the flour with the salt. Add the cold butter and process just until the butter is the size of peas, about 5 seconds. Sprinkle the ice water over the mixture and process just until moistened, about 5 seconds. Transfer the dough to a lightly floured work surface and knead 2 or 3 times, just until it comes together. Pat the dough into a disk. On a lightly floured surface, roll out the dough into a 16- to 17-inch round.

2. Line a large unrimmed baking sheet with parchment paper. Roll the dough around the rolling pin and unroll it onto the prepared baking sheet.

3. In a bowl, combine 2 tablespoons of the sugar with the remaining 1 tablespoon of flour and sprinkle over the dough. Arrange the apple slices on top in overlapping concentric circles up to 3 inches from the edge. Fold the dough free-form over the apples. Brush the apples with the melted butter and sprinkle with the remaining 1½ tablespoons of sugar. Refrigerate the unbaked tart until slightly chilled, about 10 minutes.

4. Preheat the oven to 400°. Bake the tart in the center of the oven for 1 hour, or until the apples are tender and the crust is deep golden. Brush the apples with the preserves. Slide the parchment onto a wire rack and let the tart cool slightly before serving. —*Jacques Pépin*

MAKE AHEAD The baked tart can be stored overnight at room temperature. Reheat in a 325° oven before serving.

Pumpkin Cheesecake Tart with Cranberry Gelée
ACTIVE: 50 MIN; TOTAL: 4 HR 30 MIN
MAKES ONE 11½-INCH TART ● ●
PASTRY

6 **tablespoons blanched almonds**
1½ **cups plus 1 tablespoon all-purpose flour**
1½ **sticks (6 ounces) unsalted butter, at room temperature**
¾ **cup plus 2 tablespoons confectioners' sugar**
1 **large egg**
¾ **teaspoon pure vanilla extract**
Pinch of salt

FILLING

12 ounces cream cheese, at room
temperature

½ cup packed light brown sugar

½ teaspoon cinnamon

¼ teaspoon ground ginger

⅛ teaspoon ground allspice

⅛ teaspoon ground cardamom

⅛ teaspoon ground cloves

Pinch of freshly ground white pepper

Pinch of freshly grated nutmeg

Pinch of salt

1¼ cups canned pumpkin puree
(10 ounces)

¼ cup heavy cream

3 tablespoons pure maple syrup

1½ teaspoons pure vanilla extract

2 large eggs, at room temperature

GELÉE

2 cups fresh cranberries (½ pound),
rinsed and patted dry

½ cup sugar

¼ cup orange juice

1½ teaspoons unflavored gelatin

I. MAKE THE PASTRY: In a food
processor, pulse the almonds until
coarsely ground. Add ½ cup of the flour
and process to a fine powder; transfer
to a bowl. In the food processor, pulse
the butter and confectioners' sugar until
creamy. Pulse in the egg and vanilla.
Pulse in the remaining 1 cup plus 1
tablespoon of flour, the almond flour and
the salt until a soft dough forms. Pat the
pastry into a disk, wrap in plastic and
refrigerate until firm, at least 1 hour.

2. Preheat the oven to 325°. On a very
lightly floured work surface, roll out the
prepared pastry to a 14-inch round
about ⅛ inch thick. Roll the pastry onto
the rolling pin and unroll it over an
11½-inch fluted tart pan with a removable bottom. Gently press the pastry
into the rim. Fold in the overhanging
dough and press gently to reinforce the
side; the side should be twice as thick
as the bottom. Trim off any excess and
refrigerate the tart shell until firm.

3. Line the tart pastry with parchment
paper and fill it with pie weights or
dried beans. Bake the pastry for about
25 minutes, or until set. Remove the
parchment and weights and bake the
pastry for 10 minutes longer, until the
crust is golden and cooked through. Let
cool slightly.

4. MEANWHILE, MAKE THE FILLING:
In a large bowl, combine the cream
cheese, brown sugar, ground spices,
nutmeg and salt. Using an electric
mixer, beat the mixture at medium speed
until smooth. Beat in the pumpkin puree
until smooth. Beat in the cream, maple
syrup, vanilla and eggs at low speed until
well blended.

5. Put the crust on a large, sturdy baking
sheet and set it in the oven. Carefully
pour the pumpkin custard into the crust.
Bake for 30 to 35 minutes, until the
custard is just set but still slightly jiggly
in the center. Cover the edge of the tart
with foil if the crust starts to brown too
much. Transfer the tart to a rack and let
it cool completely.

6. MEANWHILE, MAKE THE GELÉE:
In a medium saucepan, combine the
cranberries with ½ cup of water and
cook over moderate heat until they
begin to pop, about 5 minutes. Let cool.
Transfer to a blender and puree until
smooth. Strain the puree through a fine
sieve. Rinse out the saucepan.

7. Add the sugar and ¼ cup of water to
the saucepan and bring to a boil, stirring, until dissolved. Let cool. Stir in the
orange juice and cranberry puree.

8. In a small bowl, sprinkle the gelatin
over 2 tablespoons of water and let stand
until softened, 5 minutes. Microwave for
10 seconds, or until completely melted.
Whisk the gelatin into the cranberry mixture and pour the gelée over the pumpkin custard; shake it gently to even it out.
Refrigerate the tart until set, at least
1 hour and up to 2 days. Remove the
tart ring and serve. —*Deborah Racicot*

Fig Tart with Pistachio Crust

ACTIVE: 45 MIN; TOTAL: 4 HR

MAKES ONE 11-INCH TART ●

The tart is most delicious one day after
it's baked.

FILLING

1 pound dried black Mission
figs, stemmed

1½ cups water

¾ cup sugar

1 tablespoon cinnamon

1 teaspoon freshly grated nutmeg

½ teaspoon ground cloves

Juice and zest of 1 lemon

Salt

CRUST

2 cups unsalted roasted pistachios

2¼ cups all-purpose flour

1 cup plus 2 tablespoons sugar

2 teaspoons baking powder

½ teaspoon finely grated lemon zest

2 sticks plus 2 tablespoons
(9 ounces) unsalted butter,
softened

1 large egg

2 large egg yolks

1 teaspoon pure vanilla extract

Vegetable oil cooking spray

I. MAKE THE FILLING: In a medium
saucepan, combine the figs with the
water, sugar, cinnamon, nutmeg, cloves,
lemon juice and zest and a pinch of salt
and bring to a boil. Simmer the figs over
moderately low heat until tender and
the liquid is thick and syrupy, about
40 minutes. Transfer the mixture to a
food processor and puree. Let cool.

2. MEANWHILE, MAKE THE CRUST:
In a food processor, pulse the pistachios
until finely ground. Transfer the nuts to
a large bowl and add the flour, sugar,
baking powder and lemon zest. Add the
butter and stir with a wooden spoon
until it is thoroughly combined; it
may be necessary to knead the dough
gently with your hands. Add the whole
egg, egg yolks and vanilla extract and
stir or knead until evenly combined.

tarts, pies + fruit desserts

Break off one-third of the dough and flatten it into a disk. Pat the remaining dough into another disk. Wrap both pieces in plastic and refrigerate until chilled, about 30 minutes.

3. Preheat the oven to 350°. Spray an 11-inch fluted tart pan with a removable bottom with vegetable oil cooking spray. Press the larger disk of dough into the bottom and up the side of the tart pan to form an even ¼- to ⅓-inch-thick crust. Trim off any excess. Spread the fig filling over the crust. Roll out the smaller disk between 2 sheets of wax paper to a 12-inch round about ¼ inch thick. Remove 1 sheet of the wax paper and invert the top crust over the filling. Press the edges together to seal and trim off any excess. Chill the tart for 15 minutes.

4. Bake the tart in the center of the oven for 50 minutes, or until golden, covering with foil if the edge becomes too brown. Let the tart cool for 30 minutes, then carefully remove the fluted ring and let the tart cool completely. —*Tom Valenti*

MAKE AHEAD The tart can kept in an airtight container at room temperature for up to 2 days.

Coconut-Custard Meringue Pie

ACTIVE: 40 MIN; TOTAL: 6 HR

MAKES ONE 9-INCH PIE ●

It is essential to prebake pie crusts before filling them with custards to prevent them from becoming soggy.

Flaky Pie Crust (recipe, p. 305)
- 2 cups whole milk
- ¾ cup sugar
- ⅓ cup all-purpose flour
- Pinch of salt
- 4 large eggs, separated
- 1½ cups sweetened shredded coconut (about 6 ounces)
- 1 teaspoon pure vanilla extract
- Pinch of cream of tartar

I. Preheat the oven to 350°. Line a 9-inch glass pie plate with 1 rolled-out round of the Flaky Pie Crust. Trim the overhang to 1 inch, fold it under itself and crimp decoratively. Refrigerate until chilled, about 15 minutes.

2. Line the pastry with aluminum foil and fill with pie weights or dried beans. Bake for 30 minutes, or until nearly cooked through and dry to the touch. Carefully remove the foil and weights. Bake for 10 minutes longer, until golden. Let cool completely.

3. Meanwhile, set a fine strainer over a medium heatproof bowl. In a medium saucepan, combine the milk with ½ cup of the sugar, the flour and salt; whisk until smooth. Cook over moderate heat, whisking frequently, until the mixture is the consistency of sour cream, about 8 minutes.

4. Put the egg yolks in a small bowl and gradually whisk in ½ cup of the hot milk mixture. Whisk the tempered egg mixture in the bowl into the saucepan and cook over moderate heat, whisking constantly, until thickened, about 2 minutes. Pour the custard into the strainer over the heatproof bowl and press with the back of a spoon. Stir in 1¼ cups of the coconut and the vanilla. Press plastic wrap directly onto the custard and refrigerate until chilled.

5. Spoon the custard into the baked pie crust and refrigerate for at least 2 hours.

6. Preheat the oven to 350°. In a large stainless-steel bowl, using an electric mixer, beat the egg whites with the cream of tartar at medium speed until frothy. Increase the speed to high and beat until firm peaks form. Add the remaining ¼ cup of sugar, 1 tablespoon at a time, and beat until glossy. Spoon the meringue onto the custard, spread it to the edge of the crust and swirl decoratively, using the back of a spoon. Sprinkle the remaining ¼ cup of coconut on top. Bake the pie until the meringue is golden and the coconut toasted, 7 minutes. Let cool, cut into wedges and serve. —*Grace Parisi*

Heirloom-Pear Hand Pies

ACTIVE: 45 MIN; TOTAL: 2 HR 20 MIN

MAKES 4 HAND PIES ● ●

These single-serving pies showcase heirloom pears (such as Flemish Beauty and Devoe), but firm Bartletts work well, too.

- 2 tablespoons unsalted butter
- 2½ pounds ripe but firm heirloom pears—peeled, cored and cut into ½-inch dice
- ½ cup plus 2 tablespoons sugar
- 2 tablespoons fresh lemon juice
- ½ vanilla bean, split lengthwise, seeds scraped
- ¼ cup all-purpose flour, for dusting
- 1 pound puff pastry, thawed but cold
- 2 egg whites, lightly beaten with 1 teaspoon cold water

I. In a large skillet, melt the butter over high heat. Add the diced pears and cook, stirring occasionally, until they are golden around the edges, about 5 minutes. Add ½ cup of the sugar, the lemon juice and the vanilla bean and seeds and cook until the pears are tender and the liquid in the skillet has reduced to about 2 tablespoons, 4 to 5 minutes. Spread the diced pears on a baking sheet and let them cool, about 25 minutes. Discard the vanilla bean.

2. Lightly flour a work surface. Roll out the puff pastry to a scant ⅛-inch thickness. Using a plate as a template, carefully cut out four 7-inch rounds. Transfer the rounds to a large baking sheet lined with parchment paper (they will overlap slightly).

3. Preheat the oven to 425°. Spoon one-fourth of the pear filling over half of a pastry round, leaving a ½-inch border at the edge. Brush the border lightly with the egg-white wash. Fold the top half of the round over and press the edges together firmly to seal. Repeat with the remaining pear filling and pastry rounds. Refrigerate the hand pies for 30 minutes. Reserve the remaining egg-white wash.

COCONUT-CUSTARD MERINGUE PIE

tarts, pies + fruit desserts

4. Brush the tops of the hand pies lightly with the remaining egg-white wash. Sprinkle the tops all over with the remaining 2 tablespoons of sugar. Bake the hand pies for 15 minutes in the middle of the oven, then reduce the oven temperature to 400° and bake the hand pies for about 15 minutes longer, until they are a deep golden brown color. Let the hand pies cool for 20 minutes, then serve them slightly warm. —*Maria Helm Sinskey*

MAKE AHEAD The hand pies can be made 1 day ahead and kept at room temperature. To serve, reheat the pies in a 350° oven for 10 minutes.

SERVE WITH Vanilla ice cream or other ice cream of your choice.

Banana Cream Pie

ACTIVE: 35 MIN; TOTAL: 6 HR 30 MIN

MAKES ONE 9-INCH PIE ●

PASTRY

- 1¼ cups all-purpose flour
- 2 tablespoons confectioners' sugar
- ⅛ teaspoon salt
- 1 stick (4 ounces) unsalted butter, chilled
- ¼ cup heavy cream
- 1 teaspoon cider vinegar
- 3 tablespoons apricot preserves, melted and strained

FILLING

- 2 cups milk

BAKING TIP

chocolate curls

THE BANANA CREAM PIE on this page is garnished with beautiful chocolate curls. To make them, spread melted chocolate onto the back of a baking sheet or a marble pastry board. When the chocolate has cooled completely, push forward with a pastry scraper to shave thin curls.

- 3 large egg yolks
- ½ teaspoon pure vanilla extract
- ¾ cup granulated sugar
- 2 tablespoons all-purpose flour
- 2 tablespoons cornstarch

Pinch of salt

- ¼ teaspoon freshly grated nutmeg
- 2 tablespoons unsalted butter
- 3 tablespoons light rum
- ½ teaspoon unflavored gelatin
- 2 tablespoons cold water
- 1 cup heavy cream, chilled
- 2 tablespoons superfine sugar
- 3 ripe bananas, cut into ¼-inch-thick slices
- 2 ounces chocolate curls

I. MAKE THE PASTRY: In a food processor, pulse the flour, confectioners' sugar and salt. Add the butter; pulse until the mixture resembles small peas. In a bowl, combine the heavy cream and vinegar; pour over the crumbs and pulse until moistened. On a floured surface, knead the pastry 2 or 3 times, just until it comes together. Shape into a disk, wrap in plastic and chill for 30 minutes.

2. On a lightly floured surface, roll out the pastry to a 12-inch round about ⅛ inch thick. Fit the round into a 9-inch glass pie plate. Trim the overhang to ½ inch and fold it under; crimp decoratively. Refrigerate until chilled.

3. Preheat the oven to 400°. Prick the crust with a fork, line the pastry with foil and fill with dried beans or pie weights. Bake for about 25 minutes, or until set. Remove the foil and beans. Press down any air bubbles and bake for about 8 minutes, until the pastry is golden; transfer to a rack and brush the bottom and side with the preserves. Let cool.

4. MEANWHILE, MAKE THE FILLING: In a bowl, mix ¼ cup of the milk, the egg yolks and vanilla. In a saucepan, combine the granulated sugar, flour, cornstarch, salt and nutmeg. Add the remaining 1¾ cups of milk and bring to a simmer, whisking constantly. Add the

butter and stir over moderate heat until thick and smooth, 2 to 3 minutes. Remove from the heat and whisk about half into the egg mixture. Return the mixture to the saucepan and cook over moderately high heat, stirring constantly, until thickened, about 3 minutes. Strain through a fine sieve set over a bowl and add 2 tablespoons of the rum. Press a piece of wax paper on the custard; refrigerate until chilled.

5. In a small glass bowl, sprinkle the gelatin over the cold water; let stand until softened. Microwave on high until melted, 15 seconds; let cool. In a bowl, beat the cream with the superfine sugar, the remaining 1 tablespoon of rum and the melted gelatin until soft peaks form. Arrange the bananas in overlapping layers on the crust and pour the custard on top. Tap the pie once on the counter. Spread the whipped cream on top and make deep swirls with the back of a spoon. Refrigerate until firm, 4 hours. Garnish with the chocolate curls and serve. —*Joyce White*

Lemon Meringue Pie

ACTIVE: 35 MIN; TOTAL: 5 HR

MAKES ONE 9-INCH PIE ●

PASTRY

- 1⅓ cups all-purpose flour
- ½ teaspoon salt
- 4 tablespoons cold unsalted butter, thinly sliced
- 4 tablespoons cold lard or solid vegetable shortening
- 3 tablespoons ice water

FILLING

- 1½ cups sugar
- ¼ cup plus 1 tablespoon cornstarch
- ½ teaspoon salt
- 4 large eggs, separated
- ¾ cup fresh lemon juice
- 2 cups cold water
- 1½ teaspoons finely grated lemon zest
- 5 tablespoons unsalted butter, cut into tablespoons

I. MAKE THE PASTRY: In a bowl, combine the flour and salt. Using a pastry blender or 2 knives, cut in the butter and lard until the mixture resembles coarse meal. Add the ice water, tossing with a fork. Form the dough into a ball; knead briefly until evenly moistened. Pat into a 6-inch disk, wrap in plastic and refrigerate for at least 1 hour.

2. Preheat the oven to 425°. On a floured surface, roll out the chilled pastry into a 12-inch round 1/8 inch thick. Fit it into a 9-inch glass pie plate and trim the overhang to 1/2 inch; fold the overhang under and crimp decoratively. Line the pie shell with foil and fill with pie weights.

3. Bake the pie shell on a baking sheet for 10 minutes, or until the edge has set. Remove the foil and weights and bake the shell for 15 minutes longer, or until the bottom is firm and light golden; tap the bottom with a spoon if it bubbles up. If the crust begins to brown too quickly, loosely cover the edge with foil. Transfer to a wire rack and let cool.

4. MAKE THE FILLING: Meanwhile, in a medium saucepan, combine 1 cup of the sugar with the cornstarch, 1/4 teaspoon of the salt, the egg yolks and lemon juice. Whisk in the cold water and cook over moderate heat, whisking constantly, until the mixture comes to a boil. Boil, stirring, for 1 minute. Remove from the heat and add the lemon zest and butter, stirring until the butter is melted. Pour the filling into the pie shell, cover with wax paper and let cool to room temperature.

5. Preheat the oven to 350° and position a rack in the upper third. In a large stainless steel bowl, beat the egg whites with the remaining 1/4 teaspoon of salt until soft peaks form. Gradually add the remaining 1/2 cup of sugar and beat until stiff and glossy peaks form.

6. Remove the wax paper from the filling. Scrape the meringue onto the pie and gently spread it over the filling all the way to the crimped edge. Make decorative swirls with the back of a spoon.

7. Bake the pie until the meringue is golden, about 7 minutes. Transfer to a wire rack and let cool, then refrigerate until chilled and set, at least 3 hours. To cut the pie, use a sharp knife dipped into hot water. —*Jim Fobel*

MAKE AHEAD The recipe can be made through Step 4 and refrigerated overnight. Top with the meringue and bake, then let cool before serving.

Blackberry Pie

ACTIVE: 40 MIN; TOTAL: 6 HR
MAKES ONE 9-INCH PIE ●
6 half-pints blackberries
1½ cups sugar
6 tablespoons cornstarch
¼ teaspoon pure almond extract
Pinch of salt
Flaky Pie Crust (recipe, p. 305)
1½ tablespoons unsalted butter, cut into small pieces

I. Preheat the oven to 350°. Set a baking sheet lined with foil on the bottom rack. In a large bowl, toss 1 half-pint of the blackberries with the sugar, cornstarch, almond extract and salt; lightly crush the berries. Fold in the remaining berries and let stand for 5 minutes.

2. Spoon the fruit and any accumulated juices into a 9-inch glass pie plate lined with 1 round of the Flaky Pie Crust. Dot the filling with the butter. Lightly brush the pastry rim with water. Position the rolled-out top crust over the filling and press the edges together to seal. Trim the overhang to 1/2 inch, fold it under itself and crimp decoratively.

3. Bake the pie in the center of the oven for 1½ hours, or until the filling is bubbling and the crust is deep golden. Cover the edge with strips of foil halfway through baking to prevent overbrowning. Transfer to a wire rack and let cool for at least 4 hours before cutting. —*Grace Parisi*

Vanilla-Ginger Peach Pie

ACTIVE: 50 MIN; TOTAL: 6 HR
MAKES ONE 9-INCH PIE ●
Choose ripe yellow peaches rather than white ones for pie filling; they are juicier and sweet-tart. Cut them into thick wedges, which add texture to the filling and are less likely to lose their shape.
¼ cup quick-cooking tapioca
1 vanilla bean, split lengthwise, seeds scraped
1 tablespoon minced candied ginger
3 pounds firm, ripe yellow peaches, peeled and cut into ¾-inch wedges
¾ cup plus 3 tablespoons sugar
Flaky Pie Crust (recipe, p. 305)

I. Preheat the oven to 350°. Set a baking sheet lined with foil on the bottom rack. In a spice grinder, combine the tapioca and the vanilla bean seeds and grind to a fine powder. Add the candied ginger and pulse until finely ground and well combined.

2. Transfer the tapioca mixture to a large nonreactive bowl. Add the peach slices and ¾ cup plus 2 tablespoons of the sugar and toss gently to mix. Let the peach filling stand for 10 minutes, or until slightly juicy.

3. Spoon the peach filling into a 9-inch glass pie plate lined with 1 disk of Flaky Pie Crust. Lightly brush the rim of the pastry with water. Position the rolled-out top crust over the filling and press the top and bottom edges together to seal. Trim the overhang to 1/2 inch, fold it under itself and crimp decoratively. Lightly brush the top crust with water and sprinkle with the remaining 1 tablespoon of sugar.

4. Bake the pie in the center of the oven for 1 hour and 45 minutes, or until the filling is bubbling and the crust is deep golden. Cover the edge of the pie with strips of foil halfway through baking to prevent overbrowning. Transfer the pie to a wire rack and let cool for at least 4 hours before cutting. —*Grace Parisi*

LEMON RIPPLE CHEESECAKE BARS

Tangy Rhubarb Pie

ACTIVE: 50 MIN; TOTAL: 6 HR

MAKES ONE 9-INCH PIE ●

¼ cup plus 2 tablespoons
  quick-cooking tapioca
1½ cups sugar
Pinch of freshly grated nutmeg
2 pounds rhubarb (stalks only),
  cut into 1-inch lengths
½ teaspoon finely grated lemon zest
Flaky Pie Crust (recipe follows)
2 tablespoons unsalted butter,
  cut into small pieces

1. Preheat the oven to 350°. Set a baking sheet lined with foil on the bottom rack. In a spice grinder, coarsely grind the tapioca. Add ¼ cup of the sugar and the nutmeg and grind to a fine powder.

2. In a large bowl, toss the rhubarb with the tapioca mixture, lemon zest and the remaining 1¼ cups of sugar. Let stand for 10 minutes, or until slightly juicy.

3. Spoon the rhubarb and any accumulated juices into a 9-inch glass pie plate lined with 1 round of the Flaky Pie Crust. Dot the filling with the butter. Lightly brush the rim of the pastry with water. Position the rolled-out top crust over the filling; press the edges together to seal. Trim the overhang to ½ inch, fold it under itself and crimp decoratively.

4. Bake the pie in the center of the oven for 1½ hours, or until the filling is bubbling and the crust golden. Cover the edge with foil strips halfway through to prevent overbrowning. Transfer to a wire rack and let cool for at least 4 hours. —*Grace Parisi*

Flaky Pie Crust

ACTIVE: 20 MIN; TOTAL: 50 MIN

MAKES TWO 9- TO 10-INCH PIE
CRUSTS ●

If you need only half of this recipe to make one crust, freeze the other half of the dough for up to 1 month for future use. Let the dough thaw in the refrigerator for a few hours before using.

3 cups all-purpose flour
1 teaspoon sugar
¾ teaspoon salt
½ cup cold solid vegetable
  shortening, cut into 4 pieces
1 stick (4 ounces) cold unsalted
  butter, cut into ½-inch pieces
½ cup plus 1 tablespoon ice water

1. In a food processor, combine the flour, sugar and salt and pulse several times. Add the vegetable shortening and pulse 5 or 6 times, until the shortening is the size of peas. Add the butter and pulse 5 or 6 times, until the butter is also the size of peas. Pour the ice water evenly over the top. Replace the processor lid and pulse 5 or 6 times, just until moistened.

2. Transfer the pastry to a lightly floured work surface and knead lightly several times, just until it comes together. Divide the pastry in half and pat it into two 6-inch disks; wrap the disks in plastic wrap and refrigerate until firm, at least 30 minutes, or overnight; or freeze the pastry dough.

3. Work with 1 disk of pastry at a time. On a lightly floured work surface, gently tap the pastry all over with a rolling pin to flatten it slightly. Dust the dough very lightly with flour and roll it out into a 13½-inch round ⅛ inch thick. To line a pie plate, roll the pastry around the rolling pin, then unroll it over a 9- or 10-inch glass pie plate. Press the dough gently into the pan, being careful not to tear the dough (you can patch a tear with a scrap of dough).

4. If making a double-crust pie, refrigerate the bottom crust in the pan while you prepare the top. Roll out the second piece of pastry into a 13½-inch round ⅛ inch thick. Transfer the round to a wax paper–lined baking sheet. Using a ½-inch cutter, stamp out a vent hole in the center or prick the pastry all over with a fork. Refrigerate the dough until ready to use. —*G.P.*

Lemon Ripple Cheesecake Bars

ACTIVE: 35 MIN; TOTAL: 3 HR

MAKES 16 BARS ● ●

CRUST

1 cup all-purpose flour
¼ cup sugar
1 teaspoon finely grated lemon zest
⅛ teaspoon salt
1 stick (4 ounces) unsalted butter,
  cut into ½-inch pieces and chilled

FILLING

1 tablespoon plus 2 teaspoons
  cornstarch
½ cup cold water
2 large egg yolks
1¾ cups sugar
¼ cup fresh lemon juice
1 teaspoon finely grated lemon zest
1¼ pounds cream cheese, softened
2 tablespoons all-purpose flour
3 large eggs, at room temperature
¼ cup sour cream
1 teaspoon pure vanilla extract

1. MAKE THE CRUST: Preheat the oven to 325° and position a rack in the center. Butter a 9-inch-square nonstick baking pan. In a food processor, pulse the flour with the sugar, lemon zest and salt. Add the butter and pulse until a soft, crumbly dough forms. Press the dough evenly over the bottom and a scant ½ inch up the side of the pan. Bake the crust for 20 minutes, or until golden and firm.

2. MEANWHILE, MAKE THE FILLING: In a small bowl, dissolve the cornstarch in the water. In a medium saucepan, whisk the egg yolks with ¾ cup of the sugar and the lemon juice. Whisk in the cornstarch mixture and cook over moderate heat, whisking gently, until the sugar is dissolved and the lemon mixture is hot, about 4 minutes. Boil over moderately high heat for 1 minute, whisking constantly, until the mixture is thick and glossy. Strain the lemon mixture into a heatproof bowl. Stir in the lemon zest and let cool.

tarts, pies + fruit desserts

3. In a bowl, using an electric mixer, beat the cream cheese and remaining 1 cup of sugar until smooth. Beat in the flour. Add the eggs, 1 at a time, beating well between additions. Add the sour cream and vanilla and beat until smooth. Pour the batter over the crust and smooth the surface with a spatula. Dollop the lemon mixture on the cheesecake batter and swirl it into the batter; take care not to cut into the crust.

4. Bake the cheesecake for about 40 minutes, or until golden around the edge and just set. Run the tip of a knife around the edge to loosen the cheesecake from the side of the pan. Let cool on a wire rack for 1 hour, then refrigerate the cheesecake until thoroughly chilled. Cut into 16 bars and serve. —*Elinor Klivans*

MAKE AHEAD The cheesecake bars can be covered and refrigerated in the pan for up to 3 days.

INGREDIENT TIP

a to z of apples

FOR STRAIGHT SNACKING, pick apples with crunchy, juicy flesh, a fragrant aroma and sweetness with a touch of tartness. New varieties include Honeycrisp, Cameo and Pink Lady.

FOR BAKING WHOLE, choose sweet, firm apples that won't collapse: Braeburn, Idared, Jonagold, Jonathan, Northern Spy, Stayman or Winesap.

FOR PIES, combine hard, tart apples like Granny Smiths with a sweeter variety like Empire.

FOR APPLESAUCE, mix different apples, adding some that fall apart easily when cooked but have good body: Braeburn, Gala, Golden Delicious, Melrose, Mutsu and Newtown Pippin.

Ginger and Pear Upside-Down Cake

ACTIVE: 40 MIN; TOTAL: 1 HR 25 MIN

MAKES ONE 10-INCH CAKE ●

- 2 sticks (8 ounces) unsalted butter, softened
- 4 medium, very firm Bosc pears— peeled, cored and cut into eighths
- ½ cup packed light brown sugar
- ¼ cup plus 2 tablespoons honey
- 2 tablespoons minced crystallized ginger
- 2 cups all-purpose flour
- 1½ teaspoons baking powder
- 1 teaspoon cinnamon
- ¼ teaspoon ground ginger
- ¼ teaspoon freshly grated nutmeg
- ¼ teaspoon salt
- 1¼ cups granulated sugar
- 3 large eggs
- 1 teaspoon pure vanilla extract
- ¾ cup milk

I. Preheat the oven to 350°. In a 10-inch cast-iron skillet, melt 4 tablespoons of the butter. Add the pears and cook over high heat, stirring, until crisp-tender. Add another 4 tablespoons of the butter, the brown sugar and the honey and stir over moderate heat until melted. Off the heat, arrange some of the pears in an overlapping ring, with the pointed ends facing the center. Fill the center with the remaining pears and sprinkle with the crystallized ginger.

2. In a bowl, whisk the flour, baking powder, cinnamon, ground ginger, nutmeg and salt. In a large bowl, cream the remaining stick of butter. Beat in the granulated sugar until light and fluffy. Beat in the eggs, 1 at a time, and the vanilla. Beat in the dry ingredients in 3 additions, alternating with the milk. Spoon the batter evenly over the pears.

3. Bake the cake on the bottom oven rack for 30 minutes, or until golden and a toothpick inserted in the center comes out clean. Let cool for 10 minutes, then invert a plate over the skillet. Quickly invert the skillet to release the cake. Replace any pears that stick to the skillet and drizzle any remaining syrup over the cake. Let cool. —*Grace Parisi*

MAKE AHEAD The unmolded cake can be refrigerated for up to 2 days.

Plum—Brown Sugar Upside-Down Cake

ACTIVE: 35 MIN; TOTAL: 1 HR 30 MIN

MAKES ONE 12-INCH CAKE ●

- 1½ sticks (6 ounces) unsalted butter, softened
- ¾ cup light brown sugar
- 2 pounds medium plums— halved, pitted and cut into ½-inch-thick wedges
- 1½ cups all-purpose flour
- 2 teaspoons baking powder
- ½ teaspoon salt
- 1 cup granulated sugar
- 2 large eggs, separated
- 1 teaspoon pure vanilla extract
- ½ cup milk

I. Preheat the oven to 350°. In a 12-inch ovenproof skillet, melt 4 tablespoons of the butter. Sprinkle the brown sugar evenly in the skillet. Turn off the heat and arrange the plum wedges in the skillet in 2 concentric circles.

2. In a bowl, whisk the flour, baking powder and salt. Using an electric mixer, beat the remaining stick of butter with the granulated sugar until fluffy. Beat in the egg yolks, 1 at a time, and the vanilla. Beat in the dry ingredients in 3 additions, alternating with the milk.

3. In a medium bowl, beat the egg whites until firm peaks form. Using a rubber spatula, stir one-third of the egg whites into the batter to lighten it, then fold in the remaining whites. Spread the batter over the plums and bake until a cake tester inserted in the center comes out clean, about 55 minutes. Let the cake cool for 15 minutes, then turn it out onto a plate. Serve warm or at room temperature. —*Fanny Singer*

Fallen Prune and Armagnac Soufflé

ACTIVE: 45 MIN; TOTAL: 2 HR 30 MIN, PLUS 2 DAYS SOAKING TIME

MAKES ONE 10-INCH SOUFFLÉ ● ● ●

- 36 pitted prunes (about 13 ounces)
- 1 vanilla bean, split lengthwise
- ½ teaspoon crushed fennel seeds, tied in a piece of cheesecloth
- 1½ cups fruity red wine
- 1½ cups Armagnac
- ⅓ cup sugar, plus more for dusting
- ¾ cup milk
- 2 tablespoons all-purpose flour
- 8 large egg yolks
- 10 large egg whites

Pinch of salt

Sweetened whipped cream, for serving

1. In a heatproof bowl, combine the prunes, vanilla bean and fennel seed bag. In a medium saucepan, bring the wine and Armagnac to a boil. Pour over the prunes; let cool. Cover with plastic and let the prunes macerate for 2 days.

2. Preheat the oven to 375°. Butter a 10-inch springform pan and lightly dust it with sugar. In a medium saucepan, bring the prunes and their soaking liquid to a boil. Reduce the heat to low and simmer until a syrup forms, about 25 minutes. Strain the prunes over a bowl; remove the fennel seed bag and squeeze the syrup back into the pan. Remove the vanilla bean; scrape the seeds into the syrup and stir. Reserve 12 plump prunes in the syrup. Finely chop the remaining prunes.

3. In a small saucepan, bring the milk to a simmer. Pour it into a large bowl. Whisk in the flour and 8 egg yolks, 1 at a time. Stir in the chopped prunes.

4. In a bowl, beat the egg whites until soft peaks form. Gradually beat in the ⅓ cup of sugar with the salt; beat until the whites are stiff and glossy. Fold one-third of the beaten whites into the prune-egg mixture, then fold in the rest.

5. Scrape the batter into the pan and bake in the center of the oven for 40 minutes, or until risen and golden. Let cool on a rack for at least 30 minutes.

6. Increase the oven temperature to 400°. Run a knife around the soufflé and remove the ring. Reheat the soufflé for 15 minutes, or until warmed through. Slice with a serrated knife and transfer to plates. Drizzle with the Armagnac syrup. Serve warm with the whole prunes and sweetened whipped cream. —*Marcia Kiesel*

MAKE AHEAD The soufflé can be prepared through Step 5 earlier in the day.

Souffléed Apple Pancake

ACTIVE: 10 MIN; TOTAL: 20 MIN

2 SERVINGS ● ●

- ½ cup all-purpose flour
- 2 teaspoons sugar

Pinch of salt

- ½ cup skim milk
- 2 large eggs, beaten
- 2 tablespoons vegetable oil
- 2 baking apples (1 pound), peeled and cut into 8 wedges each, the wedges cut in half
- 1 teaspoon fresh lemon juice
- ⅛ teaspoon cinnamon

Maple syrup, for serving (optional)

1. Preheat the oven to 500°. In a medium bowl, whisk the flour with the sugar and salt. Gradually mix in the milk, eggs and 1 tablespoon of oil.

2. Heat the remaining 1 tablespoon of oil in a 10-inch ovenproof nonstick skillet. Spread the apples in the pan, add the lemon juice and cinnamon and cook over moderately high heat until lightly browned, about 5 minutes.

3. Strain the batter through a sieve over the warm apples in the skillet, pressing with a spatula. Bake the pancake for 8 to 10 minutes, or until the edge is puffed and browned and the center is set. Serve immediately, with maple syrup. —*Scott Campbell*

Apples Baked in Pastry with Plum Sauce

ACTIVE: 1 HR; TOTAL: 3 HR

6 SERVINGS ●

These apple pastries can be prepared using 2 pounds of thawed frozen all-butter puff pastry.

PASTRY

- 3¾ cups all-purpose flour
- 3 tablespoons sugar
- ¾ teaspoon salt
- 1 stick plus 7 tablespoons cold unsalted butter, cut in small pieces
- 1 large egg
- 1 large egg yolk
- ½ cup plus 3 tablespoons ice water
- 6 Golden Delicious apples, cored

Three 3-inch cinnamon sticks, broken in half

- 1 large egg beaten with 1 tablespoon water

PLUM SAUCE

- 2¼ pounds Italian prune plums, or other red or black plums, pitted and cut into ½-inch wedges
- ½ cup sugar
- 2 tablespoons Armagnac

1. MAKE THE PASTRY: In a large bowl, whisk the flour with the sugar and salt. Using a pastry blender, cut in the butter until the mixture resembles coarse meal. In a small bowl, whisk the egg with the egg yolk, then whisk in the water. Drizzle the egg over the flour mixture and stir with a fork to lightly blend the ingredients. Squeeze gently until a smooth dough forms. Divide it in half, pat each half into a disk and wrap in plastic. Refrigerate until firm, about 1 hour.

2. Preheat the oven to 350°. On a lightly floured work surface, roll 1 of the chilled pastry disks into a rough 9-by-24-inch rectangle about ⅛ inch thick. Using a plate as a guide, cut out three 8-inch rounds. Transfer the rounds to a large baking sheet with plastic wrap between them to prevent sticking. Repeat the procedure with the remaining pastry.

APRICOT-BERRY CRUMBLE

MACAROON SANDWICH WITH POACHED PEARS

Cut out leaf decorations from the scraps with a cookie cutter or by hand to use for garnish. Transfer to the baking sheet as well. Refrigerate the rounds and decorations until firm, at least 20 minutes. Remove from the refrigerator and let stand until pliable, about 2 minutes.

3. Lightly oil a large rimmed baking sheet. Drape a pastry round over each apple and wrap the apples without stretching the pastry, tucking it around and underneath to form a neat package. Transfer the apples to the baking sheet. Using a small knife, make a hole in the pastry at the top of each apple and press the cinnamon sticks on the diagonal through the holes and into the apples, creating stems. Place a leaf decoration on each apple, brush the pastry with the beaten egg and bake the apples for about 1 hour, or until they are cooked through.

4. MAKE THE PLUM SAUCE: In a large skillet, sprinkle the plum wedges with the sugar and bring to a simmer over moderately high heat. Stir well, cover and reduce the heat to moderate. Simmer, stirring occasionally, until the plums are just tender, about 8 minutes. Using a slotted spoon, transfer the plums to a large heatproof bowl.

5. Add the Armagnac to the skillet and simmer over moderately high heat, stirring occasionally and scraping the bottom of the skillet, until the cooking liquid is syrupy, about 3 minutes. Add the Armagnac syrup to the plums. Let the plum sauce cool slightly.

6. Let the apples cool on the baking sheet for about 5 minutes. Using a metal spatula, transfer the apples to plates. Serve with the plum sauce.

—Christophe Côte

Macaroon Sandwiches with Poached Pears and Devon Cream

ACTIVE: 40 MIN; TOTAL: 1 HR 30 MIN

MAKES 6 SANDWICHES ●

Devon (also known as Devonshire) cream is the thick layer of cream that is spooned off the surface of heated and cooled unpasteurized milk. It is a traditional accompaniment at English tea, served with scones. Here it adds a creamy, slightly tangy dimension to a pear-and-cookie dessert.

PEARS

2 cups unsweetened Concord grape juice

1 cup dry red wine

⅓ cup sugar

¼ cup fresh lemon juice

3 large ripe, firm Bartlett pears, peeled

MACAROONS

- ¾ cup walnut halves (3 ounces)
- 1 cup plus 2½ tablespoons confectioners' sugar, plus more for dusting
- 2 large egg whites

Fleur de sel (French sea salt)

CREAM

- ¾ cup Devon clotted cream (one 6-ounce bottle) or crème fraîche
- 1½ tablespoons sugar
- ¾ cup heavy cream

I. POACH THE PEARS: In a medium saucepan, combine the grape juice with the red wine, sugar and lemon juice and bring to a boil. Turn off the heat and let cool slightly. Add the pears and simmer over moderate heat until they are tender, about 20 minutes; let cool slightly. Using a slotted spoon, transfer the pears to a plate. Simmer the poaching liquid over moderate heat until thickened slightly, about 15 minutes.

2. MAKE THE MACAROONS: Preheat the oven to 350° and line a large baking sheet with parchment paper. Spread the walnut halves on another baking sheet and toast them until they are golden and fragrant, about 9 minutes. Transfer the walnuts to a plate and let cool completely. Coarsely chop the walnuts in a food processor. Add the 1 cup plus 2½ tablespoons of confectioners' sugar and pulse until all of the nuts are very finely ground, scraping down the sides of the bowl frequently. Transfer the walnut sugar to a bowl and whisk it to break up any lumps. Increase the oven temperature to 425°.

3. In a medium bowl, using an electric mixer, beat the egg whites at medium speed until they are frothy. Increase the speed to high and beat until firm peaks form. Add the walnut sugar all at once and fold the mixture together with a large rubber spatula until no streaks of white remain. (The meringue will de-flate, so don't worry.)

4. Transfer the meringue to a large pastry bag fitted with a ½-inch plain round tip or to a sturdy plastic bag with a corner cut off. Pipe out 12 meringue mounds on top of the parchment-lined baking sheet, leaving at least 1 inch between each of them. Gently tap the baking sheet once on the work surface to smooth the tops. Sprinkle each of the macaroons with a tiny pinch of fleur de sel and then bake them for 4 minutes. Reduce the oven temperature to 350° and carefully prop the door open about 2 inches with a spoon or pot holder. Continue to bake the macaroons for about 12 minutes, or until the tops are brown and dry but the cookies are still soft. Let the macaroons cool on the baking sheets for 5 minutes, then carefully transfer the macaroons to a wire rack to cool completely.

5. PREPARE THE CREAM: In a medium bowl, using an electric mixer or whisk, beat the clotted cream with the sugar until smooth and runny. Add the heavy cream and beat until soft peaks form.

6. ASSEMBLE THE DESSERT: To get 2 even slabs from each pear, first trim a thin slice from the bottom and trim off most of the top of the pear; cut the remainder in half horizontally. Using a small knife or melon baller, remove the pear core.

7. Place 6 of the macaroons, flat side up, on plates. Top each cookie with a pear half and drizzle the pears with some of the grape reduction. Spoon the whipped cream on top and cover with another macaroon. Lightly dust with confectioners' sugar and serve at once.
—*Yvan-David Lemoine*

MAKE AHEAD The poached pears and grape reduction can be covered and refrigerated separately overnight. The macaroons can be stored overnight in an airtight container (handle carefully to prevent crushing).

Apricot-Berry Crumble

ACTIVE: 25 MIN; TOTAL: 1 HR 10 MIN

8 SERVINGS ●

Adapted from Greg Patent's definitive *Baking in America,* this homey fruit dessert is exceptionally delicious. The apricots, the thickened juices of the fruit and the toasty, oaty topping all meld together in each bite.

- 2 pounds firm, ripe apricots, halved and pitted
- 8 whole almonds
- 1 cup (packed) light brown sugar

Finely grated zest of 1 lemon

- 1½ cups raspberries
- 1½ cups blueberries
- 2 tablespoons fresh lemon juice
- 1 cup all-purpose flour
- 1 teaspoon ground cinnamon
- ¼ teaspoon salt
- ¾ cup old-fashioned or quick-cooking (not instant) rolled oats
- 1 stick plus 2 tablespoons (5 ounces) cold unsalted butter, cut into tablespoons

I. Preheat the oven to 375° and set a rack in the bottom third. Place the apricots in a shallow 2½-quart baking dish, such as a 10-inch round dish.

2. In a food processor, grind the almonds with ¼ cup of the brown sugar until fine, about 30 seconds. Add the lemon zest and process for 5 to 10 seconds. Scrape the sugar mixture over the apricots and toss. Scatter the raspberries and blueberries over the apricots and drizzle with the lemon juice.

3. In the food processor, combine the flour, cinnamon, salt, oats and the remaining ¾ cup of light brown sugar; process for 10 seconds. Add the butter and pulse just until the mixture resembles coarse crumbs. Sprinkle the topping evenly over the fruit and bake for 55 minutes, or until the topping is browned and the filling is bubbling. Let the crumble cool on a wire rack and serve. —*Greg Patent*

tarts, pies + fruit desserts

Crispy Apple and Pine Nut Fritters

TOTAL: 45 MIN

MAKES 30 SMALL FRITTERS

- ¼ cup raisins
- 1 tablespoon dark rum, warmed over low heat
- ½ cup pine nuts
- 1 cup all-purpose flour
- 1 teaspoon baking powder
- ½ teaspoon kosher salt
- 2 large eggs
- 2 tablespoons sugar
- ½ cup milk
- ½ teaspoon finely grated lemon zest
- ½ teaspoon finely grated orange zest
- 1 Golden Delicious apple—peeled, cored and cut into ¼-inch dice

Vegetable oil, for frying

Confectioners' sugar, for dusting

1. Preheat the oven to 350°. In a small bowl, cover the raisins with the warm rum. Let the mixture stand for about 10 minutes, or until the raisins are completely softened.

2. Meanwhile, spread the pine nuts in a pie plate and toast for 4 minutes, or until lightly browned. Let cool.

3. In a small bowl, whisk the flour with the baking powder and salt. In a medium bowl, whisk the eggs with the sugar until pale. Whisk in the milk and the citrus zests, then whisk in the dry ingredients. Fold in the apple, pine nuts and the raisins with their soaking liquid.

4. In a medium saucepan, heat about 1½ inches of oil to 350°. Drop level tablespoons of the batter into the hot oil, about 6 at a time. Fry until the fritters are golden, about 4 minutes. Transfer the fritters to a rack set over a baking sheet to drain, then follow the same procedure with the remaining batter to make more fritters. Dust the warm fritters with confectioners' sugar and serve immediately. —*Marika Seguso*

Apple Crisp with Granola Topping

ACTIVE: 20 MIN; TOTAL: 1 HR 45 MIN

12 SERVINGS ●

- 1 cup plus 2 tablespoons all-purpose flour
- ½ cup packed light brown sugar
- ½ teaspoon baking powder

Pinch of salt

- 1 stick (4 ounces) unsalted butter
- 2 cups granola without dried fruit
- 3½ pounds Granny Smith apples, peeled and cut into ¾-inch pieces
- 1 cup granulated sugar
- 1 tablespoon fresh lemon juice
- 2 teaspoons cinnamon
- ½ teaspoon freshly grated nutmeg

1. Preheat the oven to 350°. Butter a shallow 3-quart baking dish. In a food processor, pulse 1 cup of the flour with the brown sugar, baking powder and salt. Pulse in the butter. Pulse in the granola. Transfer the topping to a bowl.

2. In a large bowl, toss the apples with the granulated sugar, lemon juice, cinnamon, nutmeg and the remaining 2 tablespoons of flour, then spread in the baking dish. Sprinkle on the topping and bake for 1 hour, or until the topping is golden and the filling is bubbling. Let cool for 20 minutes, then serve.

—*Grace Parisi*

MAKE AHEAD Cover and store the crisp overnight at room temperature. Reheat before serving.

Strawberry Shortcake with Star Anise Sauce

ACTIVE: 40 MIN; TOTAL: 2 HR 20 MIN

MAKES ONE 9-INCH LAYER CAKE ●

- 3 ounces white chocolate (preferably Valrhona), chopped
- 2 cups cake flour
- 1 teaspoon baking powder
- ½ teaspoon baking soda
- ⅛ teaspoon salt
- 1½ sticks unsalted butter, softened
- 1½ cups plus 1 tablespoon sugar
- 1 teaspoon pure vanilla extract
- 4 large eggs, at room temperature, separated
- 1 cup buttermilk, at room temperature
- 1½ cups heavy cream, chilled
- ½ cup crème fraîche, chilled
- 3 pints strawberries, quartered

Strawberry Star Anise Sauce (recipe follows)

1. Preheat the oven to 350°. Butter two 9-inch round cake pans and line the bottoms with parchment paper; butter the parchment paper. Coat the pans with flour, tapping out any excess.

2. Melt the white chocolate in a saucepan set over a pot of barely simmering water, stirring occasionally. In a medium bowl, whisk the flour with the baking powder, baking soda and salt. In a large bowl, using an electric mixer, beat the butter with 1¼ cups of the sugar until fluffy, about 2 minutes. Add the vanilla, then beat in 1 egg yolk at a time. Beat in the melted white chocolate. Mix in the dry ingredients in 2 batches, alternating with the buttermilk.

berry boost

IN A STUDY CONDUCTED AT TUFTS UNIVERSITY in Boston, berries ranked first among 50 fruits and vegetables as sources of antioxidants, compounds that may help prevent heart disease, cancer and stroke. According to Gary Stoner, a researcher at Ohio State University, strawberries, blackberries and cranberries are extraordinary sources of ellagic acid, an antioxidant that may help prevent some kinds of cancer. All berries deliver notable amounts of vitamin C, potassium and fiber, but strawberries are particularly high in C; half a cup provides 75 percent of the recommended daily amount.

3. In a medium bowl, beat the egg whites until soft peaks form. Gradually beat in ¼ cup of the sugar until the whites are glossy and firm. Stir one-third of the beaten egg whites into the batter, then fold in the rest until no white streaks remain. Scrape the batter into the prepared pans and smooth the tops. Bake for about 35 minutes, or until springy and golden and a toothpick inserted in the centers comes out clean. Let the cakes cool in the pans for 10 minutes, then run a knife around the edges and invert them onto a wire rack to cool. Peel off the parchment paper.

4. In another bowl, beat the cream and crème fraîche with the remaining 1 tablespoon of sugar until firm peaks form. Place 1 cake layer on a plate and spread with half of the whipped cream. Top with half of the strawberries and the second layer. Spoon the remaining whipped cream over the cake, swirling it decoratively. Top with the remaining berries. Serve with the strawberry sauce. —*Sherry Yard*

MAKE AHEAD The assembled cake can be refrigerated for up to 2 hours.

Strawberry Star Anise Sauce

TOTAL: 30 MIN

MAKES ABOUT ¾ CUP ● ● ●

2 pints strawberries, thickly sliced
½ cup fresh orange juice
¼ cup sugar
1 teaspoon finely grated orange zest
1 tablespoon Cointreau
2 whole star anise pods

In a medium saucepan, combine all of the ingredients and crush lightly with a potato masher. Bring to a boil, then simmer over moderate heat until the strawberries lose their bright red color, about 2 minutes. Strain the sauce through a fine sieve into a heatproof bowl, pressing hard on the solids to extract as much of the juice as possible; refrigerate until chilled. Transfer to a pitcher. —*S.Y.*

Pear and Almond Cream Tart

ACTIVE: 45 MIN; TOTAL: 1 HR 30 MIN

MAKES TWO 9-INCH TARTS ●

PASTRY

2 cups all-purpose flour
1 teaspoon sugar
¼ teaspoon salt
1 stick plus 2 tablespoons cold unsalted butter, cut into pieces
1 large egg yolk mixed with ¼ cup ice water

FILLING

1 cup milk
¼ cup sugar
3 tablespoons cornstarch
3 large eggs
Pinch of salt
1 stick plus 6 tablespoons (7 ounces) unsalted butter, softened
2½ cups sliced almonds
1½ cups confectioners' sugar
2 tablespoons brandy
6 ripe medium Bartlett pears— peeled, quartered and cored
Vanilla ice cream, for serving

1. MAKE THE PASTRY: In a food processor, pulse the flour with the sugar and salt. Pulse in the butter until it is the size of small peas. Sprinkle the egg mixture on top; pulse just until a dough forms. Scrape the pastry onto 2 sheets of plastic wrap and form into 2 disks. Wrap and refrigerate until chilled.

2. MEANWHILE, MAKE THE FILLING: Bring the milk to a simmer in a medium saucepan. In a medium bowl, whisk the sugar with 1 tablespoon of the cornstarch. Whisk in 1 egg and the salt. Gradually whisk in the hot milk, then return it to the saucepan and cook over moderate heat, whisking, until thickened and just beginning to bubble around the edge, about 4 minutes. Strain the custard into a bowl and let cool slightly. Whisk in 2 tablespoons of the butter.

3. Using an electric mixer, beat the remaining 12 tablespoons of butter with the sliced almonds at medium-low speed until the almonds are slightly crushed. Beat in the confectioners' sugar and the remaining 2 tablespoons of cornstarch and 2 eggs, then beat in the custard and brandy.

4. Preheat the oven to 350°. On a lightly floured surface, roll out each pastry disk to a 12-inch round ⅛ inch thick. Fit the pastry into two 9-inch fluted tart pans with removable bottoms. Fold the overhang onto itself. Using a sharp knife, trim off any excess pastry.

5. Spoon the filling into the tarts. Place 1 pear quarter in the center of each tart; arrange the remaining quarters in a circle around it. Bake the tarts in the center of the oven for 1 hour and 10 minutes, or until the pears are very tender and the custard and pastry are deep golden. Let the tarts cool for 30 minutes, then unmold and serve warm or at room temperature with vanilla ice cream. —*Elisabeth Prueitt*

MAKE AHEAD The tarts can be stored overnight in airtight containers.

Pineapple Foster

TOTAL: 20 MIN

4 SERVINGS ●

4 tablespoons unsalted butter
½ cup light brown sugar
Pinch of cinnamon
½ ripe pineapple—peeled, cored and cut into 8 long spears
½ cup dark rum
Vanilla ice cream, for serving

In a large skillet, cook the butter over high heat until lightly browned, 1 to 2 minutes. Stir in the brown sugar and cinnamon. Add the pineapple and cook over moderate heat, shaking the skillet, until the sugar is melted and the pineapple is slightly tender, about 2 minutes. Flip the pineapple spears. Add the rum, carefully ignite and cook until the flames subside. Serve with ice cream. —*Grace Parisi*

tarts, pies + fruit desserts

Caramel Apple Parfaits

ACTIVE: 1 HR 30 MIN; TOTAL: 2 HR 30 MIN

MAKES 12 PARFAITS ●

The parfait can also be assembled in one large glass bowl.

CAKE

- 2½ cups all-purpose flour
- 1½ teaspoons baking soda
- ½ teaspoon salt
- ½ teaspoon cinnamon
- ¼ teaspoon ground cloves
- ¼ teaspoon ground allspice
- 1 stick (4 ounces) unsalted butter, softened
- 1 cup packed dark brown sugar
- 1 tablespoon unsulfured molasses
- 1 large egg, beaten
- 1 cup buttermilk

CARAMEL SAUCE

- 1 cup sugar
- ¼ cup water
- 1½ cups heavy cream
- 1 teaspoon cinnamon

APPLES

- 1 stick (4 ounces) unsalted butter
- 8 large Granny Smith apples— peeled, cored and thinly sliced (12 cups)
- ½ cup granulated sugar
- ¼ cup packed dark brown sugar
- 1 quart chilled heavy cream

1. MAKE THE CAKE: Preheat the oven to 350°. Butter and lightly flour a 12-by-17-inch rimmed baking sheet. In a medium bowl, whisk the flour with the baking soda, salt, cinnamon, cloves and allspice. In a large bowl, using an electric mixer, beat the softened butter with the brown sugar and molasses at medium speed until combined. Add the egg and beat until blended, then add the dry ingredients in 3 batches, alternating with the buttermilk. Using a rubber spatula, scrape the batter onto the prepared baking sheet and evenly smooth the surface.

2. Bake the cake in the center of the oven for about 20 minutes, or until springy. Let cool in the pan for 10 minutes, then invert onto a wire rack and let cool completely.

3. MEANWHILE, MAKE THE CARAMEL SAUCE: In a medium saucepan, combine the sugar and water and cook over moderately high heat, stirring, until the sugar dissolves. Cook without stirring until a deep amber caramel forms, 5 to 6 minutes. Remove from the heat and carefully add the cream. Once the bubbling subsides, return the caramel to moderate heat and cook, stirring occasionally, until the sauce is slightly thickened, 5 to 6 minutes. Whisk in the cinnamon. Transfer the caramel to a heatproof pitcher.

4. PREPARE THE APPLES: In a large skillet, melt 4 tablespoons of the butter. Add half of the apples and cook over high heat, tossing occasionally, until lightly browned, about 4 minutes. Add half each of the granulated and brown sugars and cook, stirring occasionally, until the apples are caramelized and very tender, about 6 minutes. Transfer the apples to a plate, rinse out the skillet and repeat the procedure with the remaining butter, apples and granulated and brown sugars.

5. In a large bowl, using an electric mixer, beat the cream until medium-soft peaks form. Using a 2½-inch biscuit cutter, stamp out 24 rounds of the cake. Spoon 1 tablespoon of caramel sauce into each of 12 large glasses. Add about 2 tablespoons of apples and ¼ cup of whipped cream to each glass. Place a cake round in each glass. Repeat with the remaining ingredients, ending with whipped cream. Refrigerate for at least 30 minutes or overnight. Let stand at room temperature for 15 minutes; serve.
—Tom Valenti

MAKE AHEAD The parfaits can be assembled early in the day and refrigerated. Let stand at room temperature for 15 minutes before serving.

Tangy Strawberry Parfait with Lime Gelée

TOTAL: 35 MIN

MAKES 4 PARFAITS ● ●

- 1 teaspoon unflavored gelatin
- ½ cup sugar
- ¼ cup fresh lime juice
- 1 teaspoon finely grated lime zest
- 2 pints strawberries, hulled and thinly sliced
- ½ vanilla bean, split lengthwise, seeds scraped
- ½ cup heavy cream, chilled

Vanilla ice cream, for serving

1. Set 4 martini glasses or shallow dessert bowls in the freezer. In a small cup, sprinkle the gelatin over the cold water and let stand until softened, about 3 minutes. Fill a medium bowl half full of ice water.

2. In a small saucepan, combine ¼ cup of the sugar with 2 tablespoons of water and simmer over moderate heat just until the sugar is dissolved. Remove the sugar syrup from the heat and whisk in the softened gelatin until dissolved. Stir in the lime juice and ½ teaspoon of the lime zest. Set the saucepan in the ice-water bath and stir the gelée until cooled. Pour the gelée into the chilled glasses and freeze until firm, about 15 minutes.

3. Meanwhile, in a medium saucepan, combine 1 cup of the strawberries with 2 tablespoons of sugar and ¼ cup of water and bring to a boil. Let cool slightly. Transfer the strawberry mixture to a blender and puree until smooth. Pour the puree into a bowl and stir in the remaining strawberries and half of the vanilla bean seeds; let cool.

4. In a bowl, whisk the cream with the remaining 2 tablespoons of sugar, ½ teaspoon of lime zest and vanilla seeds until soft peaks form. Spoon the strawberry puree over the lime gelée. Top with a dollop of ice cream and whipped cream; serve. *—Daniel Boulud*

CARAMEL APPLE PARFAIT

tarts, pies + fruit desserts

Melon and Mango Salad with Toasted Coconut and Pistachios

TOTAL: 30 MIN

4 SERVINGS ● ● ●

¼ cup unsweetened shredded coconut

⅓ cup roasted salted pistachios, coarsely chopped

¼ cup fresh lime juice

1 tablespoon minced candied ginger

1 tablespoon packed mint leaves

½ teaspoon crushed red pepper

Kosher salt and freshly ground white pepper

½ medium honeydew melon, cut into ½-inch chunks

½ large cantaloupe, cut into ½-inch chunks

1 mango, cut into ½-inch chunks

1. In a small skillet, toast the coconut over moderately high heat, stirring, until golden, about 2 minutes. Transfer to a bowl and let cool. Mix in the pistachios.
2. In a blender, puree the lime juice, ginger, mint and red pepper; season with salt and white pepper. Toss with the fruit. Sprinkle the coconut-pistachio mixture on top. —*Megan Moore*

MAKE AHEAD The fruit salad can be covered and kept at room temperature for up to 2 hours. Sprinkle on the coconut-pistachio mixture right before serving.

Roasted Peaches, Nectarines and Cherries with Sabayon

ACTIVE: 35 MIN; TOTAL: 1 HR 25 MIN

8 SERVINGS ●

Chef Michael Tusk infuses the sugar for this recipe overnight with sprigs of lemon verbena. Here we give a quicker and easier alternative that uses lemon zest and mint.

8 white peaches

4 nectarines

2 pounds Bing cherries, pitted and stemmed

1½ teaspoons finely grated lemon zest

⅔ cup plus ¼ cup sugar

8 large mint sprigs or lemon verbena sprigs

4 large egg yolks

½ cup Moscato d'Asti or German Riesling

½ cup heavy cream

1. Preheat the oven to 425°. Butter two 9-by-13-inch baking dishes. Bring a large pot of water to a boil. Add the peaches and nectarines and blanch just until the skins loosen, about 20 seconds. Drain in a colander, refresh under cold running water and drain again. Peel the peaches and nectarines and cut them into quarters.
2. In a large bowl, toss the peaches and nectarines with the cherries. In a small bowl, rub the lemon zest into the ⅔ cup of sugar. Add 4 mint sprigs and half of the fruit to each baking dish. Sprinkle half of the lemon sugar over the fruit in each baking dish and bake in the upper third of the oven for about 30 minutes, or until the fruit is bubbling and caramelized in spots. Let the fruit rest for 10 minutes before serving.
3. Meanwhile, in a large saucepan, bring 1 inch of water to a simmer over low heat. In a medium stainless steel bowl, whisk the egg yolks with the remaining ¼ cup of sugar, then whisk in the wine. Set the bowl over the simmering water and whisk constantly until the sabayon is pale yellow and fluffy, about 8 minutes. There should be no dark yellow streaks visible. Remove the bowl from the heat and continue to whisk a few times to cool down the sabayon. Refrigerate the sabayon, whisking often, until it is slightly chilled, about 20 minutes.
4. In a medium stainless steel bowl, whip the cream until firm, then fold it into the chilled sabayon. Spoon the baked fruit into shallow bowls, top with the sabayon and serve. —*Michael Tusk*

MAKE AHEAD The sabayon can be refrigerated separately overnight. Stir well before serving.

Raspberry Baked Custard

ACTIVE: 10 MIN; TOTAL: 1 HR 15 MIN

8 SERVINGS ●

3 large eggs

2 large egg whites

⅓ cup granulated sugar

1½ teaspoons pure vanilla extract

½ teaspoon finely grated lemon zest

1¼ cups heavy cream

3 tablespoons all-purpose flour

2 cups raspberries

2 tablespoons superfine sugar

1. Preheat the oven to 325°. Lightly butter a shallow 2-quart baking dish.
2. In a large bowl, whisk the whole eggs and egg whites with the granulated sugar, vanilla and lemon zest until pale, about 1 minute. Whisk in the cream. Sift the flour on top and whisk just until blended. Pour 1 cup of the custard into the baking dish and bake for 12 minutes, or just until set.
3. Scatter the raspberries all over the baked custard and sprinkle with the superfine sugar. Pour the remaining

custard on top and tamp down any floating raspberries with a spoon. Bake for 50 minutes longer, until the custard is lightly golden on top and nicely set in the center. Let the custard cool slightly and then serve warm or at room temperature. —*Alexandra Angle*

Rosy Summer-Berry Puddings

TOTAL: I HR

MAKES 6 PUDDINGS ●

- 4 half-pints raspberries, plus more for garnish
- 6 tablespoons superfine sugar
- 1½ tablespoons Chambord liqueur
- ¾ teaspoon rose water (optional)
- 1¼ cups mascarpone cheese
- 3 tablespoons rose jam

One ½-pound loaf brioche, crusts trimmed, bread cut into twelve ⅓- to ½-inch-thick slices

I. Line six 8 ounce ramekins with plastic wrap, leaving 2 inches of overhang.

2. In a blender, puree 3 half-pints of raspberries with 5 tablespoons of the sugar, the Chambord and the rose water. Strain through a fine sieve.

3. In a bowl, toss the remaining half-pint of berries with the remaining 1 tablespoon of sugar. In another small bowl, combine the mascarpone with the jam.

4. Using a 3¼-inch round cookie cutter, stamp out a round from each brioche slice. Dip 6 rounds in the berry puree to coat completely; place 1 in each prepared ramekin. Spoon the mascarpone mixture over the rounds, spreading it evenly. Scatter the sugared raspberries on top. Dip the 6 remaining rounds in the remaining puree and place in the ramekins. Fold the overhanging plastic wrap over the top, pressing hard to compact the puddings. Refrigerate for at least 30 minutes and for up to 24 hours.

5. To serve, peel back the plastic and invert the puddings onto dessert plates. Garnish with raspberries and serve. —*Melissa Clark*

Orange-Figgy Steamed Pudding

ACTIVE: I HR; TOTAL: 3 HR

12 SERVINGS ● ●

- ½ pound dried black Mission figs, stems discarded
- ¼ cup Cognac or Armagnac

Zest of 1 orange in 1-inch strips

- ¾ cup water
- ¼ cup molasses
- ½ cup low-fat (1%) milk
- ¼ cup nonfat sour cream
- ¼ cup applesauce
- 2 tablespoons canola oil
- 1½ teaspoons pure vanilla extract
- 2½ cups all-purpose flour
- 1 teaspoon baking powder
- 1 teaspoon ground cinnamon
- 1 teaspoon ground ginger
- ¼ teaspoon salt
- 1 stick (4 ounces) unsalted butter
- ¾ cup dark brown sugar
- 1 large egg
- 2 large egg whites
- 1 cup minced mixed dried fruit

Vegetable oil cooking spray

- 6 candied orange slices (6 ounces)
- 2 tablespoons low-sugar apricot preserves

Boiling water

I. In a large glass bowl, combine the figs, Cognac, zest and water. Cover with plastic; microwave on high for 2 minutes. Let stand for 5 minutes. Reserve 4 figs. In a food processor, puree the contents of the bowl with the molasses.

2. In a measuring cup, mix the milk, sour cream, applesauce, oil and vanilla. In a bowl, whisk the flour, baking powder, cinnamon, ginger and salt. In the large glass bowl, using an electric mixer, beat the butter and brown sugar until fluffy. Add the whole egg and egg whites, 1 at a time, beating well between additions. Beat in the pureed fruit. In 2 alternating batches, beat in the dry and wet ingredients at low speed just until combined. Stir in the minced dried fruit.

3. Spray a 6- to 8-cup steamed pudding

mold or soufflé dish with vegetable oil cooking spray. Arrange the candied orange slices in an overlapping pattern in the bottom of the mold. Halve the reserved figs lengthwise and tuck them in between the orange slices. Dollop the apricot preserves over the fruit. Pour the batter into the mold; tap the mold gently.

4. Cover the mold with a piece of oiled parchment paper, followed by a piece of foil, and then secure the lid. If using a soufflé dish, tie the parchment and foil in place with kitchen string.

5. Set the pudding on a rack in a large pot. Pour enough boiling water into the pot to reach two-thirds of the way up the side of the pudding. Cover the pot and bring to a boil. Reduce the heat to low and simmer for 2 hours; add more boiling water if the water evaporates.

6. Carefully remove the pudding from the pot and let cool slightly. Uncover the pudding and invert it onto a plate. Replace any figs or orange slices that are stuck to the mold. Slice the pudding and serve warm.
—*Stephana Bottom*

Blueberry-Peach Tequila Popsicles

ACTIVE: 20 MIN; TOTAL: 2 HR 35 MIN

MAKES 4 POPSICLES ● ●

- 2 large ripe peaches, pitted and sliced
- 5 tablespoons sugar
- 3 tablespoons tequila
- 1 tablespoon plus 2 teaspoons fresh lemon juice
- 1 pint blueberries

I. Puree the peaches in a food processor. Strain the puree into a bowl and stir in 3 tablespoons of the sugar, 2 tablespoons of the tequila and 1 tablespoon of the lemon juice. Pour 3 tablespoons of the puree into four 5 ounce popsicle molds or paper cups. Freeze until almost firm, about 25 minutes. Poke a popsicle stick into the center of each.

TANGELO CREAMSICLES

2. Meanwhile, puree the blueberries in a food processor. Strain through a sieve into a bowl and stir in the remaining 2 tablespoons of sugar, 1 tablespoon of tequila and 2 teaspoons of lemon juice. Pour 2 tablespoons of the blueberry puree into each mold and cover with plastic wrap. Freeze until almost firm, 25 minutes. Pour the remaining peach puree on top and freeze until almost firm, 25 minutes. Finish with a blueberry layer and freeze for 1 hour. Unmold and serve. —*Janie Hibler*

Quick Coconut Milk Ice Cream with Tropical Fruit

ACTIVE: 15 MIN; TOTAL: 3 HR 15 MIN

4 SERVINGS ●

In this recipe, coconut milk pureed with frozen tropical fruit creates an almost-instant soft ice cream.

- 2 cups ½-inch chunks mixed peeled ripe tropical fruit, such as mango, papaya and banana, plus ½ cup ¼-inch dice of mixed peeled ripe tropical fruit
- ½ cup unsweetened coconut milk, chilled (see Note)

About 2 tablespoons superfine sugar
About 1 tablespoon fresh lime juice
A few drops of dark rum (optional)

I. Line a baking sheet with plastic and spread with the fruit chunks. Cover and freeze until solid, at least 1 hour. Refrigerate the diced fruit until chilled.

2. Transfer the frozen fruit to a food processor. Puree for 2 minutes; as the fruit thaws, the puree will become creamy. Drizzle in the coconut milk, sugar, lime juice and rum and process until combined; do not overprocess. Taste and add more sugar and lime juice if desired. Transfer to an airtight container and freeze for at least 2 hours or for up to 6 hours. Right before serving, fold in the diced fruit. —*Sally Schneider*

NOTE Stir the canned coconut milk well; it separates during storage.

Minted Melon with Vanilla Granita and Citrus Yogurt

ACTIVE: 40 MIN; TOTAL: 2 HR 40 MIN

6 SERVINGS ●

GRANITA

- ¾ cup water
- ¼ cup sugar
- ½ vanilla bean, split lengthwise, seeds scraped
- 1 teaspoon fresh lemon juice

MELONS

- ¼ cup plus 1 tablespoon fresh orange juice
- ¼ cup sugar
- 3 tablespoons fresh lime juice
- 1½ teaspoons finely grated fresh ginger
- 1 teaspoon finely chopped mint
- ½ teaspoon finely grated lime zest
- ½ small honeydew melon, seeds discarded, melon scooped into large and small balls (2½ cups)
- ½ large cantaloupe, seeds discarded, melon scooped into large and small balls (1½ cups)

CITRUS YOGURT

- ½ teaspoon unflavored gelatin
- 1 tablespoon cold water
- 1 cup plain whole milk yogurt, at room temperature
- 1 tablespoon sugar
- 1 tablespoon honey
- 1 teaspoon finely grated orange zest

I. MAKE THE GRANITA: In a small saucepan, combine the water with the sugar, the vanilla bean and its seeds and simmer over low heat until the sugar is dissolved. Let cool. Discard the vanilla bean and stir in the lemon juice.

2. Transfer the mixture to a shallow baking dish and freeze for 2 hours stirring with a fork every 30 minutes, until the granita is light and snowy. Transfer the granita to a plastic container, cover and freeze.

3. MARINATE THE MELONS: In a large bowl, combine the orange juice with the sugar, lime juice, ginger, mint and lime zest and stir until the sugar is dissolved. Add the melon balls and let stand at room temperature for 2 hours or refrigerate overnight.

4. MAKE THE CITRUS YOGURT: In a small microwavable cup, sprinkle the gelatin over the water and let stand until softened, about 5 minutes. Microwave on high power for 10 seconds, just until the gelatin is dissolved. In a medium bowl, combine the yogurt with the sugar, honey, orange zest and gelatin and stir until smooth. Chill the citrus yogurt just until set, about 30 minutes.

5. Spoon the yogurt into bowls. Drain the melon balls and mound them on the yogurt. Spoon the granita on top and serve right away. —*Michael Laiskonis*

MAKE AHEAD The recipe can be prepared through step 3 up to 1 day ahead.

Tangelo Creamsicles

TOTAL: 15 MIN

MAKES 10 CREAMSICLES ●

- 2 quarts vanilla ice cream
- 3 cups fresh tangelo or orange juice

Put 2 scoops of ice cream in each of 10 tall glasses. Add about ¼ cup of the citrus juice to each and serve right away. —*Kimberly Sklar*

Honey-Caramelized Apricots

TOTAL: 10 MIN

4 SERVINGS ●

- 8 ripe apricots, halved and pitted
- ½ cup fragrant honey, such as lavender

Vanilla ice cream

Preheat the broiler. Arrange the apricot halves, cut side up, on a rimmed baking sheet. Spoon ½ tablespoon of honey into each apricot half. Broil the apricots 4 inches from the heat for 3 to 4 minutes, rotating the sheet once, until bubbling and caramelized. Transfer 4 apricot halves to each plate and serve with a scoop of ice cream. —*Tony Maws*

ANGEL CAKE, P. 322

cakes, cookies + other desserts

WARM APPLE CIDER CAKE

CITRUS-GLAZED YOGURT CAKE

Warm Apple Cider Cake with Pumpkin Seed Brittle

ACTIVE: 40 MIN; TOTAL: 1 HR 45 MIN

8 SERVINGS ● ◐

CIDER SAUCE

- 4 cups apple cider, preferably fresh
- ⅓ cup bourbon
- ⅓ cup lightly packed dark brown sugar
- ¼ cup dark corn syrup
- 2 tablespoons cider vinegar
- 1 cinnamon stick
- ½ vanilla bean, split lengthwise, seeds scraped
- 1 cup heavy cream

CAKE

- 1¾ cups plus 1 tablespoon all-purpose flour
- 1 teaspoon salt
- 1 teaspoon baking powder
- ¼ teaspoon baking soda
- ¾ cup plus 2 tablespoons apple cider
- 3 tablespoons canola oil
- ¼ cup bourbon
- 7 tablespoons unsalted butter, softened
- ¾ cup dark brown sugar
- ½ vanilla bean, split lengthwise, seeds scraped
- 2 large eggs

Vanilla ice cream, for serving

Pumpkin Seed Brittle (recipe follows)

I. MAKE THE CIDER SAUCE: In a medium saucepan, combine the cider, bourbon, brown sugar, corn syrup, vinegar, cinnamon stick and vanilla bean and vanilla seeds. Bring the mixture to a boil, then simmer for 10 minutes.

2. Stir the cream into the cider mixture. Cook over moderately high heat until reduced to about 1 cup, about 25 minutes. Transfer the sauce to a pitcher;

let cool slightly. Discard the vanilla bean and cinnamon stick.

3. MAKE THE CAKE: Preheat the oven to 350°. Butter and flour a 9-inch round cake pan. Line the bottom of the pan with parchment paper; butter and flour the paper. In a bowl, whisk the flour, salt, baking powder and baking soda. In a glass measuring cup, mix the apple cider with the canola oil and bourbon. In a large bowl, using an electric mixer, beat the butter until creamy. Add the brown sugar and vanilla seeds and beat until completely smooth. Add the eggs, 1 at a time, beating well between each addition. Beat in the dry ingredients in 3 batches, alternating with the cider-bourbon mixture, until smooth.

4. Spread two-thirds of the batter in the prepared cake pan. Drizzle half of the cider sauce over the batter. Dollop the remaining batter on top, then spread the batter over the cider sauce, being careful not to mix them together. Bake the cake in the center of the oven for about 40 minutes, or until springy when touched. Let cool for 10 minutes in the pan, then turn the cake out onto a wire rack and let cool for 15 minutes. Peel off the parchment paper.

5. Rewarm the remaining cider sauce. Cut the cake into wedges and serve warm with vanilla ice cream, Pumpkin Seed Brittle and the cider sauce. —*Vicki Wells*

MAKE AHEAD The cake and cider sauce can be refrigerated for up to 3 days.

Pumpkin Seed Brittle

ACTIVE: 15 MIN; TOTAL: 1 HR

MAKES ABOUT 7 OUNCES ●

- ⅓ cup sugar
- 2 tablespoons light corn syrup
- 2 tablespoons water
- ¼ cup plus 2 tablespoons toasted unsalted pumpkin seeds
- ⅛ teaspoon baking soda dissolved in 1 teaspoon water

1. Line a baking sheet with parchment paper and butter the paper. In a medium saucepan, combine the sugar, corn syrup and water and bring to a boil over moderately high heat, stirring with a wooden spoon just until the sugar dissolves. Continue to cook, undisturbed, until a deep amber caramel forms, 8 to 9 minutes. Remove the caramel from the heat.

2. Add the pumpkin seeds and the dissolved baking soda to the caramel and stir until combined, then quickly pour the mixture onto the prepared baking sheet, spreading it into a thin layer with a spatula. Let cool until completely hardened. Break the brittle into shards and serve. *V.W.*

MAKE AHEAD The Pumpkin Seed Brittle can be kept in an airtight container at room temperature for up to 1 week.

Citrus-Glazed Yogurt Cake

ACTIVE: 50 MIN; TOTAL: 4 HR

MAKES ONE 9-INCH CAKE ●

The cake must be glazed while it is still hot, so be sure to make the glaze while the cake is baking.

- 3 cups sifted cake flour
- ½ teaspoon baking soda
- ½ teaspoon salt
- 2 sticks (½ pound) unsalted butter, softened
- 2 cups sugar
- 3 large eggs, at room temperature
- 1 cup plain low-fat yogurt
- ½ teaspoon pure vanilla extract

Finely grated zest of 2 scrubbed organic lemons

Finely grated zest of 2 scrubbed organic oranges

Finely grated zest of 1 scrubbed organic grapefruit

- 2 tablespoons fresh lemon juice
- 2 tablespoons fresh orange juice

Citrus Glaze and Candied Zest (recipe follows)

1. Preheat the oven to 350° and position a rack in the lower third. Butter and flour a 9-inch tube or Bundt pan.

2. In a large bowl, whisk the cake flour with the baking soda and salt. In another large bowl, using an electric mixer, beat the butter until nice and creamy. Add the sugar and beat at medium speed until light and fluffy. Add the eggs, 1 at a time, beating well between each addition.

3. In a small bowl, whisk the yogurt with the vanilla and citrus zests and juices. At low speed, beat the dry ingredients into the batter in 3 batches, alternating with the yogurt mixture. Scrape the batter into the prepared cake pan and bake for 1½ hours, or until the cake is golden and a cake tester inserted in the center comes out clean. Let the cake cool in the pan for 5 minutes, then turn out the cake while still fairly hot and place it right side up on a wire rack.

4. Prick the hot cake all over with a fork. Brush the Citrus Glaze all over. Scatter 2 tablespoons of the Candied Zest on top of the cake and let the cake cool completely. Slice the cake and serve the remaining Candied Zest alongside. —*Gail Monaghan*

MAKE AHEAD The cake can be stored at room temperature for up to 3 days.

Citrus Glaze and Candied Zest

ACTIVE: 20 MIN; TOTAL: 3 HR

MAKES ENOUGH FOR ONE 9-INCH CAKE OR 12 CUPCAKES ●

- 1 organic navel orange, scrubbed
- 1 large organic lemon, scrubbed
- 1 small organic grapefruit, scrubbed
- 2½ cups sugar

1. Using a sturdy vegetable peeler, remove the zest from the orange, lemon and grapefruit. Cut the zest into fine julienne strips.

2. Fill a medium saucepan with cold water. Add the zest and bring to a boil. Remove from the heat and let stand for 15 minutes. Drain the zest and rinse under cold water.

3. Return the zest to the saucepan. Add ½ cup of the sugar and 1 cup of cold water and bring to a boil, stirring until the sugar dissolves. Simmer over low heat until the glaze is slightly thickened and the zest is softened and translucent, about 20 minutes.

4. Strain the glaze into a heatproof bowl, pressing on the zest to extract as much glaze as possible. Return 2 tablespoons of the zest to the glaze.

5. Spread the remaining 2 cups of sugar on a large plate. Scatter the remaining zest over the sugar and toss to coat completely. Scatter the sugared zest on a wax paper–lined plate and let stand until dry, about 2 hours. —*G.M.*

MAKE AHEAD The glaze and candied zest can be stored separately in airtight containers at room temperature for up to 2 days. Reheat the glaze before using.

cakes, cookies + other desserts

Angel Cake

ACTIVE: 45 MIN; TOTAL: 1 HR 45 MIN

MAKES ONE 9-INCH LAYER CAKE ●

- 3 cups all-purpose flour
- 1 tablespoon baking powder
- ¼ teaspoon baking soda
- ¼ teaspoon salt
- 2 sticks (½ pound) unsalted butter, at room temperature
- 2 cups sugar
- 4 large eggs, at room temperature
- 1 cup buttermilk
- 1 teaspoon pure vanilla extract

Marshmallow Icing (recipe follows)

Silver dragées, for decorating

1. Preheat the oven to 350°. Butter and flour two 9-inch cake pans. On a sheet of wax paper, sift the flour, baking powder, baking soda and salt.

2. In a large bowl, using an electric mixer, beat the butter at medium speed until creamy. Beat in the sugar until fluffy, about 2 minutes. Add the eggs, 1 at a time, beating well between additions. Beat in the dry ingredients at low speed, in 3 additions, alternating with the buttermilk. Beat in the vanilla.

3. Spoon the batter into the prepared pans and bake in the center of the oven for about 35 minutes, until golden and a cake tester inserted in the centers comes out clean. Let the cakes cool on a rack for 10 minutes. Unmold the cakes and let cool completely on the rack.

4. Transfer a cake layer to a plate and frost the top generously with icing. Cover with the second cake layer and spread the top and sides with the remaining icing. Decorate with dragées and serve.
—*Peggy Cullen*

MAKE AHEAD Although it's best when freshly made, the cake can be refrigerated overnight.

Marshmallow Icing

TOTAL: 25 MIN

MAKES ABOUT 6½ CUPS ●

- 5 large egg whites
- 1⅔ cups sugar
- 2 tablespoons cold water
- 1½ cups light corn syrup

Pinch of cream of tartar

- 2 teaspoons pure vanilla extract

1. Bring 1 inch of water to a boil in a wide saucepan. In a large stainless steel bowl, whisk the egg whites with the sugar, cold water and corn syrup until blended. Set the bowl over the saucepan and whisk the whites until the sugar is completely melted, 4 to 5 minutes. Rub some of the mixture between your fingers to be sure it's not gritty.

2. Remove the bowl from the saucepan and add the cream of tartar to the whites. Using a standing electric mixer, beat the egg whites at medium speed for 1 minute to break them up. Gradually increase the speed to high and beat until the icing is fluffy, firm and no longer warm to the touch, about 10 minutes. Beat in the vanilla extract. Use the icing right away.—*P.C.*

Yogurt-Semolina Cake

ACTIVE: 20 MIN; TOTAL: 2 HR 30 MIN

MAKES ONE 9-INCH CAKE ●

This dense and chewy dessert from Turkey is closer to a syrupy baklava than a spongy cake. Baking it in a ceramic vessel, such as a shallow clay baking dish (a Spanish *cazuela* is a good option) or a porcelain pan, produces a crisp bottom crust.

- 1 cup plain whole milk yogurt
- ½ teaspoon baking soda
- 1½ cups semolina
- 1½ cups sugar
- ½ teaspoon baking powder
- ½ teaspoon pure vanilla extract
- 3 tablespoons unsalted butter, melted and cooled slightly
- 16 blanched almond slivers
- ½ cup water
- ½ lemon, washed and quartered

1. In a small glass bowl, combine the yogurt and the baking soda and let stand for 10 minutes.

2. In a medium bowl, combine the semolina with ¾ cup of the sugar and the baking powder. Slowly stir in the yogurt and the vanilla until blended.

3. Brush a 9-inch square porcelain baking dish or a medium *cazuela* with 1 tablespoon of the melted butter. Scrape the batter into the baking dish and spread evenly. Using a thin knife, mark 16 squares on the top of the batter by scoring lines ¼ inch deep. Place an almond sliver in the middle of each square. Let stand for 1 hour.

4. Preheat the oven to 375°. Bake the cake for 25 minutes, or until it is golden brown and pulls away from the dish.

5. In a saucepan, mix the the remaining ¾ cup of sugar with the water and lemon. Simmer until the sugar dissolves and the liquid has thickened slightly. Squeeze the lemon juice into the syrup; discard the seeds and peels.

6. Remove the cake from the oven and run a knife along the score lines. Brush the top of the cake with the remaining 2 tablespoons of melted butter and spoon the lemon syrup on top. Cover the cake and let stand for a few minutes until the syrup is completely absorbed. —*Paula Wolfert*

SERVE WITH Crème fraîche.

BAKING TIP

egg whites

WHEN MAKING MERINGUE (or just beating egg whites for a cake batter), make sure the bowl and beaters are clean and dry. Even a trace of water, oil or egg yolk can interfere with the formation of the foam. Also, be careful not to overbeat the whites, as this will ruin the texture of the meringue and result in a tough cake. As soon as stiff peaks form, stop beating.

cakes, cookies + other desserts

Golden Yuca-and-Coconut Cake

ACTIVE: 30 MIN; TOTAL: 3 HR

MAKES ONE 10-INCH CAKE ●

Known as *enyucado* in Colombia, this cake is traditionally cooked in a skillet and browned on both sides like a Spanish tortilla; some Colombian cooks like to bake it in the oven. The result is a dense, chewy cake that is cut into wedges and served as a side dish with savory foods or as a dessert.

- 1¾ pounds yuca, peeled and finely grated (about 3 cups; see Note)
- ¾ cup plus 2 tablespoons finely grated fresh or frozen coconut (from 1 small coconut)
- 1½ cups coarsely shredded queso blanco or Monterey Jack cheese (about 7½ ounces)
- ¾ cup unsweetened coconut milk
- ¾ cup plus 2 tablespoons sugar
- 2 teaspoons anise seeds, lightly crushed
- ¼ teaspoon kosher salt
- 1½ tablespoons unsalted butter, melted

1. Preheat the oven to 350°. In a large bowl, mix the yuca with the grated coconut, queso blanco, coconut milk, sugar, anise seeds, salt and melted butter. Let stand for 15 minutes.

2. Butter the bottom of a 10-by-2-inch nonstick round cake pan and line it with parchment paper; butter the paper. Pour the yuca mixture into the prepared pan. Bake the cake for 2 hours, or until it is deeply browned and pulls away from the side of the pan. Transfer to a wire rack and let cool for 10 minutes. Run a knife around the edge of the cake and invert it onto the rack. Peel off the parchment; invert the cake onto a platter. Cut into wedges and serve warm.

—*Maricel Presilla*

NOTE Yuca, also known as cassava and manioc, is a starchy root vegetable available at many supermarkets. The skin is usually waxed to prevent moisture loss.

If you get an older yuca root, you'll have to grate around the tough core.

MAKE AHEAD The cake can be stored at room temperature or refrigerated for up to 3 days. Reheat in a 325° oven.

Robiola Cheesecake with Shortbread Crust

ACTIVE: 30 MIN; TOTAL: 4 HR 30 MIN

MAKES ONE 9-INCH CHEESECAKE ●

CRUST

- 6 tablespoons unsalted butter
- 3 tablespoons sugar
- ½ teaspoon pure vanilla extract
- ½ cup all-purpose flour
- ¼ cup rice flour

Pinch of salt

- ¼ cup plus 2 tablespoons coarsely chopped dried fruit, such as cherries, apricots, figs and dates

FILLING

- 6 ounces fresh Robiola cheese (see Note), without the rind, at room temperature
- 6 ounces cream cheese, at room temperature
- ½ cup sugar
- ½ vanilla bean, split lengthwise, seeds scraped
- 2 large eggs
- 2 tablespoons sour cream
- 3 tablespoons apricot nectar
- 2 tablespoons sherry
- ½ teaspoon cornstarch

1. **MAKE THE CRUST:** Preheat the oven to 325°. Line a baking sheet with parchment paper. In a medium bowl, using an electric mixer, beat the butter with the sugar and vanilla until smooth. Add the all-purpose flour, rice flour and salt and beat just until combined. Quickly beat in the dried fruit. Pat the dough in an even layer ¼ inch thick on the parchment paper. Bake for about 30 minutes, or until the shortbread is barely golden. Transfer the baking sheet to a rack and let cool. Increase the oven temperature to 375°.

2. Break the shortbread into small pieces and transfer to a food processor. Pulse until fine crumbs form.

3. Generously butter a 9-inch nonstick springform pan. Press the crumbs evenly over the bottom and ⅓ inch up the side of the pan.

4. **MAKE THE FILLING:** In a large bowl, using an electric mixer, beat the Robiola cheese with the cream cheese until smooth. Beat in the sugar and vanilla seeds, then add the eggs, 1 at a time, beating well between additions. Beat in the sour cream, nectar and sherry until blended. Beat in the cornstarch.

5. Pour the filling into the crust. Bake for about 15 minutes, then lower the oven temperature to 325° and bake for 15 minutes longer, until the center of the cake is still slightly jiggly. Transfer to a rack to cool, then refrigerate for at least 3 hours or overnight. Serve cold.

—*Vicki Wells*

NOTE Robiola is an Italian cheese; be sure to choose a mild form, such as Osella or Bosina.

MAKE AHEAD The cheesecake can be refrigerated for up to 2 days.

Raspberry and Kirsch Jelly Roll

ACTIVE: 30 MIN; TOTAL: 2 HR

8 TO 10 SERVINGS ●

When the season for fresh berries is over, use IQF (Individually Quick Frozen) raspberries for the coulis. IQF berries are available in the freezer section of most supermarkets.

- 6 large eggs, separated
- ½ cup sugar
- 1 teaspoon pure vanilla extract
- ½ cup all-purpose flour
- 1½ tablespoons kirsch
- 1½ cups raspberry preserves
- 1 pound fresh or thawed IQF raspberries
- 1 cup chilled sour cream

1. Preheat the oven to 350°. Evenly butter a 15½-by-10½-inch jelly-roll pan.

CHOCOLATE MARBLE POUND CAKE

MOLTEN CHOCOLATE CAKE

Line the jelly-roll pan with parchment paper; press the paper into the corners and up the sides of the pan. Lightly butter the parchment paper.

2. In a large bowl, using an electric mixer, beat the egg yolks, sugar and vanilla at high speed until fluffy and lemon colored, about 5 minutes. Using a large rubber spatula, fold the flour into the batter.

3. In a glass or stainless steel bowl, using clean beaters, beat the egg whites at high speed until firm peaks form. Using a clean large rubber spatula, fold one-fourth of the beaten whites into the batter until incorporated, then fold in the remaining whites. Spread the batter in the prepared jelly-roll pan.

4. Bake the cake in the center of the oven for 10 to 12 minutes, or until it is pale golden yellow and a cake tester

inserted in the center comes out clean. Let the cake cool on a rack for 15 minutes. Using the edge of the parchment paper, carefully slide the cake onto a work surface.

5. Sprinkle the kirsch over the jelly roll cake and spread ½ cup of the preserves over the surface. Starting at a short end, grasp the parchment paper with both hands and push and roll the cake into a neat, tight scroll, peeling off the parchment paper as you go. Wrap the rolled cake in the parchment and refrigerate until firm, at least 1 hour.

6. Meanwhile, in a food processor, puree the raspberries with the remaining 1 cup of raspberry preserves. Strain the coulis through a fine sieve.

7. Spoon about 3 tablespoons of the coulis onto each dessert plate; tilt the plates to spread the coulis out. Using a

serrated knife, cut the jelly roll into 1-inch-thick slices. Set the jelly-roll slices in the center of the plates and serve with the sour cream.

—Jacques Pépin

MAKE AHEAD The rolled cake can be refrigerated overnight. Bring almost to room temperature before slicing and serving. The coulis can be refrigerated for up to 5 days.

Chocolate Marble Pound Cake

ACTIVE: 20 MIN; TOTAL: 2 HR

MAKES ONE 8-BY-4-INCH LOAF ●

Vegetable oil cooking spray

  2 cups all-purpose flour

  2 teaspoons baking powder

¼ teaspoon salt

1½ sticks (6 ounces) unsalted butter, softened, plus 3 tablespoons melted

2 tablespoons unsweetened cocoa powder, preferably Dutch process (see Note)

1⅓ cups granulated sugar

2 large eggs

1 teaspoon pure vanilla extract

½ cup heavy cream or milk

Confectioners' sugar, for dusting

1. Preheat the oven to 350°. Spray an 8-by-4-inch loaf pan with vegetable oil cooking spray and line it with parchment paper. Spray the paper.

2. In a bowl, whisk the flour, baking powder and salt. In another bowl, combine the melted butter and cocoa until smooth.

3. In a food processor, combine the softened butter with the granulated sugar. Add the eggs and vanilla and process until smooth. Add the dry ingredients and pulse just until combined. Add the cream and process until smooth. Transfer 1 cup of the batter to the bowl with the cocoa and stir until smooth.

4. Spoon half of the remaining batter into the prepared pan and smooth the surface. Spread the chocolate batter in the pan, then cover with the remaining plain batter. Using a table knife, cut 5 swirls in the batter. Bake the pound cake for 25 minutes. Reduce the temperature to 325° and bake for 25 minutes more. Cover loosely with foil and bake for 15 to 20 minutes longer, or until the cake is lightly browned and a toothpick inserted in the center comes out with moist crumbs attached. Let the pound cake cool in the pan for 10 minutes, then unmold and let cool completely on a wire rack. Dust with confectioners' sugar before serving. —*Marcy Goldman*

NOTE Buy pure unsweetened cocoa powder that says "Dutch process" on the label. This means the cocoa has been treated with an alkali, which helps neutralize cocoa's natural acidity.

MAKE AHEAD The cake can be wrapped in foil and refrigerated for 1 week or frozen for up to 2 months.

Molten Chocolate Cake

ACTIVE: 20 MIN; TOTAL: 35 MIN

4 SERVINGS ●

It seems as though every restaurant in America offers a version of this cake created by New York master chef Jean-Georges Vongerichten. But his rich and chocolaty original is in a class by itself.

1 stick (4 ounces) unsalted butter, plus more for buttering

6 ounces bittersweet chocolate, preferably Valrhona, chopped

2 large eggs

2 large egg yolks

¼ cup sugar

Pinch of salt

2 tablespoons all-purpose flour, plus more for dusting

1. Preheat the oven to 450°. Butter and flour four 6-ounce ramekins, tapping out the excess.

2. In a double boiler set over simmering water, melt the butter with the chocolate. In a medium bowl, using a handheld electric mixer, beat the whole eggs with the egg yolks, sugar and salt at high speed until pale and thickened.

3. Whisk the chocolate until smooth. Quickly fold it into the egg mixture along with the flour. Spoon the batter into the prepared ramekins. Set the ramekins on a baking sheet and bake for 12 minutes, or until the sides of the cakes are firm but the centers are soft.

4. Let the cakes cool for 1 minute. Run a knife around the edge of each cake; cover with an inverted dessert plate and turn it over. Let the cakes stand for a few seconds before unmolding, then serve. —*Jean-Georges Vongerichten*

Chocolate Sour Cream Pound Cake

ACTIVE: 30 MIN; TOTAL: 2 HR 30 MIN

8 TO 10 SERVINGS ●

2½ cups all-purpose flour

1 cup unsweetened cocoa powder, preferably Dutch process

1 teaspoon baking soda

½ teaspoon salt

3 sticks (12 ounces) unsalted butter, softened

3 cups granulated sugar

5 large eggs

2 teaspoons pure vanilla extract

1 cup sour cream

1 cup boiling water

Confectioners' sugar, for dusting (optional)

1. Preheat the oven to 350°. Butter and flour a 10-cup Bundt pan. In a large bowl, sift the flour with the cocoa powder, baking soda and salt. In a standing electric mixer fitted with the paddle attachment, beat the softened butter until creamy. Add the granulated sugar and beat at medium speed until light and fluffy. Add the eggs, 1 at a time, beating well after each addition. Beat in the vanilla extract. At low speed, beat in the dry ingredients in 3 additions, alternating with 3 additions of the sour cream. Gradually beat in the boiling water.

2. Pour the cake batter into the prepared pan and bake in the lower third of the oven for about 65 minutes, or until a toothpick inserted in the center comes out clean. Let the cake cool in the pan for 5 minutes, then turn out onto a wire rack and let cool completely. Dust it lightly with confectioners' sugar before slicing and serving. —*Sandy Carpenter*

baking pans

EQUIPMENT TIP

TO ELIMINATE GUESSWORK when you're in the middle of a baking project, consider marking the measurements on the bottoms of your new baking pans and cake tins. Using a thin permanent marker, copy the volume and/or measurements from the packaging label.

cakes, cookies + other desserts

Chocolate Layer Cake with Peppermint Ganache Frosting

ACTIVE: 40 MIN; TOTAL: 2 HR 30 MIN

MAKES ONE 9-INCH LAYER CAKE ●

If peppermint isn't your favorite, there are many different flavored extracts that would be equally delicious in the frosting on this cake. Besides hazelnut and coffee, orange, raspberry or even maple extract can transform the recipe into something different each time you make it. Look for extracts (we like Boyajian brand) in supermarkets and specialty food shops.

CAKE

Unsweetened cocoa powder, for dusting

½ pound unsweetened chocolate, coarsely chopped

3 tablespoons unsalted butter

2½ cups plus 2 tablespoons all-purpose flour

¾ teaspoon salt

6 large egg yolks

3 cups sugar

1 teaspoon pure vanilla extract

2¾ cups milk

1½ teaspoons baking soda

FROSTING

1½ pounds bittersweet chocolate, chopped

2 cups heavy cream

4 tablespoons unsalted butter, cut into ½-inch slices

1 tablespoon pure peppermint extract

3 ounces mini nonpareil candies

I. MAKE THE CAKE: Preheat the oven to 325°. Butter three 9-inch round cake pans. Line the bottoms with parchment paper, butter the paper and dust the pans with cocoa, tapping out any excess.

2. In a small saucepan, melt the coarsely chopped chocolate with the butter over low heat; let cool.

3. In a medium bowl, whisk the flour with the salt. In a large bowl, using an electric mixer, beat the egg yolks with 1 cup of the sugar at medium speed until light and fluffy, about 3 minutes. Add the cooled chocolate and the vanilla and beat until blended. Gradually beat in half of the milk. In a bowl, dissolve the baking soda in the remaining milk; add this to the chocolate batter along with the remaining 2 cups of sugar and beat at medium speed until combined. Beat in the dry ingredients at moderately low speed.

4. Pour the chocolate batter into the prepared pans. Bake the cakes on the lower and middle racks of the oven for 35 minutes, or until a toothpick inserted in the centers comes out with a few moist crumbs attached. Let the cakes cool in the pans for 5 minutes. Run the tip of a knife around the inside rims of the pans and invert the cakes onto wire racks. Peel off the parchment paper, then invert the cakes again and let them cool completely.

5. MAKE THE FROSTING: Put the chocolate in a large heatproof bowl. In a small saucepan, bring the cream to a boil. Pour the hot cream over the chocolate and let stand for 5 minutes, then whisk until smooth. Whisk in the butter and peppermint extract. Transfer half of the ganache to a large bowl and refrigerate it for 15 minutes, or until barely set and slightly cool. Using an electric mixer, whip the chilled ganache at medium speed until thick, creamy and pale, about 3 minutes.

6. Place 1 cake layer upside down on a cake plate. Spread the top of the cake with half of the whipped chilled ganache. Top with another cake layer and spread with the remaining whipped ganache. Set the third cake layer on top. Spread most of the reserved unwhipped ganache on the top and side of the cake and refrigerate until just set, about 10 minutes. Spread the remaining unwhipped ganache all over the cake. Press the nonpareils around the bottom edge of the cake and press more nonpareils onto the top in a snowflake pattern. Refrigerate the cake for 20 minutes before serving.

—Claudia Fleming

MAKE AHEAD The cake layers can be wrapped tightly in plastic and frozen for up to 1 month. The finished cake can be refrigerated for up to 2 days. Bring to room temperature before serving.

Chocolate Soufflé Cakes with Vanilla-Thyme Ice Cream

ACTIVE: 35 MIN; TOTAL: 1 HR

8 SERVINGS ●

These soft, chocolaty sponge cakes are a cross between an angel food cake and a firm soufflé.

¾ cup confectioners' sugar, sifted, plus more for dusting

4½ ounces bittersweet chocolate, finely chopped

4 tablespoons unsalted butter, cut into tablespoons

6 large eggs, separated

Salt

¼ cup all-purpose flour

Vanilla ice cream, for serving

1 tablespoon plus 1 teaspoon thyme leaves, coarsely chopped

SERVING TIP

ice cream mix

CREATE YOUR OWN ICE CREAM combinations. Soften a good quality vanilla (we love Häagen-Dazs); then, using a small, flat spatula, mix in flavorings of your choice, such as chopped candy, mixed nuts, crushed pralines, toasted coconut, candied fruit, diced fresh fruit or even chopped fresh herbs. Freeze the ice cream again until it is firm, then serve with toppings of your choice.

cakes, cookies + other desserts

1. Preheat the oven to 425°. Butter eight 1-cup ramekins and line the bottoms with parchment paper. Butter the paper and dust the bottoms and sides of the ramekins with confectioners' sugar.

2. In a glass bowl, melt the chocolate and butter in a microwave oven, checking every 10 seconds. Stir until smooth.

3. In a large stainless steel bowl, using a handheld electric mixer, beat the egg whites with a pinch of salt at high speed until soft peaks form. Add ¼ cup of the confectioners' sugar and beat the egg whites until they are firm and glossy peaks form.

4. In another large stainless steel bowl, whisk the egg yolks with the remaining ½ cup of the confectioners' sugar until the mixture is thoroughly blended. Whisk the melted chocolate and butter mixture into the egg yolks, then gradually whisk in the all-purpose flour. Using a large, clean rubber spatula, fold in one-third of the beaten egg whites to lighten the mixture, then fold in the remaining beaten whites until almost no white streaks remain.

5. Spoon enough soufflé cake batter into each of the prepared ramekins to reach three-fourths of the way up the side. Bake the cakes for about 15 minutes, or until they are puffed and just set in the middle. Leave the oven on.

6. Let the soufflé cakes cool in the ramekins for about 5 minutes, or until the edges of the cakes start to pull away from the sides of the ramekins. Invert the cakes onto a large baking sheet, then peel off the parchment paper and set the cakes upright on the baking sheet. Reheat the cakes in the oven for 2 minutes.

7. Transfer the soufflé cakes to plates and serve them with vanilla ice cream that has been sprinkled with the chopped thyme. —*Adolfo Muñoz*

MAKE AHEAD The chocolate soufflé cakes can be prepared through Step 5.

Store the soufflé cakes right in their ramekins at room temperature for up to 3 hours. Proceed with the remainder of the recipe, reheating the soufflé cakes as directed.

Mexican Chocolate and Dulce de Leche Crêpe Torte

ACTIVE: 1 HR 30 MIN; TOTAL: 4 HR

12 SERVINGS ● ●

- 2 cups all-purpose flour
- 2 tablespoons granulated sugar

Pinch of salt

- 2½ cups plus 2 tablespoons milk
- 1 teaspoon pure vanilla extract
- 6 large eggs, lightly beaten
- 4 tablespoons melted butter, plus more for brushing
- 1 cup plus 2 tablespoons heavy cream
- 10 ounces bittersweet chocolate, chopped
- 1 teaspoon cinnamon
- 4 large egg yolks
- 1½ cups dulce de leche (see Note)

Confectioners' sugar, for dusting

1. In a medium bowl, whisk the flour with the granulated sugar and salt. Whisk in the milk, vanilla, 6 whole eggs and the 4 tablespoons of melted butter and let stand for 30 minutes.

2. Heat a 10-inch nonstick skillet and lightly brush with melted butter. Pour ⅓ cup of the crêpe batter into the skillet and immediately swirl the batter around until it reaches halfway up the side of the skillet. Pour any excess batter back into the bowl. Cook the crêpe over moderate heat until it is golden at the edge and set in the center, about 1 minute. Flip the crêpe and cook for about 15 seconds longer, or just until the bottom is lightly browned in spots. Transfer the crêpe to a baking sheet lined with wax paper. Repeat the procedure with the remaining crêpe batter, brushing the skillet with butter only as needed.

3. In a medium saucepan, bring 1 cup of the cream to a boil. Remove the pan from the heat and add the chocolate and cinnamon. Let stand for 5 minutes, then whisk until smooth. Whisk in 2 of the egg yolks. In a medium bowl, whisk the dulce de leche with the remaining 2 tablespoons of cream and 2 egg yolks.

4. Preheat the oven to 350°. Butter a 9-inch round cake pan, line the bottom with parchment paper and butter the paper. Fit a crêpe in the bottom of the pan, pressing to flatten it. Halve 2 crêpes and line the side of the pan with them, placing the cut sides down and slightly overlapping the bottom crêpe; the rounded part of the halved crêpes will hang over the edge of the pan a bit.

5. Spoon a slightly heaping ½ cup of the chocolate filling into the pan and spread to the edge of the crêpe. Top with another crêpe, pressing to flatten it. Spoon a slightly heaping ½ cup of the dulce de leche filling on top, spread it to the edge and top with a crêpe. Repeat this layering with the remainder of the fillings and 4 more crêpes, ending with a crêpe. Any leftover crêpes can be frozen between sheets of wax paper for later use. Fold the overhanging crêpes over the top. Press a round of buttered parchment paper directly onto the torte and cover the pan with foil.

6. Bake the torte for 1 hour, or until puffed. Remove the foil and let cool for 1 hour. Remove the parchment and run a knife around the edge of the pan. Invert a plate over the pan and then invert the torte onto the plate. Remove the pan and parchment and let cool completely. Sift confectioners' sugar on top just before serving. —*Grace Parisi*

NOTE Dulce de leche is a caramel-like boiled sweetened milk. Smuckers is a good supermarket brand.

MAKE AHEAD The baked torte can be refrigerated for up to 2 days. Reheat slightly in a 350° oven.

CHOCOLATE-MINT ICEBOX CAKES

Molded Mocha-Marsala Semifreddo

ACTIVE: 1 HR; TOTAL: 9 HR

8 SERVINGS ●

This creamy multilayered frozen dessert uses a simple zabaglione (known as sabayon in French) of whipped egg yolks, sugar and Marsala as its base. The addition of bittersweet chocolate and strong espresso to the sweet zabaglione brings the flavors of the semifreddo into perfect balance.

- 5 large eggs, separated
- ⅓ cup plus ½ cup sugar
- ¼ cup dry Marsala
- 3 tablespoons Cognac or dark rum
- 1 cup heavy cream
- ½ teaspoon cream of tartar
- 1 tablespoon instant espresso powder dissolved in 2 tablespoons hot water
- 2 ounces bittersweet chocolate, finely grated

1. Line a 2-quart loaf pan with plastic wrap. In a medium stainless steel bowl, whisk the egg yolks with ⅓ cup of the sugar. Set the bowl over a medium saucepan filled with 1 inch of barely simmering water, and, using a large whisk, beat constantly until the mixture is pale and fluffy and doubled in volume, about 5 minutes; do not let the eggs get too hot or they will scramble. Add the Marsala and Cognac and whisk constantly until thickened, very warm to the touch and triple the original volume, about 5 minutes longer. Remove the bowl from the saucepan and let the zabaglione cool to room temperature.

2. In a large stainless steel bowl, using an electric mixer, beat the heavy cream until soft peaks form. Fold in the zabaglione. In another large stainless steel bowl, beat the egg whites until foamy. Add the cream of tartar, beat until soft peaks form. Add the remaining ½ cup of sugar very gradually; beat until the egg whites are very stiff and shiny.

3. Using a large rubber spatula, fold one-third of the beaten whites into the zabaglione cream. Gently fold in the remaining beaten whites in 2 additions, until only a few streaks of white remain. Spoon one-third of the semifreddo mixture into each of 2 bowls. Fold the dissolved espresso into the semifreddo mixture in one bowl and the grated chocolate into that in the other. Cover and refrigerate both semifreddo mixtures.

4. Spoon the remaining plain semifreddo mixture into the prepared loaf pan and smooth the surface. Freeze until firm, about 30 minutes. Spread the chocolate semifreddo mixture over the plain semifreddo and smooth the surface. Freeze until firm, about 30 minutes. Repeat with the espresso semifreddo mixture and freeze for 1 hour, then cover with plastic and freeze for at least 6 hours or for up 24 hours.

5. To unmold, run the sides of the loaf pan under hot water for a few seconds. Invert onto a platter. Thickly slice the semifreddo with a warm serrated knife, rinsing the knife in warm water and drying it between cuts. Set the slices on chilled plates and serve.

—*Sergio Sigala*

MAKE AHEAD The semifreddo can be frozen for up to 5 days.

Chocolate-Mint Icebox Cakes

ACTIVE: 25 MIN; TOTAL: 4 HR 30 MIN

8 SERVINGS ● ●

- ¼ cup heavy cream
- 1½ teaspoons sugar
- ¼ teaspoon pure peppermint extract
- ¾ cup light or reduced-fat sour cream (not nonfat)
- One 9-ounce package chocolate wafers
- 1 teaspoon cocoa powder

1. In a medium stainless steel bowl, mix the heavy cream with the sugar. Place the bowl of heavy cream and 2 beaters from a handheld electric mixer in the freezer for 10 minutes.

2. In another medium bowl, stir the peppermint extract into the sour cream. Remove the heavy cream from the freezer and whip to stiff peaks. Using a rubber spatula, fold the whipped cream into the sour cream.

3. On a work surface, spread 1 teaspoon of the cream topping on each chocolate wafer and assemble them in stacks of 5; position any broken wafers in the middle of the stacks. Spread the remaining cream on top of each stack. Transfer the stacks to a large platter and position several juice glasses around them. Cover the platter with plastic wrap. Refrigerate the cakes for at least 4 hours or for up to 8 hours.

4. Transfer the cakes to plates. Sift the cocoa over the tops and serve.

—*Sally Schneider*

Candied Orange Sugar Cookies

ACTIVE: 15 MIN; TOTAL: 1 HR 30 MIN

MAKES 4 DOZEN COOKIES ●

Chef Suzanne Goin adapted these sugar-edged cookies from the *Chez Panisse Dessert* cookbook.

- 2 sticks (½ pound) unsalted butter, softened
- 1 cup sugar
- 1 large egg yolk
- 1 teaspoon pure vanilla extract
- 2 cups all-purpose flour
- ⅛ teaspoon salt
- 2 tablespoons julienned candied orange peel (see Note)

1. In a large bowl, using an electric mixer, beat the butter until creamy. Add ¾ cup of the sugar and beat until fluffy. Beat in the egg yolk and vanilla. At low speed, beat in the flour and salt. Shape the dough into 2 logs, each about 1½ inches in diameter. Roll the logs in the remaining ¼ cup of sugar. Wrap in plastic and refrigerate until firm, 1 hour.

2. Preheat the oven to 350°. Using a thin knife, cut the logs into ¼-inch-thick slices. Arrange on 2 baking sheets.

cakes, cookies + other desserts

Press a few slivers of orange peel in the center of each slice. Bake on the upper and lower racks of the oven for about 22 minutes, until golden around the edges and on the bottoms. Let cool for 10 minutes on the baking sheets, then transfer to racks to cool completely. —*Suzanne Goin*

NOTE Whether you use candied peel or candied zest (or even crystallized ginger), make sure it's moist so it doesn't dry out while baking. You can order candied peel from Dorothy McNett's Place (831-637-6444) or VineTree Orchards (800-936-5128).

MAKE AHEAD The cookie dough can be frozen for up to 1 month. The baked cookies can be stored in an airtight container at room temperature for 1 week.

Toasted Walnut Cookies

ACTIVE: 10 MIN; TOTAL: 1 HR

MAKES ABOUT 2 DOZEN COOKIES ●

- 1 cup walnut pieces
- 1 stick (4 ounces) unsalted butter, softened
- 1½ cups confectioners' sugar
- 1 cup all-purpose flour
- 1 teaspoon pure vanilla extract

Pinch of salt

I. Preheat the oven to 350°. Spread the walnuts in a pie plate and bake for 6 minutes, or until golden. Let cool, then finely chop. Leave the oven on.

BAKING TIP

measuring sugar

WHEN A RECIPE CALLS FOR packed brown sugar, scoop it out with a measuring cup, then pack it (or tamp it down) with a smaller measuring cup. It should hold its shape when turned out of the cup. To measure granulated sugar, spoon it into a measuring cup, then level it off with a straight edge.

2. Using a handheld electric mixer, beat the butter with ½ cup of the sugar at medium speed until creamy. Beat in the flour, toasted walnuts, vanilla and salt at low speed.

3. Shape the dough into 1-inch balls and transfer them to a baking sheet. Bake for 15 to 20 minutes, or until firm, then let cool on the baking sheet for 5 minutes. Roll the warm cookies in the remaining 1 cup of sugar, then transfer to wax paper. Roll 2 or 3 more times in the sugar and let cool completely until set. —*Joshua Wesson*

MAKE AHEAD The cookies can be stored for 4 days in an airtight container.

Ginger Brandy Snaps

ACTIVE: 20 MIN; TOTAL: 30 MIN

MAKES ABOUT 30 COOKIES ● ●

- 4 tablespoons unsalted butter, plus more for buttering the baking sheets
- ¼ cup dark brown sugar
- ¼ cup plus 2 tablespoons all-purpose flour
- 2 tablespoons finely chopped candied ginger
- 1 tablespoon brandy

I. Preheat the oven to 350°. Lightly butter 3 large baking sheets.

2. In a medium saucepan, melt the butter with the brown sugar over moderate heat. Remove from the heat. Add the flour, candied ginger and the brandy and stir until a smooth batter forms.

3. Drop level teaspoons of the batter 3 inches apart on the prepared baking sheets. Bake the brandy snaps for about 8 minutes, or until they are lacy and nicely browned. Let the cookies cool on the baking sheets just until firm, about 2 minutes; then, using a thin metal spatula, transfer them to a rack to cool completely. —*Alexandra Angle*

MAKE AHEAD The Ginger Brandy Snaps can be stored in an airtight container for up to 3 days.

Soft Molasses-Spice Cookies

ACTIVE: 30 MIN; TOTAL: 2 HR

MAKES ABOUT 7 DOZEN COOKIES ● ●

- 5¾ cups all-purpose flour
- 1 tablespoon plus 1 teaspoon baking soda
- 2 tablespoons ground ginger
- 2 teaspoons cinnamon
- ¼ teaspoon salt
- ¼ teaspoon freshly ground pepper
- 3 sticks (12 ounces) unsalted butter, softened
- 2 cups unsulfured molasses
- ½ cup granulated sugar
- 1 large egg, lightly beaten
- 1 cup turbinado sugar, for rolling

I. Preheat the oven to 375°. Line 7 large baking sheets with parchment paper. In a large bowl, whisk the flour with the baking soda, ginger, cinnamon and salt and pepper.

2. In a large bowl, using a handheld electric mixer, beat the butter until creamy. Add the molasses and granulated sugar and beat until pale, about 3 minutes. Beat in the egg thoroughly. At low speed, gradually beat in the flour mixture. Chill the dough in the freezer just until firm, about 45 minutes.

3. Scoop the dough into 2-tablespoon-size mounds and roll into balls, then roll in the turbinado sugar. Set the molasses cookies 2 inches apart on the prepared baking sheets. Bake 1 sheet in the upper third of the oven and 1 sheet in the lower third for 15 minutes, or until the tops of the cookies are cracked and the centers are just set; shift the pans from top to bottom and front to back halfway through. Transfer the cookies to wire racks to cool completely. Repeat the procedure with the remaining cookies. —*Deborah Snyder*

MAKE AHEAD The cookies can be stored between sheets of wax paper in an airtight container for up to 1 week or frozen for up to 1 month.

Oatmeal-Gianduja-Chip Cookies

ACTIVE: 45 MIN; TOTAL: 1 HR 30 MIN

MAKES ABOUT 5 DOZEN COOKIES ●
Gianduja, a tasty blend of hazelnut paste
and chocolate, is available at specialty
food stores.

- 3½ cups old-fashioned rolled oats,
  finely ground in a food processor
- 2¼ cups all-purpose flour
- 1¼ teaspoons baking soda
- ½ teaspoon salt
- 3 sticks (12 ounces) unsalted
  butter, softened
- 2 cups packed light brown sugar
- ⅔ cup granulated sugar
- 2 tablespoons light corn syrup
- 3 large eggs
- 2 tablespoons pure vanilla extract
- 1¼ pounds milk chocolate
  gianduja, cut into ⅓-inch
  pieces, or 4 cups milk
  chocolate chips

1. Preheat the oven to 375°. Line 5 large
baking sheets with parchment paper.
In a bowl, whisk the ground rolled oats
with the flour, baking soda and salt.

2. In a large bowl, using a handheld
electric mixer, beat the butter until
creamy. Beat in the brown sugar, granulated sugar and corn syrup until light
and fluffy. Add the eggs, 1 at a time,
beating well between additions. Add
the vanilla extract. Beat in the dry ingredients at low speed. With a wooden
spoon, stir in the gianduja.

3. Spoon 2-tablespoon-size mounds of
the cookie dough 2 inches apart on the
prepared baking sheets. Bake 1 sheet of
the cookies in the lower third of the oven
and 1 in the upper third for 14 to 16 minutes, or until the edges of the cookies
are browned and the tops are lightly
cracked; shift the baking sheets from
top to bottom and front to back halfway
through. Slide the parchment paper off
the baking sheets onto wire racks. Let
the cookies cool. Repeat with the
remaining cookies. —*Deborah Snyder*

MAKE AHEAD The cookies can be stored
between sheets of wax paper in an airtight container for up to 4 days or frozen
for up to 1 month.

Crunchy Peanut Butter Cookies

TOTAL: 25 MIN

MAKES 2 DOZEN COOKIES ● ●

- 1 cup smooth peanut butter
- 1 cup sugar
- 1 teaspoon baking soda
- 1 extra-large egg, lightly beaten
- 2 tablespoons finely chopped
  peanuts (optional)
- ¼ cup mini chocolate chips
  (optional)

1. Preheat the oven to 350° and position 2 racks in the upper and lower thirds
of the oven. In a medium bowl, mix the
peanut butter with the sugar, baking
soda and egg. Stir in the peanuts and
chocolate chips.

2. Roll tablespoons of the dough
smoothly into 24 balls. Set the balls
on 2 baking sheets and, using a fork,
make a crosshatch pattern on each
cookie. Bake the cookies for 15 minutes, shifting the baking sheets from
front to back and bottom to top for even
cooking, until the cookies are lightly
browned and set. Let the cookies cool
on a wire rack. —*Elizabeth Woodson*

Peanut Butter Shortbreads with Chocolate Ganache

ACTIVE: 20 MIN; TOTAL: 1 HR 30 MIN

MAKES ABOUT 3 DOZEN COOKIES ●

- 4 cups all-purpose flour
- ½ teaspoon baking powder
- ¼ teaspoon salt
- 3 sticks (12 ounces) unsalted
  butter, softened
- 1¾ cups confectioners' sugar
- 1 cup creamy peanut butter
- 1½ teaspoons pure vanilla extract
- 6 ounces bittersweet
  chocolate, chopped
- ½ cup heavy cream

1. Preheat the oven to 325°. Line 3 large
baking sheets with parchment paper.
In a medium bowl, whisk the flour with
the baking powder and salt.

2. In a large bowl, using a handheld
electric mixer, beat the butter until
creamy. Add the confectioners' sugar
and peanut butter and beat until light
and fluffy. Add the vanilla extract. Beat
in the dry ingredients at low speed.
Scrape the dough onto 3 sheets of
plastic wrap and roll into logs about
2½-inches in diameter. Refrigerate the
logs until firm.

3. Cut the logs into ⅓-inch-thick slices
and arrange the cookies 1 inch apart on
the baking sheets. Slightly flatten the
cookies with your fingertips. Bake
1 sheet in the upper third of the oven
and 1 sheet in the lower third for 20
minutes, or until just golden; shift the
sheets from top to bottom and front to
back halfway through. Using a pestle or
the bottom of a shot glass, gently make
a 1½-inch-round indentation in the
center of each baked cookie. Let cool
on the baking sheets. Repeat with the
remaining cookies.

4. Meanwhile, put the chopped chocolate in a medium heatproof bowl. In a
small saucepan, bring the cream to a
boil. Pour it over the chocolate and let
stand until melted, then whisk until
smooth. Let the ganache cool to room
temperature, then spoon it into the
cookie indentations. —*Deborah Snyder*

MAKE AHEAD The cookies can be stored
in an airtight container in the refrigerator for up to 1 week.

Nutty Chocolate Chip Cookies

TOTAL: 45 MIN

MAKES ABOUT 42 COOKIES ● ●
This cookie has a crisp, crinkly top and
a chewy center. The recipe here offers
alternatives for anyone who wants
either a perfectly chewy or completely
crisp version.

cakes, cookies + other desserts

2 cups plus 2 tablespoons all-purpose flour
1 teaspoon baking soda
½ teaspoon salt
1½ sticks (6 ounces) unsalted butter, softened
1 cup lightly packed light brown sugar
½ cup granulated sugar
2 large eggs, at room temperature
1½ teaspoons pure vanilla extract
12 ounces semisweet chocolate chips (2 cups)
1 cup coarsely chopped walnuts or pecans, lightly toasted (optional)

1. Preheat the oven to 350° and position racks in the middle and lower thirds of the oven. In a medium bowl, whisk the flour with the baking soda and salt until combined.

2. In a large bowl, using a handheld electric mixer, beat the softened butter at medium speed until smooth and creamy. Add the brown sugar and granulated sugar and beat thoroughly until light and fluffy. Add the eggs and vanilla and beat until completely smooth. At low speed, gradually beat in the reserved dry ingredients. Stir in the chocolate chips and chopped nuts by hand until incorporated.

3. Arrange rounded tablespoons of the chocolate chip cookie dough at least 1½ inches apart on 2 large baking sheets. Bake in the oven for about 11 minutes for soft and chewy cookies, about 13 minutes for chewy cookies or about 16 minutes for crisp cookies.

4. Transfer the baking sheets to wire racks and let the cookies cool for 2 minutes. Then, using a metal spatula, transfer the cookies directly to the wire racks to cool completely. —*Grace Parisi*

MAKE AHEAD The Nutty Chocolate Chip Cookies can be stored in an airtight container between sheets of wax paper for up to 2 days.

Chocolate-Mint Sandwich Cookies

ACTIVE: 1 HR; TOTAL: 2 HR 30 MIN
MAKES ABOUT 30 SANDWICH COOKIES ●

3 cups all-purpose flour
¾ cup unsweetened Dutch process cocoa
2½ teaspoons baking powder
½ teaspoon salt
2½ sticks (10 ounces) unsalted butter, at room temperature
1¼ cups sugar
1 large egg, lightly beaten
1 large egg yolk
1½ teaspoons pure vanilla extract
Peppermint candies, colored sugar or sprinkles, for decorating
4 tablespoons cream cheese, softened
2 cups confectioners' sugar
½ teaspoon pure mint extract or fresh lemon juice

1. Preheat the oven to 375°. Line 6 baking sheets with parchment paper. In a bowl, sift the flour, cocoa, baking powder and salt. In a large bowl, using a handheld electric mixer, beat 2 sticks of the butter until creamy. Add the sugar and beat until light and fluffy. Beat in the egg, egg yolk and 1 teaspoon of the vanilla extract until blended. Add the dry ingredients and beat at low speed until a stiff, crumbly dough forms. Scrape onto plastic wrap, pat into a disk, wrap and refrigerate until chilled.

2. Divide the dough into quarters. On a lightly floured surface, working with 1 piece at a time and keeping the rest refrigerated, roll out the dough ⅛ inch thick. Using a 2¾-inch round cookie cutter, stamp out as many cookies as possible and transfer to the baking sheets. Decorate half of the cookies with peppermint candies or decorate all of the cookies with colored sugar or sprinkles. Repeat with the remaining dough and decorations.

3. Bake 1 sheet of the cookies in the upper third of the oven and 1 sheet in the lower third for 14 minutes, or until firm; shift the pans from top to bottom and front to back halfway through. Slide the parchment onto wire racks and let the cookies cool completely. Repeat with the remaining cookies.

4. In a medium bowl, beat the remaining 4 tablespoons of butter with the cream cheese until smooth. Beat in the confectioners' sugar, mint extract and the remaining ½ teaspoon of vanilla extract. If you used the peppermint candies, spread 1½ teaspoons of the filling on the undecorated cookies and top with the peppermint candy–decorated cookies. If you used the colored sugar or sprinkles, spread 1½ teaspoons of the filling on the undecorated side of the cookies; top the filling with the remaining cookies. —*Deborah Snyder*

MAKE AHEAD The wafers can be stored in an airtight container for up to 2 weeks or frozen for up to 1 month. The filled cookies can be stored at room temperature for up to 2 days.

Simple Meringues

ACTIVE: 15 MIN; TOTAL: 1 HR 30 MIN
MAKES ABOUT 40 MERINGUES ●

3 large egg whites
⅔ cup superfine sugar
1 teaspoon pure vanilla extract

1. Preheat the oven to 225°. In a medium bowl, beat the whites at low speed until foamy, then beat at high speed until firm peaks form when the beaters are lifted. Beat in the sugar 2 tablespoons at a time, beating well between additions. Beat in the vanilla.

2. Spoon or pipe the meringue onto a foil-lined baking sheet in 1½-inch mounds, or stripes. Bake for 1 hour and 15 minutes, or until firm. Let cool completely before serving. —*Tina Ujlaki*

MAKE AHEAD The cookies can be stored in an airtight container for up to 2 weeks.

Q+A
sugar cookies

Q: Can you recommend a simple, foolproof sugar cookie recipe? One where the dough isn't so soft that it's hard to roll out but is still buttery and delicious?

A: Here's a recipe for sugar cookies from *Rose's Christmas Cookies* by Rose Levy Beranbaum, one of F&W's all-time favorite holiday cookbooks. We hope you like the cookies as much as we do.

Christmas Sugar Cookies

ACTIVE: 30 MIN; TOTAL: 2 HR 20 MIN

MAKES ABOUT 4 DOZEN
2½-INCH COOKIES ●

- 2¼ cups bleached all-purpose flour
- ¼ teaspoon salt
- ¾ cup sugar
- 1½ sticks (6 ounces) unsalted butter, cut into pieces
- 1 large egg
- 2 teaspoons finely grated lemon zest (optional)
- 1 teaspoon pure vanilla extract
- Colored sugars and silver dragées

1. In a small bowl, whisk the flour with the salt. Put the sugar in a food processor and process until very fine. Add the butter and process until the mixture is smooth and creamy. Add the egg, lemon zest and vanilla and process until smooth. Add the flour mixture and pulse just until a dough forms.
2. Transfer the dough to a sheet of plastic wrap and pat it into a disk 1 inch thick. Chill until firm, about 1½ hours.
3. Preheat the oven to 350°. On a lightly floured surface, roll out the dough ⅛ inch thick. Stamp out shapes, cutting the cookies as close together as possible. Sprinkle the cookies with colored sugars or dragées. Transfer the cookies to nonstick or greased baking sheets, leaving 1 inch between them. Bake for 10 to 12 minutes, or until lightly browned around the edges. Transfer the cookies to racks and let cool.

MAKE AHEAD The cookies can be stored in an airtight container between sheets of wax paper for 1 month.

Q: I made the cookies, and I have a question: Why do I need to process the sugar?

A: According to Rose, processing the sugar until it's superfine gives these cookies an even crumb and keeps them from cracking during baking.

Q: One other thing: When the recipe calls for processing the butter and sugar until creamy, what does that look like? I'm afraid I might have overbeaten them.

A: Beating the butter and sugar together lightens the dough and makes a foundation for the other ingredients. In this recipe, neither underbeating nor overbeating should have an adverse effect on the dough. As soon as the butter and sugar are blended and fluffy, you can stop mixing.

Q: Once I made the dough, I chilled it overnight. It was hard as a brick and impossible to work with. After clonking it a few times with my rolling pin, I finally got it loosened up a bit. What should I do next time?

A: If you're in a huge rush, grate the dough coarsely, gather it together and roll it out. Otherwise, quarter the dough and let it soften on the counter until just pliable, about 15 minutes.

Q: When I was baking the cookies, it was hard to tell when they were done, because the bottoms browned faster than the tops.

A: Maybe you baked the cookies on the bottom rack of the oven, where the heat's strongest, or maybe your cookie sheets are very thin. Try baking cookies on the middle racks of the oven and switching the pans from top to bottom and front to back halfway through; as soon as the cookies lose their raw sheen and feel quite set, they're done.

cakes, cookies + other desserts

Cashew Snowballs

ACTIVE: 30 MIN; TOTAL: 1 HR 30 MIN

MAKES ABOUT 6 DOZEN COOKIES ●

- 2 sticks plus 2 tablespoons (9 ounces) unsalted butter, softened
- ½ cup confectioners' sugar, plus more for rolling
- 1½ teaspoons pure vanilla extract
- 2 cups all-purpose flour
- 2¼ cups unsalted roasted cashews (11 ounces), finely ground in a food processor
- ½ teaspoon salt

I. Preheat the oven to 375°. Line 2 large baking sheets and 2 wire racks with parchment paper. In a large bowl, using a handheld electric mixer, beat the butter with ½ cup of the confectioners' sugar at medium speed until creamy. Add the vanilla extract. At low speed, beat in the flour, ground cashews and salt. Scrape the dough onto 4 sheets of plastic wrap and form into 1-inch logs. Wrap the logs and refrigerate until firm, at least 20 minutes.

2. Cut the logs into 1-inch lengths and roll the lengths into balls. Arrange the balls on the baking sheets about ¾ inch apart. Bake the cookies in the lower and upper thirds of the oven for 20 minutes, or until golden and set; shift the baking sheets from top to bottom and front to back halfway through.

3. Fill a pie plate with about 2 cups of confectioners' sugar. Immediately roll the hot cookies, a few at a time, in the confectioners' sugar to coat; then transfer to the parchment-lined racks to cool completely. Reroll the cooled cookies in the confectioners' sugar and transfer to a plate. —*Deborah Snyder*

MAKE AHEAD The sugar-coated cookies can be stored between sheets of wax paper in an airtight container for up to 1 week or frozen for up to 1 month. Redust the cookies with confectioners' sugar before serving.

Profiteroles with Caramel-Chocolate Sauce

ACTIVE: 1 HR; TOTAL: 2 HR 10 MIN

8 SERVINGS

It's hard to improve on profiteroles—pastry puffs filled with cream, custard or vanilla ice cream and drizzled with chocolate sauce—unless you add caramel to the sauce and sprinkle candied pistachios over the top.

PUFFS

- 1 cup milk
- 1 stick (4 ounces) unsalted butter, cut into tablespoons
- 1 teaspoon pure vanilla extract
- ¼ teaspoon salt
- 1⅓ cups all-purpose flour
- 5 large eggs, plus 1 egg beaten with 2 tablespoons water

CANDIED PISTACHIOS

- 1 tablespoon white sugar
- 1 tablespoon hot water
- 1 cup shelled unsalted pistachios (¼ pound)
- ¼ cup turbinado sugar, such as Sugar in the Raw

CARAMEL-CHOCOLATE SAUCE

- 1 cup sugar
- 1 cinnamon stick
- ½ cup light corn syrup
- 1 cup heavy cream
- 6 ounces bittersweet chocolate, chopped
- 2 pints vanilla ice cream, slightly softened (see Note)

I. MAKE THE PUFFS: Preheat the oven to 400°. In a medium saucepan, combine the milk with the butter, vanilla and salt and bring to a boil over moderately high heat. Add the flour and, using a wooden spoon, beat until a smooth dough forms. Reduce the heat to low and cook the dough for 3 minutes, stirring constantly to dry it out. Remove the pan from the heat and beat in the 5 eggs, 1 at a time.

2. Line 2 rimmed baking sheets with parchment paper. Drop 1½-tablespoon-size mounds of batter onto the baking sheets, spacing them 2 inches apart. You will need 24 puffs. Brush the puffs with the beaten egg wash and bake on the 2 lower oven racks for 30 minutes. Reduce the oven temperature to 250° and bake for about 20 minutes longer, or until the puffs are browned and dry. Let the puffs cool to room temperature on the baking sheets.

3. MAKE THE CANDIED PISTACHIOS: Raise the oven temperature to 325°. Lightly oil a large rimmed baking sheet. In a medium bowl, stir the white sugar into the water until dissolved. Stir in the pistachios, then the turbinado sugar. Spread the coated nuts on the baking sheet in an even layer and bake for about 10 minutes, or until shiny. Let the candied nuts cool completely on the baking sheet, then break apart.

4. MAKE THE CARAMEL-CHOCOLATE SAUCE: In a medium saucepan, combine the sugar, cinnamon stick and corn syrup. Bring to a boil over moderate heat, stirring a few times to dissolve the sugar, and simmer until a deeply colored caramel forms, about 10 minutes. Meanwhile, in a saucepan, bring the cream just to a simmer. Remove the caramel from the heat. Slowly and carefully pour in the hot cream, stirring constantly; the caramel will bubble up, but keep stirring until the bubbles subside. Return the pan to the heat and stir to dissolve any hardened bits of caramel. Remove the pan from the heat, stir in the chocolate and let stand for a few minutes to melt. Discard the cinnamon stick and whisk the sauce until smooth.

5. Cut each puff in half and set 3 bottom halves on each plate. Generously fill the profiteroles with ice cream and cover with the puff tops. Pour the caramel-chocolate sauce over the puffs, sprinkle with the candied pistachios and serve immediately. —*Allison Levitt*

PROFITEROLES WITH CARAMEL-CHOCOLATE SAUCE

NOTE To make assembling the profiteroles easy, prepare the ice cream ahead: Soften the ice cream slightly, scoop it onto a baking sheet in 24 neat balls and freeze. Just before serving, cut the puffs in half and drop in the frozen balls of ice cream.

MAKE AHEAD The puffs can be frozen for up to 1 month. The sauce can be refrigerated for up to 5 days. The candied pistachios can be kept in an airtight container overnight.

Ricotta Fritters with Plum Puree

ACTIVE: 1 HR 5 MIN; TOTAL: 3 HR 30 MIN

MAKES ABOUT 20 FRITTERS ●

Italian ricotta is made from whey drained off while making cheese, often a sheep's-milk cheese like pecorino. American ricotta is made from a combination of whey, cow's milk and curds. Sheep's-milk ricotta from Campania, in Italy, can be mail-ordered from Buonitalia (212-633-9090 or www.buonitalia.com). You can also use a supermarket ricotta to make these crispy fritters. Just drain off any excess moisture before using commercial brands.

- ½ **pound ricotta cheese**
- ½ **cup all-purpose flour**
- 3 **tablespoons brandy**
- 1 **tablespoon granulated sugar**
- 2 **teaspoons baking powder**
- 1 **teaspoon finely grated lemon zest**
- 1 **large egg, beaten**

Pinch of salt

Vegetable oil, for frying

Confectioners' sugar, for dusting

Blood Plum Puree (recipe follows), for serving

1. In a large bowl, mix the ricotta with the flour, brandy, granulated sugar, baking powder, lemon zest, egg and salt. Cover and refrigerate for 1 hour.

2. In a medium saucepan, heat 2 inches of vegetable oil to 300° on a candy thermometer. Without crowding, drop tablespoons of the batter into the hot oil and fry over moderate heat until golden brown and cooked through, 1½ to 2 minutes per side. Drain the fritters on a rack set over a baking sheet and repeat with the remaining batter. Dust the fritters with confectioners' sugar and serve hot or warm with the Blood Plum Puree. —*Eugenia Bone*

Blood Plum Puree

ACTIVE: 45 MIN; TOTAL: 2 HR 10 MIN

MAKES 5 PINTS ●

This recipe was created by the late Venis Ewing, a Colorado home cook who made a conserve by adding walnuts to plum puree. You can make this with any large, very sweet plum. You can also add this puree to deglazed game or pork drippings to make a fabulous sauce.

- 6 **pounds red or black plums, pitted and coarsely chopped**
- 4 **pounds sugar (8 cups)**
- ⅓ **cup fresh orange juice**
- ⅓ **cup fresh lemon juice**
- 2 **tablespoons finely grated orange zest**

1. Puree the plums in a food processor. In a large, heavy pot, mix the plum puree with the sugar and bring to a boil over moderate heat, skimming as necessary. Cook uncovered over low heat for 40 minutes, stirring occasionally.

2. Stir the orange and lemon juices and the orange zest into the hot plums. Simmer over moderately low heat until thickened, about 10 minutes longer. Pour the plum puree into 5 hot sterilized 1-pint jars, stopping ¼ inch from the top. Wipe the glass rims and close the jars. Set the jars in a water bath and bring them to a boil. Boil the jars for 20 minutes. —*E.B.*

Crêpes with Ricotta and Chestnut Honey

ACTIVE: 50 MIN; TOTAL: 1 HR 50 MIN

MAKES 16 CRÊPES ●

Chestnut honey has a pungent and unmistakable flavor, so a little goes a long way. Its aftertaste is reminiscent of the bitter almond flavor in the kernels of stone fruits. Chestnut flour adds another layer of flavor to this dessert; if you can't find it, increase the all-purpose flour to ¾ cup.

CRÊPES

- 2 **tablespoons unsalted butter**
- 1 **cup milk**
- ¼ **teaspoon sugar**
- ⅛ **teaspoon salt**
- ½ **cup all-purpose flour**
- ¼ **cup chestnut flour (see Note)**
- 2 **large eggs**
- 1 **tablespoon peanut oil, plus more for the crêpe pan**
- ¼ **cup amber beer**

FILLING AND TOPPING

- 1 **cup ricotta cheese, preferably sheep's-milk**
- 2 **tablespoons sugar**
- ¼ **cup clover honey**
- ¼ **cup chestnut honey (see Note)**
- 1 **stick (4 ounces) unsalted butter, cut into 4 chunks**

1. MAKE THE CRÊPES: In a small saucepan, combine the butter, milk, sugar and salt and warm over low heat, stirring occasionally with a wooden spoon, until the butter melts. Let the mixture cool slightly.

COOKING TIP

pureeing fruit

RIPE OR SLIGHTLY OVERRIPE fruit is ideal for making sauces. Puree cleaned fruit (such as peeled peaches or nectarines, strawberries, pitted cherries or blackberries) until smooth. Strain and add sugar or fresh lemon juice to taste. Use the purees in sorbets, smoothies and cocktails or as toppings for desserts. You can freeze fruit purees for up to 2 months.

2. In a medium bowl, whisk the flours with the eggs and 1 tablespoon of peanut oil. Whisk in the milk mixture until smooth, then whisk in the beer. Strain the batter through a fine sieve. Cover and let stand at room temperature for at least 1 hour.

3. Preheat the oven to 375°. Heat a 6-inch crêpe pan or nonstick skillet over moderate heat. With a paper towel, rub the pan with peanut oil. Pour in 2 tablespoons of crêpe batter and quickly tilt the pan to distribute the batter evenly over the bottom. Pour any excess back into the bowl. Cook the crêpe until browned on the edge, about 1 minute. Flip the crêpe and cook the second side until lightly browned, about 30 seconds. Invert the crêpe onto a baking sheet. Repeat with the remaining crêpe batter, rubbing the pan with oil as needed. You should have about 22 crêpes. Set aside 16 crêpes and refrigerate the rest.

4. MAKE THE FILLING AND TOPPING: In a bowl, blend the ricotta with the sugar. Lightly oil a large rimmed baking sheet. Lay a crêpe on a work surface and spoon 1 tablespoon of the ricotta filling in the center. Fold the crêpe in half and then in half again to form a triangle; press to flatten slightly. Transfer the filled crêpe to the baking sheet. Repeat with the remaining crêpes and filling. Bake for about 5 minutes, until the crêpes are crisp around the edges and the ricotta is warm.

5. Meanwhile, in a saucepan, bring the honeys to a simmer. Off the heat, whisk in the butter, 1 piece at a time. Place 2 crêpes on each serving plate, drizzle with sauce and serve. —*Paul Bertolli*

NOTE Chestnut flour and chestnut honey are available at Italian markets.

MAKE AHEAD The crêpes can be filled early in the day and refrigerated; bring to room temperature before baking. The sauce can also be made early in the day; reheat it gently, whisking constantly.

Panettone Bread Pudding

ACTIVE: 30 MIN; TOTAL: 2 HR 30 MIN
12 SERVINGS ●

- 2 pounds panettone, cut into 1½-inch-thick slices
- 1 stick (4 ounces) unsalted butter
- 3 large eggs
- 1 cup sugar
- 2 teaspoons pure vanilla extract
- 1 teaspoon ground cinnamon
- ½ teaspoon freshly grated nutmeg

Pinch of salt
- 2 cups heavy cream

One 12-ounce can evaporated milk

1. Preheat the oven to 400°. Butter a 2-quart baking dish. Toast the panettone on the oven racks for 8 to 10 minutes, or until golden; cut into 1½-inch cubes and transfer to the prepared baking dish.

2. In a saucepan, cook the butter over moderately low heat until nutty and the milk solids are brown, 4 to 5 minutes. Toss the butter with the panettone.

3. In a medium bowl, using an electric mixer, beat the eggs and sugar at medium speed until pale and thick, 2 minutes. Beat in the vanilla, cinnamon, nutmeg and salt, then beat in the heavy cream and evaporated milk. Pour the custard over the panettone; let stand for 1 hour, gently tossing now and then, until the custard is absorbed.

4. Preheat the oven to 400°. Bake the bread pudding for 25 to 30 minutes, until the top is golden and the custard is set. Let cool for 30 minutes before cutting into squares. —*Ken Oringer*

MAKE AHEAD The pudding can be refrigerated overnight. Rewarm before serving.

SERVE WITH Vanilla ice cream.

Mocha Fudge Pudding

ACTIVE: 10 MIN; TOTAL: 30 MIN
4 SERVINGS ● ●

- ½ cup heavy cream
- 2 teaspoons instant espresso
- 6 ounces bittersweet chocolate, coarsely chopped

- ¼ cup sugar
- 1 large egg, at room temperature (see Note)
- 1 teaspoon pure vanilla extract

Pinch of salt

1. Freeze 4 ramekins. In a small saucepan, bring the cream and espresso powder to a boil over high heat, stirring.

2. Meanwhile, in a food processor, combine the chocolate and sugar and pulse until the chocolate is finely ground. Add the egg, vanilla and salt and pulse to a paste. With the machine on, add the hot cream in a steady stream and blend until smooth and silky, about 1 minute.

3. Transfer the pudding to the ramekins and freeze until firm, at least 20 minutes. —*Jan Newberry*

NOTE The silky texture of this pudding depends on the inclusion of the raw egg.

MAKE AHEAD The puddings can be refrigerated overnight.

SERVE WITH Lightly sweetened whipped cream and chocolate curls.

Bittersweet Chocolate Puddings

ACTIVE: 25 MIN; TOTAL: 1 HR
8 SERVINGS ●

This is not the usual velvety whole-egg stovetop pudding. While the ingredients are virtually the same, folding the beaten whites into the mixture and baking the puddings in a water bath gives this dessert a mousse-like consistency and a lovely crust.

- ¾ cup milk
- 5½ ounces bittersweet chocolate, 5 ounces chopped, ½ ounce finely grated (see Note)
- 3 tablespoons unsalted butter
- 3 large eggs, separated
- ½ cup plus 3 tablespoons sugar

Pinch of salt
- 3 tablespoons all-purpose flour
- 1½ teaspoons pure vanilla extract
- ½ cup heavy cream
- ½ teaspoon coffee liqueur, such as Kahlúa or Tia Maria (optional)

BLACK-AND-WHITE COCONUT RICE PUDDING

CHOCOLATE GANACHE BREAD PUDDING

1. Preheat the oven to 325°. Butter eight ½-cup ramekins and set them in a large roasting pan. In a small saucepan, heat the milk until bubbles appear around the edge, then pour it into a glass measuring cup. Wipe out the pan and add the chopped chocolate and the butter. Cook over very low heat until the chocolate is barely melted, about 2 minutes. Whisk in the hot milk and remove the pan from the heat.

2. In a large bowl, beat the egg whites to firm peaks. Add 2 tablespoons of the sugar and continue beating until glossy.

3. In a large mixing bowl, using a handheld mixer, beat the egg yolks with ½ cup of the sugar and the salt at high speed until pale, about 4 minutes. Add the flour and vanilla and beat until smooth. Beat in the chocolate mixture, then fold in the beaten egg whites until

incorporated. Pour the batter into the prepared ramekins.

4. Pour enough hot water into the roasting pan to reach halfway up the sides of the ramekins. Bake the puddings for about 35 minutes, or until puffed and set. Transfer the ramekins to plates and let cool to warm.

5. In a mixing bowl, whip the heavy cream to soft peaks. Add the remaining 1 tablespoon of sugar and the liqueur and whip until firm. Spoon a dollop of whipped cream on each pudding, sprinkle with the grated chocolate and serve.
—*Joshua Wesson*

NOTE Two excellent and widely available brands of bittersweet chocolate are Lindt and Valrhona.

MAKE AHEAD The chocolate puddings can be baked up to 4 hours ahead and served lightly chilled.

Black-and-White Coconut Rice Pudding
ACTIVE: 20 MIN; TOTAL: 2 HR

4 SERVINGS ●

BLACK RICE PUDDING

½ **cup black rice**

2½ **cups water**

1 **cup unsweetened coconut milk**

¼ **cup sugar**

½ **teaspoon pure vanilla extract**

JASMINE RICE PUDDING

½ **cup jasmine rice**

2 **cups water**

1¼ **cups unsweetened coconut milk**

¼ **cup sugar**

1 **cup finely diced fresh pineapple, preferably golden**

Pinch of freshly grated nutmeg

1. MAKE THE BLACK RICE PUDDING: In a medium saucepan, combine the black rice and water and bring to a boil.

Cover and simmer over low heat until the water has been absorbed and the rice is almost tender, about 40 minutes. Add the coconut milk and simmer, stirring occasionally, until the rice is tender and pudding-like, about 12 minutes. Stir in the sugar and vanilla and let cool to room temperature.

2. MEANWHILE, MAKE THE JASMINE RICE PUDDING: In a medium saucepan, combine the jasmine rice and water and bring to a boil. Cover and simmer over low heat until the water is absorbed and the rice is tender, about 25 minutes. Add 1 cup of the coconut milk and the sugar and simmer, stirring occasionally, until the rice is thickened, about 1 hour. Stir in the diced pineapple, nutmeg and the remaining ¼ cup of coconut milk and let the jasmine rice pudding cool to room temperature.

3. Layer the puddings in 4 glasses, alternating 3 layers of jasmine rice with 2 layers of black rice. Serve at room temperature or chilled. —*Marcia Kiesel*

MAKE AHEAD The layered puddings can be refrigerated overnight. Let stand at room temperature for 20 minutes or longer before serving.

Chocolate Ganache Bread Pudding with Port Caramel

ACTIVE: 40 MIN; TOTAL: 1 HR 45 MIN

8 SERVINGS ● ●

- 5   ounces bittersweet chocolate, coarsely chopped
- 1¼ cups heavy cream
- 6   tablespoons unsalted butter
- ½   pound challah, crust removed, bread cut into ¾-inch dice (6 cups)
- 1   cup milk
- ¾   cup sugar
- 6   large egg yolks
- 3   tablespoons unsweetened Dutch process cocoa powder
- 2   teaspoons pure vanilla extract
- ¼   teaspoon salt

Port Caramel Sauce (recipe follows)

1. Preheat the oven to 325°. Put 2 ounces of the bittersweet chocolate in a small heatproof bowl. Heat ¼ cup of the heavy cream in a small saucepan over moderately low heat. Pour the warm cream over the chopped chocolate and let stand for 5 minutes, then stir until the chocolate ganache is smooth. Let the chocolate ganache stand at room temperature until set.

2. Butter an 11-by-8-inch baking dish. In a saucepan, melt the butter. In a large bowl, toss the butter with the diced challah. Spread the bread on a baking sheet in an even layer and toast for about 15 minutes, or until the bread is golden brown. Wipe out the bowl.

3. In a small saucepan, combine the remaining 1 cup of heavy cream with the milk and 6 tablespoons of the sugar and bring just to a boil. Remove the heavy cream mixture from the heat. Stir in the remaining 3 ounces of chopped bittersweet chocolate and let stand for 5 minutes, then whisk until the chocolate is melted.

4. In the bowl used for the bread, whisk the remaining 6 tablespoons of sugar with the egg yolks, cocoa, vanilla and salt until a paste forms. Slowly whisk in the warm chocolate cream until smooth. Strain the custard into a clean bowl. Add the toasted bread and toss to coat with the warm chocolate cream. Let stand for 10 minutes, or until most of the chocolate cream is absorbed.

5. Pour the bread mixture into the prepared baking dish. Using a large spoon, dollop the chocolate ganache on top. Bake the bread pudding for about 35 minutes, or until it is cooked through. Let the chocolate bread pudding stand for 15 minutes, then serve with the Port Caramel Sauce on the side. —*Vicki Wells*

MAKE AHEAD The chocolate bread pudding can be refrigerated overnight. Rewarm before serving.

Port Caramel Sauce

TOTAL: 20 MIN

MAKES ABOUT 1⅓ CUPS ● ●

- ½   cup plus 2 tablespoons granulated sugar
- ½   cup light brown sugar
- ⅓   cup plus 1 tablespoon ruby port
- 1   cup heavy cream
- 1   tablespoon pure vanilla extract

In a heavy, medium saucepan, cook the granulated sugar over moderately high heat, stirring occasionally, until melted. Continue to cook, without stirring, until an amber caramel forms, about 3 minutes. Remove from the heat. Add the light brown sugar and stir until smooth. Return the caramel to the heat and carefully add the port; the caramel will harden slightly. Cook, stirring, until the sugar dissolves. Add the cream and cook, stirring occasionally, until the sauce thickened, about 6 minutes. Remove from the heat and stir in the vanilla. Transfer the caramel sauce to a pitcher and serve warm. —*V.W.*

MAKE AHEAD The sauce can be refrigerated for up to 1 month; rewarm.

Cardamom Pots de Crème

ACTIVE: 20 MIN; TOTAL: 6 HR 20 MIN

4 SERVINGS ●

Cardamom adds a warm, sweet, spicy flavor to this creamy dessert.

- ½   cup half-and-half
- 16 whole cardamom pods, crushed
- 4   large egg yolks, plus 1 large whole egg
- ⅓   cup sugar
- 1¼ cups heavy cream
- ½   teaspoon pure vanilla extract

1. Preheat the oven to 325°. Set four ½-cup ramekins in a baking dish just large enough to hold them. In a small saucepan, heat the half-and-half with the cardamom over moderate heat just until small bubbles appear around the edge, about 2 minutes. Remove from the heat.

2. In a medium stainless steel bowl, whisk the egg yolks with the whole egg and sugar. Whisk in the heavy cream and vanilla, then slowly whisk in the cardamom cream. Strain the custard into a glass measuring cup and pour it into the ramekins.

3. Pour enough hot water into the baking dish to reach halfway up the sides of the ramekins. Cover the ramekins with aluminum foil and bake for about 50 minutes, or until the custards are set but still a bit wobbly in the centers. Transfer the pots de crème to a wire rack and let them cool to room temperature, then refrigerate until chilled, at least 4 hours or overnight. —*Ming Tsai*

MAKE AHEAD The pots de crème can be refrigerated for up to 3 days.

Crème Caramel

ACTIVE: 15 MIN; TOTAL: 9 HR 20 MIN

4 SERVINGS ●

Throw out any recipe you may have in your card file for crème caramel. It doesn't get any better than this one.

- 1 cup sugar
- ¼ cup water
- 2 cups milk
- 1 vanilla bean, halved lengthwise, seeds scraped
- 4 large egg yolks, plus 2 large eggs

I. Preheat the oven to 325°. Set four 8-ounce ramekins in a small roasting pan. In a small saucepan, combine ½ cup of the sugar with the water and bring to a boil over moderate heat, stirring to dissolve the sugar. Simmer over moderate heat until a rich brown caramel forms, about 15 minutes. Quickly pour the caramel into the ramekins to coat the bottoms.

2. In a medium saucepan, combine the milk with the vanilla bean seeds and bring to a boil over moderate heat, stirring occasionally with a wooden spoon; reserve the bean for another use. Remove the saucepan from the heat.

3. In a medium bowl, whisk the remaining ½ cup of sugar with the egg yolks and eggs. Slowly whisk in the hot milk. Strain the custard through a fine sieve back into the pan and pour it into the ramekins.

4. Add enough hot water to the roasting pan to reach halfway up the sides of the ramekins. Bake the custards for about 50 minutes, or until barely set. Transfer the ramekins to a rack and let cool to room temperature. Cover and refrigerate overnight.

5. Run a thin knife around the edges of the custards, top with plates and invert, letting the caramel run onto the plates. —*Rob Larman*

MAKE AHEAD The custards can be refrigerated for up to 3 days.

Lychee Panna Cotta with Sugared Basil Leaves

ACTIVE: 20 MIN; TOTAL: 6 HR

8 SERVINGS ●

Three 15-ounce cans lychees in syrup, drained (see Note)

- 2 cups heavy cream, at room temperature
- 1½ teaspoons unflavored gelatin
- 2 tablespoons water
- ½ cup granulated sugar
- 1 large egg white
- 8 basil leaves
- ¼ cup superfine sugar

I. In a blender, puree the drained lychees until smooth. Add 1 cup of the heavy cream and puree until smooth. Strain the lychee puree through a fine sieve set over a medium bowl, pressing hard with the back of a spoon to extract as much of the puree as possible.

2. In a small bowl, sprinkle the gelatin over the water and let stand until softened, about 5 minutes. Scrape the gelatin into a small saucepan. Add the granulated sugar and the remaining 1 cup of cream and cook over very low heat, stirring occasionally, to combine.

Cook just until the sugar is dissolved, about 2 minutes. Let cool completely, then whisk in the lychee puree. Pour the panna cotta into 8 Champagne flutes and refrigerate them until they are set, about 4 hours.

3. Meanwhile, in a small bowl, whisk the egg white until frothy. Using a pastry brush, lightly brush the basil leaves on both sides with the egg white, then sprinkle them all over with the superfine sugar. Shake off any excess sugar and transfer the basil leaves to a wire rack to dry, about 6 hours.

4. Garnish each glass of panna cotta with a sugared basil leaf and serve right away. —*Fabio Trabocchi*

NOTE Canned lychees in syrup are available in the Asian section of most supermarkets.

MAKE AHEAD The panna cotta can be refrigerated for up to 2 days.

Buttermilk Creamsicle Panna Cotta

ACTIVE: 40 MIN; TOTAL: 9 HR 30 MIN

4 SERVINGS ● ●

- 2 large navel oranges
- ½ cup sugar
- ½ cup water
- 2 bay leaves
- ½ teaspoon whole black peppercorns
- 1 envelope (2¼ teaspoons) unflavored gelatin
- ¾ cup fresh orange juice, strained
- 2 tablespoons heavy cream
- 2 cups buttermilk

I. Peel the zest from 1 of the oranges in 1-inch-wide strips. In a small saucepan, combine the orange zest strips with the sugar, water, bay leaves and peppercorns and simmer over moderate heat until the sugar is dissolved. Pour the mixture into a heatproof bowl and let steep for 2 hours. Strain the syrup.

2. Meanwhile, in a small nonreactive bowl, sprinkle ¾ teaspoon of the gelatin over ¼ cup of the orange juice.

ESPRESSO GRANITA WITH WHIPPED CREAM

BUTTERMILK CREAMSICLE PANNA COTTA

Let stand until the gelatin softens, about 10 minutes. Scrape the orange gelatin into the small saucepan and set over low heat, stirring, until melted. Stir in the remaining ½ cup of orange juice. Pour the orange gelatin into wine glasses or parfait glasses and refrigerate until completely set, at least 1 hour.

3. In the small saucepan, combine the cream with ¼ cup of the sugar syrup. Sprinkle the remaining 1½ teaspoons of gelatin over the cream and let stand until softened, about 10 minutes. Heat, stirring, just until melted, then pour the mixture into a glass measuring cup. Add the buttermilk and ¼ cup of the syrup and let cool to room temperature. Gently pour the buttermilk mixture over the orange gelatin in each glass and refrigerate the panna cotta until very firm, at least 6 hours or overnight.

4. Working over a bowl, peel the oranges with a sharp knife, removing all of the bitter white pith. Cut in between the membranes to release the sections into the bowl. Stir in any remaining orange sugar syrup and refrigerate until the panna cotta is chilled. Spoon the orange sections into the glasses just before serving. —*Grace Parisi*

MAKE AHEAD The panna cotta and orange compote can be refrigerated separately for up to 2 days.

Espresso Granita with Whipped Cream

ACTIVE: 10 MIN; TOTAL: 2 HR 30 MIN
8 SERVINGS ●
3 cups freshly brewed espresso
About ¼ cup sugar
Lightly sweetened whipped cream, for serving

I. In a medium stainless steel bowl, combine the espresso with ¼ cup of the sugar and stir until the sugar dissolves. Taste and add more sugar if desired. Let cool slightly, then refrigerate until chilled.

2. Pour the espresso into a 9-by-9-inch square baking dish and freeze until ice crystals begin to form around the edges, about 45 minutes. Using a fork, stir to break up the crystals. Return the granita to the freezer and stir again after it begins to harden, 30 minutes. Continue freezing, stirring every 15 minutes, until the granita is completely frozen, with a texture of light shards, about 1 hour. Spoon the granita into glasses, top with whipped cream; serve. —*Sergio Sigala*

MAKE AHEAD The granita can be frozen for up to 2 days. If it solidifies, thaw it slightly and break it up with a fork.

cakes, cookies + other desserts

Jasmine Floating Island

TOTAL: 30 MIN

4 SERVINGS ●

- 2 cups heavy cream
- 1 vanilla bean, split lengthwise, seeds scraped
- 1 teaspoon jasmine tea leaves
- ¼ cup granulated sugar
- 4 large eggs, separated
- ¼ teaspoon cream of tartar
- ½ cup superfine sugar
- ½ teaspoon pure vanilla extract

Mint leaves or small sprigs, for garnish

1. In a medium saucepan, combine the heavy cream with the vanilla bean and seeds and the tea leaves and bring to a simmer over moderate heat. In a medium bowl, whisk the granulated sugar with the egg yolks until combined. Slowly whisk one-third of the warm cream into the egg yolks, then whisk that mixture back into the remaining warm cream in the saucepan.

2. Cook the sauce over moderate heat, stirring gently with a wooden spoon or heatproof rubber spatula, until thickened, 2 to 3 minutes. Set a fine strainer over a medium bowl set in an ice-water bath. Strain the sauce into the bowl and let the custard sauce cool, stirring occasionally.

3. In a large bowl, using an electric mixer, beat the egg whites with the cream of tartar until foamy. Gradually beat in the superfine sugar at high speed until the whites are glossy and hold soft peaks. Beat in the vanilla extract.

4. Fill a deep skillet with 1½ inches of water and bring to a simmer. Using a large spoon, dollop 4 mounds of the meringue into the simmering water and cook over moderate heat until just set on the bottoms, 2 minutes. Gently flip the meringues and cook for 2 minutes longer; do not let the water boil.

5. Pour the sauce into 4 bowls. Place the meringues on top, garnish with mint and serve at once. —*Anne Quatrano*

Floating Islands

ACTIVE: 25 MIN; TOTAL: 55 MIN

4 SERVINGS ●

What's innovative about the meringue here is that it's baked, not poached, so it's simple and quick.

CRÈME ANGLAISE

- 2 cups milk
- 1 vanilla bean, halved lengthwise
- 5 large egg yolks
- ⅓ cup sugar

MERINGUE

- 5 large egg whites
- ½ cup sugar

1. Preheat the oven to 200°. MAKE THE CRÈME ANGLAISE: In a heavy, medium saucepan, bring the milk to a boil; remove from the heat. Using a small knife, scrape the seeds from the vanilla bean into a medium stainless steel bowl. Whisk in the egg yolks and sugar, then slowly whisk in the hot milk. Pour the mixture back into the pan and cook over moderately low heat, whisking constantly, until starting to thicken, about 6 minutes; do not let it boil. Strain the sauce through a fine sieve set over another stainless steel bowl. Set the bowl in a slightly larger bowl of ice water. Whisk the sauce often until chilled, about 5 minutes. Cover and refrigerate.

2. MAKE THE MERINGUE: Line the bottom of an 8-inch square baking dish with parchment paper. In a large stainless steel bowl, beat the egg whites with 2 tablespoons of the sugar at high speed until they start to turn white and fluffy, about 2 minutes. Gradually add the remaining 6 tablespoons of sugar and beat until the whites hold firm peaks, about 1 minute. Spread the meringue in the prepared dish and bake for about 30 minutes, or until just set.

3. Pour the crème anglaise into shallow bowls. Cut the meringue into 4 squares. Using a spatula, transfer the squares to the bowls and serve.

—*Christophe Morvan*

MAKE AHEAD The meringue can stand at room temperature, covered with plastic wrap, for 2 hours. The crème anglaise can be refrigerated for up to 3 days.

White Fudge Sundae

TOTAL: 20 MIN

6 SERVINGS ●

- 6 ounces white chocolate, coarsely chopped
- 2¼ cups heavy cream
- 2 tablespoons light corn syrup
- 1 teaspoon raspberry liqueur
- 1 tablespoon unsalted butter
- ½ cup confectioners' sugar
- ¼ cup unsweetened cocoa powder
- 1½ pints chocolate ice cream
- 2 cups mixed berries

1. Put the white chocolate in a microwavable bowl and heat at high power for 30 seconds at a time until half melted. Alternatively, put the white chocolate in the top of a double boiler over barely simmering water and stir until half melted, about 2 minutes.

2. In a small saucepan, combine ¼ cup of the heavy cream with the corn syrup and raspberry liqueur and bring just to a simmer. Pour the hot cream mixture over the white chocolate and whisk gently until smooth. Add the butter and whisk vigorously until slightly thickened and fudgelike, about 1 minute.

3. Pour the remaining 2 cups of heavy cream into a large chilled bowl. Sift the confectioners' sugar and cocoa over the heavy cream. Beat at medium speed until soft peaks form.

4. Scoop the chocolate ice cream into bowls and top with the hot white chocolate fudge sauce and a generous dollop of the cocoa whipped cream. Garnish with the berries and serve.

—*Wayne Harley Brachman*

MAKE AHEAD The sauce can be refrigerated for up to 2 days; rewarm in a microwave oven. The cocoa whipped cream can be refrigerated overnight.

WHITE FUDGE SUNDAE

cakes, cookies + other desserts

Praline—Chocolate Chip Ice Cream

ACTIVE: 10 MIN; TOTAL: 1 HR 30 MIN

MAKES ABOUT 1½ QUARTS ●

- 2 cups whole milk or half-and-half
- 1 vanilla bean, split lengthwise, seeds scraped
- 4 large egg yolks
- ⅔ cup sugar
- 1 cup heavy cream
- 6 tablespoons praline paste (see Note)
- ¾ cup bittersweet chocolate chips

1. Prepare an ice-water bath and set a stainless steel bowl in it. In a saucepan, simmer the milk with the vanilla bean and seeds. In a bowl, whisk the yolks and sugar. Slowly whisk in half of the hot milk. Pour back into the saucepan and cook over moderate heat, whisking, until thickened, about 6 minutes. Strain the custard into the bowl in the ice-water bath and stir in the heavy cream; chill.

2. Transfer the custard to an ice cream maker and freeze according to the manufacturer's instructions. When set, add the praline paste and chocolate chips to the ice cream maker and churn until evenly distributed. Transfer the ice cream to a plastic container and freeze until serving. —*Grace Parisi*

NOTE Top-quality hazelnut praline paste is available from The Baker's Catalogue (800-827-6836).

MAKE AHEAD The ice cream can be frozen for up to 1 month.

Ginger Ice Cream Vacherin with Chocolate-Rum Sauce

ACTIVE: 20 MIN; TOTAL: 2 HR 20 MIN

6 SERVINGS

Whether the meringue is simply layered with ice cream, as here, or formed into the shell for an elaborate ice cream cake, *vacherin* is a magnificent dessert.

MERINGUES

- ½ cup hazelnuts (2 ounces)
- 4 large egg whites
- ¼ teaspoon cream of tartar
- ½ cup granulated sugar
- ½ teaspoon pure vanilla extract
- ½ cup confectioners' sugar

ICE CREAM

- 1 pint vanilla ice cream, softened
- ¼ cup minced candied ginger

SAUCE

- 3 tablespoons unsalted butter
- ½ cup water
- ⅓ cup heavy cream
- 2 tablespoons honey
- ½ pound bittersweet chocolate, coarsely chopped
- 2 tablespoons dark rum
- ½ cup sweetened whipped cream, for serving

1. **MAKE THE MERINGUES:** Preheat the oven to 350°. In a pie plate, bake the hazelnuts until lightly browned, about 8 minutes. Let cool, then rub the nuts together in a kitchen towel to remove the skins. Finely chop the nuts.

2. Reduce the oven temperature to 225°. Line a large rimmed baking sheet with parchment paper. Using a 3-inch cookie cutter as a guide, trace six 3-inch circles on the paper, spacing them equally. In a medium stainless steel bowl, using a handheld mixer, beat the egg whites with the cream of tartar at medium speed until soft peaks form. Gradually add the granulated sugar and beat until the meringue is firm and glossy, about 3 minutes. Stir in the vanilla. Set a fine sieve over the bowl and sift the confectioners' sugar over the meringue while folding it in with a rubber spatula. Fold in the hazelnuts.

3. Drop a large spoonful of meringue inside each of the circles and spread until the circle is filled, then top with more meringue until the *vacherin* is about 1 inch tall. Repeat. Bake for about 2 hours, or until the meringues are dry, crisp and barely colored. Let cool completely, then gently lift the meringues off the parchment.

4. **MAKE THE ICE CREAM:** Put the softened ice cream in a large bowl and blend in the candied ginger. Cover and freeze until firm, about 1 hour.

5. **MAKE THE SAUCE:** Melt the butter in a medium saucepan. Add the water, cream and honey and bring to a simmer over moderately high heat. Put the chocolate in a medium bowl and pour the hot cream on top. Let stand until the chocolate melts, 1 minute, then stir until smooth. Stir in the rum.

6. Set a meringue on each of 6 plates and top with a scoop of ice cream. Pour the sauce over the ice cream, top with a dollop of whipped cream and serve. —*Wolfgang Puck*

MAKE AHEAD The hazelnut meringues can be stored overnight in an airtight container.

the nut pantry

ALMOND MILK is made from ground blanched almonds that have been steeped in hot water overnight, then pressed to extract a milky liquid. It can be used to make soups and desserts.

PRALINE In French confectionery, praline means almonds or hazelnuts that have been caramelized with sugar and coarsely ground, or turned into a sweetened nut butter to make a smooth flavoring for candies and pastries.

ALMOND PASTE is produced from blanched almonds that have been ground and cooked with no more than 50 percent of their weight in sugar or sugar syrup.

ALMOND BUTTER is made from roasted almonds that have been finely ground. It can replace any nut butter.

Tequila-Cilantro Sorbet

ACTIVE: 15 MIN; TOTAL: 1 HR 45 MIN

8 SERVINGS ●

1¼ cups whole milk
1¼ cups water
1 cup sugar
1 cup coarsely chopped cilantro
1 cup fresh lime juice
¾ cup *plata* or silver tequila
   (see Note)
Pinch of salt

1. In a saucepan, bring the milk, water, sugar and cilantro to a boil; stir to dissolve the sugar. Transfer to a stainless steel bowl set in an ice-water bath; stir occasionally until cool.

2. In a blender, puree the cilantro mixture. Strain through a fine sieve set over a bowl. Stir in the lime juice, tequila and salt and mix well.

3. Freeze the sorbet in an ice cream maker according to the manufacturer's instructions. Transfer the sorbet to a shallow bowl, cover with plastic wrap and freeze until very firm, about 1 hour.
—*Deborah Racicot*

VARIATION To prepare a granita, pour the sorbet mixture made in Steps 1 and 2 into a chilled 9-by-13-inch baking dish. Freeze the mixture until ice crystals form around the edges. Using a fork, break up the crystals. Freeze the mixture until it begins to harden; break up the crystals again. Continue freezing and breaking up the crystals until the granita is completely frozen into a mass of soft, icy shards.

NOTE The *plata* tequilas—also called *blancos* or silvers—aren't aged, meaning the earthy, peppery flavor of the agave plant is still intense. While the tequilas can be sipped, their relative harshness makes them more suitable for mixing— which is why they're perfect for this sorbet recipe. Look for these premium tequilas in a well-stocked liquor store.

MAKE AHEAD The sorbet can be frozen for up to 3 days.

Dessert Couscous with Raisins and Almonds

TOTAL: 25 MIN

8 SERVINGS ● ●

Although this rich Moroccan couscous dessert is traditionally reserved for special occasions, it's simple enough to make anytime.

Two 10-ounce boxes couscous
1 tablespoon vegetable oil
4½ cups water
4 tablespoons unsalted butter
Salt
¼ cup granulated sugar
½ cup golden raisins
½ cup blanched almonds
1 teaspoon cinnamon, plus
   more for serving
Confectioners' sugar, for serving

1. In a medium bowl, mix the couscous with the oil, rubbing the grains between your palms until evenly coated.

2. In a large saucepan, combine 3½ cups of the water with the butter and a pinch of salt and bring to a boil. Remove the pan from the heat. Add the couscous, cover and let stand for 5 minutes.

3. Meanwhile, in a small saucepan, combine the remaining 1 cup of water, granulated sugar and raisins and simmer over moderate heat for 5 minutes; drain.

4. Stir the raisins into the couscous and fluff with a fork. Mound the couscous in a deep platter and flatten the top slightly. Decorate with vertical stripes of whole almonds, cinnamon and confectioners' sugar. Serve the couscous, passing small bowls of confectioners' sugar and cinnamon on the side.
—*Hajja Halima*

Fragrant Fennel Brittle

TOTAL: 15 MIN

MAKES ABOUT 1 CUP ● ●

Roasted fennel seeds mixed with sugar candies are a kind of digestif after Indian meals. Here, the seeds are caramel-coated to make a unique candy.

3 tablespoons fennel seeds
½ cup sugar
2 tablespoons water

1. Line a heavy baking sheet with a 10-by-15-inch sheet of parchment paper. In a small skillet, toast the fennel seeds over high heat, stirring occasionally, until lightly browned and fragrant, about 3 minutes.

2. In a small saucepan, cook the sugar and water over moderate heat until richly browned, about 13 minutes. Remove from the heat and stir in the fennel. Immediately pour the mixture onto the baking sheet and spread it ⅛ inch thick with a heatproof spatula. Break the warm brittle into rough 1-inch pieces.
—*Jehangir Mehta*

Puffed Rice Crunch

ACTIVE: 10 MIN; TOTAL: 25 MIN

10 SERVINGS ● ●

In India, the *chicki wallah* (sweets vendor) knows to set up shop near a school: Children find this crunch irresistible.

¾ cup light brown sugar
1 tablespoon fresh lemon juice
2 cups unsweetened puffed rice

1. Set a 12-by-18-inch sheet of parchment on a large baking sheet and oil the paper. Have a kitchen towel ready.

2. In a medium saucepan, cook the brown sugar with the lemon juice over moderately high heat, stirring occasionally, until the sugar melts, about 2 minutes. Reduce the heat to low and cook, stirring constantly, until richly browned, 3 to 4 minutes. Working quickly, stir in the puffed rice until coated, then immediately scrape the mixture onto one end of the baking sheet.

3. Fold the paper over the rice, cover with the kitchen towel and roll into a tight 3-inch log. Unwrap and let cool to room temperature, about 15 minutes. Using a serrated knife, gently cut the log crosswise into ½-inch-thick slices and serve. —*Jehangir Mehta*

BRANDY-WINE PUNCH, P. 349

beverages

BLOOD ORANGE MARGARITA WITH GINGER

SANGRITA

Blood Orange Margarita with Ginger

TOTAL: 5 MIN

MAKES 1 DRINK ●

- ¼ teaspoon finely grated fresh ginger
- ¼ cup plus 1 tablespoon fresh blood orange juice
- 3 tablespoons tequila
- 1 tablespoon Cointreau
- 1 tablespoon fresh lime juice

Cracked ice

Lime slice, for garnish

Put the grated ginger in a small sieve set over a small bowl and press to extract the juice. Combine the ginger juice with the orange juice, tequila, Cointreau and lime juice in a cocktail shaker filled with cracked ice and shake vigorously for 10 seconds. Strain into a chilled cocktail glass, garnish with the lime slice and serve. —*Alexandra Angle*

Sangrita

TOTAL: 40 MIN

MAKES 4 DRINKS ● ●

Sangrita is the traditional chaser for shots of tequila. When you're drinking tequila straight, go for premium, not bargain, versions.

- 2 medium cucumbers, each about 1½ inches in diameter
- ½ dried ancho chile, stemmed and seeded
- ½ cup fresh orange juice
- ½ cup tomato juice
- 2 tablespoons fresh lime juice
- 1 tablespoon minced onion
- ½ teaspoon Worcestershire sauce

Salt and freshly ground pepper

1. Cut two 3½-inch lengths from each of the cucumbers to use as cups. Peel the pieces partially, leaving a 1½-inch band of peel at one end of each. Using a melon baller, scoop out the seeds, stopping just before reaching the bottom of the cucumber. Refrigerate the cups for at least 10 minutes.

2. Meanwhile, in a small skillet, toast the ancho chile over moderate heat until it begins to blister, about 1½ minutes per side. Transfer the ancho to a work surface to cool.

3. In a blender, combine the orange, tomato and lime juices with the onion and Worcestershire sauce; crumble in the toasted ancho and puree. Strain through a coarse sieve. Season the sangrita with salt and pepper and chill for 20 minutes.

4. Carefully pour the sangrita into the cucumber cups and serve at once.
—*Arunas Bruzas*

MAKE AHEAD The sangrita can be refrigerated overnight.

Lynchburg Lemonade

TOTAL: 35 MIN

MAKES 20 DRINKS ● ●

Shaking up the drink in a jar makes it frothy. If you don't want your lemonade to be frothy, mix all the ingredients together in a large pitcher and add ice.

- 1 cup sugar
- 1½ cups water
- 2½ cups fresh lemon juice
- 2 cups Jack Daniel's (16 ounces)
- ½ cup pineapple juice
- ½ cup fresh orange juice

Ice

- 2 lemons, cut into thick slices

1. In a medium saucepan, mix the sugar and water and boil over moderately high heat until the sugar dissolves, about 5 minutes. Let cool completely.

2. In a very large jar with a tight-fitting lid, combine the syrup with the lemon juice, Jack Daniel's and pineapple and orange juices. Shake vigorously. Add ice and shake again.

3. Fill tall glasses with ice. Strain the lemonade into the glasses, garnish with the lemon slices and serve.

—*Matt Williamson*

MAKE AHEAD The ingredients can be mixed and refrigerated overnight.

Peruvian-Style Pisco Sour

TOTAL: 5 MIN

MAKES 1 DRINK ● ●

Juice of ½ lime

- 1 tablespoon pasteurized egg white
- 2 tablespoons sugar, or more to taste
- 2 ounces Peruvian pisco (¼ cup)
- 1 tablespoon pasteurized egg white
- ¼ cup crushed ice

Angostura bitters

In a blender, combine the lime juice with the sugar and mix to dissolve the sugar. Add the pisco, egg white and ice and blend at high speed until frothy. Pour into a sour glass, add a few drops of bitters and serve. —*Maricel Presilla*

Brandy-Wine Punch

TOTAL: 20 MIN

MAKES 4 QUARTS ●

- 1 cup fresh lemon juice
- ½ cup superfine sugar
- 1½ cups brandy
- 1½ cups amontillado sherry
- ¼ cup ruby port
- ¼ cup Cointreau
- 2 chilled 750-ml bottles sparkling wine
- 1 liter well-chilled club soda

Ice cubes

Orange and lemon slices, for garnish

In a large punch bowl, stir the lemon juice with the sugar until the sugar dissolves. Add the brandy, sherry, port, Cointreau, sparkling wine and club soda and stir gently until blended. Add the ice and garnish with the fruit.

—*Tom Colicchio and Sisha Ortuzar*

Black-Raspberry Gimlet

TOTAL: 5 MIN

MAKES 1 DRINK ●

- 2 teaspoons fresh lime juice
- 1 teaspoon superfine sugar

Ice cubes

- ¼ cup plus 2 tablespoons gin
- ½ tablespoon Chambord liqueur

In a chilled martini glass, using the handle of a wooden spoon, muddle the lime juice with the sugar. Fill a shaker with ice. Add the gin and Chambord and shake well. Strain the gimlet into the glass and serve. —*William Loob*

Passion Fruit Batida

TOTAL: 5 MIN

MAKES 6 SHAKES ●

- 1½ cups passion fruit juice
- ¼ cup sweetened condensed milk
- 3 ounces cachaça or white rum (¼ cup plus 2 tablespoons)
- 2 cups crushed ice

Combine the ingredients in a blender. Mix at high speed until smooth. Pour into 6 tumblers and serve. —*Maricel Presilla*

Caipirinha

TOTAL: 10 MIN

MAKES 1 DRINK ●

- 1 lime
- ¼ cup superfine sugar, or more to taste
- 4 ounces cachaça (½ cup)
- 2 cups crushed ice

Trim the ends off the lime and halve it lengthwise. Cut each half into 8 slices. In a cocktail shaker, using a wooden spoon or a pestle, muddle the lime with the ¼ cup of sugar until juicy and the sugar dissolves. Add the cachaça and the crushed ice and shake for about 10 seconds; taste and stir in a little bit more sugar if desired. Pour the drink into an old-fashioned glass or tumbler and serve. —*Maricel Presilla*

Spiced Apple—Calvados Cocktails

ACTIVE: 10 MIN; TOTAL: 1 HR

MAKES 12 DRINKS ● ●

This seasonal cider can be poured over ice or warmed and served in mugs with cinnamon sticks as a garnish.

- 1 quart apple cider
- 2 tablespoons sugar
- 1 teaspoon whole cloves
- 1 cinnamon stick
- ⅓ vanilla bean, seeds scraped

Salt

- 4 cups Calvados or other apple brandy

Ice

Apple slices, for garnish

In a large saucepan, combine the cider, sugar, cloves, cinnamon stick, vanilla bean and seeds and a pinch of salt and bring to a simmer, stirring, until the sugar dissolves. Remove from the heat, cover and let stand until cool. Strain into a large pitcher; stir in the Calvados. Serve over ice, garnished with apple slices. —*Tom Valenti*

MAKE AHEAD The spiced cider can be refrigerated for up to 3 days.

beverages

Watermelon-Lime Frozen Agua Fresca

ACTIVE: 30 MIN; TOTAL: 1 HR 30 MIN

MAKES 6 DRINKS ●

½ large seedless watermelon, rind removed, flesh cut into 1-inch dice (10½ cups)

½ cup plus 1 tablespoon fresh lime juice (5 limes)

½ cup plus 1 tablespoon sugar

¼ cup plus 2 tablespoons dark rum, preferably Jamaican

1. Put 9 cups of the watermelon cubes on a rimmed baking sheet, wrap with plastic and freeze until solid, about 1 hour. Meanwhile, freeze 6 highball glasses. Chill the remaining 1½ cups of watermelon.

2. In a blender, combine half of the chilled watermelon with half of the frozen watermelon and half of the lime juice, sugar and rum. Blend until smooth. Pour into 3 of the frozen glasses. Repeat with the remaining chilled and frozen watermelon, lime juice, sugar and rum. Serve the agua fresca at once. —*Fanny Singer*

DRINK TIP

apple drinks defined

SWEET CIDER Raw, unfiltered apple juice.

HARD CIDER Fermented apple juice. Outside the United States, beverages called cider are usually the hard (alcoholic) variety.

CALVADOS An apple cider brandy from France's Normandy region. To make it, eau-de-vie that is produced by distilling cider is aged for at least two years in oak; the best are aged four or more years.

APPLEJACK This American spirit is a blend of apple brandy and neutral grain spirits.

Rosemary-Mint Highball

TOTAL: 5 MIN

MAKES 1 DRINK ●

Ice cubes

½ lime

½ tablespoon superfine sugar

2 mint leaves

1 rosemary sprig

¼ cup tequila

Fill an 8-ounce highball glass with ice cubes. In a cocktail shaker, using a pestle, crush the lime with the sugar, mint leaves and 2 rosemary leaves. Add the tequila and shake well; strain into the highball glass. Garnish the drink with the rest of the rosemary sprig and serve. —*Jehangir Mehta*

Cranberry Sparkler

TOTAL: 5 MIN

MAKES 1 DRINK ●

¼ cup Stoli Cranberi vodka

2 tablespoons fresh lime juice

2 tablespoons Rose's lime juice

Splash of seltzer

Ice cubes

Lime slice and fresh cranberries, for garnish

In a cocktail shaker, mix the vodka, fresh lime juice, Rose's lime juice and seltzer. Pour into a tall glass filled with ice, garnish with a lime slice and cranberries and serve. —*Grace Parisi*

Dirty Martini

TOTAL: 5 MIN

MAKES 1 DRINK ●

Ice cubes

⅓ cup vodka

1 tablespoon green olive juice from the jar

3 pitted medium green olives, speared on a cocktail skewer

Fill a cocktail shaker with plenty of ice. Add the vodka and olive juice and shake vigorously. Strain into a chilled martini glass, add the olives and serve at once. —*Jehangir Mehta*

Blood Orange Cosmo

TOTAL: 5 MIN

MAKES 1 DRINK ●

In winter you can use half blood orange juice and half cranberry-raspberry juice with unflavored vodka.

1 twist of lemon peel

Ice cubes

⅓ cup cranberry-raspberry juice

¼ cup blood orange vodka, such as Charbay

2 tablespoons triple sec

Rub the rim of a chilled martini glass with the lemon twist and drop it into the glass. Fill a cocktail shaker with ice. Add the juice, vodka and triple sec and shake. Strain into the glass and serve. —*Jehangir Mehta*

Bourbontini

TOTAL: 5 MIN

MAKES 1 DRINK ●

Ice cubes

¼ cup bourbon

1 tablespoon Grand Marnier

1 tablespoon fresh lemon juice

Dash of Angostura bitters

1 clementine or tangerine section

Fill a shaker with ice. Add the bourbon, Grand Marnier, lemon juice and bitters. Shake well and strain into a chilled martini glass. Garnish with the clementine and serve. —*William Loob*

Hot Chocolate with Rum

TOTAL: 10 MIN

6 SERVINGS ●

5½ cups whole milk

½ cup heavy cream

2 tablespoons dark rum

9 ounces bittersweet chocolate, coarsely chopped

In a saucepan, combine the milk, cream and rum and bring to a simmer. Remove the pan from the heat, add the chocolate and let stand until melted. Whisk until smooth, pour into warmed mugs and serve. —*Christophe Côte*

Strawberry Lemonade

ACTIVE: 15 MIN; TOTAL: 25 MIN

MAKES 6 CUPS ● ● ● ●

- 1 quart water
- 1 cup sugar
- 3 large lemons, zest removed in long strips, lemons juiced
- Ice water for chilling, plus ice for serving
- 2 pints strawberries, quartered

1. In a saucepan, combine 2 cups of the water, the sugar and the lemon zest and bring to a simmer over moderate heat, stirring frequently. Pour the hot syrup into a stainless steel bowl, stir in the remaining 2 cups of water and the lemon juice and set in a bowl of ice water, stirring occasionally, until chilled, about 10 minutes.

2. Puree the strawberries in a food processor. Stir the puree into the chilled lemonade and strain through a fine sieve. Serve in tall glasses over ice. —*Janie Hibler*

Moroccan Fruit Smoothies

TOTAL: 2 HR 30 MIN

MAKES 8 SMOOTHIES ● ●

- ½ cup dried apricots, chopped
- ½ cup warm water
- 1 large banana
- 6 strawberries
- ½ cup sugar
- ½ teaspoon pure vanilla extract
- 1 quart fresh orange juice
- Mint sprigs, for garnish

1. In a small bowl, soak the dried apricots in the water until softened, about 20 minutes. Drain and transfer to a blender. Add the banana, strawberries, sugar and vanilla and pulse until chopped. Add half of the orange juice and puree until smooth.

2. Pour the smoothie into a pitcher and stir in the remaining orange juice. Refrigerate until very cold, about 2 hours. Serve the smoothie in small glasses garnished with mint. —*Hajja Halima*

Prune Whip Shakes

TOTAL: 25 MIN

MAKES 4 SHAKES ● ● ●

- 12 pitted prunes
- 1 cup hot water
- 2 cups low-fat plain yogurt
- 1 cup cracked ice
- ½ cup pure maple syrup
- 1 teaspoon pure vanilla extract
- 1 teaspoon dark rum (optional)

1. In a bowl, cover the prunes with the hot water and let soften for about 20 minutes. Reserve the soaking water and coarsely chop the prunes.

2. In a blender, mix the yogurt with the ice, maple syrup, vanilla and rum. Add the prunes and their soaking water and blend. Serve. —*Marcia Kiesel*

MAKE AHEAD The shakes can be refrigerated overnight. Shake before drinking.

Rose Petal Tea

TOTAL: 5 MIN

4 SERVINGS ● ●

- 4 cups boiling water
- 2 tablespoons Darjeeling or Ceylon tea leaves
- ½ teaspoon rose water (see Note)
- Organic rose petals, for garnish (see Note)
- Sugar, for serving

In a teapot, pour the boiling water over the tea leaves and let them steep for 3 minutes. Stir in the rose water and mix well. Strain the tea into cups, garnish with rose petals and serve with sugar. —*Alexandra Angle*

NOTE Rose water is available at Middle Eastern and Asian markets. Organic rose petals are available at specialty food stores.

---

hot chocolate

Hot chocolate helps take the edge off raw winter nights. F&W editors sampled several cocoas available in stores or by mail order. We liked these four so much we'd happily drink them any time of year.

PRODUCT	F&W COMMENT	INTERESTING BITE
Bernard Callebaut ($9 for an 18-oz. bag; 888-388-9927)	"What espresso is to American coffee, this is to regular hot chocolate."	Callebaut won a Grand Prize as Artisan Chocolatier at France's International Festival of Chocolate.
Scharffen Berger Natural Cocoa Powder ($8 for a 6-oz. can; 800-930-4528)	"For those who like their hot chocolate a little less sweet. Dark, with depth."	Scharffen Berger is one of the few brands made without alkali, an additive that alters flavor.
Ghirardelli Double Chocolate ($6 for a 16-oz. can; 800-877-9338)	"A bit sweet, but good chocolate flavor and great texture."	Domingo Ghirardelli patented the popular Broma process for manufacturing powdered chocolate.
Schokinag European Drinking Chocolate ($15 for a 16-oz. can; 866-972-6879)	"A little honeyed taste, and nice spiciness, too."	This 17th-century-style drink uses bits of both dark and milk chocolate, with a dusting of cocoa powder.

● FAST   ● HEALTHY   ● MAKE AHEAD   ● STAFF FAVORITE

menu

goat cheese cros

rosé - steamed

caramelized on

lamb shanks, '

rutabaga m

bittersweet

toasted wa

wine glossary

Elin McCoy, a contributing editor at FOOD & WINE, has created
the ultimate user-friendly guide to pairing wine and food. Her
glossary here, with descriptions of the key wine varieties and advice
on pairing specific bottles with specific recipes, is both flexible
and focused. We know you'll find it handy.

champagne + sparkling wine

The most famous sparkling wine is, of course, Champagne, which comes from the region of the same name northeast of Paris. Champagne is usually a blend of Pinot Noir, Chardonnay and sometimes Pinot Meunier grapes, and it's produced in a wide spectrum of styles, ranging from dry (Brut) to sweet (Doux), and from austere and light-bodied to full, toasty and rich.

The very best French Champagnes have both more elegance and more complexity than the sparkling wines produced elsewhere in the world. Nevertheless, California, the Pacific Northwest and Australia all make wonderful New World versions using the same grapes and the same method as traditional French Champagne. Italian Prosecco and Spanish Cava are good, inexpensive alternatives.

The brisk, appetite-stimulating acidity of sparkling wine, whether Champagne or another selection, makes it an ideal aperitif. Sparkling wine also pairs nicely with salty, smoky and spicy dishes.

DRY, LIGHT, CRISP CHAMPAGNE
Pommery Brut Royal (France)
Lanson Black Label (France)
PAIRINGS
• Spicy Cocktail Shortbreads, 12
• Mini Herb Frittatas with Smoked Salmon, 26
• Veal Scallops with Scotch Whisky Pan Sauce, 180
• Crispy Cod with Lima Beans, Crab and Corn, 192
• Curried Crab and Watermelon Salad with Arugula, 214

DRY, RICH CHAMPAGNE
Moët et Chandon Brut Imperial (France)
Pol Roger Brut (France)
PAIRINGS
• Chickpea Fries with Sage and Parmesan, 16
• Smoked Salmon and Herbed Egg Salad Involtini, 26
• Grilled Chicken Paillards with Cilantro-Mint Dressing, 105
• Herbed Pork Tenderloin with Strawberry Salsa, 163

DRY, FRUITY SPARKLING WINE
Roederer Estate (California)
Mumm Cuvée Napa (California)
PAIRINGS
• Egg Salad Crostini with White Anchovies, 18
• Spicy Chickpea Chat, 22
• Spicy Korean Pork Buns, 31
• Chile-Glazed Chicken Wings, 105
• Roasted Salmon with Spaghetti-Squash Salad, 184
• Curry-Roasted Shrimp with Chutney and Yogurt, 200

DRY, CRISP SPARKLING WINE
Bouvet Brut Signature (France)
Mionetto DOC Prosecco (Italy)
Bodegas Jaume Serra Cristalino Cava (Spain)

wine glossary

PAIRINGS
- Crispy Asiago Frico, 12
- Classic Hummus, 20
- Stir-Fried Noodles and Pork, 94
- Crab Cakes with Bloody Mary Gazpacho, 210

whites

albariño + vinho verde

Spain's most exciting white wine, and one of its most fashionable, is the zesty and aromatic Albariño. Made predominantly in the Rías Baixas region, the wine has seductive aromas of citrus, honey and kiwi and flavors of fresh ginger, lemon and almond. The texture is creamy and at the same time crisp and light—all complete with a lively acidity. All this makes it a perfect partner for scallops and other seafood. The Albariño grape is called Alvarinho in Portugal, where it's used to make the best Vinho Verdes. These slightly fizzy bottlings, light and refreshing, go beautifully with oily fish like sardines.

AROMATIC, ZESTY ALBARIÑO

Bodegas Martín Códax Albariño (Spain)
Vionta Albariño (Spain)
Bodega Salnesur Condes de Albarei Albariño (Spain)
Aveleda Quinta da Aveleda Vinho Verde Alvarinho (Portugal)
Sogrape Morgadio da Torre Vinho Verde Alvarinho (Portugal)

PAIRINGS
- Herb-Roasted Olives, 10
- Steamed Squid and Shrimp Salad with Arugula, 26
- Halibut Roasted in Grape Leaves with Lemon Vinaigrette, 191
- Seafood Stew in Saffron Broth, 196
- Monkfish Stew with Fried Garlic Sauce, 197
- Sautéed Jumbo Shrimp with Passion Fruit Dressing, 204
- Portuguese Clam and Chorizo Stew, 209

chardonnay + white burgundy

The world's most popular white wine originally came from the Burgundy region of eastern France, but it's now made successfully in just about every wine-growing country in the world, in an enormous range of styles and flavors. In France, the best white Burgundies are elegant, complex and rich, with flavors of earth, nuts and minerals; the simpler wines from Mâcon and Rully suggest green apples and lemons. Californian and Australian versions are often higher in alcohol and lush with tropical fruit flavors. Most Chardonnays (Chablis is generally an exception) are aged in oak barrels, which tend to give them a buttery richness and toasty vanilla aromas and flavors. The biggest and oakiest Chardonnays can be tricky to match with food, but they are marvelous partners for sweet corn, rich fish and poultry dishes made with cream, butter, cheese or coconut.

FRUITY, LOW-OAK CHARDONNAY

Louis Latour Pouilly-Fuissé (France)
Mâcon-Lugny Les Charmes (France)

PAIRINGS
- Prosciutto and Marinated Artichoke Involtini, 28
- Ricotta Cavatelli with Bacon and Zucchini, 92
- Sautéed Chicken Breasts with Cucumber Salad, 102
- Spicy Korean Glazed Pork Ribs, 171
- Lobster Capellini with Leek-Tarragon Cream Sauce, 206
- Scallops with Avocado Salsa, 206

FLINTY, HIGH-ACID CHABLIS

Christian Moreau Père et Fils (France)
William Fevre (France)

PAIRINGS
- Venetian Spaghetti with Sardines, 86
- Savory Cabbage and Mushroom Pancakes with Pork and Shrimp, 164
- Salt-Baked Salmon with Prosecco Butter Sauce, 185
- Halibut with Fried Capers and Lemon, 190
- Sea Scallops with Peas, Bacon and Carrots, 209

RIPE, CREAMY-TEXTURED CHARDONNAY

Penfolds Koonunga Hill (Australia)
Rosemount Estate Show Reserve (Australia)
Morgan Monterey (California)

PAIRINGS
- Red Potato and Green Pea Samosas, 22
- Fregola with Grilled Red Onions and Pine Nuts, 78
- Spaetzle with Gruyère and Caramelized Onions, 83
- Spicy Garlic Shrimp and Tomato Spaghetti, 86
- Buttermilk Fried Chicken, 106
- Turkey with Apple-Chestnut Stuffing and Cider Gravy, 127
- Maple-Roasted Pork Spareribs, 171
- Fisherman's Stew, 196
- Maine Lobster Rolls, 206
- Soft-Shell Crab and Bacon Sandwiches, 213

SUBTLE, COMPLEX WHITE BURGUNDY

Domaine Olivier Leflaive Puligny-Montrachet (France)
Louis Jadot Meursault-Genevrières (France)

chenin blanc

This underappreciated grape is grown widely in the Loire region of France, where it's used to make dry Vouvray and Savennières, as well as delicious sweet wines and a few sparkling ones. But it has also found a home in South Africa, California and Washington State, which typically turn it into a light dry or semidry white with overtones of green apples and peaches and an acidity that can range from soft to zesty. It's an interesting aperitif and a good partner for light fish dishes. Distinguished dry examples have a pleasant underlying mineral chalkiness.

LIGHT, SOFT CHENIN BLANC

Hogue Cellars (Washington State)
Dry Creek Vineyard (California)

DRY, MINERAL-FLAVORED CHENIN BLANC

Ken Forrester (South Africa)
Chappellet Napa Valley (California)
Domaine Huët Vouvray Sec (France)

gewürztraminer

The great examples of this flamboyant, fragrant white wine come from Alsace; most of them are bone-dry, but they can range all the way to very sweet (labeled *vendange tardive*— late harvest). Regardless of style, they have an irresistible, heady scent of lychees and cloves; concentrated, spicy (*Gewürz* is the German word for "spice") apricot and ginger flavors; and a rich, while low-acid, texture. They are superb companions for Muenster cheese, chicken liver pâté, smoked fish and baked ham. New World bottlings from California and Washington State are usually lighter, with a hint of sweetness; they go well with curries and dishes flavored with ginger, coriander, cloves or lemongrass.

SPICY ALSACE GEWÜRZTRAMINER

Muré (France)
Lucien Albrecht (France)

SPICY NEW WORLD GEWÜRZTRAMINER

Geyser Peak (California)
Navarro Vineyards Anderson Valley (California)

pinot blanc

Sometimes called the poor man's Chardonnay, Pinot Blanc is undervalued in its French stronghold, Alsace, and over-looked elsewhere—which is too bad, because this mild wine is dependable, easy to like and reasonably priced. As with most Alsace wines, there's no oak or excessive alcohol screaming for attention. In Austria, Pinot Blanc is called Weissburgunder; it's also produced, on a small scale, in California, Oregon and Italy (where it's dry, light and leafy and known as Pinot Bianco). Pinot Blanc's apple and pear flavors, mineral edge and crisp acidity marry well with vegetables and fish dishes.

wine glossary

MEDIUM-BODIED, ROUND PINOT BLANC
Hugel Cuvée Les Amours (France)
Pierre Sparr Pinot Blanc d'Alsace Reserve (France)
Chalone Vineyard Monterey (California)
PAIRINGS
- Gruyère Toasts with Caramelized Onions and Sherry, 15
- Bruschetta of Spring Vegetables, 16
- Shrimp Fritters, 24
- Penne with Red Pepper Sauce, 76
- Egg Noodle Gratin with Gruyère, 80
- Crispy Garlic Chicken with Dipping Salt, 111
- Crab Cakes with Lemongrass Mayonnaise, 213

pinot gris + pinot grigio
The region or country where the Pinot Gris grape grows makes all the difference in the wine's style and flavor. In Alsace, it's a high-impact wine with a musky aroma and bold, concentrated flavors of bitter almonds, spice and honey. It's available in dry and opulently sweet *(vendange tardive)* versions; the dry ones are good with smoky and creamy dishes. In Oregon, where the grape is an emerging star, pear and mango flavors prevail, along with a scent of honeysuckle. The best bottlings here are lighter and less intense than those from Alsace, with a creamy yet slightly crisp character that's versatile with food and ideal with salmon. The Italian version, the popular Pinot Grigio, is light, simple and crisp, with bright, clean, lightly spicy flavors. It works best as an aperitif or with fresh seafood.

DRY, MEDIUM-BODIED PINOT GRIS
Domaine Schlumberger Les Princes Abbés (France)
Domaine Weinbach Cuvée Laurence (France)
King Estate (Oregon)
Elk Cove Willamette Valley (Oregon)
PAIRINGS
- Sardine and Celery Salad, 24
- Fusilli Salad with Grilled Chicken and Zucchini, 86
- Chicken Skewers with Fresh Herb Vinaigrette and Feta, 112
- Cod with Creamy Nut Sauce, 193
- Scallops with Saffron Cream and Turnip Greens, 207
- Scallops with Endives and Lemongrass Glaze, 207

LIGHT, SPICY PINOT GRIGIO
Doro Princic (Italy)
Alois Lageder Alto Aldige (Italy)
PAIRINGS
- Melted Taleggio Flat Breads with Three Toppings, 14

- Two-Cheese Panini with Tomato-Olive Pesto, 19
- Prosciutto-Wrapped Shrimp with Orange Marmalade, 28
- Linguine with Fresh Tomatoes, Basil and Garlic, 76
- Toasted Orzo and Chicken Pilaf with Green Olives and Peas, 86
- Thai Chicken with Mushrooms, Green Beans and Basil, 112
- Turkey Breast Escabeche with Onions and Poblanos, 123
- Jerk Seafood Packs, 215

riesling
The versatile Riesling grape produces striking wines that range from pale, dry and delicate to apricot-scented and honey-sweet; the latter can age for decades. The lighter German ones have a pinpoint balance of fruitiness and mouthwatering acidity. Those from Alsace are weightier and very dry, with steel and mineral flavors. Other regions also make good, if less complex, Rieslings. Austria's are vibrant and powerful; Australia's have zingy lime scents and flavors; Washington State's are soft, with a touch of sweetness. Riesling's fruit, its acidity, its low alcohol and its lack of oak make it one of the most food-friendly of wines, a lovely complement to delicate fish, to spicy Asian and Latin dishes and to all smoked and salty foods.

BRIGHT, CITRUSY RIESLING
Dr. H. Thanisch Erben Müller Burggraeff Classic (Germany)
Annie's Lane Clare Valley (Australia)
PAIRINGS
- Shrimp and Green Papaya Summer Rolls, 24
- Vegetarian Red Curry Noodles, 77
- Chicken with Fresh Apricots, Ginger and Cracked Almonds, 105
- Asian-Style Orange Chicken, 111
- Pot-Roasted Pork and Apples, 165
- Smoked Trout and Apple Salad, 192
- Caribbean Mango and Steamed Shrimp Salad, 201

SOFT, OFF-DRY RIESLING
Trefethen (California)
Jekel Johannisberg (California)
PAIRINGS
- Citrus Chicken with Habanero Honey, 103
- Asian-Style Chicken Breasts and Bacon, 112
- Spicy Pineapple-Glazed Ham, 177
- Papillotes of Sea Bass in Red Curry Sauce, 187
- Smoked Trout Hash with Potatoes and Corn, 191
- Thai Tuna Burgers with Ginger-Lemon Mayonnaise, 194
- Shrimp and Sausage Gumbo, 200

DRY, FULL-FLAVORED ALSACE RIESLING
Domaine Trimbach (France)
Domaine Marcel Deiss (France)

PAIRINGS
- Farfalle with Lobster, Favas and Peas, 84
- Soba with Lemon, Cream and Prosciutto, 89
- Chicken with Riesling, 113
- Crispy Pork Tenderloin with Fried Apple Rings, 162
- Pork with Sweet Riesling Sauce and Toasted Almonds, 164
- Spicy Fish and Vegetable Stew, 197
- Coconut Shrimp with Crispy Shallot, Basil and Sesame Sprinkle, 202

sauvignon blanc

Tart acidity, aromas of fresh-cut grass and herbs, green pepper and sometimes citrus flavors give Sauvignon Blancs the world over a character people either love or hate. Sancerre and Pouilly-Fumé from France's Loire Valley have flint and mineral flavors. The lively New Zealand bottlings taste of passion fruit and gooseberries. South Africa's are elegant and bright, California's are lighter, and all are fresh and crisp. When the grape is blended with rounder, heavier Sémillon, as it typically is in Bordeaux, the result is mellow and full-bodied. The riper, oak-aged Sauvignon Blancs hint of melons and toast. The lighter versions of the wine go beautifully with salads and with almost all fish and green vegetables—even asparagus.

LIVELY, ASSERTIVE SAUVIGNON BLANC
Brancott Estate Marlborough (New Zealand)
Fleur du Cap (South Africa)
Robert Mondavi Fumé Blanc (California)
Pascal Jolivet Pouilly-Fumé (France)
La Poussie Sancerre (France)

PAIRINGS
- Fried Green Tomatoes with Anchovy and Lemon, 15
- Eggplant and Goat Cheese Crostini, 20
- Tomato-Cilantro Raita, 22
- Frisée Salad with Baked Goat Cheese and Bacon, 31
- Chicken Simmered in Spiced Yogurt, 100
- Grilled Quail with Green Papaya Salad, 119
- Warm Cured-Cod Salad with Orange and Basil, 193
- Shrimp and Avocado Salad with Citrus Dressing, 201

ROUND, RICH SAUVIGNON BLANC
Simi (California)
Château Carbonnieux Blanc Pessac-Léognan (France)

PAIRINGS
- Herb-Stuffed Zucchini, 11
- Walnut Pesto and Goat Cheese Dip, 16
- Green Olive and Walnut Crostini, 20
- Artichoke and Goat Cheese Bruschetta, 21
- Creamy Goat Cheese and Asparagus Orecchiette, 83
- Clay-Roasted Chicken Stuffed with Serrano Ham and Olives, 99
- Seared Scallop Salad with Asparagus and Scallions, 208

sémillon

Often blended with Sauvignon Blanc to add weight and richness, the Sémillon grape's flavor is round and almost waxy-textured on its own. The wine's stony, mineral and melonlike attributes are a perfect foil for crab and rich seafood dishes that are prepared with cream-based sauces. The grape is widely planted in France, where it makes both dry and sweet whites. In Australia, Sémillon has come into its own in a rich, oak-aged style. Likewise, both Napa Valley and Washington State have produced distinguished examples of this wine.

ROUND-TEXTURED SÉMILLON
Moss Wood (Australia)
Château de Chantegrive Blanc Cuvée Caroline (France)
Signorello (California)
L'Ecole No. 41 (Washington State)

PAIRINGS
- Prosciutto and Foie Gras Roulades with Fig Compote, 28
- Fettuccine with Wilted Escarole and Mushrooms, 78
- Creamy Spaghetti Carbonara, 90
- Sweet and Salty Pork Chops with Beef Jerky, 167
- Pork Scallopine with Spicy Cherry-Pepper Sauce, 172
- Swordfish Sicilian-Style, 187

soave+ similar whites

Italy produces many delicious light white wines; three of them are particularly well known and universally loved. Soave, from Veneto, is a pleasant, fruity—as well as inexpensive—wine. Verdicchio, from the Marches, has a sharp acidity followed by a tangy finish. Finally, Gavi, from Piedmont, is a delicate wine marked by citrus and mineral notes.

LIGHT, DRY SOAVE OR SIMILAR WHITE
Anselmi San Vincenzo Soave (Italy)
Pieropan Soave Classico (Italy)
Verdicchio San Floriano Monte Schiavo (Italy)
Coppo Gavi La Rocca (Italy)

wine glossary

vermentino

Vermentino is assertive and savory, with a salty, lemony edge and razorlike acidity—all of which make it a perfect partner for any kind of shellfish. Though the grape grows throughout Italy, the Vermentinos of Tuscany and Sardinia generally have the most character and the most complexity.

HIGH-ACID, SAVORY VERMENTINO
Antinori (Italy)
Argiolas Costamolino (Italy)

vernaccia di san gimignano

Vernaccia di San Gimignano is, according to Tuscan tradition, "the wine that kisses, bites and stings." It's also the best known of the many wines made from the Vernaccia grape that flourishes throughout Italy. The grapes for this version—generally considered Tuscany's finest white wine—grow on the hillsides surrounding San Gimignano, the medieval town famous for its picturesque bell towers. The wine is fresh and reliable, with no oak. Its tangy mineral and citrus flavors and its crisp acidity pair beautifully with pasta and with shellfish.

TANGY, CRISP VERNACCIA DI SAN GIMIGNANO
Teruzzi & Puthod (Italy)
Fattoria San Quirico (Italy)
Melini Lydia (Italy)

viognier

Whether it's the classic bottling from the northern Rhône Valley appellation of Condrieu in France or one of the newer versions from California and, now, Australia, the appeal of Viognier is its exotic honeysuckle aroma, its intense ripe-peach and ripe-apricot flavors and, most of all, its fleshy, mouth-filling texture. The aroma leads you to expect sweetness, but in the mouth it's bone-dry. Low in acid and often high in alcohol, Viognier is typically rich and powerful. Opulent dishes with tropical or dried fruit and those with curry or smoky flavors are good matches.

FULL-BODIED, FRAGRANT VIOGNIER
Bonterra Mendocino County (California)
Arrowood Vineyards Saralee's (California)
Calera Mount Harlan (California)
Yalumba Eden Valley (Australia)
Jean-Luc Colombo Côtes-du-Rhône Blanc,
  Les Figuières (France)

rosés

Rosés are as refreshing as white wines while offering the body and fruit of light reds. They come from many lands and from many different grapes and range in style from simple summer thirst-quenchers to sophisticated marvels. The best, from Provence and the Tavel appellation of the Rhône Valley, are savory, bone-dry bottlings made from Syrah, Grenache and Cinsaut grapes. Italy, Spain and California produce their own delectable versions. What they all have in common is zesty fruit and acidity that make them delightful with the smoky, sweet and hot spices of Chinese, Thai, Middle Eastern, Cajun and Southwestern dishes.

BRIGHT, FRUITY ROSÉ
Château Routas Côteau Varois Rosé Rouvière (France)
Château d'Acqueria Tavel (France)
Mas de Gourgonnier Rosé (France)
Iron Horse Rosato di Sangiovese (California)
Castello di Ama Rosato (Italy)
La Palma Rosé Rapel Valley (Chile)

wine glossary

reds

barbera

The second-most-planted grape in Italy (after Sangiovese), Barbera produces its finest wines—tart, bright and medium-bodied, with very little tannin—in the Piedmont areas of Asti and Alba. (A few California wineries also make Barbera, with mixed results.) Both simple styles (fresh, fruity and without oak) and more serious bottlings (plummy and oaky) have a deep, ruby color and a high acidity that gives this versatile wine vibrancy and zip. Licorice, berries and cherries are typical flavors; the taste is straightforward, mouth-filling and, for a red, quite refreshing. Barbera's tartness combines superbly with antipasti, tomato-sauced pastas and bitter greens.

TART, LOW-TANNIN BARBERA
Michele Chiarlo Barbera d'Asti (Italy)
Bruno Giacosa Barbera d'Alba (Italy)
Coppo Pomorosso Barbera d'Asti (Italy)

beaujolais

This fruity and famously charming wine is made from the Gamay grape in the Beaujolais region of France. Bottlings range from the simple Beaujolais-Villages, best when it's young, to deeper, more complex *cru* examples from villages with their own appellations, such as Moulin-à-Vent, which age well. What they all share is a smooth texture and an exuberant juicy fruitiness, with strawberry-cherry flavors. Though Beaujolais isn't as fashionable as it once was, its low tannin, fresh, enticing acidity and lack of oak still enable it to pair well with a variety of foods. It traditionally accompanies roast chicken, and it's also excellent with turkey and most cheeses.

LIGHT, FRUITY BEAUJOLAIS
Georges Duboeuf Beaujolais-Villages (France)
Château de La Chaize Brouilly (France)
Joseph Drouhin Moulin-à-Vent (France)

cabernet sauvignon + bordeaux

Cabernet Sauvignon is not merely the classic grape of Bordeaux; it is really the king of grapes, producing some of the world's most complex, elegant, powerful and long-lived red wines. In Bordeaux, where it's often blended with Merlot and Cabernet Franc, it dominates the wines of the Médoc and Graves regions, playing a smaller role in St-Émilion and Pomerol. Those made with a larger proportion of Cabernet Sauvignon typically have black currant and plum aromas and flavors; herbal, olivelike and even minty elements all add complexity. Mouth-puckering tannins, enhanced by aging in oak barrels, give the wines astringency and bite when they're young; aging smooths out the tannins and brings out aromas and flavors of cedar and cigar boxes. Many California bottlings are also blends. The fruit in New World Cabernets tends to be sweeter and riper than in the classic Bordeaux. Cabernet Sauvignon has a particular affinity for the pungent flavors of lamb; it also pairs well with roasts and steaks.

TANNIC, COMPLEX CABERNET
Columbia Crest (Washington State)
Beringer Knights Valley (California)
Markham (California)
Wynns Coonawarra Estate (Australia)
Montes Alpha (Chile)

Château Beycheville (France)
Château Talbot (France)

PAIRINGS

- Madeira-Braised Turkey with Fried Sage
  Stuffing, 121
- Steak Bordelaise, 132
- Beef with Red and Yellow Bell Peppers, 137
- Roast Beef Tenderloin with Morel Cream
  Sauce, 140
- Rosy Rack of Lamb with Garlic, 150
- Spiced Pork Tenderloin with Wilted Arugula, 163
- Veal Tournedos with Cellophane Noodles,
  Chanterelles and Coconut-Corn Sauce, 181

chianti + sangiovese

Italy's best-known wine—a medium-bodied, brightly
flavored, smooth-textured red—is made primarily from the
Sangiovese grape in the Chianti region of Tuscany. Wines
simply labeled "Chianti" tend to be soft and simple, with
cherry flavors and a touch of fresh thyme; those labeled
"Chianti Classico" and "Riserva" are more intense and
complex, with deeper licorice, sweet-sour dried cherry and
earthy flavors and a considerable hit of tannin. Chianti's
acidity and its suggestion of saltiness make it an excellent
partner for many foods, especially olives and garlic,
tomato-sauced pastas, grilled steaks and pecorino and
other tangy cheeses. A clone of the Sangiovese grape is the
base for Brunello di Montalcino, which is deep, rich and
marvelously full-bodied. Many producers also make big, rich
Sangiovese—Cabernet Sauvignon blends, which are known
as Super-Tuscans.

SIMPLE, FRUITY CHIANTI OR SANGIOVESE

Castello di Gabbiano Chianti (Italy)
Antinori Santa Cristina (Italy)
Atlas Peak Sangiovese (California)

PAIRINGS

- Pan-Fried Cheese with Salsa Verde, 11
- Roast Beef and Watercress Involtini, 28
- Eggplant, Tomato and Fresh Ricotta Farfalle, 77
- Spinach Cannelloni with Bacon and Walnuts, 90
- Chicken and Sun-Dried-Tomato Meatballs, 115

COMPLEX, SAVORY CHIANTI CLASSICO OR RISERVA

Castello di Ama Chianti Classico
Castello dei Rampolla Chianti Classico Riserva

PAIRINGS

- Spaghettini with Pesto Tomatoes and Grilled Eggplant, 77

- Penne with Cauliflower, Bacon and Creamy Tomato
  Sauce, 91
- Roast Chicken, 98
- Grilled Lamb Chops with Tahini Sauce, 153
- Sweet Sausage, Onion and Pepper Skewers, 175

dolcetto

Italy's answer to Beaujolais: a plummy, grapey, delicious
low-acid wine from Piedmont (and now from a few wineries
in California, too). It is light and spicy, with a juiciness
reminiscent of cranberries, and best when it's young (most
of these wines are designed to be drunk when they are two
or three years old). It's a versatile wine that's lovely with
osso buco and most meaty pasta dishes as well as many
creamy cheeses.

LIGHT, ZESTY, FRUITY DOLCETTO

Roberto Voerzio Dolcetto d'Alba Priavino (Italy)
Aldo Conterno Dolcetto d'Alba (Italy)
Niebaum-Coppola Dolcetto Napa Valley (California)

PAIRINGS

- Mushroom and Fontina Crostini, 19
- Pasta with Parmesan and Fried Eggs, 79
- Three-Cheese Baked Pasta with Porcini and Radicchio, 82
- Parmesan-Crusted Chicken with Arugula Salad, 103
- Smoky Turkey Chili, 126
- Greek-Style Lamb Burgers with Yogurt-Cucumber
  Sauce, 158

grenache

Although Grenache is the world's most widely planted red
grape variety, few wine lovers give it much thought. But it's
a mistake to overlook Grenache. Rhône wine enthusiasts
know it as one of the main grapes used in sturdy, deep-

KITCHEN TOOL

corkscrew

**High-tech efficiency:
Le Creuset's Lever
Model Classic Screwpull
($100 at Bloomingdale's;
800-232-1845).**

wine glossary

flavored Châteauneuf-du-Pape and the delicious rosés of the Tavel region. France's plantings, however, are dwarfed by Spain's. There the grape is known as Garnacha Tinta, important in Rioja blends; it also makes the concentrated, high-alcohol, heady, powerful reds of Priorat. In California, South Africa and Australia, it has been used to make everything from port-style wines to simple rosés, though many of these are undistinguished. Recently, however, some Australian winemakers have sought out top old-vine Grenache vineyards to make mouth-filling, assertively fruity versions that are best enjoyed young in their lusty prime and are superb with grilled meats.

ASSERTIVE, HEADY GRENACHE
Clos Mogador Priorat (Spain)
Clarendon Hills Clarendon (Australia)
D'Arenberg The Custodian (Australia)
Vieux Télégraphe Châteauneuf-du-Pape (France)

PAIRINGS
- Latin-Spiced Rib Eye with Sautéed Onions and Cilantro, 133
- Roast Beef with Spicy Yogurt-Walnut Sauce, 141
- New Mexican Chile-Sirloin Burgers with Salsa Verde, 146
- Grilled Lamb with Radicchio and Black-Olive Oil, 149
- Spice-Dusted Lamb Chops with Cherry Tomatoes, 153
- Korean Barbecued Pork, 166
- Garlic-Rubbed Spareribs, 170

merlot

Merlot, Bordeaux's major red grape variety after Cabernet Sauvignon, is similar in flavor but less assertive; because of its softer texture, it's often blended with Cabernet to tame that grape's hard tannins. When Merlot is the dominant grape, as in Bordeaux's Pomerol and St-Émilion, or when it's bottled on its own, the result has a rich, velvety texture and a come-hither juiciness, with aromas and flavors of plums and black cherries. The smooth texture and the luscious fruit combine well with medium-weight meats—duck, pork, veal—especially in dishes with a hint of sweetness. Washington State and California's Napa and Sonoma regions also make delightful Merlots.

RICH, VELVETY MERLOT
Swanson (California)
St. Supery (California)
Waterbrook (Washington State)
Château de Sales (France)

PAIRINGS
- Chipotle Chicken and Bell Pepper Casserole, 118
- Tea-Spiced Beef Short Ribs, 136
- Brisket with Onion-and-Chile Jam, 142
- Beef Stew, 144
- Lamb and Sweet Potato Shepherd's Pies, 159
- Roasted Veal Chops with Red Grapes, 178

nebbiolo + barolo + barbaresco

Barolo and Barbaresco are the most famous reds of Italy's Piedmont region. Made from the Nebbiolo grape, these big, dry, tannic wines are named for the districts where the fruit is grown. Barolo is heavier and more pungent than Barbaresco, but both share distinctive aromas of berries and mushrooms and a hint of tar or licorice that carries through in the flavor. Often, a scent of violets adds elegance to their earthiness. Mouth-puckering tannins contribute to the impression of dryness, making these reds ideal with Italian dishes—game, saltimbocca, garlicky roasts and strong cheeses—whose richness needs the balance of a dry, astringent wine. These grand, powerful wines are good at four to six years of age, but the most concentrated bottlings can develop for a decade or more. Nebbiolo is also produced as a varietal wine in Piedmont, but in a lighter style than Barolo or Barbaresco. California has experimented with Nebbiolo with mixed results.

DEEP, PUNGENT, TANNIC BAROLO
Ceretto Bricco Rocche Brunate (Italy)
Giacomo Conterno Cascina Francia (Italy)
Pio Cesare (Italy)

PAIRINGS
- Spaghetti with Bolognese Sauce, 89
- Lavender-Marinated Leg of Lamb, 151
- Lamb Shanks Osso Buco–Style, 155
- Peppered Pork Chops with Vegetable Fricassee, 167

TANNIC, FULL-BODIED BARBARESCO
Gaja (Italy)
Prunotto (Italy)
Vietti (Italy)

PAIRINGS
- Gemelli with Sweet Sausage and Spinach, 92
- Beef Brisket with Mustard and Rye Crumbs, 142
- Pancetta-Wrapped Roast Leg of Lamb, 150
- Hearty Lamb Ragù with Rigatoni, 159
- Pork Medallions with Prosciutto, Arugula and Tomatoes, 164

pinot noir + red burgundy

The most sensual and beguiling of all red wines, the best Pinot Noirs are from Burgundy, but California, Oregon and New Zealand have all done wonders with this difficult grape. Though Pinot Noir appears in many different styles, its hallmarks are seductive scents and flavors that suggest cherries, strawberries and damp earth or mushrooms, and, above all, a silky texture. Bottlings range from light- to medium-bodied and from simple to complex, but very few are tannic, and almost all can be drunk young. California's Pinot Noirs are beginning to rival Burgundy's for elegance and complexity; Oregon's have delicacy, charm and bright cherry fruit, though a few wineries there are also making bigger wines. The wine's low tannin, tart fruitiness and subtle flavors make it flexible with food. Fruity styles work well with Asian flavors and fish; earthier ones respond beautifully to mushrooms and game.

LIGHT, FRUITY PINOT NOIR
Firesteed (Oregon)
Echelon (California)
PAIRINGS
• Pan-Roasted Chicken and Leeks, 99
• Roasted Capons with Herb Butter and Mushroom-Madeira Sauce, 120
• Lamb Tagine with Artichokes and Peas, 156
• Pork Tenderloin with Rhubarb-Shallot Compote, 162
• Veal Stew with Rosemary and Lemon, 180
• Salmon with Arugula Cream and Soy-Braised Beets, 185

RICH, EARTHY PINOT NOIR
Acacia Carneros (California)
Au Bon Climat (California)
Ponzi (Oregon)
PAIRINGS
• Three-Cheese Linguine with Chicken and Spinach, 89
• Herb-Roasted Game Hens, 119
• Pancetta-Wrapped Beef Tenderloin, 139
• Pork Tenderloin with Wild Mushrooms, Ginger and Scallions, 163
• Pot-Roasted Veal, 179
• Roasted Veal Loin, 179

COMPLEX, SILKY RED BURGUNDY
Labouré-Roi Gevrey-Chambertin (France)
Domaine Faiveley Nuits-St-Georges Les Porets (France)
PAIRINGS
• Stir-Fried Chinese Noodles with Roast Pork, 93
• Summer Vegetable Stew with Braised Rabbit, 149
• Veal Blanquette, 178
• Osso Buco with Asian Flavors, 179
• Broiled Bacon-Basted Salmon with Mushroom-Oyster Sauce, 186

rioja + tempranillo

Tempranillo, which reigns supreme among Spanish grapes, gives the renowned red blends of the Rioja region their herbal scent, earthy flavor and elegant texture. Riojas made in a modern style have forward fruit and just a little oak; the more traditional, more complex ones are mellower and oakier. The newly fashionable Ribera del Duero region produces delicious blends in a bigger, richer, fruitier style. In both places, the younger versions, labeled "Crianza," are spicy, easy-drinking wines; "Reservas" and "Gran Reservas" are more subtle and refined, with flavors of leather and earth. These are big red wines; hearty bean and spicy sausage stews, grilled meats and earthy dishes (for instance, with wild mushrooms) have flavors and textures that make apt matches.

SOFT, EARTHY RIOJA
Bodegas Martinez Bujanda Conde de Valdemar Crianza (Spain)
Marqués de Cáceres (Spain)
Cune Imperial Gran Reserva (Spain)
Montecillo Reserva (Spain)
PAIRINGS
• Spaghetti with Garlicky Marsala Mushrooms, 80
• Chicken Pot-au-Feu, 101
• Fried Chicken with Tomato Gravy, 106
• Chicken Tagine with Sweet Tomato Sauce, 115
• Melted Edam with Beef, 147
• Herbed Pork Involtini, 166

shiraz + syrah

The intense and concentrated wines that are made from Syrah grapes are packed with blueberry and blackberry fruit and with spicy, peppery, sometimes smoky accents. Syrah is the star grape in France's northern Rhône Valley, where it goes into dense, powerful wines that take on a chocolaty, leathery character. Elsewhere in the Rhône, it is one of several grapes in softer, rounder, less tannic blends such as the much-loved Châteauneuf-du-Pape. In California, where the grape is gaining popularity, it's often blended with other Rhône varietals. It's also widely planted in Australia, where it goes by the name Shiraz and yields wines that range from

wine glossary

solid all the way to superb. Many of the Australian bottlings are thick, chocolaty and jammy, with notes of sweet vanilla from oak aging. Syrah's big, spicy-peppery flavors demand robust, flavorful foods. Grilled meat and game are a match, and the Rhône blends pair with spicy dishes and barbecue.

RICH, SMOKY-PLUMMY SHIRAZ

Greg Norman Estates Limestone Coast (Australia)
Grant Burge Miamba (Australia)

PAIRINGS
- Baked Pasta with Four Cheeses, 82
- Ropa Vieja with Capers, 134
- Braised Meat-and-Potato Pie, 141
- Beef Stew with Red Currant Jelly and Cream, 144
- Cumin Lamb Kebabs with Fresh Mango Chutney, 155

ROUND, SUPPLE, FRUITY SYRAH AND BLENDS

Domaine St. Luc Coteaux du Tricastin Syrah (France)
Hess Select (California)

PAIRINGS
- Macaroni and Cheese with Buttery Crumbs, 82
- Crisp Indian-Spiced Chicken with Cucumber-Tomato Raita, 109
- Mediterranean-Style Chicken and Bean Stew, 114
- Ancho-Chipotle-Spiced Duck Breasts with Mango Salsa, 129
- Beef Sirloin with Piquillo Peppers and Capers, 136
- Stir-Fried Beef with Oven-Fried Potatoes, 140
- Lamb Chops with Spicy Thai Peanut Sauce, 152

POWERFUL, SPICY SYRAH

Jaboulet Crozes-Hermitage Domaine de Thalabert (France)
Qupé (California)

PAIRINGS
- Chile-Roasted Turkey with Chorizo–Corn Bread Stuffing, 126
- Steak with Shallots and Lyonnaise Potatoes, 135
- Korean Barbecued Short Ribs with Sesame Salt, 136
- Indian-Spiced Butterflied Leg of Lamb, 151
- Roast Leg of Lamb Provençal, 152
- White Wine–Braised Lamb Shoulder with Red Wine Jus, 154

zinfandel

Though it's generally believed to have first traveled over to the United States from Italy, Zinfandel is really California's own grape. And it's an enormously versatile one that is used to make everything from bland, semisweet blush wines to jammy, highly intense reds. The Zinfandels that go best with most foods are the medium- to full-bodied bottlings that emphasize the grape's characteristic raspberry-boysenberry, often spicy fruit. These bright berry flavors and the wine's lively acidity make it a good partner for hearty food. Grilled or barbecued meats are excellent choices; so are spicy, salty dishes.

INTENSE, BERRY-FLAVORED ZINFANDEL

The Terraces (California)
Ridge Geyserville (California)
Rabbit Ridge (California)
Seghesio Sonoma County (California)

PAIRINGS
- Grandma's Lasagna, 94
- Chicken Chilaquiles, 118
- Chilled Duck with Zinfandel Sauce, 129
- Grilled Chile-Rubbed Flank Steak, 133
- Peppered Rib-Eye Steaks with Pan-Fried Watercress, 133
- Grilled Steak Tacos, 139
- Classic Beef Burgers, 145
- Pepper Jack Cheeseburgers with Jalapeño-Cumin Sauce, 146
- Lamb Steaks with Shallot-Anchovy Relish, 154
- Pork Chili with Beans and Hominy, 174
- Italian Sausage Heroes with Peppers and Onions, 177

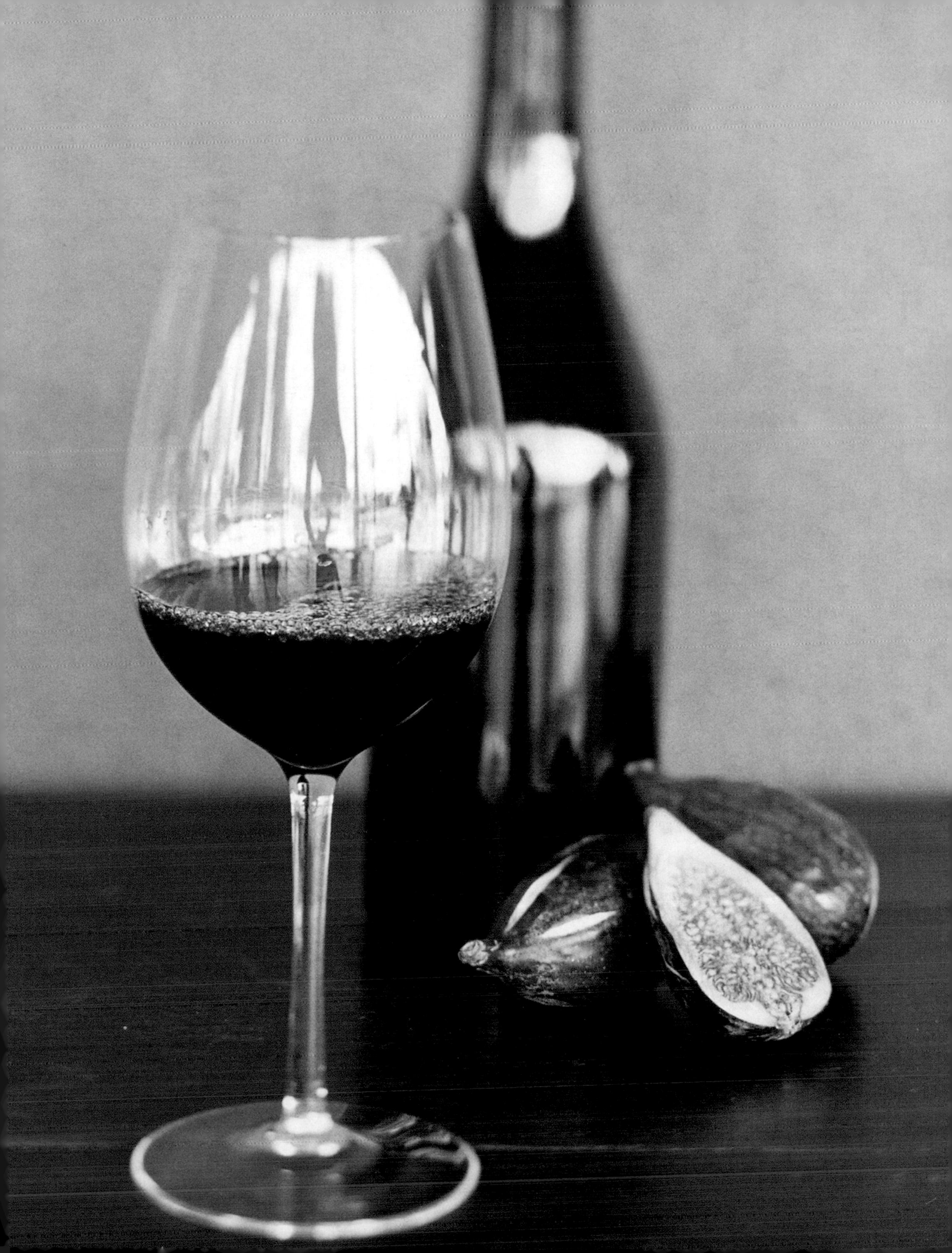

menu index

easter

STARTERS

Bruschetta of Spring Vegetables, 16

Lettuce Soup with Watercress-Herb Puree, 57

WINE Medium-bodied, round Pinot Blanc

MAIN COURSE

Shaved Asparagus Salad with Oranges and Pecorino, 36

Three-Cheese Baked Pasta with Porcini and Radicchio, 82

Spicy Pineapple-Glazed Ham, 177

Broccoli with Brown Butter Crumbs, 225

WINE Light, zesty, fruity Dolcetto

DESSERT

Coconut-Custard Meringue Pie, 300

Candied Orange Sugar Cookies, 329

passover

STARTERS

Potato, Leek and Radish Green Vichyssoise, 65

Smoked Trout and Apple Salad, 192

Beet Tartare with Horseradish and Caraway, 233

WINE Bright, citrusy Riesling

MAIN COURSE

Veal Stew with Rosemary and Lemon, 180

Green Beans with Mustard-Seed Butter, 229

Potato and Fennel Gratin, 240

WINE Light, fruity Pinot Noir

DESSERT

Tangy Strawberry Parfait with Lime Gelée, 312

Fragrant Fennel Brittle, 345

fourth of july

STARTERS

Chunky Guacamole with Cumin, 12

Two-Cheese Panini with Tomato-Olive Pesto, 19

Sangrita, 348

Strawberry Lemonade, 351

WINE Tangy, crisp Vernaccia

MAIN COURSE

Baby Romaine with Green Goddess Dressing, 39

Green Tomato, Scallion and Corn Bread Panzanella, 40

Mom's Marinated Tomato Salad, 40

Classic Beef Burgers, 145

Maine Lobster Rolls, 206

WINE Lively, assertive Sauvignon Blanc/Intense,
berry-flavored Zinfandel

DESSERT

Lemon Meringue Pie, 302

Strawberry Shortcake with Star Anise Sauce, 310

Chocolate-Mint Sandwich Cookies, 332

thanksgiving

STARTERS

Melted Taleggio Flat Breads with Three Toppings, 14

Curried Winter Squash Soup with Cheddar Crisps, 61

Spiced Apple–Calvados Cocktails, 349

WINE Light, spicy Pinot Grigio

MAIN COURSE

Fennel, Apple and Celery Salad with Watercress, 46

Madeira-Braised Turkey with Fried Sage Stuffing, 121

TOAST THE FOURTH OF JULY WITH A STRAWBERRY LEMONADE, P. 351

Instant Spiced Apple Cider–Cranberry Sauce, 124

Sautéed Leeks with Chestnuts, 226

Chipotle and Tamarind–Braised Collard Greens, 235

Maple Whipped Sweet Potatoes, 241

Sausage, Pine Nut and Oyster Stuffing, 267

WINE Light, fruity Beaujolais

DESSERT

Pumpkin Cheesecake Tart with Cranberry Gelée, 298

Warm Apple Cider Cake with Pumpkin Seed Brittle, 320

christmas

STARTERS

Porcini Mushroom Tartlets, 12

Green Olive and Walnut Crostini, 20

WINE Round, rich Sauvignon Blanc

MAIN COURSE

Roast Beef Tenderloin with Morel Cream Sauce, 140

Roasted Butternut Squash with Onions, Brown Butter
and Sage, 223

Sautéed Chard with Pancetta, 234

Baked Polenta with Parmesan, 251

WINE Tannic, complex Cabernet

DESSERT

Fallen Prune and Armagnac Soufflé, 307

Chocolate Layer Cake with Peppermint Ganache Frosting, 326

new year's eve

STARTERS

Spicy Cocktail Shortbreads, 12

Prosciutto and Foie Gras Roulades with Fig Compote, 28

Alain Ducasse's Gougères, 265

Black-Raspberry Gimlet, 349

WINE Dry, light, crisp Champagne

MAIN COURSE

Fennel and Apple Salad with Blue Cheese and Pecans, 46

Roast Leg of Lamb Provençal, 152

Lobster Capellini with Leek-Tarragon Cream Sauce, 206

Baked Endives with Bacon and Mascarpone, 230

WINE Fruity, low-oak Chardonnay / Powerful, spicy Syrah

DESSERT

Lemon Tart with Chocolate-Almond Crust, 297

Ginger Brandy Snaps, 330

Espresso Granita with Whipped Cream, 341

staff favorites

starters

Porcini Mushroom Tartlets, 12

Chickpea Fries with Sage and Parmesan, 16

Mushroom and Fontina Crostini, 19

Crostini of Squid Stewed in Red Wine, 20

Pancetta-Wrapped Mushrooms, 29

salads

Midsummer Market Salad, 35

Baby Romaine with Green Goddess Dressing, 39

Spicy Asian Tofu with Cucumber Salad, 42

Sweet Pepper Salad with Manchego and Almonds, 49

soups

Smoked Tomato Soup, 57

Creamy Asparagus Soup with Lemon Dumplings, 58

Tunisian Chickpea Soup with Harissa, 62

Bok Choy and Rice Noodle Soup with Turkey Meatballs, 66

Tortilla-Crab Soup with Tomatillo Crème Fraîche, 68

pasta

Three-Cheese Baked Pasta with Porcini and Radicchio, 82

Macaroni and Cheese with Buttery Crumbs, 82

Spaetzle with Gruyère and Caramelized Onions, 83

Venetian Spaghetti with Sardines, 86

Spaghetti with Bolognese Sauce, 89

poultry

Clay-Roasted Chicken Stuffed with Serrano Ham and Olives, 99

Roast Chicken with Grapes, Chestnuts and Tarragon Butter, 100

Parmesan-Crusted Chicken with Arugula Salad, 103

Chicken with Fresh Apricots, Ginger and Cracked Almonds, 105

Buttermilk Fried Chicken, 106

Crispy Garlic Chicken with Dipping Salt, 111

Chicken Tikka Masala, 113

Chicken with Riesling, 113

Herb-Roasted Game Hens, 119

beef, lamb + game

Beef Sirloin with Piquillo Peppers and Capers, 136

Roast Beef Tenderloin with Morel Cream Sauce, 140

Summer Vegetable Stew with Braised Rabbit, 149

Lamb Chops with Spicy Thai Peanut Sauce, 152

Lamb Steaks with Shallot-Anchovy Relish, 154

pork + veal

Crispy Pork Tenderloin with Fried Apple Rings, 162

Pork Tenderloin with Rhubarb-Shallot Compote, 162

Spicy Korean Glazed Pork Ribs, 171

Tofu with Spicy Meat Sauce, 173

Spicy Pineapple-Glazed Ham, 177

fish

Roasted Salmon with Spaghetti-Squash Salad, 184

Swordfish Sicilian-Style, 187

Sole Meunière, 189

Thai Tuna Burgers with Ginger-Lemon Mayonnaise, 194

shellfish

Sweet Shrimp with Creamy Semolina, 203

Creamy Shrimp Casserole with Buttery Crumbs, 203

Portuguese Clam and Chorizo Stew, 209

Soft-Shell Crab and Bacon Sandwiches, 213

Curried Crab and Watermelon Salad with Arugula, 214

LEMON RIPPLE CHEESECAKE BARS, P. 305

SWORDFISH SICILIAN-STYLE, P. 187

index

a

contributors

bruce aidells is a food writer, cooking teacher, cookbook author and the founder of Aidells Sausage Company.

colin alevras is co-owner, with his wife, Renee, of The Tasting Room in New York City.

pam anderson is the author of several cookbooks, including, most recently, *CookSmart*.

chip angell is co-owner, with his wife, Gail, of the Brooklin Inn in Brooklin, Maine.

alexandra angle and her husband, Eliot, are the owners of Aqua Vitae, a Los Angeles–based event and interior design company, and the authors of *Cocktail Parties with a Twist*.

dave arnold is a sculptor and Web designer who is also an obsessive home cook.

dan barber was named one of F&W's Best New Chefs in 2002. He is a chef and owner of Blue Hill in New York City and Blue Hill at Stone Barns in Tarrytown, New York.

nancy verde barr is a cooking teacher and the author of several cookbooks, including *We Called It Macaroni* and *Make It Italian*.

gianfranco becchina is the producer of Olio Verde, a flavorful Italian olive oil.

rose levy beranbaum is the author of several cookbooks, including *The Cake Bible, Rose's Christmas Cookies, The Pie and Pastry Bible* and, most recently, *The Bread Bible*.

paul bertolli is the executive chef and co-owner of Oliveto in Oakland, California, and the author of *Cooking by Hand*.

eugenia bone is the author of *At Mesa's Edge: Cooking and Ranching in Colorado's North Fork Valley,* which will be published in 2004.

stephana bottom is a food stylist, writer and recipe developer in New York City.

daniel boulud was named one of F&W's Best New Chefs in 1988. He is the chef and owner of Daniel, Café Boulud and db Bistro Moderne restaurants in New York City and Café Boulud Palm Beach at the Brazilian Court in Palm Beach, Florida. He is also the author of several books, including *Daniel's Dish: Entertaining at Home with a Four-Star Chef.*

wayne harley brachman is a pastry chef and cookbook author.

sophie braimbridge is a chef, food consultant and cookbook author.

terrance brennan was named one of F&W's Best New Chefs in 1995. He is the chef and proprietor of several New York City restaurants and the owner of Artisanal Cheese Center, also in New York City.

stuart brioza was named one of F&W's Best New Chefs in 2003. He is a former chef at Tapawingo in Ellsworth, Michigan.

jesse browner is a novelist, historian, United Nations translator and avid home cook.

arunas bruzas is a former bartender at Adobo Grill in Chicago.

david bull was named one of F&W's Best New Chefs in 2003. He is the chef at Driskill Grill in Austin, Texas.

scott campbell is the chef and owner of @SQC in New York City.

floyd cardoz is the executive chef at Tabla in New York City.

maile carpenter is the Eat Out editor for *Time Out New York*.

sandy carpenter is a first-grade teacher and home cook.

jeannie chen is a food stylist and recipe developer and tester.

laura chenel, founder and owner of Laura Chenel's Chèvre in Sonoma, California, was the first producer of French-style goat cheese in the United States.

younhee choi is a photographer who enjoys cooking her native Korean recipes at home.

paul chung is a self-taught cook specializing in Jamaican and Chinese cooking.

josiah citrin is the executive chef at Melisse in Santa Monica, California.

melissa clark is a freelance food writer who contributes regularly to F&W Magazine. She has authored 14 cookbooks, including *East of Paris,* with David Bouley.

tom colicchio was named one of F&W's Best New Chefs in 1991. He is the chef and owner of several restaurants in New York City and Las Vegas as well as the author of two cookbooks, including *Craft of Cooking.*

scott conant is the chef at L'Impero in New York City.

christophe côte is the chef at Les Fermes de Marie, a resort in Megève, France.

peggy cullen is a baker, candy-maker and the author of *Got Milk? The Cookie Book* and *Caramel.*

eric czerwinski is the chef and owner of Café Out Back in South Brooksville, Maine.

barbara damrosch is co-owner of Four Season Farm in Penobscot Bay, Maine.

jason denton is the owner of 'ino and 'inoteca restaurants and a partner at Lupa and Otto restaurants in New York City.

arif develi is the owner of Develi restaurant in Istanbul, Turkey.

paula disbrowe is the chef at Hart & Hind Fitness Ranch in Rio Frio, Texas. Her food and travel articles have appeared in F&W Magazine and the *New York Times.*

alain ducasse owns several highly acclaimed restaurants throughout Europe and in New York City.

claudia fleming is the author of *The Last Course* and a former pastry chef at Gramercy Tavern in New York City.

jim fobel is a former F&W Test Kitchen director.

nobuo fukuda was named one of F&W's Best New Chefs in 2003. He is the chef and co-owner of Sea Saw in Scottsdale, Arizona.

cornelius gallagher was named one of F&W's Best New Chefs in 2003. He is the chef at Oceana in New York City.

christophe gerard is the chef at Angèle in Napa Valley, California.

george germon was named one of F&W's Best New Chefs in 1988. He and his wife, Johanne Killeen, are the chefs and owners of Al Forno in Providence, Rhode Island, and the authors of *Cucina Simpatica.*

suzanne goin was named one of F&W's Best New Chefs in 1999. She is the chef and co-owner of Lucques and A.O.C. in Los Angeles.

marcy goldman is a Montreal pastry chef, cookbook author and host and creator of the online magazine *BetterBaking.com.*

laurent gras was named one of F&W's Best New Chefs in 2002. He is the chef at Fifth Floor in San Francisco.

grateful palate is a wine-importing and mail-order epicurean-foods company founded by F&W Magazine contributing editor Dan Philips.

anupam gulati is a chef at Amarvilas, an Oberoi resort and spa in Agra, India.

hajja halima lives in Morocco, where she is the personal chef for *Masculin* magazine editor Nawal Slaoui and her family.

sam hayward is the chef at Fore Street Grill in Portland, Maine.

marcella hazan teaches cooking classes and has authored several definitive cookbooks on Italian cuisine, including *Essentials of Classic Italian Cooking* and *Marcella's Italian Kitchen.*

lee hefter was named one of F&W's Best New Chefs in 1998. He is the chef and a partner at Spago Beverly Hills and Brasserie Vert in Hollywood.

janie hibler is a food writer and a cookbook author. Her most recent book, *The Berry Bible,* is being published in April, 2004.

john hikade is the chef at Arborvine in Blue Hill, Maine.

scott howell is the chef and owner of restaurants in Durham and Raleigh, North Carolina.

thomas john was named one of F&W's Best New Chefs in 2002. He is the chef at Mantra in Boston and the consulting chef at The Hartwell House in Lexington, Massachusetts.

joyce jue is a cooking teacher, writer and the author of three cookbooks, including *Savoring Southeast Asia*.

tom kee is the chef at The Rail Stop in The Plains, Virginia.

marcia kiesel is the F&W Test Kitchen supervisor and a co-author of *The Simple Art of Vietnamese Cooking*.

johanne killeen was named one of F&W's Best New Chefs in 1988. She and her husband, George Germon, are the chefs and owners of Al Forno in Providence, Rhode Island, and the authors of *Cucina Simpatica*.

elinor klivans is a pastry chef, food writer, culinary educator and author or co-author of several cookbooks. Her most recent book is *Fearless Baking*.

jason knibb is the chef at Nine-Ten in The Grande Colonial Hotel in La Jolla, California.

gabriel kreuther was named one of F&W's Best New Chefs in 2003. He is the chef at Atelier at the Ritz Carlton, New York, Central Park.

jenny kwak is co-owner and manager at Do Hwa in New York City.

michael laiskonis is the pastry chef at Tribute in Farmington Hills, Michigan.

rob larman is the chef and owner of La Poste in Sonoma, California.

yvan-david lemoine is a former pastry chef at New York City's Fleur de Sel.

david lentz is a former chef at Opaline in Los Angeles.

jean lentz is an inspiring home cook.

dale levitski is the chef at La Tache in Chicago.

allison levitt is the pastry chef at Marché in Chicago.

william loob is the assistant managing editor at F&W Magazine.

laurent manrique is the executive chef at Aqua in San Francisco and the corporate executive chef for the Aqua Development Corp., which owns several restaurants in California and Las Vegas.

bruce marder is the chef and owner of Capo, Cora's Coffee Shoppe and Broadway Deli in Santa Monica, California, and of Brentwood Restaurant and Lounge in Brentwood, California.

priscilla martel is a chef, food consultant and co-author of *Best Bread Ever*.

tony maws is the chef and owner of Craigie Street Bistrot in Cambridge, Massachusetts.

jehangir mehta is the pastry chef at Aix and the chef and owner of Partistry, both in New York City.

gail monaghan is a cooking teacher, cookbook editor and the author of *Perfect Picnics for All Seasons*.

megan moore is the owner of Moore Fine Foods catering in Great Barrington, Massachusetts.

christophe morvan is the chef at Tournesol in Queens, New York.

bryan moscatello was named one of F&W's Best New Chefs in 2003. He is the executive chef and partner at Adega in Denver, Colorado.

eberhard müller is the chef at Bayard's in New York City. He and his wife own Satur Farms on the North Fork of Long Island.

adolfo muñoz is the chef and owner of Adolfo in Toledo, Spain, as well as the host of a cooking show, a caterer, a winemaker and an olive grower.

david myers was named one of F&W's Best New Chefs in 2003. He is the chef and co-owner of Sona in Los Angeles.

elizabeth and sompon nabnian run the Chiang Mai Thai Cookery School in Chiang Mai, Thailand.

jan newberry is the food and wine editor at *San Francisco* magazine.

david norman is the baker and ranch manager at Hart & Hind Fitness Ranch in Rio Frio, Texas.

ken oringer is the chef and co-owner of Boston's Clio and Uni restaurants.

sisha ortuzar is the chef and manager of New York City's 'wichcraft.

angel palacios, formerly of La Broche in Miami and Madrid, was named one of F&W's Best New Chefs in 2003.

grace parisi is the senior associate in the F&W Test Kitchen and the author of a book on sauces, due out in fall 2004.

greg patent is the author of several cookbooks, including *A is For Apple, New Frontiers in Western Cooking* and the exhaustive baking book *Baking in America.*

cindy pawlcyn is the executive chef and owner of Mustards Grill and Cindy's Backstreet Kitchen restaurants in Napa Valley, California. She is the author of *Mustards Grill Cookbook.*

françois payard is the pastry chef and owner of Payard Patisserie & Bistro in New York City and Manhasset, Long Island.

scott peacock is the chef at Watershed in Decatur, Georgia, and a co-author, with Edna Lewis, of *The Gift of Southern Cooking.*

gloria pépin, the wife of Jacques Pépin, is a talented home cook.

jaques pépin, F&W Magazine contributing editor, master chef, TV personality and cooking teacher, is the author of numerous cookbooks, including *Jacques Pépin's Kitchen: Encore with Claudine and Julia, Jacques Cooking at Home* and, most recently, *The Apprentice: My Life in the Kitchen.* He is also co-host, with his daughter, Claudine, of the PBS television series *Jacques Pépin Celebrates.*

bob petersen is the pastry chef at Cuvée World Bistro in Tucson.

charles pierce is a cookbook author and editor.

andrew j. powning is a produce specialist for Greenleaf, a San Francisco wholesale produce distributor.

david pratt is the chef at Mirabeau in Dana Point, California.

maricel presilla is the author of several cookbooks as well as the chef and co-owner of two Hoboken, New Jersey, restaurants.

elisabeth prueitt is the pastry chef and co-owner, with her husband, Chad Robertson, of Tartine, a bakery in San Francisco.

wolfgang puck is a celebrity chef, restaurateur, television personality and the author of several cookbooks.

anne quatrano was named one of F&W's Best New Chefs in 1995. She is co-chef and co-owner of Bacchanalia and Floataway Café, and co-owner of the retail market Star Provisions, all in Atlanta.

patricia quintana is a cookbook author and the chef and co-owner of Izote in Mexico City.

deborah racicot is the pastry chef at Gotham Bar & Grill in New York City.

steven raichlen is the author of several cookbooks, including *The Barbecue! Bible, How to Grill* and, most recently, *Barbecue USA: 425 Fiery Recipes from All Across America.*

eric ripert is the executive chef and co-owner of Le Bernardin in New York City and the author of several cookbooks.

hans röckenwagner is the chef and owner of Röckenwagner in Santa Monica, California, and Ballona Fish Market in Marina Del Rey, California.

michael rosen is a chef and partner at Zeke's Smokehouse, a Los Angeles barbecue joint.

david rosengarten is a chef, TV personality, cookbook author, teacher and writer. His latest cookbook is *It's All American Food.* He is also the editor in chief of *The Rosengarten Report,* a food newsletter.

sally sampson is a food writer and the author of several cookbooks.

sally schneider is a food stylist, cookbook author and a longtime contributor to F&W Magazine. Her most recent book is the award-winning *A New Way to Cook.*

leonard schwartz is a chef and partner at Zeke's Smokehouse, a Los Angeles barbecue joint.

marika seguso co-owns Acquolina, a catering and event management company in New York City.

bruce sherman was named one of F&W's Best New Chefs in 2003. He is the chef and a partner at North Pond in Chicago.

jane sigal is a senior food editor at F&W Magazine.

sergio sigala is the chef at Casa Tua, a boutique hotel in Miami.

fanny singer, the daughter of culinary visionary Alice Waters, is an undergraduate at Yale University.

maria helm sinskey was named one of F&W's Best New Chefs in 1996. She is the culinary director of Robert Sinskey Vineyards and the author of *The Vineyard Kitchen.*

kimberly sklar is the former pastry chef at Lucques in Los Angeles.

deborah snyder is the pastry chef at Lever House in New York City.

annie somerville is the chef at Greens in San Francisco and the author of *Everyday Greens: Home Cooking from Greens, the Celebrated Vegetarian Restaurant* and *Fields of Greens: New Vegetarian Recipes from the Celebrated Greens Restaurant.*

richard stephens is the chef and owner of the restaurant La Gamella in Madrid, Spain.

diana sturgis, a former F&W Test Kitchen director, is a food writer, recipe developer and an adjunct lecturer at the City University of New York.

fabio trabocchi was named one of F&W's Best New Chefs in 2002. He is the chef at Maestro at the Ritz-Carlton Tysons Corner in McLean, Virginia.

jerry traunfeld is the chef and owner of The Herbfarm in Woodinville, Washington.

ming tsai is the chef and owner of Blue Ginger in Wellesley, Massachusetts, the host of *Simply Ming* on PBS and a cookbook author.

michael tusk, formerly of Chez Panisse and Oliveto, is the chef at Quince in San Francisco.

scott tycer was named one of F&W's Best New Chefs in 2003. He is the chef and co-owner of Aries restaurant and Kraftsmen Baking in Houston, Texas.

tina ujlaki is the executive food editor at F&W Magazine.

tom valenti was named one of F&W's Best New Chefs in 1990. He is the chef and co-owner of Ouest and 'Cesca in New York City and the author of *Welcome to My Kitchen* and *Tom Valenti's Soups, Stews and One-Pot Meals.*

ruth van waerebeek is a cooking teacher and the author of *Everybody Eats Well in Belgium* and *The Chilean Kitchen.*

anya von bremzen is a food writer and the author of several cookbooks, including *Please to the Table: The Russian Cookbook* and, most recently, *The Greatest Dishes: Around the World in 80 Recipes.*

jean-georges vongerichten is a contributing editor at F&W Magazine. He is the chef and owner of numerous restaurants around the world, including Jean-Georges in New York City. He has co-authored *Simple Cuisine, Cooking at Home with a Four-Star Chef* and *Simple to Spectacular.*

david waltuck co-owns, with his wife, Karen, the four-star restaurant Chanterelle and the bistro Le Zinc, both in New York City. He is also a co-author of *Staff Meals from Chanterelle.*

vicki wells is the pastry chef at Mesa Grill and Bolo restaurants in New York City.

joshua wesson is co-founder of the Best Cellars wine stores. He is co-author of *Red Wine with Fish* and a contributor to foodandwine.com.

joyce white is the author of two cookbooks, including *Brown Sugar: Soul Food Desserts from Family and Friends.*

michael white is the chef and a partner at Fiamma Osteria and Vento Trattoria in New York City and Fiamma Trattoria in Las Vegas and Scottsdale, Arizona.

jody williams is the chef at Giorgione in New York City.

matt williamson is the former bartender at Lucques in Los Angeles.

paula wolfert, a contributing editor at F&W magazine, is the author of many cookbooks, including *Mediterranean Cooking, Mediterranean Grains and Greens* and *The Slow Mediterranean Kitchen.*

elizabeth woodson is a former F&W art director who writes about cooking and crafts. She co-authored *Lemons: Growing, Cooking, Crafting.*

sherry yard is the executive pastry chef at Spago Beverly Hills and the author of *The Secrets of Baking.*

sang yoon is the chef and owner of Father's Office, a restaurant in Santa Monica, California.

kate zuckerman is the pastry chef at Chanterelle in New York City.

photo credits

akiko & pierre 14 (bottom), 205 (top), 365

anthony masterson/food pix 227

bacon, quentin 25 (left), 59 (right), 107 (bottom), 135 (bottom), 158 (right), 160, 182, 198, 260, 272 (left), 276, 308 (right), 320 (left), 338 (right)

baigrie, james 38 (right), 63 (bottom), 73, 85, 107 (top), 117, 135 (top), 138, 152 (left)

barr, edmund 262 (right)

davis, reed 212, 316, 367 (left)

duisterhof, miki 32, 320 (right)

franco, jim 46 (bottom), 96, 162 (right), 221 (bottom), 262 (left), 278 (left), 281 (right), 286 (right)

french, andrew 27

gallagher, dana 43, 67, 70 (top), 76 (right), 122, 158 (left), 176, 184 (left), 211 (right), 236, 278 (right), 281 (left), 324 (left), 338 (left), 341 (right)

gentl & hyers 157, 222 (left)

janisch, frances 17 (left), 25 (right), 166 (left), 200 (right), 243 (right), 272 (right), 333

kachatorian, ray 4, 18 (bottom)

kernick, john 60, 127 (left), 205 (bottom), 208 (left), 211 (left), 216, 248 (left), 313, 341 (left), 352

lew, rick 34 (right), 37 (bottom), 301

loftus, david 13

lung, geoff 59 (left), 93 (right), 110

mccaul, andrew 94, 108, 136, 190, 266, 284, 298

mcconnell, ericka 70 (bottom), 93 (left), 238 (right), 269

meppem, william 8, 10 (right), 14 (top), 18 (top), 23, 34 (left), 37 (top), 38 (left), 41, 52 (left), 74, 79 (bottom), 88, 98, 104 (top), 127 (right), 143, 166 (right), 192 (right), 218, 248 (right), 253 (top), 275, 296 (right), 308 (left), 318, 324 (right), 328, 346, 367 (right), 370

paul, michael 55 (bottom), 63 (top), 130, 221 (top)

pearson, victoria 232 (right), 348 (left)

piasecki, eric 348 (right)

pond, edward 10 (left), 46 (top), 184 (right), 200 (left)

poulos, con 30, 132 (left), 335

robledo, maria 283

rupp, tina 17 (right), 55 (top), 76 (left), 79 (top), 81, 87, 104 (bottom), 132 (right), 152 (right), 162 (left), 173, 195, 208 (right), 238 (left), 286 (left), 289, 369 (right)

sanchez, hector 82, 265, 361

tinslay, petrina 232 (left), 244

tsay, david 243 (left), 253 (bottom)

watson, simon 188

webber, wendell t. 125, 168, 222 (right), 224

williams, anna 50, 52 (right), 148, 192 (left), 228, 247, 258, 294, 296 (left), 304, 343, 369 (left)

woffinden, andrew 114

p.359 courtesy of park hyatt mendoza